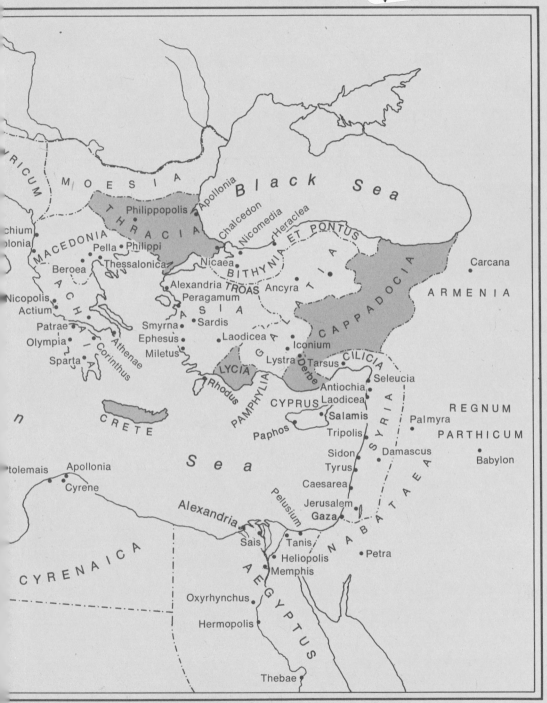

M O E S I A

THRACIA

Philippopolis • Apollonia

Chalcedon

Nicomedia • Heraclea

Black Sea

MACEDONIA

Pella • Philippi

Beroea • Thessalonica

Nicaea

BITHYNIA ET PONTUS

A

Ancyra

T

I

A

ARMENIA

Carcana

Nicopolis

Actium

Alexandria TROAS

Peragamum

A S I A

Smyrna • Sardis

CAPPADOCIA

Patrae

Olympia

Athenae

Ephesus • Laodicea

Iconium

Corinthus

Miletus

G

Lystra

Sparta

LYCIA

Derbe • Tarsus

CILICIA

Rhodus

PAMPHYLIA

Antiochia

Seleucia

CRETE

CYPRUS Laodicea

Salamis

REGNUM

PARTHICUM

Paphos

Tripolis

S

Y

R

I

A

Palmyra

Babylon

Sea

Sidon

Damascus

Tyrus

N

Caesarea

A

Ptolemais

Apollonia

Cyrene

Pelusium

Jerusalem

Gaza

B

A

T

A

E

A

Petra

Alexandria

CYRENAICA

Sais • Tanis

Heliopolis

Memphis

A

E

G

Y

P

T

U

S

Oxyrhynchus

Hermopolis

Thebae

...ORLD IN JESUS' DAY

The New Testament

**An Introduction to Its
History, Literature, and Thought**

The New Testament

**An Introduction to Its
History, Literature, and Thought**

C. Milo Connick

Whittier College

Dickenson Publishing Company, Inc.

Encino, California and Belmont, California

Library of Congress Catalog Card
Number: 76-180754

ISBN: 0-8221-0007-X

Printed in the United States of America

10 9 8 7 6 5 4 3 2 1

Designed by Dale Smith

To some of my mentors with appreciation beyond measure:

Irwin R. Beiler
Edwin P. Booth
Edgar S. Brightman
Ralph W. Decker
F. Gerald Ensley
William H. P. Hatch
William E. Hocking
Albert C. Knudson
Elmer A. Leslie
William J. Lowstuter
Robert H. Pfeiffer

PART

4

Conflict and Consolidation in the Christian Community
317

List of Maps

This book is the result of over a quarter century of teaching and research. It does not claim to tell its readers all they need to know about the New Testament. No book (or library) could do that. Its purpose is to provide a balanced account of the New Testament—one that is accurate, up-to-date, and absorbing. Since the interpretations of experts often differ, a variety of views is presented. Controversial issues are probed from different vantage points. Although we do not hesitate to express our personal convictions, we have vigorously resisted special pleading. Major positions are included, but space limitations prohibit the consideration of every informed opinion.

The New Testament: An Introduction to Its History, Literature, and Thought is not a substitute for Scripture, but, rather, an invitation to its thoughtful examination. Copious references direct the reader to pertinent Biblical passages. For each New Testament book such topics as authorship, date, destination, and purpose are treated, and the message of each composition is delineated and interpreted. Footnotes point to classical and current discussions of vital subjects. An extensive bibliography provides a rich and varied field for further exploration. The evaluative comments enable the reader to continue his quest at the level of his own background and interest.

The New Testament is a product of the Christian community. Neither can be understood apart from the other. Both influenced and were influenced by their environment. Our somewhat protracted examination of the background of the Christian community (Part 1) is an essential prelude to the comprehension of the literature that this community produced. The conception and birth and growth of the community (Parts 2–3) created the conditions that called for written records. Many of the New Testament books were offsprings of conflict. Conflict forced the community to define the contents of its faith and to develop forms of organization so it could cope with threats to its security from within and without. These factors receive particular attention in my discussion of the conflict and consolidation in the Christian community (Part 4).

A book of this kind would be impossible apart from the insightful work of hundreds of scholars, many of whom are mentioned in the footnotes and bibliography. To these scholars, and to the publishers who generously granted permission to quote from their valuable books and articles, I am deeply indebted. I would also like to thank Dr. Kenneth Kuntz, Dr. John Anderson, Prof. Fred O. Francis, Prof. Richard Hiers, Prof. Robert C. Tannehill, Prof. Joseph A. Grispino, and Dr. Keith Beebe for their helpful reviews of the manuscript. Others to whom I owe special thanks are: Whittier College (for research grants); Chairman of the Board of Directors Richard W. Hansen and President Richard J. Trudgen of Dickenson Publishing Company, Inc., and their able associates, Jane Johnson, Janet Greenblatt, and Jack Reid (for encouragement and skillful editorial assistance); Doris Hollembeak and my daughter, Nancy (for expert typing); and my wife, Genevieve (incomparable critic, patient and perceptive proofreader, and companion *par excellence*).

C. MILO CONNICK

The New Testament

**An Introduction to Its
History, Literature, and Thought**

1

Background of the Christian Community

The New Testament was the unplanned child of the church. The church had been a going concern for about twenty years before Paul penned I Thessalonians. It was another century before the contents of the little library reached completion. None of the twenty-seven books that eventually gained admission to the canon was written for inclusion in a Bible. They were composed in response to the practical needs of the church. If there had been no church, there would have been no canon.[1] The canonical books are those that the church chose as representative of its early life, work, and faith. The New Testament was produced in the church, by members of the church, for the use of the church. Apart from this historical truth, the literature makes little sense.

The church itself did not spring to life in a vacuum. If its conception was celestial, its birth and development were terrestrial. What was the world like at the turn of time? What aspirations motivated men? What anxieties undermined their security? What political, philosophical, and religious forces fought for their allegiance? We need to examine the environment of early Christianity if we are to understand how the Christian community came into being.

---

[1]"Canon" originally meant a "reed" used in measuring. It now stands for those books or writings that are accepted as authoritative.

The Greco-Roman World

Two tributaries vitalized the soil of the early church. They were the cultures of the Greco-Roman and the Jewish worlds. Each tributary, of course, was a blend of earlier streams with their own distinctive histories. Since what is known about the tributaries is so vast as to be staggering, our treatment must of necessity be selective. We shall cover only those matters that seem to have a rather direct bearing on Christian origins. The broad picture of the Greco-Roman world will be painted first. Then in Chapters 2 and 3 we shall sketch the diverse and dynamic Jewish world and Jewish religion from which the Christian community arose.

Alexander the Great (356–323 B.C.)

Alexander of Macedonia, who ruled from 336 to 323 B.C., first conquered the city-states of Greece; then he conquered the known world. His path to phenomenal military power and prestige had been paved for him by centuries of extensive Greek colonization and commerce. Greeks had occupied the Aegean Islands, Crete, and most of Cyprus. They had penetrated the coastlands of Asia Minor and the Black Sea and had crossed the Mediterranean to Libya, Cyrenaica, and Egypt. In the west, they had settled in large numbers in Southern Italy, Sicily, Sardinia, and Corsica, and they possessed thriving colonies in Gaul and Spain.

The world was custom-made for Alexander when he headed east. Persian power was on the wane, and Rome was still an adolescent. Alexander defeated the Persian potentate (Darius III) on the plains of Cilicia in 333 B.C. Then he turned south to Syria. When the coastal city of Tyre capitulated, Jewish resistance crumbled and the Jerusalem priests reversed themselves and pledged their loyalty. The Holy City was spared. Egypt succumbed without protest and crowned the conqueror Pharaoh. When Alexander appeared at the famous shrine of Amon, the oracle declared him to be Amon's son. Such an ascription was altogether congenial to the Eastern mind. Alexander reorganized the Egyptian government and founded a city on the Mediterranean that bears his name.

To Amon. The wall of a tomb at Karnak in Upper Egypt depicts
in still luxurious colors suitable offerings to Amon, the sun god.

Alexander finally marched his armies as far east as the Indus River
in modern Pakistan. There, according to legend, he wept for want
of more worlds to conquer. His tears soon turned to trouble. Climate
became a more formidable adversary than his deadliest enemy. His
men mutinied, and he was forced to withdraw. He died in Babylon
while planning yet another expedition. At the age of thirty-three he
had made himself master of the far-flung Persian Empire.

Alexander's thirst for territory was not stimulated solely by a military
mania. He was impelled by a devout faith in the superiority of Greek
culture. Aristotle had quickened in him the love of learning and
a compelling curiosity. A coterie of scholars accompanied him on
his campaigns to observe and record the wonders of the world. They
also assisted in establishing and populating seventy Greek cities—
camels' noses under the tents of alien cultures.

Alexander's dream of one world, held together by the glue of Greek learning, might well have materialized had it not been for his untimely death. The peoples of the East, long addicted to divine kingship, had paid him great personal respect. Their response to Greek culture had also been impressive. They had built theaters, gymnasiums, and hippodromes. They had altered the names of their temples to honor local deities masquerading under freshly acquired Greek titles. They had even aped Greek dress. But the cultural penetration had never succeeded in depositing more than a thin veneer on the Oriental portions of Alexander's empire. The great mass of people continued to adhere to their country's customs as though the mighty conqueror had never lived. The facade of unity so carefully constructed by the great commander vanished with his death, and his generals plunged into a power struggle for the decedent's domain.

Despite the fact that Alexander's empire fell apart the moment his firm hand faltered, he had set in motion two tendencies that would long endure. First, Greek gradually became the common language of commerce and international communication. People continued to speak their native tongues among themselves, but they quickly adjusted to the realities of the power structure. Many non-Palestinian Jews adjusted with such alacrity that they soon lost the ability to speak their native language. A Greek version of their scriptures became imperative. In Alexandria, about the middle of the third century B.C., Jews began to translate their sacred writings and scriptures into Greek. They came to be called the Septuagint (from its Latin title) and carried the identifying symbol LXX. Legend had it that seventy scholars, working independently, had produced identical translations! The Septuagint served to publicize Judaism in the ancient world, and it later became the favorite version of the Hebrew Scripture for New Testament writers. Like the Septuagint, the New Testament itself was composed in the nonclassical language of commerce made popular by Alexander's conquests. Second, provincialism gradually gave way to universalism. A common language greatly facilitated the exchange of customs and thought. Alexander sponsored the superiority of all things Greek, but he was no racist. He believed in the co-mingling of diverse peoples on the basis of equality. He and thousands of his men married Asian women—thus becoming both the symbol of and the incentive for the meeting of East and West. Three centuries later the forces that Alexander set in motion provided a fertile field for a new religion as it proclaimed to the world in a universal tongue that in Christ "there is no distinction between Jew and Greek" (Rom. 10:12).

From Alexander to Augustus (323–30 B.C.)

The period from Alexander to Augustus is commonly called the Hellenistic Age because of the cultural penetration which characterized it. (Hellas was an ancient name for Greece, and the Greeks were called Hellenes.) The designation is a useful one if it is not taken too literally. Greek culture had penetrated its birth boundaries long before Alexander arrived on the scene. His conquests merely accelerated a movement well under way, and it remained for his successors to put Hellenization into orbit.

Alexander's death sparked a bitter struggle among his several generals for his empire. Antigonus I established a short-lived dynasty through control of the Greek peninsula and Asia Minor. After his demise, rival Greek states struggled for supremacy. Rome finally offered the part of Protector in 196 B.C. When her mighty legions crushed the Macedonians, the Greeks hailed their benefactor with glee. Fifty years later, however, the glee turned to gloom. Corinth chafed under foreign domination, and the Protector destroyed the city and sold her citizens into slavery. A hundred years elapsed before Julius Caesar rebuilt the ruins and populated the city. Corinth rapidly regained the status of a commercial center. When Paul visited there about the middle of the first century A.D., she was keeping heady company with Alexandria, Antioch, Ephesus, and Rome as chief cities of the Mediterranean world.

Seleucus I gained control of most of the eastern portion of Alexander's territory. He began with Babylon, added Syria (with help from Ptolemy), relocated the capital at Antioch, and then expanded to the south and west. While his successors continued to rule at Antioch over territories of variable dimensions, they seldom managed to exert vigorous control of the extremities. Frequent uprisings and dynastic difficulties so weakened the Seleucid kingdom that Pompey was able to annex it to the Roman Empire in 64 B.C. with comparative ease. Syria promptly became an important imperial province.

Ptolemy I inherited Egypt and Palestine. Egypt was providentially located. Desert on three sides and the Mediterranean on the fourth made her relatively immune to attack. Productive agriculture, made possible by the annual overflow of the Nile, and profitable trade created wealth and insured stability. With its capital at Alexandria, the Ptolemaic kingdom lasted until 30 B.C.

The real heirs of Alexander were not the Seleucids and the Ptolemies but the Romans. They were latecomers to the councils of the mighty. The lofty civilizations that had flourished in the Nile and Tigris-Euphrates Valleys had barely brushed them. The cultural shock waves set in motion by the commerce and colonization of the Phoenicians and the Greeks elicited only studied indifference. When "the glory that was Greece" was at its zenith, the Romans were mere infants

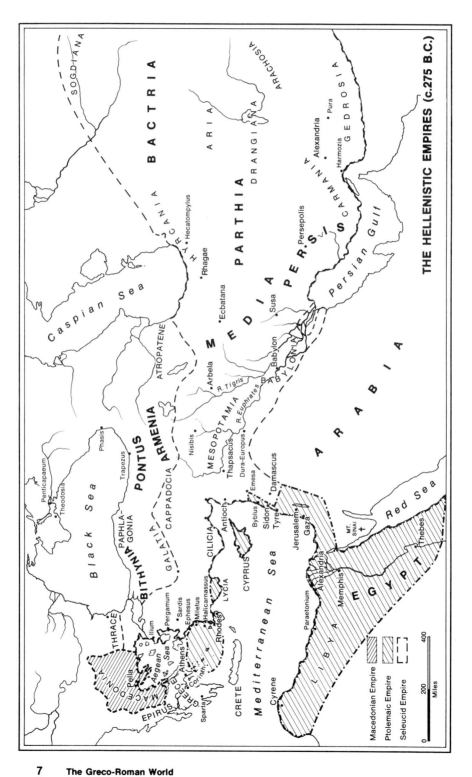

THE HELLENISTIC EMPIRES (c.275 B.C.)

SOGDIANA

BACTRIA

ARIA

ARACHOSIA

DRANGIANA

GEDROSIA

• Pura

• Alexandria

Harmozia

CARMANIA

Persian Gulf

PARTHIA

HYRCANIA

• Hecatompylus

• Rhagae

MEDIA

PERSIS

Persepolis

• Ecbatana

Susa

Caspian Sea

ATROPATENE

• Arbela

R. Tigris

Babylon

BABYLONIA

R. Euphrates

ARMENIA

Nisibis

MESOPOTAMIA

Thapsacus

Dura-Europus

PONTUS

Phasis

Trapezus

CAPPADOCIA

GALATIA

PAPHLA-
GONIA

BITHYNIA

Penticapaeum

Theodosia

Black Sea

Emesa

• Damascus

Byblus

Sidon

Tyre

Jerusalem

Gaza

MT.
SINAI

ARABIA

Red Sea

Antioch

CILICIA

CYPRUS

LYCIA

Halicarnassus

Miletus

Ephesus

Sardis

Pergamum

Ilium

THRACE

Rhodes

Aegean
Sea

Athens

Corinth

Sparta

MACEDON

Pella

EPIRUS

CRETE

Mediterranean Sea

Cyrene

LIBYA

Paraetonium

Alexandria

Memphis

EGYPT

Thebes

Macedonian Empire

Ptolemaic Empire

Seleucid Empire

0   200   400

Miles

content with tribal life. When Alexander began his conquests, they were blissful adolescents unconcerned about his growing power. Had he lived a few years longer, he would doubtless have added them to his lengthening list of lackeys. His untimely death and the dissolution of his empire bought the Romans the time they needed to reach maturity.

The unification of Italy was advancing in Alexander's day. When Roman soldiers overran the wealthy Greek settlements in the southern part of the country, their eyes bulged at hitherto undreamed-of treasures. Sicily, Sardinia, and Corsica, as we have noted, were dotted with glittering cities. Across the sea, on the mainland of Northern Africa, Carthage beckoned. This Phoenician colony outranked Rome in longevity and lucre. Her ships covered the Mediterranean like a blanket and controlled commerce from Sicily to Spain. A clash between Carthage and Rome was clearly in the cards. The prolonged struggle (264–146 B.C.) culminated in the destruction of Carthage. Meanwhile, Rome had gained control of the southern coast of France and Spain, the Greek mainland, Illyria (Yugoslavia), and Asia Minor as far east as the Taurus Mountains. Victory over Carthage left Rome without a peer in the West. Her closest competitors were Syria and Egypt.

Roman expansion continued during the first century B.C. Pompey, the great Roman general, subdued Syria in 64 B.C. When civil war threatened Palestine a year later, he made it a Roman province. Pompey's considerable popularity continued to grow; his only real rival was Julius Caesar. Caesar's conquest of Gaul (France) elicited a hero's welcome when he returned to Rome in 49 B.C. A showdown was inevitable, and Pompey's defeat came the following year. Meanwhile, Egypt had managed to remain independent under the Ptolemies. Caesar sided with Egypt's teen-age queen, Cleopatra, who had been expelled by her guardians. Although this deed deposited Egypt in the Roman camp, it remained for Augustus to convert the country into a Roman province. Caesar was murdered in 44 B.C., and Augustus became his heir and eventual successor. The struggle for power reached a climax at Actium in 31 B.C. Mark Anthony, supported by Cleopatra's fine fleet, suffered a humiliating defeat. Augustus pursued the two lovers to Egypt where they both committed suicide. Anthony's death left Augustus in sole command. The Republic was dead, and the mightiest Empire the world had ever known was in the making. Rome was the undisputed mistress of the Mediterranean world.

As architect of the Roman Empire, Augustus ruled from 27 B.C. to 14 A.D. He was called consul, tribune, and general, but he carefully avoided accepting the crown. He fostered the fiction that he was simply the leading citizen (*Princeps*), the first among equals. The preservation of the form of the republic permitted him to subvert its substance. Nevertheless, his sagacious rule struck a responsive chord in the hearts of subjects whose memories were saturated with the bloody turbulence of yesteryears. He chased pirates from the seas and made the waterways safe for trade and travel. He guaranteed the borders of the Empire, which had long been subject to dispute. He lived a simple life and adopted a firm stance against the immorality that festered among the elite. Peace and prosperity characterized his reign, and the acclaim of the people thundered in his ears. After his death in 14 A.D., a grateful populace built temples in his honor and offered incense and sacrifices in his name. He could posthumously lay claim to a triple inheritance from Alexander the Great—his kingdom, his divine kingship, and a visible unity masking invisible unrest. Perhaps the greatest monument to his memory, however, was an incidental reference on the part of an obscure first-century historian: "In those days a decree went out from Caesar Augustus that all the world should be enrolled" (Lk. 2:1). The reference reminds us that Jesus' birth took place during the reign of Augustus.

Concepts and Commitments: Philosophy

Change was the only constant from Alexander to Augustus. Governments rose and fell in rapid succession. As men became more mobile, ideas slipped their moorings. Frozen class structures began to thaw. Past certitudes came under a cloud, and the face of the future became a blur. As the people stood between two worlds, the old one dying and the new one as yet unborn, they were plagued with uncertainty. Some clung to shopworn beliefs in the desperate hope that they had not been drained of their power. Others courted newfangled ideas with a vengeance. It was a time of transition—unsettled and unsettling—made to order for philosophies and religions that promised security.

Christianity originated in the Orient, and the first Christians were all Orientals. Their approach to life was primarily religious. They did not marshal evidence for God's existence; they accepted Him on faith. Revelation was their road to truth, and they paid great heed to voices, visions, and inspiration. The Greeks, on the other hand, usually sponsored a philosophical path to knowledge. They stressed the primacy of reason. These two largely contrasting attitudes toward reality skirmished during the Hellenistic Age, but the real battles were fought when Paul plunged into Asia Minor and Europe. The new religion was forced to come to terms with the competing philosophical concepts and religious commitments of the Greco-Roman world.

Plato (428–348 B.C.) Plato marked the crest of classical Greek philosophy. He taught that for every class of objects or activities (such as trees or good deeds) there exists in the metaphysical world a perfect idea. Only the idea is real. It exists quite apart from whether a particular tree exists or a particular good deed is done. Ideas are eternal; particular objects are temporary. Ideas are perfect; particular objects are imperfect copies of reality. What little reality they seem to possess is derived from their perfect and invisible ideas or forms.

Plato's thought underwent considerable modification in the hands of his successors. By the time it had filtered down into the Christian era, it was all but unrecognizable. Nevertheless, a number of early Christians found his filtered ideas useful in formulating their faith. The author of Hebrews, for example, expressed the conviction that earthly things are only copies and shadows of those in heaven (8:1–5; 12:22–23).

Stoicism Stoicism was the most attractive and influential philosophy in the Hellenistic era. The school was founded in Athens by Zeno (c. 336–264 B.C.), a native of Cyprus. Its name described neither its principal personage nor its philosophical position; it was derived from the place where Zeno taught. Other teachers addressed their students in lecture halls, but he instructed his followers in an open colonnade (*stoa*) connected with the Agora or market place.

The Stoics rejected the Platonic notion that reality exists apart from man and the material world. God and nature cohabit. God is the rational element within nature that insures nature's purposive character. Reason (or Logos) pervades all things; it is simply another name for God. Zeus (or a suitable synonym) is a symbol for the impersonal and predestining power (itself highly refined matter) that shows itself in the world as creative fire or Reason. Man (and other animals and inanimate objects to a lesser degree) has within his nature a spark of the divine rationality. As an offshoot of Reason, he is admirably equipped to understand the world in which he lives.

The Stoics claimed that the chief end of man is the pursuit of virtue. Virtue is not the amassing of merit; it is living in harmony with nature—one's own nature and the nature of the universe. Good men subordinate their will to the will of the world. The world and everything in it are determined by destiny. Real freedom consists in accepting what is ordained, conforming to the purpose (Reason, Logos, God) that pervades the planet. Those who embrace virtue are fortified by apathy (freedom from passion). They are indifferent to pleasure and pain, plenty and poverty, fortune and misfortune.

The discipline of the Stoics was severe, and their denial of the emotions was unwholesome. Despite these decided disadvantages, their philosophy flourished. Their morality pierced the darkness of declining standards like a beacon light. People admired their sturdy character and perceptive minds. They were also attracted by the movement's implicit universalism. If the world is a perfect organism infused by Reason and the divine spark of rationality resides in every man, then men are sons of God and brothers of each other.

Sterling representatives of Stoicism during the infancy of Christianity included such disparate opinion-makers as Nero's tutor, Seneca (4–65 A.D.), the celebrated slave and younger contemporary of Paul, Epictetus (60–110 A.D.), and the philosopher-emperor Marcus Aurelius (121–180 A.D.). Christian writers themselves were not altogether impervious to the Stoics. Paul quoted their poets approvingly when he addressed Athenians at the Areopagus (Acts 17:28). The author of the Fourth Gospel uses a concept akin to the Stoic Logos as a bridge between the Semitic and the Greco-Roman worlds (Jn. 1:1–14). Some passages in Hebrews also suggest affinity with Stoic thought (4:12).

Epicureanism

Epicureanism bears the name of its founder. A contemporary of Zeno, Epicurus (341–270 B.C.) lived most of his adult life in Athens where friends and followers provided him with a house and garden. The garden became a center for all sorts of people—male and female, slave and free, of high and low repute. From there disciples carried their master's message of liberation throughout the Greek world and beyond.

Epicurus was a practical atheist. He argued that the gods exist, but they have no relevance. They live a joyous life in realms remote from men. They demand no service, and they bestow no favors. The human goal is pleasure with the delights of the mind far outshadowing sensual thrills. Fear of the gods is the root of evil. Religion is based on superstition and spawns manifold anxieties. Ultimate reality is the material atom. Atoms move about constantly, and they can change direction at will. The resultant forms of life require no First Cause as an explanation. The soul, like the body, is composed of atoms. Although the soul's atoms are made up of more refined substance, both the soul and body disintegrate at death. There is no divine retribution (since the gods are indifferent to men), and there is no immortality (since death marks the end of life).

The Epicurean denial of religion tended to restrict its appeal. Many sophisticated people in the Hellenistic world, however, did embrace the movement. The poets Lucretius and Horace were among its most articulate champions. When Paul addressed followers of this philosophy in Athens concerning the resurrection, it is safe to assume that their response was derisive (Acts 17:32).

Concepts and Commitments: Astrology and Gnosticism

Astrology

For many centuries in Mesopotamia men studied the movements of the stars and planets. As the rapidly-changing climate of the Hellenistic Age maximized uncertainty, more and more people turned (as in our day) to the pseudoscience of astrology in search of meaning. Astrologists claimed that they could foretell the future of men and nations by "reading" the stars. They argued that the particular configuration of stars present at a person's birth determines his destiny. He will be happy when he comes to understand the stars and adjusts to their decrees.

Plato's conviction that the stars are gods served as a bridge between astrology and Greek philosophy. This mode of thought was markedly accelerated by other Hellenistic thinkers who encouraged the marriage of mathematics and star study. The consequent belief in the massive power of the stars to control human affairs multiplied anxiety. People intensified their scanning of the skies in order to insure their welfare.

Superstition and magic sprout in the same soil that nourishes philosophy and religion. People attempted to placate the star spirits and other hostile forces as best they could. They devised formulas to prevent pain, ward off evil, and avoid accidents. They invoked the names of multiple deities in an effort to guarantee a favorable outcome. Societies that promised astral knowledge enjoyed brisk business. Conjurations, love potions, evil eyes, and statuettes of the gods became popular. They were considered the perfect antidote for astrological fatalism.

Astrology never made much headway among the Hebrews, but Biblical writers were well aware of its influence. Isaiah scornfully derides "those who divide the heavens, who gaze at the stars, who at the new moons predict what shall befall you" (47:13). Jeremiah admonishes the people not to be terrified "at the signs of the heavens" because the other nations are dismayed by them (10:2). The "wise men from the East" who came to Bethlehem in response to a star to worship the Babe born "king of the Jews" are widely held to have been Babylonian astrologers. Before they departed for home, they were instructed by an oracle to return by another way (Mt. 2:1–12).

Gnosticism

During the second century A.D. a group of people called Gnostics claimed to possess superior knowledge about God and His purposes.

The term was derived from *gnosis*, a Greek word meaning "knowledge." Until recently, little was known about Gnosticism except through the writings of its detractors. Irenaeus, a weighty church father and bishop of Lyons, wrote *Against Heresies* about 180 A.D. He made use of an earlier work by Justin (*c.* 150 A.D.) and also used oral and written testimony from the Gnostics themselves. He presented a complicated mythological picture of various forms of Gnosticism stressing the emanation of "aeons," intermediary beings between the supreme being and the world. Sophia, the twelfth and lowest of the aeons, is said to have fallen into outer darkness where she spontaneously gave birth to a premature child. The child, who created the universe out of his mother's solidified emotions, regarded himself as the only god. Since his mother had inserted a divine spark into men, he constantly fought with her for the control of mankind. In order to redeem both Sophia and mankind, Jesus was sent down to gather the spiritual seeds and to restore them to the "pleroma" of spiritual being, the aeons above. Irenaeus appealed to Scripture and church tradition to refute the Gnostic claims. Tertullian, Hippolytus, Epiphanius, and other church leaders later took up the battle.

A number of manuscripts were discovered in a large clay jar near Nag-Hammadi in upper Egypt in 1945. They were part of a Coptic library belonging to a monastery or church whose ruins lay near the discovery site. Investigation soon revealed that among the forty-nine treatises in the collection, several were thorough-going Gnostic originals. Others displayed Gnostic tendencies. Some of the works had been known previously only by title, and others had been quoted by church fathers, either directly or in translation. Still others were brand new discoveries. One of the writings, the *Gospel of Truth*, was composed by Valentinius, a heretic condemned by Irenaeus. The work is much simpler than Irenaeus would have us believe. It places little emphasis on the heavenly aeons, and the supreme god is not separated from the creator. The *Gospel of Thomas*, found near Nag-Hammadi in its complete form, is a misnomer. Since it contains no ministry, miracles, passion, or correlation with the Old Testament, it is not a genuine gospel. It portrays Jesus as the revealer of the secret sayings (all spoken after his death), as Son of the Living One, and himself the Living One. Many of the sayings parallel those found in the canonical New Testament, but there is no reason to suppose that any passage in Thomas provides an earlier or more reliable version of Jesus' thought.

The Nag-Hammadi manuscripts and the separate systems described by Irenaeus emphasize the amorphous nature of Gnosticism. It was not a monolith; it included a bewildering variety of thought. The Nag-Hammadi discoveries cannot be confined to a single intellectual straitjacket. Where these writings parallel the systems "refuted" by Irenaeus, startling discrepancies appear. Differences are compounded when the thoughts of Simon Magus, Saturninus, Marcion, Valentinius, and Basilides are compared.

It is beyond our purpose to deal in detail with the variform expressions that cluster around the Gnostic stem. A skeletal outline of some basic Gnostic beliefs, however, should be illuminating. (1) The affirmation of a radical dualism between the visible and the invisible world is the chief characteristic of Gnosticism. Spirit and matter, light and darkness, and good and evil are sharply contrasted. Ultimate reality (Spirit, Light, Good, or God) is supramundane and alien to the visible world (matter, darkness, evil, or the devil). (2) The creation of the world is often denied to God since spirit and matter are at odds. The world is the creation or emanation of intermediary beings (angels, demons) who rule the universe. (Valentinius, as we have noted, did not separate the supreme god from the creator.) (3) Man is a divided being. While his ultimate source is the supreme deity, his immortal spirit or spark is imprisoned in the world of matter. (4) By secret knowledge (*gnosis*) and appropriate worship, man's spirit can win freedom from matter and ascend to the realm of light. Many Gnostic systems featured a redemptive figure who had descended from the heavens. Entrapped in the material world, he experienced great suffering. Triumph over his troubles enabled him to point the way for the faithful back to the spirit world from whence they had originally come. (5) The secret knowledge that results in salvation comes from supernatural revelation.

This outline of Gnostic notions is not applicable in every instance. Significant exceptions can be found to most of the points made. The simple truth is that Gnosticism is so varied and complex that it defies definition and description. Its origin is also difficult to determine. Some scholars claim that it existed in pre-Christian times. Pagan philosophical and religious ideas doubtless influenced the movement. Its characteristic dualism owes much to Persian thought transmitted through Judaism. All of our Gnostic documentation, however, stems from the Christian Era. The writings, despite their heterodox views, resort to Jewish-Christian vocabulary. The names of angels and demons and the intricate descriptions of celestial realms remind one of Jewish apocalyptic writings. Jewish sects "beyond the Jordan" were infected by the Gnostic virus as early as the second century A.D. Such data suggest that—whatever its derivation—Gnosticism as a discernible movement arose after Christ. Perhaps the catalytic agent was that the New Age proclaimed by many Jews and early Christians failed to materialize. Gnosticism transferred the place of man's hope of redemption from human to cosmic history and its date from the future to the timeless present. Its message was cogent and convincing to many, both inside and outside the church, and the competition it provided developing Christian orthodoxy was severe. Some defenders of the faith attempted to blunt the cutting edge of the Gnostic thrust by making use of Gnostic modes of interpretation. More often than not the Gnostic framework eclipsed the Christian message. Then the church had no option but to condemn Gnosticism as heretical.[1]

Concepts and Commitments: Religion

When Paul addressed Stoic and Epicurean philosophers at Athens, he asserted that the Athenians were "very religious" (Acts 17:22). Few statements are more easily documented. Greek polytheism was so luxuriant it fathered the legend that the population of the pantheon dwarfed that of Greece. Chief of the pantheon was Zeus, father of both gods and men. Although he remained the supreme being and retained control of the heavens, he shared his dominion with his two brothers. Poseidon ruled the sea, and Hades governed the underworld. All the gods had access to the earth. Their number was legion, and the responsibilities assigned to them were both specific and shifting.

A comprehensive treatment of Greek religion would be interesting and instructive, but it would take us far afield. We shall confine

The Temple of Jupiter (Zeus) at Baalbek. Only six of these graceful three-sectioned columns remain of the fifty-four which once surrounded the temple. Each column measures 65 feet from base to capital with a diameter of about 7⅓ feet.

[1]Two penetrating studies of Gnosticism are Hans Jonas, *The Gnostic Religion* (Boston: Beacon Press, 1958) and Robert M. Grant, *Gnosticism and Early Christianity* (New York: Columbia Univ. Press, 1959). For a brief but excellent survey of Christianity in its religious and cultural milieu, see Rudolf Bultmann, *Primitive Christianity in Its Contemporary Setting*, trans. R. H. Fuller (New York: Meridian Books, 1956).

our discussion to the mystery cults that attained wide popularity in the Roman Empire prior to and during the rise of Christianity. They were called "mysteries" because they received initiates by secret rites that the converts were not permitted to divulge. The secret knowledge the participant derived from the ceremonies supposedly enabled him to secure special blessings both in the present life and beyond the grave. The myths on which the mysteries were based changed from country to country, but a common thought pattern underlies them all. A wife (or mother) mourns the loss of a husband (or child). After a time of suffering, the lost one is restored (usually from the dead) to the mother (or wife) and starts a new life.

Demeter Prominent in the mystery cults was Demeter, goddess of vegetation. One day while her daughter Persephone (Kore) was picking flowers, she was captured by Hades (Pluto) and carried off to the nether world to be his wife. Demeter's grief caused her to neglect the earth, and all vegetation died. Zeus finally intervened, and Persephone was restored to her mother. However, since Persephone had eaten food while she was with Hades, she had to spend part of each year with him. When she descended to Hades, nature wasted away. When mother and daughter were united, the earth rejoiced and vegetation sprang to life. The many shrines built in honor of Demeter throughout the Greek world vividly underscored the importance of agriculture in the life of the people.

Eleusis The most influential of the Greek mysteries was celebrated at Eleusis, located on the coast about twelve miles west of Athens. The annual

Symbols of the Eleusinian Mystery Religion. The rose represents Persephone whose descent to Hades to be with Pluto caused her mother, Demeter, to mourn and to neglect the care of life in nature. When Persephone returned to her mother, the rebirth of nature, symbolized by the wheat, occurred.

The Hole to Hades. According to the Eleusinian myth, Persephone descended to Hades through this opening in the earth.

rituals began with a colorful procession from Athens and continued with the reenactment of Demeter's sorrow, Persephone's descent to the underworld, and her joyous return. The original motif of the mystic drama was the death and resurrection of the plant world, but the initiates soon saw in the crops' cycle of life and death the symbol of their own eternal destiny. Just as nature was reborn to beauty in the springtime, so they were assured of a blessed new life. The personal nature of the Eleusinian mysteries sharply distinguished them from the largely agricultural rituals connected with the worship of Demeter elsewhere. At first only residents of Eleusis were allowed membership. When Athens became dominant, Athenians were included. Later all Greeks became eligible. Finally, people of approved moral character were admitted irrespective of geography. Initiation was open to all classes—including women and slaves. Roman Emperors Augustus, Marcus Aurelius, and Commodus were accepted, but Nero was apparently rejected.

Dionysus   The cult of Dionysus (Bacchus) was second in popularity among the Greek mysteries. Dionysus, son of Zeus, was captured and consumed by the Titans, but his heart was saved by Semele, one of his father's wives. She subsequently presented Zeus with another Dionysus. Since it was believed that the human race sprang from the Titans, the divine spark that they acquired by devouring Dionysus inheres in all men. When devotees of Dionysus ate the raw flesh of the sacrificed animal and drank its warm blood, they experienced a frenzied ecstasy inspired by the very presence of the deity within the worshipers. This mystical union peeled away the mundane aspects of their existence, fanned the divine spark into a leaping flame, and enabled them to share in the life of the gods.

The Temple of Dionysus (Bacchus) at Baalbek. This most beautiful of the surviving Roman temples in Lebanon was once surrounded by fifty Corinthian columns each of which measured nearly 60 feet in height. The temple itself measured about 65 feet by 115 feet. Two-thirds of the area was reserved for the people. The rest of it, the sanctuary, was elevated about 12 feet and was reached by a stairway the width of the temple itself.

Although Dionysus, like Persephone, was a vegetation spirit who died and rose again, he was primarily the god of wine. As Demeter brought the grain from the ground, so Dionysus produced the inspiring wine. When devotees consumed the new wine, they were filled with his spirit. Women were especially attracted to the all-night ceremonies punctuated by wine-drinking and ecstatic dancing.[2]

A priceless fringe benefit of the cult of Dionysus was the theater. The two most important festivals of this god were celebrated in winter and spring. Greek comedy was designed to cheer the people during the dreary winter months; tragedy gave voice to their hopes and fears

[2]See *The Bacchae* by Euripides.

Theater of Dionysus, Athens. This theater was built within the sacred precincts of Dionysus Eleuthereus, whose cult was introduced into Athens in the sixth century B.C. The festival of the god included dances and choirs, dialogue and mime, which gave birth to ancient drama. Extensive changes were introduced into the theater during the second half of the fifth century to accommodate the finest drama of the ancient world, including the works of Sophocles, Euripides, and Aristophanes. The completed stone auditorium dates from about 330 B.C.

A Reconstruction of the Theater of Dionysus, Athens. This drawing was made after recent excavations made possible a more accurate reconstruction of the famous theater. To the left are seats for spectators and part of the colonnade. In the foreground are the orchestra, proscenium, and stage. [Courtesy of Historical Pictures Service—Chicago]

in springtime. When Paul arrived in Athens, he doubtless saw the 14,000-seat outdoor theater of Dionysus located on the southeast side of the Acropolis. There the finest drama of the ancient western world was produced, including the works of Sophocles, Euripides, and Aristophanes. An altar of Dionysus stood in the center of the orchestra.

Cybele and Attis

Greece was not the only mother of religion in the ancient world. India, Persia, Egypt, Palestine, Mesopotamia, Syria, and Asia Minor all had their own cults long before they came in contact with Greece. The Phrygian mysteries of Asia Minor centered around the mother goddess Cybele and the youthful male deity Attis. Cybele was a wild nature goddess who mourned the death of Attis until he rose to life again in the springtime. His triumph over death was the central theme of the spring festival. Devotees believed that by their attachment to Attis they certified a similar victory for themselves. The cult spread widely about the Mediterranean world and attained prominence in Rome during the first and second centuries of the Christian Era.

Aphrodite and Adonis

Aphrodite and Adonis played the Cybele-Attis role in the Syrian mysteries. Aphrodite personified mother-life in nature, and the male Adonis represented the dying and awakening vitality in vegetation. A mystic drama vividly portrayed lamentation due to Adonis' death and unabashed rejoicing upon his return to life. His followers confidently expected to enjoy his gracious favor both here and in the hereafter.

Isis and Osiris

The Isis-Osiris mystery developed in Egypt. Isis was the mother-goddess, and Osiris was her brother-husband responsible for vegetation. Osiris was slain by his wicked brother, Set, who deposited his body in the Nile. Heartbroken at her husband's demise, Isis searched far and wide for the body. Her efforts were finally crowned with success, and she returned with the body to Egypt and concealed it. One night while hunting, Set discovered the corpse, tore it limb from limb, and scattered the pieces throughout the land. The myth is told with many variations. According to some of them, Osiris was restored to life and made ruler of the underworld. What began as an interpretation of Egyptian agriculture, intended to insure the fertility of the soil, became an account of the death and resurrection of a deity. The transformation of the myth made it into a religion of personal redemption. Those who were initiated into its secret rites could triumph over death as had Osiris. The Ptolemies made Alexandria the center of the cult from whence it penetrated most of the Mediterranean world.

Mithra

Mithraism was the last mystery religion to achieve popularity in the Roman Empire. It was the only mystery made exclusively for men.

Roman Carvings at Baalbek. The rose symbolizes joy, the dart
suggests death, and the egg stands for eternal life.

Mithra was first worshiped by the ancient Aryans who took him with
them to India and Persia. When Pompey conquered the Cilician coast
of Asia Minor in 67 B.C., he returned to Rome with some prisoners
who honored the Aryan deity. Worship soon spread to the Roman
soldiers among whom it became as popular as conquest. Since Mithra
had long been associated with the bright sky, the Romans identified
him with the sun god and regarded him as the guardian of covenants
and the insurer of loyalty. It was noted that the sun waned during
late autumn, rested briefly (solstice), and then recovered its vigor.
Mithraists celebrated the sun's victory on December 25, the birthday
of their god. When Christianity defeated its competitor, the church
adopted the date of the pagan festival and declared it to be the
birthday of Christ.

Once Mithra had been a hero deity on earth who devoted himself
to the service of mankind. After a last supper, which highlighted

the success of his redemptive labors, he ascended to heaven. From there he continued to assist faithful followers in their earthly struggle against Satan and his demons. Initiation rites were elaborate. Candidates passed through seven grades that preenacted the passage of their souls through the seven heavens to the abode of the blessed. Entrance into each grade was made possible by the observance of washings, sacred meals, and other sacramental rites. Shrines of Mithra have been found wherever Roman soldiers were stationed. The mystery became so popular that it constituted Christianity's most formidable rival during the second and third centuries.

The mystery religions and Christianity shared common virtues. (1) They were international and universal in character. Membership was open to all (except in Mithraism) irrespective of sex, clan, city, state, or race. This feature was especially attractive during the fluid social situation that characterized the Roman Empire. People were reduced to their own responsibility, and they required a religion that would meet their needs under varying conditions of life. (2) They provided devotees with meaningful fellowship. Vital emotional entrance ceremonies and commonly held certitudes erased class consciousness and cemented the bonds of brotherhood. (3) They offered personal redemption through the favor of a suffering but victorious savior.

The rivalry that developed between the two systems was real and rigorous, but the advantages of hindsight make it clear that Christianity's victory was assured. It triumphed not because of what it shared with the mysteries, but because of its peculiar assets. Its four compelling advantages were novelty, antiquity, simplicity, and historicity. (1) It came upon the scene after the mysteries were well established. (2) It pointed to an honored and productive past despite its novelty. Its mother was Judaism, and it passed on to the world the rich moral heritage of that faith. (3) Its one God was a welcome relief from the waning and confusing diversity of deities that populated the ancient world. (4) The one God's incarnation in Christ was supported by the fulfilled prophecies of the Hebrew Scriptures and the manifold memories of eyewitnesses. The well-established superiority of Christianity over the mysteries, however, should not blind us to reality. The victor owed much to the work of the mysteries in preparing the soil for Christian planting.

The Jewish World

Abraham is the traditional ancestor of the Hebrews. He was also a Semite. Semites comprised the larger division of the Caucasian race that included the Babylonians, Assyrians, Aramaeans, Phoenicians, Arabs, and other peoples of southwest Asia. The term "Jew," which is often used to describe a person's religious commitment, did not achieve common coinage until the sixth century B.C.

The Oaks of Mamre. These trees are popularly believed to be the ones near which, according to Genesis 13:18, Abraham pitched his tent at Hebron.

The Much-Conquered Community

The power, prestige, and independence that the Hebrews enjoyed under the leadership of Saul, David, and Solomon diminished after 922 B.C. At Solomon's death, the kingdom was split in two. The ten northern tribes (called Israel) fell to the Assyrians in 721 B.C. Destruction, dispersion, and assimilation terminated their existence and caused them to be remembered as "the lost tribes of the house of Israel." In the South, Judah (and Benjamin, whose territory was probably held by Judah after 926 B.C.) managed to survive until the Babylonian conquest of 587 B.C. Then many of the Hebrews were taken into captivity. Since the Holy Temple was now destroyed and they were cut off from the Holy Land, circumstances compelled the Hebrews to develop new forms of religious expression and organization. The layman's religion of the synagogue eventually resulted.

Cyrus conquered the Babylonians in 539 B.C. and inaugurated a two-hundred-year period of Persian power. Although he gave the Hebrew exiles permission to return to their homeland, many were content to remain where they were. A tiny band did make their way to Jerusalem in 538 B.C., and slow migration continued for a century. The Jerusalemites soon observed the changed religious practices of the returnees. Since they had originally come from Judah, they were dubbed "Jews." From that time onward, "Jew" specified a man's religious commitment.[1]

The returned exiles promptly erected an altar, installed the Levites, and laid the foundation of the Second Temple. A dispute with the Samaritans terminated construction for a time, but at the insistence of the prophets Haggai and Zechariah, work was resumed in 520 B.C. Five years passed before the Temple was finished. About seventy years later, under the leadership of Nehemiah, the city walls were completed, and Jerusalem once again became the center of Jewish national and religious life. Although the Jews were unable to flex their political muscles, the Persians allowed them considerable freedom in domestic affairs.

The spectacular conquests initiated by *Alexander the Great* in 333 B.C. sounded the death knell of Persian domination and provided the Jews with a new master. At Alexander's death, his dominion was divided. Palestine was left sandwiched between the powerful Ptolemies of Egypt and the Seleucids of Syria. Since both sponsored Hellenism at the expense of local cultures, it mattered little to the Jews who was in control. (See pp. 3–5.) Egypt ruled throughout the third century B.C. Then Ptolemy V was decisively defeated by the Syrian Seleucid, Antiochus III, in 198 B.C. Antiochus III was eventually succeeded by his son, Antiochus IV.

[1]This is the *religious* definition. The *cultural* definition applies to those who, without formal religious affiliation, regard the teachings of Judaism (its literature, ethics, and folkways) as their own. The *practical* definition applies to people who consider themselves to be Jews or who are so considered by others.

Antiochus IV (175–163 B.C.) posed the greatest peril to the Jewish community since the Babylonian Exile. He called himself Epiphanes ("The Manifest" of Zeus), but his subjects soon tagged him Epimanes ("The Madman"). Just what motivated the Madman is a matter of dispute among historians. He was a fanatical devotee of the Greek way of life, and he doubtless resented Jewish resistance to Hellenization. He may well have bridled at the pro-Ptolemaic spirit in Palestine. Probably economic difficulties also stimulated his demonical deeds. Significant sums were required to control his far-flung holdings and to secure protection from his Egyptian enemies. But whatever his motives, his oppressive manners were unmistakable. Soon after his accession, he deposed the legitimate High Priest (Onias III) and sold the office to the highest bidder (Joshua). Joshua adopted the Greek name Jason and became the enthusiastic in-residence promoter of the Seleucids and all things Greek. He built a gymnasium in Jerusalem where young Jews followed Greek custom and exercised in the nude. Some even submitted to surgery to remove the marks of circumcision. Jason's successor permitted Antiochus to plunder the Temple. Such flagrant violations of the Law horrified the faithful and caused them to form an opposition movement called the Hasidim (pious It finally dawned upon Antiochus that he could not control the Jews until he destroyed their religion. An edict issued in 168 B.C. was designed to do precisely that. Temple rites were abolished. Circumcision, Sabbath observance, and possession of a copy of the Law were decreed capital offenses. An altar to Zeus was set up in the Temple, and swine were sacrificed upon it. This desecrating act (called "the abomination that makes desolate" in Daniel 11:31) bolstered the spine of Jewish resistance.

The Maccabean Revolt

When a Syrian officer came to the village of Modein to enforce the royal decrees, he compelled a Jew to worship Zeus. *Mattathias*, a Jewish priest, killed them both. Then Mattathias, together with his five sons and other sympathizers, took refuge in the rugged hill country of Judea. He persuaded the Hasidim to join him. Since they had been stunned by the slaughter of more than a thousand of their fellows who declined to defend themselves on the Sabbath, a soft sell was sufficient inducement. The combined forces resisted the Syrians in the name of their religion and their Law.

The Syrians scoffed at the anemic Jewish uprising. The patriots were hopelessly outnumbered, and their deficiencies in training, arms, and shekels bordered on the bizarre. But Antiochus underestimated the psychic strengths of the resisters. What they lacked in numbers, skill, and substance they more than compensated for with bravery, ingenuity, and religious dedication. Like so many emerging countries in the twentieth century, they turned from orthodox warfare to guerrilla tactics.

Mattathias died in 166 B.C., and his son *Judas* (166–160 B.C.) assumed command of military operations. Judas proved to be such a ferocious fighter that he was named Maccabeus ("The Hammerer"),[2] and the resistance movement that he led became known as the Maccabean Revolt. Against insuperable odds, Judas and his men turned initial defeats into victory. Near the close of 165 B.C., they captured the Temple in Jerusalem, rebuilt the altar, and restored the worship of the Lord. Each year (about the time Christians celebrate Jesus' birth) Jews commemorate this triumphal event through their ceremony of Hanukkah (Dedication), the Feast of Lights.[3]

Now that religious freedom had been assured, many of the Hasidim were ready to terminate the revolt. The Maccabees, though, were in no mood to surrender. Judea was not free, Syrian armies posed intermittent danger, Jews were maltreated in some places, the enemy controlled the Acra (a military fortress overlooking the Temple area), and a vigorous group of Jewish Hellenists continued to covet the high priesthood and court the Seleucids. So Judas and his followers valiantly continued the fight until his death. Since the Hasidim preferred the leadership of the Maccabees to that of the pro-Syrian priestly families, they had little choice but to render lukewarm support. What had begun as a struggle for religious freedom soon developed into a drive for political independence.

Jonathan (160–142 B.C.) succeeded his brother Judas as military leader. He proved to be a wily warrior and a daring diplomat. He capitalized on Syrian weakness to enlarge the territory under Jewish control and enhance his family name. Despite his proven ability and noteworthy accomplishments, he was lulled by flattery and seduced by pseudo promises. When he met death at the hands of a contender for the Syrian throne, Simon stepped in to fill the void.

Simon (142–135 B.C.) was the last surviving son of Mattathias. He rebuilt the fortresses of the land, filled them with food, and backed the successful contender for the Syrian throne. The Syrian king reciprocated by renouncing all claims to Judea. Simon's followers gratefully proclaimed him High Priest even though he was not a member of the priestly family. That same year (142 B.C.), they began to date their documents and contracts "In the first year of Simon, the great high priest and commander and leader of the Jews."[4] A year

---

[2]The word from which "Maccabeus" was probably derived means a small mallet used by a skilled workman. It thus suggests the rapier-like attacks that characterized Judas' early tactics.

[3]C. Milo Connick, *Jesus: The Man, the Mission, and the Message* (Englewood Cliffs, N.J.: Prentice-Hall, 1963), p. 17.

[4]I Maccabees 13:42.

later, they bestowed upon him the title of ethnarch or governor and granted his heirs the right of hereditary succession. The seed of the Hasmonean dynasty (named after Hashmon, a Maccabean forebear) had now been planted.

Succeeding generations of ruler-priests devoted themselves to the task of transforming Judea into a Jewish nation. Simon's son, John Hyrcanus, ruled from 135 to 105 B.C. After a bungling beginning, he made marked progress toward recovering the territory that once had comprised the Davidic kingdom. He marched east "beyond the Jordan," north to ravage the Samaritans and destroy their temple atop Mt. Gerizim, and south to subdue Idumea. He switched his sympathies from the popular and pious "Pharisees" to the noble and politically oriented "Sadducees." He symbolized his Hellenistic proclivities by changing the names of his three young sons from Judas, Mattathias, and Jonathan to Aristobulus, Antigonus, and Alexander Janneus.

Aristobulus I (105–104 B.C.), the first to claim the title of king, had a brief and brutal rule. He was succeeded by a brother he had imprisoned, Alexander Janneus (104–78 B.C.). Alexander had inherited a double portion of his father's desire to conquer and convert Northern Palestine, and he set to work at once to satisfy his desire. Success crowned his efforts on the west coast from Gaza to Mt. Carmel (excepting Ashkelon) and east of the Jordan in Gadara and other cities. Under his leadership, the Hasmonean dynasty reached its territorial height. His insatiable appetite for expansion and his ruthless extermination of many Jewish leaders, however, cost him the support of the Pharisees—whose spiritual ancestors (the Hasidim) had made possible the original Maccabean rise to power. He had to resort to mercenaries to fight his battles since most Jews regarded him with distaste. His worldly ways offended sensitive religionists and stimulated a redirection of the people's hopes. Many began to mute the figure of priest and to trumpet that of the Son of Man—a preexistent, supernatural being who would descend from the clouds at the end of the age to institute Final Judgment. Such a being could never be mistaken for a Hasmonean! Sometime during the tenure of John Hyrcanus and his sons, an ultra-pious group of Jews retired to the hills overlooking the Dead Sea. They founded a semimonastic community at Qumran devoted to rigorous religious practices. From their scriptorium came the now-famous Dead Sea Scrolls.

Alexandra (78–69 B.C.), widow of Alexander Janneus, ruled shrewdly and sensibly for nine years. She made peace with the Pharisees and granted them a large measure of authority in local matters.

Since she could not serve as High Priest, she appointed her hapless son, Hyrcanus II, to that office. This infuriated his able and more ambitious brother, Aristobulus II. When the aged lady became ill and desired to leave the throne to Hyrcanus, Aristobulus recruited an army. At the Queen Mother's death, Aristobulus drove Hyrcanus from Jerusalem and moved into the palace.

Aristobulus II (69–63 B.C.) was soon stung by the intrigue of Antipater, an influential Idumean. He persuaded the effeminate Hyrcanus to purchase insurance against his hostile brother. Aretas III, king of Petrine Arabia, gladly issued the policy. The premium for the promised protection was the return to the Arabians of a dozen cities wrested from them by Alexander Janneus. The scheme worked wonderfully. Aretas, with generous assistance from disgruntled Pharisees, defeated Aristobulus whose men deserted him. Bitter civil strife ensued. Since Rome was now in control of the collapsed Syrian domain, Hyrcanus (backed by Antipater) and Aristobulus sent separate delegations to Damascus in 63 B.C. to seek the support of Pompey. A third delegation, probably dispatched by the Pharisees, argued for abolition of the monarchy and return to pre-Maccabean nonpolitical priestly rule. While Pompey cogitated, Aristobulus acted. He captured the fortress of Alexandrium. The Roman commander interpreted the brash act as a threat, subdued the fortress, and marched his men toward Jerusalem. The fate of the Jews seemed to be sealed.

The ignominious end of a hundred years of Hasmonean rule could not erase several of its distinguished and lasting accomplishments. (1) The Jewish nation and the Jewish religion became forces to be reckoned with even by the major powers. Minor nations were subdued by the Jews and forced to wear their religious yoke. (2) Temple worship was restored, the study of the Law was intensified, and the role of the scribes was greatly expanded. (3) The Pharisees and Sadducees developed as religious and political parties. (4) Belief in the resurrection of the dead and the hope of a meaningful life after death achieved prominence.

Roman Rule: The Herodians[5]

Pompey besieged Jerusalem for three months in 63 B.C. A breach in the city wall opened the way to terrible butchery. Although he spared the Temple treasures and allowed Temple worship to continue, he appalled the inhabitants by barging into the Holy of Holies. This sacred spot, which popular theology considered the dwelling place of the Lord, could be entered only once a year by the High Priest.

[5]Connick, *Jesus: The Man, the Mission, and the Message,* pp. 17, 18, 41–44.

Pompey's victory erased the last vestige of Jewish independence. The land fell under Roman control, Samaria and Galilee were appended to the Roman province of Syria, the Greek cities along the seacoast and beyond the Jordan were freed, and the shrunken Jewish state was subjected to the administration of the Roman legate of Syria. Pompey abolished the kingship and established Hyrcanus II as High Priest and ethnarch. The real power behind Hyrcanus, however, was Antipater, the wealthy and potent Idumean governor. Antipater scrupulously carried out Roman policies and managed to retain the favor of a succession of leaders during the terrible years of the civil war in Rome. Rome gratefully granted him citizenship and named his son, Herod, prefect of Galilee. Herod soon distinguished himself by capturing and executing some "bandits." Rome's response was larger responsibilities for her efficient servant. Antipater's son was further rewarded in 40 B.C. when the Roman Senate appointed him "king of the Jews." For three years disturbances in Jerusalem thwarted him from ascending the throne.

Herod (40–4 B.C.) *Herod* was extremely successful as a Roman vassal. He switched sides with the alacrity of his father, and his kingdom expanded until it included all of Palestine. As a promoter of Hellenism he had no peer. He rebuilt old cities in the Greek image and named them after relatives. New cities, like Caesarea, became the talk of the times. Hippodromes, theaters, amphitheaters, and stadiums were constructed. But by far the most famous of Herod's edifices was the rebuilt Temple in Jerusalem. He gilded its stones with gold and stretched its size with courts and porticoes until it swelled the pride of pilgrims. One of Jesus' disciples was so awed by its magnificence that he exclaimed, "Look, Teacher, what wonderful stones and what wonderful buildings!" (Mk. 13:1). Herod also supported emperor worship and built temples in honor of the divine Augustus.

Herod's place in history is a matter of dispute. Some scholars acclaim him Israel's greatest king; others accuse him of destroying all that the Maccabees had valued. He doubtless deserved his political title, "The Great." He maintained peace, promoted the arts, and gave unstinting loyalty to Rome. But his capability was often clouded by his cruelty and cunning. Most Jews saw him as a self-seeking, bloodthirsty tyrant. They despised his Idumean ancestry, and they decried his devotion to Hellenism, polygamy, and fratricide. His ambitious building programs induced monetary migraines, and his suspicious nature flooded the land with secret police in search of the slightest scent of disloyalty. He coldly executed his mother-in-law, his favorite wife (one of ten), and three of his sons because of their alleged designs on the throne. All were Hasmoneans, which provided logic for his madness. According to Matthew 2:16, he also massacred all of the male children of Bethlehem who were two years old or under. It is small wonder Josephus wrote that the lot of those who survived Herod's sword made them envy those who were slain.[6] Herod's half-Hebrew heritage, marriage to the Hasmonean princess Mariamne, Temple construction, reduction of taxes during difficult times, and provision of food during famine failed to neutralize his people's hatred. If a certain Babe had not been born in Bethlehem shortly before his death, he might long since have become a minor memory in the Western World.

Herod's Sons   The death of Herod the Great in 4 B.C. plunged Palestine into a power struggle. In his last will, Herod had divided his kingdom among his three sons—half to Archelaus and a quarter each to the other two. Archelaus was named king of Judea, Idumea, and Samaria. Herod Antipas was made tetrarch of Galilee and Perea. Herod Philip was designated tetrarch of the region northeast of Galilee (including Trachonitus, Batanea, Gaulinitus, and other small areas). Since their father had stipulated that Augustus must approve the will, the rush to Rome was on. Archelaus hastened to the emperor as soon as he had cruelly crushed a revolt. Antipas and Philip quickly followed to press their respective claims. A delegation of Jews from Jerusalem also appeared. They cataloged the deceased Herod's crimes, lodged charges against Antipas, and pleaded for self-government under Roman supervision. While Augustus deliberated, Judea rioted. The rebellion spread like wildfire, and the prompt intervention of Roman legions was required to halt the holocaust. Thousands of Jews reaped the reward of slavery or death. Augustus finally decided to approve Herod's will with a single exception. He demoted Archelaus to ethnarch until such time as he should prove to be worthy of being king. Some scholars believe that Archelaus' quest for a kingdom suggested to Jesus the allegory recorded in Luke 19:11–27: "A nobleman went into a far country to receive kingly power and then return."

Herod Antipas (4 B.C.–39 A.D.) served as tetrarch of Galilee and Perea while Jesus grew to manhood and conducted his ministry. Since Antipas shared his father's cleverness and conceit, Jesus aptly characterized him as "that fox" (Lk. 13:32). He had a bent for building, too. He rebuilt Sepphoris, the ancient capital located a short distance from Nazareth. His most ambitious and imposing project, though, was the city of Tiberias. Named after Emperor Tiberius, it was constructed in part over the remains of an old cemetery. Jews regarded it as ritually unclean and shunned it as they would a Samaritan. Antipas was forced to import Gentiles to provide the place with a

[6]*Antiquities*, XVII. 11, 2.

Entrance to Petra. Notice the sheer cliffs which bound the gorge leading to the rose-red city, capital of the Nabateans, which the poet described as "half as old as time."

population. What irony that of all the lakeside cities, Tiberias alone should see the twentieth century!

Herod's forty-three-year tenure as tetrarch testifies to his Roman worth. The Jewish people gave him a considerably lower rating. Most of his difficulties were domestic. Threatened by the Nabateans, a vigorous Arab people whose rose-red capital at Petra is said to be the Eighth Wonder of the World, he married the daughter of their king. All went well until Herod lost his head over Herodias, who was described by Mark as "his brother Philip's wife" (6:17–18).[7]

_____

[7]Herodias, in fact, was not married to Philip. She was the wife of Herod II, a half-brother of Antipas, who lived in Rome as a private citizen. This union produced a daughter, Salome; she was Antipas' "brother Philip's wife." Herodias was the daughter of another half-brother, Aristobulus, and hence Antipas' niece. Niece-marriage was

The Khazneh or Treasury at Petra. Carved out of the multicolored sandstone cliffs, which remind one of Utah's Zion National Park, the Khazneh is the best preserved of the monuments at Petra.

When he brazenly decided to marry her, his Nabatean princess ran home to King Aretas. Antipas decapitated John the Baptist because he denounced the tetrarch's marital muddle.[8] War broke out between Antipas and Aretas in 36 A.D., and the army of Antipas was demolished. The Jews saw Herod's defeat as divine punishment for the beheading of John the Baptist.

Herod's harsh treatment of John may have disturbed the tetrarch's conscience. As Jesus increased in favor with men, Herod reasoned that Jesus was John the Baptist raised from the dead (Mt. 14:1–2). Later it was rumored that Herod determined to kill Jesus (Lk. 13:31).

---

not the issue. What was disapproved, under the circumstances, was Herodias' marriage to Herod II, who was still living. Even if they had been divorced, her marriage to Antipas was clearly contrary to Leviticus 20:21: "If a man takes his brother's wife, it is impurity." Such a sister-in-law marriage would have been proper only if the Roman Herod had died and his marriage to Herodias had been childless.

[8]Josephus, contrary to the Gospels, attributes the deed to fear of rebellion.

On the night before Jesus was crucified, Herod grilled the Galilean to no avail. All the while the real danger resided in the bosom of Herod's overly ambitious wife. Herodias persuaded her husband to travel to Rome to demand a royal title. Damning charges tarnished his image, the demand was refused, Herod was banished, and his tetrarchy was turned over to his wife's brother, Agrippa.

Herod Philip (4 B.C.–34 A.D.), tetrarch of the region northeast of Galilee, ruled without renown or reproach. Peace and tranquility characterized his reign. He was content with one wife, Salome, the daughter of Herodias and Herod II. His subjects were largely Gentile, and they apparently regarded him with genuine affection. Like the other Herods, he indulged his desire to build. For his capital, he constructed a splendid city near the headwaters of the Jordan River and called it Caesarea in honor of the emperor. "Philippi" was added to the name to distinguish it from the more important city on the seacoast. It was in the region of Caesarea Philippi that Peter acknowledged Jesus to be the Christ (Mk. 8:27–33). Philip also built Bethsaida, a city situated on the east bank of the Jordan where it enters the Sea of Galilee. He called it Julias in honor of the daughter of Augustus. It was probably to Bethsaida Julias that Jesus retired to escape the clutches of Herod Antipas (Lk. 9:10). When Philip died without issue in 34 A.D., his tetrarchy was united with Syria for three years. Then it was assigned for a like period to Agrippa I.

Archelaus (4 B.C.–6 A.D.) quickly revealed himself to be the blackest of Herod's sheep by ruling Judea, Idumea, and Samaria with reckless and despotic abandon. He shocked Jewish sensibilities by marrying his brother's widow.[9] His vast building projects impoverished the people, and his high-handed dismissal of high priests dismayed them. When Joseph "heard that Archelaus reigned over Judea in place of his father Herod, he was afraid to go there" (Mt. 2:22). A decade of malpractice prompted his subjects to protest. Augustus banished him to Gaul, his ethnarchy was reduced to an imperial province, and Judea was placed under the direct rule of a succession of procurators. The only significant break in their administration occurred when Herod Agrippa I (41–44 A.D.) ruled over virtually all of the kingdom of his grandfather, Herod the Great.

Roman Rule: The Procurators (6–66 A.D.)[10] Rome sent at least fourteen procurators to Judea from 6 to 66 A.D., but only three of them (Pilate, Felix, and Festus) are mentioned in the New Testament. They made Caesarea their capital and usually came to Jerusalem only during the great religious festivals when disorders might be brewing. At their disposal were cohorts of soldiers

---

[9]Josephus, *Antiquities*, XVII, 13,1.
[10]Connick, *Jesus: The Man, the Mission, and the Message*, pp. 42, 43, 47.

recruited from non-Jewish cities. Although they possessed complete administrative, judicial, financial, and military authority, their primary responsibilities were to keep the peace and to speed the flow of tax money into the imperial treasury. They doubtless beamingly approved Jesus' admonition to "render therefore to Caesar the things that are Caesar's" (Mt. 22:21).

The popular picture of Judea writhing for sixty years beneath the boots of sadistic and predatory procurators is a libelous legacy from bygone days. Financial abuses, which had once ravaged the provinces, no longer prevailed. Procurators received a fixed salary. Tax collectors were also salaried officials whose books were subject to microscopic scrutiny. One fly remained in the ointment. Internal revenue or customs was still farmed out to the highest bidders. These creatures are called "publicans" in the Gospels and regularly linked with prostitutes and sinners.

The procurators usually respected local customs, and they granted the Jews a maximum of local control. The Jews ruled themselves through their Sanhedrin, a court composed of seventy priests, scribes, and elders. At only one point was its authority restricted: the death penalty apparently required the procurator's ratification. The Sanhedrin was presided over by a high priest who owed his appointment to the Roman administrator. By the simple expedient of withholding or releasing the sacred vestments, Rome made the office a political prize to be grasped. The Law of Moses governed the Sanhedrin and regulated all phases of existence. (A local Sanhedrin had jurisdiction over each of Judea's eleven districts.) Sanhedrin authority was technically confined to Judea, but its influence on Jewish life and practice was far more extensive.

The first four procurators are merely names to most of us, but the fifth played a prominent role in the Christian drama. *Pontius Pilate* (26–36 A.D.) presided at Jesus' trial, and he alone was legally responsible for the Galilean's death. These facts have blackened his image beyond repair in Christian circles. Unfortunately, they do not stand out as isolated incidents of stupidity or malice. Pilate found it difficult to respect Jewish sensitivities. He smuggled military insignia bearing the emperor's image into Jerusalem by night. Such stubborn defiance of the commandment that forbade images enraged the populace. When protesting Jews were threatened with death, they boldly bared their necks and Pilate's soldiers were forced to withdraw. On another occasion, at the cost of many lives, he took money from the Temple treasury to build an aqueduct to Jerusalem. He mingled the blood of Galileans with their sacrifices (Lk. 13:1). Although he could find no crime in Jesus, in order to placate the crowd he reportedly made the illegal suggestion that Jesus be chastized. When the crowd protested such mild treatment, he washed his hands of Jesus and justice (Mt. 27:11–26). What really brought about Pilate's downfall was a ruthless attack upon a credulous crowd of Samaritans. They had come to Mt. Gerizim to inspect some sacred objects believed to have been hidden there by Moses. What they saw instead was the sword. Pilate was summoned to Rome and dismissed for his brutality. Eusebius states that the procurator was forced to become his own slayer.[11]

Pilate is often viewed through prisms of prejudice, but scholars tend to regard him with mixed emotions. They readily acknowledge his occasional heavy-handed clashes with his subjects, but they also point to his vigorous maintenance of order and his sincere desire to better his province. He held office longer than any other procurator. For ten years Tiberius, who kept a close watch on his subordinates and tolerated no unrest or malmanagement, found no serious fault in Pilate's administration.

The role of the procurators was not altogether enviable. Judea was a troublesome territory. The Jews resented foreign domination, and they resisted Hellenization. Minor "prophets" repeatedly surfaced and promised the people relief from Roman rule. Open hostility flared up under Felix (c. 52–58 A.D.) before whom the Apostle Paul was summoned for a hearing. The procurator was so ruthless in suppressing his opponents (called Sicarii because of their concealed knives) that he managed to make them martyrs. This caused more people to join their ranks. An Egyptian led 4,000 Sicarii out into the wilderness.[12] The revolutionaries were quickly dispersed by the Romans, who slaughtered several hundreds of them. Festus (c. 58–62) was a champion of milder measures, but the two remaining procurators resorted to strong-arm methods. Albinus (62–64 A.D.) compounded the confusion by releasing a flock of prisoners prior to his recall to Rome to face charges of graft and harsh treatment of innocents. Brigands then roamed the country at will. Florus (64–66 A.D.) plundered the Temple treasury. When the Jews protested, he ordered many of them crucified. By 66 A.D., the seeds of revolt had sprouted.

Revolts Against Rome (66–135 A.D.) A rash of revolts proved to be contagious. Zealots stormed Roman strongholds in search of weapons. The Syrian legate made an ill-fated attempt to subdue Jerusalem late in 66 A.D. Then Rome played her trump card. She sent the perceptive and prestigious commander,

---

[11]*Ecclesiastical History*, II, 7.
[12]Acts 21:38; contrast Josephus, *Wars*, II, 2.

Vespasian, to quell the rebellion. Nero's death in 69 A.D. halted the hostilities for several months. Vespasian returned to Rome to become emperor, and his son, Titus, resumed the war. The catastrophic end came in 70 A.D., although remnants of resistance remained for three years more. Jerusalem was badly damaged, the Temple lay in ruins (there was not left "one stone upon another" [Mk. 13:2]), and for the third time in their turbulent history the Jews suffered such a crushing defeat that survival seemed to be unlikely.

Jewish Christians fled to Pella in Perea during the dark days of inevitable defeat. It seemed to them that the impending destruction would be a fitting punishment upon the people who had murdered their Master. Mainstream Jews, in turn, found it hard to forgive the deserters who sat out the war in the safety of Perea. This mutual misunderstanding contributed to the growing separation between the church and the synagogue. Pharisee Johanan ben Zakkai also left the fated city before its fall. At Jamnia, according to a long-standing tradition, he called a council of rabbinical scholars about 90 A.D. This "Council of Jamnia" has been credited with commendable accomplishments: preserving the Jewish religion, canonizing its sacred texts, and substituting the study of ritual law for the sacrificial system. Although a school of scholars did exist at Jamnia, there is no convincing evidence that there was a Council of Jamnia or that the canon was closed at that time. Some writings (such as Canticle of Canticles and Ecclesiastes) were discussed by the scholars, but arguments about their status persisted for decades.

Two additional attempts were made by Jews to wrest freedom from Rome. Rebellions broke out in Egypt, Mesopotamia, and other places during Trajan's reign (98–117 A.D.). Thousands of Jews sacrificed their lives in the lost cause. The second and final revolt occurred in Palestine during Hadrian's rule (117–138 A.D.). The Emperor planned to build a stately new city on the ruins of Jerusalem. As long as the Holy City lay prostrate, a restored Zion was a live option. The construction of a heathen metropolis there would doom this dream forever. Imagine a temple to Zeus where God's house had once dominated the landscape! Hadrian also prohibited circumcision. The edict was part of a general ban against bodily mutilation, and it was primarily aimed at castration—a common practice in the sect of Cybele, which enjoyed rapid growth on Roman soil. The Jews thought Hadrian was a latter-day Antiochus Epiphanes, and the fat was in the fire. Under the leadership of Simon ben Kosibah (or bar Cocheba), a three-year rebellion began in 132 A.D. The venerable Rabbi Akiba viewed Simon as Messiah. Akiba rallied his countrymen to Simon's colors, but the champions of circumcision never had a chance. At the close of the disastrous struggle, Jerusalem was rebuilt

Jamnia (Jabneel, Modern Yebna). Located nine miles north-northeast of Ashdod, Jamnia was the traditional site of the alleged council of rabbinical scholars about 90 A.D. which is said to have reviewed the collection of Jewish sacred writings and reached conclusions which had great significance for both Jews and Christians in matters pertaining to the canon of the Old Testament.

as a Roman city (Aelia Capitolina), and Jews were prohibited from entering it on pain of death. Years later the ban was lifted ever so slightly; they were permitted to enter its gates once a year for a day of mourning.

The Dispersion While modern man is accustomed to Jews residing in concentrated numbers in many parts of the world, he is often surprised to learn that there are more Jews who live in New York City than in Israel. His surprise turns to astonishment when he discovers that in Jesus' day more Jews lived in Alexandria than in Jerusalem, more outside of Palestine than in it. Mesopotamia, Egypt, and Asia Minor-Syria each counted a million in their midst.

Many Jews continued to pay the half-shekel to support the Temple and traveled great distances to participate in the major festivals there. Acts 2:9-11 indicates that Jews came from Parthia, Media, Persia, Mesopotamia, Judea, Cappadocia, the Pontus, Asia, Phrygia, Pamphylia, Egypt, parts of Libya, Cyrene, Rome, Crete, and Arabia to attend Pentecost. They had been away so long that they were foreigners in the Fatherland. They no longer spoke the native tongue; they babbled in the vernaculars of their places of residence.

Several factors contributed to the Jewish dispersion. (1) War provided the initial stimulus. The rapid military expansion that occurred during the reigns of David and Solomon prompted Jews to go into many parts of Africa and Asia—as administrators, colonists, and tradesmen. The Assyrian and Babylonian exiles multiplied the dispersed many-fold. Contrary to popular belief, most of the exiles never did return. They became permanent residents of their adopted country. (2) Commercial interests enticed Jews to far-away lands from the beginning of Israel's history. Fascinated by personal and financial profit, sizable numbers elected to stay abroad where they were joined by those transplanted by war. (3) The trend toward universalism in Jewish thought gave theological support to foreign residence. The authors of II Isaiah, Ruth, and Jonah proclaimed that all nations are on an equal footing before God.

Centuries of subjugation, intermittently broken by brief periods of relative independence, profoundly affected the faith of the Jews. That faith, in turn, enabled the Jews to triumph over tragedy and—perhaps even more startling—to survive the repeated and ultimate downfall of their nation. Since it was Israel's religious commitment that made her a peculiar people, we shall consider in the following chapter the faith of the Jews that sustained the community throughout its periods of peril.

The Jewish Religion

The sacred story of the Hebrews began with the Exodus. It was the decisive historical happening that transformed a people into a self-conscious community. Two compelling facts make this clear. (1) The four books of the Bible that deal with the Exodus and the Wanderings (Exodus through Deuteronomy) cover a comparatively short time span. Yet they are nearly as lengthy as the account of the next six hundred years. (2) The Exodus was an ever-recurring theme of several prophets. Hosea 11:1, for example, declares: "When Israel was a child, I loved him, and out of Egypt I called my son."

The Biblical account indicates that Moses was the central figure of the Exodus. Born of humble Hebrew parents and brought up as an Egyptian, he early identified himself with his people. Years later, God called him from his desert asylum to free the Hebrew slaves. The reluctant recruit finally consented, and a full-fledged power struggle with the Egyptian Pharaoh resulted. The Lord empowered Moses to plague the Pharaoh into submission. Success came after nine failures. When the angel of death *passed over* the Hebrews and struck dead the firstborn of the Egyptians, the Pharaoh yielded. But his melting heart soon hardened again, and he sent his chariots in hot pursuit of the fleeing Hebrews. The sea parted for Moses and his company, but it closed in on the Egyptians. "Thus the Lord saved Israel that day . . . and the people feared the Lord; and they believed . . . in his servant Moses" (Exod. 14:30–31).

The Covenant Community[1] When the Hebrews plunged into the wilderness, their faith began to flicker. Food and water were in as short supply as patience with Moses' leadership. Disciplined by daily dependence on manna and distraught by enemy attacks, they finally staggered into the Sinai oasis. There the Lord offered them a special relationship. It was not a bargain struck by equals; it was a suzerainty Covenant akin

[1]C. Milo Connick, *Jesus: The Man, the Mission, and the Message* (Englewood Cliffs, N.J.: Prentice-Hall, 1963), pp. 7, 8.

to that made by a king with his vassals. Out of gratitude for God's deliverance from Egypt, the Hebrews accepted His offer and obligated themselves to live in accordance with His Commandments. The bond's prospective rewards and potential punishments were directed toward the community. If a person did not share in the life of the group, he did not share in the Covenant.

It is said that for forty years the Hebrews wandered in the wilderness. Actually most of their time was spent in the region of Kadesh-barnea, an oasis in southern Palestine. The older generation passed away. Joshua succeeded Moses. Sons of the wanderers, disciplined by divine denials and driven by a renewed commitment to the Covenant, turned their faces toward the Promised Land. The conquest was neither sudden nor total. The successful assault on the highlands had to be followed after Joshua's death by a protracted struggle for possession of the bulk of Canaan. The Hebrews operated in a loose confederation during the prolonged probing; the twelvefold tribal pattern stemmed from the twelve sons of Jacob (Israel). The tribes held festivals at a central sanctuary (Schechem, then Shiloh), rehearsed their history, recalled their deliverance from Egypt, renewed their commitment to the Sinai Covenant, and recited their common regulations and obligations. They called their covenant community "Israel" to signify that they had personally participated in the Exodus. Others were welcomed to the community if they were willing to adopt that tradition as their own.

The Canaanite Compromise

Agriculture was the basis of Canaanite culture, and agriculture and religion were intimately intertwined. The gods governed fertility. El headed the pantheon, and Asherah was his consort. Next in rank was Baal, a storm god who wed his sister, Anath (Ashtart), renowned for her sexual passion. The union of Baal and Anath symbolized the fertility of the fields. Since reproductive powers were associated with particular towns or localities, there were as many Baals and Ashtarts as there were cities. Each was regarded as an earthly manifestation of the great Baal and Ashtart who dwelt in heaven. Since life was precarious at best in the so-called Fertile Crescent, it came naturally for the inhabitants to equate fertility and faith. They saw agriculture in a divine dimension. The ground was the locus of divine power; the Baal of a given area was its "Lord" or "Owner." Productivity depended upon sexual union between the Baal and his "Lady." Canaanite agriculture would have shriveled and died without rain. Rain fell from heaven. Earth and water mingled. Parched Palestine sprang to life once again, and a fruitful harvest was assured.

The divine drama was not a spectator sport. Canaanites were convinced that if they personally participated in it they could assist the cosmic powers in reaching their goal. So the people gathered in their temples to reenact the Baal epic, including the practice of sacred prostitution. The male played the role of Baal, the woman that of Ashtart. By the simple process of imitative magic, human mates were believed capable of triggering the divine partners into productive union.

Israel took a candid camera shot of Canaanite culture and blushed. As time passed, however, she learned to take a time exposure without blinking an eye. Her nomadic ways were unsuited to a settled life. If she was to survive in an agrarian economy, she reasoned, it would be necessary to adopt the ways of the natives. Baal was the lord of the land, the giver of rain, and the guarantor of fertility. Israel could anticipate a bountiful harvest only if she worshipped him according to the customs of the Canaanites. So parents began to name their children after Baal and bring statuettes of Ashtart into their homes. No affront to the Exodus-Covenant God was intended. The Israelites still remembered him in times of military crisis, but they looked to Baal to insure the fertility of their fields.

The two religions were as compatible as horseradish and candy. Canaanite gods were sexual, and sex played a decisive part in their worship. The purpose of piety was to control the gods for the benefit of man. Israelite worship was based upon obedience and service. The Lord was jealous; He would tolerate no rivals. His lordship was unconditional; it permeated every aspect of life. When Israel commenced to compartmentalize life—asserting that her God was the lord of history and Baal the lord of the land—she violated the terms of the Covenant: "You shall have no other gods before me" (Exod. 20:3). For centuries her spiritual leaders would find it necessary to remind her of this truth.

The tribal confederacy proved to be too weak to cope with Israel's enemies. The people clamored to keep up with the Canaanites. They, too, wanted a king. Samuel reluctantly agreed, and the United Kingdom's ship of state was launched. David captured Jerusalem and made it the political capital. Then he moved the sacred Ark there to make Jerusalem the Holy City as well. Solomon built the first Temple during his reign.

Worship was not centralized in the Holy City, but as time passed the Temple and its priests grew in importance and influence. Animal sacrifice was the principal rite, both in the Temple and in the village shrines. Although its purposes were many, one object was to reconcile the sinner to the Lord. The worshiper offered the animal's life in place of his own, and the Lord accepted it as a fitting substitute.

Cedars of Lebanon. The mountains of Lebanon provided the major source of cedar in Biblical times. Cedars grow only one inch in twenty years. Their hard wood was prized for its carving qualities and its fragrance. Solomon used huge quantities of cedar wood for the construction of the Temple. [Courtesy of Culver Pictures]

Another aim was communion. Part of the slain animal was burned on the altar; the rest was eaten by the worshipers. The ceremony cemented the bond of fellowship between the Lord and His people. Springtime and harvest festivals, also occasions for worship, were not merely agricultural rites. They served as mighty memorials to the decisive events in Israelite history.

After Solomon's death in 922 B.C, the land was divided into the Northern Kingdom of Israel and the Southern Kingdom of Judah. For two centuries Israel overshadowed her smaller, less populous and prosperous sister to the south. War between the two gave way to close collaboration when Omri became king of Israel. Omri built the city of Samaria and restored much lost territory beyond the Jordan. Ahab, his son and successor, married Jezebel—a dedicated devotee of the Phoenician deity, Melkart (Baal). Jezebel promoted her faith with calculated zeal. Had it not been for Elijah's successful challenge of the alien cult atop Mt. Carmel, she might have converted the country. A century later, the prophet Amos appeared from the South and denounced the nation's social insensitivity, callous corruption, and religious syncretism. Shortly before the final phase of Assyrian expansion, Hosea added a note of hope to Amos' message of doom. He declared that the Lord would forgive Israel and love her. Damascus fell to Assyria in 732 B.C., and, after a three-year struggle, Israel's capital of Samaria succumbed in 721 B.C. The lament of Amos had been actualized: "Fallen, no more to rise, is the virgin Israel" (5:2).

The Deuteronomic Reform[2]

While Israel was violently dashing from dynasty to dynasty, the single royal line of David sat on Judah's throne. This made her transition from tribalism to town life less traumatic. The summit of her success was reached under King Uzziah (738–742 B.C.). When he died, the atmosphere was clouded with foreboding. Who could succeed him? Judah's prophet-priest, Isaiah, trumpeted the answer: "My eyes have seen *the* King, the Lord of hosts!" (6:6). The added italics retains the prophet's emphasis. Judah's real dependence was not on the dynasty of David but upon the King of Kings!

Assyria reached the pinnacle of her power during the seventh century. For forty-two years Hezekiah's son, Manasseh, occupied Judah's throne and dutifully complied with the commands of his Assyrian superiors. With clocklike precision he promoted paganism, including sacred prostitution and child sacrifice. No prophet's voice was heard during his reign. His son succeeded him for two years; then a court coup placed the eight-year-old Josiah on the throne. The mute fell from the prophet's horn, and the kingdom soon reverberated to the cries of Zephaniah and Jeremiah (625–587 B.C.).

King Josiah's early efforts at reform were soon accelerated by a momentous discovery. While the Temple in Jerusalem was undergoing repairs designed to erase all alien symbols, a remarkable manuscript was uncovered. It condemned Canaanism, underscored unswerving loyalty to the Lord, and demanded that His worship be centralized. The manuscript (probably Deuteronomy 5:1b–28:68) was purportedly written by Moses. Josiah was so impressed that he summoned his subjects to the Temple, read the newly discovered "book of the covenant," and renewed their commitment to the Lord. The royal reform that followed received the enthusiastic support of Jeremiah. It went far beyond Temple-cleansing. High places in the hinterland, centers of worship of foreign gods, were demolished and most of their priests assassinated. Reform even reached the former land of Israel (now under nominal Assyrian control), and the temple at Bethel was destroyed. This deed left the Jerusalem Temple as the only authorized place of worship.

Josiah's purification program, commonly called the Deuteronomic Reform, provoked public piety. What it failed to produce was ethical fruit, and Jeremiah was quick to find the flaw. He denounced "the

[2]Connick, *Jesus: The Man, The Mission, and The Message*, pp. 10–12.

book of the covenant" as "deceptive words" (7:4) and pleaded for a "new covenant" that would be engraved "upon their hearts" (31:33). The challenge lay largely dormant for six centuries. Meanwhile, Josiah died, and his successors, chafing against semiservitude, suffered from independence fever. Nebuchadnezzar, powerful head of the fast-rising Babylonian Empire, stormed Jerusalem in 597 B.C. and carted thousands of Judah's finest leaders and craftsmen home with him. When Judah's king subsequently revolted, the Babylonians crushed the participants and destroyed Jerusalem. The victors then effected a still greater exodus of Judah's citizens.

Insights in Exile[3]   Life in Babylonia proved to be far less arduous than the exiles had feared. Since many of Nebuchadnezzar's recently acquired subjects were skilled artisans, he permitted them to live in their own communities, practice local autonomy, and prosper. They built houses, planted gardens, reared families, and sought the welfare of the city as Jeremiah had advised (29:4–7). When the Exile finally ended, many refused to return to Judah. It would have been painful to part with their creature comforts.

The most pressing problem the exiles faced was religious. Had the Lord been defeated by the Babylonian Marduk? Or had the Lord defaulted on His promise to protect His people? Could He be worshiped in a pagan city? Josiah's Deuteronomic Reform had insisted that the Lord could be worshiped only in the Temple in Jerusalem. Now the Holy Temple was reduced to ruins, and the Lord's people were removed from the Holy Land. Prophetic answers came to the rescue. Jeremiah's words convinced the skeptics that the Lord could be reached through prayer despite the loss of the temple (29:12–14). He had not deserted His people; they had abandoned Him. They had succumbed to idolatry, worshiped impurely, and broken the commandments. Consequently, the Lord was using Marduk's devotees to punish them. Ezekiel asserted that they could no longer hide behind heredity and chorus the comforting proverb: "The fathers have eaten sour grapes, and the children's teeth are set on edge" (18:2). In concert they had sinned, and in community they were being disciplined. They need not dread the consequences, for the Lord is just. Only "the soul that sins [and refuses to repent] shall die" (Ezek. 18:4). This doctrine of individual responsibility freed the exiles from the grip of determinism and paved the way for Ezekiel's striking portrait of the restored community.

The Persian king, Cyrus, embarked on an expansionist program about the middle of the sixth century B.C. When he made menacing gestures

---

[3]Connick, *Jesus: The Man, The Mission, and The Message,* pp. 13–17.

toward Babylonia, an anonymous Hebrew prophet was quick to read the signs of the time. II Isaiah (a convenience label for the author of much of Isaiah 40–55) boldly predicted a New Exodus. He called Cyrus the Lord's "messiah" (anointed one) who would shortly capture Babylonia, release the exiles, and rebuild Jerusalem and the Temple. Few prophecies have been implemented with greater dispatch. A small band of transplants headed for Jerusalem in 538 B.C. Despite the desolate sight that greeted them, they began almost at once to build an altar, install the Levites, and lay the foundation of the Second Temple.

Work on the Temple was interrupted when Jewish leaders spurned the Samaritans' offer to assist in the construction. Although the Samaritans were descendants of the Israelites who once formed the Northern Kingdom, they had mixed their blood with foreigners whom the Assyrians had settled in the area. They were declared unfit to share in the sacred task. The rebuke added bricks to the wall of separation between the two peoples. The Samaritans countered by building a rival temple on Mt. Gerizim overlooking Shechem and Jacob's Well. Centuries later, when a Galilean prophet asked a Samaritan woman for a drink from the well, his request elicited a question: "How is it that you, a Jew, ask a drink of me, a woman of Samaria?" (Jn. 4:9).

The prodding of the prophets Haggai and Zechariah prompted resumption of the work on the Jewish Temple in 520 B.C. It was completed five years later, but the prosperity promised by Haggai and Zechariah failed to materialize. The sorry state of affairs eventually reached the ears of Nehemiah, cup-bearer to the Persian king. He persuaded his sovereign to send him to the Holy City as governor in 445 B.C. and again in 432 B.C. He roused the dispirited Jews, rebuilt the Jerusalem wall, instituted tithing and Sabbath observance, and banned marriage with "the people of the land."

Not long after Nehemiah's governorship, a priest named Ezra journeyed to Jerusalem to assess the religious climate. He brought with him a copy of "the book of the law of Moses" (Neh. 8:1) and read it to the assembled people. There followed a covenant-renewal ceremony reminiscent of those conducted earlier by Josiah and Joshua. Ezra so exalted Moses' Law that he came to be called "Father of Judaism." Under his influence prophecy receded, and the Law molded the minds and manners of the Jews. The restrictive measures imposed by Nehemiah were multiplied. Ezra not only denounced mixed marriages; he declared that foreign wives (and their children) should be cast aside. Two notes of subtle protest were subsequently sounded against the parochialists. The book of Ruth recalled that a foreigner was actually the ancestress of David, Israel's greatest king. The book of Jonah dramatized the Lord's abiding concern for the salvation of aliens.

The Jews prospered for nearly a century after Nehemiah and Ezra. The tiny theocracy headed by a High Priest restoréd Jerusalem to a position of prominence and prestige in Jewish national and religious life. The military and cultural conquests of Alexander and his successors finally provoked the Maccabean Revolt.[4] A tract for the times, the book of Daniel, appeared shortly after the resistance began. Its author was shocked by Hellenism's infection of the Jews. His aim was to rekindle his people's faith and to renew their loyalty in the face of severe persecution. His theme was that history is in the hands of the Lord, that His kingdom is near, and that steadfastness is required of those who would have a place in it. He expressed his convictions in an idiom called apocalypse (revelation), and his work fanned the fires of Judah's faith once again.

Between the Covenants

The Protestant canon contains no source book of history after Ezra. It would be a mistake, however, to conclude from this that Jewish literary activity atrophied between the Covenants. Roman Catholic, Orthodox, and Anglican canons include the Apocrypha, Jewish writings composed between 200 B.C. and 100 A.D. The Apocrypha ("hidden") consists of fourteen or fifteen books or parts thereof found in the Septuagint[5] but not in the Hebrew Bible as finally canonized. According to the Revised Standard Version, they are I and II Esdras, Tobit, Judith, Additions to Esther, The Wisdom of Solomon, Ecclesiasticus (or the Wisdom of Jesus the Son of Sirach), Baruch, The Letter of Jeremiah, The Prayer of Azariah and the Song of the Three Young Men, Susanna, Bel and the Dragon, The Prayer of Manasseh, and I and II Maccabees. All of these writings were composed in Greek except I Maccabees.

The Jews rejected the marginal books of the Greek canon because they bore the stigma of compromise with pagan culture and were the special possession of a competing faith, Christianity. No classification of the material is altogether satisfactory. Some might rest comfortably under several different headings. I Maccabees is a historical writing of a high order, but II Maccabees is a mixture of history and legend. Tobit and Judith are romantic tales, and The Prayer of Manasseh is a magnificent liturgical psalm. Ecclesiasticus and The Wisdom of Solomon are splendid representatives of the wisdom school, and II Esdras is an apocalyptic work.

---

[4]See pp. 24–25.
[5]Except for II Esdras. See p. 5.

A large group of writings outside the Old Testament and the Apocrypha are often called the Pseudepigrapha ("false writings"). The title stems from the fact that certain of the works are respectfully but incorrectly attributed to such ancient Biblical worthies as Adam, Enoch, Moses, and Isaiah. Because many of the writings are anonymous, and because pseudonymous works appear both in the Old Testament and the Apocrypha, the designation is misleading. The so-called false writings, written between 200 B.C. and 200 A.D., were originally in Hebrew, Aramaic, and Greek. They include apocalypses, legendary histories, collections of psalms, and wisdom works. No agreement exists as to how many writings should be included in the Pseudepigrapha. The famous edition by R. H. Charles contains Jubilees, Letter to Aristeas, Book of Adam and Eve, Martyrdom of Isaiah, I Enoch, Testament of the Twelve Patriarchs, Sibylline Oracles, Assumption of Moses, II Enoch, II Baruch, III Baruch, IV Ezra, Psalms of Solomon, IV Maccabees, Pirke Aboth (Sayings of the Fathers), Story of Ahikar, and Fragment of a Zadokite Work.

The writings of Flavius Josephus (together with I Maccabees and portions of II Maccabees from the Apocrypha) provide the principal authority for Jewish history for Hasmonean and Herodian Palestine. Josephus was born about 38 A.D. and died after the turn of the century. He was the son of a priest, and he could boast of Hasmonean blood on his mother's side. Early attracted to the study of Jewish sects, he joined the popular Pharisees at the age of nineteen. He journeyed to Rome in 64 A.D. to secure the release of some priests that the procurator Felix had sent there to be tried. The success of Josephus' mission was exceeded only by the impression the splendor and might of the Eternal City made upon him. When he returned to Judea, the country was in control of those who favored revolt. Unable to dissuade the foolhardy rebels, he joined them and even exercised military leadership for a time. Roman victories led to his capture. His prediction that Vespasian would become emperor came true in 69 A.D. Josephus' reward was freedom, and for the rest of the war he served the Romans as interpreter and mediator. Titus later took him to Rome where he enjoyed Roman citizenship and an imperial pension. He was then free to devote himself to a literary career.

Four of Josephus' works owe their survival to their popularity among Christian writers. *The Jewish Wars* (seven books) was penned shortly after the fall of the Jewish state. It traces Jewish history from 175 B.C. to 70 A.D. Twenty years later *The Antiquities of the Jews* (twenty books) appeared. It covers Jewish history from the patriarchs to the revolt against Rome in 66 A.D. *Vita*, a sequel to the *Antiquities*, constitutes a vigorous defense of Josephus' career and character. *Against Apion* (two books) is an eloquent apology for Judaism. The author's Roman patronage and his transparent apologetic interests have contributed to a credibility gap. His biases have to be discounted, but when he is judged according to his peers and allowance is made for the limitations of his sources, he still ranks among the greatest of ancient historians.

The writings of Philo Judeus furnish us with an invaluable source for calculating the impact of Hellenism upon Judaism. His words have survived to a greater degree than those of any other non-Palestinian Jew of the time. Although many of his treatises are known only by name, those that are extant consist of at least a dozen volumes. An Alexandrian Jew of prominent parents, Philo was supposedly born about 20 B.C. and died in the middle of the following century. His philosophical stance was Neoplatonic, but he saw no incompatibility between philosophy and the revelation of the Hebrew Scriptures. Most of his thirty-eight writings are either allegorical commentaries upon the Law or treatments of themes selected from it. Moses was his hero, the wisest of all men. Philo's Bible was the Septuagint, which he considered verbally inspired. One of his works (apparently consisting of five books) is made up of apologetic compositions addressed to Gentiles. Only two of these have survived: *Against Flaccus* (who attempted to force cult images of the mad emperor Gaius upon Alexandrian Jews) and *Embassy to Gaius* (headed by Philo to secure protection from the emperor). Eusebius indicates that one of the lost books included a description of the Jewish sect, the Essenes. Fortunately, another treatment of this group is preserved in Philo's *Every Good Man is Free*. In *Contemplative Life*, he describes the customs of an Essene-like group of ascetics in Egypt.

Other Jewish writings of the time are the Qumran works (which are discussed later in this chapter) and numerous books known only by references to them in patristic literature. No one can possibly understand the rich religious development of Judaism between the covenants apart from knowledge of the Apocrypha, the Pseudepigrapha, the works of Josephus and Philo, and the Qumran materials. They serve as a bridge between the Old Testament and the New—supplementing much that is found in the former and pointing to new ideas that appear in the latter. We shall have occasion to refer to writings from all of these sources, but enough has already been said to dispel the notion that Jewish thought was motionless between Malachi and Matthew.

Hebrew Expectations[6]   "Messiah" translates a Hebrew word that means "anointed." It appears as "Christos" in Greek and "Christ" in English. In the Old

[6]Connick, *Jesus: The Man, the Mission, and the Message*, pp. 286–294.

Testament, the term is nearly always used as an adjective rather than as a noun (contrast Zech. 4:14). The usual phrase is "anointed of the Lord." It is never the prerogative description of a single person. It is applied to all sorts of people (patriarchs, priests, kings, the nation, and even a Persian worshiper of Marduk) through whom God asserts his sovereignty.

The expectation of blessedness that pious Jews cherished is often called "the messianic hope." The designation is doubly dubious. (1) It suggests that there was only *one* such expectation. The fact is that there were many. They ranged all the way from a determined nationalism that anticipated a political restoration with a descendant of David occupying an earthly throne to the more generic conviction that all men one day would acknowledge God's supremacy. (2) It gives undue prominence to the figure of the Messiah. Many forms of the Jewish hope did not involve a Messiah at all. God Himself would be king in the New Age. To numerous traditional hopes there must be added the apocalyptic expectation of a cataclysmic end to the Present Age. It featured a preexistent supernatural being who would descend from heaven with the clouds to institute Final Judgment. Clearly it is misleading to lump together such diverse and frequently discordant views about the future under the simple and singular phrase, "the messianic hope." Different segments of the community sponsored divergent expectations simultaneously. A hope that was prominent in one period might be peripheral in another. Many Hebrews may have been without hope. When peace and prosperity prevailed, they were content with the world as it was.

Covenant Oriented   All Hebrew hopes were rooted in the covenant concept. God had made a Covenant with Abraham, promising the Patriarch that his descendants would be many and would occupy the land from the Nile to the Euphrates (Gen. 15:18). At Sinai the Covenant was renewed. God promised the refugees from Egypt, "If you will obey my voice and keep my covenant, you shall be my own possession among all peoples" (Exod. 19:5). Then he gave to Moses the Law that was to be binding on the covenant community (Exod. 19:9–20:20). From that time forward devout Hebrews (now called Israelites) were convinced that future blessings were in store for them. They were God's chosen people, and He would be faithful to His Covenant.

The conquest of Canaan and the period of the Judges laid the foundation for the United Kingdom, Israel's Golden Age. For a century the nation enjoyed remarkable status and success under the leadership of "the Lord's anointed," Saul, David, and Solomon. When the Divided Kingdoms eventually fell to the Assyrians and the Babylonians,

Israelite hopes were dampened but not dashed. God, according to a poet, had made a Covenant with David and his descendants: "Once for all I have sworn by my holiness; I will not lie to David. His line shall endure for ever, his throne as long as the sun before me" (Ps. 89:35–36). Later generations, in times of distress and deportation, looked back to their own past and saw the days of David as a pledge for the future. Many of their dreams did not involve a single messianic figure. Hosea and Amos envisaged the renewed glory of the house of David and the reunion of the twelve tribes (Hos. 3:5; Amos 9:11–12)[7]. Jeremiah foresaw the restoration of a succession of kings (Jer. 17:25; 22:4)[8].

A Descendant of David? Some Hebrew hopes did focus upon a single descendant of David. Isaiah pleaded with King Ahaz to cancel the royal plan to secure Assyria's aid for beleaguered Judah. The prophet was convinced that the Lord would summarily deal with the Syro-Israelite attackers. He even promised the king that God's intent would be confirmed by a sign that the king might choose. But Ahaz, who had apparently already approved another course, declined to put the Lord to a test. The prophet proclaimed that the Lord would provide a sign anyway. The promised sign was the birth of a child who would be called Immanuel. The language of Isaiah 7:14 presupposes that the mother was already pregnant, or soon would be, and that the babe would be born shortly. Otherwise the child would have had no significance for Ahaz. Before the child would reach the age of choice, the Syro-Israelite alliance would disintegrate and Assyria would bring havoc upon Judah (Isa. 7:1–17). The manner of the child's birth was incidental; the sign was the child himself. The babe was to be born to a particular family, since the definite article is used in the Hebrew: "*The* woman shall conceive." Was the woman the queen and the child the future king of Judah, Hezekiah? No one can be sure, but the prophet certainly had a son of the house of David in mind. He predicted the advent of a child-king who would in time faithfully perform the tasks of government that the faithless Ahaz had fumbled. At first the child would live in a time of woe (the Assyrian invasion), but once that domination had passed, he would ascend the throne as God's agent. Then the meaning of Immanuel ("God [is] with us") would be self-evident. The words of Isaiah 9:6–7 plunged into the stream of prophetic consciousness only to surface centuries later in a transformed state in the Christian gospel (Mt. 4:15–16).

Israel, the Righteous Remnant, or an Individual? Near the close of the Babylonian Exile, II Isaiah prophesied a New Exodus for his people. He saw Israel's redemption as a part of the redemption of all nations. As the Lord's Servant, she would not only

[7]Many scholars regard "and David their king" in Hosea 3:5 and all of Amos 9:11–12 as later editorial additions.
[8]Jeremiah 17:19–27 may also be a later editorial insertion.

restore her own people; she would also be a light to the nations that His salvation should reach to the end of the earth (Isa. 49:6). The Servant is described in four particular passages. At times Israel is clearly indicated (49:3), while at other times, even in the same poem, the Servant seems to be the ideal Israel, the righteous remnant. The Servant (ideal Israel) has a mission to the rest of Israel (49:5). In still other instances, the concrete descriptions of the Servant suggest that the prophet has an individual in mind (53). Whether the Servant is seen as an individual or in a collective sense, as one who works in the present or in the messianic future, his task is of an unusual nature. He will not prophesy in the streets (42:2-3); he will establish justice universally by quiet and gentle means (49:1-6). His close fellowship with God will enable him to sustain the weary and to submit to gross afflictions (50:4-9). He will be exalted through suffering. The contrast between his repugnant present appearance and his ultimate triumph will astonish the nations (52:13-15). People will be astounded that such a revolting figure is the chosen agent of God (53:1-3). Although the Israelites supposed the Servant was suffering for his own sins, in reality he was suffering in their stead and for the nations (53:5). He did not protest. He was judged, executed, and buried in a criminal's grave (53:7-9). But the apparent victim will actually be a victor. His mission will end in triumph and exaltation, and he will look back with satisfaction on the successful result of his suffering (53:10-12).

The moving description of the Servant's sacrifice related in II Isaiah has markedly influenced Christian theology. Mark 10:45 serves as a splendid example: "For the Son of man also came not to be served but to serve, and to give his life as a ransom for many." Although Jewish thought did not conceive of the Messiah in terms of the suffering Servant until the first century, if then, it is the suggestion of many New Testament scholars that Jesus found the model for his mission in the words of II Isaiah. For this reason, we have included this prophet in our discussion of the messianic hope. Whether or not the prophecy was originally messianic, it did express an important hope of the Hebrews, and it was used messianically later on—perhaps in the Qumran community, possibly by Jesus, certainly by the early church.

Apocalyptic and Eschatological

The dreams of a glorious kingdom cherished by the postexilic Jewish community were doomed to disintegration. Palestine was subject to Persian power for two centuries (538–330 B.C.). When the Persian Empire finally folded, the Greeks took over. After the Greeks came the Egyptians and then the Syrians. Continuous domination by foreign powers provoked a profound pessimism among the Jews, but their prolonged contact with the Persians had provided them with a view of the world tailored to their mood. According to the Persian religion (Zoroastrianism), the world was a battleground of two opposing spiritual forces: God and his angels, and the devil and his demons. Evil resulted from the activity of the demonic forces. Some day in the future, Persian priests proclaimed, God would destroy the devil and his demons, the dead would be raised and judged, the wicked would be punished, and the righteous would be revived and rewarded in the New Age. As pious Jews meditated on their miseries, they began to see in this Persian dualism the explanation for their misfortune. Paradise Postponed was not due merely to God's delay in punishing the conquerors of the Jews; it was also attributable to the cosmic conflict that raged behind the visible phenomena. This Age was controlled by Satan. At a predetermined date, God would destroy Satan; then the New Age of deliverance and reward would come. It would be preceded, though, by a period of trial and calamity during which the forces of evil would make their final assault against God and His followers.

The type of Jewish thought that developed under Persian tutelage is called *apocalypticism.* "Apocalyptic" is a term derived from a Greek word meaning "revelation." Apocalyptists were dualistic. The Persian version posited two coequal opposing gods—Ormazd (good) and Ahriman (evil). The dualism was cosmic because the whole cosmos was involved—heaven, earth, and the underworld. All living creatures, natural and supernatural, owed their allegiance either to Ormazd or Ahriman. In Judaism, Yahweh was the good God and Satan (or his equivalent) was His foe and man's seducer. Since the hammer of monotheism blunted the doctrinal dualism derived from the Persians, Satan was seen not as God's coequal but as His inferior. The cosmic dualism was combined with an *eschatological* element. "Eschatology" comes from a Greek word meaning "last things." Two separate and distinct ages were affirmed. This Age, under Satan's domination, provoked pessimism. Evil rode in the saddle, and the righteous suffered oppression and persecution. Before their lot improved, it would become worse. Their only hope lay in the future. God would one day defeat Satan in a cosmic struggle, and His victory would inaugurate a New Age. Then the righteous would share a blessed existence under His control.

A Collective Concept

The first completely apocalyptic book to be included in the Bible was Daniel. Its author wrote about 167–165 B.C. under the stress of persecution initiated by Antiochus Epiphanes. Forced Syrian Hellenization had blackened Jewish skies, and the prospects of a military victory under Judas Maccabeus seemed slim indeed. It appeared that only God could save the Jews, and this thesis was advanced by Daniel's visions. Several awesome beasts, representing the evil nations that had smothered Hebrew hopes, passed before him. The doom of these nations was sealed. Daniel gazed into heaven and glimpsed what was to come. The old order had been judged, and the new era was commencing. The figure who symbolized the new era had a human form ("one like a son of man" [Dan. 7:13]). Some scholars think this phrase points to an individual, but most regard the reference as collective in character—the new Israel, ideal and glorified. This seems to be the sense of Daniel 7:17–18 where it is indicated that "the saints of the Most High [God]" shall receive the kingdom and possess it forever. Apocalyptic tales present men as beasts and celestial beings as having human form. The kingdom given to "one like a son of man" or "the saints of the Most High" is God's kingdom and His answer to a situation that seemed hopeless by all earthly standards.

Preexistent, Human, or God Himself?

Another apocalyptic work, the parables (or Similitudes) of Enoch, appeared nearly a century after Daniel. Confined to chapters 37–71 of I Enoch, the writing contains frequent references to the Son of Man, usually with the demonstrative—*this* or *that* Son of Man. The reference is not to Daniel's "saints of the Most High" (Dan. 7:13, 18) but to a personal Messiah.[9] This Messiah is unlike any known before in Judaism. He is a preexistent heavenly being hidden with God prior to the world's creation.[10] At the End of the Age, he will come to judge the world and rule over it.[11] Earlier Jewish thought never assigned the judging of the world to the Messiah; this was a function reserved for God Himself.[12]

A markedly different picture of the Messiah was painted by the author of the so-called Psalms of Solomon about the middle of the first century B.C. Four passages in particular delineate the central concepts of the collection—Israel's corruption, her God-directed punishment by the Gentiles, and her restoration by God through His "anointed."[13] While this Messiah is endowed with divine gifts, he is a man and nothing more.[14]

Sometime during Jesus' lifetime, The Assumption of Moses made its appearance. In this apocalyptic work, the kingdom was to be ushered in by a day of repentance.[15] Israel's national enemies would be punished, and she would be exalted to heaven. From that comfortable vantage point, she would see her enemies in Gehenna.[16] No

[9]Enoch 48:10; 52:4.
[10]Enoch 48:6.
[11]Enoch 51:1–5
[12]The messianic hope of the Qumran community will be discussed later in this chapter.
[13]Psalms of Solomon 8:27–30; 11; 17; 18.
[14]Psalms of Solomon 17:36; 18:6, 8.
[15]Assumption of Moses 1:18.
[16]Assumption of Moses 10:8–10.

mention is made of the Messiah; God would intervene "alone" in Israel's behalf.[17] From the middle of the first century B.C., when the Psalms of Solomon was written, until the fall of Jerusalem in 70 A.D., we have no rabbinic writings that deal with the Messiah or the messianic age.

Earth, Transformed Earth, or Heaven?

The pristine prophets of Israel foretold the establishment on earth of a kingdom in which the Hebrews would be compensated for their calamities. But a sharp separation between the Present Age and the Age to Come was introduced by the author of Daniel. For the first time, he clearly set forth the hope of a resurrection of the dead. Citizenship in the coming kingdom would not be limited to the last generation; many would be raised from the dead to participate in it. This startling idea stimulated a radical change in the concept of God's kingly rule. Although some apocalyptists were willing to settle for a transformed earth, most looked forward to paradise, a heavenly Jerusalem, or some other kind of transcendental salvation. The rabbinic teaching that survived Jerusalem's destruction agrees with the apocalypses of IV Ezra (II Esdras) and II Baruch. A double form of the hope was sponsored. Between the Present Age and the Age to Come (separated by the resurrection and the judgment), the "days of the Messiah" fall. These days are sometimes called "the Jewish good times." This hope constituted a halfway house between the dreams of national power and prestige and the concepts of salvation devoid of earthly limitations.

Our summary treatment of Hebrew expectations supports a single thesis: thoughts about the future were many and varied. Some hopes involved a Messiah; others announced that God Himself would be king in the New Age. Even when a Messiah was featured, there was no monolithic notion of the Coming One. Would he be one person (Isaiah) or one among a succession of kings (Jeremiah)? Would he be a Servant, and if so, the nation or the righteous remnant (II Isaiah)? Would he have a collective character ("the saints of the Most High" of Daniel)? Would he be a preexistent, supernatural savior from heaven (Parables of Enoch) or a second and superior David (Psalms of Solomon)? Any first-century prophet who harbored messianic ambitions certainly had a wide range of options.

The Temple and the Priesthood[18]

After the Deuteronomic Reform of 621 B.C., the Temple was the only legal place of sacrificial worship. Upon their return from Babylonia, the exiles soon started to rebuild the sacred edifice. Priests who presided over the final edition of the Law of Moses (Torah) thoughtfully

---

[17]Assumption of Moses 10:7.
[18]Connick, *Jesus: The Man, the Mission, and the Message*, pp. 45–47.

included detailed instructions concerning proper Temple structure and worship forms. Herod the Great added to the size and splendor of the complex.[19] It faced the east, and its twenty-five-acre area was set off from the rest of Jerusalem by porticoes, gates, and chambers for the priests. Gentiles had access to an outer court, but signs warned them not to venture beyond it. If they should trespass, the penalty would be death. The white stone sanctuary was divided into sections, each one thought to be holier than the one before. The Court of Women lay beyond the eastern gate. To the west was the Court of Men. Then came the Court of Priests. Here twice-daily sacrifices were offered—at dawn and in midafternoon. Special sacrifices accompanied by more elaborate rituals occurred on festival days such as Passover and Pentecost. In addition, private offerings were made daily by individuals in keeping with the myriad commands of the Torah. Consequently, the Temple area resembled a bargain basement during a January clearance sale. It was crowded with priests and penitents, with sacrificial animals and their salesmen, and at times with money changers and their tables. Beyond the Court of Priests lay the Holy of Holies, the so-called dwelling place of the Lord, separated from the Court of Priests by a curtain. Only the High Priest could go behind the curtain, and he was restricted to a yearly entrance on the Day of Atonement. The privileged character of the Holy of Holies excited Gentile curiosity and spawned scandalous stories concerning the contents of the room and the conduct of its visitors. Mark (15:38) and Matthew (27:51) indicate that on the day that Jesus was crucified "the curtain of the Temple was torn in two, from top to bottom."[20]

Different types of religious leaders arose during the hectic history of the Hebrews. Patriarchs, kings, judges, and prophets were prominent in the early days, but by the first century they no longer exercised authority. The Jews took their cues from priests, Levites, and scribes. Tradition traces the origin of the priesthood to Sinai. Moses' brother, Aaron, and his sons were consecrated there, and the rest of the tribe of Levi were designated priestly assistants. In fact, the priesthood underwent several stages of development. In the primitive period, any Israelite could perform priestly functions. During the Deuteronomic stage, priestly prerogatives were restricted to members of the tribe of Levi. Then a time of transition developed, illustrated by Ezekiel 40-48, when Zadokite priests were favored. Finally, after the Exile and continuing on into the Christian era, only supposed descendants of Aaron were permitted to function as priests. Other Levites served as priestly assistants. Musicians, choristers, doorkeepers, and other functionaries completed the retinue.

[19]See p. 29.
[20]Compare Isaiah 25:7.

The priests were supported by tithes and portions of the offerings. In return, they cared for the sanctuary and its utensils, presided at the altar, consulted the oracle and delivered judgment, preserved the purity and holiness of the people, performed rites of atonement, and pronounced the priestly blessing. They wielded great power through their professional monopoly. They numbered 23,000 in David's time and were arranged in twenty-four divisions.[21] Each division was assigned Temple duties for one week semiannually; then another division would be called into service. When the priests were off duty, they secured other kinds of employment.

At the top of the priestly pyramid stood the High Priest. He became a powerful figure in Jewish life during the Persian period. As nominal head of his people, he negotiated with the various nations to which they were subject. At least as early as the second century B.C., he served as head of the Sanhedrin.[22] When the Maccabean kings assumed the office, its political significance blurred its religious character. The Herods and Procurators diminished the power and prestige of the high priests, but they continued to exercise considerable authority and influence until the destruction of the Temple in 70 A.D. Some priestly families succeeded in amassing great wealth.

The Synagogue and the Scribes

The origin and early development of the synagogue is shrouded in mystery, but it is usually supposed that it arose spontaneously during the Babylonian Exile. Bereft of the Holy Land and the Holy Temple, the people came together to sustain their faith, study the Law (Torah), and worship. Synagogue means "assembly," and it exists whenever ten or more adult male Jews come together for religious instruction. The place of assembly bears the same name. In New Testament times, synagogues were scattered throughout Palestine and the Dispersion. It was a democratic laymen's organization. An elder of the community served as ruler. A paid attendant acted as custodian of the building and the sacred scrolls, and sometimes he doubled as schoolmaster. The synagogue was open daily, and meetings were held on several weekday evenings. Attendance was considered mandatory only on the Sabbath and on special holy days. In Palestine, as long as the Temple remained, the synagogue building resembled a Quaker meetinghouse in its simplicity. (Jews of the Dispersion, deprived of direct Temple contact, endowed their synagogues with features of the Temple.) The ark or chest that housed the scrolls was located on a raised platform. From a lectern, appointed selections from the Law and free-choice passages from the prophets were regularly read in Hebrew. Since most of the Jews did not understand this language, an interpreter

[21]Josephus, *Antiquities*, VII, 14, 7.
[22]See p. 34.

translated the selections into Aramaic. Any adult male Jew was permitted to act as reader. Jesus and Paul availed themselves of the privilege (Lk. 4:16; Acts 13:13–16). Priests did, too, but not in fulfillment of their priestly office; animals were not sacrificed in the synagogue. The people sat on benches facing the ark; opposite them sat the scribes. The seat nearest the ark was called "Moses' seat" (Mt. 23:2) and was considered the place of honor. The Sabbath service consisted of the Shema ("*Hear*, O Israel: The Lord our God is one Lord."),[23] prayers (which became known as the Eighteen Benedictions), Scripture readings, a homily or sermon that interpreted the Scripture, and the singing of psalms. Different persons delivered the sermon, although the scribes were regarded as best fitted for the task. In contrast with the Temple, the synagogue service stressed religious education rather than sacrificial worship.[24]

The first scribes were probably priests. They specialized in the Torah and guarded it against corruption. As a unique group, however, they owed their existence to conditions that prevailed during the Exile. It was then that the Law became the center of the Jewish faith, and the people studied it with unremitting zeal. Under Ezra, the scribes (*Sopherim*) emerged as a distinct and influential class of teachers and interpreters of the Law. When priests became preoccupied with the activities of the Second Temple and their interests took on political coloration, the field of specialized and scholarly study was increasingly preempted by the scribes. To train them, schools were set up in the homes of wise men or in synagogues. Scribes were not merely copyists; they interpreted and applied the commandments of the Torah to the full spectrum of life. Their verbal commentaries, called "the tradition of the elders" (Mk. 7:3), became as binding to their admirers as the written Law itself. The Hellenization of many priests under the Seleucids and their subsequent corruption under the Romans hastened the transfer of spiritual authority over the populace from priests to scribes. A certain scribe, called a "Teacher of Righteousness," profoundly influenced the people associated with the Damascus Document and the Qumran Scrolls. Although priests were doubtless numbered among the scribes in Jesus' day, the majority were laymen who happily allied themselves with their ideological cousins, the Pharisees.

The synagogue was the special province of the scribes, and they were its natural leaders. Their vocation was to study the Law, teach it to others, and act as judge and jury. As legal experts, they regulated both civil and religious life. When a certain lawyer asked Jesus what he should do to inherit eternal life, he made no idle inquiry. His

[23]Deuteronomy 6:4–9, italics added.
[24]Connick, *Jesus: The Man, the Mission, and the Message*, p. 47.

whole life was devoted to the subject. Jesus' response was singularly appropriate: "What is written in the law? How do *you* read?"[25] The scribe was the accepted authority on the topic. He taught without pay and supported himself by practicing a trade or profession. Priestly influence, already on the wane, terminated with the temple's destruction in 70 A.D. It was the scribe who rode the wave of the future. His successor, the rabbi, continues to give leadership in Judaism today.[26]

Sectarian Judaism
The party spirit was prominent in Jesus' day. Josephus mentions four "philosophies"—Sadducees, Pharisees, Essenes, and Zealots. The classification is a convenient one, but it cannot be regarded as fixed or final. The historian wrote for non-Jews; he probably did not want to burden them with the detailed groupings his own people would have required. The Apocrypha and Pseudepigrapha, the Cairo-Damascus Document, and the sensational discoveries at Qumran strongly point to a rich diversity of Jewish thought and practice in the first century. Josephus' groupings are generalizations; they represent open-ended categories rather than card-carrying membership.

The Sadducees
"Sadducee" is a term of disputed origin. Some scholars believe that it was derived from "Zadok," Solomon's priest (I Kings 2:35).[27] The Old Testament indicates that the legitimate priestly office of Aaron was given to Zadok and his descendants. Since the chief claim of the Sadducees was the exclusive right to preside over sacrificial worship in the Temple, this derivation of the name has considerably merit. The first mention of the sect was made by Josephus. He spoke of the Sadducees as a party supported by John Hyrcanus (135–104 B.C.) after his dispute with the Pharisees. Since no certain Sadducean literature has survived, our knowledge of the group stems from the writings of its opponents and should be evaluated accordingly.

The influence of the Sadducees was disproportionate to their limited numbers. Their ranks were filled with priests, drawn from the top echelon of the Temple hierarchy, and landed laymen who lived in and near Jerusalem. Their religious outlook was conservative. They denied that the Prophets and the Writings were authoritative commentaries on the Law, and they found in the Pentateuch all of the rules required for the control of the priesthood, care of the Temple, and performance of the sacrifices. They rejected such doctrines as resurrection, judgment, future life, angels, demonic spirits, and fate— apparently because these ideas were not found in the Torah. They

[25]Luke 10:25–26, italics added.
[26]Connick, *Jesus: The Man, the Mission, and the Message*, p. 46.
[27]But David appointed priests himself (II Sam. 20:25).

repudiated the oral law that the Pharisees endorsed. This was the major bone of contention between the two groups.

The interests and influence of the Sadducees were by no means confined to the Temple and its activities. They played a dominant role in the Sanhedrin and served as official representatives for the Jews in their relations with Rome. They were the party of compromise. As astute political opportunists, they practiced coexistence with the Romans. Their motives may well have been pure—the preservation of the theocratic state (headed by the High Priest) and uninterrupted Temple services. Their popularity plummeted, though, because of their alliance with the Oppressor and their accumulation of earthly treasures. Their interpretation of the Torah was too wooden to meet changing circumstances, and their faith was too narrowly focused on the Temple. When the Temple was destroyed in 70 A.D., their *raison d'être* was demolished. They soon disappeared from the scene, and the triumph of the Pharisees, their chief rivals, was assured.

The Pharisees

The Pharisees were the authentic sons of their spiritual ancestors, the Hasidim. These "Pious Ones" joined the Maccabean Revolt to protest the Hellenization zealously promulgated by Antiochus Epiphanes.[28] Like the Hasidim, the Pharisees were deeply devoted to the Law. They regarded Ezra as their founding father, but their roots reached back into the preexilic period. When the Pharisees first appear in the historical record, they are already an established religious-political entity. Josephus indicates that they were one of three parties existent at the time of Jonathan (c. 145 B.C.) and that they first broke with the Hasmonean dynasty during the reign of John Hyrcanus.[29] The historian records their contempt for Alexander Janneus, his persecution of them, and his subsequent repentance. Alexandra granted the party a large share in government, but its power swiftly atrophied under Roman domination. Henceforth, most Pharisees were content to concentrate on their religious vocation and leave politics to the Sadducees. They adopted a policy of passive resistance to the Romans and the Herods until the national crisis of 66 A.D.

The derivation of the name "Pharisee" is uncertain. Many scholars think it stems from a Hebrew word meaning "one who is separate." If this is the case, then from what (or whom) were they separated? Theories abound, but the most common one is also the most cogent. In their punctilious practice of the Law, especially its Levitical requirements, they separated themselves from all that is ritualistically un-

[28]See pp. 24–25.
[29]*Antiquities*, XIII, 5,9; 10,5–6.

clean—particularly from the "people of the land" who were careless about minutiae. Whether the name was a self-designation or a derisive label invented by their enemies cannot be determined.

The Pharisees were lay religionists. They respected the supreme authority of the Law of Moses, but they were more progressive than the Sadducees. They enlarged the canon of Scripture to include the Prophets and the Writings (sometime after 90 A.D.), forming what Christians call the Old Testament. They endorsed new Temple rites and sponsored new religious festivals (Hanukkah and Purim). They urged the baptism of converts and the hallowing of the Passover meal. To their expanded Scripture they added a second authority, the oral law of "the tradition of the elders." This far more detailed and extensive body of legislation contained the verdicts of the rabbis concerning the Pentateuch. Later codified in the Mishna and Talmud, the oral law assumed the same place in pharisaic thought that court decisions interpreting our Constitution hold for us. It was as binding as Scripture. The genius of the oral law was that it permitted the Pharisees to adjust the written Law to changed conditions; its flaw, according to the Synoptics (Matthew, Mark, and Luke), was that it reduced religion to a list of do's and don'ts. Thirty-nine kinds of work were banned on the Sabbath; each kind was extensively defined. Six hundred and thirteen prohibitions baffled the ordinary layman. It took a Philadelphia lawyer (a scribe) to make sense out of the perplexing situation.[30]

The enlarged Scripture and the oral law enabled the Pharisees to incorporate into their thinking many apocalyptic and eschatological ideas that attained prominence after 200 B.C. Such concepts as angels and demons, the coming of the Messiah, the resurrection, judgment, and future life soared in value. Jews had long divided time into two parts—the Present Age and the Age to Come. Prompted by Persian dualism, they believed that the Present Age was under the control of the Devil and his demons. They dominated human happenings and caused men to act contrary to God's purposes. The only way their hold could be broken was for people to live according to the commands of the Torah. At a time of God's own choosing, He would usher in the "Age to Come" by reasserting his sovereignty "on earth" and destroying the wicked. Then the righteous would enjoy a new order of existence akin to that experienced by Adam and Eve in Eden.

The Pharisees fasted frequently, tithed above and beyond the call of duty, practiced ritualistic washings, ate only "kosher" food, attended

[30]Connick, *Jesus: The Man, the Mission, and the Message*, p. 48.

synagogue and Temple services, abstained even from the appearance of work on the Sabbath, and avoided contact with Gentiles. Their aim was not prudery but piety. Strict obedience to the Law, both written and oral, brought them life and joy. Their disdain for the common people, among whom they numbered Jesus and his disciples, was triggered by the multitude's ignorance of the Law and carelessness about observing it. The Gospels picture the Pharisees as sanctimonious hypocrites and egomaniacs (Mt. 23:23–24; Lk. 18:11). Some of them doubtless deserved such caustic criticism, but for most it constituted rank injustice. The ancient world knew no higher standard of righteousness than theirs. While they numbered only about 6,000,[31] their influence was enormous. They enjoyed great prestige and were the real leaders of Jewish life. Jesus had far more in common with them than is generally supposed. After the Temple's destruction in 70 A.D., Judaism was mostly pharisaic.[32]

The Essenes Until rather recently, knowledge of the Essenes was dependent upon secondary sources. The most productive mines of information were found in the writings of Philo, Josephus, and Pliny the Elder.

Discoveries at Qumran. A startling discovery was made at Qumran in the spring of 1947. Two shepherd lads, tending a mixed flock of goats and sheep at the base of the crumbling cliffs near the Dead Sea on the northwest, began to search for a stray animal. One of the shepherds tossed a stone into a small opening in the rock. The sound that resulted was heard round the world. He had inadvertently broken a jar filled with an ancient manuscript, a portion of the now-famous Dead Sea Scrolls. Since that day, many more caves[33] have yielded hundreds of manuscripts and tens of thousands of fragments. Although the work of publication and evaluation is far from complete, enough progress has been made to permit specialists to reach at least tentative conclusions.[34]

An impressive group of Jewish and Christian scholars now hold that the people who composed and preserved the Qumran Scrolls were Essenes. These scholars readily acknowledge their critics' claim that omissions and differences exist between the Philo-Josephus-Pliny accounts and the Scrolls. (1) The Teacher of Righteousness, so central to the Scrolls, is not mentioned in the secondary sources. (2) The secondary sources contain no hint that the Essenes considered themselves the people of the "new covenant." (3) Although the Qumran community taught an eschatological bliss for the righteous and eternal

---

[31]Josephus, *Antiquities,* XVII, 2, 4.
[32]Connick, *Jesus: The Man, the Mission, and the Message,* pp. 48–49.
[33]Eleven are of major significance.
[34]Connick, *Jesus: The Man, the Mission, and the Message,* p. 50.

Qumran. In these caves northwest of the Dead Sea some of the celebrated Qumran Scrolls were discovered.

fire for the wicked, no equivalent of the Essene paradise is found in the Scrolls. (4) Attitudes toward the Temple and its animal sacrifices conflict. (5) It is difficult to harmonize Philo's picture of Essene pacifism with the militant spirit and organization for war depicted in "the War Scroll."

The omissions and differences between the Qumran Scrolls and the Essene writings must be viewed in perspective. Many such discrepancies have resulted from faulty interpretations of the secondary sources. Their authors were non-Essenes. They wrote for Gentiles unfamiliar with sectarian Judaism. It is small wonder that their descriptions appear to be incomplete and incongruous. Allowances must be made, moreover, for developments in Essene doctrines over the years and for some diversity within the order at any given time. Finally, it is strange that Philo, Josephus, and Pliny should have overlooked such a significant sect if the Covenanters at Qumran and the Essenes were actually different groups.

Objective examination of the evidence reveals that the similarities between the inhabitants of Qumran and the Essenes far outweigh omissions and differences. They lived in the same area at the same time. They adhered to common beliefs and disciplines. They read (and composed?) the same books. On balance, then, we are forced to conclude that the two groups were one and the same, or they were so similar as to make distinction exceedingly difficult if not impossible. The significance of this conclusion, if accepted, is considerable. We now possess extensive firsthand sources for the study of Essene beliefs and practices.

Origin and history of the sect. The Essenes are not mentioned in the New Testament or in the Qumran Scrolls. Their New Testament omission can be explained by their lack of hostility toward the Jesus movement. The Sadducees and the Pharisees appear principally in polemic passages. The absence of the term "Essene" from the Scrolls suggests that it was not a self-designation. The origin of the name is uncertain, and the history of the sect must be sketched with considerable caution and conjecture.

The Essenes, like the Pharisees, seem to have been the spiritual kin of the Hasidim. Just when the Essenes attained separate existence is debatable. Jewish tradition pictures them active in Jerusalem until 105 B.C., and archeological data place them at their Qumran headquarters no later than the reign of Alexander Janneus (104–78 B.C.). They deeply resented the Hellenistic tendencies of the Hasmoneans and their absurd claims to the office of High Priest. The hateful happening that hastened their departure to the desert was the persecution of the "Teacher of Righteousness" by the "wicked priest." The persecutor was undoubtedly a Hasmonean, and an increasing number of scholars believe that he was Alexander Janneus. The identity of the Teacher of Righteousness is far more mysterious. Concrete references to him are infrequent and sometimes confusing. That he was a formative figure in the faith of the Essene sect seems certain. His followers regarded him, rather than the Hasmonean pretenders, as the authentic representative of the Zadokite priesthood. This helps to explain the priestly character of the Essenes and their antipathy toward the Temple hierarchy. Since their Teacher possessed the Spirit of Truth, he was able to speak with authority. The community he founded was the only one that held the legitimate priestly offices and preserved the correct interpretation of the Torah.

The Essenes remained at Qumran until the Herodians ended Hasmonean rule in 36 B.C. Archeological evidence indicates that at this time they abandoned their desert headquarters. They probably returned to Jerusalem, where their anti-Hasmonean attitude would have been extremely helpful to Herod the Great. The King allowed them unrestricted religious freedom, which they capitalized on to establish Essene communities throughout Judea. After Herod's death, they returned to Qumran as archeological data again testify. Motivation for the move was probably supplied by the slaying of 3,000 worshipers during the Passover or the crucifixion of 2,000 Jews by Syrian-sent Gentile soldiers. Either would have freshened their memories of Alexander Janneus.

Number, distribution, and nature of the sect. The Essenes numbered about 4,000.[35] Only a few hundred regularly lived in the wilderness retreat. The entire group may have gathered at Qumran for such special occasions as Pentecost, but most of them were scattered throughout the small towns and villages of Judea. Large cities were generally shunned since their inhabitants welcomed Gentiles and were careless about ceremonial cleanness. An Essene writing called the *Damascus Document* describes the organization of the dispersed communities. They were founded with a minimum of ten people, providing one was a priest. Since they did not enjoy the privacy of Qumran, certain accommodations in religious practices were necessary. As far as possible, though, they conformed to the monastic mold of the mother movement.

It was not easy to become an Essene. Prospective members were required to serve a rigorous three-year probation period before they were admitted to full rank. The *Rule of the Community* describes in detail the initiation rite in which priests, Levites, and laymen participated. Candidates were sworn to secrecy and compelled to take "tremendous vows." Established members reviewed their obedience and renewed their commitment. The climax came with baptism and cleansing by the Holy Spirit.

Essenes began their day at sunrise with special prayers for the community. Then they were dismissed by their superiors to work at the various crafts until about eleven o'clock.[36] After a purification bath,[37] they assembled for breakfast. The single-course meal began and ended with a priestly blessing. Then they returned to their labors

---

[35]Josephus, *Antiquities*, XVIII, 1, 5.
[36]The remains of a bakery, grain mills, storage silos, pottery kilns, and smith shop have been discovered.
[37]Some of the cisterns in their intricate system were designed for this purpose.

until the evening repast. Participation in the common meal was reserved for full-fledged members, and at least some of the meals had eschatological significance. They were eaten in anticipation of the messianic banquet that would follow God's final victory over the forces of evil.

The Essenes spent time every day studying the Scriptures, but the Sabbath was especially devoted to this activity. The large scriptorium at Qumran and the multitude of Biblical texts found there underscore their zeal for reading, copying, commenting upon, and preserving the sacred writings. They were driven by the conviction that the promises of God articulated by the prophets were actually being fulfilled in the history of their own community. Their retreat to Qumran was seen as a righteous response to the call of Isaiah 40:3: "In the wilderness prepare the way of the Lord, make straight in the desert a highway for our God." They searched the Scriptures to understand the present and to discern the future. They believed that they were the people of the New Covenant. This was not merely the Old Covenant renewed; it was also the Eternal Covenant that would be established in the Age to Come. God would soon defeat His enemies and reestablish His sovereignty. The Covenanters, as the Righteous Remnant or the New Israel, would dwell in the New Eden. In the meantime, they lived as though they were on the periphery of the Promised Land preparing to penetrate it once again. Under an overseer, they submitted to the strictest discipline. They held all things in common, generally avoided marriage and strangers, opposed oaths, slavery, and anointing with oil, wore white garments, and ritualistically bathed after any kind of pollution. They constituted a kind of Salvation Army with battle divisions and a liturgy of Armageddon. So scrupulously did they observe the Sabbath that they disregarded even normal bodily needs on that day.

The Essenes sent into the Temple what they had dedicated to God, but because of their radical requirements concerning ceremonial purity and their opposition to the Jerusalem priesthood, they refused to participate in the Temple sacrifices. Whether they performed sacrifices at Qumran[38] or spiritualized the concept of sacrifice[39] is uncertain. They did celebrate the great religious festivals of the Jews at Qumran. This was done according to a solar calendar, however, not the lunar calendar as used in Jerusalem.

Messianic hopes thrived among the Essenes. Nowhere is this fact more evident than in their *Testimonia Document.* It is a collection

---

[38]As Josephus, *Antiquities,* XVIII, 1, 5 and some archeological data seem to suggest.
[39]As Philo indicates in *Every Good Man Is Free,* XII.

of Biblical proof texts designed to support the Messiah's advent. Although messianic fever was not uncommon among the Jews, the Qumran version was characterized by two distinctions. The Covenanters were infected with an extremely virulent strain, and they anticipated the arrival of not one Messiah but two! The Messiah of Aaron, the more prestigious of the two, would come from the priestly line.[40] His assignment would be to establish the New Jerusalem and the New Temple. The Messiah of Israel, a descendant of the royal line, would lead the community to victory in its holy war. Early scholarly speculation that the Teacher of Righteousness himself was viewed as Messiah is now rather generally discounted.

End of the community. The Essenes continued to live at Qumran until the siege of Jerusalem. Sometime during that fateful offensive, probably in 68 A.D., Roman soldiers sacked and destroyed the settlement. Many of the Covenanters, spurred on by the mistaken notion that this was the Holy War for which they had been preparing, were slaughtered. Those who managed to escape death soon suffered disillusionment. They had erred in their interpretation of the Torah. Some of them subsequently became Jewish Christians, later called Ebionites. Before death and disillusionment had their day, the Essenes had managed to conceal in nearby caves a mighty monument to their zeal for Zion and their consuming conviction that they were, as the title of one of their works suggests, the *Community of the New Covenant.*

The Scrolls and Scripture.[41] Striking similarities exist between the thought patterns of the Scrolls and those of the New Testament. The Essenes thought the world was a battleground of two warring spirits, the Spirit of Truth and the Spirit of Wickedness. They believed that they were living in the last days; in some sense a new age had already appeared. They regarded themselves as the people of the New Covenant and anticipated the coming of a priestly Messiah. Their community pattern roughly corresponded to that of the democratic assembly, council of twelve, and episcopal overseer that prevailed in the early church. Some scholars declare that John the Baptist "was certainly a kind of Essene, and since Jesus was baptised by John and took over his mission, he too must have been closely related with this group."[42] To support this contention, they cite such items

---

[40]His prominent position was probably predicated upon the central place the priesthood held in Israel's early theocracy.
[41]Connick, *Jesus: The Man, the Mission, and the Message,* p. 52.
[42]Otto Betz, "Dead Sea Scrolls," in George Arthur Buttrick, ed., *The Interpreter's Dictionary of the Bible* (New York: Abingdon Press, 1962), A–D, 801. Reprinted by permission of Abingdon Press.

as Jesus' single state, his sharp attitude toward wealth and the wealthy, his conflict with the Pharisees and the Sadducees, and his silence concerning the Essenes. They believe that some of Jesus' sayings are illuminated by the Scrolls and think it highly probable that he numbered Essenes among his disciples.

Were John and Jesus, then, Essenes? Was the church merely a mature Qumran community? Marked similarities between John-Jesus and the Essenes and between the Scrolls and Scripture can be matched with decided differences. The Covenanters lived in the same conceptual world as John, Jesus, and New Testament writers. They all drank from the same theological well. They accepted or rejected institutions found in their common environment, and in this environment they developed new solutions for the perennial problems of faith. Beyond this it is hazardous to speculate.

The Zealots

The fourth philosophy described by Josephus has usually been equated with the Zealots. They were pious cutthroats who longed to slaughter Romans on sight. Their slogan was "The sword and not sparingly; no king but the Lord." They did not appear as a specific party until 66 A.D. Josephus identified them as followers of the doughty John of Gischala, a leader of the disastrous revolt against Rome. Zealot roots reached back many centuries. The mentality originated in the exclusive worship of the one true God of Israel. By Maccabean times, zeal for the covenantal God was transferred to His Law, and the foundation of later Zealotism was firmly laid. As strict interpreters of the Law, Zealots defended it unto death. Support of the Law sired nationalistic yearnings. Revolutionary groups spontaneously sprang into existence—at Herod's death, ten years later at the time of the census, etc. As long as life remained reasonably tolerable, their movements were minimal. But when oppression became overt, as it often did, simmering patriots threw caution to the winds. They were ever present, eager to detect abuses, and ready to goad their more moderate brethren into open revolt.

The superpatriots found it difficult to arouse the nation. The Pharisees saw their own mission largely in the religious sphere. The Essenes were convinced that only God could overthrow Rome, so they repaired to the desert to await the Holy War. Many Sadducees loved lucre too much to endanger their privileged position. The masses suffered from apathy. Therefore, the liberty-under-Law lovers had to go it alone. When at times their enthusiasm outdistanced their power, they were swiftly and severely subdued. Even with popular support, the uprising they sparked in 66 A.D. was cruelly crushed.

The Sadducees, Pharisees, Essenes, and Zealots were not the only sectarian groups in first-century Palestine. The others were relatively unimportant, though, except as witness to the rich diversity within Judaism. The religious parties collectively did not comprise even ten per cent of the total population. The great mass of people (*'Am Ha' arez*, or "People of the Land") belonged to no party; many were nominal Pharisees. Most of them doubtless lived good lives, but their reputation was stained by their failure to practice ceremonial correctness. Priests and Pharisees, according to the Fourth Gospel, judged them to be accursed (Jn. 7:49).[43]

The focal points of the Jewish faith were God and His Torah. Loyalty to the Law, real or expected, provided the Jewish people with unmatched cohesiveness. Some outsiders were attracted by the religious zeal and moral standards of the Jews; more were repelled by the exclusiveness that their togetherness seemingly generated. Consequently, Jewish attempts to be "a light to the nations" were largely unsuccessful. Most Hellenized heathen of the Greco-Roman world who yearned for the security of a religious fellowship were forced to look elsewhere. Many found what they were looking for in the Christian community that emerged from Judaism. We shall turn our attention now to the new sect and the sources that tell us about it.

[43]Connick, *Jesus: The Man, the Mission, and the Message*, pp. 52–53.

2

Conception of the Christian Community

Substantial shock waves activated the religious seismograph of Palestine about 30 A.D. A small band of Jews audaciously announced that the New Age, long promised by the prophets, had begun. For proof of their proposition they pointed to God's decisive act in Jesus of Nazareth. The Creator had raised the Christ from the dead. There was nothing novel about resuscitated corpses; both the Old and New Testaments furnish evidences of them (I Kings 17:22; II Kings 4:18–37; Matthew 9:18–26; Luke 7:11–15). In each of these instances, however, the revived was subject to a second death. Not so with Jesus! His resurrection was distinctive—God had enabled him to enter a life that was permanent. Jewish leaders had successfully conspired to have Jesus condemned as a common criminal, but God had turned the tables on them. He had chosen the Rejected One to inaugurate the New Age. He had made Jesus "both Lord and Christ" (Acts 2:36).

Those who experienced the resurrected Jesus became convinced that evil had spent its power and death had lost its sting. They regarded themselves as the New Israel, heirs of the promises made to the Israel of old. Soon the New Israelites were called "Christians" after their leader.

The resurrection of Jesus was clearly the catalytic agent that triggered the birth of the Christian community, but the conception of that community occurred during the earthly sojourn of the Galilean. When we turn to the earliest New Testament writings to discover how the conception took place, we are at first surprised to learn that the subject is surrounded by a wall of silence. After some reflection, we realize why this is so. Although Paul's letters were written many years before the Gospels, the apostle's career actually followed that of Jesus. Paul assumed both the conception and the birth of the Christian community. The community had already attained public identity, experienced rapid numerical and geographical growth, and become the object of persecution before he wrote his letters.

If we are to understand how the Christian community was conceived, we must turn to the only records that deal with the subject—the Gospels. Since they are of a relatively late date, we shall need to know something about their nature and development. Then we shall be in a position, in so far as is possible, to look *through* the Gospels to Jesus. A study of the man, his mission, and his message should reveal how the Christian community was conceived. It should also enable us to treat more intelligently the birth and growth of the Christian community and the life and letters of its resolute champion, Paul (Part 3).

IV

The Records
(Matthew,
Mark, Luke)

Western man reveres records. Physicians are fond of case histories, lawyers like testimony, librarians prize books, and Internal Revenue representatives respect dated documents. Such people do not accept records at their face value, though. Long exposure to modern science has taught them to subject their sources to serious scrutiny. Printed matter can be false and verbal witness misleading. Researchers must rely on impartial observers and objective evidence.

The rigorous evaluation of records is of rather late origin. It was not until the eighteenth century that the Bible was exposed to "objective" examination. It was then that obscurities and contradictions in the Gospels led to the denial of Jesus' existence. Some scholars claimed that he was a solar deity. Others argued that he was the creation of the church, the consequence rather than the cause of Christianity. Still others, under the influence of an ancient Semitic myth, saw him as the latest manifestation of a divinity called Joshua. Later on, Marxists (who regard Christianity as a mere social phenomenon) maintained that Jesus resulted from contact between Jewish messianic hopes and the oppressed Roman proletariat.

Jesus—Man or Myth?

Christian records cannot be used to settle the question of Jesus' existence. They were written and preserved by partisan observers and would properly be considered biased. Since no such stigma is attached to non-Christian witnesses, they will be given greater weight in the matter of whether Jesus was man or myth. We shall focus our attention on three Roman and two Jewish sources.

Pliny, the Younger

Pliny, the Younger, who governed the province of Bithynia in north central Turkey from 111 to 115 A.D., wrote to Emperor Trajan.[1] He

The material in this chapter is a condensed, updated, and at times expanded version of material found in C. Milo Connick, *Jesus: The Man, the Mission, and the Message* (Englewood Cliffs, N.J.: Prentice-Hall, 1963), and is used by permission of the publisher.
[1]Pliny, *Letters,* XCVII.

solicited the emperor's advice concerning the methods used at the trial of Christians. Believers in this "absurd and extravagant superstition" had become sufficiently numerous to create a problem. Pliny's practice was to pardon those who renounced Christ, invoked the gods, and offered incense before Trajan's statue. Christians who maintained their faith were executed unless they were Roman citizens. In that case, the death penalty was left to the discretion of the emperor. Pliny's observation that on a stated day Christians addressed a form of prayer to Christ as they would to a divinity suggests that the governor believed Christ to be different from the gods other men worshiped. The difference was that Christ had lived upon the earth.

Tacitus

Tacitus, an aristocratic historian and contemporary of Pliny, described the awful fire that raged in Rome in 64 A.D. He reported that Nero, who was accused of setting the fire, had blamed it on the Christians and had had them tortured severely. By way of explanation, Tacitus indicated that Christians derived their name from Christus who had suffered the extreme penalty under Tiberius and Pontius Pilate.[2] Two considerations indicate that the information about Jesus' death stems from non-Christian sources. (1) Tacitus treated the nationalistic outbreak in Judea (which precipitated the war with Rome) and the alleged arsonist activities of Christians in Rome as one and the same movement. No Christian would have done that. (2) No Jew would have called Jesus "Christus." Clearly Tacitus provides untainted evidence for the existence of Jesus.

Suetonius

Suetonius, biographer and reporter, wrote about 120 A.D. He reported that Claudius (41–54 A.D.) expelled all Jews from Rome because they had created disturbances at the behest of "Chrestus."[3] The spelling of Chrestus and the implication that he was present in Rome create difficulties. The reference may have been to an unknown Jewish agitator. Since Tacitus wrote of "Christus" and Christians commonly spoke of Christ in the present tense, it is usually assumed that Chrestus is merely another spelling of Christus.

Josephus

Josephus, a first-century Jewish historian, twice referred to Jesus.[4] Since he simultaneously wished to flatter the Romans and favor the Jews, his writings reflect a strong bias. The first passage that mentions Jesus is also overladen with subsequent Christian additions, but this is not true of the second. While the first passage makes the historian bear a Christian witness to Jesus, it does not obscure Josephus' conviction that Jesus really lived.

[2]Tacitus, *Annals*, XV, 44.
[3]Suetonius, *The Lives of the Twelve Caesars*, XXV.
[4]*Antiquities*, XVIII, 3,3; XX, 9,1. Josephus and the Talmud are superior in value to the Roman sources.

The Talmud is an encyclopedia of Jewish tradition designed to supplement the Hebrew Bible. Its occasional polemic and vituperative references to Jesus also affirm his existence.

Neither Roman nor Jewish sources yield anything new about Jesus. They simply confirm what we already know from Christian writings. The confirmations are of paramount importance, however, since they do underscore the simple truth that Jesus lived. Even the far-out claims and caricatures embedded in Talmudic literature assume that he was a real antagonist. The distinguished Jewish scholar, Joseph Klausner, rightly appraises the situation: "It is unreasonable to question . . . the existence of Jesus."[5]

Jesus never wrote a book. On one occasion he reportedly wrote with his finger on the ground (Jn. 8:6), but time soon erased the marks. Jesus followed Jewish custom and communicated the Good News (gospel) to his disciples by word of mouth. No stenographer or tape recorder preserved a verbatim account. The only record of his message and mission was the memory of his followers. Although he remained unforgettable, much of what he taught was undoubtedly forgotten.

For twenty years the Good News remained in an oral state. Jesus' death occurred at the beginning of the period, but even this terrible trauma did not tempt his followers to record his words and works. His disciples were on hand to provide a rich storehouse of information for the curious and the concerned. Thousands of eyewitnesses in Galilee and Judea supplied a ready-reserve memory bank. The fervent conviction that Jesus would soon return in judgment telescoped time and made permanent records as useless as a boat without a bottom. Besides, the Christian community already had a Bible. They scanned the Hebrew Scriptures to discern and to declare the significance of Christ.

By mid-century, the followers of Jesus were forced to reappraise the need for written records. Eyewitnesses were either aged or dead, and there was fear that information about Jesus might perish with them. The expected return of Jesus had failed to materialize. People who had discounted the future began to take time seriously. Debates about the nature and practice of the faith called for the formulation of an authoritative standard. When Paul campaigned for Christ in Asia

[5]Joseph Klausner, *Jesus of Nazareth*, trans. Herbert Danby (New York: The Macmillan Co., 1925), p. 20. Reprinted by permission of the publisher. Klausner presents a cogent and convenient review and evaluation of the material concerning Jesus on pp. 18–60. Quotations from relevant historical sources can be found in C.K. Barrett, ed., *New Testament Background: Selected Documents* (New York: Harper & Row, 1959), pp. 14–16.

Minor and Europe, a dramatic shift in membership and interest occurred. Gentiles soon outnumbered Jews. A brief for evangelism, education of converts, and the defense of the gospel against its enemies—in a language all could understand—became imperative.

Initial Writings (50–65 A.D.)

Paul furnishes the first known written witness to Jesus. His undisputed letters were penned between 50 A.D. and 62 A.D. Unfortunately, they contain only scattered and fragmentary information about the earthly career of Jesus. This is not surprising. Paul's primary concern, according to Acts 26:9-20, was the risen Christ who had confronted him on the Damascus road and had changed him from a persecutor to a proclaimer of "the Way." He presupposed the existence of the church and its apostolic leadership, and he addressed his communications to established Christian communities. Although he repeatedly referred to Jesus' death and resurrection, he made no effort to write a gospel. His aim was to supplement his readers' understanding of their faith and to assist them in sustaining it.

Paul was a contemporary of Jesus. According to Acts, he studied for many years in Jerusalem at the feet of the distinguished Rabbi Gamaliel. The chances are that he did not know Jesus in the flesh. If this assumption is correct, then he was not an eyewitness. This circumstance, however, would not invalidate his testimony. After his conversion, he was in close touch with many notable firsthand observers—including Peter, John, and James, the brother of Jesus (Gal. 2:9).[6] He not only preached the gospel in their presence, but he received the right hand of fellowship from them. His frequent traveling companion, if Acts is a reliable guide (see pp. 232–233), was Luke, who had ample opportunity to gather data about Jesus while Paul languished for two years in a Caesarean prison (Acts 23:33).[7] He also worked closely with Mark during the initial and terminal phases of his missionary campaign. Perhaps the most valuable testimonies of Paul concern the Lord's Supper (I Cor. 11:23-25) and the resurrection (I Cor. 15:3-8).

Q is a hypothetical source. Modern man has never seen it, but a careful study of Matthew and Luke has caused many scholars to assume its existence. These two Gospels have in common about 207 verses that are missing in Mark.[8] Sometimes the parallel passages suggest that different versions of an identical source were used (Mt.

[6]Contrast 1:15–20 and 2:1-10 where Paul stresses his independence of their tradition and authority.
[7]See p. 86 and p. 77 on the questions of who actually wrote Luke and Mark.
[8]Most of the content of Luke 3:2–4:16; 6:20–7:35; 9:57–10:24; 11:2–12:59; 13:18–35; 17:20–37 and Matthew's parallel material. A few scattered parallels are found elsewhere.

5:3-12; Lk. 6:20-22). Generally, though, the language is so similar (indeed, often exactly the same for many consecutive verses) that a single document is required to explain the phenomenon. The hypothetical document is commonly called *Q* after the German word *Quelle*, which means "source."

Q was not a gospel, which is a literary form in which the good news of Jesus' life, death, and resurrection was narrated. *Q* consisted largely of a collection of miscellaneous sayings arranged topically. Its affirmative moral and religious character suggests that it was designed to serve as a manual of instruction on the responsibilities of the Christian life. Who reduced the contents to writing is uncertain. Matthew is a likely candidate on the basis of a statement made by Papias, bishop of Hierapolis, about 140 A.D.: "Matthew composed his history in the Hebrew (Aramaic) dialect. . . ."[9] Matthew's composition could not have been the direct source of Matthew and Luke, however, since both seem to have used a Greek document. The fact that these Gospels relied so heavily on *Q* testifies to the high esteem in which this document was held in the early church. *Q* probably ceased to circulate independently after it was incorporated in Matthew and Luke.

L stands for another hypothetical source. There are about 300 verses in the Gospel of Luke, excluding the first two chapters, which have no parallel elsewhere. The supposition is that they came from an independent source. They contain both narrative and teaching material and include such memorable parables as the Good Samaritan and the Prodigal Son. Incidents in the ministry of Jesus from the preaching of John the Baptist to the ascension of Jesus are related with little concern for chronology. L is usually dated about 60 A.D., but no one knows who collected the material. Both Luke and Philip the Evangelist have been suggested. Actually, L may stand for several sources instead of one, and it may include oral tradition incorporated into the Gospel by its author. It is Luke's' usual faithfulness to his sources and his custom of using them in blocks that have prompted scholars to refer to his independent tradition as L.

M stands for a third hypothetical source, the material peculiar to Matthew. It contains about a dozen quotations from the Hebrew Scripture, a like number of narratives (Nativity, Peter Walking on the Water, etc.), and many parables and sayings. Its spirit is markedly Jewish, and it exhibits a keen interest in Jesus' relation to Judaism. Jesus is pictured as a second Moses. This characteristic has fostered

---

[9]Eusebius, *Ecclesiastical History,* III, 39.

speculation that Jerusalem was the birthplace of the collection. M is dated about 65 A.D.[10]

**Completed Writings
(65–100 A.D.)**
The Jewish revolt against Rome from 66 to 70 A.D. sealed the nation's fate. Jerusalem was destroyed, tens of thousands of Jews were slaughtered, and larger numbers were dispersed. These frightful happenings profoundly affected the Christian community. The church was wrenched from its Palestinian moorings. All of the apostles were dead (except John, perhaps), and eyewitnesses had become scarce. Hope for the imminent return of Jesus had faded. The need for more adequate records was urgent.

Mark was the first extant written Gospel.[11] This conclusion is supported by several facts. (1) Matthew and Luke used Mark as a major source. Matthew incorporated about 90 percent of Mark in his Gospel and Luke about one-half. When a passage from Mark fails to appear in either Matthew or Luke, it is usually found in the other Gospel—a solid argument against the notion that Mark was a later abridgment of Matthew. A stronger case can be made for the supposition that Matthew and Luke abridged Mark in order to secure room for their substantial non-Markan material. (2) Matthew and Luke normally follow the order of Mark. When either departs from Mark's order, the other usually remains steadfast. (3) Matthew and Luke frequently improve on Mark's grammar and refine his style of writing. (4) Matthew and Luke often modify or omit phrases in Mark that they deem offensive. In the incident of the Stilling of the Storm, Mark's "Teacher, do you not care if we perish?" (4:38b) is reduced to a simple factual exclamation in Luke 8:24 and a plea for help in Matthew 8:25. More serious modifications occur elsewhere. Jesus'

[10]Although no two reconstructions of *Q*, M, and L are alike, representative ones may be found in A.M. Hunter, *The Work and Words of Jesus* (Philadelphia: The Westminster Press, 1950); F.C. Grant (for *Q*), *Harper's Annotated Bible* (New York: Harper & Row, 1955); C.S.C. Williams (for M and L) in Peake's *Commentary on the Bible*, rev. ed., ed. M. Black and H. H. Rowley (New York & Edinburgh: Thomas Nelson & Sons, 1962).

[11]Irenaeus believed that Matthew was written first (Eusebius, *Ecclesiastical History*, IV, 8), and this has remained the official position of the Roman Catholic Church until recently. Since *Divino Afflante Spiritu* (1943) and *De Revelatione* (1965, Vatican II), Catholic scholars have been completely free (as long as they respect the teaching authority of the Church and do nothing contrary to declared dogma) to interpret the 1911 and 1912 decrees of the Pontifical Biblical Commission. Currently most of them support the solution of the Synoptic Problem that assumes the priority of Mark and the dependence of Matthew and Luke on that Gospel. This is the position taken by the latest and best Catholic exegetical work, R.E. Brown, J.A. Fitzmyer, and R.E. Murphy, eds., *The Jerome Biblical Commentary*, vols. I and II (Englewood Cliffs, N.J.: Prentice-Hall, Inc., 1968), pp. 4–5 (11–18); p. 63 (5). See also Alfred Wikenhauser, *New Testament Introduction* (New York: Herder & Herder, Inc., 1963), pp. 239–253. Perhaps the best case for Mark's alleged dependence on Matthew is made by W.R. Farmer, *The Synoptic Problem* (New York: The Macmillan Co., 1964).

encounter with the Rich Young Ruler is a case in point. Mark reports that when the young man addressed Jesus as "Good Teacher," he replied, "Why do you call me good? No one is good but God alone" (10:18). Matthew rewrites Jesus' response to read, "Why do you ask me about what is good?" (19:17). Proof that Matthew revised Mark's account is furnished by Luke, who follows Mark's version faithfully (Lk. 18:18–19).

The authorship of Mark is a matter of conjecture. Papias, venerable bishop of Hierapolis, wrote about 140 A.D. that John Mark was the author, and Irenaeus later confirmed this view.[12] The early disciples assembled in the house of Mark's mother (Acts 12:12), and Mark accompanied Barnabas and Paul on part of their first missionary campaign. He withdrew from them at Perga and returned to Jerusalem (Acts 13:13). Much later he was reconciled with Paul and became a useful worker in Rome (Col. 4:10; II Tim. 4:11; Philem. 24). He is referred to in I Peter 5:13 as "my son Mark" and is associated with Babylon (Rome). Papias called him Peter's "interpreter" and stated that Mark wrote down what he remembered from Peter's preaching.

The evidence for John Mark's authorship might seem to be irrefutable, but recent studies have multiplied skepticism. (1) The title was not attached to the Gospel when it first appeared, and nowhere does the Gospel suggest its author's name. (2) "Mark" (or "Marcus") was a common Roman name, and the man that Papias mentioned had neither heard nor followed the Lord. (3) The Gospel does not appear to stem from a memory source supplied by a single apostolic preacher. Form critics have demonstrated that the individual units which the author fashioned into a Gospel had a long history in the oral state. (4) The author betrays an anti-Jewish bias, unfamiliarity with the geography and topography of northern Palestine (7:31), and ignorance regarding certain Jewish practices (7:3–4; 10:12) and procedures connected with Jesus' trial. Could such a Gospel be the work of a Palestinian Jewish-Christian?

The date of Mark is as hidden as its author's identity. The apocalyptic discourse in chapter 13 provides the only clue. When four disciples asked Jesus when the Temple would be destroyed and the accompanying catastrophes accomplished, his reply included a reference to the desecration of an undesignated holy place (Mk. 13:14). Matthew's parallel passage indirectly identifies the holy place as the Jerusalem Temple (24:15), and Luke's comparable material clearly links the

---

[12]Eusebius, *Ecclesiastical History*, III, 39, and VI, 8.

prophecy with the siege of Jerusalem (21:20). Roman armies attacked the Holy City from 67 to 70 A.D. Since Mark's account of the prediction of the desecration specifically mentions neither the Temple nor Jerusalem, some scholars conclude that it must have been written prior to the siege. They regard the passage as an authentic prophecy and usually date the Gospel in the early sixties. Other scholars view the passage as a "prophecy after the event" and date Mark in the early seventies. They assert that the shadowy language employed precludes precise dating, and they point to the apocalyptists' time-honored habit of describing historical happenings as though they lay in the future. The data for dating Mark are inconclusive, although the vividness of chapter 13 suggests that the event described was not far distant. It seems most likely that the Gospel was written between 65 and 70 A.D.

Tradition indicates that Mark was written in Rome, but nothing in the Gospel clearly suggests its place of origin. The author's careful explanation of Aramaic words and Jewish customs (Mk. 5:41; 7:3–4, 11, 34; 15:22) implies a Gentile readership, but his use of Latin words transliterated into Greek (Mk. 5:9; 12:15, 42; 15:16, 39) no more proves that he wrote in Rome than our use of *hoi polloi* would certify that this book was written in Athens. Nor is it a convincing argument that nonapostolic Mark would never have been included in the New Testament unless it had a special connection with Rome. Some scholars maintain that Mark originated in Syrian Antioch; others favor Alexandria. Under such circumstances, it is the course of wisdom to accept this Gospel as it is and to refrain from pontificating on such disputed and insoluble matters as authorship and place of origin.

The purpose of Mark, unlike the Gospels of Luke and John, is not explicitly stated. Some of the author's reasons for writing, though, are not difficult to detect. (1) He wanted to confirm and strengthen the faith of fellow believers who stood on the threshold of suffering.[13] Nero had blamed Christians for the fierce fire that raged in Rome during the summer of 64 A.D. Many were condemned and compelled to confess. Then they were forced to fight wild beasts in the arena, become tar-coated incendiary torches in the emperor's gardens, or experience the agonizing torture of crucifixion.[14] The martyrdoms of Peter and Paul were recent. Although things were relatively quiet at that time, Nero still sat on the throne. Any day the readers might be put to the test. (2) He wanted to persuade the faithful that the

[13]The use of the technical word "gospel," the introduction of characters without explanation, and the assumption that Jesus' teachings are known suggest that the Gospel is addressed primarily to Christians.
[14]Tacitus, *Annals* XV, 40,44.

impending destruction of Jerusalem was a sign of the Consummation of the Age. His eschatological interests frequently manifest themselves in the Gospel (4:29; 9:1; 12:1–12), but they are most cogently articulated in chapter 13. The passage delineates the suffering, persecution, and natural disturbances that will precede the End. After the tribulation, the Son of Man will come in the clouds and dispatch the angels to "gather his elect from the four winds" (13:27). (3) He wanted to assure his readers that the Coming Son of Man and the Crucified Christ were one and the same. Jesus' humiliation and rejection rankled early Christians, but the author confidently declared that his death was a divine necessity: "For the Son of Man also came not to be served but to serve, and to give his life as a ransom for many" (10:45).

The sources of Mark were many. Whether they were oral or written is debated, but it is safe to assume that some of the material had been grouped together before it reached the author. His most evident sources were: Peter, as Papias stated; the Passion Story; a collection of teachings, parables, and sayings somewhat similar to Q; stories of conflict between Jesus and his opponents (Mk. 2:13–3:6); stories such as the one describing the death of John the Baptist; and the Little Apocalypse (Mk. 13:1–37).

Mark's structure is clear-cut. The Gospel falls into two main parts of almost equal length. The first division (1:14–8:26 concerns Jesus' Galilean ministry. His conflict with the demons and the religious and civil authorities is accompanied by a corresponding surge of popularity among the crowds. The common people heard him gladly, but their understanding of his mission and message was minimal. Even his intimate disciples failed to grasp his teachings and his true significance. The second division (11:1–16:8) describes Jesus' Jerusalem ministry, the machinations of the power structure that provoked the crucifixion, and the surprising resurrection. The two divisions are preceded by an introduction (1:1–13) and followed by an ending added by a later hand (16:9–20), and they are linked by Peter's "confession," the Transfiguration, and a summary version of the journey to Jerusalem (8:27–10:52).

The characteristics of Mark help to distinguish it from the other Gospels. (1) It is the shortest, simplest, and oldest of them all. (2) It gives the most candid account of Jesus. He is pictured as one who is limited both in knowledge (5:9, 30; 6:38; 9:16, 21) and in power (6:5). While the author acknowledges Jesus as Son of God, he frankly faces his humanity. Jesus hungers, tires, becomes angry, wonders, groans, pities, prays, cries, and dies. (3) It is action-packed. Jesus is a doer. He calls disciples, collects crowds, heals the sick, disputes adversaries, travels, teaches, and touches. (4) It is geared to Gentiles. Roman coins are used (6:37; 12:42; 14:5) and Roman laws are cited (10:12). Jewish customs and Aramaic words are explained (3:17; 5:41; 7:11, 34; 15:22). (5) It advances the messianic-secret motif (followed, in part, by Matthew and Luke). Jesus' messiahship, which is never clearly and convincingly disclosed to the public, is revealed in five successive stages. (a) Jesus is informed at his baptism (1:11). (b) The demons recognize who he is (1:24). (c) Peter, near Caesarea Philippi, perceives that Jesus is the Messiah (8:29). (d) Jesus quietly affirms who he is by his symbolic ride into Jerusalem (11:1–10). (e) The climax is reached on the final day of Jesus' life. In a secret session, the High Priest asks Jesus, "Are you the Christ, the Son of the Blessed?" Jesus replied, "I am" (14:61–62).[15]

Mark's peculiar ending has puzzled scholars. In the two most reliable texts,[16] the Gospel terminates with *ephobounto gar,* "for they [the women who visited the empty tomb] were afraid" (16:8). The conjunctive conclusion appears abrupt and ungrammatical. Was something intended to follow, as in 11:18 and Luke 22:2? The author was certainly aware of the resurrection. Perhaps he was interrupted before he could complete his work, or maybe the end of his scroll suffered mutilation. In any case, the early church concluded that the Gospel was incomplete and added to it two different endings.[17] The Longer Ending (16:9–20), which contains three appearances of Jesus, probably dates from the second century. It is found in most of the existing manuscripts of Mark and in all of the ancient versions. The Shorter Ending, which may be nearly as old as the Longer Ending, is found in a few manuscripts—following either 16:8 or 16:20. If

---

[15]At the beginning of our century, the distinguished German scholar, Wilhelm Wrede, attributed the scheme of secrecy in Mark to its author. Wrede reasoned that the idea of Jesus' messiahship had occurred to no one prior to the resurrection. As soon as the Easter faith was proclaimed, however, believers tended to interpret Jesus' non-messianic ministry in messianic terms. The absence of any claim to messiahship by Jesus and his disciples during his historical career caused the church to sponsor "the dogma of intentional secrecy." Since the church's post-resurrection insight that Jesus was the Messiah had never publicly been proclaimed by him, it was concluded that he must have secretly taught his disciples his true identity. Mark did not invent the secrecy motif; it was current in the church of his day. He simply fixed it in the Synoptic tradition.

Markan research has developed considerably since Wrede's day. Although his thesis received strong support in Rudolf Bultmann's work (*Theology of the New Testament,* vol. I), significant modifications were made by post-Bultmannian scholars. See James M. Robinson, "The Recent Debate on the 'New Quest,' " *The Journal of Bible and Religion,* XXX, 3 (1962), 198–208. The Conzelmann-Robinson position is "refuted" by Lewis S. Hay, "Mark's Use of the Messianic Secret," *Journal of the American Academy of Religion,* XXXV, 1 (1967), 16–27.

[16]*Vaticanus* and *Sinaiticus.*

[17]See the passages printed after Mark 16:8 in the Revised Standard Version.

the evidence of vocabulary, style, content, and manuscript is taken seriously, neither ending could have been part of the original Mark.

Numerous attempts have been made to reconstruct the "lost ending" of Mark from the concluding sections of Matthew and Luke, or even from John and Acts.[18] The results have been less than convincing. Mark may have felt that his previous promises of the resurrection were sufficient (8:31; 9:31; 10:34; 14:28; 16:7).[19] Consequently he chose to end his Gospel as we now have it—on the high-pitched note of expectation. Parallels have been found to his "abrupt ending," and an increasing number of specialists are persuaded that "for they were afraid" marked the original ending of his work. In this conclusion they can claim the support of the venerable Eusebius, the most widely read Christian scholar of antiquity.

Mark remained the sole Gospel for nearly twenty years. Then Matthew and Luke incorporated massive amounts of it into their more inclusive works. It was a telltale tribute to the status the Second Gospel enjoyed in the early church. Since little more than a generation separated the writing of Mark from the death of Jesus, the earliest Gospel was highly esteemed. The pattern its author created started a trend. Every known gospel of early times, canonical or otherwise (except, perhaps, John), used Mark as a major source.

Matthew, according to church tradition, was written by the converted tax collector and disciple of that name. The tradition stems from a statement by Papias that Matthew composed the oracles (sayings?) in Hebrew and everyone interpreted (translated?) them as he was able.[20] Similar statements are made by Irenaeus,[21] Origen,[22] Eusebius,[23] and Jerome.[24] The substitution of the name "Matthew" (Mt. 9:9) for "Levi" (Mk. 2:14) seems to some a confirmation of the tradition. Many modern scholars, however, remain unconvinced. (1) Matthew was not written in Hebrew (Aramaic?) but in Greek. Its author used Greek sources and addressed a predominantly Gentile church. (2) Papias' words probably refer only to the sayings of Jesus (*Q*), not to the entire Gospel of Matthew. (3) Jewish authors fre-

---

[18]See H.D.A. Major, T.W. Manson, and C.J. Wright, *The Mission and Message of Jesus* (New York: E. P. Dutton & Co., 1938), pp. 208–211.
[19]N.Q. Hamilton, "Resurrection Tradition and the Composition of Mark," *Journal of Biblical Literature*, LXXXIV, Part IV (1965), 415–421, argues that Mark wanted to reinterpret the traditional resurrection.
[20]Eusebius, *Ecclesiastical History*, III, 39.
[21]*Against Heresies*, III, 1, 1.
[22]Eusebius, *Ecclesiastical History*, VI, 25.
[23]*Ecclesiastical History*, III, 24.
[24]*Commentary on Matthew*, Prooem., 5.

quently wrote under the names of past notables. (4) Matthew's author reinterprets Jesus' ethical teachings, codifies them, and applies them to situations that probably originated beyond the life-span of the Twelve. (5) An apostle would not have relied so extensively on Mark, a nonapostolic source.

If Matthew's authorship of the First Gospel is indefensible, it is no matter for despair. We can treat it as anonymous, as we must Mark, and discover what the Gospel suggests concerning its author. He was a second-generation Christian of Hebrew extraction. His native tongue was Greek, and he used Greek sources. He derived his knowledge of Jesus not from personal recollections as an apostle but from oral and written traditions that circulated in his own community.

The date of Matthew cannot be fixed with precision. The latest possible time would be about 115 A.D., when the Gospel was used by Ignatius of Antioch. Since Ignatius regarded Matthew as authoritative, it must have been in circulation for many years—perhaps by 100 A.D. or sooner. On the other hand, Matthew's use of Mark makes a date earlier than 65–70 A.D. unlikely. A date later than 70 is supported by Matthew's clear reference to the conquest and burning of Jerusalem (22:7), the addition of the word "desolate" (23:38), the alteration of Mark 13:14 (24:15), and the presence of the phrase "to this day" (27:8). When time is allowed for Mark's dissemination and acceptance, the years of probability are reduced to between 75 and 100 A.D. Theological and ecclesiastical considerations indicate 80 to 85 A.D. as the most likely date.[25]

Matthew gives no clear-cut indication of its place of origin, but it does furnish its readers with several helpful clues. We have already noted that its author wrote in Greek and employed Greek sources, including Mark. His quotations from the Old Testament are usually derived from the Septuagint, a Greek translation popular among Hellenized Jews. A center of Greek-speaking Christians with a Hebrew background would seem to be a probable place for the composition of Matthew. Alexandria and Caesarea have been suggested, but scholarly consensus has settled on Syrian Antioch.[26] Not only does this city meet the general specifications but it was there that Matthew was first quoted by Ignatius.

[25]Sherman E. Johnson, "The Gospel According to St. Matthew: Introduction and Exegesis," in George A. Buttrick, ed., *The Interpreter's Bible* (New York: Abingdon Press, 1951), VII, 240–241, argues for a date not far from 100 A.D. Some scholars of a conservative bent date Matthew and Luke in the sixties.
[26]See the seminal work by B. H. Streeter, *The Four Gospels: A Study of Origins* (London: The Macmillan Co., 1924). Streeter locates each Gospel at one of the four centers of early Christianity.

Many purposes apparently prompted Matthew to write his Gospel. (1) He wished to supplement Mark, which was deficient in the teachings of Jesus, by adding to Mark's "deeds" the sayings of Jesus found in Q and other sources. (2) He wanted to affirm that Jesus was the predicted Messiah of Jewish prophecy and apocalypticism. The family tree he records shows symbolically and substantively that Jesus is a descendant of David. Isaiah, Micah, and Jeremiah foretold his birth. Matthew repeatedly introduces the Christ concept into his sources (11:2; 16:20; 24:5; 26:68; 27:17, 22), and he increases considerably the Son-of-David references (1:1; 9:27; 12:23; 15:22; 21:9, 15). His use of Old Testament prophecies corresponds to that of the Qumran scribes. The testimonies were understood in the context of the eschatological convictions of the Christian community, and the eschatological beliefs, in turn, tended to correct and expand the gospel tradition. Once Matthew has established Jesus' first advent as Messiah, he moves on to a second and more compelling theme: Jesus will soon come again as the glorified Son of Man to judge and rule the world. (3) He wanted to proclaim that the church is the New Israel. The Jews forfeited their claim to the covenant relationship when they rejected Jesus as the Messiah and accepted responsibility for his crucifixion (27:25). The troubled state of their nation was the logical consequence. The "church" (the word appears in no other Gospel) is comprised of all who share Peter's confession that Jesus is the Christ (16:16). It has been given the power to interpret the Law and to evangelize the world (18:17; 24:14; 28:16–20). (4) He wanted to provide the church with a manual of instruction and administration. He pictures Jesus as a second Moses and his teachings as New Law. Even the structure of his Gospel incorporates this idea. Jesus' sayings are arranged into five formal discourses apparently patterned after the five books of Moses. Like Moses, Jesus escapes death in infancy, is called out of Egypt, is tempted in the wilderness, and proclaims the Law from a mountaintop. His teachings are authoritative, and obedience to them brings automatic rewards. The church is an organized society of both good and bad people. It is separate from the synagogue and hostile toward it (17:24–27; 23:1–36). It has its own disciplinary procedure (18:15–17), and it acknowledges a double standard of discipleship. Less is required of common Christians than of those who would be perfect (19:3–12, 16–22).

Matthew's principal source was Mark. He reproduced about 90 percent of the earliest Gospel, making his own writing a second edition of Mark, revised and enlarged. Although he usually followed Mark's order, he was not a slave to the earliest Gospel. He abbreviated it, added to it, omitted from it, and corrected it to suit his purposes. In addition to Mark, he used Q, M (material found only in Matthew), a list of Old Testament quotations, a genealogy of Jesus' ancestors, and a nativity narrative. From these diverse and sometimes discordant parts, he fashioned an artistic and memorable whole.

Matthew's fondness for structure shows throughout his Gospel. Jesus' genealogy is artificially arranged in three groups of fourteen ancestors each (1:1–17). Five blocks of Jesus' teaching material are introduced at intervals into Mark's basic chronology. The fivefold pattern is probably a conscious imitation of the fivefold Torah. Each of the extended discourses is introduced by a series of narratives that relate the activities of Jesus, and each is concluded by some such phrase as "And when Jesus had finished these sayings . . ." The first narrative-discourse is preceded by an account of Jesus' birth and infancy, and the fifth is followed by the Passion and Resurrection. In the outline of Matthew that follows, the five blocks of teaching material are italicized.

I.	Introduction:	The Nativity	1:1–2:23
II.	Jesus' Life and Law		
	Book One	Baptism and Temptation	3:1–4:25
		Sermon on the Mount	5:1–7:29
	Book Two	Jesus' Mighty Works	8:1–9:34
		Instructions to Disciples	9:35–11:1
	Book Three	Questions and Controversies	11:2–12:50
		Parables of the Kingdom	13:1–53
	Book Four	More Mighty Works and Teachings	13:54–17:27
		On Sin and Forgiveness	18:1–19:2
	Book Five	Teachings and Happenings in Judea	19:3–23:39
		The End of the Age	24:1–26:2
III.	Conclusion:	Jesus' Death and Resurrection	26:3–28:20

The characteristics of Matthew lie close to the surface of this impressive work. (1) It is topical in arrangement. What chronology it does possess stems largely from Mark. (2) It has a textbook quality about it. Materials are grouped in threes, fives, sevens, and other numbers apparently to make memorization easy. There are three sections to the genealogy, three temptations, three miracles (leprosy, palsy, fever), three denials by Peter, three parables about the future, and three wonders at the crucifixion. There are five major discourses and five searching questions on a given day in Jerusalem. There are seven parables in chapter 13. (3) It occasionally magnifies the miraculous. From Jesus' supernatural birth and star-guided visitors to the convulsions of nature and the resurrection of the saints that accompanied his death, readers are alerted to God's power at work in the world. Matthew includes most of the miracle stories found in his sources, sometimes heightening the miraculous element (9:18; 20:30). (4) It tends to idealize the disciples and Jesus. References to the disciples' ignorance or bewilderment are diminished (Mk. 18:17-21; Mt. 16:9-12) or deleted (Mk. 9:6, 10, 32; Mt. 17:4-5, 9-10, 22-23). The self-serving question about special seats in the kingdom is transferred from the mouths of James and John to their mother (Mk. 10:35; Mt. 20:20). References to Jesus' sternness, anger, and alleged insanity are omitted (Mk. 1:43; 3:5; 10:14; 3:21). The fact that he *could* do no mighty works in Nazareth is altered to read that he *did* not do many mighty works there (Mk. 6:5; Mt. 13:58). (5) It emphasizes the fulfillment of prophecy. Jesus is pictured as the Davidic Messiah foretold by Scripture. The Old Testament is quoted or alluded to about 130 times to prove a point. Frequently the author uses the phrase "that it might be fulfilled" as spoken by some prophet or psalmist. One of these prophecies (2:23) cannot be found in the Hebrew Bible. Others are accorded higher historical value than Mark (Mk. 14:10-11; Mt. 29:3-10. Mk. 15:23; Mt. 27:34). In still another prophecy, Matthew misunderstands the nature of Hebrew poetic parallelism[27] and interprets Zechariah 9:9 to mean that Jesus rode into Jerusalem on *two* animals instead of one (21:5). Few, if any, of the prophecies in their original setting meant what they are made to mean in Matthew's context. "Out of Egypt have I called my son" in Hosea 11:1, for example, historically referred to Israel's Exodus from Egypt. Matthew (who alone records the flight of Joseph, Mary, and the Babe into Egypt) understood the passage to be a prediction of God's call to the infant Jesus, after the death of Herod the Great, to return from his temporary abode in the land of the Pharaohs (2:15).[28] (6) It looks upon Jesus as a second Moses and upon his teachings as New Law. Jesus did not come to destroy Moses' Law but to fill it with its divinely intended meaning. He both universalized and internalized its ethical demands. (7) It contains both pro-Jewish and anti-Jewish material. Pharisees are praised and blamed. Sabbath observances and fasting are accorded favorable and unfavorable treatment. Stories and sayings that presuppose and preclude a Gentile mission are placed side by side. Apparently Matthew candidly compiled his data. Although he modified his varied sources occasionally, for the most part he accurately reflected the thinking of a segment of the church in his day. (8) Its style is smoother and more flowing than Mark's. The use of such words as "lo" and "truly" helps to

---

[27]In which the second line of a couplet repeats the thought of the first.

[28]Some scholars see a school of interpretation responsible for Matthew's formula quotations. Qumran parallels are often cited. See Krister Stendahl, *The School of St. Matthew* (Philadelphia: Fortress Press, 1968). See also the stimulating article by S. Vernon McCasland, "Matthew Twists the Scriptures," *Journal of Biblical Literature*. LXXX, Part II (1961), 143-148.

make it so. While Matthew compresses Mark's narratives, he also omits ambiguities (Mk. 6:5-6; Mt. 13:58), redundancies (Mk. 1:32; Mt. 8:16; Mk. 4:39; Mt. 8:26b), and tasteless or tortured speech forms (Mk. 1:12-13; Mt. 4:1).

Matthew quickly displaced Mark at the top of the Christian best-seller list. Under the circumstances, Mark's surprising survival is a tribute to its vivid and fast-moving account of the gospel. Matthew included most of Mark and much more. Its convenient arrangement, so easily separated into sections, made it a first-class manual for church study and worship. Its fluid style aroused interest, and its adroit treatment of delicate questions[29] dissolved doubts. Second-century authors quoted Matthew more than any other Gospel. When the four Gospels began to circulate together, Matthew was placed first, a position it has never relinquished. Perhaps the claim that Matthew's masterpiece is the most important book in the world suffers from only slight exaggeration.

Luke, according to tradition, bears the name of its author, the beloved physician and the traveling companion of Paul. Of course the Gospel did not originally carry his name, and Papias does not mention him. Irenaeus, writing about 180 A.D., indicates that Luke, an attendant of Paul, wrote Acts.[30] This view was confirmed by the Roman church, according to the Muratorian canon, near the end of the second century. An ancient introduction to the Gospel, called the anti-Marcion prologue, identifies Luke as a doctor, a disciple of apostles, and author of Luke and Acts. These conclusions rest primarily upon the preface of Luke, Paul's reference to Luke by name (Col. 4:14; Philem. 24), and the so-called "we sections" which present a first-person account of travels with Paul (Acts 16:10-17; 20:5-15; 21:1-18; 27:1-18:16). Evidence for Luke's authorship, however, is by no means conclusive. Word studies do not support the claim that the author was a physician. A technical medical language was nonexistent in antiquity, and nearly all of the alleged medical terms found in Luke were used by nonmedical writers of his age. Yet a clear medical interest does permeate Luke-Acts. Attention is directed to the care and healing of the sick, cures performed by the apostles, and protection of the reputation of the medical profession (Mk. 5:26-Lk. 8:43). The author may well have been a physician, but whether he was Dr. Luke is an open question. All we really know about the author is revealed in his work.

[29]Such as "Why did a sinless Jesus submit to a baptism for the remission of sins?"
[30]*Against Heresies*, III, 13, 3.

Luke was probably written about 80–85 A.D. This date is suggested by several items. (1) Luke's author made extensive use of Mark (65–70 A.D.), reproducing at least fifty per cent of that Gospel. (2) Jesus had predicted that Jerusalem would be destroyed. This fateful happening occurred in 70 A.D. Luke's author records passages that seem to indicate that Jesus' prophecy had already been fulfilled (19:41–44; 21:20–24). (3) Luke makes no use of Matthew (80–85 A.D.), and vice versa. (4) Luke's author wrote a second volume, the Acts of the Apostles, during the last decade of the first century (Acts 1:1–2). (5) Luke shows no knowledge of the collected letters of Paul, which were in circulation after 100 A.D.

Luke's place of composition is unknown. A second-century tradition suggested Achaia (Greece) or Alexandria. Modern speculation includes Caesarea, Ephesus, Rome, Syria, and Palestine. The very multiplicity of proffered municipalities underscores the uncertainty. It is fortunate that an interpretation of Luke (and Acts) does not depend upon sure knowledge of its place of origin.

The purposes of Luke were numerous. (1) In the preface, the author states that he wrote to communicate more fully and accurately the truth of the gospel (1:1–4). He was the first historian of the Christian movement; another (Eusebius) would not appear for three centuries. The Gospel (and Acts) is addressed to Theophilus ("lover of God"), probably a practicing Christian. The singular form of the address and the deferential title ("most excellent") suggest that he was a Roman governmental official.[31] Perhaps he was Luke's patron and publisher. But no one seriously maintains that this Gospel was written for only one person. Its formal preface was patterned after those used for the general reading public. Luke was a trade book. It was intended to inform and inspire fellow Christians and to attract Gentiles. Other motives that led to its birth can be gleaned from the work itself. (2) He wanted to show that Christianity was not subversive. During its infancy, the Jesus movement was regarded by Rome as a Jewish sect. Since Judaism was a legal religion, this identification was an altogether happy one. It guaranteed Christians freedom from harassment and freedom for propaganda. Their movement spread and their numbers multiplied. Success stimulated Jewish hostility and rejection and Roman suspicion. Christians were shorn of their natal security and subject to sporadic local persecution as under Nero in 64 A.D. Luke attempted to forestall further violence by stressing such items as Jesus' political loyalty, Pilate's assurance

---

[31]Some scholars argue that the deferential address and Theophilus' need "to know the truth" indicate that he was not a Christian but a Gentile "God-fearer" who had to some degree resisted Christian persuasion.

of Jesus' innocence, and Herod Antipas' failure to find legal grounds for Jesus' death. (3) He wanted to indicate that Christianity was a universal religion devoid of racial prejudice. He traces Jesus' genealogy to Adam (Father of the human race) rather than merely to Abraham (Father of the Hebrews). He casts a hated Samaritan as the hero in one of Jesus' most compelling parables. All references to the strictly Jewish mission of Jesus are absent (Mt. 10:5; 15:24). He alone records Jesus' mission charge to "the seventy," traditional number for all the nations of the earth (10:1–20). (4) He wanted to show that the church had superseded the synagogue as the true eschatological community of Israel. He emphasized that Jesus was the acknowledged Christ of Jewish expectation who had been resurrected "to give repentance to Israel and forgiveness of sins" (Acts 5:31). It was the stubborn refusal of the chosen people to recognize and accept their own Messiah that caused God to call into being a new community. This community, the church, possessed all of the rights and privileges once held by the Jews. Luke was the first gospel writer to see the church in its theological setting. Mark had envisaged an interval of evangelism among the Gentiles prior to the End of the Age (Mk. 13:10). Matthew described the establishment of the church, its apostolic authority, and its disciplinary procedure (Mt. 16:18–19; 18:15–17). Luke mutes Markan passages that trumpet the imminence of the End, and he looks askance at people hooked on the hope of instant Eden. He views the lengthening time before the End as providential. It enables the church to play its necessary role in the divine drama of redemption.

Luke credits his material to "eyewitnesses and ministers of the word" (1:2). Scholars believe that he employed three principal sources. He reproduces over half of Mark, strangely omitting 6:45–8:26.[32] He generally adheres to Mark's order, quoting him at length and interspersing the quoted blocks with other material. He deals more drastically with Mark's language than does Matthew, telescoping his tales and refining his style. Such Semitisms as Golgotha, Gethsemane, Boanerges, Iscariot, abba, and hosanna are shunned. Numerals and adverbs are often omitted. Specific Semitic terms are replaced by more general designations (scribe becomes lawyer; rabbi becomes master). Luke also presumably used Q which he usually quotes in order and with fidelity. Most of Luke's Q tradition is found in 6:20–8:3 ("the lesser interpolation") and 9:51–18:14 ("the greater interpolation"). About one-third of Luke stems from a special source (or sources), L. It probably never circulated as a separate document.

---

[32]Was this passage missing from his copy of Mark? Was he merely conserving space for other data? (The convenient size of a scroll might have been the deciding factor.) Or did he regard his own material as sufficient?

The birth and infancy stories found in the first two chapters differ in style and language from the rest of L; they doubtless existed independently. Much of L's passion and resurrection material probably sprang from oral tradition. Even the central block of L material is not blessed with homogeneity. Despite these facts, L is a convenient symbol for Luke's special tradition (as is M for Matthew's special source). L is laden with parables (seventeen of them) including such favorites as the Good Samaritan, the Pharisee and the Publican, the Rich Fool, the Rich Man and Lazarus, the Prodigal Son, and the Dishonest Steward. Except for the miracle material, L rivals Q in early origin. Caesarea advances the most compelling claim as the place where Luke's special source was collected and preserved. It was a Hellenistic city on the fringe of Palestine, the place of Peter's first Gentile convert, and the home of Philip the Evangelist.

Luke's structure is simple, and it shows how the author's sources were used. Mark's order and large blocks of his material provide the framework. Q is largely confined to 6:20–8:3 and 9:51–19:27 (the latter shared with L). Luke's special source is used exclusively for the first two chapters.

1. Preface   1:1–4
2. Birth and Boyhood of John and Jesus   1:5–2:52
3. John's Mission; Jesus' Baptism and Temptation   3:1–4:13
4. The Galilean Ministry   4:14–9:50
5. Journey to Jerusalem   9:51–19:27
6. Final Days in the Holy City   19:28–24:53

The characteristics of Luke serve to emphasize its distinctiveness. (1) Its author was a Gentile. (2) It has a formal preface. (3) It is Volume One of a larger work (Luke-Acts). The Gospel's preface also covers Acts. Both books are addressed to Theophilus. "In the first book" (Acts 1:1) refers to the Gospel. Both books share common purposes, concerns, and vocabulary. (4) It is the longest and most complete Gospel. (5) It highlights the work of the Holy Spirit. Everyone connected with Jesus' supernatural birth is "filled with the Holy Spirit" (1:15, 35, 41, 67, 80; 2:25), Jesus' ministry is inaugurated by "the Spirit of the Lord" (4:18), and the guidance of the Holy Spirit is evident throughout his life and the lives of his followers (9:29; 10:21; 21:36; 22:40; 24:49). (6) It stresses the universal nature of the gospel. Color, class, and culture count for naught: "All flesh shall see the salvation of God" (3:6). (7) It contains the best Greek and displays the most polished style of any Gospel. Luke had a way with words; his imagery is vivid and arresting. His contrasts are particularly captivating: Mary and Martha, "Dives" and Lazarus, the

Pharisee and the Publican, the Priest-Levite and the Good Samaritan. (8) It preserves the first Christian hymns, best known by their Latin titles: Ave Maria (1:28–33), The Magnificat (1:46–55), The Benedictus (1:68–79), The Gloria in Excelsis (2:14), and The Nunc Dimittis (2:29–32). (9) It evidences special interest in particular subjects: the perils of wealth (the rich fool, the rich ruler, the rich man), concern for outcasts,[33] prayer, women, the poor, miracles, and the Spirit.

The Gospel of John differs markedly from Matthew, Mark, and Luke. Although the latter were also written to nourish faith, John far surpasses them in this purpose and accomplishment (Jn. 20:31). In his work, history and interpretation are so skillfully intermingled as to defy separation. Jesus' words are clothed in the idiom of the author. Parables are replaced by allegories, and symbolism reigns supreme. The end result is essential biography—the portrayal of the permanent aspects of the thought and the meaning of Jesus. Consequently, we cannot be as confident of finding in John the actual or approximate words and works of Jesus as we can in Matthew, Mark, and Luke. We shall, therefore, postpone in-depth treatment of the Fourth Gospel to a later chapter.

The Synoptic Problem

Since Matthew, Mark, and Luke "look together" at the mission and message of Jesus, they are called the Synoptic Gospels. These Gospels reveal not only a considerable similarity of viewpoint and content but also a rather astonishing variety. How can the similarities and differences be explained? This is the Synoptic problem. Proposed solutions attribute the paradox to oral tradition, written documents, or both.

The oral theory accounts for the Synoptic similarities by positing a common oral Aramaic source. The idea was once rather popular, but it has now fallen into general disrepute. It explains some of the similarities but none of the differences. It ignores startling likenesses that can be explained only on the basis of the Greek language. It fails to account for Mark's omission of so much material included by Matthew and Luke.[34]

The documentary theory holds that the Synoptics were composed from earlier written sources (or copied from each other). The theory has many variations; we shall treat the three in current favor. (1) *The two-document theory* states that the authors of Matthew and Luke used *Q* and Mark as main sources. Their common use of *Q* accounts

---

[33]Chapters 15–19 have been called "the gospel to the outcasts."
[34]The theory of a *written* Aramaic gospel is burdened with the same deficiencies.

for the remarkable parallels between the sayings of Jesus in their Gospels; their use of Mark explains the fact that they independently follow Mark's order, smooth his style, and together, reproduce almost all of his Gospel. The differences between Matthew and Luke are explained by their departure from Q or Mark (or the use of somewhat different versions of each) and their use of independent traditions. The two-document theory assumes the priority of Mark,[35] connected Greek sources for the Synoptics, and the unfamiliarity of Matthew and Luke with each other's writing. The theory, which has received widespread scholarly support,[36] is outlined in the following diagram.

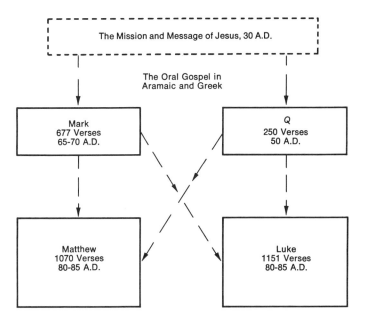

[Adapted from C. Milo Connick, *Jesus: The Man, the Mission, and the Message*, p. 85.]

(2) *The four-document theory* has replaced the two-document hypothesis in the thinking of some scholars. Two documents seem to them to be too narrow a base for the Synoptics. Matthew and Luke contain material not found in Q or Mark. Each Gospel has parts peculiar

[35]See pp. 76–77.
[36]There are notable exceptions. The Roman Catholic Pontifical Commission declared on June 26, 1912, that the theory lacks the support either of history or tradition. Recent Roman Catholic scholarship, however, looks with greater favor upon the two-source theory. See Wikenhauser, *New Testament Introduction.* Conservative Protestant scholars hold that each gospel writer, guided by the Holy Spirit, wrote an independent account which was unrelated to any other Gospel; his work was based on direct knowledge, oral teachings, and brief written records. See H. C. Thiessen, *Introduction to the New Testament* (Grand Rapids, Mich.: Wm. B. Eerdmans Publishing Co., 1943), pp. 101–129.

to itself. B. H. Streeter studied the special materials and concluded that they represent documents. He assigned each of the Synoptic sources to a special church. Mark was born in Rome, Matthew's special source (M) was in Jerusalem, Luke's (L) in Caesarea, and *Q* in Antioch. These four (plus a first edition of Luke called Proto-Luke) were collected and arranged in the pattern indicated below.[37]

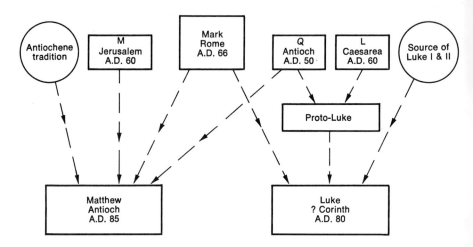

[Reprinted from B.H. Streeter, *The Four Gospels: A Study of Origins* (New York: St. Martin's Press, 1924), p. 150. Reprinted by permission of St. Martin's Press, Inc., Macmillan Co. of Canada, and Macmillan & Co., Ltd., London, England.]

(3) *The multiple-document theory* was a natural consequence of the two- and four-document hypotheses. Luke declared in his preface that many had undertaken to compile a narrative of Jesus while eye-witnesses still lived (1:1–2). Perhaps there was an assortment of written documents. Frederick C. Grant claims to have isolated seven sources: Syrian, Roman, General (Traditional Petrine narrative), Palestinian-Syrian (*Q*), Palestinian-Caesarean (L), Palestinian-Judean (Special Passion Story), and Judean (Lukan infancy story).[38]

[37]See Streeter, *The Four Gospels: A Study of Origins*, pp. 150–181, 485–562. Streeter discovered five sections of Luke (3:1–4:30; 6:12–8:3; 9:51–18:14; 19:1–27; 22:14–24:53) that are largely or wholly independent of Mark. They formed a "Gospel" similar to Mark in length and scope, composed of alternating blocks of *Q* and L materials. Streeter reasoned that to this first edition (Proto-Luke), Luke prefixed the birth stories and inserted narratives from Mark to form the Gospel of Luke. Since evidence points to Mark as the framework of the whole of Luke's Gospel and several Proto-Luke passages probably represent Luke's editing and expansion of Mark, the Proto-Luke theory has not won significant scholarly support.
[38]*The Growth of the Gospels* (New York: Abingdon Press, 1933), p. 66.

The Synoptic Problem is a highly complicated one, and the more one studies it, the more intricate it becomes. Although some form of the documentary theory is generally regarded as the best possible solution, none is altogether adequate and convincing. Q is a cogent hypothesis that falls somewhat short of certitude. M is attractive but speculative. L is doubtful in documentary form. The work of the form critics, as we shall shortly see, has bolstered the claim that both written and oral traditions were used. It is sometimes excruciatingly difficult to determine where one leaves off and the other begins. Our preference, consequently, is for a modified four-*source* theory (Mark, Q, L, and M) rather than a four-*document* theory. It is uncertain whether Q was one document or several, whether L was a continuous document (including the passion story) or a collection of documents. M rather clearly displays diverse lines of development. "Though considerations of simplicity favor limitation of the number of common sources, the separate sources may have been numerous, and either written or oral."[39] Probably all of the evangelists used oral tradition more extensively than is commonly believed.[40]

Before the Gospels After World War I, interest shifted to oral sources of the Synoptics. Decades of intense searching for written sources had largely exhausted the possibilities. Scholars wondered if the Gospels could be penetrated to their very beginnings. Careful scrutiny of Mark revealed imprecise indications of time[41] and place.[42] Clearly the chronological and topographical connective narratives had been supplied by the author. Further study suggested that even the selection and arrangement of gospel material had been governed by Mark's religious orientation and objectives. The traditions that he had included in his work had evidently reached him largely lacking in any framework. This insight demolished a long-standing scholarly premise—that Mark had preserved in his Gospel an historically accurate and dependable chronological account of the mission and message of Jesus. Now it was evident that Mark himself had furnished the time, place, and sequential pattern. Study of the other Synoptics confirmed that they had followed suit. They were all composed of separate, unrelated anecdotes and other pieces of tradition. Nearly any one of the paragraphs could be removed from its surroundings and allowed to stand alone, complete and self-explanatory. The evangelists had woven the fragments into a more or less connected narrative. But each of the authors had been conscious that the individual units were really self-contained; he had not hesitated to rearrange them to suit his purpose.

---

[39]A.M. Perry, "The Growth of the Gospels," in George A. Buttrick, ed., *The Interpreter's Bible* (New York: Abingdon Press, 1951), VII, 66. Reprinted by permission of Abingdon Press.

[40]Vincent Taylor, *The Life and Ministry of Jesus* (New York: Abingdon Press, 1955), p. 24.

[41]"Now after John was arrested," 1:14; "One sabbath," 2:23; 3:1; 8:1; etc.

[42]"Galilee," 1:14; "by the Sea of Galilee," 1:16; 1:35; 2:13; 2:23; 3:7; 6:1; etc.

The independent and fragmentary nature of the Synoptic material is not surprising. Extensive and connected accounts point to written records, yet for a double decade or more the gospel was preserved by word of mouth. Short, self-contained materials facilitate memory. This truth was trumpeted by a new trend in scholarship. It was called "form history" (from the German, *Formgeschichte*) or "form criticism" (in English-speaking countries).

Form Criticism Form critics applied the results of folklore study to the gospel materials. Their assumptions were several. (1) Folklore literature develops certain rather fixed forms such as the conundrum or limerick. (2) These forms are transmitted with relatively little alteration; where alterations do occur, they can be traced. (3) The forms stem from the situation in which the tradition was fixed. (4) The history of the tradition (its relative age and historical value) can be discovered from the form. On the basis of these assumptions, the form critics attempted to "look through" the Synoptics to the oral period. They used the written records as clues, and they isolated and classified each individual unit (called a "pericope"—a "cutting around," a section) according to its form.[43] Then they evaluated each unit historically and endeavored to recover the purpose of the people who had produced the first stories about Jesus and applied them to their own situation.

Foremost of the early form critics were Martin Dibelius of Heidelberg and Rudolf Bultmann of Marburg. Dibelius advanced the principles of form criticism in 1919.[44] Two years later Bultmann wrote an extensive analysis of the gospel materials.[45] Both attempted to learn the setting in which the gospel tradition developed. Dibelius concluded that the tradition arose in the missionary activity of the church. When the followers of Jesus proclaimed that he was the Messiah and Savior who would soon return, a compelling demand for further information arose. Bultmann believed that the tradition was more broadly based. He attributed the origin of the forms in the Gospels more to the controversies of the church and its educational activities.

Types of Forms Form critics generally agree that the Passion Story had a connected sequence almost from the start. It was vital to evangelism. A crucified Christ was "a stumbling-block to Jews and folly to Gentiles" (I Cor.

[43]The Fourth Gospel has few of the forms found in the Synoptics. This is one of the strongest evidences that it was composed at a later date.
[44]Martin Dibelius, *From Tradition to Gospel*, trans. B.L. Woolf (New York: Charles Scribner's Sons, 1935).
[45]Rudolf Bultmann, *History of the Synoptic Tradition*, trans. John March (New York: Harper & Row, 1963).

1:23). Christians countered that Jesus' death had been willed by God, and they appealed to historic revelations in Law and prophecy to substantiate their point (Acts 2:23–31; 3:18; 10:43; I Cor. 15:3). Against the charge that Jesus was a criminal and a blasphemer, they declared his innocence by recounting the circumstances of his arrest, trial, and crucifixion. Soon the Passion Story approximated its present arrangement. It served to remove the stigma of the cross and to make plain the way of salvation. Aside from it, form critics believe, the independent units or pericopes of the Synoptics exhibit five main forms. The choice of names to describe the forms varies; we shall follow the terminology advanced by Vincent Taylor.[46]

Pronouncement stories[47] are brief narratives in dialogue form. They purport to describe an encounter between Jesus and others. They are frequently of a controversial nature and are sometimes connected with a miracle. The setting is characteristically general and vague. Only minimum details are furnished to provide the distinctive feature of the story: a culminating striking statement of Jesus that can be applied generally. The overriding interest is in Jesus' pronouncement, not in the persons or the details of the related incident. The stories were remembered and transmitted not primarily to perpetuate accounts of past happenings but to provide the Christian community with an authoritative standard for its life in the world. The pericope concerning payment of tribute to Caesar is a good example (Mk. 12:13–17).

Miracle stories[48] are generally longer, more detailed, and more dramatic than pronouncement stories. They usually manifest a threefold pattern of development. Some difficulty is described, the method used to overcome it is related, and the miracle's effect is reported. The story's interest is in the display of power. Sometimes narratives seem to be a blend of miracle and pronouncement stories (Mk. 2:3–12), and on one occasion two miracle stories are combined in one narrative (Mk. 5:21–43). Mark 1:40–45 illustrates a miracle story in its pure form. Although the miracle stories, like the pronouncement stories, at first circulated independently, they may well have circulated in collections during the latter part of the oral period.

Sayings[49] of Jesus often circulated alone in the oral period. They were devoid of any narrative framework linking them to their original

[46]*The Formation of the Gospel Tradition* (London: The Macmillan Co., 1933).
[47]Dibelius uses *paradigm* and Bultmann *apothegm* to describe this form.
[48]Dibelius calls them *Novellen* and Bultmann *Wundergeschichten.*
[49]Dibelius uses the term *Paranesis*; Bultmann's inclusive term is *Logia.*

occasion in Jesus' ministry. Even after many of them had forfeited their independence by joining small collections, some continued to be autonomous. Proof of this is supplied by their floating nature. The same saying appears in different contexts in the Synoptics (Lk. 14:11; 18:14; Mt. 23:12). Some of the collections of sayings may date from Jesus himself,[50] but the great majority owe their existence to the Christian community. Dibelius thinks that they were preserved for the purpose of instructing new converts. Mark 8:34—9:1 constitutes a collection of sayings that deal with a common theme.

Parables[51] are found in profusion in the Synoptics. The Hebrew equivalent for parable stands for nearly any kind of verbal image— metaphor, simile, allegory, example story, proverb, etc. Synoptic usage is usually restricted to the simile (a succinct statement of likeness), the narrative parable (an extended simile), and the example story (like the Good Samaritan or the Rich Fool). The simile and narrative parable teach by analogy; the example story teaches directly what is to be imitated or avoided. The basic function of a parable is to compare. It places a familiar or convincing incident or story alongside something less well-known in order to shed light on the latter. The truth it sponsors is almost always singular and independent of the parable itself. During the oral period, a tendency developed to allegorize the parables by finding figurative or hidden meanings in them. Two main factors were responsible. (1) The original setting of many of the parables was soon forgotten, and the stories circulated in splendid isolation from the circumstances that gave them birth. Yet their original context often determined their proper meaning. What would be more natural than to allegorize them? Then the symbolic stories would derive their meaning from the situation that prevailed in the early church. (2) Early Christians delighted in hunting for hidden meanings in the message of Jesus. Sometimes the allegorical interpretation simply supplemented the original parable (Mk. 4:1–9, 13–20); more often it altered its internal structure (Mt. 22:1–14).

The nonparabolic teachings of Jesus are considerably more difficult to classify according to form. Bultmann sorts them according to wisdom sayings of the proverbial type (Mt. 6:34b; 12:34b), prophetic (Lk. 10:23–24) and apocalyptic (Mk. 13:24–27) utterances, sayings about the Law and its traditional interpretations (Mk. 7:15; 10:11–12), and first-person singular sayings that suggest Jesus' sense of authority (Mt. 10:16; Lk. 10:19–20).

[50]Such as Luke 6:20–22.
[51]Dibelius and Bultmann use the term *Gleichnis.* Taylor's term is intended to designate a wide range of stories of varying subject matter which does not submit to easy classification under other headings.

Stories about Jesus [and others][52] is Taylor's title for the fifth and final class of pericopes. Although his preference for this euphemism is understandable, it does not describe a literary *form*. Most critics prefer the terms "legends" and "myths." The form of legends resembles the stories saints and holy men in all cultures. Legends usually concern the associates of Jesus and evidence a distinct biographical interest (Mt. 14:28-33; Lk. 5:1-11; 19:1-10). Their practical value is minimal and, according to the form critics, so is their historical worth. Dibelius includes the Nativity Stories in this category. Luke's account of Jesus at the age of twelve also illustrates the legendary form (2:41-49). Myths describe stories in which the agent is divine rather than human. The accounts of the Temptation and Transfiguration serve as good examples (Mt. 4:1-11; Lk. 4:1-13; Mk. 9:2-8). Dibelius finds only a few myths, including such sayings as Matthew 11:28; Bultmann's list is much longer.[53]

Results and Limitations of Form Criticism

The form critics virtually paralyzed the search for the historical Jesus. They demonstrated, at least to their own satisfaction, that the Synoptics had been arranged like pearls on a string. The pearls (the independent, unrelated pericopes) "had been selected, polished and valued, even created at times, in the living environment of the church in the course of its preaching, controversy, teaching, persecution, and worship."[54] The string and the position of the pearls on it had been supplied by the evangelists. Since the pearls had been colored and shaped by the day-to-day needs and doctrinal convictions of the church, form critics despaired of finding reliable information about Jesus in them. Bultmann declared that "we can now know almost nothing concerning the life and personality of Jesus, since the early Christian sources show no interest in either, are moreover fragmentary and often legendary; and other sources about Jesus do not exist."[55]

Not all New Testament scholars enthusiastically embraced the new skepticism. As time passed, the form-critical tool for penetrating the Gospels came in for some searching criticism. (1) Prominent form critics disagree on the classification of gospel material. (2) Classifications are based on style and subject matter as well as form. This

---

[52]Called *Mythen* and *Legende* by Dibelius and *Geschichtserzählung* and *Legende* by Bultmann.

[53]For excellent, concise treatments of form criticism see A.M. Perry, "The Growth of the Gospels," in *The Interpreter's Bible*, VII, 68-72; E.V. McKnight, *What is Form Criticism?* (Philadelphia: Fortress Press, 1969).

[54]Dwight Marion Beck, *Through the Gospels to Jesus* (New York: Harper & Row Publishers, Inc., 1954), p. 56. Reprinted by permission of the publisher.

[55]Rudolf Bultmann, *Jesus and the Word*, trans. L.P. Smith and E.H. Lantero (New York: Charles Scribner's Sons, 1958), p. 8. Reprinted by permission of the publisher. Dibelius was far less skeptical.

compromises the claimed objectivity of the critics. (3) Pure forms are hard to come by. Many pericopes have a mixed form. Was form, then, the decisive factor in the development of the tradition? (4) The assumption that the form created the tradition ignores the fact that communities are more apt to shape and conserve than to create. (5) The results of literary criticism have often been neglected. (6) Questionable assumptions have been made concerning the needs and requirements of the early church. (7) The interest of the early church in the mission of Jesus has been negated. If second-generation Christians had a consuming concern for an outline of Jesus' ministry, is it not reasonable to assume that first-generation Christians desired and probably possessed an overall view of his work? (8) Full weight has not been given to the presence of eyewitnesses in the Christian community when the traditions were recalled, interpreted, and transmitted. (9) The history of the form and the history of the subject matter have sometimes been confused. (10) Many factors other than form operated in the growth and control of tradition. (11) The identity of a particular form does not disclose its history.[56]

Quest for the Historical Jesus Renewed

Growing concern over the limitations of form criticism failed to awaken in the Bultmann "school" an interest in the quest for the historical Jesus. Silence on the subject reigned for nearly thirty years (1926–1956).[57] Ernst Käsemann's address at Marburg in 1953 began the new quest. Then Günther Bornkamm's *Jesus von Nazareth* appeared in 1956. Bornkamm did not share the conviction of form critics who believe that the actual history of Jesus has been lost. Although he readily acknowledged that the gospel materials had been filtered through the post-Easter faith of the church, he argued that they cannot be dismissed as the mere product of pious imagination. They are considerably concerned with the pre-Easter history of Jesus. The tradition "points beyond itself to him whom the Church has encountered in his earthly form and who proves his presence to her as the resurrected and risen Lord. In every layer, therefore, and in each individual part, the tradition is witness of the reality of his history and the reality of his resurrection. Our task, then, is to seek the history *in* the kerygma of the Gospels, and in this history to seek the kerygma."[58] The Gospels tell Jesus' story in pericopes. Each one contains the person and history of Jesus in their entirety. The same

---

[56]Taylor, *The Formation of the Gospel Tradition*, gives a balanced evaluation of form criticism. A conservative critique is found in B.S. Easton, *The Gospel Before the Gospels* (New York: Charles Scribner's Sons, 1928).

[57]C.C. McCown, *The Search for the Real Jesus* (New York: Charles Scribner's Sons, 1940) depicts the quest that went on elsewhere in the twentieth century.

[58]Günther Bornkamm, *Jesus of Nazareth*, trans. Irene and Fraser McLuskey with J.M. Robinson (New York: Harper & Row Publishers, Inc., 1960), p. 21. Reprinted by permission of the publisher. "Kerygma" (proclamation) stands for the "essence" of the gospel proclaimed by the early Christians.

can be said for his words. Each one is self-contained, exhaustive in itself, independent of context for its meaning. Bornkamm concedes that the origin and purpose of the gospel tradition were governed by the practical needs of the church, that the tradition is often silent where we seek answers, and that naïve generalizations obscure particulars. These factors tend to blur the distinction between history and interpretation and make the historian's work more difficult. Nevertheless, Bornkamm insists that "precisely in this way of transmitting and recounting, the person and work of Jesus, in their unmistakable uniqueness and distinctiveness, are shown forth. . . . Understood in this way, the primitive tradition of Jesus is brim full of history.[59]

It became increasingly evident to scholars that early tradition did not run rampant. Many factors were at work to control it and to preserve its validity. (1) The Christian faith was based upon the remembered words and works of an actual historical person. Jesus was not a myth or legend but a figure whom many had encountered. (2) The leaders of the Christian community and many of their followers were themselves eyewitnesses of the happenings (Lk. 1:1). They were fully competent to correct errors that crept into the tradition. Their testimony was highly regarded and put to good effect. (3) Eyewitnesses were also numerous among the critics of Christianity. They were able to correct errors, and they doubtless pointed out departures from fact with alacrity. They thus served as a built-in hedge against falsification. (4) The folklore analogy is not altogether appropriate. There were well-educated people in the church almost from its inception. It is erroneous to assume that all oral "literature" was illiterate.[60]

When stories are told and retold, they are stripped of nonessentials. In its oral stage, the gospel material was no exception to this rule. Christian teachers and preachers tapped a vast reservoir of memories about Jesus. Their selections were usually spontaneous. They simply responded to the practical needs of the church. As the reminiscences were repeated, they assumed the most functional form. The form did not create the content, nor did it extensively alter the content. The form actually conserved the content. Once the form had been fixed, modification of the material became exceedingly difficult. Rather than undermining the historical reliability of the pericopes,

---

[59]McCown, *The Search for the Real Jesus*, pp. 25–26. For other illuminating discussions see J.M. Robinson, *A New Quest of the Historical Jesus* (Naperville, Ill.: Alec R. Allenson, 1959) and the excellent recent treatment by Harvey K. McArthur, ed., *In Search of the Historical Jesus* (New York: Charles Scribner's Sons, 1969).
[60]See A.M. Perry, "The Growth of the Gospels," in *The Interpreter's Bible*, VII, 71, on which these insights are based.

form criticism actually underscored it. The essential history was preserved by means of the forms.

Synoptic sources go back no further than 50 A.D. The double decade of development between Jesus and the first writings is surrounded by a wall of silence. The imaginative and concerted attempts of the form critics to breach that wall and to reconstruct the lost period of gospel tradition were altogether salutary. They can be faulted for subjective speculation, excessive skepticism, and the attribution of too much to the early church and too little to its founder, but their solid accomplishments cannot be slighted. They established the independent and self-contained nature of much of the gospel material. Interpreters can no longer rely with confidence on the immediate context of a particular passage or saying. The context was probably supplied by the evangelist and might actually conflict with the original setting. The form critics also demonstrated the dominant role the church played in the selection and shaping of the tradition.

Redaction Criticism

Form critics viewed the authors of the Synoptics primarily as collectors and transmitters of traditions that they had received. The form critics paid small attention to such questions as the controlling concepts and the unity of individual gospels. They directed their attention to the gospel material itself—its forms, life situation, and the history of its transmission. Their removal of older traditional material from its secondary setting convinced them of the composite nature of the writings commonly attributed to Matthew, Mark, and Luke.

World War II brought a virtual halt to literary activity. After 1945, however, Synoptic research resumed and began to take a new direction. Interest in small units was replaced by an examination of each of the Synoptics as a whole. It was recognized that the evangelists were not merely collectors and transmitters of traditional material, as the form critics claimed, but redactors (editors and revisors). They arranged and altered the material they had received to express their own theology, a theology often quite different from that found in the original. They were, to a considerable degree, authors in their own right.

The term "redaction criticism" was coined by the German scholar, Willi Marxsen, in 1954 although Günther Bornkamm and others had employed the redaction-critical method of study several years earlier. Bornkamm selected Matthew's account of the pericope of the Stilling of the Storm (8:23–27) to illustrate how the evangelists functioned as authors.[61] He compared Matthew's version with its parallels in Mark (4:35–41) and Luke (8:22–25). It was evident that the story in Matthew does not stand in a biographical context. It is one of a series of miracles designed to reveal Jesus as the "Messiah of deed" as the Sermon on the Mount (Mt. 5–7) had shown him to be the "Messiah of the word." The graphic and full-bodied account in Mark displays the characteristics of a typical miracle story, but Matthew omits the storytelling details and forces the pericope to sponsor a new theme. He accomplishes this by placing the story after two sayings about discipleship (8:19–22). In both instances the word "follow" (as a disciple) is used, and this word is repeated in the pericope concerning the storm on the lake (8:23). By prefacing the Stilling of the Storm with the sayings about "following," the evangelist endows the pericope with exemplary significance. The turbulent ride of the disciples with Jesus in the boat and the stilling of the storm typify the tribulations of discipleship and the small ship of the church. Matthew, then, has not merely collected and transmitted traditional material. By placing it in a context different from the one he found in Mark, Matthew has become the pericope's earliest known interpreter.

Matthew's authorship role is not limited to his placement of the pericope. He also alters its substance. Several instances of this fact could be cited but one will suffice. Bornkamm called attention to the evangelist's choice of the word used by the disciples to address Jesus when they call to him for help. Matthew replaces Mark's "Master" (διδάσκαλε) with "Lord" (κύριε). "Lord" is a respectful human title in Mark and Luke, but it is not a common form of address in Matthew. It is a divine predicate of majesty—at once a prayer and a declaration of discipleship!

Bornkamm's interpretation of the Stilling of the Storm did not constitute a repudiation of the principles of form criticism. Quite the contrary. He and other redactionists simply insisted that the form critical emphasis on individual units should be supplemented by awareness of the general conception and composition of each Synoptic as a whole. Only the contents of a given gospel, not that gospel in its entirety, can be considered composite material. The redaction of a gospel (its arrangement and composition into a particular framework) is the work of the evangelist. His selection of the traditional material, the order in which he used it, and his alterations of it were dictated

---

[61]Günther Bornkamm, "*Die Sturmstillung* in *Matthäusevangelium*," *Wort und Dienst, Jahrbuch der Theologischen Schule Bethel NF* (1948), pp. 49–54; reprinted in G. Bornkamm, Gerhard Barth, and H.J. Held, *Tradition and Interpretation in Matthew*, trans. Percy Scott (Philadelphia: The Westminster Press, 1963), pp. 52–57.

by his theology. He was a theological author operating from theological perspectives.[62]

After the Gospels Publication of the Synoptics did not exhaust the supply of gospel tradition. Perhaps no one was more cognizant of this than the person who penned the appendix of the Fourth Gospel. He observed that Jesus had done "many other things" besides those recorded in John. Then, with pardonable hyperbole, he opined: "Were every one of them to be written, I suppose that the world itself could not contain the books" (Jn. 21:25). Some of the tradition was preserved in early writings that have only recently come to light.

Agrapha ("unwritten" things) is a term used to describe purported sayings of Jesus not contained in the accepted text of the canonical Gospels. The agrapha run the gamut from terse, aphoristic utterances to extended discourses. Their sources are several. (1) Some appear in ancient manuscripts of the New Testament. After Luke 6:5, in the sixth-century Codex Bezae (which contained the gospels and Acts in two languages with the Greek and Latin texts facing each other on opposite pages) Jesus responds to a man working on the sabbath as follows: "Man, if indeed you know what you are doing, you are blessed; but if you do not know, you are cursed and a transgressor of the Law." (2) Others are found in the New Testament outside the Gospels. The author of Acts records Jesus' statement, "It is more blessed to give than to receive" (20:35), and Paul quotes Jesus' words in connection with the institution of the Lord's Supper (I Cor. 11:24–25). (3) A larger number are found in the writings of the Apostolic Fathers. These words, which are far from homogeneous, were composed by authors reputed to have been associates of the original apostles or their immediate disciples. They include the so-called Epistle of Barnabas, two epistles attributed to Clement of Rome, seven letters ascribed to Ignatius (bishop of Syrian Antioch), the Epistle and the Martyrdom of Polycarp (bishop of Smyrna), the Shepherd of Hermas, extant fragments from the works of Papias (bishop of Hierapolis), the Didache (or Teaching of the Twelve Apostles), and the Epistle of Diognetus. (4) Egyptian papyri discovered during the past hundred years contain numerous agrapha. The most fructifying find is contained in a collection called the Oxyrhynchus Papyri. The agrapha do not appear as a continuous discourse but as separate, unrelated sayings, preceded by the stereotyped introduction, "Jesus

[62]Redaction criticism has been applied principally to the Synoptics and the Acts of the Apostles. Two helpful studies in English are Joachim Rohde, *Rediscovering the Teachings of the Evangelists*, trans. Dorothea M. Barton (Philadelphia: The Westminster Press, 1968), and Norman Perrin, *What is Redaction Criticism?* (Philadelphia: Fortress Press, 1969).

says." The following is an example from papyrus 1: "Jesus says: . . . Lift up the stone and you shall then find me; cleave the wood and I am there." (5) Extracanonical gospels offer many alleged words of Jesus. Scholars first became aware of these writings from references to them in Christian literature of the second and third centuries. When Matthew, Mark, Luke, and John joined the canon, many competing gospels were neglected. Survivors have been discovered in ancient manuscripts of varying dates and states of repair. Apocryphal gospel material tends to exhibit one of two characteristics: amplification of a tradition found in the canon or heavy indebtedness to some special interest group in the Christian community.[63] Examples of the latter are the Gospel of Thomas, the Gospel of Truth, and the Gospel of the Egyptians.

Scholarly assessment of the agrapha has been as variable as the weather. Early experts certified many of the sayings as genuine and traced their source to the oral gospel from which our canonical Gospels drew heavily. Later specialists concluded that the historical utterances of Jesus had been so successfully smothered by legend and fantasy as to be rendered worthless. Current authoritative opinion is characterized by an attitude of openness. Some scholars make bold to suggest that we now possess a few agrapha as authentic as sayings of Jesus in the Synoptics. The suggestion is a seminal one, but it raises a question that screams for an answer: "Which sayings in the Synoptics?" Several Synoptic sayings seem themselves to be later additions and thus quite as dubious as those external to the canonical Gospels. Clearly every saying attributed to Jesus, whether canonical or apocryphal, must be evaluated individually. When this is done, no substantial revision of the Jesus presented in the Synoptics is required.

In this chapter we have determined and discussed the main sources of data concerning Jesus, and we have established the nature of the gospel tradition. Now, within the limitations and possibilities provided by modern scholarship, we shall see what the records say about Jesus of Nazareth.

[63]See *The Apocryphal New Testament*, corrected ed., trans. M.R. James (Oxford: Clarendon Press, 1955).

Jesus and His Mission
(Matthew, Mark, Luke)

The popular mind is filled with details about Jesus. Sunday School children confidently recite the circumstances of his nativity. He was born in a crude wooden stable on December 25th, in the year 1 A.D. Shortly thereafter, he was visited by shepherds and by three Oriental kings named Gaspar, Melchior, and Balthasar. Each of the potentates presented the Bethlehem Babe with an expensive gift that symbolized some aspect of his adult ministry.

The Gospels do not support such familiar declarations. They are the product of pious imaginations, and their historical value is nil. The circumstances of Jesus' birth cannot be gleaned from fantasy. Neither can they be unraveled from the tapestry of a single Christmas Story woven from separate gospel accounts. Matthew and Luke record different data, and they disagree on the sequence of events. It is in the midst of this diversity that truth must be sought.

Ancestry and Birth   Matthew begins his Gospel with an account of Jesus' genealogy (1:1–17). Luke introduces this subject in connection with the start of Jesus' ministry (3:23–38). Since prevailing opinion decreed that the Messiah would be a descendant of David,[1] both evangelists endeavor to provide Jesus with the proper credentials. But, alas, they don't present the same genealogies. The family trees are not only different; they conflict with each other and with the story of Jesus' virgin birth.[2] Matthew, who lists forty-six names, traces the ancestry from Abraham (Father of the Hebrews) to Jesus. Luke, using seventy-seven names, begins with Jesus and ends with Adam (Father of all men). Beginning with David, the genealogies travel different roads. Matthew routes

The material in this chapter is a condensed, updated, and at times expanded version of material found in C. Milo Connick, *Jesus: The Man, the Mission, and the Message* (Englewood Cliffs, N.J.: Prentice-Hall, 1963), and is used by permission of the publisher.
[1]Notable exceptions are *The Testament of the Twelve Patriarchs* and the Qumran Scrolls. There Jewish speculation envisages a Messiah who would come from a priestly line.
[2]See *Gospel Parallels*, 2nd ed. rev. (New York: Thomas Nelson & Sons, 1957), pp. 1–2, where the two accounts are conveniently arranged in parallel form. F.W. Beare, *The Earliest Records of Jesus* (New York: Abingdon Press, 1962) provides an excellent analysis of the first three gospels.

the royal line through Solomon (1:6), and Luke traces it through Nathan (3:31). They cross again at Shealtiel and Zerubbabel, thereafter to part permanently. They are even at odds as to the name of Jesus' grandfather. Matthew calls him Jacob (1:16), and Luke calls him Heli (3:23).

The artificial character of Matthew's genealogy is transparent. The evangelist divides his list of names into three sections of fourteen generations each.[3] It was a clever device designed to enshrine Jesus' Davidic descent in the schematic arrangement. The Hebrew alphabet was devoid of vowels. Each consonant had a numerical equivalent. "David," minus vowels, would be spelled Dvd. "D" (daleth) had the value of four, and "v" the value of six: D (4) + v (6) + d (4) = 14. Such a contrived family tree naturally necessitated the telescoping of time and the omission of numerous names well known to us from the Old Testament.

Conflicts between the genealogies and the claims of virgin birth compound the confusion. Both Matthew and Luke declare that Jesus was virgin born, yet both record genealogies which trace Jesus' ancestry through Joseph. If Joseph had nothing to do with Jesus' conception, as the virgin birth stories testify, why did the evangelists bother to reconstruct Joseph's ancestry? The purpose of the family trees is to prove that Jesus was a descendant of David, hence a person with proper messianic credentials. Perhaps the evangelists (or later editors) were aware of the difficulty. Matthew abruptly changes the ancestral line from Joseph to Mary: "Jacob the father of Joseph the husband of Mary, of whom Jesus was born" (1:16). Luke cares for the problem with a parenthetical comment: "Jesus, when he began his ministry, was about thirty years of age, being the son (as was supposed) of Joseph" (3:23). While these attempts at reconciliation are noteworthy, they do not diminish the difficulty. The real purpose of the genealogies is to demonstrate that Jesus is a descendant of David *through Joseph.*

The difficulties presented by the genealogies were detected early,[4] and over the centuries three main solutions have been proposed. (1) Matthew gives the genealogy of Joseph, and Luke gives the genealogy of Mary. Roman Catholics, Luther, and others have looked favorably on this proposal, but the theory is suspect. Joseph's Davidic

---

[3]Only thirteen appear in the third section, indicating that a name has been lost. Fourteen were clearly intended (1:17).

[4]See Eusebius, *Ecclesiastical History*, I,7, where a third-century solution is advanced by Julius Africanus. He accounted for the discrepancies on the basis of the levirate law by which a dead brother's childless widow might be married to a living brother to raise up children in the name of the deceased. This would permit the natural and legal ancestors to differ at points and result in two equally valid family trees. Note the variant readings of Matthew 1:16.

descent is well established (Mt. 1:20; Lk. 1:27), but the records contain no hint that Mary shared this heritage. Quite the contrary. Luke 1:36 suggests that Mary was a relative of Elizabeth, a member of the tribe of Levi. Since most people expected the Messiah to be "of David," for Luke to trace Jesus' line through Mary would strip Jesus of his eligibility. This was assuredly not his intent. (2) Matthew gives Jesus' legal descent, and Luke gives his natural descent. A number of eminent scholars have endorsed this view.[5] It leaves unexplained, however, why Luke would make a double departure from tradition and trace Jesus' ancestry through his *mother* who was probably a *Levite*. Since Matthew and Luke believed that Jesus' birth stemmed from a special act of God, is it not more credible that they both understood the lineage of Jesus in legal rather than literal terms? (3) The genealogies represent separate traditions that originated in different sections of the early church. This view, which is enjoying accelerated acceptance among scholars, has two distinct advantages. It coheres with knowledge of how the tradition developed, and it eliminates the necessity of harmonizing conflicting accounts.

The birth stories themselves reveal few agreements and many divergencies. Matthew and Luke both indicate that Jesus was born in Bethlehem and that the three central participants were Mary, Joseph, and Jesus. Beyond these commonalities their accounts are at odds.

Matthew	Luke
Mary and Joseph reside in Bethlehem (2:1).	Mary and Joseph reside in Nazareth (2:4).
	Couple travel to Bethlehem in connection with Roman census (2:4–5).
Jesus born in Joseph's house (2:11).	No room in the inn; Jesus placed in a manger (2:6–7).
King Herod learns of Jesus' birth; consults star-guided wise men (2:3–7).	
Wise men from East visit Babe; warned in a dream (2:8–12).	Shepherds from nearby fields visit Babe (2:8–19).
	Jesus circumcised on eighth day and given name (2:21).
Joseph warned; flight into Egypt (2:13–15).	
Herod slaughters innocent children (2:16–18).	
Herod dies; angel tells Joseph to return (2:19–20).	
Family heads for Bethlehem; Archelaus' reputation and a dream divert them to a new home, Nazareth (2:21–23).	Family returns to their home in Nazareth (2:22–40).

[5]See J.G. Machen, *The Virgin Birth of Christ* (New York: Harper & Row, 1930) for the definitive exposition of this position.

Even the declaration of Matthew and Luke that Jesus was born in Bethlehem has been challenged. Although their common witness cannot be cavalierly cast aside, no other evidence supports it. Some scholars are convinced that Jesus was born in Nazareth. (1) The evangelists refer to him as Jesus of Nazareth (Mk. 1:24; Lk. 4:34; Jn. 1:45), the official Roman inscription on the cross read "Jesus of Nazareth (Jn. 19:19), and his early followers were called Nazarenes (Acts 24:5). Then, as now, a man was known by the place of his birth rather than his residence. (2) After Jesus was rejected at Nazareth, Mark 6:4 indicates that he said of himself, "A prophet is not without honor, except in his own country." The Greek word for country (*patris*) customarily meant either a person's ancestral home or his birthplace.[6] Since Joseph was of Davidic descent, Jesus' ancestral home was Bethlehem. For Jesus to call Nazareth his *patris* would seem to indicate that he was born there. (3) Jesus was reared in Nazareth, an obscure village with no messianic associations. (4) The birth stories were originally private; they played no part in Jesus' public ministry. They arose after Jesus became the acknowledged Messiah. The purpose of the Bethlehem nativity tradition was to provide Jesus with the proper credentials. The Scriptures had prophesied that the Messiah would come from Bethlehem. Few expected anything good to come out of Nazareth (Jn. 1:46; 7:40-44).[7]

What, then, can be concluded about the virgin birth of Jesus? The idea is deeply rooted in Christian tradition and belief. As Matthew and Luke indicate, accounts containing the concept circulated at an early date and were widely accepted. Jesus' virgin birth was incorporated in the Apostles' Creed, and it is a necessary article of faith for Roman Catholic and Orthodox Christians and a personal article of faith for many Protestants. Despite these formidable considerations, however, scholarly judgments have increasingly questioned the virgin birth tradition. Matthew implies that Jesus is the son of a carpenter (13:55), and John assumes that he is the son of Joseph (6:42). Mark records the names of Jesus' four brothers and refers to his unnamed and unnumbered sisters (6.3).[8] The earliest New Testament writings (the letters of Paul) and the earliest Gospel (Mark)

[6]Philo of Alexandria, however, did call Jerusalem his *patris*. See Robert M. Grant, *A Historical Introduction to the New Testament* (New York: Harper & Row, 1963), pp. 276, 303.
[7]Despite the cogency of these arguments, a majority of scholars still accept the double witness of Matthew and Luke and affirm Jesus' Bethlehem birth. Perhaps the best statement of their case is found in William Ramsay, *Was Christ Born at Bethlehem?* (London: Hodder & Stoughton, 1898).
[8]Roman Catholics, who believe in Mary's perpetual virginity, correctly argue that the Greek word translated "brothers" did not have a precise meaning; it could include relatives beyond the closest blood ties. They regard Jesus' "brothers" as (1) sons of Joseph by a previous marriage, the theory of Epiphanius, or (2) cousins, sons of another Mary (Mt. 27:56), the suggestion of Jerome.

do not mention the virgin birth. Jesus never made belief in the virgin birth a condition of discipleship. The first preaching about Jesus, the kerygma, does not contain it. The nativity narratives are confined to the first two chapters of Matthew and Luke, and neither Gospel ever refers back to them. If the twenty-seven books of the New Testament had originally circulated together, the failure of twenty-five of them to deal with the nativity would be understandable. But since each book originally circulated alone, it seems clear that for the earliest Christians the idea of Jesus' virgin birth was either unknown or considered to be of little importance.[9]

The birth stories sprang from the theology of the church near the close of the first century. Although they provide an appropriate theological preface to a life that was climaxed by resurrection from the dead,[10] they cannot be relied upon for historical information about Jesus. The church knew Jesus as "the Son of God" (Mk. 1:1, 11; 3:11; 5:7; 14:61; 15:39). Some of its members, represented by Matthew and Luke, supposed that this implied a miraculous birth. Others, like Paul, Mark, and John, understood the phrase in a spiritual sense. Jesus' manhood depended on a normal conception and birth. His sinlessness stemmed not from the manner of his birth but from his decision to follow the will of God. Jesus was "descended from David according to the flesh and designated Son of God in power according to the Spirit of holiness by his resurrection from the dead" (Rom. 1:3–4). The real miracle "was the actual appearance in the world of one who in his mind and spirit completely expressed and embodied the reality of God."[11]

The Baptism The church showed slight interest in Jesus' life between his birth and his baptism. Only one incident of his boyhood was preserved (Lk. 2:41–52).[12] Aside from this, readers of the Gospels are confronted with thirty years of silence. Some data about Jesus' youth, however, can be gleaned from his public ministry and from known facts about life in first-century Palestine. Jesus lived in the frontier village of Nazareth as a member of a family that numbered no less than nine (Mk. 6:3). His father was a carpenter, a craftsman who worked both in wood and stone. Justin Martyr tells us that Jesus himself fashioned yokes and plows in his father's shop.[13] Whether Jesus attended a

[9]Perhaps the most dispassionate treatment of the subject is Vincent Taylor, *The Historical Evidence of the Virgin Birth* (Oxford: Clarendon Press, 1920).
[10]See A.M. Hunter, *The Work and Words of Jesus*, (Philadelphia: The Westminster Press, 1950), p. 30.
[11]Walter Russell Bowie, "Exposition, The Gospel According to St. Luke," in George A. Buttrick, ed., *The Interpreter's Bible* (New York: Abingdon Press, 1952), VIII, 39. Reprinted by permission of Abingdon Press.
[12]The passage is in legend form, according to the form critics.
[13]Justin Martyr, *Dialogue with Trypho*, 88.

synagogue school is uncertain,[14] but somewhere he learned the Palestinian equivalent of the "three R's" in Aramaic. He also knew Hebrew well enough to read from the sacred scrolls in public (Lk. 4:16–19), and he probably had a carpenter's command of common Greek. His home was poor,[15] but like former President Dwight D. Eisenhower, Jesus apparently did not know it. Lost coins were sorely missed (Lk. 15:8–9), and clothes were scarce and plentifully patched (Mt. 9:16), but Jesus knew that if he asked his father for a fish, he would not be given a serpent (Mt. 7:10).

The paucity of hardcore information about Jesus between his birth and his baptism points to an inescapable conclusion. For the evangelists, the real history of Jesus begins neither with the christologically colored birth stories nor with the wildly speculative tales of his boyhood found in the Apocryphal Gospels;[16] it begins with the account of his baptism.

John, the Baptist (1–5)[17] John was born into a priestly family (Lk. 1:5), but he eventually abandoned his priestly prerogatives to become a wilderness wanderer. He may have been motivated by a feeling of revulsion for a secularized segment of Jerusalem's "holy" hierarchy. But his drastic decision was doubtless prompted by another factor as well. The forebears of his faith had found the supernatural in the wilderness—Moses at Sinai and Elijah under the broom tree (I Kings 19:4–8). John's desire to receive insight and understanding in the presence of the Divine must have played a decisive part.

John's sojourn in the wilderness was a striking success. He emerged from seclusion about 28 or 29 A.D. (Lk. 3:1–2) [18] to conduct a religious revival along the banks of the Jordan River.[19] What a forbidding

---

[14]Did a synagogue school exist in Nazareth? For opposite answers to this question see H.D.A. Major, T.W. Manson, and C.J. Wright, *The Mission and Message of Jesus* (New York: E.P. Dutton & Co., 1938), p. 271, and A.T. Olmstead, *Jesus in the Light of History* (New York: Charles Scribner's Sons, 1942), p. 12.

[15]Luke 2:22–24 describes the sacrifice required of poor people.

[16]See M.R. James, trans. *The Apocryphal New Testament* (Oxford: Clarendon Press, 1955).

[17]Throughout Chapters 5, 6, and 7, numbers in parentheses following subtitles refer to sections in *Gospel Parallels* (see footnote 2 of this chapter), where the Synoptic material may be read in parallel form. Scripture references are given in footnotes. For sections 1–5, see Matthew 3:1–12, Mark 1:1–8; Luke 3:1–20.

[18]If "the fifteenth year of the reign of Tiberius Caesar" is calculated from the regency of Tiberius instead of from the death of Augustus (when Tiberius became sole emperor), then the date would be 26 or 27 A.D. Maurice Goguel, *The Life Of Jesus*, trans O. Wyon (London: George Allen & Unwin, Ltd., 1933), p. 224, argues for a date between October 1, 27 and September 30, 28.

[19]Matthew 3:1 places John in the "wilderness of Judea," the wasteland east of Jerusalem. John locates him at "Bethany beyond the Jordan" (1:28) and at Aenon near Salim (3:23), places certainly to be preferred. They were close to well-traveled routes (which provided the prophet with a captive audience) and an ample supply of water (required for baptism by immersion).

figure the bearded, sun-blackened priest-turned-prophet must have presented to the passersby! His message matched the man. He proclaimed the imminence of a long-awaited event in Judaism: the final, universal judgment of God. He announced the coming of a transcendent Messiah who would purge men of evil and obliterate the unrepentant. His thoughts were couched in the fashionable language of eschatology and punctuated by such phrases as "the wrath to come" (Mt. 3:7) and "the ax is laid to the root of the trees" (Mt. 3:10). He pictured a heavenly Messiah whose "winnowing fork is in his hand, to clear his threshing floor, and to gather the wheat into his granary; but the chaff he will burn with unquenchable fire" (Lk. 3:17). Not since the days of Malachi had such a fierce and foreboding message shattered the placidity of the people. Lest anyone mistake John for the Messiah, the prophet's secondary role was made crystal clear. He was a mere "voice," unfit even to be a slave of the Mightier One through whom God's judgment would be executed.[20]

In view of the impending distress, John made three demands upon his hearers. (1) They should repent of their sins. No one was exempt from this requirement. Faith in imminent judgment fractured conventional religious practices and rendered claims of patriarchal descent null and void (Mt. 3:9). Only the repentant could face the coming of the Mightier One with equanimity. (2) They should be baptized. The Levitical Law prescribed washings for the purpose of purification, and Josephus and the Qumran Scrolls confirm that various sects in the Jordan Valley practiced daily lustrations.[21] Converts to Judaism were required to submit to baptism. John's baptism of converts in the Jordan River was predicated on repentance and accompanied by the confession of sins. It differed from the customary ceremonial washings in several ways. It was not to be repeated, was required of all men including the Jews, and it was preparatory. When a person submitted to John's baptism, he preenacted his own judgment. He acknowledged God's sovereignty, confessed his sins, and trusted in divine forgiveness and deliverance. (3) They should behave ethically. Those who had more than they needed were to share with the underprivileged. Tax collectors were to curb their desire to enrich themselves and soldiers were to avoid plundering.

Jesus' Call (6)[22] Matthew and Mark agree that Jesus was baptized by John, but only Matthew states that Jesus made the journey to the Jordan for this purpose (3:13). The historicity of the incident seems assured; it is certified by ecclesiastical embarrassment. The church would not have

[20]See Luke 3:16.
[21]Josephus, *Life*, 2: *Rule of the Community*, 5:13; 3:4–9.
[22]See Matthew 3:13–17; Mark 1:9–11; Luke 3:21–22.

invented a story that resulted in so much consternation and required so much subsequent explanation. Why was Jesus baptized by someone whom Christians regarded as his inferior? How could one who was believed to be sinless submit to "a baptism of repentance for the forgiveness of sins" (Mk. 1:4)? Matthew resolves the dilemma by indicating that Jesus was baptized as an example to the Jews (3:14–15).[23]

What happened to Jesus at his baptism, according to Mark, was strictly private. Not even John shared in the secret revelation. Jesus saw the heavens open, experienced the descent of the Spirit, and heard a heavenly voice declare, "*Thou* art my beloved Son; with thee I am well pleased."[24] The later Synoptics modify Mark. Luke preserves the private nature of the disclosure but names, objectifies, and materializes the Spirit. Matthew makes the revelation a public pronouncement: "*This* is my beloved Son."[25] The Fourth Gospel contains no account of the baptism, but it does mention that the Spirit descended on Jesus (1:32–34).

The revelation to Jesus was based on a Psalm and on a section from II Isaiah, modified to suit the situation. The Psalm celebrates a royal coronation. In it the king recalls a message received from the Lord on the day of his installation: "You are my son, today I have begotten you" (Ps. 2:7). The words are those that were used by people legally adopting a child.[26] The section from II Isaiah was quoted often in the early church and understood messianically: "Behold my servant, whom I uphold, my chosen, in whom my soul delights; I have put my spirit upon him, he will bring forth justice to the nations" (Isa. 42:1).

Did the baptism, then, mark the birth of Jesus' messianic consciousness? Not according to the Fourth Gospel. Its author pictures Jesus as aware "in the beginning" that he was the Incarnate Logos (1:1, 14). The birth stories of Matthew and Luke disclose Jesus' messiahship, but only Matthew makes the baptism an occasion for the public announcement of Jesus' status (3:17). In Mark, however, Jesus' messiahship is a secret that is gradually revealed in five successive stages.[27] The conflicting gospel records have caused specialists to

---

[23]For a discussion of the origin and development of the concept of Jesus' sinlessness, see C. Milo Connick, *Jesus: The Man, the Mission, and the Message* (Englewood Cliffs, N.J.: Prentice-Hall, Inc., 1963), pp. 140–141.
[24]Mark 1:11, italics added.
[25]Matthew 3:17, italics added.
[26]Code of Hammurabi, 170–171.
[27]See p. 80.

adopt diverse views concerning Jesus' Messianic consciousness. Some deny that he ever thought of himself as Messiah.[28] Others maintain that some experience of divine vocation lay back of Jesus' ministry, but they reject the idea that the baptism marked the beginning of his messianic consciousness.[29] Still others believe that Jesus was conscious of his messianic role at the baptism, but he had no clear-cut idea of the direction it would take.[30] Yet others assert that Jesus was not only conscious of his messianic mission at his baptism, but he also had a well-defined concept of what that mission involved.[31] It is our conviction that at the baptism Jesus experienced the divine call to herald the coming of God's kingdom.[32] When the incident was told by the early church, it was understood in the light of the church's conviction that Jesus was the Son of God who fulfilled prophetic expectations (Mk. 1:1, 11; Isa. 42:1; 44:2).

Jesus and the Baptist
(64–65)[33]

A baffling relationship exists between Jesus and John in the Gospels. Luke's nativity narratives unite the two by blood and prophecy. He pictures the future Forerunner greeting the future Messiah in their prenatal state. Matthew connects neither the families nor the births of Jesus and John, but his account of the baptism indicates that John is completely cognizant of Jesus' messianic mission. Later both evangelists introduce material that seems to be contrary to their theory. "Now when John heard in prison about the deeds of the Christ [sic], he sent word by his disciples and said to him, 'Are you he who is to come, or shall we look for another?' " (Mt. 11:2–3).[34] The inquiry is hard to harmonize with blood relationship, prenatal prophetic knowledge, prolonged association, and at-the-baptism awareness of who Jesus really was. It is altogether consonant, though, with Mark's implication that Jesus and John were strangers prior to the baptism. It also dovetails with the writings of Josephus, who in no way associates John with Jesus.[35]

Jesus' reply to John's question is instructive: "Go and tell John what you hear and see: the blind receive their sight and the lame walk, lepers are cleansed and the deaf hear, and the dead are raised up, and the poor have good news preached to them" (Mt. 11:4–5). This indirection threw the responsibility back on the questioner. John must

[28]C. Guignebert, *Jesus* (London: Kegan Paul, Trench, Trubner & Co., 1935), p. 155.
[29]F. C. Grant, "The Gospel According to St. Mark: Exegesis," in *The Interpreter's Bible*, VII, 654.
[30]Major, Manson, and Wright, *The Mission and Message of Jesus*, p. 338.
[31]Hunter, *The Work and Words of Jesus*, p. 37.
[32]For Mark, the stress is not upon Jesus' inner experience but upon the divine declaration of who Jesus really is.
[33]See Matthew 11:2–19; Luke 7:18–35; 16:16.
[34]Compare Luke 7:18–19.
[35]*Antiquities*, XVIII, 5, 2.

decide for himself. Jews believed that all illness would be healed prior to the Messianic Age. Jesus does not explicitly claim to be the Messiah; he rests his case on his words and works. From his comments to John's disciples two deductions seem legitimate. Jesus saw his work in connection with the coming of God's kingdom, and he sensed significant differences between John's view of the kingdom and his own.

It would be rewarding to explore in depth the difference between Jesus and John, the Baptist's alleged connection with Qumran, the cause and consequence of his martyrdom, and a host of other topics. Unfortunately, such a study would consume more space than is at our disposal.[36] One further subject, however, does merit minimal mention. It is the tendency of the Synoptics to subordinate John to Jesus. Matthew and Luke modify Malachi 3:1 (where the messenger, Elijah, is the forerunner of God Himself) to make the prophecy refer to John as the herald of Jesus, the Messiah (Mt. 11:10; Lk. 7:27). John is permitted no independent role or self-validating ministry. He is only "Elijah who is to come" (Mt. 11:14). The subservience of John is even more severe in the Fourth Gospel. He is a mere "voice," and his disciples are belated but eager converts of Jesus (1:23, 35-51). Twice in the prologue the hymn about the Logos (Word) is interrupted to underscore John's inferior function and status (1:6-8, 15). Jesus must increase, but John must decrease (3:30).

John's followers probably regarded him as the eschatological prophet whose appearance signaled the start of the New Age. He was the herald preparing the way for God to reassert His sovereignty on earth. From this estimate it was only a short step for John's devotees to think of him as both prophet and Messiah who acted in God's stead.[37] Among the Mandaeans, John was considered a genuine prophet in messianic dress and Jesus was judged a false Messiah. It is small wonder, then, that the evangelists depicted John as a herald and placed on his lips the flat denial that he was the Christ (Jn. 1:20). The two groups were locked in competition. "From a Christian view the sun soon dimmed the moon, but both John and his movement had remarkable significance and even rivalry for beginning Christianity."[38]

[36]A scholarly work of top-drawer quality is Carl H. Kraeling, *John the Baptist* (New York and London: Charles Scribner's Sons, 1951). See also W. H. Brownlee, "John the Baptist in the New Light of Ancient Scrolls," in K. Stendahl, ed., *The Scrolls and the New Testament* (New York: Harper & Row, 1956), pp. 33–53; Connick, *Jesus: The Man, the Mission, and the Message*, pp. 132–135; 145–148.

[37]See the *Testament of Levi* 8:15–16, where the two roles are merged. In the *Manual of Discipline* ix, II, from Qumran, three eschatological figures are envisaged—prophet, lay Messiah, and priestly Messiah.

[38]Dwight Marion Beck, *Through the Gospels to Jesus* (New York: Harper & Row, Publishers, Inc., 1954), p. 115. Reprinted by permission of the publisher.

Jesus and John espoused different messages and appealed to different followings, but Jesus never questioned God's wisdom in choosing John to do His work (Mt. 11:19). John's baptism was heaven-sent (Mt. 21:23–27). When the early church proclaimed John as the forerunner of Jesus, it laid hold of a towering truth. In the light of Jesus' ministry, death, and resurrection, the church saw God at work in John's ministry—pointing to His climactic revelation in Christ. John's work paved the way for the Good News that was destined to supersede it.

The Temptation (8) [39]   The Synoptics present the baptism and the temptation of Jesus as twin phases of a single experience. Mark indicates that the Spirit "drove" Jesus into the wilderness after the baptism; Matthew and Luke soften Mark's abrupt and forceful verb to "led." Mark specifies neither the nature nor the number of the temptations and says nothing about a fast. Matthew and Luke agree that Jesus fasted and list three temptations in different orders.

It was commonly expected among the Jews that a man of God should undergo a time of testing. Jesus had been empowered by the Spirit at the baptism; now in the wilderness he was called upon to wage war with a wily adversary, Satan (Mk.) or the devil (Mt., Lk.).[40] The battle raged for forty days, a round number for an extensive but indefinite period of time. Two of the devil's suggestions were prefaced with the phrase, "If you are the Son of God." In Jewish thought, "Son of God" had multiple meanings. It was used to describe the whole nation of Israel (Exod. 4:22), the godly and upright in Israel (Hos. 1:10), an anointed king (Ps. 2:7), heavenly servants (Job 1:6) and the Messiah. Since it was applied to the Messiah only in a few apocalyptic works and occasionally in late rabbinical writings,[41] "Son of God" was never a standard term for the Messiah. In the Old Testament it stressed function rather than supernatural conception or birth. It called attention to the moral relationship of love and filial obedience that was supposed to exist between a father and his son.[42]

The first temptation[43] was preceded by a prolonged period of fasting. The devil lunged for the jugular: "If you are the Son of God, command these stones to become loaves of bread" (Mt. 4:3). Palestine provided

---

[39]See Matthew 4:1–11; Mark 1:12–13; Luke 4:1–13.
[40]See pp. 51–52.
[41]Enoch 105:2; II Esdras 7:28–29; 13:32, 37, 52.
[42]See Johnson, "The Gospel According to St. Matthew: Introduction and Exegesis," in *The Interpreter's Bible*, VII, 270.
[43]Matthew's order is followed for the temptations.

an inexhaustible supply of rocks awaiting conversion into bread, and its people were convinced that the Messianic Age would be characterized by material abundance. If Jesus was the Son of God, surely he would be able to produce one of the signs of the Messiah's coming. Perhaps so, but he did not elect to do it. Instead, he recalled God's dealings with Israel during her wilderness sojourn. God had allowed his people to hunger before He had fed them with manna. His object had been to impress them with their primary dependence upon Him. From this experience of his ancestors, Jesus drew ammunition to pierce the devil's armor: "Man shall not live by bread alone, but by every word that proceeds from the mouth of God" (Mt. 4:4; Deut. 8:3).

The second temptation occurred in Jerusalem. The devil took Jesus to the pinnacle of the Temple where tradition had decreed that the Messiah would appear and proclaim deliverance to the people. Since the devil had previously been wounded by Scripture, he tried a text himself: "If you are the Son of God, throw yourself down; for it is written, 'He will give his angels charge of you,' and 'On their hands they will bear you up, lest you strike your foot against a stone'" (Mt. 4:6; Ps. 91:11–12). This satanic suggestion differed from the first. Jesus was not asked to use miraculous power to deliver himself or his people from an existing danger; he was urged to court disaster in a deliberate attempt to test the validity of God's promised protection. As Jesus gazed from the dizzy height of the royal cloister into the deep chasm below,[44] he perhaps pondered the instant advantage of an injury-free jump. Would it not be convincing proof to the crowd of his call? But he recalled the feverish efforts of the Israelites to coerce God into providing them with water during their wilderness wanderings and Moses' stern rebuke: "You shall not tempt the Lord your God" (Mt. 4:7; Deut. 6:16; Exod. 17:1–7). Jesus had not been called to command God but to trust and obey Him. "If the way of obedience means leaping over a precipice—or going to the Cross—that is another matter; but to thrust oneself into peril, merely to provide God with the occasion for a miracle, is not faith but presumption."[45]

The third proposal of the devil was not prefaced by the words, "If you are the Son of God." He took Jesus to a very high mountain[46] and showed him a panoramic view of the world and its glory. Then he declared, "All these I will give you" (Mt. 4:9). Matthew disdained

---

[44]See Josephus, *Antiquities*, XV, 11, 5.
[45]T.W. Manson, in H.D.A. Major, T.W. Manson, and C.J. Wright, *The Mission and Message of Jesus.* Copyright 1938 by E. P. Dutton & Co., Inc. Renewal © 1966 by H. D. A. Major. Published by E. P. Dutton & Co., Inc., and reprinted with their permission.
[46]Luke's phrase "in a moment of time" (4:5) suggests a visionary experience.

the devil's ownership claim and refused to mention it. Most Jews, though, believed that the devil controlled the world and could dispose of it as he wished (Lk. 4:6). There was, of course, some fine print in the devil's contractual proposition. Jesus could gain control of the world *if* he would fall down and worship his benefactor.[47] But Jesus spurned the dazzling prospect with a note of finality: "Begone, Satan! for it is written, 'You shall worship the Lord your God and him only shall you serve'" (Mt. 4:10). Submission to Satan would have shattered Jesus' sonship; the first and final loyalty of the Son was to the Father.

Satan obeyed the command to depart, but he did not stay away for long. Luke states that "he departed from him until an opportune time" (Lk. 4:13). The wilderness ordeal was no isolated incident for Jesus; throughout his life he was "tempted as we are" (Heb. 4:15). The temptation narrative both anticipates and summarizes Jesus' frontal attack on Satan's domain. Final victory was not assured until Easter Sunday.

Some scholars regard Jesus' temptation as legendary[48]. They point to the highly stylized nature of the narrative and the fact that the account is not authenticated by ecclesiastical embarrassment as was the baptism. The majority of scholars, however, continue to accept the essential historicity of the temptation. Their belief is buttressed by the common witness of the Synoptics, the close connection of the temptation with the baptism (a happening of high historical likelihood), and the surprising absence of any mention of the cross in relation to the temptation, which almost surely would have been the case if the church had created the story. We accept the latter view and see in the temptation experience three aspects of a single concern. That concern was the use of power that the Son of God had received at the baptism. The dialogue with the devil did not disclose the positive features of Jesus' future work, but it did enable him to reject several satanic suggestions.[49] Jesus probably departed from the desert without a master plan of his mission, but we have every right to believe that he had full knowledge of who his Master was.

[47]Ernest W. Saunders, *Jesus in the Gospels* (Englewood Cliffs, N.J.: Prentice-Hall, Inc., 1967), p. 73, interprets this temptation as a revival of the Maccabean ideal in the revised apocalyptic editions of the Zealots and the Essenes at Qumran.

[48]Goguel, *The Life of Jesus*, omits the temptation experience entirely. Guignebert, *Jesus*, p. 158, judges the temptation completely legendary. Walter E. Bundy, *Jesus and the First Three Gospels* (Cambridge, Mass.: Harvard Univ. Press, 1955), p. 64, agrees.

[49]We cannot accept the view that the temptations are closely connected with specific political and religious parties of the day. Although Jesus did not reject Satan's suggestions in a cultural vacuum, the poetic account of Satan's triple enticement cannot be decoded into the platforms of three separate parties.

The Message in Shorthand (9)[50]

Mark states that after John's arrest, Jesus came into Galilee preaching the gospel (1:14). A cursory examination of Mark indicates that Jesus' public ministry was confined almost exclusively to Galilee, that it lasted for about one year,[51] and that it abruptly terminated with Jesus' first and final journey to Jerusalem. The Fourth Gospel, on the other hand, indicates that Jesus began his ministry before John was put in prison (3:24), that he alternated his activity between Judea and Galilee (1-6), but that he spent the bulk of his time in Judea (7-19). His campaign lasted for a period of three or four years.[52] Even the Synoptics, on further reflection, seem to supply grist for the mill of a more extensive ministry. Mark 1:14 does not exclude activity by Jesus prior to his arrival in Galilee; and Jesus' lament over Jerusalem (Mt. 23:37), the presence of friends there, and the pious custom of celebrating Passover within its sacred walls actually support the idea. Attempts to construct a chronology of Jesus' ministry on the basis of these and other data found in the four Gospels, however, are counterproductive. The Gospels are not finely-honed historical treatises; they are literary creations, of a theological nature, composed from traditions that formerly had an independent existence. They cannot be commandeered to provide what they do not contain. A precise chronological reconstruction of Jesus' ministry is impossible; we shall have to be content with broad outlines and probabilities.

Galilee was ideally suited for Jesus' campaign. The inhabitants were of mixed origin, in close contact with the outside world, and receptive to new thought patterns. More than 100,000 people ringed the Sea of Galilee and represented potential converts.[53]

Mark records a threefold summary of Jesus' message (1:15).[54] *"The time is fulfilled"* refers not to the clock but to the Creator. It is the time fixed in God's foreknowledge and foreseen by the prophets, the decisive moment for the accomplishment of His eternal purpose. The phrase is eschatological, but its verb has been misunderstood by the

---

[50]See Matthew 4:12-17; Mark 1:14-15; Luke 4:14-15.

[51]It is spring (2:23); it is spring again (14:1), the Passover of the Passion.

[52]Three Passovers are mentioned (2:13; 6:4; 12:1) and two others (1:29, 41-42; 4:35) may be assumed. Ethelbert Stauffer, *Jesus and His Story*, trans. R.&C. Winston (New York: Alfred A. Knopf, Inc., 1960), p. 6, n. 5, argues for a four-year ministry. For a trenchant criticism of Stauffer's efforts to write a chronologically historical account of Jesus' life, see Hugh Anderson, *Jesus and Christian Origins* (New York: Oxford Univ. Press, 1964), pp. 57-61.

[53]George Adam Smith states that there were nine cities around the lake with reportedly not less than 15,000 inhabitants each. See *The Historical Geography of the Holy Land*, 14th ed. (New York: A. C. Armstrong & Sons, 1908), p. 447.

[54]The fourth proclamation ("believe in the gospel") is clearly a later Christian addition. Jesus stressed faith in God, not belief in the gospel.

---

devotees of "realized eschatology," who believe that the End has arrived. "Is fulfilled" (Mk. 1:15) or "is at hand" (Mt. 4:17) cannot mean "has arrived."[55] The Greek word (*ēggiken*) means "has drawn near." Jesus taught his disciples to pray that the kingdom come, and his evangelistic campaign assumed that there was still opportunity for repentance to prepare for its arrival. His subsequent mighty works were viewed by Mark as signs of its coming, but Mark did not think that the kingdom had arrived.

The second aspect of Jesus' message concerns "*the kingdom of God.*" The phrase is not found in the Old Testament, but the idea of God as King is featured there (Isa. 43:15; Ps. 103:19; etc.). Once His sovereignty had been supreme; now it was only partial. Sin had separated Him and His people. When an Israelite obeyed the Law or recited the Shema (Deut. 6:4–9), God's sovereignty was reasserted. But as long as sin prevailed, Satan exercised authority and God's reign was incomplete. Hope grew that God would one day establish full control. Prophets proclaimed that He would defeat the forces of evil, punish the wicked, and institute His reign on earth (Isa. 9:7; Zech. 14:9). Some thought He would act directly; others believed that He would work through a Messiah. In either case, the New Age would follow with rewards for the righteous. Apocalyptists took a different tack. They spoke of a supernatural Messiah and a transformed earth or a transcendental heaven.

Since Jesus never defined what he meant by "the kingdom of God" (Mk.) or "the kingdom of heaven" (Mt.),[56] its nature and nearness have been hotly disputed. It has been equated with such diverse concepts as the church, the rule of God in human hearts, a miraculous new order of God, a spiritual commonwealth composed of those who obey God's will, and human society ordered by love. As to the nearness of the kingdom, three basic positions have found favor. Albert Schweitzer popularized the futurist position.[57] He held that "consistent eschatology" provides the key to Jesus' message and mission. Jesus was inspired by an apocalyptic vision, and he felt that the birth pangs of the New Age were imminent. The Son of Man would soon appear with the clouds and execute God's final judgment. Satan

---

[55]See Hunter, *The Work and Words of Jesus*, p. 43. The foremost representative of realized eschatology is C. H. Dodd. See his illuminating book, *The Parables of Jesus*, rev. ed. (New York: Charles Scribner's Sons, 1961). See also p. 119.

[56]The two phrases have the same meaning. Matthew simply follows pious Jewish practice and avoids use of the divine name.

[57]Albert Schweitzer, *The Quest of the Historical Jesus* (New York: The Macmillan Co., 1948) was published in German in 1906. An earlier work by Johannes Weiss, *Die Predigt Jesu vom Reiche Gottes* (Göttingen: Vandenhoeck and Ruprecht, 1892), markedly influenced the scholarly world.

would be rendered impotent, the dead would be raised, and all men would be rewarded according to their deeds. As the Messiah-designate, Jesus identified himself with the Son of Man and strove to set in motion the apocalyptic program of events. When he dispatched the Twelve on their evangelistic mission, he expected the End to come before they could return (Mt. 10:23). When his calculation proved erroneous, he revised the timetable and his role in the divine scheme. He concluded that his death would be the catalytic agent that would trigger the End. Antithetical to Schweitzer's futurist position is that of "realized eschatology." C. H. Dodd, a foremost exponent of this school of thought, argues that Jesus never implied an early end of the world. On the contrary, the Carpenter's claim that the kingdom of God "had come" smashed the old eschatological scheme and made way for a new set of ideas. The once prospective eschaton was now present. In parable after parable Jesus pointed to the "zero hour" in human experience. The kingdom confronted men with a crisis and called for decisive action. Jesus' mighty works demonstrated its power in the world. The kingdom was not something that happens after something else; it was that to which men awaken when the space-time order no longer restricts their vision.[58] Most scholars have rejected both consistent and realized eschatology in favor of tension eschatology. They hold that Jesus' thought centered about two foci, and both of them must be given their due. In some sense the kingdom was a present reality during Jesus' lifetime, but its full manifestation was yet to come.

Although Jesus did not define the kingdom, he did profusely illustrate it by means of parables. Final conclusions regarding its nature and nearness will be given in a later chapter of this book, but several preliminary comments concerning the kingdom may prove to be productive. (1) It is *God's* kingdom. The stress is on the King, not the kingdom. The realm or sphere of the King is secondary. (2) It is God's *gift*, and He bestows it upon whom He wills. Men cannot build or earn it; neither can they hasten or hinder its coming. (3) Jesus is its herald. (4) The qualifications for membership are moral and spiritual, not racial or national. (5) The characteristics of those who will be in the kingdom are delineated in the Beatitudes (Mt. 5:3–11). (6) Men should prepare for the kingdom's coming, despite its gratuitous nature, by repentance and by living as though the kingdom had already arrived. (7) It exceeds all else in value.

The third part of Jesus' message in shorthand was the demand to *repent*. Repentance was a common concept in Judaism. It was taught

---

[58]See Dodd, *The Parables of Jesus*. See also pp. 117–118.

in every synagogue and assumed in every Temple sacrifice. It involved remorse for sins, restitution (when possible), and resolution not to repeat the offenses. Although repentance did not unlock the door of the kingdom, it did prepare people for the day when God would open it.

Mighty Works (12–17, 45–48)[59] Jesus began his Galilean campaign solo, but he soon conformed to custom and sought special disciples. His first invitations were extended to four fishermen[60] and a customs collector for a foreign government.[61] Tradition finally fixed the total number of intimates at twelve, one for each of the twelve tribes of Israel. Thus the character of the campaign was defined; the disciples would be sent on a national (not an international) mission. The four New Testament lists of the Twelve differ, and attempts to reconcile them have been less than convincing.[62] The number in the inner circle doubtless varied from time to time, and the figure "twelve" should be regarded as symbolic and approximate. All of the Twelve were drawn from the ranks of unofficial Judaism, and all were probably Galileans. To these common men Jesus gave uncommon opportunities and responsibilities.[63]

When Jesus spoke in the synagogue at Capernaum, the people were astonished at the manner of his teaching. Unlike the scribes, he seldom appealed to precedent. He acted as though authority resided in him. At the close of his comments, he drove an unclean spirit from a man. Later the same day he cured Simon's mother-in-law of a fever. At sundown, when Mark's sample Sabbath was over, they brought to Jesus all who were sick or possessed with demons, and he healed many and cast out many demons. Before daybreak the next morning, the helpless invaded a lonely place where Jesus was praying. They, too, wanted to be healed. Jesus' response to his disciples laid bare his primary priority: "Let us go on to the next towns, that I may preach there also; for that is why I came out" (Mk. 1:37–38). Whatever else may be said about his signs, wonders, and mighty works, one thing is crystal clear. They were of secondary importance.[64] Jesus was first and foremost a herald of the Good News.

[59]See Matthew 4:23–25; 7:28–8:17; Mark 1:21–45; Luke 4:31–44; 5:1–16; 7:1–10.
[60]Simon (Greek) or Simeon (Hebrew) or Peter (nickname) and his brother, Andrew, and James and his brother, John, sons of Zebedee.
[61]Matthew (Mt. 9:9) or Levi (Mk. 2:14; Lk. 5:27) or Matthew-Levi?
[62]See Mark 3:16–19; Matthew 10:2–4; Luke 6:14–16; Acts 1:13. One effort to harmonize the lists equates Thaddaeus (Mt., Mk.) with Judas the son of James (Lk.) and Judas not Iscariot (Jn.).
[63]See sections 11, 53, and 58 of *Gospel Parallels* or Matthew 4:18–22; 9:9–13; 9:35–10:16; Mark 1:16–20; 2:13–17; Luke 5:27–32; 10:1–2.
[64]Their nature and meaning are discussed on pp. 151–156.

Partially Restored Synagogue at Capernaum. The colonnade of pillars once supported a balcony used by women worshipers. The synagogue probably dates from the second century A.D. Jesus made his Galilean headquarters in Capernaum (Village of Nahum) and taught in its synagogue (Mk. 1:21).

A precise itinerary of Jesus' Galilean campaign has been constructed by some scholars on the basis of Mark's references to places,[65] but Mark's chronology is not that reliable. Matthew and Luke use the same sources in a different order. Either the evangelists had scant knowledge of the proper sequence of events[66] or they elected to disregard it. Although it is possible to arrive at a tentative chronological arrangement of key happenings in the Galilean ministry, the topical method must generally be followed. The occasion and background of most of the parables and miracles in the Synoptics were provided by the early church. The Sermon on the Mount consists of summaries of Jesus' teachings taken from different periods of his mission (Mt. 5:1—7:29).[67] We shall therefore postpone treatment of the parables, miracles, and Sermon until later.

Popularity and Opposition (52–54, 69–70)[68]

Jesus' campaign, according to the Synoptics, greatly stirred Galilee and environs. As he moved from synagogue to synagogue, large numbers responded to his words and works. They came from as far

[65]See the illustration in Connick, *Jesus: The Man, the Mission, and the Message*, p. 166.
[66]This is the dominant view among scholars.
[67]Compare the Sermon on the Plain in Luke 6:20 49.
[68]See Matthew 9:1–17; 12:1–14; Mark 2:1–3:6; Luke 5:17–6:11.

north as Tyre and Sidon, as far south as Judea and Idumea, and from east of the Jordan River (Mk. 3:7–8). So great was their clamor to hear and to be healed, Mark indicates, that they forced Jesus to transform a boat into a lectern lest they crush him (Mk. 3:9). At the apex of his popularity 5,000 men plus women and children dined as his guests in the desert (Mk. 6:35–44; Mt. 14:21).

The surge of popularity soon stirred opposition. The antagonism of the scribes and Pharisees[69] is summarized by Mark in a block of five conflict stories.

On Forgiving Sins (Mk. 2:1–12) One day while Jesus was at home in Capernaum, a crowd collected. As Jesus taught, his audience overflowed the house into the courtyard. When four men approached carrying a paralytic on a pallet, they found the doorway blocked. They mounted the outside stairway, removed a section of the roof, and lowered the pallet and the paralytic into Jesus' presence. Jesus was so impressed by the intruders' faith that he declared, "My son, your sins are forgiven" (2:5). Some of the startled scribes pronounced the saying blasphemous. Only God could forgive sins. Jesus was guilty of a double error. He had usurped God's authority, and he had failed to require repentance from the paralytic.

Jesus countered the scribal charge with a question: "Which is easier, to say to the paralytic, 'Your sins are forgiven,' or to say, 'Rise, take up your pallet and walk'?" (2:9). Obviously the deed would surpass the declaration. Sin and suffering were regarded as cause and consequence in the ancient world (Job 4:7; Ps. 103:3). If Jesus could cure the man's paralysis, prima facie proof that his sins had been forgiven would exist. Presence of the paralysis, however, made any claim of forgiveness patently absurd. "But that you may know that the Son of man has authority on earth to forgive sins," Jesus continued, "I say to you [the paralytic], rise, take up your pallet and go home" (2:10–11). The paralytic did as he was commanded and the astounded crowd exclaimed that they had never seen anything like it.[70]

On Eating with Sinners (Mk. 2:13–17) A despised customs collector named Levi was on duty at the northern end of the Sea of Galilee. Jesus passed by and invited him to become a special disciple. Levi promptly accepted and soon found himself

---

[69]See pp. 175–178.
[70]Did Jesus actually forgive the paralytic's sins, or was his pronouncement the customary Jewish circumlocution designed to avoid the use of God's name? If the latter, then the meaning would have been, "Your sins *are* forgiven [by God]." Mark, of course, reflects the faith of the early church that Jesus did have authority to forgive sins.

a dinner guest in Jesus' house.[71] Many customs collectors and sinners were present. The privilege of collecting customs was sold to the highest bidder, and winners managed to charge as much above their cost as the traffic would bear.[72] Sinners, from the standpoint of the Pharisees, were those who were careless about observing the minutiae of the Mosaic Law. Many pious Jews lumped the two groups together and treated them like Samaritans. It was a scandal to associate with such disreputables, and it was sacrilegious to host them at a banquet. The stiff-necked scribes of the Pharisees demanded to know of Jesus' disciples why their master ate with them. Jesus replied for his followers: "Those who are well have no need of a physician, but those who are sick; I came not to call the righteous, but sinners" (2:17).

On Fasting (Mk. 2:18–22)

The disciples of John the Baptist and of the Pharisees were observed fasting above and beyond the requirements of the Law, but the followers of Jesus were conspicuous because they failed to follow suit. Since voluntary fasting was an integral aspect of Jewish religious life, it was only natural that people asked why Jesus' disciples did not participate. Jesus' reply struck at the heart of the matter: "Can the wedding guests fast while the bridegroom is with them?" (2:19). He had nothing against fasting *per se* (Mt. 6:16), but he did object to the timing. Fasting was a sign of sorrow. Now the kingdom of God was approaching. The forces of evil were being overthrown. Mourning should be replaced by rejoicing.[73]

On Sabbath Observance: Reaping (Mk. 2:23–28)

When Jesus and his disciples passed through grainfields on the Sabbath, the disciples paused to pluck heads of grain.[74] The omnipresent Pharisees protested. Such conduct was unlawful on the Sabbath. God had provided six days for labor, and those who worked on the Sabbath were liable to death by stoning (Exod. 34:21; 31:14). The Pharisees, moreover, honored "the tradition of the elders" as highly as the written Law. The tradition prohibited thirty-nine classes of work on the Sabbath, two of which were reaping and threshing.[75] Since the right of travelers to help themselves to grain in order to satisfy their hunger was well established, this issue was not involved (Deut. 23:24–25). What galled the Pharisees was anti-Sabbath conduct.

[71]The feast took place in Levi's house according to Luke 5:29.
[72]See p. 34.
[73]Mark 2:20 appears to have been written in the perspective of the crucifixion when the figure of the bridegroom had been identified with Jesus and influenced by his death. If Jesus informed his disciples early in his ministry that the day would come when the bridegroom would be taken from them, they failed utterly to grasp the point. When much later he told them of his certain doom, they were incredulous (8:32).
[74]Luke 6:1 indicates that they not only reaped the grain but also threshed it by rubbing the grain between their hands.
[75]Shabbath 7:2.

Jesus defended his disciples with an appeal to Scripture. He recalled the time when David, returning from battle, was hungry and asked for bread from the High Priest. The only bread on hand was "the bread of the Presence." These loaves, one representing each of the twelve tribes of Israel, were placed on the holy table early on the Sabbath. There they remained for a week in the presence of God. Then they would be removed, replaced, and eaten only by the priests. In this particular emergency, however, the High Priest gave David and his men the sacred bread and they ate it (I Sam. 21:1-6). It was a cogent example. If a paragon of virtue like David could eat the bread of the Presence to satisfy his hunger, surely Jesus' disciples could pluck grain on the Sabbath to satisfy theirs. Then Jesus capped the climax with a pithy proclamation: "The sabbath was made for man, not man for the sabbath" (2:27).[76]

On Sabbath Observance: Healing (Mk. 3:1-6)

One Sabbath Jesus was in a synagogue where he noticed a man with a withered hand. The Pharisees stood ready to pounce on Jesus should he decide to practice the healing art. Rabbinical thought decreed that it was contrary to the Law to heal on the Sabbath unless the case constituted a dire emergency. Obviously the man with the withered hand could not be so classified. His cure could wait until the Sabbath was over. Jesus evidently perceived the intent of his critics; nevertheless, he directed the victim to come into his presence. Then he addressed a double-barreled question to the Pharisees: "Is it lawful on the sabbath to do good or to do harm, to save life or to kill?" (3:4). The Pharisees fell silent while Jesus' anger mounted with his grief at their insensitivity. He commanded the cripple to stretch out his hand, the man obeyed, and he was healed. The Pharisees were furious. They rushed out and joined forces with the Herodians to plot Jesus' demise.

Mark's five controversy stories highlight the hostility of the scribes and Pharisees toward Jesus. The alliance of convenience between the Pharisees and the Herodians in 3:6 is undoubtedly premature. It indicates too decisive an action at too early a stage in Jesus' campaign. But Mark's order is more topical than chronological. The conflict stories are not to be thought of as having transpired in rapid succession. They are intended to suggest the growth in opposition to Jesus as the seaside account that follows explicates Jesus' rising popularity with the crowds (3:7-12).

[76]This is an excellent example of a paradigm or pronouncement story. The historicity of 2:28 has been questioned. If "Son of man" means "man," what Jew would declare that man is lord of the Sabbath? Matthew and Luke, who omit Mark 2:27, understand that Jesus as Messiah regulates the Sabbath. Was the church, that equated Jesus with the heavenly Son of Man, responsible for the saying?

Prophet Without Honor (10, 85, 89)[77]   Opposition to Jesus was not confined to the scribes and Pharisees. Mark reports several incidents that indicate that hostility was also a home-grown product. Jesus was at home one day in Capernaum when such a large crowd gathered that eating became impossible. When his friends (or family) heard about it, they attempted to seize him because they thought he was mad (Mk. 3:19b–22).[78] On another occasion Jesus was seated on the ground in oriental fashion addressing a crowd. When his mother and brothers approached, he took no notice. After their presence was announced to him, he declared: "Who are my mother and my brothers?" (Mk. 3:33).[79] The casual role Jesus' family played in his ministry has caused comment. Were they embarrassed by his activity? Did they regard his proclamations as lunatic language? His brothers rejected his claims and took no part in his campaign although they later played supportive roles in the drama of the early church (Jn. 7:5; 1 Cor. 9:5). The Synoptics assign Mary a nondescript part and exclude her entirely from the crucifixion scene. The Fourth Gospel places her at the crucifixion and portrays her as faithful but lacking full understanding of her son (2:4–5; 19:25).[80]

When Jesus had completed a rather extensive evangelistic campaign in the vicinity of the Sea of Galilee, according to Mark, he headed home to Nazareth where he encountered still further opposition. As a visiting dignitary, he was invited by the ruling elders to participate in the synagogue service on the Sabbath. The service included the recitation of the Shema, a set reading from the Law, a free-choice reading from the Prophets (accompanied by explanation and application of one or both passages), and a blessing or prayer. The townsmen were astonished at Jesus' teaching, they were amazed at his wisdom and his mighty works, and they registered surprise that such a person could come from the family that they knew so well. Suddenly their surprise turned to offense. Perhaps they thought the Carpenter was putting on airs. In any case, the evangelist records Jesus' response and his own commentary: " 'A prophet is not without honor, except in his own country [Nazareth], and among his own kin [uncles, cousins, and others], and in his own house [mother, brothers, sisters].' And he *could* do no mighty work there, except that he laid his hands

---

[77]See Matthew 12:22–24, 46–50; 13:54–58; Mark 3:19b–22, 31–35; 6:1–6; Luke 4:16–30; 8:19–21; 11:14–16.
[78]Compare II Kings 9:11.
[79]Many commentators equate Jesus' mother and brothers with his "friends" in 3:21.
[80]Whatever the family's intent concerning Jesus, Mark's motive in recording the incident in 3:31–35 is clear. He included the pericope in order to introduce the pronouncement in 3:35: "Whoever does the will of God is my brother, and sister, and mother." It stresses the fact that the real relationships of life are not biological but spiritual.

upon a few sick people and healed them. And he marveled because of their unbelief."[81]

Luke treats the Nazareth incident more extensively, and he places it much earlier in the Galilean campaign than it is in Mark or Matthew. According to Luke, when Jesus stood up in the synagogue to read, he was given a scroll of the prophet Isaiah. Jesus unrolled the scroll and found the place where it was written, "The Spirit of the Lord is upon me, because he has anointed me to preach good news to the poor. He has sent me to proclaim release to the captives and recovering of sight to the blind, to set at liberty those who are oppressed, to proclaim the acceptable year of the Lord" (Lk. 4:18–19). Then Jesus sat down to teach: "Today this scripture has been fulfilled in your hearing" (Lk. 4:21). The people registered surprise, but they spoke well of him. Their hostility did not develop until later when Jesus suggested that the benefits of his mission would be reserved for foreigners (Lk. 4:25–27). Then the infuriated congregation attempted to throw him headlong over a hill, but he was able to escape.

Attempts have been made to use Luke's fuller account to explain Mark's briefer one. The hostility of the synagogue congregation in Mark is viewed as the consequence of Jesus' messianic claim in Luke.[82] Such efforts are questionable. Luke's version is tightly controlled by a literary purpose. He presents the Nazareth incident as the inauguration of Jesus' ministry. "He has anointed me" refers to Jesus' baptism, "the acceptable year of the Lord" refers to the Messianic Age, and "today this scripture has been fulfilled in your hearing" is Jesus' first public pronouncement. His career conforms to prophetic prediction. He is the Messiah, and the Messianic Age is at hand. His rejection by his fellow townsmen "prepares the reader for the rejection of Christ by the Sanhedrin, and the rejection of the gospel by the Jewish nation."[83]

The Mission of the Twelve and the Seventy (58–63, 109, 139–140)[84]

After Jesus' rejection in Nazareth, Mark relates the mission of the Twelve, although their appointment occurred much earlier (3:14–15).[85] Luke lists two appointments (of the Twelve and of the Seventy) and two missions. Mark's account of the mission of the

---

[81]Mark 6:4–6, italics added. See p. 107.
[82]See Major, Manson, and Wright, *The Mission and Message of Jesus*, p. 81.
[83]S. MacLean Gilmour, "Exegesis: The Gospel According to St. Luke," in George Arthur Buttrick, ed., *The Interpreter's Bible* (New York: Abingdon Press, 1952), VIII, 95–96. Reprinted by permission of Abingdon Press.
[84]See Matthew 9:35–11:1; 16:24–25; 18:5; 24:9, 13; Mark 6:6–13; 8:34–35; 9:37; 13:9–13; Luke 9:1–6, 23–24, 48; 10:1–16; 12:2–9, 51–53; 14;26–27; 21:12–17, 19; Acts 1:13.
[85]The mission directly follows the appointment in Matthew.

Twelve is probably more nearly historical, but even so, it contains a mixture of Jesus' commands and practices of the early church. The staff and sandals, which clearly suggest a *world* mission, are permitted by Mark (6:8-9) but prohibited by Matthew (10:10).[86] Matthew adds much to Mark's record, and the end result is a set of directions geared to the mission of the church. He alone attributes to Jesus the command that the disciples should confine their campaign to the Jews (10:5-6). Since Jesus worked almost exclusively in Jewish territory, such an injunction would hardly have been necessary. Nor would nonaffluent disciples need to be cautioned against taking gold or silver with them (10:9).[87] Persecutions that plagued Christians after Matthew's composition are suggested by 10:21-22.

Luke's lone account of the mission of the Seventy has elicited varied explanations. Some think it is just another version of the sending out of the Twelve. Others take the Seventy to symbolize the later Gentile mission as the Twelve symbolized the mission to the Jews. Jewish literature frequently spoke of seventy as the number of Gentile nations.[88] Still others believe that the Seventy were messengers sent ahead by Jesus to arrange lodging for his party in the towns and villages en route to Jerusalem. They also obtained a colt on which Jesus rode into the Holy City and an upper room where he and his disciples ate the Passover meal.[89]

What, then, may reasonably be concluded about the mission of the Twelve? Jesus did not draw a blueprint of an organized church; neither did he structure a world-wide campaign. Sometime during his Galilean ministry he sent his disciples out on a mission. Perhaps there were several missions, and the one described in the Synoptics was intended to be a sample. The object was to arouse the nation, the message was the imminence of the kingdom, and the summons was to repent. The missionaries traveled in pairs, and they depended upon the hospitality of their hearers for support. They cast out demons, healed the sick, and stayed only where they were welcome. Time was of the essence.

A Messianic Meal In Miniature (110–112, 118)[90]   The Synoptics do not state how long the mission of the Twelve lasted, but it may have ground to a halt with the beheading of John the Baptist. Their campaign had aroused both Galilee and Galilee's ruler,

[86]Luke 9:3 forbids the staff.
[87]Mark mentions only copper coin in the Greek.
[88]If Luke had this in mind, why did he imply that the Seventy were sent only to Jewish or Samaritan centers? And why did they return so soon?
[89]Why would it take so many advance men to accomplish these objectives?
[90]See Matthew 14:1-21; 15:32-39; Mark 6:14-44; 8:1-10; Luke 9:7-17.

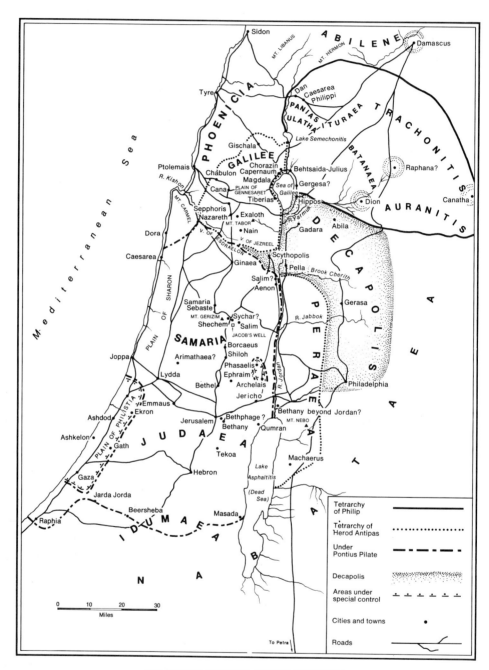

PALESTINE DURING JESUS' MINISTRY

Sidon

ABILENE

MT. LIBANUS

MT. HERMON

Damascus

Tyre

Dan

Caesarea
Philippi

PHOENICIA

PANIAS

ULATHA · ITURAEA

TRACHONITIS

Lake Semechonitis

Gischala

GALILEE

BATANAEA

Ptolemais

Chorazin

Behtsaida-Julius

Raphana?

Chábulon

Capernaum

Gergesa?

Cana

Magdala

PLAIN OF
GENNESARET

Sea of
Galilee

Hippos

Dion

Canatha

Sepphoris

Tiberias

AURANITIS

Dora

Nazareth

Exaloth

R. Yarmuk

Abila

MT. TABOR

Nain

Gadara

MT. CARMEL

V. OF JEZREEL

Caesarea

Ginaea

Scythopolis

PLAIN OF SHARON

V. OF ESDRAELON

Pella

Brook Cherith

Salim?

DECAPOLIS

Aenon

Samaria
Sebaste

Gerasa

MT. GERIZIM

Sychar?

R. Jabbok

Shechem

Salim

PEREA

JACOB'S WELL

SAMARIA

Borcaeus

Joppa

Arimathaea?

Shiloh

Lydda

Phasaelis

Bethel

Ephraim

R. Jordan

Archelais

Philadelphia

Jericho

Emmaus

Ekron

Bethphage ?

Bethany beyond Jordan?

Ashdod

Jerusalem

Bethany

MT. NEBO

Ashkelon

Gath

Qumran

JUDAEA

Tekoa

Machaerus

Gaza

Hebron

Lake
Asphaltitis

Jarda Jorda

(Dead
Sea)

Beersheba

Masada

Raphia

IDUMAEA

NABAT

Mediterranean Sea

To Petra

Legend	
Tetrarchy of Philip	———
Tetrarchy of Herod Antipas	·············
Under Pontius Pilate	—·—·—
Decapolis	░░░░░
Areas under special control	+ + + +
Cities and towns	•
Roads	———

0   10   20   30
Miles

Herod Antipas. Escalating opposition of religious leaders had slammed the door of the synagogue in Jesus' face and forced him to teach out in the open. The shift of location simply served to advertise his popularity, and the crowds flocked to hear him in ever increasing numbers. Rumors ran rife. Some thought Jesus was John the Baptist raised from the dead, a speculation with which Antipas concurred. Others opined that he was Elijah, the personage expected to return before "the great and terrible day" (Mal. 4:5). Still others likened him to one of the prophets of old. No one seems to have surmised that he was the Messiah.

When the Twelve returned to Capernaum, they related to Jesus all that had happened on their mission. Since the press of people (and perhaps a hostile Herod Antipas who had already disposed of John the Baptist) invaded their leisure, Jesus invited them to come away to a lonely place for a rest. They traveled by boat, and upon arrival they discovered that a crowd had already gathered.[91] Jesus began to teach them many things, but the day is remembered because of what transpired at its close. The crowds grew hungry, and the disciples suggested that Jesus send the people into nearby villages where they could purchase food. Jesus countered with the astounding command that the disciples should feed them—as though they could produce 200 denarii on the spot. Jesus suggested that they inventory the crowd to see how much food they had. The five loaves and two fish that were found seemed grossly inadequate, but Jesus commanded the crowds to sit down in groups of fifty or one hundred. Then he began to recite the traditional Jewish table blessing. "Blessed art thou, O Lord, King of the world, who bringest forth bread from the earth." As the sun sank on the horizon, he broke the tortilla-type loaves and divided the fish and had the disciples distribute the minuscule pieces to the people. When the distribution was done, five thousand men (Mk.) plus women and children (Mt.) ate until satisfied, and there were enough food scraps left over to fill a dozen reed baskets.

This is the only miracle story found in all four Gospels, and Matthew and Mark appear to record it twice.[92] Numerous theories have been developed to explain the feeding, but none has won scholarly consensus. Some accept the story at face value. As God incarnate, Jesus multiplied the food exactly as described. Others see the feeding as a miracle of sharing. John 6:9 states that there was a lad present

---

[91]The location of the landing is unspecified. See G. H. Dalman, *Sacred Sites and Ways* (New York: The Macmillan Co., 1935) p. 173, and Connick, *Jesus: The Man, the Mission, and the Message*, p. 180, for contrasting views.

[92]All of the accounts, including the feeding of the four thousand in Mark 8:1–9 and Matthew 15:32–38, seem to be variant forms of the same tradition.

who had five barley loaves and two fish. He offered to share with others who had come without supplies. Onlookers emulated his example. When the potluck ended, there was food left over. Still others argue that the crowds were fed with spiritual food. Jesus so filled them with thoughts about the kingdom of God that their physical hunger vanished. Some claim the feeding had an Old Testament origin. Moses, Elijah, and Elisha had all fed people miraculously (Exod. 16; I Kings 17:8–16; II Kings 4:42–44). Now one greater than they was here. Others see the feeding as the first Lord's Supper. They accept the account as is except for the reference to the twelve baskets full of food that remained.

Perhaps the feeding should be regarded as a dramatized parable by which Jesus alerted his hearers to the messianic meal in their future. The evangelists frequently employ the figures of eating and drinking to convey religious truth, and they depict the Kingdom of God in terms of a banquet (Mt. 22:1–14; Lk. 14:16–24). The Lord's Supper of the early church was a messianic meal in miniature. Parallels between the Lord's Supper and the feeding of the thousands are remarkable—the blessing of God, the breaking of the bread, the distribution of the bread by the disciples as by the deacons in the church. When Jesus provided a meal for the people, he intended that they see in it a promise of the kingdom's coming and experience in it a foretaste of its manifold blessings.[93]

Withdrawal (113–117, 121)[94]

The messianic meal in miniature marked the virtual end of Jesus' Galilean campaign. Shortly thereafter, according to Mark, Jesus departed to the region of Tyre and Sidon, Phoenician cities located on the Mediterranean coast to the north of Galilee. Although no reason for the withdrawal is given, several theories have been advanced. Some say that he penetrated the area to conduct a Gentile mission. This motivation is contradicted by his desire for seclusion and his reluctance to heal (Mk. 7:24–27). Others explain the withdrawal as a flight from the hostile Herod Antipas. The tetrarch had made short shrift of John, and he believed that Jesus was the Baptist brought back to life (Mk. 6:16). Still others think the withdrawal was more a flight from the dangerous enthusiasm of friends than from the malevolence of his foes.[95] Jesus' teaching had aroused the crowds, and the feeding had multiplied their fervor. Galled by Roman

---

[93]A parabolic interpretation of the feeding eliminates the necessity of explaining how the food was multiplied. The bits of bread and fish were intended to symbolize the messianic meal, not to satisfy ravenous physical hunger. The disciples' lack of understanding (Mk. 6:52) is no more difficult to explain here than elsewhere.

[94]See Matthew, 14:22–15:31; Mark 6:45–7:37; 8:22–26.

[95]See T.W. Manson, *The Servant-Messiah* (Cambridge: At the University Press, 1956), p. 71.

rule, they longed for the restoration of David's kingdom (Mk. 11:10). Immediately after the meal served to many, Jesus "made" his disciples get into a boat and go before him to Bethsaida while he dismissed the crowds (Mk. 6:45). He evidently thought it would be easier to persuade the people to disperse after the disciples had departed. The disciples seem to have shared the crowd's conviction, and the Fourth Gospel makes plain what that conviction was: "Perceiving then that they were about to come and take him by force to make him king, Jesus withdrew again to the hills by himself" (6:15). The crisis that caused the flight from friends was not metaphysical (the miracle of multiplication) but political. This theory is vitiated by several Synoptic data. Mark maintains the messianic secret to the very end, Jesus never appeals to his messianic authority, and when a poll is taken of his true identity, no one mentions that he is the Messiah. Evidently Jesus did not arouse in the popular mind the notion that his mission was messianic. Remaining theories are that Jesus withdrew from Galilee for rest and prayer, to permit the hostility of his critics to moderate, or because his Galilean mission had failed. Actually, as in the case of modern men, he may have operated from mixed motives.

Just how long Jesus stayed in Phoenician territory is unknown. Mark indicates that his sojourn there was followed by visits to two other territories outside of Galilee: the Decapolis and the Bethsaida-Caesarea Philippi area, ruled by the more tolerant Herod Philip (7:31; 8:22, 27). Since Mark's section is omitted entirely by Luke, some scholars consider it to be of questionable value.[96]

Peter's "Confession" (122, 127, 191)[97]

The Synoptics report a crucial conversation between Jesus and his disciples near Caesarea Philippi. The Carpenter, concerned about the interpretation placed on his campaign by others, inquired of his disciples, "Who do men say that I am?" (Mk. 8:27). The answers they supplied cohered with the rumors rehearsed in Mark 6:14–16. Then Jesus personalized his inquiry: "But who do *you* say that I am?"[98] Peter, perhaps speaking for the Twelve, replied, "You are the Christ" (Mk. 8:29).[99] Then Jesus instructed his disciples to tell no one about him.

The Nature of Jesus' Mission

Did Jesus understand his mission in messianic terms? Many scholars respond in the affirmative. They interpret the baptism as his call,

[96]See Saunders, *Jesus in the Gospels*, p. 233, n1.
[97]See Matthew 16:13–23; 17:22–23; 20:17–19; Mark 8:27–33; 9:30–32; 10:32–34; Luke 9:18–22, 43b–45; 18:31–34.
[98]Mark 8:29, italics added.
[99]See pp. 48–49. Matthew and Luke add interpretations for the benefit of their readers.

the temptation as his commitment, and the meal for many as a fore-taste of the messianic banquet. Jesus caught the fancy of the crowds so completely, they claim, that people tried to make him king. When Peter called him Messiah, Jesus did not reject the title; his command "to tell no one" was dictated by political connotations the title evoked in the minds of others. The Triumphal Entry and the Anointing at Bethany were definite messianic demonstrations, and Jesus was con-demned and crucified as a pretender to the Jewish throne. Despite these well-marked signposts, an increasing number of scholars deny that Jesus thought of himself as Messiah. They contend that this conviction was the credo of the early church read back into the records.[100] The issue is too crucial to be decided by a single saying such as the one by Peter. We shall return to the subject of Jesus' alleged messianic consciousness in a subsequent chapter when the various titles applied to him are considered. Meanwhile, we should keep in mind the division among scholars on the topic and the multiple meanings attached to the word "Messiah."

Matthew's Special Tradition

Matthew alone contains the disputed passage that follows Peter's affirmation.

And Jesus answered him, 'Blessed are you, Simon Bar-Jona! For flesh and blood has not revealed this to you, but my Father who is in heaven. And I tell you, you are Peter, and on this rock I will build my church, and the powers of death shall not prevail against it. I will give you the keys of the kingdom of heaven, and whatever you bind on earth shall be bound in heaven, and whatever you loose on earth shall be loosed in heaven.' (16:17–19)

Raging storms of controversy have swirled over the meaning of these words, and a sharp separation of viewpoints has been provoked.

Acceptance. Some scholars accept the passage as historical. Since the text is found in all Greek manuscripts and ancient versions, they regard it as stronger than the Rock of Gibraltar. The charge that the text must be spurious because it appears only in Matthew scarcely scratches their armor. If all single-source sayings were discarded, many of Jesus' most memorable words would descend to the depths. These scholars call attention to the distinctively Aramaic images and construction of the passage and to the prominence given to Peter throughout the Synoptics. Peter's "confession" clearly came from God

---

[100]See Rudolf Bultmann, *Jesus and the Word*, trans. L.P. Smith and E.H. Lantero (New York: Charles Scribner's Sons, 1958), p. 9.

("My Father"). When Jesus called Simon "Peter," he gave him a new name. When he said, "And on this rock [*petra*] I will build my church [*ekklēsia*]," he established the primacy of Peter. The church founded on Peter, the man, is a living, perpetual institution ("the powers of death shall not prevail against it"). When Jesus gave Peter "the keys of the kingdom" with the power to "bind" or "loose," he equated the church with the kingdom and delegated to Peter the authority to forgive sins. Peter became the first Pope, passed on his prerogatives to his successor who in turn passed them on to his successor, and so forth. The church founded on Peter, called the Catholic Church by its members, is the true church. Other churches were man-made (founded by Luther, Calvin, Wesley, and others). Insofar as they depart from the authoritative teachings of the Catholic Church, they are false or separated, a term popularized by the ecumenically minded Pope John XXIII.

As widespread as this position is among Roman Catholics, it is by no means universally held. Roman Catholic experts in dogmatic theology differ as to where their Church has spoken authoritatively about the literal sense of Scripture. Vatican I seems to have done so when it insisted that Christ gave Peter primacy among the apostles, but some scholars deny that this is the case. The extent to which the Church and the kingdom can be equated also elicits vigorous discussion. Some Roman Catholic exegetes think that Matthew 16:17–19 has been removed from its original context, which was postresurrectional. They doubt that Jesus ever used the word *ekklēsia* (church). They believe that Peter is the rock on which the Church is built, but they assert that the passage from which this idea is derived does not make clear in what sense he is the foundation. The true-church claim of the Roman Catholic Church has not been abandoned, but the relationship of this claim to the truth claims of other churches (Eastern Orthodox, Lutheran, and others) is currently undergoing fruitful reexamination.[101]

[101]See John L. McKenzie, S. J., "The Gospel According to Matthew," in R.E. Brown, J.A. Fitzmyer, and R.E. Murphy, eds., *The Jerome Biblical Commentary* (Englewood Cliffs, N.J.: Prentice-Hall, Inc., 1968), II, 91–93 (113–117); compare p. 602 (87) and pp. 783–784 (102–105). See also Edmund F. Sutcliffe, S. J., "St. Peter's Double Confession in Matthew 16:16–19," in M. Rosalie Ryan, C. S. J., ed., *Contemporary New Testament Studies* (Collegeville, Minn.: Liturgical Press, 1965), pp. 260–269; Hans Küng, *The Church*, trans. Ray and Rosaleen Ockenden (New York: Sheed & Ward, 1967). A popular conservative presentation is found in Daniel-Rops, *Jesus and His Times*, rev. Catholic ed. (New York: Image Books, 1958), I (especially pp. 271–274) and II. The authenticity of Matthew 16:17–19 is defended by L.K. Schmidt, "The Church," in J.R. Coates, ed., *Bible Key Words* (New York: Harper & Row, 1951), pp. 33–50. Oscar Cullmann, a distinguished Protestant scholar, accepts the genuineness of the passage but suggests that the Last Supper was probably the original setting of the pronouncement. He believes that Peter was promised authority over the whole church but that authority terminated when he set out on his missionary activity. See Cullmann, *Peter—Disciple, Apostle, Martyr*, trans. F.V. Filson (Philadelphia: The Westminster Press, 1953).

Conditional acceptance. Other scholars accept the essential historicity of the passage, but they place a different interpretation on it. They claim that "this rock" does not refer to Peter. He was a weak, vacillating, impetuous character, an uncertain foundation on which to build anything. The reference is either to Jesus himself (the view of several early church fathers) or to Peter's affirmation that Jesus is the Christ. It is questionable that Jesus intended to establish a perpetual institution. The word "church" appears in no Gospel other than Matthew, and it is found there only twice. The church is a unique fellowship that sprang to life after the resurrection. Jesus announced the coming of the kingdom of God, but he did not identify the church with the kingdom. The "keys to the kingdom" symbolize authority rather than raw power to control entrance to the church-kingdom. "To bind" and "to loose" in rabbinical language meant to pronounce certain actions prohibited or permitted according to the Law.[102] The primacy of Peter is not established by this passage. The power to bind and loose is possessed by all the disciples who one day will sit on thrones of apparently equal value (Mt. 18:18; Jn. 20:23). James and John are not refused privileged positions in the kingdom because the primacy of Peter prohibits, but because it is not in Jesus' power to bestow them (Mk. 10:35–45). With due allowance for denominational differences and emphases, the viewpoint just described may be considered a consensus of current Protestant thought and reflects a segment of Roman Catholic thought as well.

Rejection. Still other scholars hold that the passage is unhistorical. They attribute it to the evangelist or some section of the early church. Since the books of the New Testament originally circulated separately, it is strange that so important a pronouncement appears only in Matthew. Papias states that Mark served as Peter's interpreter. Surely Mark would not have been so careless as to omit such a bedrock truth as the founding of the church on Peter. The use of the word "church" in the passage reflects the conditions of a later time when it properly meant the whole body, of which local groups were but parts.[103] In the Synoptics, Jesus characteristically speaks not of the coming of the church but of the kingdom, and he does not equate the two. Paul betrays no knowledge of Peter's primacy, and on one occasion he actually reprimands Peter for his errant ways (Gal. 2:11). James, not Peter, seems to have dominated Mother Church in Jerusalem (Acts 15:13–21). If Jesus had given Peter special authority, would he have called Peter "Satan" (Mt. 16:23)? Would the disciples have argued about who was the greatest (Mt. 18:1)? Would they have asked for preferential treatment (Mk. 10:37)? Would Peter have inquired what he would get for following Jesus (Mt. 19:27)? This third

---

[102]Terumoth 5:4. Compare Acts 10:44–48.
[103]In Matthew 18:17 the reference is to the local community of believers.

position, to which we subscribe, is endorsed by an increasing number of scholars.[104]

Passion Predictions

Three passion predictions are related in relatively rapid order after Jesus charged his disciples to tell no one about him (Mk. 8:31; 9:31; 10:32–34). They indicate that Jesus foresaw in some detail his suffering, rejection, death, and resurrection, and they state that he plainly taught his intimate associates about the tragic and triumphant events that would follow. Although it is probable that Jesus recognized that a journey to Jerusalem involved a calculated risk, it is unlikely that he foresaw the detailed happenings that would occur or that he repeatedly instructed his disciples concerning them. Except for Peter's spontaneous rebuke in Mark 8:32, the disciples betray no knowledge of the predictions. If Jesus had repeatedly forecast the future for them, why were they crushed by the crucifixion and astonished by the resurrection? Jesus' own attitude as depicted in the Synoptics, moreover, does not cohere with a precise foreknowledge of events. The predictions are better understood as a dramatic technique employed by Mark to advance his purpose.

The passion predictions introduce the idea that the Son of Man will *suffer* many things. Although Jesus frequently refers to himself as Son of Man in *Q*, it is never in connection with his future glory. When he speaks of the Son of Man as future judge, he does not specifically identify himself with that figure. *Q* never states that the Son of Man must suffer. Consequently, many scholars reject the notion that Jesus claimed to be the coming Son of Man. The evangelists, however, never use Son of Man except in words ascribed to Jesus. They picture Peter as reacting violently to Jesus' prediction of his suffering and death. How could the Messiah suffer and die? The two ideas are as congenial as water and oil. When the Messiah comes, he will live forever! So Peter rebuked Jesus and received a rebuke in return: "Get behind me, Satan! For you are not on the side of God, but of men" (Mk. 8:33). The Rock had not moved beyond the comfortable conception that the Messiah could act only in terms of triumph.

Jesus' Transfiguration (124–125)[105]

About a week after Peter's affirmation, Jesus took his three intimates (Peter, James, and John) up a high mountain to be alone. There the Master was transfigured before them. His garments turned gleam-

---

[104]See Major, Manson, and Wright, *The Mission and Message of Jesus*, pp. 494–497; Johnson, "The Gospel According to St. Matthew: Introduction and Exegesis," in *The Interpreter's Bible*, VII, 448–449; H.C. Kee, F.W. Young, and K. Froehlich, *Understanding the New Testament*, 2nd ed. (Englewood Cliffs, N.J.: Prentice-Hall, Inc., 1965), pp. 288–289.
[105]See Matthew 17:1–8, Mark 9:2–8; Luke 9:28–36.

ing white, and Moses and Elijah appeared and spoke to him. Luke alone records the subject of their conversation. The two most prestigious figures in Israel, representing the Law and the prophets, talked to Jesus about his impending death in Jerusalem. The disciples noted Jesus' glory, his changed countenance, and his glistening garments. Peter was so dazzled by the sight that he proposed the construction of three booths like those used at the Feast of Tabernacles to commemorate the occasion. Suddenly a luminous cloud, ancient symbol of the divine Presence, overshadowed them all. An echo of the voice of God came from the cloud and confirmed the message heard by Jesus at his baptism: "This is my beloved Son; listen to him" (Mk. 9:7). Then there was no one save Jesus.

The Transfiguration account has been called a myth, a legend, a postresurrection appearance of Jesus read back into his ministry, and a theological construction of the early church. Jesus reportedly called it a vision (Mt. 17:9). The story is replete with symbolic references to Israel's wilderness wanderings—Mt. Sinai and the cloud that hovered over it, the voice that spoke from the cloud, Moses' radiant face as he descended the mountain clutching the Ten Commandments, and the like (Exod. 24:12-18; 34:29). The Exodus theme was prominently featured in prophetic and rabbinic thought as a pattern for the anticipated ultimate redemption of Israel. The Transfiguration symbolism suggests that a second Moses is at hand who will lead the people of God in a New Exodus to the Promised Land of the kingdom of God.

The Transfiguration experience marks a continental divide in the Synoptic account of Jesus' ministry. From it readers can, Janus-like, look in opposite directions. They can look backward through the various events of Jesus' mission to the commitment, call, and the Baptist's work of preparation. Or they can look forward through the journey to Jerusalem to the tragic and triumphant events that are yet to come. Before we descend the Mount of Transfiguration, however, we shall pause to consider some of Jesus' teachings, his mighty works, and his titles.

VI

The Message and the Messenger
(Matthew, Mark, Luke)

Jesus was a carpenter by trade, a preacher by vocation, and a healer by choice, but he was commonly called a teacher. This title is applied to him nearly fifty times in the Synoptics. Yet, according to the accepted standard of the day, he was not a teacher at all. Rabbis and scribes spent many years studying in schools. They learned Hebrew, memorized the Law and the Prophets, and acquired a minute knowledge of the oral law as well. Jesus had neither the scribal training nor the scribal viewpoint. His primary task was to proclaim the imminence of the kingdom of God and the necessity of repentance. Such a mission required more than the mere repetition of the proclamation. Kingdom concepts were many and varied. In order to clarify what he meant by the kingdom and its righteousness, Jesus became a teacher. His extraordinary skills, especially in the use of parables, soon made him a celebrated figure.

The Parables

Purpose of the Parables

The primary function of the parable is to force the hearers to make a comparison. It places a familiar or convincing story or incident next to something less familiar. The aim is to shed light on the latter. Usually only one truth is highlighted, and that truth is independent of the parable itself.[1] Matthew states that Jesus said nothing to the crowds without a parable, but Mark indicates that Jesus adopted the parabolic technique after the Galilean campaign had been launched for some time (Mt. 13:34; Mk. 4:2). Mark further suggests that Jesus resorted to parables in order to conceal rather than reveal the truth of the kingdom.[2] This conclusion rests on a mistaken interpretation of Isaiah 6:9–10. These verses summarize the *results* of Isaiah's career.

The material in this chapter is a condensed, updated, and at times expanded version of material found in C. Milo Connick, *Jesus: The Man, the Mission, and the Message* (Englewood Cliffs, N.J.: Prentice-Hall, 1963), and C. Milo Connick, *Build on the Rock, You and the Sermon on the Mount* (Westwood, N.J.: Fleming H. Revell, 1960). Material based on *Jesus: The Man, the Mission, and the Message* is used by permission of Prentice-Hall.

[1]See p. 96.

[2]See *Gospel Parallels* (New York: Thomas Nelson & Sons, 1949), sections 90–91, 93, 99; Matthew 13:1–15, 18–23, 34–35; Mark 4:1–20, 33–34; Luke 8:4–15.

In spite of the prophet's heroic efforts, the people stubbornly rejected his message. Years later, as Isaiah reflected on his call, he concluded that his work had been foreordained to failure. Would he have persisted in his prophesying had he known from the beginning that it would be fruitless? Mark, influenced by a faulty understanding of Isaiah, saw the divine intentions in the consequences of Jesus' ministry. The parable of the Sower disclosed the dullness of Jesus' hearers. Some heard but paid no heed. Others luxuriated in a surface response. Still others allowed the kingdom to be choked by many interests. Jesus intended the secrets of the kingdom for the elect alone, Mark reasoned, and he used parables to screen the truth from others. The reasoning is specious. The time-honored purpose of a parable was to persuade. That Jesus deliberately clothed his teaching in unintelligible forms to prevent the public from comprehending his message contradicts every canon of custom, common sense, and scholarly reading of the Synoptics. It also clashes with a later comment in Mark that Jesus spoke the word with many parables as the people were able to hear it (Mk. 4:33).[3]

Modification of the Parables

Almost from the beginning the parables were provided with two different settings: the original one connected with Jesus' ministry and the later one furnished by the early church. When Jesus delivered the parables, they sprang from specific situations and were directed toward particular audiences. No scribe recorded them; their content and context were either remembered or forgotten. The remembered parables circulated singly or in pairs, and for a double decade they knew no home except the oral tradition of the church. The church collected the parables, arranged them according to subject matter, and created a new setting for them in order that she could press them into service in support of her work of evangelism, education of converts, and defense of the gospel against her enemies.

The parables experienced considerable modification in the custody of the church. Some were embellished: Mark's lone "fig tree" (13:28) was joined by "all the trees" in Luke (21:29). Others were given a different audience. The Lost Sheep, in its more nearly original setting in Luke, is addressed to Jesus' opponents (15:3–7). Its object is apologetic; it offers a vigorous defense of Jesus' ministry to the religiously disinherited. The stress of the story falls on the shepherd's joy in finding the strayed sheep. Matthew's secondary version of the parable is aimed at the disciples who are urged to emulate the shepherd and be faithful pastors to erring church members (18:12–14).

---

[3]A. M. Hunter, *The Work and Words of Jesus* (Philadelphia: The Westminster Press, 1950), p. 45, presents four different interpretations of Mark 4:11–12. See also H. C. Kee, F. W. Young, and K. Froehlich, *Understanding the New Testament* (Englewood Cliffs, N.J.: Prentice-Hall, Inc., 1965), pp. 264–265, for a contrary view.

Threshing as in Biblical Times. Lebanese farmers attach stones
to the underside of their drag. When the drag is pulled, the stones
knock the grain from the stalks. Toward evening the farmers pitch
the dragged grain into the air, and the rising wind separates the
wheat from the chaff.

The stress is on the shepherd's persistent search. Still others were
made vehicles of exhortation. The Defendant, originally designed
to alert people to the imminence of the kingdom, is transformed into
a call to Christians to become reconciled with an estranged brother
(Lk. 12:58–59). Some, like the Weeds (Mt. 13:24–30), the Net (Mt.
13:47–48), and the Sower (Mt. 13:3–8; Mk. 4:3–8; Lk. 8:5–8), were
allegorized. A few, like the Wedding Garment (Mt. 22:11–13) and
the Marriage Feast (Mt. 22:2–10), were fused. Finally, generalized
conclusions, which sometimes miss the point of the parables, were
added (Mt. 20:16).[4]

Message of the Parables

Recognition that the parables have undergone modifications makes
possible the recovery of their original content and context. The process
is necessarily speculative, and absolute certainties are precluded. Yet
the imaginative, informed, and disciplined conjecture that accompa-
nies all historical inquiry can yield reasonably accurate results. When
the parables are stripped of excess baggage and placed in their primary
setting, a remarkable fact appears—many of them sponsor the same
point. Jesus apparently never wearied of communicating a few basic
kingdom concepts in ever-changing images. Taken together they provide a rather comprehensive compendium of his message.

[4]For a fascinating discussion of the development of the parables from their primary
to their secondary settings, see Joachim Jeremias, *The Parables of Jesus*, revised (New
York: Charles Scribner's Sons, 1963), to which our general outline is indebted.

The gift of the kingdom is the point of the parable of the Laborers in the Vineyard (190).[5] The Jewish working day extended from sunrise to sunset. An estate owner hired some laborers early one morning to work in his vineyard for the generous and agreed-upon wage of one denarius. Later in the day (about nine, twelve, three, and five o'clock) other workers were hired and promised a just wage. When the day was done, each worker received a denarius. The early birds grumbled because they had borne the burden of the day and the scorching heat. The owner replied to the protest: "Friend, I am doing you no wrong; did you not agree with me for a denarius? Take what belongs to you, and go; I choose to give to this last as I give to you. Am I not allowed to do what I choose with what belongs to me? Or do you begrudge my generosity?" (Mt. 20:13–15).

The scribes and Pharisees strenuously objected to Jesus' preaching to the "people of the land." Such folk were careless about keeping the Law and the oral traditions. Special consideration should be reserved for those who had earned it. By the parable of the Laborers in the Vineyard, Jesus justifies his work with the religious outcasts, and he exposes the self-serving concern of his critics. He makes clear that the rewards of the kingdom are not rationed according to man's desert. They are the free gift of God's grace; He bestows them on whom He wills.

The newness of the kingdom is sponsored by the twin parables of the New Cloth and the New Wine (54).[6] No one sews a piece of new cloth on an old garment. The first washing would rend the garment, and the resultant tear would exceed the first. Neither does a person put new wine in old, brittle wineskins. Fermentation would cause the nonelastic containers to burst, and the wine would be lost. Jesus evidently intended those parables to indicate that the approaching kingdom would shatter the framework of the old order.

The nearness of the kingdom is the burden of a host of parables.[7]

---

[5]See Matthew 20:1–15. Matthew 20:16 is a generalized conclusion that clashes with the point of the parable (see Mk. 10:31; Lk. 13:30). Other parables making the same point are the Places at Table (169), Lk. 14:7–10, and the Servant's Duty (181), Lk. 17:7–10.

[6]See Matthew 9:16–17; Mark 2:21–22; Luke 5:36–38.

[7]The Budding Fig Tree (220), Mt. 24:32–33; Mk. 13:28–29; Lk. 21:29–31; the Supervising Servant (158), Mt. 24:45–51a; Lk. 12:42–46; the Talents and the Pounds (195), Mt. 25:14–18; Lk. 19:12–27; the Watchful Servants (158) and its variant the Watchful Doorkeeper (222), Lk. 12:35–38; Mk. 13:34–36; the Speck and the Log (36), Mt. 7:3–5; Lk. 6:41–42; the Blind Guides (76), Mt. 15:14; Lk. 6:39; the Lamp and Bushel and the Body's Lamp (153), Mt. 5:15; 6:22–23; Lk. 11:33–36; the Tree and the Fruit (41), Mt. 7:16–20; Lk. 6:43–45; the Savorless Salt (132), Mt. 5:13; Mk. 9:49–50; Lk. 14:34–35; and the Barren Fig Tree (162), Lk. 13:6–9.

It is picturesquely presented in the parable of the Rich Fool (156).[8] Although the story is often taken as a stark warning against greed, it is more likely a parable of "the times." A bumper crop bulged a farmer's barns. In order to care for his surplus and to insure against future crop failures, he resolved to tear down his barns and build bigger ones. Then he would live it up in luxury. What a fool! He failed to include God in his plans. The kingdom was near. "This night," God informed the farmer, "your soul is required of you" (Lk. 12:20. All the while he was scheming to husband his harvest and maximize his creature comforts, the sword of Damocles hung over his head.

The inevitability of the kingdom is advanced by the twin parables of the Mustard Seed and the Leaven (97–98).[9] They assure their hearers that the kingdom's coming is certain. The mustard seed's smallness is proverbial—no larger than the period at the end of this sentence. Yet when it is planted in the ground, surprising results follow. It grows to the height of ten to twelve feet and becomes the greatest of all shrubs. The leaven also produces spectacular results. A housewife hides a tiny bit of it in three measures of meal. Then she covers the receptacle with a cloth and allows the mass to stand overnight. By morning the whole loaf is leavened. Contrary to the thinking of earlier days, neither of these parables supports the notion that the kingdom grows gradually. Mustard seed matures rapidly, and leaven does its work overnight. The stress in the stories is not on the process but on the prospect. The nub of these parables lies in the contrast between minute beginnings and magnificent ends. God is reasserting his sovereignty. The seed has been sown, and the leaven has been placed in the lump. Soon the mighty consequences will be present for all to see. The kingdom's coming is inevitable. Nothing man can do will hasten or hinder its arrival.

The inclusiveness of the kingdom is the subject of many parables.[10] The Physician and the Sick (53) is a case in point.[11] Jesus sat at

---

[8]See Luke 12:16–20. Luke 12:21 is a generalized conclusion that distorts the parable's thrust.

[9]See Matthew 13:31–33; Mark 4:30–32; Luke 13:18–21. Other parables that support the same teaching are the Seed Growing Secretly (95), Mk. 4:26–29, and the Sower (90), Mt. 13:18–23; Mk. 4:13–20; Lk. 8:11–15.

[10]The Lost Sheep, The Lost Coin, and the Lost Son (172–173), Mt. 18:12–14; Lk. 15:3–32; the Two Debtors (83), Lk. 7:41–43; the Two Sons (203), Mt. 21:28–31; the Pharisee and the Publican (186), Lk. 18:10–14a; the Unjust Judge (185), Lk. 18:2–5; the Friend at Midnight (147), Lk. 11:5–8; The Great Banquet-Marriage Feast (205), Lk. 14:16–24; Mt. 22:2–10; the Wicked Tenants (204), Mt. 21:33–43; Mk. 12:1–11; Lk. 20:9–18.

[11]See Matthew 9:12; Mark 2:17; Luke 5:31.

table with sinners and tax collectors. The reputation of these people was darkly stained. They were considered immoral (adulterers, swindlers), practitioners of callings involving dishonesty (tax collecting) or infractions of the Law (tanning), or otherwise lax about keeping the rules and regulations of religion. The scribes of the Pharisees, noted for their scrupulous observance of the food regulations and other requirements, protested to Jesus' disciples. Since the scribes avoided all contact with nonobserving Jews lest they themselves be contaminated, they found it difficult to understand why Jesus would eat with such people. Jesus' reply struck to the heart of the matter: "Those who are well have no need of a physician, but those who are sick; I came not to call the righteous, but sinners" (Mk. 2:17). He was no doubt concerned about "the righteous"; they were also sinners and stood in need of repentance. But the kingdom he proclaimed was not confined to the respectable; its primary interest centered on those believed to be beyond the pale of Providence.

The supreme value of the kingdom is accented by the twin parables of the Hidden Treasure and the Precious Pearl (101). Jesus said, "The kingdom of heaven is like treasure hidden in a field, which a man found and covered up; then in his joy he goes and sells all that he has and buys that field. Again, the kingdom of heaven is like a merchant in search of fine pearls, who, on finding one pearl of great value, went and sold all that he had and bought it" (Mt. 13:44–46). There is no significance to the different methods of discovery employed here. These are parables, not allegories. Neither should the stories be seen as calls to complete self-surrender. They do not stress what is given up; they stress what is found. The man who discovered the buried treasure did not sit down and calculate the cost of purchase. He joyously went at once, sold all that he had, and bought the field. He had found wealth that devalues all other currencies.[12]

The cost of discipleship is emphasized by the companion parables of the Tower Builder and the Warring King(171).[13] Jesus asked, "For which of you, desiring to build a tower, does not first sit down and count the cost, whether he has enough to complete it? Otherwise, when he has laid a foundation, and is not able to finish, all who

---

[12]A paraphrase of T. W. Manson's pregnant comment in H. D. A. Major, T. W. Manson, and C. J. Wright, *The Mission and Message of Jesus* (New York: E. P. Dutton & Co., 1938), p. 488.

[13]See also the Empty House (88), Mt. 12:43–45c; Lk. 11:24–26; the Householder (103), Mt. 13:52; the Good Samaritan (144), Lk. 10:30–37; the Sheep and Goats (229), Mt. 25:31–46; The Unmerciful Servant (136), Mt. 18:23–34; the City on a Hill (20), Mt. 5:14b.

Watchtower at Jericho. At the old city of Jericho excavations (which have unearthed a wall dated about 7200 B.C.) reveal this watchtower. Watchtowers were a vital link in the security system of ancient Israel. Before a farmer planted his fields he built a watchtower. It enabled him to detect the approach of wild animals or an enemy that might ravage his crops.

see it begin to mock him, saying, 'This man began to build, and was not able to finish.' Or what king, going to encounter another king in war, will not sit down first and take counsel whether he is able with ten thousand to meet him who comes against him with twenty thousand? And if not, while the other is yet a great way off, he sends an embassy and asks terms of peace" (Lk. 14:28–32).[14]

Jesus' call is for complete commitment. If prospective disciples do not place kingdom responsibilities above the most intimate and solemn

[14]Luke 14:33 is a later, generalized conclusion.

human obligations—even above the right of self-preservation—their candidacy is denied (Lk. 14:26). They must leave the dead to bury their own dead (Lk. 9:60). Once they have placed their hands on plows, they cannot glance back (Lk. 9:62). In every instance the kingdom must have top priority (Mt. 6:33). It has no room for those who have failed to count the cost.

The challenge of the kingdom is espoused by the parable of the Two Foundations (43).[15] Jesus said, "Every one then who hears these words of mine and does them will be like a wise man who built his house upon the rock; and the rain fell, and the floods came, and the winds blew and beat upon that house, but it did not fall, because it had been founded on the rock" (Mt. 7:24–25). Rains, floods, and winds were as certain as Passover in Palestine. A wise man prepared for such certainties by building on a sure foundation. "And every one who hears these words of mine and does not do them [Jesus continued], will be like a foolish man who built his house upon the sand" (Mt. 7:26). The house he built was evidently as substantial as that of the wise man; the difference lay in the foundation. The foolish man chose the smooth sand of a river bed for his building base. When the rain fell, and the floods came, and the winds beat against his house, it collapsed. The lesson is lucid. "How happy are they who build their lives on the rock of hearing and heeding my words," Jesus says in effect, "for they will be ready when the kingdom comes."

The climax of the kingdom is the point underscored by the parable of the Net (102).[16] The allegorical interpretation that follows is clearly secondary (Mt. 13:49–50). Matthew has not only stamped his style on it,[17] but he has transformed the parable into a description of the Final Judgment. In the process, Jesus' original point, a plea for patience, has been virtually obscured. Jesus compared the kingdom of heaven to a large fishing net. Sometimes such a net was dragged between two boats; at other times it was placed in the water by a single boat with one end of the net attached to the shore by long ropes. In either case, when the net was brought to shore, it contained "fish of every kind" (Mt. 13:47). The kingdom is not compared to the net that catches and keeps the fish of every kind; it is compared to the sorting that follows the fishing. The fishermen "sorted the

---

[15]See Matthew 7:24–27; Luke 6:47–49. Other parables making the same point are the Defendant (161), Mt. 5:25–26; Lk. 12:58–59; the Dishonest Steward (174), Lk. 16:1–8; the Rich Man and Lazarus (177), Lk. 16:19–31; the Wedding Garment (205), Mt. 22:11–13; the Wise and Foolish Maidens (227), Mt. 25:1–13.

[16]See Matthew 13:47–48. (T. W. Manson, in Major et al, *The Mission and Message of Jesus*, p. 489, considers only vs. 47 to be original.) The parable of the Weeds (96), Mt. 13:24–30, also makes the same point.

[17]Jeremias, *The Parables of Jesus*, p. 67, notes six examples.

good into vessels but threw away the bad" (Mt. 13:48). The bad fish were either inedible or "unclean," without "fins and scales" (Lev. 11:10). The parable is church oriented and eschatological. It concerns (but it does not describe) the Final Judgment. Those who hanker to separate "the good guys" from "the bad guys" in the church are urged to wait patiently for the climax of the kingdom. It is God's kingdom, and He has fixed the time of separation. That time has not yet arrived. Opportunity for repentance has not yet expired. "Till then, all false zeal must be checked, . . . the net must be cast widely, and everything else left to God in faith, until his hour comes."[18]

The Sermon on the Mount

Matthew's Sermon on the Mount is composed of only 107 verses (5:1–7:29), and Luke's parallel Sermon on the Plain is even shorter (6:20–49). The common assumption that Jesus delivered the sermon at a single sitting seems to make sense on the surface, but a more thorough examination of the content suggests otherwise. The Sermon on the Mount is a collection of sermon summaries supplemented by interpretative comments by the evangelist. Matthew placed this marvelous mosaic in a mountain setting to parallel Moses' reception of the Law on Mt. Sinai. The symbolism is intended to suggest that the Old Order of Judaism has been fulfilled, and the New Order of the kingdom of heaven is at hand.

The Beatitudes (19)[19]

Both Matthew and Luke begin Jesus' "Sermon" with the Beatitudes. Matthew's version, given below, contains eight sayings; Luke lists only four. The first clause in each sets forth the kind of character possessed by kingdom members, and the second clause describes the consequence. Perhaps all of the Beatitudes originally ended with the declaration, "for theirs is the kingdom of heaven."

"Blessed are the poor in spirit, for theirs is the kingdom of heaven." "Blessed" meant "How happy!" and was often used to communicate hearty congratulations. It signified the well-being that flows from God's favor. In Luke, "the poor" stands for the economically disadvantaged, an emphasis that befits this evangelist's understanding of the gospel. Matthew adds to his source the words "in spirit" to clarify the meaning and designate the subject under discussion. It was a spiritual (not economic) condition to which Jesus referred. The usage

[18]Joachim Jeremias, *The Parables of Jesus*, 3rd ed., tr. S. H. Hooke (New York: Charles Scribner's Sons, 1955), p. 157. Reprinted by permission of the publisher. For treatment of those parables mentioned only in footnotes, see C. Milo Connick, *Jesus: The Man, the Mission, and the Message* (Englewood Cliffs, N.J.: Prentice-Hall, Inc., 1963), pp. 203–233.
[19]See Matthew 5:3–12; Luke 6:20–23.

stems from the Psalms where poor and pious are often interchangeable (9:18; 10:9; 12:5; 34:6). The poor are the faithful who are keenly aware of their spiritual need. To them belongs "the kingdom of heaven," a shorthand phrase for God's rule and its benefits.

"Blessed are those who mourn, for they shall be comforted." The mourners are those who are sorry for personal or national sins or who weep over the woes that announce the Messiah's coming. They may also include those separated from power, possessions, or persons dear to them. The Greek word for comfort means "to strengthen much." When the mourners sin, they seek forgiveness and experience the comfort that comes with confession. When others sin, they share their suffering. When trouble torments the mourners, they bear it with courage. They are confident they can see it through because they will be fortified by the Father.

"Blessed are the meek, for they shall inherit the earth." The clue to the meaning of "meek" is found in its object. Meekness concerns a person's attitude toward God. Moses was bold and assertive among men, yet the Scripture describes him as very meek (Num. 12:3). The clauses do not clash. In the presence of God, Moses was malleable. That such people should find a foremost place in the kingdom of heaven is easily grasped, but does not the earth belong to the mighty? This Beatitude echoes the Old Testament. God promised Abraham that his descendants would occupy the land that stretched from the Nile to the Euphrates (Gen. 15:18–21). The covenant was conditional; the prerequisite of possession was faithfulness. The Israelites took literally the pledge that "the meek shall possess the land" (Ps. 37:11), and they eagerly anticipated an exchange of real estate for righteousness. But Jesus and his followers already possessed the promised real estate. His declaration that the meek shall inherit the earth must be interpreted metaphorically. The meek will bask in the blessings of the kingdom.

"Blessed are those who hunger and thirst for righteousness, for they shall be satisfied." As in the first Beatitude, the form of Luke's version seems nearer the original: "Blessed are you that hunger now, for you shall be satisfied" (6:21). Since it seems to stress a physical condition, Matthew adds "for righteousness" to his source to clarify the meaning. The addition is a happy one and firmly rooted in history. Hunger and thirst had often been used to symbolize spiritual longing (Amos 8:11). The "righteousness" sought is the character and conduct of God, the subject of the entire Sermon. Those who deeply desire the reign of God enjoy a ravenous appetite at their Father's table, and they can rest assured that His bounty will suffice.

"Blessed are the merciful, for they shall obtain mercy." Many Jews believed that all suffering was caused by sin. Men were poor because they had transgressed God's Law; women were barren because they had lost His favor. The sick, lame, halt, and blind were sowers who had reaped their reward. People hesitated to be helpful because they did not want to interfere with divine justice. The need for sympathetic loving-kindness was urgent. The benediction of this Beatitude, however, comes not from merciful men but from God. Mercy is another name for His nature. His mercy falls on the merciful and the unmerciful alike, but only the merciful can receive it. Unless mercy flows out of a man's heart, there is no room for God's mercy to flow in.[20]

"Blessed are the pure in heart, for they shall see God." The "pure" are not the well-scrubbed; neither are they the ceremonially certified. Jews believed that when they worshiped in the Temple they appeared before God. Many kinds of bodily defilement, such as contact with Gentiles or the dead, could disqualify them for the experience. So they meticulously practiced the myriad purifications prescribed by Law. Only thus could they be certain of seeing God as they worshiped. Jesus showed little sympathy for ceremonial purity. "In heart" defines the topic under discussion, as "in spirit" does in the first Beatitude. The pure are the single-minded toward God. Nothing diverts them from their controlling purpose. They love God and serve Him unstintingly. Since they are focused on God, they "see" Him. Their sight is not a matter of optics but of fellowship. Presently their sight is dim, but the day will come when they will see God "face to face" (I Cor. 13:12).

"Blessed are the peacemakers, for they shall be called sons of God." This Beatitude is a call to action. Permanent peace is the goal. The prospects for success were not bright. Galilee seethed under Roman rule, but this did not deter one of its sons from praising peacemakers. They are to seek peace and pursue it (Ps. 34:14), resolve quarrels and reconcile enemies. They are to be as much concerned with the causes of conflicts as with the cures. Their aim is peace, and their program is peaceful. Such people are "sons of God" because they share their Father's nature. He is the God of peace, and His son is the Prince of Peace. His command is "On earth peace!" (Lk. 2:14).

"Blessed are those who are persecuted for righteousness' sake, for theirs is the kingdom of heaven." What a paradox! Happy are the persecuted! The pronouncement struck a new note of wide-ranging signifi-

[20]See Hugh Martin, *The Beatitudes* (New York: Harper & Row, 1953), p. 59.

cance. Never before had disciples been told to rejoice in their misfortunes.[21] Of course not every persecution promotes happiness; it has to be "for righteousness' sake." Those who undergo hardship, suffering, or persecution while in the line of duty for God are the happy ones because they enjoy God's approval. In the life to come, their happiness will know no bounds.

The eschatological character of the Beatitudes is increasingly acknowledged.[22] Six of the eight sayings express their promises in the future tense in the Greek. Even where the present tense is used, the future reference is not ruled out (Mt. 5:3,10).[23] The form of the Beatitudes in Luke 6:21 highlights the future character of the promised rewards: "Blessed are you that hunger *now*, for you *shall* be satisfied [at the End of the Age]."[24] It is our conviction, however, that the happiness promised the people of the Beatitudes was not purely prospective. In some measure they were already blessed. Perhaps their present happiness was prompted by the prospect of future reward, but it also stemmed from the nature of their character and commitment.

The Old Order and the New (21–27)[25]

The parables of Salt and Light urge disciples to live the kingdom life described by the Beatitudes openly before the world.[26] Then life in the kingdom is compared with life under the Law. Matthew alone introduces the series of antitheses that follows with general statements about the Law attributed to Jesus.[27] Matthew 5:18–19 could not have crossed Jesus' lips. The verses declare that the Law is true and permanent down to the last dotted "i" and crossed "t," and they exclude from the kingdom all except those who teach and observe the Law in its entirety. Such a standard would have denied entrance to Jesus himself! Verses 17 and 20, however, substantially cohere with Jesus' thought. He did not come to destroy the Law but to fulfill it. He saw kingdom life as both continuous with and superior to life under the Law. John the Baptist was as great as any of the Old Order, but he was outranked by the lowest in the kingdom (Mt. 11:11). Jesus came to rescue the Law from its oral distortions and to accomplish its original intent—the realization of the will of God in

[21]See C.G. Montefiore, *The Synoptic Gospels*, 2nd rev. ed. (London: The Macmillan Co., 1927), II, 44.
[22]See Martin Dibelius, *The Sermon on the Mount*, trans, C.H. Kraeling (New York: Charles Scribner's Sons, 1940), pp. 22, 61; Hans Windisch, *The Meaning of the Sermon on the Mount*, trans. S.M. Gilmour (Philadelphia: The Westminster Press, 1951), pp. 113, 168.
[23]There would have been no verb at all in the Aramaic.
[24]Italics added. See also the corresponding "woes" in Luke 6:25.
[25]See Matthew 5:17–48; 18:8–9; 19:9; Mark 9:43–48; 10:11–12; Luke 6:27–30, 32–36; 12:57–59; 16:18.
[26]See section 20; Matthew 5:13–16; Luke 11:33; 14:34–35.
[27]See section 21; Matthew 5:17–20.

human experience. The effect of his mission, though, was to overthrow the Law as *Law* and at times to erase, contradict, or repudiate the old.[28]

There was no finer standard of righteousness in the ancient world than that sponsored by the Pharisees. It placed great stress on the twin virtues of personal holiness and social responsibility.[29] It comes as a surprise, then, to read Jesus' injunction to his followers: "Unless your righteousness exceeds that of the scribes and Pharisees, you will never enter the kingdom of heaven" (Mt. 5:20). What did he have in mind? The scribes and Pharisees had reduced religion to a list of large and small duties. Their aim was an attainable ethic adjusted to human capacity. Jesus' emphasis was not on the best possible but the impossible best. He asked his devotees to exceed the righteousness of the scribes and Pharisees by living in This Age as though they were already living in the Age to Come.

The six contrasting statements that follow in Matthew 5:21–48 detail what the higher righteousness of the kingdom is all about. A simpler, original set of contrasts, to which the evangelist has added his own comments and other sayings of Jesus, can be detected (Mt. 5:21a, 22a, 27–28, 31–32, 33a, 34a, 38–39a, 43a, 44a). A summary of the substance of the primary sayings is instructive.

Moses	*Jesus*
"You have heard . . ."	"But I say . . ."
No murder	No anger
No adultery	No lustful look
No divorce without a certificate	No divorce with re-marriage[30]
No false oath-taking	No oath-taking at all
Limited retaliation	No retaliation
Love your neighbor	Love your enemy

The radical nature of Jesus' ethic is indisputable. Although the Mosaic Law constituted a considerable advance over previous codes of conduct, its requirements were altogether reasonable. With thought and discipline, nearly everyone could observe them. But Jesus prohibited

[28]See Montifiore, *The Synoptic Gospels*, II, 47.
[29]See S.E. Johnson, "The Gospel According to St. Matthew: Introduction and Exegesis," in George A. Buttrick, ed., *The Interpreter's Bible* (New York: Abingdon Press, 1951), VII, 293–294.
[30]Matthew's qualification, "except on the ground of unchastity," is a post-Jesus concession to human frailty. It was not Jesus' habit to make exceptions. Mark (10:11–12), Luke (16:18), and Paul (I Cor. 7:10–16) know nothing about an exception. In Matthew 19:9, where the exception also occurs, Matthew clearly inserted it into his source.

anger, lust, divorce, oaths, and retaliation. Then he compounded his commands by insisting that his followers should love their enemies! These are not reasonable requirements; they are impossible imperatives. No one can say of them, as the rich young ruler did of Moses' Law, "All these I have observed from my youth" (Mk. 10:20). Their concern is not merely conduct but character. They at once internalize and universalize religion. They are radical not only because they are stringent and unyielding, but because they cure the cause of human conflict. They are grounded in the nature and purpose of God Himself. Those who love their enemies and pray for their persecutors are worthy sons of their Father who is in heaven (Mt. 5:44–45).

Current Practices and Problems (28–44)[31] In the previous section of the Sermon, Jesus contrasted life under the Law with life in the kingdom (Mt. 5:21–28). The emphasis was on the horizontal—man's relations with man. Now he proceeds to contrast life in the kingdom with certain current practices. His attention shifts to the vertical—man's relations with his Maker (Mt. 6:1–18). The theme of his thought is found in the first verse: "Beware of practicing your piety before men." Piety for publicity is contrasted with true worship in three areas: almsgiving, prayer, and fasting. Worshipers are exhorted to give alms in secret, to pray in private, and to avoid external signs of fasting. The Sermon's concern for obedience is not confined to ethical performance; it includes modes of worship as well. To the teaching on prayer, Matthew adds other sayings of Jesus that treat how not to pray (6:7–8), how to pray (the Lord's Prayer, 6:9–13), and prayer for forgiveness (6:14–15)—matters of vital concern to the church.

The Sermon next focuses the spotlight on four persistent human problems: possessions, anxiety, judgment, and prayer (Mt. 6:19—7:12). Followers are urged to bypass earthly riches and concentrate on the accumulation of imperishable heavenly treasures, to cultivate trust in God as the perfect antidote for anxiety, to judge others lovingly, and to pray persistently. The Sermon reaches its summit at this point with the proclamation of the familiar Golden Rule: "So whatever you wish that men would do to you, do so to them; for this is the law and the prophets" (Mt. 7:12).

A sharp cleavage prevails among scholars as to the extent of eschatology in the Sermon. Martin Dibelius thinks that it pervades the whole.[32] Hans Windisch, on the other hand, holds that Matthew has escalated the eschatological elements in the Sermon. Where the near-

---

[31]See Matthew 6:1–7:29 and parallels.
[32]Dibelius, *The Sermon on the Mount*, pp. 60–61, 65.

ness of the judgment and the eschatological rule of God are not explicitly articulated, the passages should not be considered eschatological.[33] Harvey K. McArthur sponsors a more moderate view. He believes that about 40 percent of the Sermon is directly dominated by eschatology, 40 percent contains no explicit eschatological reference, and the remainder defies classification. In none of the references to the End does he find emphasis on its imminence.[34] No matter which scholarly stance is adopted, it seems reasonable to suppose that eschatology played a significant role in the Sermon.

Was the Sermon's ethic, then, conditioned by its eschatology? Did Jesus proffer a purely crash program to be followed in the brief interim before the End? Would his ethical injunctions have been modified had he expected the world to continue for two millennia? If so, are modern Christians freed from the Sermon's impossible imperatives? Answers to these and related questions are numerous. McArthur has summarized and evaluated twelve "versions and evasions" of the Sermon.[35] We are convinced that Jesus did not advocate an interim ethic. The imminence of the End is not stressed in the Sermon or in Jesus' ethical demands outside of it. He certainly believed that the time was short. The assumed nearness of the End doubtless accentuated the urgency of the crisis. But the imminence of the End was not the cause of the stringency of the demands but their occasion.

When Jesus rejected the Mosaic concessions concerning divorce, he did not do so because the End was near. He grounded his teaching in Genesis. From the beginning of creation God had intended marriage to be permanent.

Signs, Wonders, and Mighty Works

The Gospels are unacquainted with miracles. "Miracle" is a modern word often used to describe a happening contrary to the known laws of nature. But our evangelists wrote in a prescientific age. Since they knew nothing about most of nature's laws, they did not think of occurrences as being either coherent with or contrary to them. Instead, the Gospels speak of "powers" (*dunameis*), "wonders" (*terata*), "mighty works" (*dunata erga*), and "signs" (*sēmeia*). Power was another name for God (Mk. 14:62).[36] When a happening was filled with power, people watched and wondered. They saw in it a manifestation of God's presence and purpose. Thus understood, of course,

---

[33]Windisch, *The Meaning of the Sermon on the Mount*, pp. 29–30.
[34]McArthur, *Understanding the Sermon on the Mount* (New York: Harper & Row, 1960), p. 91.
[35]McArthur, *Understanding the Sermon on the Mount*, pp. 105–148.
[36]"Power" is a circumlocution.

miracles abound in the Gospels. About one-third of Mark can be so classified. Matthew and Luke include most of Mark's miracles and add a few of their own. The Gospels list about thirty-five in all. Some are described in considerable detail (Mt. 8:28–34; 14:13–21), while others are briefly treated (Mt. 8:14–15; 9:32–33). A host of others are merely mentioned: Jesus healed "every disease and every infirmity among the people" (Mt. 4:23). From this wealth of miracle evidence two conclusions can be drawn. The evangelists could easily have recorded more miracles than they did, and miracles were an integral (not accidental) part of Jesus' mission and message.

Development of Miracle Material The miracle stories moved through five stages of development. (1) There was an actual happening, in most cases, in which Jesus participated. (2) Eyewitnesses interpreted what had occurred. (3) The church used the interpreted happening in its evangelistic and educational endeavors. (4) The story was reduced to writing. (5) The evangelists edited the story and incorporated it in the gospel record.

If we begin with the final stage and work backward, we can observe the process at work. Mark's versions are lifelike, individualized, and detailed. Matthew condenses Mark's stories, sometimes destroying their individuality, and occasionally doubles their statistics.[37] Although Luke usually follows Mark more faithfully, he omits some of the direct dialogue in the Earliest Gospel. Despite the later evangelists' tendency to telescope and omit, they add touches of their own to Mark's reports. The additions magnify the adequacy of Jesus' power in one of two ways. They either increase the number of people benefited or they heighten the severity of the disorder relieved.[38] During the oral period (stage three), the material was subject to the same tendencies that other miracle stories experienced. Vincent Taylor notes five of them. While the story was being shortened, explanatory or inferential points were added. Direct speech gave way to indirect speech. Personal and place names were eliminated. The story was rounded out as details were dropped. The substance of the story, however, was retained.[39] From this it follows that the shorter and more conventional stories passed through many more hands before they were recorded than did the longer and more colorful ones. The eyewitnesses to the strange happenings in which Jesus participated (stage two) were not trained and objective observers. They were first-century Palestinians: farmers, fishermen, artisans, and day laborers. Many were illiterate and superstitious. Most of them believed in a

[37]Compare Mark 5:1–20 and Matthew 8:28–34; Mark 10:46 and Matthew 20:30.
[38]Compare Mark 1:34 and Matthew 8:16; Luke 4:40; Mark 1:30 and Luke 4:38.
[39]Taylor, *The Formation of the Gospel Tradition* (London: The Macmillan Co., 1953), pp. 124–126.

three-storied, geocentric "universe" in which mental illness was attributed to demon possession and physical deformity to sin. These facts by no means invalidate their testimonies, but they do place those testimonies in a world radically different from our own. It is in the framework of that world, not our own, that they must be evaluated.

Types of Miracles A common way to classify the miracles is by subject matter. They divide rather naturally into four groups.

Exorcisms concern the casting out of demons. Since demons were associated with a wide variety of abnormalities—moral, mental, and physical—the line between exorcisms and healings is sometimes as thin as a razor's edge. Normally, though, "casting out demons" refers to the relief of mental disorders and "healing" to the curing of physical disease.

In keeping with his theological bent, Mark records several stories in which Jesus defeats the demons. The account of the Gerasene Demoniac (106) is a case in point.[40] A certain man lived among the tombs, the natural habitat of demons and the enforced habitat of the possessed. He could not be held by chains and fetters, and no one had the superstrength to subdue him. He cried out constantly and bruised himself with stones. When he saw Jesus, he sought to subvert his power. He revealed Jesus' true name, "Son of the Most High God" (hitherto unknown to sane men), and he commanded Jesus to take an oath not to torment him. Jesus responded by calling the demoniac by name, "Legion." (It was a common conviction that to speak a man's name was to exercise control over him.) Defeated at his own game, the demoniac parleyed for the best possible terms. As servile spokesman for the spirits, he begged Jesus not to send them out of the country where they were indigenous. Since they had to seek embodiment somewhere, the spirits urged Jesus to send them into the nearby swine. That way they could remain in the country. Jesus honored their request, but the demons were duped nonetheless. They failed to foresee the catastrophic consequences of their suggestion. The huge herd of swine rushed down the steep bank and were drowned in the sea. When the aroused Gerasenes came to investigate, they found the demoniac "clothed and in his right mind." Their fear skyrocketed. Jesus' awesome power might be used again. They could not disregard the possible loss of two thousand swine whenever he might war with the demons. So they begged him to practice his exorcisms somewhere else.

[40]See Matthew 8:28-34; Mark 5:1-20; Luke 8:26-39. See also Mark 1:23-38; 7:25-30; 9:14-29 and parallels.

Healings abound in the Synoptics, and they cover an astonishing variety of physical disorders: fever, paralysis, dumbness, atrophy, hemorrhage, deafness and speech impairment, blindness, epilepsy, infirmity, dropsy, and the like. The Healing of the Leper (45) conjures up a false image in the western world.[41] What we call leprosy, or Hansen's disease, is not under consideration. Biblical leprosy was a catchall term that covered a variety of skin disorders (contagious ringworm, psoriasis, leucoderma, and vitiligo) and even mildew on walls and cooking vessels. The disease was sufficiently common in Palestine that the entire tractate Negaim in the Mishnah was devoted to it. Rabbis usually held that leprosy was a direct punishment for serious sins. The Law presupposed that a cure was possible but difficult. Victims were shunned because of the double fears of contagion and ritualistic contamination. The afflicted were compelled to live apart from regular society, wear torn clothes and loose hair, and at the approach of nonlepers cover their mouths and cry out the warning, "Unclean, unclean" (Lev. 13:45–46).[42] They remained in this state until a priest pronounced them cured and their sacrifices were performed.

One day a leper approached Jesus and declared, "If you will, you can make me clean" (Mk. 1:40). Jesus, moved by compassion, threw caution to the winds. Disregarding certain ceremonial defilement and possible contagion, he stretched out his hand, touched the leper, spoke to him, and immediately healed him. Suddenly the emotional climate worsened. Jesus' compassion turned to anger. (Was it because of the leper's presumptuous demand, his illegal approach, or Jesus' foreknowledge of what the leper would do next?) He sternly charged the man to say nothing to anyone, go and show himself to the priest (in Jerusalem), and perform the proper purification ceremony. The ceremony would constitute "proof to the people" that the leper was cured. Then he could return to society. But the leper talked freely and spread the news of Jesus' deed. Jesus could no longer openly enter a town, according to Mark, because of the man's disobedience.

Resuscitations are a rarity in the Gospels. Two are found in the Synoptics and only one in John. The story of Jairus' Daughter (107) is set in Jewish territory.[43] Jesus had just crossed the Sea of Galilee by boat, and a great crowd had gathered on the western shore. Then Jairus, a synagogue ruler, saw him. Jairus fell at Jesus' feet and declared that his little daughter was near death. He implored Jesus to go and lay his hands on her that she might be made well and

[41]See Matthew 8:1–4; Mark 1:40–45; Luke 5:12–16.
[42]Note II Kings 15:5. King Azariah (Uzziah) was smitten with leprosy. He had to live "in a separate house," and his son (Jothan) had to rule for him as regent.
[43]See Matthew 9:18–26; Mark 5:21–43; Luke 8:40–56.

live. Jesus did as he was asked, but on the way he was stopped by a woman who was hemorrhaging. While he was speaking to her, word arrived that Jairus' child was dead. There was surely no need to trouble the teacher further, but Jesus reassured Jairus and urged him to believe. Before they reached the ruler's house, Jesus dismissed the crowd. When Jairus, Jesus, and his three intimates (Peter, James, and John) arrived at the house, a public wake was in process. Jesus declared that the sorrow was premature and dubious: "The child is not dead but sleeping" (Mk. 5:39). The mourners took Jesus' words literally, and they laughed at the absurd claim. Jesus hustled them all outside. Then, with his intimates and the child's parents, he entered the death chamber. He took the child by the hand and commanded her to arise. Her response was immediate; she got up and walked. The crowd was amazed.

Nature wonders also occur infrequently in the Gospels. They derive their name from the fact that the objects in which changes are wrought are impersonal—such as bread, fish, and water. The Stilling of the Storm (105) is full of concrete details in Mark.[44] Jesus had spent the day speaking his parables from a boat to the people along the shore. That evening he urged his disciples to go with him to the other side. While they were on the Sea, a great storm arose. The waves overflowed the boat and it began to fill with water. Jesus, exhausted by the strenuous day, lay asleep in the stern on a cushion. The frightened disciples rudely aroused him. " 'Teacher, do you not care if we perish?' And he awoke and rebuked the wind, and said to the sea, 'Peace! Be still!' And the wind ceased, and there was great calm" (4:38–39).[45] Jesus then chided the disciples for their lack of faith, and they were filled with awe that even the wind and sea should obey him.

Understanding the Miracles

The miracles attributed to Jesus caused no commotion among early Christians. They were not inhibited by modern notions of natural laws. They believed that Jesus and his disciples possessed unusual powers, and they accepted their mighty works as a matter of course. When the miracle stories made their way into the New Testament, their status was enhanced. Canonicity insured historicity. To deny them was to reject Jesus.

The comfortable acceptance of mighty works continued for many centuries. It was the Renaissance, with its love of individualism, followed by the Enlightenment, with its love of empiricism and rational-

[44]See Matthew 8:18, 23–27; Mark 4:35–41; Luke 8:22–25.
[45]Many scholars find the source of this sign in Psalm 107:23–30. See M.S. Enslin, *The Prophet from Nazareth* (New York: McGraw-Hill Book Co., 1961), p. 156.

ism, that forced a radical reappraisal. Scientists discovered a universe undreamed of by the evangelists. Critical methods were applied to the study of religion. The climate turned caustic, and faith in Jesus' supernatural deeds fell under attack. The evangelists were exonerated. They sincerely believed that they were reporting miracles; their error stemmed from their ignorance of natural law. Rationalists quickly filled the void and offered common-sense explanations of Jesus' mighty works. The rush of swine into the Sea as Jesus healed the demoniac and the stilling of the storm were charged to coincidence. The leper was said to have suffered from an arrested skin disease that Jesus simply certified as cured. Jairus' daughter was not really dead but in a coma from which Jesus roused her. The cases of paralysis, dumbness, atrophy, deafness, blindness, and the like were functional disorders that readily responded to faith.

Few responsible scholars accept at face value all of the miracles attributed to Jesus. The evangelists do not always agree as to what transpired. Some of the "miracles" may actually be allegories. Others may be based on coincidence, and still others may rest on psychological or spiritual factors. Some may be helped along by hyperbole. But the wholesale reduction of Jesus' wondrous works to a rational basis cannot be countenanced.[46] It is inimical to the spirit of the Gospels. The evangelists present a Savior whose power is not contingent upon knowledge of the occurrence of coincidences or the distinction between organic and functional illnesses. They betray no awareness that Jesus' deeds contravened a universal system of natural laws. Quite the contrary! The deeds were natural phenomena that possessed evidential value. They showed that God was at work in His world. They were remembered and recorded not because of their intrinsic worth but because of what they proved—the presence, the power, and the purpose of God.

Faith was the foundation of Jesus' mighty works. His own faith in God made him a channel of Paternal power. Faith on the part of those who would be healed permitted that power to accomplish its purpose. Where faith was wanting, healing was hindered (Mk. 6:5). Jesus scrupulously refused to perform mighty works to prop up his pronouncements or to swell his status. His primary task was to preach the gospel (Mk. 1:38). Miracles occupied an important but secondary place in his mission. They were signs that advertised that God was actively accomplishing His purpose in the world. "But if it is by the spirit of God that I cast out demons," declared Jesus, "then the kingdom of God has come upon you" (Mt. 12:28; Lk. 11:20).

[46]Such an attempt is made in J.M. Thompson, *Miracles in the New Testament* (London: Edward Arnold & Co., 1912).

Titles for Jesus   The Synoptics picture Jesus moving through the towns and villages of Galilee preaching the nearness of the kingdom and the need for repentance (Mk. 1:15). His message does not concern himself, and his miracles are not intended to convince and convert the crowds. He warns, persuades, and entices his hearers, but he never clearly declares who he is or what his place is in the divine drama. The Fourth Gospel is far more forthright. Its readers know Jesus' identity from the start. He is the preexistent Word incarnate in the world. He frequently debates with others concerning his own person, and he repeatedly speaks of his saving significance.

The striking differences between these two portraits are so disconcerting that modern men are tempted to cry out, "Will the *real* Jesus please step forward?" The solution, of course, is not that simple. The early church shattered the Synoptic silence by bestowing a variety of titles on Jesus. It called him "Christ" (Mk. 1:1), "Son of God" (Mk. 1:1), "Lord" (Mt. 7:21), "Savior" (Lk. 2:11), "Word" (Jn. 1:14), and "High Priest" (Heb. 7:26). Although all of these may have been apt appellations, they do not tell us what Jesus thought of himself. Only his self-designations can do that.[47]

Jesus as Prophet   Jesus referred to himself as a prophet: "A prophet is not without honor, except in his own country, and among his own kin, and in his own house" (Mk. 6:4). The self-designation was confirmed by friendly Pharisees (Lk. 7:39), the crowds (Lk. 7:16; Mt. 21:11, 46), public opinion (Mk. 8:28), the rabble (Mk. 14:65), and travelers on the Emmaus road (Lk. 24:18–19). When people proclaimed that Jesus was more than a prophet, they were rebuked or sentenced to silence (Mk. 1:24–25, 34; 3:11–12; 8:30). The seemingly messianic significance of Jesus' Jerusalem entry is smashed by his failure to defend his authority by messianic claims (Mk. 11:27–33). On the final day of his life, even false witnesses could not agree that he had claimed to be the Christ (Mk. 14:55–56). When the High Priest put the question to him, Jesus reportedly replied, "I am" (Mk. 14:62) or "You have said so" (Mt. 26:64). But the session was secret, and the answer is suspect. All three of the Synoptics agree that in his only public trial, before Pilate, Jesus' response was, "You have said so" (Mt. 27:11; Mk. 15:2; Lk. 23:3). Pilate understood it to be no answer at all (Mt. 27:12–14; Mk. 15:4).

The silence of the Synoptics concerning Jesus' messiahship has convinced some scholars that he never claimed to be the Messiah. He was a prophet and nothing more. Although he frequently spoke of

---

[47]A review of the history of Hebrew hopes should be profitable here. See pp. 48–54.

the Son of Man who would establish the kingdom at his coming, Jesus never identified himself with that glorious, cloud-carried figure. Jesus' "messiahship" was a latter-day discovery read back into the record. The messianic secret was an invention of the church to explain a paradox. The church knew Jesus to be the Messiah; yet it also knew that he had not appeared before the public in that capacity during his career. It resolved the difficulty by concluding that Jesus must have compelled his disciples to keep his messiahship a secret.[48]

Jesus as Son of Man   The term "Son of Man," the most common self-designation of Jesus, appears about eighty times in the Gospels.[49] It is used by Jesus only. His disciples, petitioners, critics, and opponents call him by many names, but they never refer to him as "Son of Man." The title is as conspicuous in the Gospels as it is scarce in the remainder of the New Testament.[50] It is nonexistent in the early creeds of Christendom.[51] It is a translation of *ben adam* (Hebrew) or *bar nasha* (Aramaic). It originally meant man in the general sense of *anthrōpos* (Greek) and *homo* (Latin). It is used scores of times in Ezekiel to stress the prophet's humanity in contrast with the Creator.[52] By the time the term reached the Gospels, however, it had taken on certain superhuman connotations. The transition started with the book of Daniel where "one like a son of man" is used to describe "the saints of the Most High" (Dan. 7:13, 19), and it was completed in the Parables of Enoch.[53] There "Son of Man" no longer stands for man in the general sense of Psalm 8:4 or Ezekiel 2:1. It stands for *"that* Son of Man"—a preexistent heavenly being who will come with the clouds to execute the Final Judgment and rule in the New Age.[54] Although the present form of the Parables of Enoch may be post-Christian, they probably reflect thinking current in pre-Christian Judaism.

The Son-of-Man sayings in the Synoptics are not uniform. Some describe the present activity of the Son of Man. Others speak of

[48]For a provocative and highly readable presentation of this position, see Enslin, *The Prophet from Nazareth.*
[49]We shall capitalize "man," contrary to the R.S.V. Bible, except when quoting Scripture.
[50]Outside the Gospels it is found only in Acts 7:56 and Hebrews 2:6. Revelation 1:13 and 14:14 contain the term "one like a son of man."
[51]Ethelbert Stauffer, *Jesus and His Story*, trans. R. and C. Winston (New York: Alfred A. Knopf, Inc., 1960), p. 163, concludes that since Jesus had reserved "Son of Man" for himself, the early church treated it as a taboo designation—just as the synagogue treated "Yahweh," God's self-designation.
[52]See Ezek. 2:1; for example.
[53]Enoch 37–71.
[54]Enoch 51:1–5, italics added. The discovery of fragments of Enoch among the Qumran Scrolls has insured the book's pre-Christian origin. Since none of the fragments comes from the Parables of Enoch (chapters 37–71), some scholars have concluded that the latter are post-Christian. The failure of the fragments to include any of the Parables, however, could be quite accidental.

the Son of Man's impending suffering. Still others concern the future coming of the exalted and glorified Son of Man.[55] The sayings that concern the Son of Man's present and future activity come from the earliest and most reliable sources, *Q* and Mark. Those that deal with the suffering of the Son of Man, strangely absent from *Q*, are derived almost exclusively from Mark.[56] They stem from the Passion predictions and the Passion Story itself. The "suffering" sayings are never joined with those that announce the future advent of the Son of Man.

The "present" sayings all occur in the public ministry of Jesus. They tend to emphasize the authority of the Son of Man as the following samples show.

But that you may know that the Son of man has authority on earth to forgive sins . . . (Mk. 2:10)
So the Son of man is Lord even of the sabbath. (Mk. 2:28)
Foxes have holes, and birds of the air have nests; but the Son of man has nowhere to lay his head. (Mt. 8:20; Lk. 9:58)

Scholars are not agreed on the meaning of Son of Man in these sayings or on the authenticity of the sayings themselves. Some take Son of Man in its original Aramaic sense of simply "man." Jesus declared that man is lord of the Sabbath and has the power to forgive sins. He saw himself as the humble, suffering Righteous One.[57] Others understand Son of Man in a far more exalted sense. As to authenticity, Reginald H. Fuller accepts the "present" sayings as genuine and messianic. Although in the popular mind Son of Man was a mysterious self-designation by the prophet, it had a precise meaning for Jesus. When he declared the eschatological forgiveness of sins and dispensed with the Sabbath, he proleptically exercised the functions of the coming Son of Man. The powers of the kingdom were present in his proclamations and in his mighty works. The three apparently divergent uses of Son of Man in the Synoptics coalesced in Jesus' thought. His activity, however, was divided into two periods—the period of earthly obedience and suffering described in the language of the Servant, and the future period expressed in terms of the Son of Man. The cross marked the dividing point between the two. It set the eschatological process in motion—the coming of the kingdom and

[55]See Connick, *Jesus: The Man, the Mission, and the Message*, p. 297. For a comprehensive and suggestive study see H.E. Tödt, *The Son of Man in the Synoptic Tradition* (Philadelphia: The Westminster Press, 1965).
[56]The exceptions may well be editorial.
[57]See Eduard Schweizer, "The Son of Man," *Journal of Biblical Literature*, LXXXIX, Part II (1960), 119–129.

the triumph of the Son of Man.[58] Rudolf Bultmann also accepts the authenticity of the "present" sayings, but he regards Son of Man on Jesus' lips to be simply an Aramaic circumlocution for "man" or "I."[59] Günther Bornkamm rules the "present" sayings unauthentic. He thinks it unlikely that Jesus would have used a term that could be taken as a messianic title or merely as "man." Neither would he have used Son of Man in a Socratic sense just to stimulate his hearers to arrive at their own conclusions.[60]

The "suffering" sayings play no part in Jesus' public ministry. After Peter's "confession" near Caesarea Philippi, Jesus began to teach his disciples privately "that the Son of man must suffer many things, and be rejected by the elders and the chief priests and the scribes, and be killed, and after three days rise again" (Mk. 8:31). The theme recurs repeatedly (Mk. 9:12, 31; 10:33). Some of the sayings are so stylized and detailed that they sound like summaries of the early church's kerygma.[61] Others are more spontaneous and less specific (Mk. 9:12; Lk. 17:25). Their claim to historicity is supported by other sayings, devoid of the Son-of-Man concept, in which Jesus appears to have anticipated his death as a part of the divine purpose. When James and John sought privileged positions in the kingdom, Jesus asked them: " 'Are you able to drink the cup that I drink, or to be baptized with the baptism with which I am baptized?' And they said to him, 'We are able.' And Jesus said to them, 'The cup that I drink you will drink; and with the baptism with which I am baptized, you will be baptized; but to sit at my right hand or at my left is not mine to grant, but it is for those for whom it has been prepared' " (Mk. 10:38–40).[62]

The "future" sayings, like the "present" ones, are firmly grounded in the earliest sources. Two illustrations will suffice.

> For as the lightning comes from the east and shines as far as the west, so will be the coming of the Son of man. (Mt. 24:27; compare Lk. 17:24)
> Therefore you also must be ready; for the Son of man is coming at an hour you do not expect. (Mt. 24:44; compare Lk. 12:40)

[58]R.H. Fuller, *The Mission and Achievement of Jesus* (London: SCM Press, 1954), especially pp. 107–108. Compare p. 98 and p. 106.
[59]*Theology of the New Testament* (New York: Charles Scribner's Sons, 1951), I, 30–31.
[30]Bornkamm, *Jesus of Nazareth*, (New York: Harper & Row, 1960), p. 230.
[61]Bultmann, *Theology of the New Testament*, I, 30–31, attributes all of the "suffering" sayings to Mark's invention.
[62]Compare Luke 12:50.

Fuller believes that Jesus thought of himself as the one who would become the future Son of Man. He was not yet that glorified figure, but the cross would take care of that. Jesus repeatedly urged his followers to wait for the advent of the Son of Man, but he never counted himself among the waiters. He was, as it were, standing on the same side as the Son of Man over against his followers.[63]

This interpretation is an attractive one, but it must clear two extremely high hurdles. The first is that the "future" sayings bear the marks of tampering. Again and again the Son-of-Man theology appears in Jesus' words where it did not exist originally.

> *Truly, I say to you, there are some standing here who will not taste death before they see the kingdom of God come with power.* (Mk. 9:1; Lk. 9:27)
> *Truly, I say to you, there are some standing here who will not taste death before they see the Son of man coming in his kingdom.* (Mt. 16:28)

> *Jesus: 'Who do men say that I am?'* (Mk. 8:27; Lk. 9:18)
> *Jesus: 'Who do men say that the Son of man is?'* (Mt. 16:13)

> *Blessed are you when men revile you and persecute you and utter all kinds of evil against you falsely on my account.* (Mt. 5:11)
> *Blessed are you when men hate you, and when they exclude you and revile you, and cast out your name as evil, on account of the Son of Man!* (Lk. 6:22)[64]

Since it can be demonstrated that the church introduced the Son-of-Man concept into several of the "future" sayings, a cloud of suspicion hovers over the whole. Harvie Branscomb believes that all of the "future" sayings are unhistorical, the postresurrection creation of the church.[65] There is one saying, though, that does not support this argument. In the "trial" before the Sanhedrin, the High Priest asked Jesus if he were the Christ, the Son of the Blessed. Jesus replied: "I am; and you will see the *Son of man* sitting at the right hand of Power, and coming with the clouds of heaven."[66] The prediction did not materialize. At the time the Synoptics were being written, the church still awaited the coming of the Son of Man. The church would hardly have fabricated a saying that caused it so much embarrassment. Its preservation in the record suggests that the Son-of-Man idea in some sense goes back to Jesus himself.

[63]Fuller, *The Mission and Achievement of Jesus*, pp. 102–103.
[64]Underscores added in each quotation.
[65]*The Gospel of Mark*, The Moffatt New Testament Commentary (New York: Harper & Row, n.d.), pp. 146–159.
[66]Mark 14:62, italics added.

Fuller's interpretation must not only clear the hurdle of the "future" sayings' authenticity, but it must also deal convincingly with the fact that Jesus does not call himself the coming Son of Man. A casual reading of the sayings in question might lead one to conclude that Jesus is simply alluding to himself in the third person when he speaks of the Son of Man, but closer examination reveals that he never *explicitly* identifies himself as the coming Son of Man.

For as the lighting comes from the east and shines as far as the west, so will be the coming of the Son of man. (Mt. 24:27; Lk. 17:24)
When they persecute you in one town, flee to the next; for truly, I say to you, you will not have gone through all the towns of Israel, before the Son of man comes. (Mt. 10:23)
Nevertheless, when the Son of man comes, will he find faith on earth? (Lk. 18:8b)

Since the church would have been more disposed to have changed Jesus' sayings so as to identify him with the Son of Man than to change "Son of Man" to "I," the weight of evidence is tipped in favor of the theory that Jesus distinguished between himself and the coming Son of Man. To "distinguish between" is not equivalent to "disassociate from." Although Jesus did not regard himself as the coming Son of Man, he did see his mission in close connection with that figure: "For whoever is ashamed of me and of my words in this adulterous and sinful generation, of him will the Son of man also be ashamed, when he comes in the glory of his Father with the holy angels" (Mk. 8:38).[67] Although Jesus here refers to the Son of Man in the third person, he links the work of the Son of Man with his own. When the Son of Man comes to judge the world and vindicate the faithful, people will be judged on the basis of their response to the mission and message of Jesus.

Jesus as Son of God   The term "Son of God" had many meanings in Jewish thought,[68] but it was never a regular synonym for the Messiah. It usually emphasized the moral relationship of love and filial obedience that should exist between a father and his son. Christians early applied the title to Jesus (Rom. 1:3–4).[69] In the Synoptics, it is used of him by Mark (1:1), the voice from heaven at the Baptism (1:11) and Transfiguration (9:7), the demons (3:11; 5:7), the High Priest (14:61), and the centurion at the cross (15:39). Evidence that Jesus used Son of God

---

[67]Compare Luke 9:26.
[68]See p. 114.
[69]Compare John 1:1–18, where the term describes a metaphysical relationship between God and His incarnate Word.

as a self-designation, however, is slim. Only two such sayings are recorded; in each instance, "of God" is implied. The first passage is so congenial in style and content with the Fourth Gospel that it has been labeled a thunderbolt from the Johannine sky: "All things have been delivered to me by my Father; and no one knows the Son except the Father, and no one knows the Father except the Son and any one to whom the Son chooses to reveal him (Mt. 11:27).[70] An imposing list of scholars judge the saying unhistorical. The second passage, however, arouses no Johannine comparisons: "But of that day or that hour no one knows, not even the angels in heaven, nor the Son, but only the Father" (Mk. 13:32).[71] Although some scholars insist that this saying is tainted by the Christology of the early church, their reasoning is faulty. Why would the church concoct such a scandalous pronouncement? It declared that there was something the Son did not know. Many manuscripts of Matthew omit "nor the Son," and Luke omits the entire verse. The saying was evidently so embarrassing to the church that it sought partially or wholly to erase it from the record.

Jesus' sense of sonship is also supported by passages where Son of God is not mentioned. He called God "Father" in a new and daring way: "Abba, Father, all things are possible to thee" (Mk. 14:36). Some have attributed this prayer to the church since the witnesses were beyond earshot and asleep. But no such onus is attached to the Lord's Prayer, in which Jesus addressed God as "Father" (Mt. 6:9; Lk. 11:2). Jesus did what no Jew had done before. He used an intimate and familiar term, one reserved for a man's human father and no other, to describe God Himself. The usage suggests not only his own unique view of God but also his own uniqueness as Son.

Jesus as Servant of the Lord

Although Jesus apparently never used the title "Servant of the Lord," a number of scholars believe that he found the key to his mission in the suffering servant figure of Isaiah 53.[72] Note the parallels between the Passion utterances and the ideas expressed by the prophet.

Mark and Luke	Isaiah
For the Son of man also came not to be served but to serve, and to give his life as a ransom for many. (Mk. 10:45)	He was wounded for our transgressions. (53:5) The Lord has laid on him the iniquity of us all. (53:6)

[70]Compare Luke 10:22. See Bornkamm, *Jesus of Nazareth*, p. 226.
[71]Compare Matthew 24:36.
[72]See Vincent Taylor, *The Life and Ministry of Jesus* (New York: Abingdon Press, 1955), pp. 148–151; T.W. Manson, *The Servant-Messiah* (Cambridge: At the University Press, 1956), p. 73; Hunter, *The Work and Words of Jesus*, pp. 80–87.

Mark and Luke	Isaiah
This is my blood of the covenant, which is poured out for many. (Mk. 14:24)	When he makes himself an offering for sin . . . (53:10)
For I tell you that this scripture must be fulfilled in me, 'And he was reckoned with the transgressors.' (Lk. 22:37)	By his knowledge shall the righteous one, my servant, make many to be accounted righteous. (53:11)
	Yet he bore the sin of many, and made intercession for the transgressors. (53:12)

Do the Synoptic sayings reflect Jesus' thought or that of the early church? Scholars have increasingly embraced the latter viewpoint. Isaiah 53 was not interpreted messianically in first-century Judaism. Jesus never called himself Servant of the Lord, and only a few faint echoes of the Isaiah chapter can be heard in the Passion narrative.[73] Mark 10:45, the only distinct echo of Isaiah 53, is transmitted in a much simpler form in Luke 22:27. This suggests that Mark's version had been colored by the church, which interpreted Jesus' life and death in the setting of Isaiah 53.[74]

Jesus as Son of David

The title "son of David" falls from Jesus' lips only once in the Synoptics: "How can the scribes say that the Christ is the son of David? David himself, inspired by the Holy Spirit, declared, 'The Lord said to my Lord, Sit at my right hand, till I put thy enemies under thy feet.' David himself calls him Lord; so how is he his son?" (Mk. 12:35–37a).[75] Bultmann regards the saying as an interpolation of the early church.[76] Those who accept the pronouncement as genuine generally see in it not a denial of Jesus' Davidic descent but a declaration that Davidic descent was not decisive. Whatever scholars may think of the saying's genuineness, they are in wide agreement that Jesus vigorously spurned the concept of political kingship connected with the title "son of David." When he was asked if people should pay taxes to Caesar, he replied in words that must be construed as an affirmative answer (Mk. 12:13–17). He counseled against retaliation and violence and warned that "all who take the sword will perish by the sword" (Mt. 26:52). He did not lift a finger to reestablish

[73]See Clarence Tucker Craig, "The Proclamation of the Kingdom," in *The Interpreter's Bible*, VII, 149. See also Craig "The Identification of Jesus with the Suffering Servant," *Journal of Religion*, XXIV (1944), 240–245. In W. Manson, *Jesus the Messiah* (Philadelphia: The Westminster Press, 1946), pp. 140–143, 155, the author's contention that a synthesis of the Son-of-God, Servant-of-the-Lord, and Son-of-Man figures had taken place in pre-Christian Judaism has not won wide acceptance.
[74]See Bornkamm, *Jesus of Nazareth*, p. 227. Bultmann, *Theology of the New Testament*, I, p. 29, had many years earlier concluded that the Passion predictions were "prophecies after the event."
[75]Compare Matthew 22:41–45; Luke 20:41–44.
[76]*Theology of the New Testament*, I, 28. See also Branscomb, *The Gospel of Mark*, pp. 222–225.

David's throne, and he never dreamed of attempting to scale that throne himself.

The kindred titles of "King of the Jews" and "King of Israel" are applied to Jesus in the Synoptics, but they never appear as self-designations (Mk. 15:32; Mk. 15:2). When Pilate asked Jesus if he was King of the Jews, the Galilean replied, "You have said so" (Mt. 27:11; Mk. 15:2; Lk. 23:3). Although the evangelists understood the response to be affirmative, Pilate thought it was noncommittal. If he had taken it to be affirmative, he would have halted the hearing instantly. There could be no king but Caesar. Instead, Pilate continued the inquiry with a question: "Have you no answer to make?" (Mk. 15:4).

At one point in the Synoptics Jesus does appear to accept the title "the Christ." Before a meeting of the Sanhedrin, the High Priest asked him,

> 'Are you the Christ, the Son of the Blessed?' And Jesus said, 'I am; and you will see the Son of man sitting at the right hand of Power, and coming with the clouds of heaven.' And the high priest tore his mantle, and said, 'Why do we still need witnesses? You have heard his blasphemy. What is your decision?' And they all condemned him as deserving death. (Mk. 14:61b–64)

Jesus' unqualified affirmative in Mark that he is the Christ finds shaky support in the other Synoptics. Matthew's "You have said so" (26:64) and Luke's "You say that I am" (22:70) are at most evasive, and they may constitute a veiled denial.[77] Since the Sanhedrin's session was held in secret, with no disciples present, the source of the evangelists' reports is an enigma. Both the question and the answer are clothed in the language of the church. The High Priest would not have asked, "Are you the Christ?" but "Are you the Messiah?" Since Jews did not view the Messiah as "Son of God," the title "the Son of the Blessed" seems to be a Christian postscript. The church was convinced that Jesus was not only the Christ but *also* the Son of the Blessed One *and* the Son of Man who would come with the clouds of heaven to judge the world. No Jewish court would have considered the claim to be Messiah blasphemous. It was the Christian assumption that virtually equated Jesus with God ("the Son of man sitting at the right hand of Power") that made it so.[78]

[77]See Oscar Cullmann, *The Christology of the New Testament* (London: SCM Press; 1959, published in the U.S.A. the same year by The Westminster Press), p. 118.
[78]Compare F.C. Grant, "The Gospel According to St. Mark: Introduction and Exegesis," in *The Interpreter's Bible*, VII, 890.

As impressive as the arguments are that Jesus did not consider himself to be the Messiah, many scholars continue to maintain that he did. Their case is not without merit. (1) They claim that Jesus' messianic consciousness is implicit in large sections of the Synoptics where no explicit messianic claim is advanced. Perhaps the evangelists did insert this element into passages where it did not belong, but there are altogether too many incidents and sayings where the messianic authority and mission unlock the understanding of a passage for it to be cast aside. The messianic claim is inherent in the stories of the baptism, the temptation, Peter's "confession," the transfiguration, and the entry into Jerusalem. If Jesus thought of himself only as a prophet, why did he ride into the Holy City in such a manner as to suggest the prophecy of Zechariah 9:9? If the messianic elements are simply Christian additions, then the Synoptics are no more credible than a James Bond mystery.[79] (2) Jesus was charged with being an insurrectionist against Rome, and he was crucified as King of the Jews (Lk. 23:2; Mk. 15:26).[80] Why would a humble Galilean peasant who had counseled his converts to pay taxes to Caesar, confined himself to ethical and religious pronouncements, and never raised a finger in civil disobedience be charged with kingly aspirations and treason unless he had given some grounds for the accusations?[81] He was put to death as a messianic pretender, and apart from such a claim the crucifixion was meaningless.[82] While he knew himself to be the Messiah, he did not advertise the fact. Quite the contrary! He silenced all who would publicize it, and for good reason. He knew he was not the Messiah of popular expectation. If he or his followers had disclosed his secret, Rome would have smothered his movement with dispatch.[83]

Jesus' Self-Identity

An avalanche of answers has been precipitated by the question, "What did Jesus think of himself?" Distinguished specialists are convinced that he considered himself to be the Messiah, and equally distinguished specialists deny it. Competent critics claim that he identified himself with the Suffering Servant of II Isaiah, and equally competent critics repudiate the notion. Able experts declare that he equated himself with the coming Son of Man, and equally able experts demur. Some think he was merely a prophet, and others hold that he was the preexistent Son of God. Speculation ranges from one end of the theological spectrum to the other. Why such diversity of informed opinion? Perhaps it is because our records are insufficient to answer

[79]See Hunter, *The Work and Words of Jesus*, pp. 80–90.
[80]Compare Matthew 27:37 and John 19:19.
[81]See Harvie Branscomb, *The Teachings of Jesus* (New York: Abingdon Press, 1931), p. 343.
[82]See Rudolf Otto, *The Kingdom of God and the Son of Man* (Boston: Beacon Press, 1943), pp. 228–229.
[83]The view of Hunter, *The Work and Words of Jesus*, p. 82.

such a question. Not enough sayings of Jesus about Jesus exist to enable independent investigators to arrive at a common conclusion.[84] Despite this disturbing fact, some comments concerning Jesus and his role can be made with reasonable assurance. (1) The theme of Jesus' message was the kingdom rather than himself as king. He was so intent on proclaiming the nearness of the kingdom and the need for repentance that he paid small attention to himself. His focus was on God. (2) Jesus acted with a unique sense of authority. He implied that he was the prophet, and he possessed the prophet's stance and inner power. But he was far more than a prophet. He dominated the devil and defeated his demons. He healed the helpless and forgave sins in God's name. He set aside the tradition of the elders and interpreted the venerable Jewish Law with sovereign freedom. He articulated his conclusions not as opinions to be considered but as commands to be obeyed as the will of God. (3) Jesus journeyed to Jerusalem, as he had previously gone to Galilee, to force a decision concerning the impending crisis—the advent of the kingdom. He was undoubtedly aware of the attendant dangers, although the passion predictions are too precise to be considered genuine. He may even have anticipated his rejection. Nevertheless, he took the calculated risk fully confident that no matter what his fate, God would ultimately vindicate him. This confidence was conceived at his baptism, born during his ministry, tested at his crucifixion, and confirmed by his resurrection.

Beyond these three conclusions, certitude turns to educated conjecture and speculation. Our own theory is probably no more reliable than many others. Easy disciples should be cautioned that our views on this topic are subject to change. It is our current conviction, however, that Jesus did not think of his mission in messianic terms. This momentous idea was a discovery of the early church. So was the concept of Jesus as the Servant who suffered for the sake of many.[85] The validity of these tardy thoughts is not determined by their timing. We often see the providence of God more in retrospect than in prospect.[86] Jesus believed his task was to prophesy the imminence of the kingdom. He talked much about the coming Son of Man, but he never mistook himself for that preexistent and exalted figure. When the Son of Man came to judge the world, Jesus declared, people would be "sorted" in accordance with how they had responded to Jesus' mission and message. The church, after Jesus' death and resurrection, meditated on the meaning of recent events. It found tempo-

[84]See Ernest Cadman Colwell, *An Approach to the Teachings of Jesus* (New York: Abingdon Press, 1947), pp. 74–75. It should be noted, however, that our records are insufficient because the question that would have prompted their creation was not asked by those to whom the gospels were addressed.
[85]Derived either from II Isaiah, the Suffering Psalms, or both.
[86]A favorite expression of the American philosopher, Borden Parker Bowne.

rary understanding in the Christ concept, but it was not content for long to call Jesus "Messiah" in the usual Jewish sense—a human being anointed to do God's will. It transposed the term into a higher key. "Messiah" came to express the conviction that Jesus would soon return to judge the world and vindicate the righteous, functions Jesus had attributed to the coming Son of Man. In Mark, "Christ" is no longer an adjective or even a title. It has virtually become Jesus' last name, and to it has been affixed the title "Son of God" (1:1). Jesus may well have used "Son" as a correlative to "Father" since the word so succinctly summed up his awareness of his intimate relationship to God.[87] But to Mark, "Son of God" meant much more than that. It "was the title above all others which expressed the growing thought of Greek-speaking Christianity, moving steadily in the direction of Nicea, Constantinople, and Chalcedon with their monumental affirmations of the doctrine of the Incarnation."[88]

In the chapter that follows we shall resume the discussion of Jesus' public ministry. The scene of his activity shifts from Galilee to Judea after the Transfiguration. Jesus' purpose is transparent. He wants to deliver his proclamations at the seat of the nation's religious life. We shall travel with him to Jerusalem, examine his words and works, and observe their fateful consequences.

[87]See pp. 162–163.
[88]Grant, "The Gospel According to St. Mark: Introduction and Exegesis," in *The Interpreter's Bible*, VII, 643.

VII

**The Mission
Resumed**
(Matthew,
Mark, Luke)

Shortly after the Transfiguration, Jesus and his disciples headed for Jerusalem (Mk. 9:30, 33; 10:1, 17, 32). They traveled secretly, according to Mark, so that Jesus could further instruct the Twelve concerning the coming crucifixion. They halted briefly at Capernaum. Then they resumed their journey by way of Perea, territory east of the Jordan controlled by Herod Antipas, where Jesus taught the crowds. The tiny band finally passed through Jericho and approached Jerusalem by way of Bethphage and Bethany (Mk. 10:46; 11:1). Mark's account is succinct and summary, greatly lacking in details. The trip is pictured as a forced march rather than a journey. The pace is rapid and the purpose is plain. The Master is marching to martyrdom.

Luke's account of the journey to Jerusalem is much longer. At first glance, it seems to flesh out Mark's skeleton with appropriate details. Closer inspection, however, does not sustain the initial impression. Luke's "great insertion" into Mark's framework, sometimes called the "travel document," is composed of many separate incidents, parables, and sayings (Lk. 9:51–18:14). Many of them may have originated in the Galilean campaign. Their connecting links are editorial rather than historical. Like Mark, Luke evidently had little information about the Jerusalem journey. The deficiency is understandable. Jesus' final days were so crucial for early Christians that the Transfiguration-Triumphal Entry period that preceded them was soon dwarfed.

**Entry into Jerusalem
(196)[1]**

When Jesus drew near to Jerusalem, he instructed two disciples to enter a certain village where they would find a tethered colt on which no one had ever sat. They were to untie the colt and bring it to him. If anyone should question their conduct, they were simply to

The material in this chapter is a condensed, updated, and at times expanded version of material found in C. Milo Connick, *Jesus: The Man, the Mission, and the Message* (Englewood Cliffs, N.J.: Prentice-Hall, 1963), and is used by permission of the publisher.
[1]See Matthew, 21:1–9; Mark 11:1–10; Luke 19:28–38.

Gethsemane and the Mount of Olives. At the left of the Church
of All Nations (popularly called the Church of Agony, Lk. 22:44)
is the traditional site of the Garden of Gethsemane on the Mount
of Olives. (Gethsemane means "oil press.") A Russian Orthodox
Church is seen at the right. [Courtesy of the Israeli Government
Tourist Office]

say that the Lord had need of the animal. When the two disciples
returned, they threw their garments on the colt, and Jesus mounted
the animal. Many people spread their garments or leafy branches
on the road. Those who preceded Jesus and those who followed him
cried out, "Hosanna! Blessed be he who comes in the name of the
Lord! Blessed be the kingdom of our father David that is coming!
Hosanna in the highest!" (Mk. 11:9–10).

"Lord" is an unusual designation for Jesus in Mark, but the early
church applied the title to him without hesitation. If Jesus had made
prearrangements for the colt, then "the Lord has need of it" could
have been the password.[2] Newness had a sacred quality to the Semites. They honored the first fruits, the new moon, the first-born
son, and the first year of marriage. The selection of an unbroken
colt by Jesus was fraught with meaning for the evangelists. A sacred
animal would bear the messianic king to the Holy City! Matthew,
misreading the poetic parallelism of Zechariah 9:9 and determined

[2]See S. MacLean Gilmour, "The Gospel According to St. Luke: Introduction and
Exegesis," in George A. Buttrick, ed., *The Interpreter's Bible* (New York: Abingdon Press,
1952), VIII, 336, for a contrary view.

to make prophecy literally come true, doubled the number of animals[3] and then had Jesus ride on both beasts at once (21:2, 7). The spreading of garments and branches on the road were acts of homage. John alone mentions palm branches (12:13). Palm trees grew in profusion along the Jordan, but they were nonexistent in the environs of elevated Jerusalem.

A comparison of Mark with the later Gospels reveals how the entry tradition developed. Matthew 21:4-5 makes explicit the prophecy of Zechariah merely hinted at by Mark. An indefinite number of disciples in Mark (11:8) swells to a crowd in Matthew (21:8), a whole multitude in Luke (19:37), and a great crowd (coming out from Jerusalem) in John (12:12-13). "Hosanna!" ("Save now!") is found in the Hallel, which was sung at Tabernacles and during Passover. It was addressed to God or to a king on behalf of God (Ps. 118:25; II Sam. 14:4; Ps. 20:9). "Blessed be he who comes in the name of the Lord!" stems from the same source (Ps. 118:26). It originally referred to a pilgrim on his way to the festival. The eschatological ejaculation of Mark 11:10 ("Blessed be the kingdom of our father David that is coming!") is altered to acclaim Jesus as "Son of David" (Mt. 21:9) and "King" (Lk. 19:38). The gospels were written in retrospect of the resurrection at a time when Jesus was joyfully exalted as Lord and Christ. It was only natural that the accounts of Jesus' entrance into Jerusalem should be infused with messianic meanings. It is doubtful, though, that the messianic significance of the occasion was apparent either to Jesus or to his traveling companions. The Jerusalem authorities were not aroused by the entry. It was Jesus' subsequent words and works in the Temple that caught their attention and increased their anxiety. If Jesus' entry had been so patently messianic, why was this fact not presented at his trial as proof of his treasonable conduct?[4]

The Synoptics mention only one visit of Jesus to Jerusalem during his ministry. It took place at the close of his career and was terminated by the crucifixion. The Fourth Gospel, on the other hand, suggests that Jesus made four or five visits to the Holy City during this period.

---

[3]"An ass" and "A colt the foal of an ass" are one and the same animal.

[4]An alternative understanding of the entry regards it as an actual fulfillment of Zechariah 9:9, which Jesus carried out in accordance with a preconceived plan. He realized that he was the messiah—from the beginning, at the Baptism, or as the result of a gradual awakening. Although he tacitly confirmed this knowledge near Caesarea Philippi, he insisted that it be kept a secret. As he approached Jerusalem, however, he threw caution to the winds. He mounted the arranged-for ass and entered Jerusalem to the messianic acclaim of the pilgrims. The entry was a deliberate symbolic act by which he publicly proclaimed to the populace the nature of his messiahship. He was not a mighty military ruler borne by a horse but a humble man of peace astride an ass.

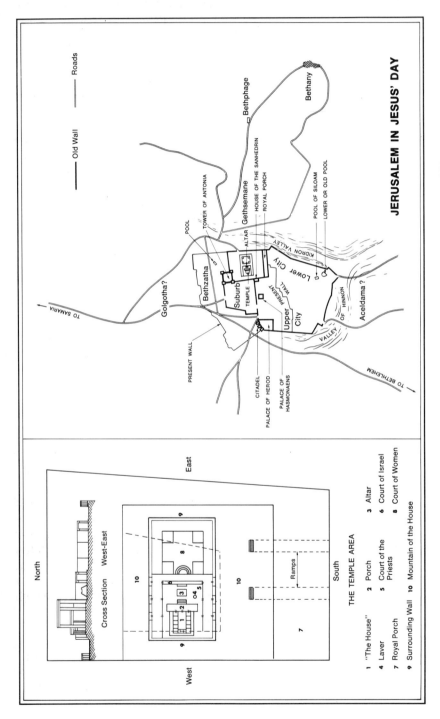

JERUSALEM IN JESUS' DAY

——— Old Wall

———— Roads

TO SAMARIA

Golgotha?

Bethzatha

POOL

TOWER OF ANTONIA

Gethsemane

HOUSE OF THE SANHEDRIN

ROYAL PORCH

Bethphage

Bethany

PRESENT WALL

Suburb

TEMPLE

ALTAR

KIDRON VALLEY

Lower City

PRESENT WALL

CITADEL

PALACE OF HEROD

PALACE OF HASMONAENS

Upper City

PRESENT WALL

POOL OF SILOAM

LOWER OR OLD POOL

VALLEY OF HINNON

Aceldama?

TO BETHLEHEM

North

West

Cross Section   West-East

East

South

THE TEMPLE AREA

1 "The House"   2 Porch   3 Altar
4 Laver   5 Court of the   6 Court of Israel
                         Priests
7 Royal Porch   8 Court of Women
9 Surrounding Wall   10 Mountain of the House

Ramps

[The Map of Jerusalem in the Time of Jesus is based upon plate XVII, B, in The Westminister Historical Atlas to the Bible, rev. ed., editors George Ernest Wright and Floyd Vivian Silson, copyright 1956 by W. L. Jenkins, published by The Westminster Press and is used by permission. The plan of the temple area is based upon the plan in Sacred Sites and Ways by Gustav Dalman, translated by P. P. Levertoss, copyright 1935 by The Macmillan Company, published by The Society for Promoting Christian Knowledge, and is used by permission of the publisher.]

The Synoptics themselves, as we have noted, seem to support a Jerusalem ministry of Jesus prior to the last week.[5] Numerous efforts have been made to reconstruct that ministry from the Transfiguration to the Triumphal Entry. Perhaps Goguel's is the most cogent. He argues that Jesus left Galilee shortly after the Feast of Tabernacles in September or October (Jn. 7:2) and taught in Jerusalem until the Feast of Dedication in December (Jn. 10:22). Soon thereafter he retired to Perea across the Jordan where he remained until shortly before the fateful Passover (Jn. 10:40; 11:54). Then he returned for his last entry, which led to his arrest and execution (Mt. 21:1; Mk. 11:1; Lk. 19:28–29; Jn. 12:1).[6] This reconstruction assumes the historicity of many statements in the Fourth Gospel. Although that Gospel is increasingly being regarded as a valid source of historical material amid its sea of interpretations, the special characteristics of John and the dearth of data in the Synoptics preclude the filling out of Goguel's skimpy outline. The theory of an extended Jerusalem ministry for Jesus receives substantial support from all four Gospels, but the precise detailing of that ministry remains a matter of speculation. What is true of the Transfiguration-Triumphal Entry segment is also true of the last week of Jesus' life. Mark's chronology differs at significant points from that of the later evangelists.[7]

Cleansing the Temple (200)[8]

When Jesus entered the Temple on the day of his entry into Jerusalem, according to Mark, he looked around at everything. Since it was already late in the day, he then went out to Bethany with the Twelve. On the following day he returned from Bethany, "cursed" the fig tree on the way, and entered the Temple and began to drive out those who sold and those who bought (Mk. 11:11, 15). Matthew and Luke evidently found it difficult to comprehend Jesus calmly looking about the Temple on the first day of the week and returning at white heat on the second. Consequently, they place the Temple Cleansing on the same day as the Entry (Mt. 21:12; Lk. 19:45). This location paid an added bonus for Matthew. It made the purge conform to prophecy. Malachi had long before predicted that the Lord would *suddenly* appear in His Temple (3:1–2). In the Fourth Gospel, the Cleansing occurs on the occasion of Jesus' visit to Jerusalem prior to the launching of his Galilean campaign (2:13–22). This dating is dramatic and doctrinal, but it is hardly historical. So strong a rebuke of the power structure at so early a stage would have aborted Jesus' campaign then and there. But if John's cleansing is too early, the

[5]See p. 117.
[6]See Maurice Goguel, *The Life of Jesus*, trans. O. Wyon (London: George Allen & Unwin, Ltd., 1933), pp. 400–428.
[7]For an outline of Mark's chronology see C. Milo Connick, *Jesus: The Man, the Mission, and the Message* (Englewood Cliffs, N.J.: Prentice-Hall, Inc., 1963), p. 327.
[8]See Matthew 21:12–13; Mark 11:15–19; Luke 19:45–48.

Dome of the Rock in Jerusalem. This beautiful octagonal structure, graced with multicolored mosaics, is a Moslem shrine erected late in the seventh century A.D. The huge sacred rock underneath the dome (on which, a tradition holds, Abraham intended to sacrifice his son, Isaac) is probably the site of the ancient Jewish altar of burnt offerings. In the foreground of the picture Moslems are performing washings required by the Koran before worshiping.

Synoptics' is too tardy. There would have been no money-changers in the Temple then, a few days before the Passover. They had to depart from the Temple area on Nisan 1, two weeks before the Passover.[9]

The Synoptics agree that Jesus drove out the merchants, overturned the tables of the money-changers and the seats of the pigeon-sellers, and proclaimed that the Temple should be a house of prayer instead

[9]See Harvie Branscomb, *The Gospel of Mark*, The Moffatt New Testament Commentary (New York: Harper & Row, n.d.), pp. 203-204.

of a den of robbers. Only Mark mentions the use of the Temple as a short cut. Jesus enforces his condemnations by appealing to the words of Isaiah 56:7 and Jeremiah 7:11. In John, the enforcing agent includes a whip of cords (2:14-16).

Those who attribute a messianic consciousness to Jesus see the Cleansing as another symbolic act by which he set forth an aspect of his messianic office—the purging of Judaism of its commercialism and materialism. Others claim that since the Cleansing occurred in the Court of the Gentiles, it reflects Jesus' concern for the Gentile world and prefigures the call of the Gentiles and the extension of Christianity to all mankind. Those who view Jesus as a prophet of the coming kingdom regard the Cleansing as a prophetic act. Prior prophets had resorted to visual aids to reinforce their message. Isaiah had gone naked and barefoot (that is, clad only in the loincloth of a war prisoner) for three years (Isa. 20:1-6), and Jeremiah had buried his waistcloth and had worn a yoke around his neck (Jer. 13:1-11; 28:10).[10] When Jesus cleansed the Temple of its abuses, he rebuked the priesthood. Just so God would judge the people unless they repented.

Whatever Jesus' intent, the consequences of the Cleansing were altogether predictable. The Temple served both as the seat of Jewish worship and as a symbol of unity for the scattered nation. Its control rested in the hands of the High Priest who held office at the pleasure of Rome. Any alteration of the status quo in Temple administration was fraught with grave religious and political implications. Official Judaism looked at Jesus with a jaundiced eye. He was a self-appointed, uncredentialed, impudent impersonator who arrogated to himself authority to purify the Temple. Such action could not be ignored. It was a brazen attack on the power, prestige, and privileges of the priesthood, which held a patent on matters involving purification. It is small wonder that henceforth the Synoptics picture the priests as actively plotting Jesus' destruction. They could not launch a frontal attack because of Jesus' soaring popularity with the populace, so they concocted an alternate course of action. They joined forces with "the scribes" and with "the principal men of the people" and attempted to persuade the Romans to rid them of their enemy (Mk. 11:18; Lk. 19:47). Rome was a willing ally. Jesus posed a threat to the peace she was determined to maintain.

Climax of the Controversies   A series of five rather stylized controversy stories follows the Temple Cleansing in Mark. Most of the questions put to Jesus are designed

[10]Such acts not only reinforced the spoken word, but they were believed to have brought the impending judgment closer.

to elicit self-incriminating statements that could be fashioned into a charge deserving the death penalty. In their present form, the incidents reflect the issues that engaged the early church and its opponents, but some of the root topics may well go back to Jesus himself.

Jesus' Authority (202)[11]   On the day after the Cleansing, according to Mark, representatives of the Sanhedrin confronted Jesus in the Temple. They wanted to know the source of his authority. Their object was to wring from him an explicit messianic claim. Jesus resorted to the rabbinical ruse of answering their question by asking another: "Was the baptism of John from heaven or from men?" (11:30). The Jerusalem authorities did not think highly of John, but the people regarded him as a real prophet. No matter which way the Sanhedrinites replied, they would impale themselves on one horn of the dilemma. Their refusal to answer meaningfully freed Jesus from replying to their initial challenge, and he emerged from the encounter victorious. He probably intended to do more than embarrass his opponents. He wanted to suggest that both his ministry and John's had heaven's seal of approval.

Tribute to Caesar (206)[12]   The Jerusalem authorities next sent to Jesus representatives of two widely divergent groups, the Pharisees and the Herodians, to entrap him in his talk. They lubricated their language with flattery to ease their thrust. "Is it lawful," they asked Jesus, "to pay taxes to Caesar, or not?" (Mk. 12:14). This was a burning issue in Judea, where a head tax had been imposed on all adult male Jews since Rome had assumed direct control of the province in 6 A.D. The tax was little more than a trifle, a day's wage, but it symbolized subservience. Jesus asked for a coin, and when it was brought to him, he inquired whose likeness and inscription it bore. When told that they were Caesar's, he said, "Render to Caesar the things that are Caesar's, and to God the things that are God's" (Mk. 12:17).

The incident is a splendid example of a pronouncement story. Everything points to the climactic saying in Mark 12:17 for the sake of which the story is told. Although the problem of paying taxes to Rome sprang from the life situation of Judea in Jesus' day, his pronouncement provided vital guidance for the early church as it struggled to survive in the increasingly hostile environment of the Roman Empire. Jesus clearly enjoined the Judeans to pay the tax![13] The fact that Jesus had to be asked the question about tax payment under-

[11]See Matthew 21:23–27; Mark 11:27–33; Luke 20:1–8.
[12]See Matthew 22:15–22; Mark 12:13–17; Luke 20:20–26.
[13]For other interpretations of the pronouncement, see Connick, *Jesus: The Man, the Mission, and the Message*, p. 339.

scores his concern for the *religious* problem, as does his answer to a question that was not put to him. He reminded his hearers that God outranks Caesar. Their primary obligation is to render unto God the things that are God's—repentance, obedience, and worship.

Resurrection of the Dead (207)[14]

The Sadducees, aware that Jesus believed in the resurrection, posed a peculiar problem for him. They cited the so-called levirate law of Moses, which required that the brother of a deceased man marry his widow (Deut. 25:5-6).[15] The first-born son would then bear the dead brother's name, the widow would be assured "social security," and the property holdings would be kept in the family. With the stage thus set, the Sadducees spun what to us is an incredible story. A certain man, one of seven brothers, took a wife. When he died leaving no children, one of his brothers married his widow. When that brother died without issue, another brother married the widow. The cycle continued until all the brothers were exhausted. Finally, the widow died. In the resurrection of the dead, the Sadducees wanted to know of Jesus, whose wife would she be? The incident is amusing, but Jesus' questioners were not comedians. They were trying to prove a point. Moses did not envisage a resurrection, else he would never have promulgated the levirate law that made the circumstances of resurrection absurd.

Jesus turned the tables on his opponents by pointing out that they knew neither the Scriptures nor the power of God. "For when they rise from the dead," he declared, "they neither marry nor are given in marriage, but are like angels in heaven" (Mk. 12:25). Marriage insured the propagation of the race on earth, but in the resurrected state (where death would not prevail) marriage would be outmoded. There people would be sexless like the angels.[16] The quotation that follows, taken from the most famous passage in Sadducean scripture, is surely a separate teaching that has become attached to the preceding one.[17] The argument is Talmudic, purely linguistic, and most uncharacteristic of Jesus.

The Primary Commandment (208)[18]

A scribe, who had overheard Jesus' encounter with the Sadducees, asked him which commandment was first of all. The climate had changed now. The questioner was not a critic—he evidenced a genuine interest in Jesus' answer to a much-debated question. Since all

[14]See Matthew 22:23-33; Mark 12:18-27; Luke 20:27-40.
[15]The Latin *levir* means "husband's brother."
[16]I Enoch 15:6-7.
[17]See S.E. Johnson, "The Gospel According to St. Matthew: Introduction and Exegesis," in *The Interpreter's Bible*, VII, 522.
[18]See Matthew 22:34-40; Mark 12:28-34; Luke 10:25-28.

commandments were obligatory, what the scribe wanted to know was which one provided a basic foundation for the rest. Jesus' answer combined two Old Testament injunctions. The command to love God came from Deuteronomy 6:5, and the command to love one's neighbor stemmed from Leviticus 19:18. The combination was not original. It had appeared in the Testaments of the Twelve Patriarchs of the previous century.[19] When the scribe repeated Jesus' words, stressing their theological implications, Jesus observed that his inquirer was not far from the kingdom of God. Matthew and Luke, who picture the scribe as hostile, omit this commendation. The Christians of their day had suffered too much at the hands of the scribes to pass on such a compliment.

David's Son (209)[20] The fifth and final question in the conflict series was raised by Jesus himself, according to the Synoptics. He asked how the scribes could say that the Christ is the son of David. David had said, "The Lord said to my Lord, Sit at my right hand, till I put thy enemies under thy feet" (Mk. 12:36). Since David had called the Christ "Lord," how could the Christ be David's son? Since we have assumed that Jesus did not apply the messianic titles to himself, he would not have spoken of himself as "the Christ," "son of David," and "David's Lord."[21] As Enslin has observed, the saying sounds like an early church answer to a Jewish gibe: "He cannot be God's anointed because he is not of Davidic descent." The Christian counter-retort: "Davidic descent is not a necessity."[22]

Condemnations (210)[23] At the close of the five conflict stories, Mark declares that a great throng heard Jesus gladly. Then he records Jesus' condemnation of the scribes for their proneness to special privileges, their exploitation of widows, and their hypocrisy (12:37b–40). Luke contains a much larger collection of condemnations from another source as well as Mark's brief one (Lk. 11:39–54; 20:45–47). Matthew combines the material in Mark and Luke, generously adds to it from his special source, and freely rewrites the whole. Matthew's expanded account begins with a general criticism of the scribes and Pharisees (23:1–12), is followed by seven "woes" (23:13–33), and concludes with a threat and lament (23:34–39).[24]

---

[19]Issachar 5:2; 7:6; Dan 5:3.
[20]See Matthew 22:41–46; Mark 12:35–37a; Luke 20:41–44.
[21]See pp. 164–165.
[22]M.S. Enslin, *The Prophet from Nazareth* (New York: McGraw-Hill Book Co., 1961), p. 136.
[23]See Matthew 23:1–36; Mark 12:37b–40; Luke 11:39–54; 20:45–47.
[24]Luke records only six "woes"—three against Pharisees and three against lawyers (scribes).

The picture drawn of the scribes and the Pharisees is a caricature. That some of these people were hypocrites is acknowledged, and they received round rebukes from the rabbis for their pretense. Scribes and Pharisees did place heavy burdens on their followers, but not for sadistic satisfaction. Their aim was to protect the faithful from transgression. Some surely sought seats of honor, but their number was probably no greater than in any other group. It would have been unconscionable for Jesus to have castigated a whole class of people for the misdeeds of a few. The scribes and the Pharisees did not "do *all* their deeds to be seen by men."[25] The Synoptics reached their final form at a time when the church and synagogue were at loggerheads. Matthew 23 tells us much about the church's attitude toward its opponents, but it reveals virtually nothing about the mind of Jesus. Contradiction in the polemical passages counsels moderation of the whole. At one place we are advised that the teaching of the Pharisees is altogether trustworthy, and in another that teaching is vigorously criticized.[26] Elsewhere Jesus is sometimes pictured in complete agreement with the Pharisees (Mt. 22:15-22). To acknowledge that the barbed and brutal attacks on the Pharisees are overdrawn is not to absolve them completely from guilt. They made their contribution to the cross along with others, and they bitterly persecuted the early church. A Pharisee of the Pharisees named Paul bears witness (I Thess. 2:15-16)!

<table>
<tr><td>**Synoptic Apocalypse**
(214–223)[27]</td><td>As Jesus emerged from the Temple, one of his disciples proudly called his attention to that magnificent complex. Jesus' response must have startled his companions: "Do you see these great buildings? There will not be left here one stone upon another, that will not be thrown down" (Mk. 13:2). Micah (3:12) and Jeremiah (26:6) had made comparable predictions, and the Babylonians had brought them to fulfillment. Jesus' prophecy concerned the Second Temple, which was burned by the Romans in 70 A.D. Some scholars regard his proclamation as a "prophecy after the event," but their conclusion hardly seems justified. A garbled form of the prediction was lodged against Jesus during his session before the Sanhedrin (Mk. 14:58).</td></tr>
</table>

Jesus' prophecy of the Temple's destruction serves to introduce the Synoptic Apocalypse.[28] The material betrays signs of modification in the light of the subsequent siege and conquest of Jerusalem by the Romans. Mark speaks of the desecration of the sanctuary with

[25]Matthew 23:5, italics added.
[26]Compare Matthew 23:2-3 with 23:4, 16-22, 25-26.
[27]See Matthew 24:4-36, 42; 25:13-15b; Mark 13:5-37; Luke 12:38, 40; 17:23-24, 37; 19:12-13; 21:8-36.
[28]Mark 13:5-37 and the expanded versions in Matthew and Luke noted in footnote 27.

an allusion to the defilement of the Temple by Antiochus Epiphanes (13:14).[29] and Matthew follows suit (24:15). Luke, on the other hand, names the siege of the city by surrounding armies as the sign of the disaster, rather than the profaning of the Temple (21:20). The entire discourse appears to be directed to Christians in general rather than to intimate disciples (Mk. 13:3). Although most of the Apocalypse purports to reveal the signs of the End, one verse flatly restricts such knowledge to the Father (Mk. 13:32). In another verse, Jesus refers to "the reader" when he is supposed to be speaking to his disciples (Mk. 13:14). Clearly Mark 13 is a composite. It contains material of an apocalyptic nature as well as sayings that stem from Jesus himself. The apocalyptic sections of that chapter, commonly called "The Little Apocalypse," include verses 6–8, 14–20, 24–27, and possibly 31. Many scholars equate them, or the whole of chapter 13, with an "oracle" that circulated among Jewish Christians in Jerusalem shortly before the siege and destruction of that city in 70 A.D. The oracle impelled the Christians to flee from Jerusalem to Pella in Perea where they safely sat out the frightful war between the Romans and the Jews.[30]

The Synoptic Apocalypse sounds strange to modern ears attuned to the notion that history is an unbroken process. But Mark's readers did not share our view. Centuries of subjugation had prepared them for apocalypticism. An earthly Eden yielded to a supernatural realm where the deferred hopes of the present would be realized. The New Age was painted in glowing imagery. At the instigation of God or His agent, it would suddenly arrive at the conclusion of a series of woes capped by supernatural signs and conflicts with evil powers. The Final Judgment would bring the condemnation of the wicked and the commendation of the righteous. The earlier hope for a son of David who would rule over a restored Jewish nation was supplemented by the glorified figure of the Son of Man who would come with the clouds of heaven. While the hopes were many and varied, they all agreed that God would terminate the Present Age and inaugurate a New Age. Mark's readers believed intensely in the imminence of the End (eschatology) and in the early advent of Jesus (parousia), as did the original Apostles and Paul. Christians were convinced that Christ's return in power and glory would validate their faith and assure their triumph over Jewish and pagan persecutors as well as Satan and his servants.

What did Jesus think about eschatology and his parousia? Mark 13 cannot tell us because it is saturated with the theology of the early

[29]See pp. 24–25.
[30]Eusebius, *Ecclesiastical History*, III, 5.

church. The sayings and stories of Jesus that are generally considered genuine are not always clear and seldom if ever comprehensive on these subjects, but they do suggest several conclusions. (1) Jesus shared the eschatological view of history that permeated his people. He believed that God had created the world, which remained "very good" until stained by man's sin (Gen. 1:31). At a time of His own choosing, God would reassert His sovereignty and bring history to an end. The Present Age would be replaced by the kingdom of God, a permanent order of righteousness and bliss. The New Age would arise neither by chance nor by human choice but by divine direction. Jesus' words and works pointed to the nearness of the kingdom. (2) Jesus disclaimed any knowledge of the precise program of events that would precede the End. Here he parted company with the apocalyptists who doted on timetables and blueprints. Jesus' motto, which cohered with traditional eschatology, was perpetual preparedness. (3) Jesus confidently expected that when God did triumph, his own mission and message would be vindicated and he would be joyously reunited with his faithful followers. The church proclaimed his Second Advent as an apocalyptic Christ, but Jesus' espousal of this doctrine is difficult to document.

Chronology of Holy Week (231, 234)[31] The Passover was a feast of prehistoric origin that originally may have concerned sacrifice of the first-born.[32] Although Israel evidently observed the feast prior to the Exodus, it took on new meaning under Moses. He smashed the Pharaoh's resistance to his liberation movement with the tenth plague. The Lord passed over Hebrew homes, whose doorposts had been smeared with lamb's blood, and smote only the first-born of the Egyptians (Exod. 12:1–30). Later on, in Canaan, the Passover was associated with the agricultural festival of Unleavened Bread. Originally the latter probably celebrated the opening of the harvest season. If this was the case, the custom of unleavened bread sprang from the use of new grain hastily converted into food at the beginning of the harvest season. For the later Israelites, however, unleavened bread had another meaning. It symbolized their hurried departure from Egypt. Since there had not been enough time for their dough to rise, they had baked and consumed their bread in an unleavened state.

Mark commences his account of Jesus' passover preparation with a curious comment: "And on the first day of Unleavened Bread, when they sacrificed the passover lamb, his disciples said to him, 'Where

---

[31]See Matthew 26:1–5, 17–19; Mark 14:1–2, 12–16; Luke 22:1–2, 7–13. Compare John 12:1–8; 13:1.

[32]See J.C. Rylaarsdam, "Passover and Feast of Unleavened Bread," in George A. Buttrick, ed., *The Interpreter's Dictionary of the Bible* (New York: Abingdon Press, 1962), K–Q, 663–668.

will you have us go and prepare for you to eat the passover?' " (14:12) The Passover lamb was sacrificed on the afternoon of Nisan 14. The Passover meal was eaten after sunset and continued on into the night. Since the Jewish day began at sundown, the meal occurred on Nisan 15 by Jewish reckoning. This date also marked the first day of the week-long Feast of Unleavened Bread, but the Passover was not technically part of that celebration (Num. 28:16–17). Luke adheres to Mark's wording, but Matthew omits his misleading phrase, "When they sacrificed the passover lamb."[33] Despite this difference, the Synoptic meaning is unmistakable. It is the Passover meal Jesus instructs his disciples to prepare (Mt. 26:17–19; Mk. 14:12–16; Lk. 22:7–13).

The Synoptic data indicate that the Last Supper coincided with the Passover Meal on Nisan 15 (shortly after sunset of the 14th), the first day of Unleavened Bread. Jesus ate the Passover meal, was arrested late the same night, was condemned to death in the early morning, was crucified, and died on the cross the same day—Nisan 15, the day before the Sabbath (Mk. 15:42). The chronology of the Fourth Gospel, however, is quite different—everything happens twenty-four hours earlier. The Last Supper was not the Passover Meal (13:1; 18:28; 19:14). Jesus died on the cross on Nisan 14 at the time the Passover lambs were being slain (1:29). John and the Synoptics agree that the crucifixion was on the day before the Sabbath. They disagree as to whether that day was Nisan 14 (when the Passover lamb was slain) or Nisan 15 (the first day of Unleavened Bread).

Which chronology is correct? No easy answer can be advanced, but most scholars favor the Johannine dating. The chief priests apparently intended to do away with Jesus before the feast (Mk. 14:1–2). So much activity on the night of the Passover meal and the first day of Unleavened Bread would have been extraordinary. Paul suggests that Christ was crucified at the same time the Passover lambs were being slain (I Cor. 5:7). None of the principal features of the Passover meal is mentioned in the Synoptic account—the roasted lamb, unleavened bread, bitter herbs, the cups of wine, and the recital of the Passover story from the Old Testament. The Lord's Supper was celebrated weekly or more frequently in the early church, a practice conditioned by its eschatological expectation. If it had originated in connection with the Passover meal, would it not have been observed on an annual basis?[34]

[33]Mark may have written with the Roman day in mind, or he may have followed a Jewish tendency to treat the two feasts as one.
[34]Attempts to reconcile the Synoptic and Johannine accounts have not been successful. Some argue that the Pharisees and the Sadducees observed Passover on different days or that day differed in their calendar calculations. Others maintain that Galilean Jews followed Exodus 12:1–14 to the letter and began Passover with the slaying of the lambs

**The Last Supper
(235–237)**[35]   Jesus' final meal with his disciples is known by many names. The early church called it the Eucharist, a practice continued in Eastern Orthodoxy.[36] Roman Catholicism named it the Mass. Protestants commonly call it Holy Communion or the Lord's Supper. The extraordinary development and significance of the sacrament contrast sharply with the simple account of Mark. Jesus "took bread, and blessed [God for the bread], and broke it, and gave it to them, and said, 'Take; this is my body.' And he took a cup, and when he had given thanks he gave it to them, and they all drank of it. And he said to them, 'This is my blood of the covenant, which is poured out for many. Truly, I say to you, I shall not drink again of the fruit of the vine until that day when I drink it new in the kingdom of God'" (14:22–25).

Matthew, mirroring meanings current in the early church, magnifies Mark's account. Jesus instructs the disciples to eat the bread and "drink" the wine, declares that his blood is poured out for many "for the forgiveness of sins," and states that he will not again drink wine until he drinks it "with them" in the kingdom of God. Luke places Jesus' words about the future first, reverses the order of the bread and cup, implies that only the disciples drank the wine, and omits reference to the blood of the covenant or the forgiveness of sins. Paul, who wrote earlier than Mark, presents an expanded tradition. He makes the Lord's Supper an *institution*. Jesus' followers are to repeat the rite *in memory* of their Master as a *new* covenant (I Cor. 11:23–25).[37]

At the gospel stage, the Last Supper story is clearly in midpassage. Alterations are still taking place. In Mark, the identity of Jesus' betrayer is one of the Twelve who dips bread in the same dish with Jesus (14:20). Since the disciples dipped from a common dish at any meal, this information reveals little. Luke merely indicates that the betrayer's hand is on the table (22:21). Matthew goes so far as to have Judas ask if it is he, to which Jesus replies, "You have said so" (26:25). John erases all doubt by specifically identifying Judas as the betrayer (13:26). Jesus may well have known who the traitor would be. But it is incredible that he could have told his other disciples about it without their attempting to thwart Judas' plan. It was the

---

and the eating of the meal on the eve of Nisan 14. Jerusalem Jews, on the other hand, are said to have observed the current and continuing practice of celebrating Passover by consuming the meal on Nisan 15.

[35]See Matthew 19:28; 20:25–28; 26:20–29; Mark 10:42–45; 14:17–25; Luke 22:14–38.
[36]From *eucharistēsas*, "when he had given thanks," of Mark 14:23.
[37]Luke's longer version of the Supper, which includes 22:19b–20, contains these same ideas. Many modern translators favor the shorter Lukan text on the ground that the longer one is derived from Paul.

epitome of perfidy to betray a companion after eating with him. The development of Judas' identity by Matthew and John appears to be "prophecy after the event."

What was the meaning of the Last Supper for Jesus? It was not the Lord's Supper of the Christian Church. The church had not yet been born; it resulted from the resurrection.[38] Neither was the Last Supper, in our view, the Passover meal with messianic overtones of the Synoptics[39] or Jesus' preenacted memorial service as envisaged by Paul. Some have seen it as a special kiddush meal designed to usher in and sanctify the sacred day. It was more likely a solemn eschatological banquet similar to those celebrated by religious brotherhoods.[40] Table fellowship played a vital role in Jewish life. Common meals had served to cement the bonds between Jesus and his disciples as they had proclaimed the kingdom's coming and the need for repentance. When they gathered for their final meal, they were exhilarated by a joyful feeling of eschatological expectation. Jesus' declaration that he would not again drink wine until he drank it new in the kingdom may at first have signaled sorrow (Mt. 26:29; Mk. 14:25; Lk. 22:18). But the central thrust of his words was not lost for long. The relationships that his impending death would rupture were renewable. The kingdom of God would soon be consummated![41]

The gap between Jesus' understanding of the Last Supper[42] and the Lord's Supper of the New Testament is not difficult to bridge. The New Covenant concept, first advanced by Jeremiah, quite naturally attached itself to Jesus' words: "This is my blood of the covenant, which is poured out for many" (Mk. 14:24). The sacrificial character of Jesus' death became evident in retrospect. His broken body and his life blood came to be symbolized by the bread and the wine. It remained for Paul to transform the whole into a suitable memorial.

Gethsemane to Golgotha

At the close of the Last Supper, Jesus and his disciples sang a hymn. Then they departed from the Upper Room and crossed the Kidron

[38]See p. 134. Some scholars believe that Jesus used "church" in the Hebrew sense of *kahal*, the gathered community of Israel in the wilderness period. Since Jesus considered himself to be the Messiah, he would have presupposed the existence of a messianic people—the New Community of God's People. See Oscar Cullmann, *Peter*, rev. ed. (Philadelphia: The Westminster Press, 1962), pp. 192–217.
[39]The view of Joachim Jeremias, *Eucharistic Words of Jesus* (Oxford: Blackwell, 1955).
[40]Compare the Qumran writing, *Rule of the Future Community*, II, 17–21.
[41]For a stimulating discussion of the distinction between the Last Supper as a Passover celebration and as an eschatological celebration, see Hans Lietzmann, *Mass and Lord's Supper* (Leiden: E. J. Brill, 1953). Compare our treatment of the messianic meal on pp. 127–130.
[42]As we have reconstructed it.

An old olive tree grows in the Garden of Gethsemane ("oil press").

to the Mount of Olives. When they arrived at the place called Gethsemane ("oil press"), Jesus asked eight of his disciples to wait while he prayed. He took with him Peter, James, and John and began to be greatly troubled: "My soul is very sorrowful, even to death," he said to his intimates. "Remain here, and watch" (Mk. 14:34).[43] Then he walked a little farther, fell on the ground, and prayed that if possible the hour might pass from him: "Abba, Father, all things are possible to thee; remove this cup from me; yet not what I will, but what thou wilt" (Mk. 14:35–36). Luke alone mentions the appearance of an angel and Jesus' agony (22:43–44). Three times, according to Mark and Matthew, Jesus returned from prayer and found the disciples asleep. "Are you still sleeping and taking your rest?" Jesus inquired. "It is enough; the hour has come; the Son of man is betrayed into the hands of sinners. Rise, let us be going; see, my betrayer is at hand" (Mk. 14:41–42).

The disciples were out of earshot and asleep while Jesus prayed in Gethsemane, and Jesus had no subsequent opportunity to tell them

---

[43]Jesus' request for the disciples to "watch" probably meant for them to share his vigil rather than to note the approach of his enemies.

of his prayer's content. These facts suggest that the Markan episode is a construct of the Christian community, and the dramatic nature of the material seems to bear this out. The three times of prayer and the three returns to the disciples match Peter's three denials and Jesus' three days in the tomb. Jesus' prayer reminds one of the Lord's Prayer, and "My soul is very sorrowful" echoes Psalm 42:6. Although the verbal accuracy of the Gethsemane episode is open to question, we are convinced of its essential historicity. The church would not have invented an incident that stressed Jesus' humanity, indecision, and limited knowledge.[44]

Arrest (240)[45] The Synoptics suggest that Jesus was arrested by a hastily armed, motley mob (including, perhaps, some Temple police) acting on orders from the Sanhedrin (Mt. 26:47; Mk. 14:43; Lk. 22:47, 52).[46] John's version identifies the arresters as a cohort of Roman soldiers evidently acting at the behest of the procurator, Pontius Pilate (18:3, 12).[47] The chances are that the Sanhedrin had ordered Temple police to assist a detachment of Roman soldiers in their task of assembling Jesus and his associates. The object was an informal interrogation preparatory to a Roman judicial decision.[48] They came armed because they regarded Jesus as a revolutionary and the precautions that they took against possible resistance proved to be partially justified (Mk. 14:47).

Judas served as guide to the group of arresters (Jn. 18:2; Acts 1:16). Since the light was dim and time was of the essence if a disturbance were to be avoided, swift and certain identification of Jesus was essential. Judas' scheme was foolproof. He kissed Jesus on the head. It was a clever camouflage—the usual way a disciple greeted his master! Judas' motive remains a mystery. Some think that he was money-mad. Matthew suggests that the thirty pieces of silver played a decisive role (26:15), and John agrees and indicates that Judas was dishonest as well as avaricious (12:6). Others attribute Judas' betrayal to malice. Judas was a Judean (based on the dubious notion that Iscariot meant "man of Kerioth"), and the rest of the disciples were Galileans. Sectional rivalry and Peter's displacement of Judas as leader of the Twelve prompted him to turn Jesus over to his enemies. Still others hold that Judas was mistaken but not malicious. He had joined Jesus'

[44]See Joseph Klausner, *Jesus of Nazareth*, trans. H. Danby (New York: The Macmillan Co., 1925), p. 332.
[45]See Matthew 26:47–56; Mark 14:43–52; Luke 22:47–53. Compare John 18:3–11.
[46]See p. 31.
[47]A cohort of approximately 600 soldiers would have constituted an "overkill."
[48]See the incisive study by the able Jewish scholar Paul Winter, *On the Trial of Jesus* (Berlin: Walter de Gruyter & Co., 1961) to which our discussion in this section is partially indebted.

movement thinking that its leader would soon declare his kingship and oust the Romans. When this did not happen, he betrayed Jesus to the High Priest to force his Master's hand. Jesus failed to act in the anticipated manner. Judas was horror-struck. He repented, returned the blood money, and hanged himself (Mt. 27:3–5). Judas may, in fact, have operated from mixed motives or for reasons other than those we have mentioned. Apparently the early church was as puzzled by the betrayal as we are. It finally fell back on the explanation that the deed was foretold by Scripture. The outline of Judas' action was filled in by details gleaned from such prophecies as Psalm 41:9 and Zechariah 11:12–13.

What Judas betrayed is more easily determined. It was not the messianic secret. Jesus did not claim to be the Messiah, in our view, either publicly or in private. Actions of his that have been interpreted messianically (such as the Entry and the Temple Cleansing) were not used against him at the trial, and Judas failed to show up with damaging testimony purchased for the occasion. What Judas betrayed was the place where Jesus slept. The authorities could not arrest Jesus during the day because of his popularity with the crowds, and Jesus did not remain in the city at night. It would have caused considerable commotion for them to have sought the Carpenter after dark amid the multitudes of pilgrims encamped outside Jerusalem. They needed a guide to direct them to the exact spot where Jesus slept. Then they could apprehend him quickly and with a minimum of fuss. Judas, for whatever reason, supplied them with the required information.[49]

Trial (241–242, 244–247)[50] The Gospels report four different "trials" of Jesus—one in John and three in the Synoptics. If the several accounts are harmonized, Jesus appeared successively before the former High Priest, Annas (John), the current High Priest and the Sanhedrin (Synoptics), the procurator, Pontius Pilate (Synoptics), and the Tetrarch of Galilee and Perea, Herod Antipas (Luke). Only the proceedings before Pilate constituted a trial in the proper sense of the term[51] Anywhere from fourteen to twenty-seven infractions of Jewish jurisprudence have been noted in connection with Jesus' Sanhedrin appearance. The meeting was held at night, in the residence of the High Priest, during a festival, under circumstances that probably precluded a full quorum of

[49]See *Gospel Parallels*, sections 233, 243; Matthew 26:14–16; 27:3–10; Mark 14:10–11; Luke 22:3–6. Compare John 12:4–6; 18:2–3; Acts 1:18–19.
[50]See Matthew 26:57–27:2; 27:11–31; Mark 14:53–15:20; Luke 22:54–23:25. Compare John 18:28–19:1; 19:4–16.
[51]Winter, *On the Trial of Jesus*, pp. 31–43, believes that the earliest form of Luke and John and the earliest chapters of Acts mistakenly identified the official High Priest at Jesus' death as Annas, probably Ananus II.

twenty-three. No defense witnesses were called, condemnation and execution occurred on the same day, and the penalty (death by crucifixion) did not cohere with the crime (blasphemy). It is a dubious argument that these and other violations of the Mishna tractate Sanhedrin are anachronistic. Although the tractate is post-Synoptics, it was composed of largely traditional materials based on earlier practice.

The Synoptic accounts of Jesus before the Sanhedrin represent a popular Christian version of what transpired between his arrest and his trial before Pilate. They reflect the heightening hostility between the churches and the synagogues and the growing tension between Christians and the political authorities. Their apologetic purpose is to shift responsibility for Jesus' death from the Romans to the Jews. This purpose reaches its pinnacle in Matthew 27:24-25. There Pilate washes his hands of *l'affaire de Jésus*, and the Jewish people ecstatically accept guilt for the Galilean's Golgotha: "His blood be on us and on our children!" Jesus' appearance before Herod Antipas (found only in Luke 23:6-16) also reflects an apologetic concern that is even more evident in Acts. Luke makes plain that Jesus and the apostles were frequently brought before the courts, but no charge against them was ever sustained. More convincing proof of the nonsubversive character of Christians could not be furnished.

Was the Jewish "trial," then, a complete fabrication? Such elements as the false witnesses, the charge of blasphemy, and the final condemnation do appear to be later developments, but these factors do not justify the dismissal of the entire story as an invention. It is likely that Jesus was escorted from the Mount of Olives to the High Priest's home and kept there until morning for private examination. Even if the arresters were Roman soldiers operating under orders from the procurator, Jesus would have been brought before the High Priest out of courtesy and respect for his right to adjudicate purely local matters. Pilate probably required a specific indictment before he would examine the prisoner. When the Sanhedrin convened in the morning, presumably in its customary council chamber, it was to confirm the nocturnal decisions of its Executive Committee (Lk. 22:66). Its members agreed to turn Jesus over to the Roman tribunal for an official trial on the charge of seditious activity. Whether the Sanhedrin had the right at this time to try a capital case for violation of Jewish Law is disputed. We think it did.[52] Where the charge involved political activity, Rome probably reserved the right to make the final decision. But the issue is largely academic. Jesus was not put to death by the Sanhedrin on the charge of blasphemy. If he

[52]See Winter, *On the Trial of Jesus*, pp. 67-74; Connick, *Jesus: The Man, the Mission, and the Message*, pp. 381-382.

had been, his death would have been by stoning. He was tried in a Roman court, condemned by Pilate on the charge of high treason, and put to death by the Roman method of crucifixion. The inscription on the cross bears witness to his alleged crime: "King of the Jews." Once more, it seemed to the Romans, the political stability of this trouble-prone area had been preserved.

The incident involving Barabbas is a puzzler. If Barabbas was an insurrectionist, as Mark seems to suggest (15:7), the clamor of the crowd for his release requires no explanation. That the crowd's insistence was stiffened by Pilate's practice of releasing a prisoner at the feast is another matter. The granting of amnesty at festival times is well known, and the Romans practiced it at the lectisternium. But there is no evidence outside of the Gospels that the Roman procurator regularly released a prisoner at Passover and permitted the people to name the one to be released regardless of the gravity of his offense. Up to this point, the crowds had smiled on Jesus, and the chief priests had had to operate surreptitiously lest Jesus' arrest spark an uproar. Suddenly they were able to stir up the populace to demand the release of Barabbas in Jesus' stead. Pilate, who could find no crime in Jesus, was compelled by the crowd to condemn him to death. The abrupt shift of sentiment arouses the suspicion that once again we have an illustration of the evangelists' tendency to absolve the procurator and blame the Jews for Jesus' death. Did they not prefer the release of a proven insurrectionist to that of an innocent Jesus?[53]

Pilate's sentence of death is not recorded in the Synoptics, but the events that follow leave no doubt that it was given. After the sentence was pronounced, Jesus was scourged. This gruesome Roman custom was inflicted on the condemned preliminary to their crucifixion.[54] Jesus was tied to a flagellation post and brutally beaten with leather whips stiffened with pieces of metal or bone. Then he was turned over to Roman soldiers to be crucified. Since he was a condemned criminal, the soldiers could do with him as they pleased. They took him to the praetorium (the government house of the procurator when in Jerusalem) where they indulged in some crude horseplay. Since Jesus had been condemned to death as King of the Jews, they treated him as royalty. Over his shoulders they threw a soldier's cloak to represent the imperial purple. On his head they placed a wreath woven from some thorny-looking plant in imitation of the laurel wreath worn by the emperor.[55] Then they parodied a royal salute,

[53]For a defense of the historicity of the Barabbas episode see F. C. Grant, "The Gospel According to St. Mark: Introduction and Exegesis," in *The Interpreter's Bible*, VII, 895.
[54]According to John 19:1, Pilate had Jesus scourged in an unsuccessful effort to prevent the crucifixion.
[55]Note any Roman coin.

struck Jesus with a reed (scepter), and knelt before him in homage. It must have reminded the onlookers of the burlesques of unpopular public officials mimed by actors in the streets of the large cities of the Roman Empire. When their fun was finished, they led Jesus away to be crucified.

Crucifixion (248–250)[56]   The Romans had practiced crucifixion since the Punic Wars of the third and second centuries B.C. It was a form of punishment reserved for rebels, runaway slaves, and common criminals. After an excruciating scourging, the condemned was forced to carry the crossbeam (*patibulum*), weighing eighty to ninety pounds, to the place of execution as part of his punishment.[57] When he reached the place of execution, which was usually near some well-traveled road, he was stripped of his clothing. His outstretched hands were then lashed to the crossbeam, perhaps with the *titulus* attached on which his crime was described[58] The crossbeam was lifted up and fastened to a permanent upright pole (*simplex*) that had been driven into the ground. Part of the condemned's body weight was supported by a peg under his crotch. His legs were lashed out in an unnatural position, and his feet were tied to the upright post so that they were a few inches from the ground. It was customary to crucify in groups. Exposure, loss of blood, pillorying by passers-by, torment by insects, impaired circulation, and hunger pyramided the pain. Death usually came in a dozen hours, but some men managed to cling to life for several days.[59]

Roman soldiers escorted Jesus from the praetorium toward the place of execution. When Jesus' strength failed from lack of sleep and the brutal scourging, the soldiers compelled Simon of Cyrene (a member of the Jewish dispersion from North Africa) to carry the crossbeam while they carried Jesus.[60] The route of the death march is uncertain. The traditional stations of the cross did not originate until about the middle of the fourteenth century. Golgotha (Aramaic) or Calvary (Latin) was located outside the city gate, far within the present walls of the Old City (Heb. 13:12). Since the time of Constantine, when a number of holy places were designated, the traditional location of Golgotha has been the site of the Church of the Holy Sepulcher. Although it remains the only place for Golgotha and the sepulcher

[56]See Matthew 27:32–56; Mark 15:21–41; Luke 23:26–49. Compare John 19:17–30.
[57]The picture of Jesus bearing the full cross is an artist's invention.
[58]The Synoptics do not indicate that Jesus' hands and feet were nailed. This detail was supplied later by John 20:25.
[59]Josephus, *Life*, 75.
[60]The verb translated "they brought" him in Mark 15:22 may be rendered "they carried" him. John 19:17, which flatly declares that Jesus bore his own cross, may have been designed to refute the Docetic claim, based on the Synoptics, that Simon had been crucified in place of the divine Christ.

with any archeological support, other locations have been proposed. Pilgrims may find "Gordon's Calvary" and the "Garden Tomb," located to the north of Herod's Gate, a more convincing picture of how the places probably appeared. Golgotha is believed to have derived its name from its rocky eminence, which resembled a skull or head.[61]

Before Jesus was hoisted to the upright pole, he was offered a drugged drink to deaden the pain. He refused it, probably because he did not want to die in a state of stupor. Here, as elsewhere, the details of the Passion Story have been colored by prophecy. Matthew 27:34 changes Mark's myrrhed wine (15:23) into wine "mingled with gall" to make it conform to Psalm 69:21. In Mark, Jesus' clothes are divided among the soldiers by the casting of lots (15:24). Christians found this to be a fulfillment of Psalm 22:18: "They divide my garments among them, and for my raiment they cast lots." Not so in John! By the time the Fourth Gospel was composed, it was observed that the psalmist had distinguished between garments (which were divided) and the raiment (for which lots were cast). So in the Fourth Gospel, the soldiers divided Jesus' garments into four parts, but they cast lots for his seamless tunic (19:23–24).

The evangelists record Jesus' agony with remarkable restraint: "And they crucified him" (Mk. 15:24). There was no need to elaborate. People were well acquainted with the horrors of crucifixion. Jesus hung on the cross from three (John) to six hours (Synoptics). What he said while there is a mystery. The disciples had fled, and the women stood at a distance (Mt. 26:56; Mk. 14:50; Lk. 23:49).[62] Matthew (27:46) and Mark (15:34) report one utterance, Luke gives three different ones (23:34, 43, 46), and John records three others (19:26–27, 28, 30). The church wove the whole into a devotional pattern of seven last words for Good Friday.

One of the words from the cross requires special comment: "My God, my God, why hast thou forsaken me?" (Mk. 15:34; Mt. 27:46).[63] Some scholars think it is secondary, but why would the church invent a saying it found so difficult to explain? It seems to suggest that Jesus felt bereft of the Father. Was he threatened with the gnawing thought that death after all was the final victor? Perhaps so, but another explanation appears more likely. Pious Jews customarily re-

[61]A less likely theory is that the name arose from the fact that the place was littered with the skulls of executed criminals.
[62]Only John 19:26 has the women (including Jesus' Mother) and a disciple "standing near."
[63]Luke (23:46) and John (19:30) substitute other sayings for this one.

cited Psalm 22 in times of adversity. It begins with a complaint, the very words attributed to Jesus: "My God, my God, why hast thou forsaken me?" It ends on a note of triumph: "I will tell of thy name to my brethren. . . . Posterity shall serve him [the Lord]; men shall tell of the Lord to the coming generation, and proclaim his deliverance to a people yet unborn, that he has wrought it" (Ps. 22:22, 30-31).[64] Although for Mark this indicates the summit of Jesus' rejection and desertion, it is no cry of despair, no sigh of relief, no last gasp of a dying organism. It is the victor's shout. Nothing less would have evoked the centurion's comment, "Truly this man was a son of God."[65]

Strange portents accompanied Jesus' death. Darkness covered the land from noon until three o'clock.[66] The curtain that separated the Holy of Holies from the rest of the Temple was torn in two from top to bottom.[67] An earthquake rent the rocks in the vicinity of Jerusalem, and deceased saints exited from their tombs and appeared to many people in the Holy City (Mt. 27:51b-53). Such phenomena were commonly reported in connection with the death of charismatic men in the ancient world. It would have been strange indeed had they not been told in connection with the demise of "Jesus Christ, the Son of God" (Mk. 1:1). It would violate the evangelists' intent, however, if these incidents were clothed in the garments of history. Their purpose was to convey the mystery and the horror that encircled the death of Jesus. Man was awe-struck, and nature was convulsed.

Burial (251–252, A 1)[68] Jesus died at midafternoon and the Sabbath began at sunset.[69] Jewish law dictated that his burial take place in the brief interim (Deut. 21:22-23; Jn. 19:32).[70] It was a praiseworthy deed to care for the dead, and the Synoptics agree that Joseph of Arimathea asked Pilate for Jesus' body. The petitioner was not a disciple[71] but a devout and influential Jew doing his duty (Mk. 15:43; Luk. 23:50).[72] He

[64]Compare the Qumran *Hymns of Thanksgiving*.
[65]The original and more accurate R.S.V. translation of Mark 15:39. Compare Luke 23:47.
[66]Another prophecy made history? See Amos 8:9.
[67]A symbol of uninterrupted access to God made possible by Jesus' death?
[68]See Matthew 27:57-66; 28:11-15; Mark 15:42-47; Luke 23:50-56. Compare John 19:38-42.
[69]The date (Nisan 14 in John; Nisan 15 in the Synoptics) and the year (anywhere from 27-33 A.D.) are disputed. See G.B. Caird, "The Chronology of the New Testament," in *The Interpreter's Dictionary of the Bible*, A-D, 599-603. Our preference is Nisan 14, 30 A.D.
[70]Roman custom permitted the crucified to hang on their crosses until they putrefied and preying birds picked their bones clean. The grisly practice served as a stark warning to potential lawbreakers. In Palestine, however, the conqueror suspended the custom in consideration of Jewish sensitivities.
[71]Contrary to Matthew 27:57 and John 19:38.
[72]Matthew's view that Joseph was "rich" (27:57) may have been derived from Isaiah 53:9.

The Garden Tomb. Some English authorities believe this is the authentic sepulcher of Jesus although archeological support for their conviction is nil. The Tomb does, however, provide a convincing picture of the kind of place in which Jesus was buried. Notice the trough which has been cut in front of the entrance. A round, flat stone was rolled in the trough to close the opening.

may also have been a secret admirer of the gritty Galilean. After Pilate had confirmed the surprising fact that Jesus was already dead, he granted Joseph's request. The body was removed from the cross, wrapped in a hastily-obtained winding sheet, and placed in a nearby rock-hewn tomb owned by Joseph. A round, flat, heavy stone was rolled in a rock groove to close the opening. Mary Magdalene and Mary, the mother of Joseph, saw where Jesus was laid (Mk. 15:47; Mt. 27:61).[73]

Who was responsible for Jesus' death? Roman Catholics were taught for centuries that the Jews were Christ-killers, and many Protestants readily shared their conviction. Pope Paul VI recently absolved the Jewish people from special guilt and transferred the onus of the crucifixion to the human race. Surely the Jewish people as a whole did not destroy Jesus. Many of them heard him gladly and learned of his death *ex post facto.* The high-priestly group cooperated in Jesus' arrest and preferred charges against him before Pilate. But it was the procurator who was primarily to blame. He held in his unwashed hands the power of life or death. That his decision was death is established by the charge (treason), the carriers (Roman soldiers carried Christ to Calvary), and the crucifixion (a Roman method of execution).

[73]Compare Luke 23:55–56 and John 19:39–40. Two incidents related by Matthew in connection with Jesus' burial bear the marks of manufacture. The Guard at the Tomb (27:62–66) and the Bribing of the Soldiers (28:11–15) were designed to refute Jewish antagonists who claimed that the disciples had stolen Jesus' body from the tomb in order to propagate the falsehood of the resurrection. See Connick, *Jesus: The Man, the Mission, and the Message,* pp. 403–404.

The Resurrection (253, A 2, B 1, 2, 3, C)[74]

Disillusionment and despair overcame Jesus' followers after the crucifixion. They had hoped that he would be the one to redeem Israel (Lk. 24:21), but that hope had turned to ashes. Dead men do not deliver. Then a strange happening was reported. Three women went to Jesus' burial place early on the first day of the week. They were startled to discover that the closing-stone had been rolled away. An angel informed them that Jesus had risen and invited them to inspect the empty tomb. Then the angel commanded them to tell the disciples that Jesus could be seen in Galilee. Trembling and astonishment seized the women, who fled from the tomb and said nothing to anyone (Mk. 16:1–8).

Mark's Ending

Mark's Gospel ends abruptly at 16:8—with the word *gar* ("for") in the Greek text. Since the evangelist knew about the resurrection, it is argued that his Gospel originally ended with an appearance of Jesus to his disciples in Galilee.[75] Numerous attempts have been made to reconstruct the ending, said to have been lost through accidental mutilation, but none has been altogether successful.[76] Mark may have regarded the previous promises of the resurrection as sufficient (Mk. 8:31; 9:31; 10:34). Early Christian scribes, however, found Mark's sudden terminus unsatisfactory. Two different conclusions were added—the Longer Ending (16:9–20, with appearances to Mary Magdalene, the Two, and the Eleven) and the Shorter Ending.[77] Neither reflects the vocabulary, style, or thought patterns of the evangelist.

The Appearances

Whether Mark originally contained post-resurrection appearances of Jesus is debatable, but there can be no uncertainty about the other Gospels. They all record appearances, and their records are at odds. (1) To whom Jesus first presented himself is not clear. Matthew indicates that after the angel at the tomb had given the two Marys the same message as in Mark, the women ran with fear and great joy to tell the disciples. On the way, Jesus met and greeted them. As they worshiped him, he calmed their fears and repeated the message for the disciples to see him in Galilee (Mt. 28:1–10). In Luke, Jesus did not appear to the women. When they reached the disciples and related their experience of the empty tomb and the angel's words, the disciples thought it was an idle tale and disbelieved them (Lk. 24:10–11). The first appearance of Jesus recorded by Luke is to Cleopas and his traveling companion on the road to Emmaus (24:13–32).

---

[74]See Matthew 28:1–10, 16:20; Mark 16:1–20; Luke 24:1–53. Compare John 20:1–18.
[75]Martin Dibelius, *From Tradition to Gospel*, trans. B.L. Woolf (New York: Charles Scribner's Sons, 1935), pp. 189–190.
[76]See H.D.A. Major, T.W. Manson, and C.J. Wright, *The Mission and Message of Jesus* (New York: E.P. Dutton & Co., 1938), pp. 206–207.
[77]See *Gospel Parallels*, p. 191.

When these two rushed to Jerusalem to report the phenomenon, they learned from the Eleven that Jesus had already appeared to Simon (Lk. 24:33-35). Paul agrees with Luke (I Cor. 15:3-8). However, in the Fourth Gospel Jesus first appeared to Mary Magdalene (20:15-17). (2) The location of the appearances is confusing. Matthew reports one appearance in the Jerusalem area and another in Galilee, but those in Luke and John occur in or near Jerusalem.[78] (3) The form in which Jesus appeared is puzzling. At times, his human nature is stressed. He eats, walks, talks, shows his wounds, and is not in the tomb visited. The body that was buried seems to have been resuscitated. At other times, the data point in another direction. His grave clothes are undisturbed (Jn. 20:6-9). He enters a room through closed doors (Jn. 20:19). He is able to appear and disappear at will (Lk. 24:13-53). These reports cohere with the earliest and most comprehensive treatment of the resurrection. Paul, who wrote long before the Gospels were composed, insisted that flesh and blood could not inherit the kingdom of God, called the resurrected body "spiritual," and declared that Christ would change our physical body to be like his glorious one (I Cor. 15:35-53).

The Empty Tomb

Although the Gospels make much of the empty tomb, Paul never mentions it. He records Jesus' appearances to "Cephas," "the twelve," the "more than five hundred brethren," "James," and "all the apostles." Then he adds his own personal experience of the risen Christ to the list (I Cor. 15:3-8).[79] Is the great apostle unaware of the empty-tomb tradition, or does he regard it as of secondary significance? Some scholars insist that while Paul does not mention the empty tomb, he implies its existence by using the triadic form—died, buried, raised (I Cor. 15:3-4). Such words are hollow unless they mean that what was buried is raised.[80] Perhaps so, but the gestalt of Paul's thought suggests otherwise. He regards Jesus' resurrection as the first fruits of those who are dead (I Cor. 15:20). It inaugurated the end-time and is the warranty and model of the resurrection of Christians (I Cor. 15:23). Paul rejects the notion of a resuscitated corpse (embraced by some Jews) and the Greek concept of a disembodied spirit. Jesus taught that life after death would be lived under radically different conditions (Mk. 12:24-25). Paul expands this thought in terms similar to the later words found in the Fourth Gospel about a grain of wheat falling into the ground (Jn. 12:24). Both a body and a seed are placed in the earth, but what comes up is different in both instances. God *gives* to both a *new* body (I Cor. 15:36-41). The body born of woman is perishable, dishonorable, weak, and phys-

---

[78]Only in the epilogue of John (ch. 21) is a Galilean appearance reported.
[79]Compare Acts 26:19 where Luke writes of Paul's "heavenly vision."
[80]See A.M. Hunter, *The Work and Words of Jesus* (Philadelphia: The Westminster Press, 1950), p. 124.

ical. The resurrection body is imperishable, glorified, powerful, and spiritual (I Cor. 15:42b–44). Paul's "spiritual body" assumes a complete metamorphosis. "Spiritual" indicates that the new life, which is a gift of God, is nonphysical; "body" suggests that the deceased is resurrected in his wholeness.

Paul's Corinthian correspondence lends strong support to the claim that the earliest Christians pointed to Jesus' postresurrection appearances rather than to the empty tomb as proof of his resurrection. The claim is further bolstered by a statement in Acts. There it is related that Jesus "presented himself alive after his passion by many proofs, appearing to them [the apostles] during forty days, and speaking of the kingdom of God" (Acts 1:3).[81] Perhaps the witness of the women was unknown (as Mark 16:8 suggests) or was disregarded (as Luke 24:11 states) until Jesus' resurrection had been confirmed by something more convincing than an empty tomb. Jewish antagonists never denied the Christian claim that the tomb was empty; they simply asserted that Galilean ghouls had desecrated the tomb and stolen the body.[82]

The conflicting details of the resurrection data may seem to sponsor skepticism. The Gospels disagree as to where Jesus appeared, who saw him first, to whom he spoke, what he said, and what form he assumed. There are some things, however, about which we may be confident. (1) The evangelists were not in collusion. The very diversity of their accounts guarantees their honesty. (2) No one expected Jesus to be resurrected. When the story circulated that he was alive, his closest associates dismissed it as an idle tale. This should give permanent burial to the accusation that the disciples' wish played father to their faith. (3) The sources unanimously testify to the witnesses' *faith* in Jesus' resurrection. (4) The earliest account indicates that the *form* of Jesus' resurrection was nonmaterial. Even the later gospel accounts lay primary stress not on the physical but the *personal* identity of the earthly Galilean and the resurrected Christ. It was the risen Christ who explained the empty tomb, not the empty tomb that explained the risen Christ.[83] (5) Faith in Jesus' resurrection impelled his followers to resume and expand the work he had initiated. Matthew's Great Commission, written from the vantage point of hindsight, formally describes the purpose, substance, and scope of their mission (28:16–20).

[81]Compare Mark 16:8.
[82]For various theories concerning the origin of the empty-tomb story, see Connick, *Jesus: The Man, the Mission, and the Message*, pp. 416–417.
[83]See Michael Ramsey, *The Resurrection of Christ* (London: Geoffrey Bles, 1946), pp. 42–44, 71–73. Rudolf Bultmann, *History of the Synoptic Tradition*, trans. John March (New York: Harper & Row, 1963), pp. 285, 290, on the other hand, regards the story of the women and the empty tomb as an apologetic legend.

Reflections on the Cross

Jesus' resurrection did more than convince his followers that he was alive and prompt them to resume his work with renewed vigor. It also enabled his enthusiasts to understand his death. From Golgotha to Easter, the cross had painfully reminded them of the tragic demise of their innocent Master. But their encounter with the living Christ soon caused them to see the cross in a new light. It was not the end but the beginning. Jesus' death was seen as a divine deed—a decisive act of God in His history of redemption. What had once been the symbol of a despicable death for the despised became the focal point of the Christian faith. Not everyone interpreted the cross in the same way. In resurrection retrospect, different meanings were discovered. Since these interpretations directly modified the Synoptic tradition, we shall consider some of the ways the cross came to be understood.

The Cross as Fulfilled Scripture

The Hebrew Scriptures were the Bible of the early church. Jesus had frequently appealed to them during the course of his ministry. "You have heard that it was said to the men of old . . ." introduced quotations from the Mosaic Law (Mt. 5:21, 27). "For I tell you that this scripture must be fulfilled in me" (Lk. 22:37) echoed Isaiah 53:12. In a postresurrection appearance to two followers on the Emmaus road, Jesus opened their eyes to the significance of his passion by interpreting the Scriptures, beginning with Moses and continuing through the prophets (Lk. 24:27). The Hebrew Scriptures were regarded as prophetic history by the early church (Rom. 15:4; I Cor. 10:6, 11), and they provided a custom-made context for comprehending the meaning of Jesus' death.

The Cross as a Divine Necessity

According to the early church, Jesus' death was not an accident but a divine necessity. "Was it not *necessary*," the Resurrected One asked his followers, "that the Christ should suffer these things and enter into his glory?"[84] This postresurrection concept also permeates the accounts of Jesus' earthly ministry. After the Transfiguration, Jesus reportedly asked his three intimate disciples, "How is it written of the Son of man, that he should suffer many things and be treated with contempt?" (Mk. 9:12).[85] The Passion predictions, composed after the impact of the resurrection, make the same point (Mk. 8:31; 9:31; 10:33–34). The thesis that Jesus must die was rooted in the assurance that the ancient prophecies must find eschatological fulfillment.

The Cross as Preparation for Glorification

Jesus' death was also seen as a prelude to his glorification. Paul put the idea succinctly in his letter to the Philippians. He observed that

[84]Luke 24:26, italics added. See also Luke 22:37; 24:7, 44–45.
[85]Compare John 3:14.

Jesus humbled himself and became obedient even unto death on the cross. As a consequence, God exalted him and gave him a name that outranks all others (Phil. 2:8–9). The same theme finds expression in the Synoptics and the Acts. It lies just below the surface in Jesus' words about losing one's life in order to save it (Mt. 16:25; Mk. 8:35; Lk. 9:24), and it is unmistakable in Luke 24:26. There it is stated that it was necessary for the Christ first to suffer, then to enter into his glory. The sermons in Acts 2, 10, and 13 evidence similar ideas.

The Cross as an Instrument of Salvation

The early Christian kerygma stressed that Jesus' death was a redemptive act. He "died for our sins in accordance with the scriptures" (I Cor. 15:3).[86] Isaiah 53 served as the primary pattern for the interpretation of Jesus' death as a vicarious and atoning sacrifice. This central concept finds expression in the early Christian Eucharistic liturgy (I Cor. 11:23–26), the letters of Paul (Rom. 4:25; 5:8; 8:34; II Cor. 5:14–15, 21; Gal. 1:4; 2:20), the Pastorals (I Tim. 2:6, Tit. 2:14), the Catholic epistles (I Pet. 2:21; 3:18), and the Johannine literature (Jn. 10:11; 11:50–51; I Jn. 2:2; 3:16a; 4:10). Its clearest and most cogent Synoptic formulation is found in Mark 10:45: "For the Son of man also came not to be served but to serve, and to give his life as a ransom for many." While the authenticity of this saying has been upheld,[87] it is our judgment that it is secondary.[88]

If there had been no resurrection, the cross of Jesus would have faded in man's memory. At most, it would have symbolized the death of a virtuous Rabbi. The resurrection transformed the cross from a question mark into an exclamation point and changed scattered followers of Jesus from dispirited individuals into a robust and rapidly expanding community of the faithful.[89] The growth of this vital and vitalizing community is described in the book of Acts and in the letters of Paul. We will now turn our attention to these records.

[86]Compare Acts 10:43.
[87]See Vincent Taylor, *Gospel According to Mark* (London: The Macmillan Co., 1953), pp. 445–446.
[88]See pp. 163–164.
[89]See Oscar Cullmann, "Death of Christ," in *The Interpreter's Dictionary of the Bible*, A–D, 804–808, to which our discussion is partially indebted, for a fuller treatment of the meaning of the cross in the New Testament.

PART

3

Birth and Growth of the Christian Community

Luke has been called the most important contributor to the New Testament, and there is much to sustain this judgment. The very massiveness of his work is alone impressive. The author of Luke-Acts composed more than one-fourth of the Christian canon. His prodigious output exceeded both the fourteen letters popularly ascribed to Paul and the five writings traditionally attributed to John.[1]

The content of Luke's contribution to the New Testament is no less significant than its bulk. The Third Gospel is much richer and more varied than the other Synoptics. It also incorporates more independent material (including a number of Jesus' most poignant and memorable parables) and more choice data concerning Jesus' postresurrection days. The book of Acts does not suffer by comparison. It provides the only extant account of Christian beginnings. Although Paul's letters were written earlier than Luke-Acts, they are mute concerning this vital topic. The postresurrection followers of Jesus had already attained public identity, experienced rapid numerical and geographic growth, and become the object of persecution before Paul became a convert. Volume II of Luke's extensive work appears to supply the necessary background for making meaningful many of Paul's passing allusions.

The place of Luke's second volume in the unfolding drama of the New Testament has been aptly stated by one of that writing's most perceptive interpreters: "The Book of Acts is the keystone linking the two major portions of the New Testament, the 'Gospel' and the 'Apostle,' as the early Christians called them, . . . the only bridge we have across the seemingly impassable gulf that separates Jesus from Paul, Christ from Christianity, the Gospel of Jesus from the gospel about Jesus."[2]

[1]The Gospel of John, I, II, and III John, and Revelation.
[2]H. J. Cadbury, *The Making of Luke-Acts* (New York: The Macmillan Co., 1927), p. 2. Reprinted by permission of the author.

In this section of our study we shall examine the Acts and the letters of Paul to see what light they shed on the origin and growth of the Christian community.

VIII

**The Age of the
Church**
([Luke–] Acts 1–15)

Modern scholars are nearly unanimous in the belief that the Gospel of Luke and the Acts of the Apostles were written by the same person. Their judgment is supported by tradition, the common dedication of the two works to Theophilus, the cross reference to the Gospel in Acts (1:1), and the similarity of vocabulary and style. The Gospel concludes with Jesus' assurance to his disciples that he will send the promise of his Father upon them, his command that they remain in Jerusalem until they are clothed with power from on high, and a notation concerning his departure from them (24:49–53). Acts opens with a reminder of the promise and command, a description of the disciples waiting at Jerusalem for the promise to be fulfilled, a more extensive account of Jesus' departure (ascension), and a stirring story of the fulfillment of the promise by the gift of the Spirit at Pentecost (1:1–2:13). Just as the first volume looks ahead to the second, the second looks back to the first. They are two premeditated parts of a single whole.

The scholarly consensus that prevails concerning the unity of Luke-Acts collapses when such questions as author, date, place of origin, and purpose are raised. Since we have discussed these matters in connection with our treatment of the Gospel of Luke, we shall move on to topics specifically related to Acts itself.[1]

**Some Questions
Concerning Acts**

Separation from Luke

The Acts of the Apostles survived for nearly a century without leaving a trace in the meager Christian writings of that period that are still extant. The first unmistakable references to the book appear about 180 A.D. in different geographical locations: by Irenaeus (Lyons), an anonymous Latin fragment (Rome?), Clement (Alexandria), and Tertullian (North Africa). By this time, Acts had been detached from the Gospel. Why did the separation take place? The character and content of the Gospel corresponded with other accounts of Jesus' mission and message. The Third Gospel was quite naturally linked

[1]See pp. 86–90.

with the three other Gospels. Like them, it was given a distinguished name, "According to Luke." The four circulated as a unit, and together they entered the New Testament canon. Volume II, thus left to itself, appeared to belong to a different category. It was given its present title, Acts of the Apostles, and related either to the Catholic or the Pauline epistles. The positioning of the Third Gospel and Acts in the Christian canon and our treatment of this Gospel in connection with the other Synoptics, however, should not blind us to the fact that Acts was intended as a sequel to the Gospel of Luke.

Sources   If Acts was written by a companion of Paul, as tradition asserts, then its author had access to considerable oral information. He could have derived much oral knowledge from Paul and his associates (and from persons like Mark, Philip, Jesus' brother James, and perhaps Peter) who were themselves present at the events described in the early chapters of his book. But source critics have long argued that variations of language, style, and viewpoint in the narrative suggest the presence of written documents. For the first half of Acts, Adolf Harnack isolated a Jerusalem Source A (3:1–5:16, which may be identical with the Jerusalem-Caesarean Source), a Jerusalem Source B (1:6–2:47; 5:17–42), a Jerusalem-Caesarean Source (8:5–40; 9:31–11:18; 12:1–24), an Antiochene Source (6:1–8:4; 11:19–30; 12:25–15:35), and a Pauline Source (9:1–30).[2] C. C. Torrey theorized that a single Aramaic document underlay Acts 1–15, but his thesis proved to be linguistically unsound.[3]

When the form critics turned their attention to Acts, they soon questioned the claim that the author relied on written sources. The most that source critics had established was the identification of blocks of material that seemed to point to independent traditions. The latter could have stemmed from oral as well as written sources. Analysis of the separate stories in Acts convinced the form critics that they bear the marks of oral tradition. The tradition acquired its fixed forms in response to the needs and interests of the early Christian community.

Before the stories in Acts were written down, they were part of an unwritten tradition. The separate episodes first existed in men's minds. When they were told and retold to others, they evidenced

[2]Harnack, *The Acts of the Apostles* (New York: G.P. Putnam's Sons, 1909), pp. 162–202. A summary of Harnack's source criticism is presented by G.H.C. Macgregor, "Acts, Introduction," in George A. Buttrick, ed., *The Interpreter's Bible* (New York: Abingdon Press, 1954), IX, 18. See the excellent work by Martin Dibelius, *Studies in the Acts of the Apostles*, ed. H. Greeven, trans. M. Ling (New York: Charles Scribner's Sons, 1956).
[3]*The Composition and Date of Acts* (Cambridge, Mass.: Harvard Univ. Press, 1916).

the earmarks of selection, alteration, and emphasis for some particular purpose of the church. These separate and self-contained pericopes eventually appeared in Acts. We cannot be certain which pericopes, if any, were first arranged by its author and which had been reduced to writing before they reached him.

Organization If the author of Acts adhered to a precise plan when he wrote his second volume, it has escaped his interpreters. Some have divided Acts into two parts.

a. Peter and the Jerusalem church (1–12).
b. Paul and his mission (13–28).[4]

Other scholars have found four parts in the book of Acts.

a. Birth of the church and Peter's preaching (1:1–8:3).
b. The church, except for the apostles, is driven from Jerusalem. Local church history is alternated with accounts of the beginnings of a world mission (8:4–15:35).
c. The Pauline mission (15:36–21:26).
d. Christianity is defended against Jewish accusations. The Christian message is taken to the world's capital (21:27–28:31).[5]

Still other interpreters have separated Acts into six parts. Each part is concluded by a summary that heralds the triumphal march of Christianity from Jerusalem to Rome—the theme of Acts 1:8: "But you shall receive power when the Holy Spirit has come upon you; and you shall be my witnesses in Jerusalem and in all Judea and Samaria and to the end of the earth."

a. Origin of the church in Jerusalem (1:1–6:6).
   Summary: "And the word of God increased; and the number of the disciples multiplied greatly in Jerusalem, and a great many of the priests were obedient to the faith." (6:7)
b. Diffusion of the church through Palestine (6:8–9:30).
   Summary: "So the church throughout all Judea and Galilee and Samaria had peace and was built up; and walking in the fear of the Lord and in the comfort of the Holy Spirit it was multiplied." (9:31)
c. Expansion of the church of Antioch (9:32–12:23).
   Summary: "But the word of God grew and multiplied." (12:24)

[4]Such a division ignores the facts that Paul's conversion is reported in chapter 9 and the Jerusalem Council is related in chapter 15 after Paul's first missionary journey.
[5]Ernst Haenchen, "The Book of Acts as Source Material for the History of Early Christianity," in L.E. Keck and J.L. Martyn, eds., *Studies in Luke-Acts* (New York: Abingdon Press, 1966), pp. 259–260.

d. Spread of the church throughout Asia Minor (12:25–16:4).
   Summary: "So the churches were strengthened in the faith and they increased in numbers daily." (16:5)
e. Extension of the church to Europe (16:6–19:19).
   Summary: "So the word of the Lord grew and prevailed mightily." (19:20)
f. Expansion of the church to Rome (19:21–28:30).
   Summary: "Preaching the kingdom of God and teaching about the Lord Jesus Christ quite openly and unhindered." (28:31)[6]

A conscious and detailed outline of Acts may not have occurred to its author. What appear to be natural divisions of his book may be due to the character of his sources, and the diverse structuring of his work by modern interpreters may result from the unity and continuity that he imposed on his materials.

Characteristics   Since Luke-Acts has a common author, the two volumes naturally share important characteristics.[7]

They are formal treatises.   The dedication of the volumes to Theophilus might indicate otherwise to the modern reader, but the opposite was true in the ancient world. The preface conforms to the custom for formal rather than for informal writings. The speeches in Acts more closely parallel speeches in Greek and Roman literature than in Biblical writings. The author's interest in chronology also befits a formal document (Lk. 3:1–2).

They stress the work of the Holy Spirit.   The Spirit that manifested itself in the ministry of Jesus made itself felt in an even more pronounced way in the mission of the apostles.[8] The series of guidances referred to in Acts 16:6–10 is especially noteworthy: the apostles were "forbidden by the Holy Spirit" to preach in Asia, but in "a vision" they learned that "God had called" them to go to Macedonia. Supernatural acts characterized the movement from its inception. They attested that God was personally involved in the life and program of the church. Its rapid growth was due to its divinely appointed mission (Lk. 10:1–16; 24:47; Acts 1:8; 2:4–11; 4:28). Those who opposed its advance wrestled with God Himself (Acts 5:39; 12:2; 23).

[6]See C.H. Turner, "Chronology of the New Testament," in James Hastings, ed., *Dictionary of the Bible* (New York: Charles Scribner's Sons, 1898), I, 421; James Moffatt, *An Introduction to the Literature of the New Testament*, 3rd ed. (New York: Charles Scribner's Sons, 1918), pp. 284–285. But what about such summary statements as 2:41 and 11:21?
[7]See pp. 89–90.
[8]Luke 1:15, 35; 2:25–27; 3:22; 4:1, 18; 10:21; 24:49; and Acts 1:2,8; 2:1–4, 38; 8:14–17, 29, 39; 10:44–47; 13:2,4,9; 15:28; 16:7; 19:1–7.

They champion the universal nature of the gospel. The insistence of Volume I that "all flesh shall see the salvation of God" (Lk. 3:6)[9] and its omission of material akin to that found in Matthew that would subvert the idea[10] clearly establish its author's broad concerns. It comes as no surprise, then, to find in his second volume the declaration that "God shows no partiality, but in every nation any one who fears him and does what is right is acceptable to him" (Acts 10:34-35).[11]

They exhibit a supple and varied style. The Synoptic parallels show how the author of the Gospel of Luke polishes and embellishes the language of Mark to a much greater degree than does Matthew. In Acts, which has no parallel, the author demonstrates an uncanny ability to vary his style to suit the situation. When the narrative moves in Palestinian circles, it is steeped in Biblical phraseology derived from the Septuagint. When the author describes Paul's appearance before the Areopagus in Athens, however, he writes like a native Hellene.. Repetition, variation, distribution, and concentration characterize his style.[12]

They advance the idea that Christianity is the legitimate fulfillment of Judaism. Christianity's founder marvelously fulfilled the Scriptures. He was the promised prophet, a descendant of David, the Suffering Servant of Isaiah 53, the Christ. His initial followers faithfully attended synagogue and Temple services, scrupulously honored the requirements of the Scriptures, and were markedly more adept at discerning the import of the Scriptures than were nominal Jews.[13] Jewish misunderstanding of Christianity sprang from a defective grasp of Judaism as God had intended it.[14] What passed for Judaism was a perversion. Corruption had caused historic Judaism to forfeit its privileges; Christianity was the true Israel.

They picture Christianity as politically inoffensive. Jesus approved payment of taxes to Caesar (Lk. 20:25), and he and his followers never advocated revolt against Rome (Lk. 4:5-8; 22:50-53; Acts 21:38-39). Jesus was innocent of the charge of sedition lodged against him (Lk. 23:1-4, 22; Acts 3:13; 13:28), and his principal followers were regularly exonerated whenever they were arraigned in Roman courts (Acts 5:17-42; 16:32-40; 17:9; 18:12-16; 19:35-41). Paul pos-

[9]Compare Luke 2:32; 4:23-27; 10:29-37; 17:15-18.
[10]See Matthew 7:6; 10:5-6; 15:21-28; 18:17.
[11]Compare Acts 13:46-47; 17:26-28; 28:28.
[12]See H.J. Cadbury, "Four Features of Lucan Style," in Keck and Martyn, eds., *Studies in Luke-Acts*, pp. 87-101.
[13]Luke 2:21-24, 27-32, 39-41; 5:14; 17:14; 21:37; 24:25-27, 44-47; Acts 2:46; 3:1; 5:30-31; 13:15; 15:15-17; 17:3; 18:19; 21:20, 26; 22:3-21.
[14]Luke 2:34-35, 38,47; 3:8-9; 4:22-30; 5:21; 6:2-11; 7:30-35; 8:19-21; 10:23-37; etc.; Acts 1:16,20; 2:16-38; 3:13-15; 4:11; 6:11; 8:3; 10:43; 13:17-41; etc.

sessed Roman citizenship, which caused him to be treated with unusual care. He traveled as a prisoner to Rome on his own volition, an innocent man seeking acquittal before the supreme tribunal of the Empire (Acts 25:10–11; 26:30–32; 28:16–20). He was never formally condemned by the Romans (Acts 28:30–31).[15] Whenever Roman officials did take hostile action, it was because of Jewish pressure (Lk. 23:23; Acts 12:2; 24:27). The Jews' own record, of course, was far from spotless. Claudius had expelled them from Rome, and Roman leaders in the provinces generally regarded the Jews as troublemakers (Acts 18:2, 16–17). Their leaders had called for the release of Barabbas in place of Jesus (Lk. 23:19, 25; Acts 3:14–15), contrived the Carpenter's death, and used as an accomplice a Jew whom Jesus trusted (Lk. 22:3, 22). Small wonder! Jesus' accusers, like Judas, had been seduced by Satan. God's repudiation of them was confirmed when their city was destroyed (Lk. 21:20–28; 23:28–31).

They modify the eschatological message of Jesus and his early followers. The clearest illustration of this modification is found in the Gospel of Luke. Mark 13:14 (followed by Matthew 24:15) contains a general prophecy concerning the End: "But when you see the desolating sacrilege set up where it ought not to be . . ." Luke's parallel (21:20) replaces this prophecy with a reference to the historical fact of the fall of Jerusalem: "But when you see Jerusalem surrounded by armies, then know that its desolation has come near." Other passages also underscore the decline in the belief that the kingdom is imminent.[16] Our author, unlike those of Mark and Matthew, repeatedly modifies the eschatological views of the disciples. According to him, the disciples mistakenly supposed that God's kingdom would appear "immediately" (Lk. 19:11). Before the resurrection, they hoped that Jesus would be the one to redeem Israel (Lk. 24:21). Even after that momentous event, the thought lingered: "Lord," they inquired expectantly, "will you at this time restore the kingdom to Israel?" (Acts 1:6). They did not understand that it was necessary that the Christ should suffer and enter into his glory (Lk. 24:26). Neither did they know that the Spirit would be given to the church, and that the church would bear witness to Jesus "to the end of the earth" (Acts 1:8).

While the author of Luke-Acts modifies the eschatological message of Jesus and Paul, he does not erase it. He agrees that the End will come, but he cautions his readers not to be duped by those who declare that "the time is at hand!" (Lk. 21:8). The eschatological

---

[15]The author of Luke-Acts omits any reference to the three occasions when Paul was flogged by lictors. See II Corinthians 11:25.
[16]Compare Mark 13:6 and Luke 21:8.

hope is still alive and an authentic part of the Christian message. The time of the End, however, has been postponed. Final Judgment lies in an imprecise future, and it has ceased to be the primary motivating force. Eschatology has been upstaged by historical development.

The Construction of Acts

Any attempts to recapture the thoughts of the author of Acts as he constructed his second volume must end in frustration. Brief passages exhibit a topical arrangement. Acts 1:8 suggests that the primary principle of organization was geographical: "You shall be my witnesses in Jerusalem and in all Judea and Samaria and to the end of the earth." Some material seems to be grouped around people—Stephen and Philip (6–8), Peter 9:32–11:18; 12:1–17), and Paul (13–28). Perhaps a parallelism between Peter (who dominates much of early Acts) and Paul was intended. When our author recounts the career of Paul, he pays close attention to the sequence of events. Yet Paul's travels are reported in such a way as to minimize his return to places and problems that have engaged him previously. The thrust is forward to new areas of conquest for Christ. In the early chapters of Acts, the author betrays scant interest in chronology. He returns to events already mentioned.[17] When he recounts happenings his first readers could have dated, such as Jewish feasts or changes in political personnel, he does not usually do so for reasons of chronology.[18] His knowledge of Jewish and Roman leaders and the various levels of government is extensive. Centurions, tribunes, proconsuls, procurators, princes, tetrarchs, and high priests are called by name (Acts 4:6; 10:1; 18:2; 23:26). They provide background music and local color, but they seldom serve as reliable signposts for the march of time.

Omissions

Acts is as noteworthy for what it omits as for what it includes. The title, "The Acts of the Apostles," although no responsibility of the author, is grossly misleading. It should read, "Some of the Acts of Some of the Apostles, Mainly of Peter and Paul." Why, except for Peter, do we hear so little about the Twelve? John, James, and Judas are barely mentioned, and the remainder are smothered with silence. Why, except for Philip and Stephen, is the narrative mute concerning the Seven (6:5–6)? Why, except for Barnabas and Paul (Saul), are we told nothing about the Five at Antioch (13:1)?[19] How did Jesus' brother, James, become a Christian? How did he rise to a position

---

[17]Compare Acts 8:1–2 and 11:19–20.
[18]Contrast Luke 3:1–2.
[19]Two names are used to describe Luke's primary hero in Acts. While he is in Palestine, he is regularly referred to by his Hebrew name, "Saul." As soon as he leaves that area, he is customarily called by his Roman name, "Paul." (See Acts 12:25; 13:9, 13.) In the interest of consistency, we shall call him "Paul."

of preeminence in the Jerusalem church? When and how was Christianity introduced into Rome and Alexandria? What was the final fate of the two main characters in Acts, Peter (12:17; 15:7–21) and Paul (28:30–31)? Many minor figures and situations suffer similar neglect.

The author of Acts must have realized that he was leaving out a great deal. His omissions, like his inclusions, may well have resulted from his interests and intentions. Nineteenth-century critics tended to favor this view. They argued that the author's partisan concerns often prompted him to select certain incidents, ignore others, and distort those he used.[20] Modern scholars are more inclined to attribute the shortcomings of Acts as a history of the early church to the limitations imposed upon the author by his sources. To be sure, he was biased; he had special reasons for writing.

Summaries

The early part of Acts consists of a series of detached episodes. The episodes remind us of the independent Synoptic pericopes that deal with healings, parables and other teachings, encounters with critics, and the like. They are self-contained, and they make their own points. The theme-thread that holds them together is the compelling conviction that the power and purpose of God are at work in the world to expand the Christian community. From time to time the void between episodes is filled with a summary statement. The statement sometimes suggests that the previous episode is simply a sample of a much more extensive activity, such as gifts of money from the sale of property (4:34–35).[21] Most of the summaries accent the rapid numerical and geographical growth of the church (2:41; 6:7; 9:31; 11:21; 12:24; 16:5; 19:20; 28:31). All of them facilitate the flow of the narrative and point to the author's awareness of the "omissions" we have mentioned.

Speeches

Over one-fourth of Acts is devoted to speeches attributed to such worthies as Peter, Stephen, James, and Paul. Stephen's reply to his accusers is the longest (7:2–53), and those by Paul are the most numerous and varied. None is intended to represent more than the gist of what was said. Representative speeches are listed below:

Peter:	At Pentecost	2:14–40
	At Solomon's Portico	3:12–26
	Before the Sanhedrin	4:8–12

[20]The so-called Tübingen school of thought and its influence are discussed in F.J. Foakes-Jackson and K. Lake, eds., *The Beginnings of Christianity* (London: The Macmillan Co., 1922), II, 363–395; 408–443. See also Macgregor, "Acts, Introduction," in *The Interpreter's Bible*, IX, 12–13.
[21]Compare Acts 5:42 and 8:25 on preaching.

	At Cornelius' house	10:34–43,47
	To Jewish Christians in Jerusalem	11:5–18
	Before the Jerusalem Council	15:7–11
James:	Before the Jerusalem Council	15:13–21
Paul:	Before the Synagogue in Pisidian Antioch	13:15–41
	At the Areopagas in Athens	17:22–31
	Before the Elders from Ephesus	20:18–35
	Before the Temple	22:3–21
	Before Felix	24:10–21
	Before Agrippa	26:2–29
	Before Jewish leaders in Rome	28:17–20

The speeches are effectively used in Acts. Professor Cadbury has observed that they interpret the narrative in much the same way the chorus does in a Greek tragedy.[22] Sometimes they repeat what has already been said in narrative form, and at other times they introduce novel material. Their aim is to lay bare the ideational content and claims of the Christian community. Some of the recurring themes are listed below.

1. Jesus is a descendant of David (2:30–32; 13:23).
2. John's preaching prepared the way for Jesus' mission (10:37; 13:24–25).
3. The divinely-approved nature of Jesus' ministry is established by the mighty works that he performed through the Holy Spirit (2:22; 10:38).
4. The Jews unwittingly fulfilled the Scriptures and God's plan when they put Jesus to death (2:23, 36; 3:13–15, 18; 4:10; 5:30; 10:39; 13:27–29).
5. God vindicated Jesus by raising him from the dead (2:32; 3:15; 4:10; 5:30; 10:40; 13:30).
6. The ministry of Jesus, as God's exalted Son, continues unhindered, as the presence of the Spirit testifies (5:31; 10:42–43).
7. God has provided for the salvation of the Gentiles (10:47; 11:15–18; 15:7–11; 22:21).
8. All men should repent and accept salvation through the name of Jesus who will one day judge the world (2:38–39; 3:19–21; 4:11–12; 10:34, 42; 17:30–31).

Even a casual examination of the speeches in Acts produces thorny problems. In the speeches attributed to Paul by the author of Acts, Jesus' death merits little importance. It is mentioned merely as proof of human sin. Yet in the letters of Paul, the death of Jesus is the central theme: "Christ died for our sins in accordance with the scriptures" (I Cor. 15:3).[23] His death has saving significance. It is the way of God's grace. Secondly, the speeches of Peter and those of

[22]H.J. Cadbury, "Acts of the Apostles," in George A. Buttrick, ed., *The Interpreter's Dictionary of the Bible* (New York: Abingdon Press, 1962), A–D, 34.
[23]Compare Philippians 2:5–11.

Paul are virtually interchangeable. If the speaker were not identified, it would be difficult to know which one is talking. Such unanimity of thought is astounding in view of sections in Paul's letters that describe relations between the two leaders as less than harmonious. When Peter came to Antioch, he unabashedly ate with Gentiles. When he was pressured by the circumcision party, he refused the Gentiles further table fellowship. His cowardice incensed Paul, who "opposed him to his face, because he stood condemned" (Gal. 2:11). Acts might logically be expected to reflect this sharp disagreement concerning the nature of the Christian faith. Instead, Acts pictures Jewish Christians (including Paul) as loyal to the Law's requirements although Gentile Christians were not expected to observe the Law in toto. Thirdly, both the Synoptics and the letters of Paul make plain the ethical implications of the gospel, but Acts is oblivious to such matters. Neither the theological emphasis nor the terminology of the speeches in Acts coheres with that of Paul in his letters. Although some scholars have attempted to demonstrate the existence of a pre-Pauline kerygma common to Paul and the sermons, their efforts have met with small success.[24]

Must the speeches in Acts be regarded as unhistorical? Not according to the criteria established by Thucydides several centuries before Christ.

As to the speeches that were made by different men . . . it has been difficult to recall with strict accuracy the words actually spoken, both for me as regards that which I myself heard, and for those who from various other sources have brought me reports. *Therefore the speeches are given in the language in which, as it seemed to me, the several speakers would express, on the subjects under consideration, the sentiments most befitting the occasion*, though at the same time I have adhered as closely as possible to *the general sense* of what was actually said.[25]

Even when Thucydides possessed reliable reports of speeches, he made no effort to reproduce them verbatim. Instead he recorded "the general sense" of what was said. Such casual concern for verbal veracity is shocking to literal-minded westerners, but it was standard procedure in that day. The widespread character of the practice is suggested by Polybius, a historian in the second century B.C. He sternly repri-

---

[24]See C.H. Dodd, *The Apostolic Preaching and Its Development in the New Testament* (New York: Harper & Row, 1951) and counterarguments by C.F. Evans, "The Kerygma," *Journal of Theological Studies*, n.s. VII (1956), 25–41.

[25]Thucydides, *History* I, 22, H. J. Cadbury's translation, *The Making of Luke-Acts*, p. 185, italics added. Reprinted by permission of the author. See Paul Schubert, "The Final Cycle of Speeches in the Book of Acts," *Journal of Biblical Literature*, LXXXVII, Part I (1968), 1–16.

manded his predecessors for inventing speeches and argued that historians were obligated to record what was actually said. Josephus, celebrated Jewish historian and contemporary of the author of Acts, reveled in the construction of appropriate speeches. One of them was supposedly delivered just before all the witnesses committed suicide!

We cannot be certain, of course, that the author of Acts followed the literary convention of his day. He may have been in possession of reliable written or oral reports. If this was the case, he thoroughly rewrote them. Scholars are generally agreed that the speeches, in their present form, are compositions of the author. They are written in his style, and they reflect his ideas. Since the speeches attributed to Paul in Acts harmonize with those assigned to Peter (despite the obvious ideological incompatibility of the two) but differ markedly in vocabulary and theology from the letters of Paul, it is reasonable to assume that they are not faithful transcriptions of the apostolic kerygma. They are "historical" only after the manner of Thucydides.

Itinerary and "We-Passages"

More continuity prevails in the latter part of Acts than in the first. As soon as the author begins to relate Paul's campaigns for Christ in Asia Minor and Europe, the reader's attention is riveted on the sequence of events. Paul's arrest and imprisonment, his several hearings, and his transfer to Caesarea and finally to Rome highlight the pattern of progression. The episodic character of the material and the inserted sermons, both features of the first part of Acts, continue. But the uninterrupted character of the account and the presence of a wealth of local detail arouse the suspicion that the author relied on a continuous written source. This suspicion is heightened by the occasional sudden shift from the third person singular to the first person plural. These "we-passages" are four in number: 16:10-17; 20:5-15; 21:1-18; 27:1-28:16. Their contents concern sea voyages. They begin without comment at the point of setting sail, and they end shortly after the party reaches land. Their style and vocabulary do not differ from the "itinerary" material that surrounds them.

The natural and widely held conclusion is that the "we-passages" are excerpts from a diary of one of Paul's companions. Numerous literary parallels can be cited that combine the use of the first person and the third.[26] When Provincial governors, military figures, or travelers made their reports, they often used the first person to stress that they had actually been present at the events being recounted. If the

---

[26]See Eduard Norden, *Agnostos Theos* (Leipzig: B. G. Teubner, 1913), pp. 313-314; Cadbury, *The Making of Luke-Acts*, pp. 144-146.

"we-passages" were lifted from a travel document of one of Paul's associates, the identity of the diarist becomes a matter of prime importance. A strong tradition, traceable back to Irenaeus about 180 A.D., points to "Luke the beloved physician" (Col. 14:4). Who was with Paul at the times and places noted in the "we-passages?" An examination of Paul's letters, it is alleged, demonstrates that Luke was the only one of Paul's companions who was present on every occasion (II Tim. 4:11) Furthermore, if the diarist was a Gentile Christian, as is commonly assumed by his interests, the case for Luke is strengthened. Finally, if the author of Acts had a penchant for medical language, the argument for Dr. Luke's authorship becomes well-nigh invincible.

There are many "ifs" in this line of reasoning. The author of Acts could have simulated the "we" style as a literary device. Another companion of Paul could have written the diary. The theory assumes that Paul wrote Colossians and that he wrote it in Rome, which is probably correct. But the use of II Timothy as a reliable source of information is questionable. The medical language hypothesis has been vitiated by experts.[27] Of the 400 medical terms listed by Hobart, 360 are found in the Septuagint! There is no more reason to suppose that our author was a physician from his use of a technical medical vocabulary than there is to conjecture that he was a sailor from the number of nautical terms found in chapter 27.[28] By far the most damaging argument against Luke's authorship of the "we-passages" (and hence of Acts 16–28 and probably of the whole) is the serious discrepancies that exist between Acts and Paul's letters. The claim that it is possible to associate intimately with another without sharing all of his views is acknowledged. But the differences between Acts and Paul's letters are so numerous and of such a substantial character, as we shall soon see, as to render the claim impotent in this instance. We shall use the name "Luke" to designate the author of Acts, as we did for the Gospel, simply for convenience. In our view, the author of Luke-Acts must be considered anonymous.[29]

Ending and Date Perhaps the most puzzling aspect of Acts is its tantalizingly inconclusive ending. The book is a cliff-hanger comparable to the *Perils of Pauline* but, alas, without a sequel. What happened to its two commanding characters? We hear nothing of Peter after chapter 15. This may be pardonable since the latter half of Acts is devoted to Paul.

[27]See W.K. Hobart, *The Medical Language of St. Luke* (Dublin: Hodges, Figgis, & Co., 1882) and its refutation by H.J. Cadbury, *The Style and Literary Method of Luke* (Cambridge, Mass.: Harvard Univ. Press, 1920).
[28]Macgregor, "Acts, Introduction," in *The Interpreter's Bible*, IX, 8.
[29]Luke's authorship is cogently upheld by Macgregor, "Acts, Introduction," in *The Interpreter's Bible*, IX, 16–21.

But what was Paul's fate? After his appeal to Caesar, he was taken to Rome for trial and remained there for two years. He preached the gospel openly and unhindered to all who came to him. Period! Was he tried, convicted, and executed? Or was he released—making possible a fourth campaign for Christ? If the latter, what was his ultimate end? Luke gives no hint of the final fate of his hero.

Numerous hypotheses have been advanced to explain the abrupt ending of Acts. They indicate, among other things, how little we know about the circumstances out of which the book arose. (1) The author died before his manuscript was finished. A later non-Lukan editor terminated Acts abruptly because his source failed him at that point. (2) The author wrote a brief for Paul's trial which, quite naturally, did not contain the outcome. (3) Paul never came to trial. He was automatically released and the case dropped because his accusers failed to appear in Rome before the statutory limit of two years had expired. (4) Theophilus, to whom Luke-Acts is dedicated, was a Roman official who already knew the results. (5) The author intended to write a third volume that would include the account of the trial, Paul's defense, perhaps other items connected with his years in Rome, and his death. (6) Acts ends abruptly in order not to cloud an apologetic aim of the author. His object was to pacify Roman opinion by showing that Roman authority consistently favored Christianity and its chief propagandist in the Empire. (7) The primary purpose of the author had been achieved. He had successfully chronicled the triumphal march of Christianity from its Judean cradle to the capital of the world.

None of these theories is altogether convincing. Thoughtful counter-arguments have been lodged against all of them.[30] If a satisfactory solution is ever found, it will probably come from a combination of (6) and (7), although (5) remains a live option. In the meantime, hypercurious readers may derive some comfort from Chrysostom, who observed that to know everything makes one sluggish and dull.[31]

The date of Acts is closely connected to that of Luke. If the Gospel was written about 80–85 A.D., as we believe, then a likely date for Acts would be 85–90 A.D.[32]

From Jerusalem to Antioch (Acts 1–12) Acts begins with a picture of Jesus' Galilean followers huddled in Jerusalem awaiting the appearance of the Holy Spirit that their Master

---

[30]See Macgregor, "Acts, Exegesis," in *The Interpreter's Bible*, IX, 351–352, on which our analysis is partly dependent.
[31]*Homilies on Acts*, 55.
[32]See p. 87.

had promised to send (Lk. 24:49; Acts 1:4–5). They numbered about 120 persons, including the Eleven, the women in Jesus' entourage, and his mother and brothers. The first act of the group was to replenish the ranks of the Twelve. They "cast lots" to determine a successor to the traitor, Judas.[33] The lot fell on Matthias, and he was listed with the Eleven (Acts 1:26). He was appointed not as an office-bearer, but rather as one who had witnessed Jesus' ministry and his resurrection. Evidently the disciples wished to preserve the national symbolism inherent in the figure twelve—telltale evidence that they envisaged neither a mission to the Gentiles nor a prolonged postponement of the parousia. The former would sap the symbolism of its significance and the latter would make it impossible to keep intact the number twelve.

The Spirit Energizes the Church (Acts 2:1–42)

Fifty days after the resurrection, Jesus' promise to his disciples was fulfilled. It was the day of Pentecost, the Hellenistic name for the Hebrew Feast of Weeks. They were all assembled in one place.

And suddenly a sound came from heaven like the rush of a mighty wind, and it filled all the house where they were sitting. And there appeared to them tongues as of fire, distributed and resting on each one of them. And they were all filled with the Holy Spirit and began to speak in other tongues, as the Spirit gave them utterance. (Acts 2:2–4)

Pentecost was not the first time that the Spirit had manifested itself. The nativity narratives reveal that the Spirit had been instrumental in preparing the way for Christ's coming. Prophecies proclaimed that John the Baptist would be filled with the Holy Spirit, and the Holy Spirit would cause Mary to conceive and bear a son. Elizabeth was filled with the Holy Spirit when Mary greeted her, as were Zechariah and Simeon before they prophesied (Lk. 1:15, 35, 41, 67; 2:25). The Holy Spirit descended on Jesus at the Baptism, led him into the desert where he was tempted, and guided him into Galilee. Jesus' ministry was Spirit-generated from its inception. At the synagogue in Nazareth, the Carpenter read approvingly from Isaiah: "The Spirit of the Lord is upon me, because he has anointed me to preach good news to the poor" (Lk. 4:18).

The central truth of Pentecost was not the newness of the Spirit but its power—power that would enable those present to "be my witnesses

---

[33]Stones with names inscribed on them were placed in a container and shaken until one fell out. That person was the one God had chosen. The Greek verb used in this instance suggests that voting may have been involved.

in Jerusalem and in all Judea and Samaria and to the end of the earth" (Acts 1:8; 2:1-6). The promise made through Joel was now being fulfilled. God's Spirit would be poured out on all humanity, and whoever would call on the name of the Lord (be he Jew or Gentile) would be saved (Joel 2:28-32; Acts 2:17-21). The miracle of simultaneous translation, called "speaking in tongues" or "glossolalia,"[34] is reminiscent of a Jewish tradition that highlights the divine power that manifested itself when the Law was given at Sinai. The legend asserts that there were seventy tongues of fire on the mountain—one for each language of the seventy nations of the world. The Law, which was entrusted to Israel, seldom served as a light unto the Gentiles. Now, Luke informs his readers, the situation had changed. The power of the Holy Spirit had been manifested to all men. The list of people who heard the Spirit-filled followers of Jesus speaking in their own native languages is intended to cover "every nation under heaven" (Acts 2:5). Ever since the Tower-of-Babel debacle, language barriers had divided men into hostile groups (Gen. 11:1-9). Now they were to be divided no more. The Spirit had enabled all men to hear the gospel each in his own tongue. The possibility of universal salvation was at hand. A new community had been born, and it would soon begin its missionary work (Acts 4:31).

Speaking in tongues was a common phenomenon in the Pauline churches, especially in Corinth (I Cor. 12-14).[35] It consisted of the outpouring of unintelligible sounds under the stress of an overpowering religious emotion. Paul spoke in tongues more than others, and he regarded it as a genuine gift of the Spirit that edified the speaker. Even so, practitioners of the art took calculated risks. Tongue-talk tended to disrupt worship, discourage unbelievers, and stimulate imitation. Consequently, the great apostle placed this gift next to the bottom of his list of charismata, and he urged his readers to concentrate on the higher ones (I Cor. 12:4-11, 31). For those who insisted on speaking in tongues, he offered several rules of conduct: (1) only one should speak at a time; (2) not more than two or three at a meeting; (3) an interpreter should be present; and (4) five understandable words are worth ten thousand words in a tongue (Acts 14:19, 26-28).

The Pentecostal phenomenon, according to Luke, was unique: the tongues spoken by the disciples were foreign languages comprehended by a bewildered and astonished crowd. But this interpretation is almost certainly erroneous. Elsewhere in Acts, glossolalia is mentioned

[34]A transliteration of two Greek words, γλῶσσα (tongue) and λαλεῖν (to speak).
[35]Although speaking in tongues has long been associated with the Pentecostal churches, a renewed interest in the practice has surfaced in such liturgical communions as the Episcopal and Roman Catholic Churches.

in the true Pauline sense. Peter equates the speaking in tongues related in Acts 10:44–47 with his own Pentecostal encounter without any hint of a linguistic miracle.[36] Long before Acts was composed, talking in tongues was known to the Pauline churches. No one thought of it as an instant language course, and Paul made quite a point of its unintelligible nature (I Cor. 14:9, 23). There is no evidence that the apostles ever made use of such a gift in their missionary labors. Indeed, such a gift would have been superfluous, because Koine Greek was almost universally understood. The charge that the disciples were drunk dovetails with known tongue-talk, but it clashes with newly found multilingual skills. Luke evidently took the older and more reliable glossolalia tradition, which stressed the ecstasy of the disciples, and transformed it to suit his theological purpose. He molded and dramatized the historical phenomenon according to the rabbinic tale of the giving of the Law in every language. This set the stage for the world mission of the church.

The Spirit that descended at Pentecost empowered the Christian community to perform its work. When the Jerusalem hierarchy sought to squelch Peter and John, the disciples were heartened by the Holy Spirit to defy the authorities and speak the word of God with boldness (Acts 4:13–31). One of the criteria used to select the seven "deacons" to perform a specialized ministry was that they must be "full of the Spirit" (6:3).[37] Stephen was able to endure death by stoning because he was Spirit-filled (7:55–58). Missionary work among the Samaritans and the Gentiles was validated by the descent of the Holy Spirit (8:17; 10:44). Paul's conversion was confirmed in like manner (9:17). The Spirit selected people to conduct particular campaigns for Christ and altered the itinerary of the evangelists (13:2, 4; 16:7; 19:21). That which taught untutored men to talk in foreign tongues continued to energize and direct them as they achieved God's purpose in the world.

Community of Goods (Acts 2:43–47; 4:32–5:11) One of the first acts of the charismatic community was the joyful and generous sharing of their material possessions. "And all who believed were together and had all things in common; and they sold their possessions and goods and distributed them to all, as any had need" (2:44–45). The Greek verb translated "sold" is imperfect. It indicates continued past action. From time to time, as the need arose, members of the community sold their possessions (real estate) and divided the proceeds among those in want. They distributed their

---

[36]Compare Acts 19:6; I Corinthians 12–13.
[37]See W. Schmithals, *Paul and James*, trans. D. M. Barton (Naperville, Ill.: Alec R. Allenson, 1965), for helpful discussions on this point and regarding Hellenists, Hebrews, deacons, Stephen, and the like.

goods (private possessions) directly. No one selfishly hoarded his resources. "There was not a needy person among them, for as many as were possessors of lands or houses sold them, and brought the proceeds of what was sold and laid it at the apostles' feet; and distribution was made to each as any had need" (4:34–35).

The origins of this community of goods may be found in the teaching of Jesus, the practice of his followers, the expectation of the coming of the End, and the contagious enthusiasm generated by the Holy Spirit (Mk. 10:21; Lk. 8:3; Acts 2:4; 4:31). The communal life of the Essenes, as described by Josephus and the Qumran Scrolls, provides interesting comparisons.[38] Sometimes the Christian phenomenon has been called "communism," but the term is unsuitable even when prefixed by the adjective "Christian." The communal life of the post-Pentecost group was grounded in God and His grace. It concerned consumption only, not the equality of property or production. It was voluntary. The sin of Ananias and Sapphira was not that they withheld part of the proceeds of their land sale. "While it remained unsold," Peter probed, "did it not remain your own? And after it was sold, was it not at your disposal?" (5:4). Their sin was prevarication. They pretended that the part was the whole.

We do not know how extensive the divine experiment was, but it seems very soon to have faded away. The causes of its early demise can be conjectured. Dissension arose between the Hellenists and the Hebrews "because their widows were neglected in the daily distribution" (6:1). The Seven who were chosen to administer the distribution as a result of the dispute were driven from the city (8:1). Perhaps the most decisive factor, however, was the burning belief of the community in the imminent return of Jesus. Their penchant for the parousia prompted them to become improvident. The movement simply ran out of funds.

Signs and Wonders
Acts 3:1–4:31; 5:12–32)

Luke has a special fondness for "miracles" (evidence of God's power and purpose at work in the world), especially those involving healing. He reports that the apostles performed many signs and wonders among the people, and there were added to the Lord multitudes of converts. Witnesses were so impressed "that they even carried out the sick into the streets, and laid them on beds and pallets, that as Peter came by at least his shadow might fall on some of them. The people also gathered from the towns around Jerusalem, bringing the sick and those afflicted with unclean spirits, and they were all healed" (5:15–16).

[38]Josephus, *Wars*, II, 8, 3–4; *Manual of Discipline* 1:12; 5:2; 6:3, 19, 22; 7:25.

One day Peter and John were headed for the Temple at the midafternoon hour of prayer. When a man lame from birth accosted them and asked for alms, Peter responded, "I have no silver and gold, but I give you what I have; in the name of Jesus Christ of Nazareth, walk" (3:6). Then the apostle took the lame man by the hand, his feet and ankles were strengthened, and he leaped up and walked into the Temple praising God. The spectators were astonished, and the Temple officials were annoyed.

On another occasion, the jealousy-laden religious leaders arrested the apostles because of their healing activities and put them in the common prison. At night an angel of the Lord released them and commanded them to stand in the Temple and speak to the people. The apostles entered the Temple at daybreak and taught. When the Sanhedrin dispatched officers to the prison to fetch the apostles, they found the prison securely locked, sentries standing at the doors—but no apostles! When the apostles were finally found in the Temple, they were brought before the Sanhedrin and reminded that they had been strictly charged not to teach in Jesus' name. The apostles countered with the ringing declaration that they must obey God rather than men (5:12–32).

Some scholars have taken such signs and wonders with a grain of salt, but wholesale skepticism is surely unwarranted. Luke had a demonstrable talent for magnifying the miraculous aspects of the tradition, but he did not make them all up out of whole cloth.[39] Jesus not only proclaimed the good news of the kingdom; by deeds he proved that God's promises were being fulfilled. His exorcisms signaled Satan's fall from heaven, and his healings demonstrated the immediacy of God's presence and power. Jesus was truly a man "attested to you by God with mighty works and wonders and signs which God did through him" (2:22). These signs and wonders were performed not only by Jesus, but also by his disciples and the church through the agency of the Spirit.[40]

The Seven (Acts 6:1–6) As the number of disciples increased, dissension arose between the Hellenists and the Hebrews. Both groups were zealous Jews, but they differed in their attitude toward Greek culture. The Hellenists, who had returned to Jerusalem after living abroad, had accommodated to their former surroundings. The Hebrews, on the other hand, had remained loyal to the customs of their forefathers.[41] The crux of

[39]Compare Mark 5:23 and Luke 8:42; Mark 5:40 and Luke 8:53.
[40]Acts 4:16, 30; 5:12; 6:8; 14:3; I Corinthians 12:9–10, 28; II Corinthians 12:12; Galatians 3:5; Hebrews 2:4.
[41]Cadbury's claim, in Foakes-Jackson and Lake, eds., *The Beginnings of Christianity,*

the dispute concerned the daily distribution of public assistance in the form of a common meal or the giving of alms. The Hellenists claimed discrimination against their widows. The Twelve solved the problem by summoning the congregation. They informed those assembled that it was not right for their leaders to forego preaching the word of God to serve tables. They urged the brethren to select seven men of good reputation, full of the Spirit and of wisdom, whom the Twelve could appoint to this duty. The idea was happily accepted, and the Seven were soon chosen. All bore Greek names, suggesting that they were somehow supposed to safeguard the interests of the Hellenists. Only Stephen and Philip are subsequently mentioned. The Seven were initially appointed to be in charge of the menial aspects of the community's life. Very soon, though, they are depicted knee-deep in evangelistic work. Tradition tabs them as the first "deacons" ("servants" or "assistants"). By the time Luke wrote, such an order did exist (Phil. 1:1). They assisted the bishops in the conduct of the Lord's Supper, the maintenance of discipline, and the administration of alms. But there is no evidence that deacons performed these advanced functions in Jerusalem near the natal day of the church. Stephen (Acts 6:7–7:60) and Philip (Acts 8:4–40) are accorded prominence rivaling that of the apostles. The distinction between the Seven and the Twelve is no longer one of rank and function but of spheres of influence. The Seven do for the Hellenists precisely what the Twelve do for the Hebrews. It would appear that Luke has altered traditional material in such a way as to italicize two convictions. The division between Jewish and Gentile Christians sprang not from deep-seated differences but from divine direction. The Jerusalem community enthusiastically endorsed the preaching of the gospel to non-Jews. The account of Stephen, which follows, discloses a third conviction of the author: Stephen's death was no accident. It was a divinely planned happening to influence Paul. It prepared the zealous persecutor of the Christian community for the decisive role he was to play as God's foremost apostle to the Gentiles.

The First Christian Martyr (Acts 6:8–8:3)

The fascinating story of Stephen is not without its problems. There seems to be little connection between the great wonders and signs that Stephen performed among the people and the disputation that follows. The real source of the acrimonious debate seems to stem from Stephen's militant missionary message delivered in the Hellenistic synagogues. Strange repetitions also characterize the narrative. Both the charge against Stephen and the stoning are stated twice (6:9–11 and 6:12–14; 7:54–58a and 7:58b–7:60). These doublets

---

V. 59–60), that Hellenists were Hellenes (Greek Gentiles) is untenable. Would Luke have introduced them into his account so early and so casually? Later he focuses the spotlight on Cornelius as the first Gentile convert and views him as the crucial point in the Christian missionary enterprise.

suggest that the material was derived from two different sources. According to one account, Stephen was hastily lynched by an infuriated mob (6:9–11; 7:54–58a). According to the other, he was duly tried by the Sanhedrin and executed (6:12–7:53; 7:58b–60). The insertion of a judicial trial scene into the more primitive account, with a consequent shifting of the guilt for Stephen's murder from the mob or the Romans to the Jewish leaders, is altogether congruent with Luke's purpose.

Stephen's entire speech, like the other speeches in Acts, is the free composition of Luke. No direct or convincing answer is made to the charges. The lengthy account of God's gracious treatment of Israel is capped by evidence of her ingratitude. No mention is made of Christ. The climax of Israel's history is reached in the construction of Solomon's Temple! The Old Testament record is freely altered and supplemented. It is small wonder that scholars have attacked the speech's historicity. It would be difficult to devise a more irrelevant defense.

As Stephen neared death, he prayed for his enemies as Jesus had done before him. When he "fell asleep," devout men of the Jews buried him. His career had been brief. His preaching, as presented by Luke, made it clear that the Christian community had already burst the bounds of sectarian Judaism. The Law stood in deadly peril. Its subverters were not the Christians but their critics.

Paul "consented" to Stephen's death (8:1). In the persecution that followed, he "laid waste the church, and entering house after house, he dragged off men and women and committed them to prison (8:3). But did he? Several times he shamefacedly confessed that he had violently persecuted the church of God, but he never indicated that he had done so in Jerusalem (Gal. 1:13, 23; I Cor. 15:9; Phil. 3:6). Galatians suggests that Damascus was the center of his hostile activity. The apostles (and presumably other indigenous Christians) were permitted to remain in Jerusalem while the persecution raged, but the Hellenists were driven in diverse directions. Probably most of them returned to their former homes and sowed the seeds of a more extensive mission. We do not know how long the persecution prevailed. Three years after Paul's conversion (Gal. 1:18),[42] Peter and James (and doubtless other Jewish Christians) were still in Jerusalem. About a decade later, the community was sufficiently numerous to provide Herod Agrippa with an opportunity to curry favor with the Jews by

---

[42]Or is Paul counting the three years from his return to Damascus?

killing James, son of Zebedee and brother of John, and putting Peter in prison (12:1–3).[43]

Philip, the Evangelist
(Acts 8:4–40)

Philip, who heads the list of the Seven, was the first to penetrate non-Jewish territory on behalf of the church. His Hellenistic background made him a natural for a mission to people who occupied a halfway house between the Jewish and the Gentile world. Although the rabbis permitted social intercourse with the Samaritans, the prevailing cold war generally prompted Jews to regard Samaritans as mixed-breed heretics.[44] Philip's initiative indicates a concern beyond normal expectations. Multitudes responded to his words and works. Many were healed, and much joy pervaded the Samaritan city. As Philip preached the good news about the kingdom of God, converts presented themselves for baptism. Among them was one named Simon, a former magician smitten with messianic notions.

When the Jerusalem apostles heard that Samaritans had accepted the word of God, they dispatched Peter and John to the scene. The two prayed that the neophytes might receive the Holy Spirit since they had merely been baptized in the name of Jesus. The Spirit came when the apostles laid their hands on them. Simon was so impressed that he offered to pay money for the privilege and power. Thus the sin of "simony" was born, and it provoked Peter's scathing denunciation.

The entire incident is couched in concepts of a later age. Luke pictures authority as centralized in an apostolic college without whose sanction no undertaking was permissible. The Holy Spirit was communicated to converts only through the apostolic rite of the laying on of hands, a privilege Philip presumably could not exercise. But it is highly questionable that the apostles ever supervised the entire church and its respective parts. Nor was the gift of the Spirit channeled through a particular office, class of men, or specific rite. Luke himself provides proof in other passages. A common disciple called Ananias laid his hands on Paul in order that he might receive the Holy Spirit (9:17). The Spirit fell on Cornelius and his companions prior to baptism or the laying on of hands—just as it had fallen on Peter and others at Pentecost (10:44; 11:15).[45]

[43]For a more comprehensive treatment of the text in Acts, see Macgregor, "Acts, Exegesis," in *The Interpreter's Bible*, IX, 23–107, to which we are indebted.
[44]See p. 45.
[45]Compare Acts 2:4.

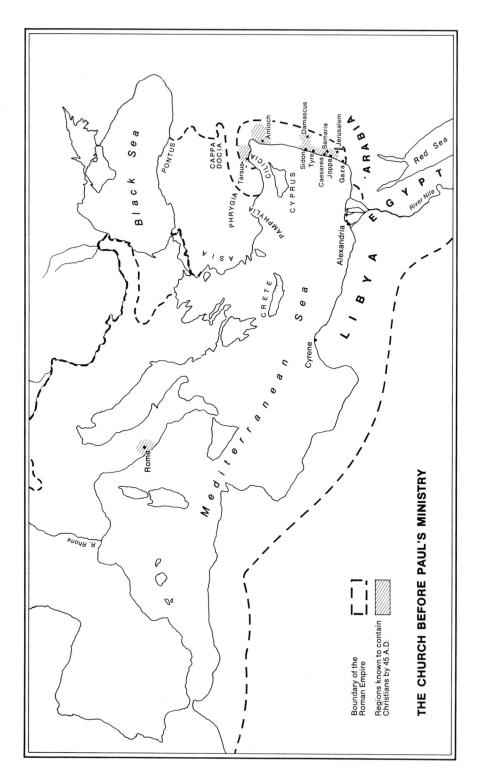

Boundary of the
Roman Empire

Regions known to contain
Christians by 45 A.D.

THE CHURCH BEFORE PAUL'S MINISTRY

Black Sea

PONTUS

CAPPA
DOCIA

PHRYGIA

Tarsus

CILICIA

PAMPHYLIA

ASIA

CYPRUS

Antioch

Sidon

Tyre

Caesarea

Joppa

Gaza

Damascus

Samaria

Jerusalem

ARABIA

Red Sea

EGYPT

River Nile

Alexandria

LIBYA

Mediterranean Sea

CRETE

Cyrene

Rome

R. Rhone

After his Samaritan campaign, Philip headed south toward Gaza. He soon overtook an Ethiopian eunuch who served as Secretary of the Treasury for his queen, Candace. According to the Law, a eunuch was excluded from "the assembly of the Lord," but the prophetic attitude was considerably more charitable (Deut. 23:1; Isa. 56:3–5). Since this eunuch was a pilgrim returning from Jerusalem and was reading from Isaiah, he was doubtless a Jewish proselyte. The Spirit prompted Philip to join the chariot, and the evangelist proceeded to interpret for the Ethiopian the Suffering Servant passage of Isaiah 53 as a prophecy concerning Jesus Christ.[46] When the two came to some water, the eunuch's request for baptism was honored. The Spirit then whisked Philip away, and the evangelist continued to preach the gospel "to all the towns" until he reached his home at Caesarea-by-the-Sea (8:40; 21:8).

Conversion of Paul
(Acts 9:1–31)

The story of the Ethiopian eunuch, like the preceding account of Philip's Samaritan campaign, has been modified by Luke to serve his purpose. It prepares the reader for the Gentile mission that begins in earnest with the conversion of Cornelius.

Acts pictures Paul as a member of the Jewish dispersion, a native of Tarsus in Cilicia, and a Roman citizen (21:39; 22:28). Tarsus was a commercial center and the seat of a famous "university" that some scholars suggest Paul may have attended. From Tarsus, he was sent to Jerusalem to study in the rabbinical schools. His major mentor there was the celebrated Gamaliel (22:3).[47] Paul consented to Stephen's death and zealously participated in the persecution that arose against the church. He was so bent on badgering Christians that he secured letters from the High Priest to the synagogues at Damascus. As Paul approached the Syrian city, he encountered the risen Christ. The experience transformed the fanatical rabbi from persecutor to campaigner, convinced him of the gospel, and placed him among the witnesses to the resurrection.

Luke provides us with three versions of Paul's conversion (9:3–30; 22:6–21; 26:12–23). Although they are in general agreement, they do differ concerning significant details. Did Paul's companions hear the voice (9:70 or did they not (22:9; 26:14)? Did they see "no one" (9:7), "the light" from heaven (22:9), or nothing (26:13–14)? How did Paul receive his call to be an apostle to the Gentiles? In 9:3–18, no specific call is issued to him. He is simply told to go to Damascus, where he will receive instructions. There the announcement about Paul's future is made not to him but to Ananias. In 26:16–18, the

---

[46]This is the first time that Isaiah 53 is specifically quoted as a Christian proof text.
[47]Compare Acts 5:34–39.

The House of Ananias in Damascus. The reported relationship between Ananias and Paul can be found in Acts 9:10–19; 22:12–16.

commission is given directly to Paul by the risen Christ. In 22:21, the revelation is connected with a later vision while Paul is in a trance in the Temple. The decisive role played by Ananias in chapters 9 and 22 is curiously absent from Paul's personal account in Galatians, and it is hard to harmonize with Paul's claim that he was an apostle "not from men nor through man, but through Jesus Christ (Gal. 1:1, 11–12).

After Paul's conversion and baptism, Acts indicates that he immediately proclaimed Jesus as the son of God in the Damascus synagogues. Such a bold thrust into the enemy camp by a turncoat taxes credulity. If Jewish leaders in Damascus had been given authority to turn over Christians to Paul, they would not have permitted him to preach unhindered the faith he had come to persecute. After "many days had passed," a Jewish plot to kill Paul prompted "his disciples" to lower him over the city wall at night in a fish basket. No mention is made of Paul's prolonged sojourn in Arabia and subsequent return to Damascus, which the apostle succinctly records in Galatians 1:17. Instead, he journeyed to Jerusalem and attempted to join the disciples. They were horrified at the thought of welcoming to their ranks so powerful an opponent until Barnabas vouched for him. Then Paul preached boldly in the name of the Lord and disputed with the Hellenists before the brethren hustled him down to Caesarea and sent him off to Tarsus.

Accounts of Paul's first visit to Jerusalem are difficult to reconcile. Whereas Paul declares that it occurred "three years" after his conversion, Luke telescopes the time to "many days" (Gal. 1:18; Acts 9:23). Paul states under oath that he saw none of the apostles (except Peter and Jesus' brother, James), that he was in the Holy City for only fifteen days, and that he was not known by sight to the churches of Christ in Judea (Gal. 1:22). Nothing is said of the intervention of Barnabas, and Luke's claim that Paul joined the Jerusalem apostles and preached boldly in the city is as mystifying as Paul's previously alleged behavior in Damascus. Some scholars attribute the discrepancies to Paul's desire to establish the immediate and independent nature of his apostleship. While this view may have some merit, there is a more likely explanation. Luke wrote at considerable distance from the events described, and he had little knowledge of the details. He filled in the picture as best he could in harmony with his apologetic purpose—that from the very beginning peace prevailed between Paul and the Twelve, and the Twelve approved the Gentile mission.

Initial Gentile Missions (Acts 9:32–11:30)

Peter at Lydda and Joppa. As Peter moved among the people, he came to Lydda, located between Jerusalem and the coastal city of Joppa. There he encountered a man named Aeneas, a paralytic who had been bedridden for eight years. Peter healed Aeneas in the name of Jesus Christ, and all the residents of Lydda and the plain of Sharon turned to the Lord.

Tabitha, a Joppa disciple noted for her good works and acts of charity, fell sick and died. Since Lydda was near Joppa, Peter was summoned. He dispersed the mourners, prayed, and commanded Tabitha to rise. She opened her eyes, saw Peter, and sat up. He presented her alive to the saints and widows. When the restoration became known throughout Joppa, many believed in the Lord. Peter stayed in Joppa for many days at the house of Simon, a tanner.

These miracles bear a striking resemblance to others featured in the Old and New Testaments. The healing of Aeneas recalls Jesus' cure of the paralytic, and the resuscitation of Tabitha resembles the raising of Jairus' daughter and the mighty works of Elijah and Elisha (Lk. 5:18–26; 8:41–42, 49–56; I Kings 17:17–24; II Kings 4:32–37). Whatever their basis in fact, Luke's purpose in recording these wonders is evident. He wants to make plain that the cures performed by Peter are simply a continuation of the miraculous activity of Jesus Christ in the age of the church.

Conversion of Cornelius. Although the Cornelius episode is followed by more material than precedes it, it stands at the center of the book of Acts in the purpose of its author.[48] Its significance lies not only in the claim that Cornelius was the first case in which the gospel was heard and received by an uncircumcised pagan, but also in the affirmation that God placed his seal of approval on this novelty by bestowing His Spirit on the new believers. From this point on, interest is focused on the gospel's success among the Gentiles, first in the cities of Asia Minor and then in Europe. Every step along the way is guided by divine direction or disapproval.

Luke emphasizes the importance of the Cornelius story by the adoption of a literary device common in epic writing: he tells the tale twice! The centurion's vision is repeated by Cornelius himself when Peter arrives at Caesarea (10:3–6; 30–32). The narrative of Peter's housetop experience is chronicled again in detail by Peter in his own defense (10:9–23; 11:4–14). Lest anyone miss the point of Peter's emancipating vision and Cornelius' conversion, God's approval is affirmed (10:44), reaffirmed (10:45), and placed in question form to refute potential critics of the practice of evangelizing Gentiles: "Can any one forbid water for baptizing these people," Peter inquires, "who have received the Holy Spirit just as we have?" (10:47) When the Jerusalem apostles heard that Gentiles had received the word of God, they listened to objections from the circumcision party and to Peter's explanation. Then they glorified their Creator because "to the Gentiles also God has granted repentance unto life" (11:18).

Perhaps the most surprising notion advanced in connection with the incidents at Lydda, Joppa, and Caesarea is the initiative attributed to Peter in pioneering the Gentile missions. This is an honor usually reserved for Paul. Paul claimed that God had entrusted him with the gospel to the Gentiles just as Peter had been entrusted with the gospel to the Jews (Gal. 2:7). If Peter's Joppa vision had convinced him that there was no distinction between kosher and nonkosher food, why did he vacillate concerning this verity at Antioch (Gal. 2:11–13)? If the dispute concerning the admission of Gentiles to the Christian fold had been settled affirmatively in the case of Cornelius, then what was the point of the later Jerusalem Summit Conference (Acts 15; Gal. 2)? Once again Luke seems to have used his material to further the idea that there was really no conflict between the Pauline and Petrine parties within the church.[49]

Barnabas and Paul in Antioch. This celebrated city, seat of the imperial legate of the province of Syria and Cilicia, ranked next to Rome

[48]See Ernst Haenchen, *Die Apostelgeschichte* (Göttingen: Vandenhoeck & Ruprecht, 1959), pp. 305–308.
[49]For a contrary view, see Macgregor, "Acts, Exegesis," in *The Interpreter's Bible*, IX, 132–133.

and Alexandria in the Roman Empire. Strategically situated on the Orontes, with a port at Seleucia, Antioch was a bustling commercial center. Greek by culture, predominantly Syrian by population, it contained a large Jewish colony. In the dispersion that resulted from the death of Stephen, devotees of Jesus traveled as far as Phoenicia, Cyprus, and Antioch speaking the word only to Jews. Some men from Cyprus and Cyrene, however, arrived at Antioch and addressed Greeks as well. Many that believed turned to the Lord. When the Jerusalem church heard the news, it promptly dispatched Barnabas to the scene. He was not an apostle, but he was imbued with apostolic authority. He rejoiced at what he saw and exhorted the new converts to remain faithful. Just as Philip's preaching to the Samaritans had been confirmed by Peter and John, and Peter's conversion of Cornelius had been approved by the Jerusalem apostles, so now a new and more momentous mission to the Gentiles was scrutinized and sanctioned by Barnabas. Luke wants his readers to realize that at each step in the rapidly expanding thrust of the Christian enterprise the innovators bore the imprimatur of Mother Church (8:14–17; 11:18, 22–24).

The success of the Gentile mission in Antioch prompted Barnabas to travel to Tarsus in search of Paul. The two returned to Antioch where for a whole year they met with the church and taught a large company of people. In Galatians, Paul makes no mention of this long and fruitful association with Barnabas. At Antioch for the first time the disciples were called "Christians." When a Jerusalem prophet named Agabus arrived and predicted that a great famine would engulf the world, a prediction which came to pass in the days of Claudius, the disciples determined to send relief to the brethren who lived in Judea. This they did by Barnabas and Paul.

Herod's persecution of Christians. Herod Agrippa I (41–44 A.D.), grandson of Herod the Great, was reared in Rome and enjoyed close contact with the imperial family. When Caligula rose to power, he bestowed the title "king" on his friend and made him tetrarch of Philip's territory northeast of Galilee. Soon Caligula added the tetrarchy of Herod Antipas, and Claudius subsequently included Judea and Samaria. Agrippa then left Rome for his new domain where he feigned great zeal for the formalities of the Jewish faith in order to secure the favor of his subjects. He laid violent hands upon some who belonged to the church, and he killed James, son of Zebedee and the brother of John.[50] When Agrippa saw that his behavior

---

[50]The prophecy of Mark 10:39, a statement by Philip of Side in the fifth century, two early martyrologies that commemorate the death of James and John on the same day, and silence concerning a later residence of the apostle John in Ephesus furnish cumulative evidence that John perished with his brother, James.

pleased the Jews, he had Peter arrested and securely placed in prison. "An angel of the Lord" engineered Peter's nocturnal escape to the disbelief and astonishment of those who were praying for his release (Acts 12:7–11). Agrippa sentenced the sentries to death, and he soon suffered a similar fate at the hands of an angel. Barnabas and Paul completed their relief mission to Jerusalem and returned to Antioch with John Mark.

Jerusalem Summit Conference (Acts 15; Gal. 2)

After effective evangelism in Antioch, Barnabas and Paul were set apart to represent the church in a larger mission. The two, accompanied by John Mark, sailed to Cyprus. The voyage marked the beginning of what is commonly called Paul's first missionary journey. At Paphos the conversion of the proconsul, Sergius Paulus, was effected. John Mark returned to Jerusalem from Perga in Pamphylia, and Paul and Barnabas continued their compaign for Christ in southern and central Asia Minor. In each community (according to Acts but not according to Paul's letters) they preached first to the Jews. The strategy was not only natural and convenient, but it was also "necessary" that the word of God be spoken to them before others. When opposition developed, Paul and Barnabas turned to the Gentiles (Acts 13:46; Rom. 1:16). At Pisidian Antioch, Iconium, Lystra, and Derbe they made many disciples. As they retraced their steps, they appointed "elders" in every church.[51] Finally they returned to Syrian Antioch, assembled the church that had dispatched them on their mission, and reported how God had opened a door of faith to the Gentiles. They remained with their fellow Christians at Antioch for no little time (Acts 13–14).[52]

Not everyone was pleased with the work of Paul and Barnabas. Certain men from Jerusalem, commonly called "Judaizers" because of their viewpoint, came to Antioch and insisted that Gentile converts to Christianity should be circumcised. They held that circumcision was the sign of membership in the covenant community and the condition of God's promised blessings. Whether they were free-lance or official inspectors is not stated. After considerable dissension and debate, Paul and Barnabas (among others) were appointed to go to Jerusalem to thresh out the question with the apostles and elders.

Acts 15 vs. Galatians 2

The "conference" described in Acts 15 appears to be the same one mentioned by Paul in Galatians 2. The issue in both instances is

---

[51]"Elder" does not appear in any of Paul's authentic writings. It is unlikely that he established a formal church organization supervised by regularly ordained "elders" at this time. Those "appointed" were probably senior converts to whom junior ones were to show deference. See I Corinthians 16:16; I Thessalonians 5:12–13.
[52]The literary purpose of Paul's "missionary journeys" is unquestioned, but most scholars deny their historicity.

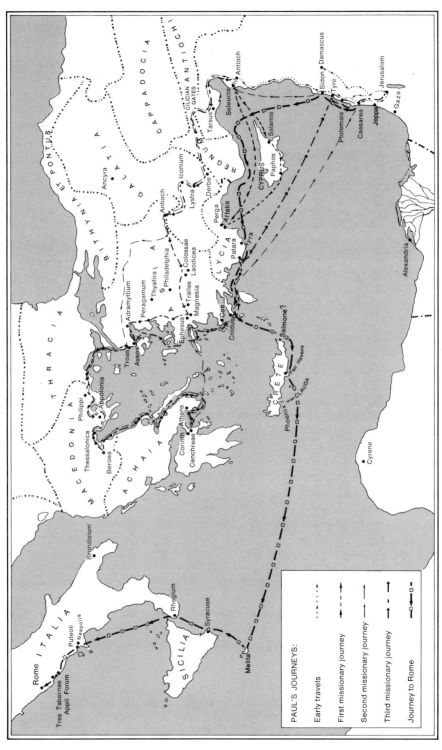

THE JOURNEYS OF PAUL

PAUL'S JOURNEYS:

Early travels	··········
First missionary journey	⟵---
Second missionary journey	⟶
Third missionary journey	⟵--
Journey to Rome	⟵□□□

the grounds of admission of Gentile converts to the Christian community. Should Gentile Christians be subject to circumcision? The answer in both accounts is no. Beneath the surface of the two reports, however, significant differences can be detected. According to Acts, all of "the apostles and the elders" were gathered together for a public and formal debate on the question. The Jerusalem Christian community was present and heard the decisions that were handed down by the leaders of the apostolic circle (Acts 15:6–21). According to Paul, the Jerusalem meeting was a private affair. Presumably only Peter, James (Jesus' brother), and John were present (Gal. 2:2.9). No mention is made of Titus in Acts, but he is present in Paul's account (Gal 2:1). According to Acts, Paul had visited Jerusalem at least twice before—once following his conversion (9:26) and again with relief for the famine-stricken Judean brethren (11:29–30),[53] Paul, on the other hand, makes it perfectly clear that the conference visit was only the second time that he had been in Jerusalem since his conversion (Gal. 1:17–18; 2:1).

More crucial than the public or private nature of the conference, the composition of the participants and spectators, and the frequency of Paul's visits to Jerusalem is the outcome of the discussion. On this subject Acts and Galatians are at even greater odds. Acts indicates that the opposing parties agreed that four restrictions should be imposed on Gentile converts. They should abstain from : (1) meat that had been sacrificed to idols; (2) unchastity; (3) meat that had been strangled; and (4) meat that contained blood.[54] Except for "unchastity," a sin to which previous pagans were particularly prone, these apostolic decrees concerned forms of unclean food that offended Jewish sensitivities. In Galatians, however, Paul paints a radically different picture of the conference's conclusions. He makes no mention of the restrictions found in Acts 15:20.[55] On the contrary, he vigorously declares that he did not yield even for a moment to those who sought to subvert the freedom of the gospel by imposing the obligations of the Law on Gentile converts. When the leaders of the Jerusalem church saw that Paul had been entrusted with the gospel to the Gentiles and Peter had been entrusted with the gospel to Jews, they extended to Paul and Barnabas the right hand of fellowship. The only obligation that the two assumed was the taking up of a collection on behalf of the poor in the Jerusalem community. This was not a legal requirement but an act of charity and compassion. Paul evi-

---

[53]Some manuscripts of Acts record a third visit in Acts 12:25.
[54]The third restriction, omitted by a number of Western authorities, refers to the same kind of food as the fourth. A strangled animal (considered a delicacy in pagan society) was forbidden to Jews because the meat contained blood, the seat of life. See Genesis 9:5; Leviticus 3:17; Deuteronomy 12:16, 23–25.
[55]Stranger still, he does not refer to them when he is later compelled to deal with the question of eating food offered to idols at Corinth. See I Corinthians 8.

dently realized that if the position of the Judaizers prevailed, Gentiles would be forced to become Jews before they could become Christians and the church would remain a stunted Jewish sect. Such an accommodation of the Christian message to the works-righteousness concept of Judaism was unthinkable—it would rob the cross of its meaning. If salvation were to be achieved by obedience to the Law, "then Christ died to no purpose" (Gal. 2:21).

Suggested Solutions How can the conflicting claims concerning the nature and outcome of the Jerusalem Summit Conference be reconciled? Several solutions have been suggested.

Acts 15 and Galatians 2 describe the same conference from different viewpoints. The Acts account is based on Jerusalem sources; Galatians represents Paul's personal witness. This theory may seem sound on the surface, but it is burdened by many handicaps. The discrepancies between the two accounts are not simply subjective; they are substantive—so flagrant as to compel one to question either the historicity of Acts or the honesty of Paul. If Paul had agreed to the apostolic decrees reported in Acts 15:22–30 (which were circulated in an encyclical), how could he write to the Galatians that the only obligation imposed by the Jerusalem leaders was that "they would have us remember the poor" (Gal. 2:10)? Would not his acceptance of the decrees have invalidated his Galatians argument? His opponents would have had only to produce the encyclical to which he had subscribed. Perhaps they did not do this because they could not do it, since there is no evidence that such a document ever circulated among the Gentiles. And how could the church at Antioch rejoice at restrictions placed on Gentiles that it had no intention of keeping (Acts 15:31)?

Galatians 2 describes the famine-relief visit of Acts 11:27–30.[56] This hypothesis voids the need to reconcile the conflicting claims of Acts 15 and Galatians 2. It also relieves Paul and Luke of the respective charges of dishonesty and ignorance of the facts. Paul did not mention the formal council described in Acts 15, it is argued, because that meeting had not yet taken place when he wrote Galatians. The thorn in this thesis is sharp and painful. The theory assumes that Galatians is the earliest of Paul's surviving letters. Yet Galatians is a soul brother of Romans, a work assuredly written toward the close of Paul's life. Hans Windisch dubs the identification of Galatians 2 and Acts 11

[56]Acts records three postconversion visits of Paul to Jerusalem: (1) the acquaintance visit of 9:26; (2) the famine relief visit of 11:27–30; and (3) the conference visit of 15:2. Galatians reports only two visits: (4) 1:18 and (5) 2:1. Unquestionably visits (1) and (4) are the same. The first solution given above equates (3) and (5), while the second solution equates (2) and (5).

"a clever and convenient exit," which he proceeds to block.[57] Even an enthusiastic sponsor of this theory is forced to acknowledge that it is not yet commonly accepted.[58]

Luke modified the account of the Jerusalem Conference in order to advance his apologetic interests. By the time he wrote, Jerusalem had fallen, both Jews and Christians had been driven from the city, and James, leader of Jewish Christians of the Law-abiding type, was dead. The question of Gentile obedience to the Law, a burning issue in Paul's letters, was passé. It had been resolved in favor of freedom. Luke glossed over such early conflicts and concentrated on the growing consensus that prevailed in the church of his day. Consequently his version of the Jerusalem Conference muted the clash between the right and left wings of the early church and showed instead how differences had been settled and unity obtained. We consider this third solution the most likely one.

The Nature of Luke-Acts

Luke as an Historian

Our discussion of Luke-Acts has at many points called into question Luke's reliability as a historian. When the word of God came to John the Baptist, Caiaphas was the only High Priest—not Annas *and* Caiaphas as Luke mistakenly reports (Lk. 3:2). Jesus could not have been born "in the days of Herod, king of Judea," who died in 4 B.C., *and* at the time of a census under Quirinius, governor of Syria, in 6 A.D. (Lk. 1:5; 2:2). The nonchronological and "rhetorical" nature of much of Luke's material is revealed in his account of Jesus' journey to Jerusalem. The evangelist uses this occasion to include data of various sorts, the bulk of which is devoid of precise time and place indications and may well belong elsewhere (Lk. 9:15–18:14). The speeches in Acts reflect Luke's style and thought and represent his free composition. Luke attributes a reference to a revolt by Theudas to Gamaliel, speaking before 36 A.D. According to Josephus, this revolt did not occur until after 44 A.D.[59] Luke also indicates that the revolt by Theudas happened prior to one by Judas of Galilee, who perished at the time of the census in 6–8 A.D. (Acts 5:36–37). The conversion of Cornelius, described as a centurion of the Italian Cohort, is placed during the reign of Herod Agrippa I when no Roman troops were stationed there (Acts 10:1; 12:1). The suspicion arises that Cornelius is a stock figure patterned after the anonymous centurion of Luke 7:1–10. The expanded version in Acts is designed to show how the Jerusalem church was responsible for the Gentile mission. Luke constantly reads into the record notions of his own time—such as the statement that Paul and Barnabas appointed "elders" in various churches (Acts 14:23; 20:17, 28).

[57]See Foakes-Jackson and Lake, eds., *The Beginnings of Christianity*, II, 321–322.
[58]Macgregor, "Acts, Exegesis," in *The Interpreter's Bible*, IX, 198–200.
[59]*Wars*, II, 8, 1; VII, 8, 1; *Antiquities*, XVIII, 1, 1; XX, 5, 1–2.

The parts of Acts that deal primarily with Paul provide information in sharp contrast to that found in his letters. A few illustrations will suffice.

Acts	Letters
Paul's home is Tarsus in Cilicia (22:3).	Paul's home seems to be Damascus. He was converted near there, and he returned there after his Arabian sojourn (Gal. 1:17).
Paul studied in Jerusalem under the celebrated rabbi, Gamaliel (22:3).	Paul was not in Jerusalem as a youth (Gal. 1:22). His exegesis was not essentially rabbinic, and his writings reflect a lifelong acquaintance with the Septuagint.
Paul spearheaded opposition to the Christian community in Jerusalem (9:1–2).	Paul was not known by sight to the Jerusalem church (Gal. 1:22).
The Jerusalem Conference was a public affair. "The apostles and the elders" were assembled for a formal debate. It marked Paul's third visit to the Holy City since his conversion. No mention is made of Titus (9:26; 11:29–30; 15:6–21).	The Jerusalem Conference was a private affair. Only Peter, James, and John were present. It marked Paul's second visit to the Holy City since his conversion. He and Barnabas were accompanied by Titus (Gal. 1:17–18; 2:1, 3, 9).
At the Jerusalem Conference, Paul accepted four restrictions on the admission of Gentiles into the Christian community (15:19–20).	At the Jerusalem Conference, Paul did not yield to the Judaizers "even for a moment." He did not accept a single legal obligation, but he did agree to raise funds to assist the Jerusalem poor (Gal. 2:4–10).

Luke's reliability as a historian is further tarnished by the irreconcilable differences that exist between Paul's theology as expressed in his letters and that attributed to him in Acts. Paul claims to have waged a vigorous and unrelenting anti-Jewish polemic against the Law, but Acts pictures him as law abiding—the true representative of Israel who confronts the hardhearted officials of Judaism. All traces of the Christology of preexistence, so central for Paul in Philippians 2, are missing in Acts. Nowhere in Acts is it stated that Christ died for our sins, yet this concept is paramount in Paul's thought. Acts removes eschatology from the core of Paul's faith and places it on the periphery. In his letters, Paul views Christ's death as having saving significance and his resurrection as the advent of the New Age. Salvation is by the redemptive event here and now. Acts, on the other hand, sees no saving significance in Jesus' death. His resurrection initiates a third stage in the history of salvation, the age of the church.[60]

Luke as a Theologian   Luke was regarded primarily as a historian prior to 1950. Then a sudden shift in sentiment occurred. New Testament specialists, long

[60] See Philipp Vielhauer, "On the 'Paulinism' of Acts," in Keck and Martyn, eds., *Studies in Luke-Acts*, pp. 33–50.

preoccupied with such perplexing problems as the quest for the historical Jesus, form criticism, and the place of Paul in the development of Christianity, began to focus their attention on Luke-Acts. This two-volume work became a veritable storm center of scholarly debate. In 1953, Ernst Käsemann declared that the appearance of Acts as a sequel to Luke's Gospel meant that a great change had taken place. An author does not write the history of the church if he expects the end of the world at any moment.[61] Hans Conzelmann's monumental work, *Die Mitte der Zeit*, appeared in 1954.[62] Another landmark, Ernst Haenchen's *Die Apostelgeschichte*, a penetrating commentary on Acts, soon followed.[63]

Conzelmann's book received immediate and influential recognition. His study led him to the conclusion that Luke wrote not primarily as a historian but as a theologian. Luke divided the history of salvation into three periods. Although he dealt directly only with the second and third, his two volumes frequently point back to the first and beyond the third to the End of the Age.

From Ancient Israel to John the Baptist. Both Matthew and Luke preserve a saying of Jesus based on *Q*. In Matthew's version, the more original of the two, John the Baptist marks the *beginning* of the new era of violence that foreshadows the coming of the kingdom (Mt. 11:12–13). Luke telescopes and modifies the *Q* saying in such a way as to show that John marks the *end* of the period of the Law and the prophets: "The law and the prophets were until John; since then the good news of the kingdom of God is preached, and every one enters it violently" (Lk. 16:16). God gave to Israel, through the prophets, the promise of salvation. The promised deliverance did not occur, however, until the second stage of salvation-history arrived.

The ministry of Jesus. The second period is the central one. The promise of salvation, fulfilled in the words and works of Jesus, is completely present and effective on earth. Luke divides Jesus' ministry into three parts. The first part begins with Jesus' inauguration at the synagogue in Nazareth. After he reads the words of promised redemption from the prophet Isaiah ("good news to the poor," "release to the captives," "sight to the blind," and "to set at liberty" the op-

---

[61]Käsemann's paper appears in English as "The Problem of the Historical Jesus," in *Essays on New Testament Themes*, trans. W.J. Montague, *Studies in Biblical Theology*, vol. XLI (London: SCM Press, 1964).

[62]The title translated means "The Mid-Point of Time." The English translation of the book is *The Theology of St. Luke* (New York: Harper & Row, 1960). Our brief outline of Conzelmann's thought is indebted to it.

[63]See footnote 49. For a helpful treatment of the history of recent Luke-Acts investigations, consult W.C. van Unnik, "Luke-Acts, A Storm Center in Contemporary Scholarship," in Keck and Martyn, eds., *Studies in Luke-Acts*, pp. 15–32.

pressed), he declares, "Today this scripture has been fulfilled in your hearing" (Lk. 4:16–21). The second part of Jesus' ministry concerns the preaching of the gospel outside the land of Galilee (Lk. 9:52), and the third takes place in Jerusalem (Lk. 19:1, 11, 28).

From the ascension to the parousia. The ascension, reported only by Luke, introduces the third period in the history of salvation—the Age of the Church and its mission to the world. Christ is seated at God's right hand waiting to judge all men at the End of the Age (Acts 2:33; 3:20–21; 10:42; 17:31). Until then, God's work in the world is accomplished by the church under the leadership of the Spirit. The message of salvation, fulfilled in Jesus' ministry, is spread from Jerusalem to all nations in order that all who will may believe in the name of Jesus. It does not matter how long the Day of Judgment is delayed. The church mediates the redemption realized in the ministry of Jesus until the End comes with the parousia of Jesus. Then salvation will once again be immediately present on earth.[64]

Each of the periods of salvation is a separate entity. The time of expectancy ends with John, the time of Jesus ends with the ascension, and the time of the church ends with the parousia. Yet each succeeding period is a continuation of the previous one and builds upon it. The history of salvation is one uninterrupted movement in which God's plan for His creatures is historically realized.[65]

Conzelmann pointed out that this threefold time-scheme was necessitated by the historical situation in which Luke lived. First-generation Christians had expected the End of the Age in the immediate future. They did not have the slightest notion that between the ministry of Jesus and the End there would lie a historical period of indefinite duration. But in Luke's day the continuation of the world was an established fact. Luke saw the theological significance of this unexpected turn of events, and from it he drew two conclusions: (1) the history of Jesus belonged to the past; and (2) Christians must take into account the possibility that the End would not arrive before a long period of time had elapsed. Consequently, Luke composed his Gospel as a history of Jesus, and in his second volume he put that history into the mouths of the apostles as the core of their preaching

[64]Conzelmann is correct when he concludes that for Luke the midpoint of time is the ministry of Jesus. Käsemann, on the other hand, believes that Luke viewed the Age of the Church as the midpoint of time. See his *"Neutestamentliche Fragen von heute,"* Zeitschrift für Theologie und Kirche, LIV (1957), 1–21.

[65]For a critique of Conzelmann's threefold time-scheme for Luke, see Helmut Flender, *St. Luke: Theologian of Redemptive History* (Philadelphia: Fortress Press, 1967) and Fred O. Francis, "Eschatology and History in Luke-Acts," *Journal of the American Academy of Religion,* XXXVII, Part 4 (1969), 49–63.

of salvation. At the same time, he perceived that the post-Jesus period had its own special meaning. It was the period in which the church carried the story of Jesus to all mankind. The writing of Acts as a sequel to the Gospel of Luke was a theological breakthrough of the first magnitude. Luke thereby placed the ministry of Jesus at the midpoint of time and underscored the existence of the church as a world-wide witness to that history as the completed redemption of God. At one fell swoop he solved the problem of the delayed parousia and placed early Christian eschatology on the periphery of the full history of salvation.

Acts as a Source Book Acts provides us with nearly all of the information we have about the beginnings of the church. It also furnishes additional data about Paul that cannot be gleaned from his letters—such as his residence in Tarsus and his education under Gamaliel. If we could accept Acts as a reasonably reliable historical record, our sources for the study of the early church and Paul would be considerably enhanced. But we are prevented from doing this by the predominantly theological character of Luke-Acts and the sharp disagreements that exist between the accounts in Acts and those in the letters of Paul. While Acts may not be wholly worthless as a historical source, it must be used with considerable caution. Where Acts and Paul's letters conflict, preference must be given to Paul's personal and primary witness. Where Acts cannot be checked by Paul's letters or other reliable sources, the information it provides may well be cited. It must not be assumed, however, that in these instances Acts reproduces history unadorned. As a theological treatise, Luke-Acts knows no peer. It furnishes the framework for understanding the Age of the Church in the long-range purpose of God. For the early history of the church, where it can be recovered at all, we must turn to Paul and his letters. These first-hand sources are admittedly woefully inadequate. Where possible, they will be judiciously supplemented by Luke's second- or third-generation testimony. Before we deal with the letters, however, we shall continue our study of the remainder of Acts.

IX

**The Age of the
Church**
([Luke-] Acts
16–28)

Paul and Barnabas parted company, according to Acts, prior to the
second campaign for Christ.[1] Luke attributes their estrangement to
a disagreement concerning Mark. Barnabas wanted Mark to accompany them, but Paul objected to taking "one who had withdrawn
from them in Pamphylia, and had not gone with them to the work"
(Acts 15:38). But the root cause doubtless lay deeper than this. Paul
had rebuked Peter and Barnabas at Antioch for shrinking from table
fellowship with Gentiles (Gal. 2:11–21). Perhaps Barnabas still had
reservations about joining Paul on a new mission to found churches
that would be completely free from Jewish legal obligations. If so,
the dispute about Mark merely ruffled feelings that were already
strained. In any case, Barnabas took Mark and sailed for Cyprus.
Paul chose Silas (Sylvanus) as his companion and went through Syria
and Cilicia strengthening the churches.

When Paul and Silas reached Lystra, retracing in reverse the first
missionary journey, they found a convert called Timothy. He was
the son of a Jewish woman who had become a Christian, but his
father was Greek. Paul wanted Timothy to accompany him. In order
to avoid needless antagonisms, Paul circumcised Timothy "because
of the Jews" (Acts 16:3). This seems like strange behavior on the
part of one who vigorously defended Gentile freedom at the Jerusalem
Summit Conference and who wrote to the Galatians, "If you receive
circumcision, Christ will be of no advantage to you" (Gal. 5:2). But
Timothy was not a Gentile. Judaism traced membership in the covenant community through a man's mother, and Timothy's mother was
Jewish when he was born. The case was not comparable to that of
Titus, who was a Greek (Gal. 2:3). Paul sacrificed no principle in
the circumcision of Timothy, and the deed served to maximize his
usefulness. It provided Timothy with a valid passport to the Jewish
synagogues en route.

[1]For details of the first campaign, see p. 228.

Acts does not mention Paul's visit to Iconium and Pisidian Antioch on this journey, but these cities are probably covered by the phrase "the region of Phrygia and Galatia" (16:6).[2] Luke was more interested in the pioneering work that led to the founding of new churches than in the subsequent development of established congregations. References to the Holy Spirit and the Spirit of Jesus prohibiting the evangelists from entering Asia and Bithynia respectively are intended to show that the mission to Macedonia was conceived by God. It had priority over any plans that Paul and his companions had concocted.

Philippi (Acts 16:11–40)
When the evangelists reached Troas, a man from Macedonia appeared to Paul in a vision and invited him to come to Macedonia.[3] The invitation was accepted as the call of God, and Paul and his party set sail for another continent. The first conversion in what is now called Europe occurred at Philippi. Some women had gathered on the Sabbath at a place of prayer by the river where ceremonial washings could take place. Paul addressed the congregation, and a woman named Lydia responded and was baptized together with her family and slaves.

On the next Sabbath, as Paul and his companions were going to the place of prayer, they were met by a mad slave girl. Insanity fascinated the ancients. They believed that the gods had stolen the sanity of such people in order to make them their spokesmen. When the deranged girl persisted in annoying Paul, he healed her. Her owners were horrified at the loss of the girl's commercial value. They seized Paul and Silas, dragged them before the local authorities, and lodged charges against them. The missionaries were beaten, cast into the inner prison, and their feet were placed in the stocks. About midnight, while they were praying and singing hymns, all of the prisoners were liberated by an earthquake. The jailer, who would forfeit his life if any prisoners escaped, was about to commit suicide. When Paul assured him that all had remained, the jailer asked what he must do to be saved. Paul seized the opportunity to tell him about the Lord Jesus, and the jailer and his family were baptized. When daylight arrived, the magistrates dispatched police to release Paul and Silas, but Paul insisted that the magistrates themselves perform this function. It was not wounded pride that prompted him to make the demand. He and Silas were Roman citizens who had been publicly beaten and imprisoned without a trial. For the sake of the gospel

---

[2]We shall discuss the North and South Galatians theories in connection with Paul's letter to the Galatians.
[3]Some scholars conjecture that the man was Luke who subsequently wrote Acts. See Wm. Ramsay, *St. Paul the Traveller and the Roman Citizen* (London: Hodder & Stoughton, 1896), pp. 200–201.

and the Philippian Christians, it was important that these wrongs be righted.[4]

Thessalonica and Beroea (Acts 17:1–15) Paul spent three weeks in the synagogue at Thessalonica explaining that it was necessary for the Christ to suffer and to rise from the dead. Some of the congregation were persuaded that Jesus was the Christ. They joined Paul and Silas as did many devout Greeks and leading women. This aroused the hostility of the Jews. They incited a crowd to attack the house of Jason, who was sympathetic to the Christian cause. When they could not find Paul and his companions, they hauled Jason and some of the brethren before the city authorities. Jason was accused of harboring men who acted against the decrees of Caesar and proclaimed that there was another king, Jesus. The authorities exacted a bond from Jason and the brethren (which would be forfeited in the event Christians caused any further trouble) and let them go. Then the brethren immediately sent Paul and Silas away by night to Beroea.

A reconstruction of the Acropolis at Athens. In prehistoric times the steep crags of the Acropolis (high place of the city) afforded a stronghold and place of refuge for the Athenians. Later it became a religious sanctuary. Persian invaders destroyed the shrines in 480 B.C. Pericles' decision to rebuild them about mid-century happliy coincided with the time of Greece's greatest artistic accomplishments. The Parthenon, which dominates the Acropolis, was named for the virgin goddess, Athena. It is often heralded as the most perfect product of Athenian art. On its left is the Erechtheum with its famous Porch of the Maidens. [Courtesy of Agora Excavations, Athens.]

[4]The details of Paul's escape from prison recall that of Peter's in chapter 12.

A Reconstruction of the Interior of the Parthenon, Athens. Religious ceremonies and public worship were conducted at altars outside the temples. The interiors were used for private prayers. There were two interior rooms. The cella, divided into three aisles by a double order of colonnades, was dominated by a 39-foot gold and ivory statue of Athena, the work of Phidias. In the square tetrastyle room to the rear was the treasure store of the goddess. Among other valuables, it contained the Persian Xerxes' silver-footed throne. [Courtesy of Historical Pictures Service—Chicago]

The evangelists enjoyed an enthusiastic reception at Beroea. The Jews received the word with eagerness and searched the Scriptures to see if the Christian claims were true. Many of them believed, including Greek men and women of high standing. But when Jews from Thessalonica learned that Paul proclaimed the word of God at Beroea, they arrived posthaste and incited the crowds. Paul was sent off to the sea at once. On the way to Athens, he doubtless saw two of the greatest glories of Greece. Majestic Mount Olympus, fabled home of the gods, dominated the Gulf of Thessalonica and much of the

Aegean Sea. As Paul approached Athens, the breathtaking Acropolis came into view. This highest point in the city was crowned by clusters of glistening marbled splendor that included the incomparable Parthenon, perhaps man's most perfect architectural creation, and the Erectheum, with its celebrated Porch of the Maidens. Those who had conducted Paul to Athens returned to Beroea with instructions to send Silas and Timothy to him as soon as possible.

Athens (Acts 17:16–34) First-century Athens was the seat of a famous university and a mecca for intellectuals, but the heyday of its literary and political creativity was a distant though proud memory. There were innumerable reminders of former accomplishments, of course, but cultural leadership had boarded ship and set sail across the Mediterranean for Alexandria. Although Paul may have been properly impressed by the glories of Greece, he had not come to Athens to take a refresher course at the university. According to Acts, he divided his time between the synagogue and the marketplace. The six acres of open market, called the *agora*, were cluttered with altars and monuments to a legion of deities. The original square was surrounded by colonnades and buildings in which the full range of Athenian public life (commercial, political, social, and cerebral) was carried on. Some of Paul's agora auditors were Epicurean and Stoic philosophers who were curious as to what "this babbler" would say. Others thought he was a preacher of "foreign divinities" because he spoke of Jesus and the resurrection. They reasoned from their pagan perspective that, like Isis and Osiris,

A Fluted Column of the Temple of Jupiter, Athens.

The Areopagus. While Paul was in Athens, according to Acts 17:22, he addressed the Athenians from the rocky foreground depicted in this picture. The place is sometimes called "Mars' Hill," but its real name is the Hill of Ares (Areopagus).

"resurrection" (*anastasis*, feminine) was a female deity and "Jesus" (masculine) was her consort! Paul's preaching was sufficiently exciting that he was taken before the judicial council that was charged with keeping order in the agora. It is uncertain whether the court met at this time in one of the chambers near the agora or in the open air atop the Hill of Ares (Areopagus).

Paul began his address to the council with a clever and ear-catching reference to the acute interest in religion Athenians evidenced by their many objects of worship. He was particularly impressed by an inscription on one altar to an unknown god. "What therefore you worship as unknown," he continued, "this I proclaim to you" (17:23). Scholars have been quick to note that neither the style nor content of this sermon coheres with what we find in Paul's letters. The familiar phrase, "In him we live and move and have our being," smacks of Stoic pantheism (17:28).[5] It pictures God as a kind of world-soul

[5]The phrase is commonly attributed to Epimenides, the semilegendary Cretan.

that permeates everything. "For we are indeed his offspring" was also apparently a stock Stoic quotation (17:28).[6] It endorses a notion repugnant to Paul—that man is by nature akin to God. The apostle sharply contrasted man's fleshly nature and the spiritual nature of the Father. Clearly the speech is a free creation of the author of Acts.[7] He saw Paul's appearance at Athens as an event of world-shaking significance. At the Areopagus, Christianity confronted the quintessence of pagan culture. The meeting and resultant rivalry were destined to continue for many centuries and shape the history of the Occidental world.[8]

Paul's emphasis on judgment and the resurrection of the dead soon alienated most of his audience. A handful of people did join him and believe, but the results of his mission proved to be ephemeral. Paul referred to the household of Stephanas, not these Athenians, as "the first converts in Achaia" (I Cor. 16:15), and no reference is made in the New Testament to a Christian church in Athens.

Corinth (Acts 18:1–22) When Paul arrived in Corinth from Athens, he stayed with Aquila and his wife, Priscilla—Jews who had recently been expelled from Rome by Claudius. Suetonius states that Claudius dispersed the Jews because they had created disturbances at the behest of "Chrestus."[9] It is possible that these disturbances were sparked by the arrival in Rome of Christian preachers who provoked dissension among the Jews. If so, Aquila and Priscilla may have heard the gospel and become devotees of Christ before they arrived in Athens. This would explain why Paul did not refer to them as his first converts in Achaia.

Corinth was a bustling commercial center by virtue of its location between two seas with a port on each. Its cosmopolitan population was decidedly syncretistic in its religious interests. The mystery cults, especially the one centered not far away at Eleusis, enjoyed great popularity.[10] Temples to Isis and other Oriental deities were numerous. Outside the city, a huge rock nearly 1,900 feet high hid the horizon. The rock was called Acrocorinth, and on its top had been constructed a temple in honor of the Hellenic goddess of love

[6]The quotation is from the *Phaenomena* of Aratus.
[7]See Hans Conzelmann, "The Address of Paul on the Areopagus," in L.E. Keck and J.L. Martyn, eds., *Studies in Luke-Acts* (New York: Abingdon Press, 1966), pp. 217–229. The substantial historicity of the speech is defended by Bertil Gärtner, *The Areopagus Speech and Natural Revelation* (Uppsala, Sweden: C.W.K. Gleerup, 1955), pp. 248–252, and G.H.C. Macgregor, "Acts, Exegesis," in George A. Buttrick, ed., *The Interpreter's Bible* (New York: Abingdon Press, 1954), IX, 231–232.
[8]See Martin Dibelius, "Paul on the Areopagus," in *Studies in the Acts of the Apostles*, ed. H. Greeven, trans. M. Ling (New York: Charles Scribner's Sons, 1956), pp. 26–77.
[9]See p. 72.
[10]See pp. 16–17.

and beauty, Aphrodite. Since the Greeks often identified Aphrodite with the wantonly sensual Phoenician deity, Astarte, bane of the Hebrew prophets, the temple served as a center for Astarte worship in the first century. According to the chronicler, Strabo, a thousand sacred prostitutes practiced their profession at the hilltop shrine and attracted a steady stream of pilgrims. It is not surprising that in the ancient world "to live like a Corinthian" was synonymous with "debauchery."[11] Paul wrote at least four letters to the Christian community in Corinth. When we examine the contents of I and II Corinthians in chapter 10, we shall discover that even the church was infected with a virulent case of immorality.

Acrocorinth. On the summit of Acrocorinth was a temple of Aphrodite, the Hellenic goddess of love. By the first century A.D. it served as a center for the worship of Astarte, the sensual Phoenician deity.

Paul may not have intended to remain long in Corinth. He was still awaiting the arrival of Silas and Timothy. Perhaps he expected them to bring word that he was once again welcome in Macedonia. When they did appear, they found him proclaiming to the Jews that the Christ was Jesus. Opposition from the Jews and, perhaps, discouraging news from Silas and Timothy caused Paul to transfer his activities to the house of Titius Justus next door to the synagogue. There he remained for eighteen months, teaching the word of God to the Gentiles. When Gallio became proconsul in 51 A.D., the Jews made a

[11]See Macgregor, "Acts, Exegesis," in *The Interpreter's Bible,* IX, 239.

united attack upon Paul, brought him before the tribunal, and charged him with persuading people to worship contrary to the Law. They presumably thought that a new official would want to win their favor, but Gallio saw through their trumped-up charge and refused to be intimidated. He declined to pass judgment on a religious squabble. This public snub of the Jews encouraged the onlookers to vent their spleen on Sosthenes, the ruler of the synagogue, but Gallio paid no heed.

A Synagogue Stone at Corinth. Some scholars date this stone from the time of Paul.

Sometime during Paul's stay in Corinth, if our calculation is correct, he wrote I and II Thessalonians. Many days after the Gallio episode, he took leave of the brethren and set sail for Syria. Priscilla and Aquila accompanied him as far as Ephesus, where Paul argued with the Jews in the synagogue. Then he sailed to Caesarea, went up to Jerusalem to greet Mother Church, and then went down to Antioch.

Mission to Asia (Acts 18:23–21:26)

After Paul had spent some time in Antioch, he departed on what is usually referred to as his third missionary journey. He went through the region of Galatia and Phrygia "strengthening all the disciples" (18:23). At this point Luke interrupts the narrative to inform his readers about an Alexandrian Jew named Apollos who had come to Ephesus.

Apollos at Ephesus and Corinth (Acts 18:24–28)

Apollos was an eloquent man, trained in rhetoric and philosophy, and well versed in the Hebrew Scripture. He had been instructed in the way of the Lord, and he taught accurately the things concerning Jesus. His only deficiency, from the Christian viewpoint, was that "he knew only the baptism of John" (18:25). This cryptic statement leaves much to conjecture. It probably means that Apollos was aware that both John and Jesus had preached about the coming judgment, the End of the Age, the necessity of repentance and ethical living, but he did not know that Jesus was the Christ, that people were baptized in his name, and that they experienced the power of the Holy Spirit. When Priscilla and Aquila, Corinthian Christians whom Paul had left in Ephesus, heard Apollos speaking boldly in the synagogue, they took him aside and expounded to him the way of God more accurately. Then Apollos knew not only the Jesus of history but the Christ of faith. Armed with the full gospel, he expressed the desire to go to Achaia. The brethren encouraged him and wrote to Achaian Christians to receive him. When he arrived at Corinth, he rewarded his hosts by powerfully confuting "the Jews in public, showing by the scriptures that the Christ was Jesus" (18:28). From the account in I Corinthians, however, it would seem that Apollos' major preaching took place before the intellectual Greek section of the community. His eloquence, erudition, and experience with the sophisticated allegorical teaching techniques of Alexandria made Paul appear to be a minimind and sparked serious splits in the Christian community. Some claimed to belong to Paul, others to Apollos, and still others to Christ (I Cor. 1:10–13; 2:1–3:4). Apollos himself probably acted innocently, and Paul apparently bore him no grudge. "What then is Apollos? What is Paul?" he asked the Corinthian Christians. "Servants through whom you believed, as the Lord assigned to each. I planted, Apollos watered, but God gave the growth" (I Cor. 3:5–6).

Paul at Ephesus (Acts 19:1–41)

While Apollos was at Corinth, Paul passed through "the upper country" and came to Ephesus.[12] This large seaport was a commercial and religious center of considerable importance. Its location at the western end of the great trade route to the Euphrates guaranteed prosperity. It was the seat both of the Roman proconsul and of the confederation of cities called the "Asiarchate." Emperor worship was promoted by the "Asiarch," the provincial high priest of the imperial cult, and a coterie of subordinates. The inhabitants boasted of such civic virtues as a commodious stadium (which catered to athletic events, gladiatorial combats, and contests with wild animals) and a 24,000-seat theater. Their principal pride, though, was showered on the temple of Artemis, Greek goddess of the moon and the chase, called "Diana" in Latin. The great marble temple, one of the Seven Wonders of the World, was built in the middle of the sixth century

[12]Devotees of the North Galatians theory interpret "the upper country" (19:1) as a reference to the northern coasts of Galatia proper, but a more likely meaning is that Paul traveled across the high ground west of Pisidian Antioch rather than along the lower road through Colossae and Laodicea.

B.C. From the few fragments which remain, archeologists have estimated that the octagonal structure measured about 180 by 360 feet. Gold rather than mortar is said to have held its marble blocks together. One hundred and twenty-seven pillars, sixty feet in height, had drums six feet high and twenty feet in circumference. Each drum was graced with eight life-size sculptured figures. An inner chamber, called the "cella," was about seventy feet wide and open to the skies.[13]

Paul spent from two to three years in "the Light of Asia," as Ephesus was popularly known.[14] When he encountered about a dozen "disciples" who were devoid of the Holy Spirit because they had experienced only "John's baptism," he baptized them in the name of the Lord Jesus. The apostle then laid his hands upon them, and they received the Holy Spirit. Proof of the Spirit's presence was supplied when they spoke with tongues and prophesied. A three-month stint in the synagogue followed. Paul spoke boldly about "the kingdom of God," but some rejected his message. When the disbelievers spoke evil about "the Way" before the congregation, Paul and his disciples withdrew to the hall of Tyrannus, where he argued daily for two years. So extensive was his preaching that "all the residents of Asia heard the word of the Lord" (19:10).[15]

Extraordinary miracles are attributed to Paul at Ephesus. Handkerchiefs and aprons taken from his body were placed on the sick, and the diseases and devils departed. When certain traveling Jewish exorcists attempted to use the name of Jesus to accomplish the same ends, they were rebuffed by the evil spirits. The demoniac overpowered the exorcists and caused them to flee away naked and wounded. Fear fell on the residents of the city, and the name of the Lord Jesus was extolled. Many new believers confessed that they had practiced magical arts. Others assembled and burned over ten thousand dollars' worth of documents inscribed with magical spells and charms, designed to insure such things as safe journeys and success in love and business. "So the word of the Lord grew and prevailed mightily" (19:20).[16]

After these events Paul resolved, under divine guidance, to pass through Macedonia and Achaia and go to Jerusalem. Acts is silent

[13]See Jack Finegan, "Ephesus," in George A. Buttrick, ed., *The Interpreter's Dictionary of the Bible* (New York: Abingdon Press, 1962), E–J, 114–118; C.M. Cobern, *The New Archeological Discoveries* (New York: Funk & Wagnalls, 1917), pp. 468–470.
[14]See Acts 19:8–10; 20:31.
[15]Here "Asia" may mean only the environs of Ephesus, but usually the term in the New Testament refers to the Roman province in Asia Minor.
[16]Note the marked similarity between the kinds of miracles ascribed to Paul in Acts 19:11–12 and to Peter in 5:12–16. Luke is intent on demonstrating the power of Jesus' name and the superiority of Christian exorcism to its rivals in Acts 19:13–20.

concerning his primary motivation for the trip, which was delivery of the collection for the support of the poor saints in the Holy City (Rom. 15:25). When this had been accomplished, he intended to visit Rome. Meanwhile, he had dispatched Timothy and Erastus to Macedonia, but he tarried in Asia for a time. During the long Ephesian mission and the visit to Macedonia, complications had arisen with the church at Corinth. Paul wrote I and II Corinthians in an effort to resolve the situation. A Letter to the Galatians probably also originated in this period.

A riot was precipitated in Ephesus by Paul's persuasive preaching. The city was the guardian of the popular pagan goddess, Artemis. The magnificent marble temple that had been erected in her honor attracted pilgrims from far and wide and small silver images of the deity were sold. When Paul proclaimed that "gods made with hands are not gods" (19:26), he threatened the very structure of Ephesian society. The triple drives of patriotism, religion, and self-interest closed ranks, and a silversmith named Demetrius was galvanized into action. He called a "union meeting" and declared, "There is danger not only that this trade of ours may come into disrepute but also that the temple of the great goddess Artemis may count for nothing, and that she may even be deposed from her magnificence, she whom all Asia and the world worship" (19:27).

The craftsmen responded with predictable rage and affirmed their loyalty to Artemis. Confusion reigned in the city. The inhabitants rushed to the theater, dragging with them two of Paul's traveling companions. Most of those present did not know why they had come together. When a certain Alexander attempted to speak, he was recognized as a Jew. For about two hours the people cried out, "Great is Artemis of the Ephesians!" (19:34). Only the intervention of the town clerk quieted the crowd and prevented a more serious melee. His speech reveals once again Luke's interest in the relation of the church to Roman civil authority: "For you have brought these men here who are neither sacrilegious nor blasphemers of our goddess" (19:37).

Return to Jerusalem (Acts 20:1–21:26)

When the uproar at Ephesus subsided, Paul departed for Macedonia. After he had visited and encouraged the churches established there on his second journey, he came to Greece (probably to Corinth), where two events marked his three-month stay. He wrote a letter to "all God's beloved in Rome" (about which Luke is curiously silent), and a Jewish plot against him was uncovered as he was about to set sail for Syria. No motive for the plot is mentioned. Paul had for some time been collecting a fund for the poor saints in Jerusalem (I Cor.

16:1-4; II Cor. 9:1-5; Rom. 15:25-29). Perhaps his antagonists planned to murder him on the high seas and make off with the money. In any case, the plot prompted Paul to alter his plans and return through Macedonia. The detour prevented him from realizing his ambition to arrive in Jerusalem in time for Pentecost (19:21; 20:16). It did, however, enable him to collect a company of companions on the way. The seven mentioned in Acts 20:4 were probably delegates chosen by local churches to carry their contributions to the Holy City. Their presence with Paul not only demonstrated the essential unity of the church, but it also proved that Paul had not promoted the collection for his personal benefit.

The most unusual incident during the return to Jerusalem occurred at Troas. On the first day of the week, Paul spoke to those who had gathered to break bread. There were many lights in the upper chamber, and a young man named Eutychus sat in the window. Paul prolonged his speech until midnight. Eutychus sank into a deep sleep, fell from the third story, and was taken up for dead. Paul dashed down to the ground level, bent over Eutychus, embraced him, and declared, "Do not be alarmed, for his life is in him" (20:10). Once again Luke assures his readers that God's power over life and death, which manifested itself through Jesus, was also at work through the apostles.

Paul and his party made several stops along the western coast of Asia Minor. Because Paul was eager to reach Jerusalem for Pentecost, they sailed past Ephesus and landed at Miletus. From there the apostle summoned the elders of the church at Ephesus. When they arrived, he delivered a touching talk. He stressed the special privilege and responsibility of church leaders, humbly reminded them of the trials he had endured while preaching among them, and shared with them two premonitions: he would never see them again, and the church would be plagued with discord and false teachings after his departure.[17]

At Tyre (and later at Caesarea) disciples sought to dissuade Paul from going up to Jerusalem. Perhaps they had heard about a plot to kill the apostle. If so, they ignored the pragmatic approach and appealed to the authority of the Holy Spirit. Paul either doubted their inspiration or regarded their dour declarations as the Spirit's way of testing his faith. In either case, he was not deterred. From

---

[17]The first premonition makes Paul's subsequent release from Roman imprisonment unlikely. Luke would not have recorded the premonition if it had not been fulfilled. The second premonition also came to pass if I Timothy 1:3-7 is authentic.

Tyre, he and his companions sailed to Ptolemais. After a day with the brethren, they departed for Caesarea where they were the guests of Philip the Evangelist and his four unmarried daughters. When some days had elapsed, the Jerusalem-bound party went up to the Holy City and were warmly welcomed by the brethren.

Paul met with James and all the elders the day after he arrived in Jerusalem, and he told them what God had done among the Gentiles through his ministry. Rumors were rife that the apostle had encouraged his Jewish converts to forsake their Law and traditions when they accepted Christ. Paul's reputation evidently caused considerable embarrassment for the Jerusalem church leaders. They proposed that he placate his critics by a public demonstration of his orthodoxy. Four men were about to complete a Nazirite vow. Paul was urged to purify himself along with them and to pay their expenses for the required sacrifices.[18] According to Acts, which pictures Paul in a conciliatory frame of mind, he readily complied with the request. Was he simply overcome by a surge of sentiment for the practices of his ancestral faith, or did he compromise his principles in a crass concession to expediency? His letters make it extremely unlikely that he could have been a party to the scheme concocted by James and his associates. Perhaps Luke recorded the incident to strengthen his oft-repeated thesis that peace prevailed between Paul and the Jerusalem church.

A Prisoner for Christ (Acts 21:27–28:31)

Near the close of the period of ritual obligation, Paul was in the Temple preparing to complete the required offerings for himself and the four men. A wall separated the Court of the Gentiles (where Gentiles and defiled Jews could congregate) from the sacred precincts. In front of the wall was a low balustrade. Stone tablets at appropriate intervals warned Gentiles that if they were caught inside the balustrade, they would be responsible for their consequent deaths. Asian Jews spread the word that Paul had brought the Gentile by the name of Trophimus into the inner courts. Jerusalemites were aroused by Paul's reported desecration. His pro-Gentile reputation widened the credibility gap, and the people rushed to the scene of the melee to witness or participate in his death. They seized Paul and dragged him out of the Temple.

Arrest and Defense (Acts 21:27–23:11)

The crowd had already begun to beat Paul when word of the disturbance reached Claudius Lysias, tribune in command of the Roman garrison stationed in the Tower of Antonia, which overlooked the Temple area. He immediately took soldiers and hurried down the

[18]See Numbers 6:1–21.

tower's stairway to the outer court of the Temple to quell the riot. As soon as the people saw the tribune and his men, they stopped beating Paul. Then the tribune arrested Paul, on the assumption that he was an Egyptian rebel who had sparked an earlier insurrection, and ordered him chained to two soldiers. When the tribune inquired of the crowd who Paul was and what he had done, some shouted one thing and some another. Since the tribune could not discern the facts because of the uproar, he ordered Paul to be taken up into the fortress. As they mounted the stairs, Paul spoke to the tribune in Greek. Straightaway he realized that he had mistaken his prisoner's identity. Paul requested permission to address the crowd, and the tribune gave him leave. A great hush fell on the people as the apostle spoke to them in the Hebrew (Aramaic) language.

Paul began his address to the crowd by emphasizing his orthodoxy. He told about his strict Jewish rearing, education, and zealous persecution of the Christians. The story of his conversion captivated his hearers, and the role the devout Jew, Ananias, had played in his transformation doubtless impressed them deeply. But when the apostle mentioned "the Gentiles," the enchantment of the throng turned to sulfuric fury. The fickle mob once again demanded Paul's death. The tribune, determined to get to the bottom of the mob's malevolence, decided to torture the truth out of his prisoner. Just before the excruciating ordeal was to begin, Paul informed the centurion in charge that it was illegal to scourge a Roman citizen. When the apostle's remark was relayed to the tribune, he interrogated Paul personally. Convinced of the genuineness of Paul's claim, the tribune stopped the proceedings forthwith.

On the following morning, the tribune made a further effort to determine the real reason for the Jewish hostility. He commanded the Sanhedrin to meet, and then he brought his prisoner before it. Paul's declaration of a clear conscience caused the High Priest to have the apostle struck on the mouth. This illegal act convinced Paul that he could not receive justice at the hands of the Council so he resorted to a tactic designed to divide the Sanhedrin and to divert it from its task. "Brethren, I am a Pharisee, a son of Pharisees;" he declared, "with respect to the hope and the resurrection of the dead I am on trial" (23:6). By taking his stand with the Pharisees and against the Sadducees on the touchy subjects of the messianic hope and the resurrection, Paul's strategy paid off. Violent dissension arose between the two sects, and the tribune and his troops were forced to intervene in order to effect Paul's escape.[19]

[19]For a discussion of the credibility of Paul's appearance before the Sanhedrin, see Macgregor, "Acts, Exegesis," in *The Interpreter's Bible*, IX, 294–297.

The Jews were only temporarily thwarted by Paul's removal from their midst. Over forty of them took an oath to refrain from eating and drinking till they had killed Paul, and they solicited the cooperation of the Sanhedrin in carrying out their plan. Paul learned of the plot from his nephew and reported it to the tribune. The tribune made arrangements to take the apostle secretly to Caesarea, capital of the province and residence of the governors. There he would be assured greater protection from his enemies. Under cover of darkness, a large military escort, with a letter of explanation for the governor, accompanied Paul to the Mediterranean city.

Paul before Felix. Shortly after Paul arrived in Caesarea, the High Priest and some elders appeared to press their case against him with Felix, the governor. Their hired advocate began his address with words calculated to win favor for his clients. Then he charged Paul with a truly indictable offense: being a pestilent fellow, a world-wide agitator among the Jews, and a ringleader of the Nazarene sect. For good measure, the advocate added another complaint—attempting to profane the Temple.

When Felix gave Paul permission to speak, Paul pointed out that he had gone up to Jerusalem to worship and to bring alms to his people. He had not been a troublemaker at all, and he challenged his enemies to prove the contrary. His only offense was membership in a law-abiding Jewish sect that believed in the resurrection. This point was a potent one. Felix had a rather accurate knowledge of the Way (an early designation of the Christian Community), possibly because his wife was a Jewess. He evidently concluded that the dispute between Paul and his enemies was a purely religious one—whether or not there was a resurrection. Roman courts had little interest and no jurisdiction in such matters.[20] Felix postponed a decision until he could talk with Lysias, the tribune in Jerusalem. Meanwhile, Paul was kept in custody but was given permission to receive his friends and their assistance.

After some days, Felix arranged for his wife to hear Paul. As the apostle spoke about Christ Jesus, he argued for justice, self-control, and future judgment. The governor, plagued by a corrupt administration and marital irregularities, became alarmed. He ordered his prisoner to go away but indicated he would summon him again. Luke is concerned to show that this Roman, like Sergius Paulus in 13:12, was deeply impressed by Paul's preaching—so impressed that he sent for Paul often and conversed with him. At the same time, according

[20]See A.N. Sherwin-White, *Roman Society and Roman Law in the New Testament* (Oxford: Clarendon Press, 1963).

to Acts, Felix hoped that Paul would give him money. The taking of money from prisoners was expressly forbidden by Roman law, but the practice was not uncommon and it cohered with Felix's character. Reports of the large sum the apostle had brought to Jerusalem from Asia and Greece may have sired the governor's hope of a bribe for Paul's release. Be that as it may, two years later Felix was unconverted, no bribe had been paid, and Paul was still in jail.[21] Felix' attempt to ingratiate himself with his Jewish subjects by leaving Paul in prison was doubtless appreciated by them, but their leaders evidently thought it was not enough.

Paul before Festus. Felix was succeeded by Porcius Festus, and the Jewish leaders asked the governor to have Paul brought to Jerusalem for a new hearing. Their intent was to ambush and murder him en route. Festus refused the request but announced that a hearing would soon take place in Caesarea. He invited Paul's critics to attend and make their accusations at that time. At the hearing, the Jewish leaders restated their earlier charges, and Paul defended himself in much the same fashion as before. Then Festus again sought to placate the Jews. He asked if Paul would like to have the trial transferred to the Holy City. The choice was frightening—Paul despaired of Jerusalem justice, and he was disgusted by provincial politics. He decided to exercise his only remaining option. He appealed to Caesar, a privilege of any Roman citizen. The response of Festus was instant and automatic: "You have appealed to Caesar; to Caesar you shall go" (25:12).

Paul before Agrippa. While arrangements were being made to take Paul to Rome, King Herod Agrippa II arrived to welcome Festus. Agrippa ruled over territory northeast of Galilee that had once been within the tetrarchy of Philip. He brought with him his profligate and domineering sister, Bernice. During their stay, Festus laid Paul's case before the king. The governor stated that he had inherited the perplexing problem from his predecessor, that only religious charges had been brought against the prisoner when the case was reopened, and that Paul had finally appealed to Caesar. Agrippa expressed an interest in hearing the man himself.

Agrippa and Bernice appeared the next day with great pomp and entered the audience hall with military tribunes and prominent men of the city. Festus commanded that Paul be brought in. The governor

---

[21]The mention of the "praetorium" as the place of Paul's imprisonment in Acts 23:35 and again in Philippians 1:13 has caused some scholars to conclude that the imprisonment letters (Philippians, Colossians, Philemon, and perhaps Ephesians) were written during Paul's two-year incarceration at Caesarea.

briefly reviewed Paul's situation, expressed the hope that Agrippa could find some suitable charge against him that could be sent to Rome, and then gave Paul permission to speak. The apostle recounted his conversion and the circumstances that led to Jewish hostility toward him. He stressed the compatibility of his message with that of the prophets, the resurrection of Christ, and his Gentile mission. So fervently did he plead his case that Festus concluded he was a madman. Paul turned to Agrippa and attempted to secure his support. He pressed the king for a personal decision concerning the Christian conviction that Christ had fulfilled prophecy. Agrippa doubtless resented the prisoner's attempt to get him to side against Festus. The king abruptly terminated the hearing with the exclamation, "In a short time you think to make me a Christian!" (26:28). Privately he confided to Festus that Paul had done nothing worthy of death or imprisonment. If he had not already appealed to Caesar, he could have been set free. Once again Luke has indicated the benign nature of the Christian community in Roman eyes.

Voyage to Rome (Acts 27:1–28:31) When the time came for Paul to set sail for Rome, he and some other prisoners were placed in the custody of a centurion named Julius. The ship was late in departing for a voyage across the Mediterranean. The summer was far spent, and winter winds were about to blow. It was late September or early October before the ship reached Crete.[22] Progress had been slow, and the prospect for improvement was nil. Shipping was at a standstill between November and March. Paul advised against continuing, but his counsel was rejected. Soon a tempestuous wind, the northeaster, struck. It threatened to drive the ship across the sea and ground it on the sand bars of North Africa. The cargo was thrown overboard to lighten the ship, and for many days the ship bobbed about on the raging sea like a cork. All hope of being saved was at last abandoned. One night Paul had a vision in which he was assured that he would stand trial in Rome, and despair was turned into confidence. Finally the ship ran aground on the island of Malta. The soldiers planned to kill the prisoners lest any should escape, but the centurion stopped them in order to save Paul.

The Maltese welcomed their unexpected visitors with a warm fire. When Paul placed a bundle of sticks on the flame, he was bitten by a viper. The natives concluded that he was a murderer who had survived storm and shipwreck only to succumb to Dike, goddess of justice, who had sent the viper to sting him. But when Paul failed to swell up or fall down dead, they changed their minds and said

[22]This dating assumes that "the fast" mentioned in Acts 27:9 is the Day of Atonement that occurred after the fall equinox.

that he was a god. Their regard for the apostle soared still further when he healed the father of the chief man of the island and others. After three months, the weather began to clear. The centurion, his prisoners, and friends of Paul who had accompanied him from Caesarea set sail on an Alexandrian ship for the Italian mainland. After stops at Syracuse and Rhegium, they reached the harbor of Puteoli where they found a community of Christians. When the brethren at the church in Rome heard that Paul was headed their way, they sent a delegation southward along the famous Appian Way to escort him to the Imperial City.

The Appian Way. This is the oldest of the famous Roman roads. Construction was begun on it in 312 B.C. According to Acts 28:15 a delegation from the church in Rome traveled south on this road to meet Paul. A tradition indicates that Peter was buried on the Appian Way although other traditions point to a Vatican site. [Courtesy of Frederick Lewis, Inc.]

Three days after Paul and his party arrived in Rome, he called together the local leaders of the Jews. He presented to them his version of the dispute with their Jerusalem counterparts. The Roman Jews stated that no letters or adverse reports about Paul had reached them, and they expressed a desire to hear his views concerning "this sect" to which he belonged. When the appointed time arrived, they came to Paul in great numbers. The response to his preaching was mixed.

Paul compared those who rejected his message to the people of Isaiah's day: "Let it be known to you then that this salvation of God has been sent to the Gentiles; they will listen" (28:28).

Paul was permitted considerable freedom during his Roman imprisonment. Although constantly attended by a Roman guard, he was a favored prisoner. He lived at his own expense, welcomed all who came to him, and preached about the kingdom of God and the teaching of Jesus "quite openly and unhindered" (28:31). All of this accords with Luke's oft-repeated thesis that Rome smiled on the Christian missionary enterprise. If the "imprisonment letters" (Philippians, Colossians, and Philemon) were written during this period, as we believe they were, Paul was also able to continue his interest in and supervision of far-distant churches.[23] We shall now turn our attention to these and other letters Paul composed during his career.

[23]These letters contain references to Paul's imprisonment. See Philippians 1:12, 17; Colossians 4:10; Philemon 23. Some scholars add Ephesians to the list (4:1) although there is no direct evidence that Paul was imprisoned in that city.

X

Paul's Correspondence for Christ
(I and II Thessalonians; I and II Corinthians)

The noun "apostle" stems from a Greek infinitive that means "to send off or out." The term appears seventy-nine times in the New Testament with various shades of meaning. Sometimes it simply denotes "messenger," without any hint of status or authority (II Cor. 8:23; Phil. 2:25). More frequently, it describes an official emissary who has been commissioned to proclaim the gospel and instruct the churches. On other occasions, "apostle" refers to one of the Twelve, the original disciples of Jesus with Judas replaced by Matthias (Acts 1:15–16). This more restricted usage is characteristic of Acts.[1]

Commissioned by Christ

Paul begins most of his letters with a common claim: "Paul, an apostle of Christ Jesus by the will of God" (II Cor. 1:1).[2] It rankled him that there were those in the Christian community who contested his right to the title. He countered their skepticism with the charge that these "superlative apostles" were false and deceitful. With scathing sarcasm, he asserted that he was not one whit inferior to them (II Cor. 11:5, 13; 12:11). His reference was not to the Jerusalem leaders, but to subordinate missionaries who had been appointed by the church to carry out its work.[3]

Paul distinguished between apostles of Christ and apostles of men (Gal. 1:1). His detractors clearly fell in the latter category. According to Acts 1:22, an apostle was one who had shared Jesus' ministry from its inception and had witnessed his resurrection. Since Paul was "untimely born," he could not meet the first condition (I Cor. 15:8). He grounded his claim to be numbered among the apostles on his confrontation by the risen Christ. Christ had personally commissioned him to be an apostle to the Gentiles (Gal. 1:16). He was not one of the Twelve, and he had no desire to crash their ranks. But they had no advantage over him, because he was also a witness to the

---

[1] The only exception is found in Acts 14:4, 14.
[2] Exceptions are Philippians and Thessalonians, but note I Thessalonians 2:6.
[3] Such as Paul's kinsmen in Romans 16:7.

resurrection. The distinction between him and the "superlative apostles" was not the word "apostle," which they both shared. It lay in the source of authority that the word represented. If Paul had been designated an apostle by the church, as they had, he would have been responsible to the church for what he taught. But like the Twelve, he had received his authority from Christ. All he wanted from his critics was the simple acknowledgement that he was what he claimed to be: "an apostle—not from men nor through man, but through Jesus Christ and God the Father, who raised him from the dead" (Gal. 1:1).

Message and Authority

Paul's message and authority are disclosed in his letters. His missive to the Galatians was partly prompted by a challenge to his apostolic authority. The situation so disturbed him that he forsook his customary literary habit and substituted censure for thanksgiving (Gal. 1:6–9).[4] Then he plunged into his central theme. He was in no way dependent upon other men, not even the apostles, for the gospel that he preached. "For I did not receive it from man, nor was I taught it, but it came through a revelation of Jesus Christ" (Gal. 1:12). It was three years after his conversion before he visited briefly with Peter and James in Jerusalem. Fourteen additional years elapsed before he consulted with an inner core of Jerusalem leaders. These two widely-spaced events constituted the whole of his contact with the apostles prior to the writing of Galatians. Clearly "those who were of repute" were responsible for neither his mission nor his message (Gal. 1:15–2:10).

Paul's fierce declaration of independence from men has sometimes been equated with his independence from church tradition. The two are not synonymous. When Paul wrote to the Corinthians, he indicated that the gospel he preached was the same as that which he had received from those who had preceded him in the faith:

For I _delivered_ to you as of first importance what I also _received_, that Christ died for our sins in accordance with the scriptures, that he was buried, that he was raised on the third day in accordance with the scriptures, and that he appeared to Cephas, then to the twelve. Then he appeared to more than five hundred brethren at one time, most of whom are still alive, though some have fallen asleep. Then he appeared to James, then to all the apostles. Last of all, as to one untimely born, he appeared also to me.[5]

[4]See p. 260.
[5]I Corinthians 15:3–8, underscores added.

The use of the verb "delivered" (*paradidōmi*) is striking. Its technical connotation is "to pass on what one has received." It is roughly equivalent to the Latin verb (*traditio*) from which the English "tradition" is derived. The correlative verb "received" (*paralambanō*) means "to receive the tradition from those who have passed it on." Paul preached nothing new; he simply transmitted the tradition that he had received from the earliest Christians. His declaration of independence was not from church tradition but from the notion that the church was the source of his mission and message. Not so! The source of both was Christ.

Paul's place among the apostles was secured not only by his commission from Christ and his sponsorship of church tradition, but also by his exercise of apostolic authority. When a Corinthian convert unashamedly lived with his stepmother, the congregation remained unconcerned. Paul castigated the church for its arrogance and commanded that the offender be excommunicated: "When you are assembled, and my spirit is present, with the power of our Lord Jesus, you are to deliver this man to Satan for the destruction of the flesh, that his spirit may be saved in the day of the Lord Jesus" (I Cor. 5:4b-5).[6] A multitude of moral problems plagued the churches, and Paul repeatedly made pronouncements concerning them. On the question of divorce among the faithful, for example, he simply paraphrased and transmitted the teaching of Jesus imbedded in the tradition: no divorce with remarriage (I Cor. 7:10-11).[7] He took pains to point out that this counsel came from Jesus and not from himself. But on the problem of a believer married to a nonbeliever, Jesus gave no guidance. On this subject Paul issued his own command with an authority no less compelling than a word from Jesus: "To the rest I say, not the Lord, that if any brother has a wife who is an unbeliever, and she consents to live with him, he should not divorce her" (I Cor. 7:12). Such exercise of authority on Paul's part was not sheer presumption. He bore all of the marks of an authentic apostle. Among the people he performed "with signs and wonders and mighty works" (II Cor. 12:12). The transformed lives he left in his wake constituted pragmatic proof of his apostleship. He needed no letters of recommendation from his converts. "You yourselves are our letters of recommendation," he wrote to the Corinthians, "written on your hearts, to be known and read by all men" (II Cor. 3:2).

Weighty Letters   One of the most effective ways that Paul exercised apostolic authority

---

[6]Some scholars think Paul asked not for excommunication of the offender but that a curse be invoked against him to bring about his death.

[7]Compare Mark 10.1-9.

was through his letters. His detractors derided his weak bodily presence and ineffectual speech, but they readily acknowledged that his letters were "weighty and strong" (II Cor. 10:10). These writings used to be called "epistles," but Paul's compositions are not formal essays addressed to the general public. They are genuine letters (although not of the private, "off-the-record" variety) directed to a particular situation. It is evident from the use of the second person plural, the allusions to various people, the greetings and salutations, and the explicit orders that Paul intended them to be read before the congregations to which they were addressed. At the close of I Thessalonians, for example, he declares: "I adjure you by the Lord that this letter be read to *all* the brethren."[8] Even Philemon, the only communication of Paul directed to an individual, is also addressed to "the church" in his house (Phm. 1–2).

Form

Paul's writings generally follow the form of private Greek letters of his day, although the nature of his mission and message caused him to make certain modifications. Greek letters began with a prescript that contained the writer's name, the name of the person or persons addressed, and a greeting. Paul enlarged the pattern to indicate the Christian status of the writer and readers, changed "greeting" (*chairein*) to "grace" (*charis*), and added the familiar Semitic "peace" (*eirēnē*). He often transformed the salutation into a joint greeting by naming one or two persons with himself. Greek letters usually followed the salutation with a word of praise, thanks, or a prayer for the health of the addressee. This practice became so characteristic of Paul that when his customary thanksgiving was missing in Galatians, scholars attributed it to the tension under which he wrote.[9]

Oral Style

Paul dictated his letters to a secretary (or amanuensis) who, on one occasion, identified himself: "I Tertius, the writer of this letter, greet you in the Lord" (Rom. 16:22). Unlike his modern counterpart, the secretary did not take dictation word for word. His crude shorthand enabled him to record only the essence of what was said. He would reconstruct the letter from his notes and present it to Paul for approval and the addition of his final words. How much Paul's secretary influenced the vocabulary and style of the finished product is difficult to determine, although he assuredly played a far more creative role than that of a twentieth-century stenographer. He might be compared to a presidential speechwriter.

[8] I Thessalonians 5:27, italics added. Compare Colossians 4:16.
[9] On the style of Paul and the literary characteristics of his letters, see Adolf Deissmann, *Light from the Ancient East* (New York: Harper & Row, n.d.), pp. 146–251; Martin Dibelius, *A Fresh Approach to the New Testament and Early Christian Literature* (New York: Charles Scribner's Sons, 1936), pp. 142–143; A.D. Nock, *St. Paul* (New York: Harper & Row, 1968), pp. 233–237.

The dictated nature of Paul's letters accounts for their oral style. The heat of controversy caused his thought to outdistance his words and forced him to pause and correct himself: "I am thankful that I baptized none of you except Crispus and Gaius; lest any one should say that you were baptized in my name. (I did baptize also the household of Stephanas. Beyond this, I do not know whether I baptized any one else.)" (I Cor. 1:14–16). He allowed extraneous ideas to sandwich themselves between two halves of an exposition and force him to restate his opening clause lest the sequence be lost: "So we are always of good courage; we know that while we are at home in the body we are away from the Lord, *for we walk by faith, not by sight.* We are of good courage."[10] A rough-and-ready style, dangling participles, and incomplete sentences also support the generally extemporaneous character of the compositions (Rom. 5:12). To taste their full flavor, the letters should be read aloud.

Polished Passages

Not all passages in Paul's letters were dictated spontaneously. Some exhibit a stunning lyrical quality and bear the marks of careful and precise composition. The discourses on love (I Cor. 13) and the incarnation (Phil. 2:5–11), if original, have all the characteristics of hymns or poems, including the delicate and deliberate balancing of clauses and words. The expositions on wisdom (I Cor. 2:6–16), separation from God (Rom. 8:35–39), and the primal significance of Christ (Col. 1:15–20) are not tip-of-the-tongue treatments. Like any experienced evangelist, Paul evidently made use of material that had been independently composed. His extended exegesis of Old Testament materials (Rom. 15:7–12; Gal. 3:10–13; 4:21–31) probably first appeared in his sermons. The exhortations of a general nature that often appear near the end of his letters (Rom. 12:9–13; II Cor. 13:1–12; Phil. 4:8–9) and the "household lists" (Col. 3:5–4:6) suggest dependence on conventional collections. Paul Christianized them by inserting references to "the Lord."

Certified Authenticity

Paul customarily took the stylus from his amanuensis near the close of his letters and added a few words in his own handwriting (I Cor. 16:21; Gal. 6:11; Col. 4:18; Phm. 19). Lest anyone be in doubt as to the reason for this practice, he spelled it out: "I, Paul, write this greeting with my own hand. This is the mark in every letter of mine; it is the way I write" (II Thess. 3:17). Others had been writing letters in his name. Paul's personal postscript was intended to insure the authenticity of his own communications. With this accomplished, he rolled up the papyrus scroll, tied it with a string secured by hot wax,

---

[10]II Corinthians 5:6–8, italics added.

and handed it over to a helper to deliver.[11] If the destination was far distant, then a trader or shipmaster would be pressed into service.

Modern Parallel Paul's missives were genuine letters rather than epistles. This can be seen not only by comparing them to ancient Greek letters, but also by noting their remarkable similarity to the modern letter form. The beginning and ending of Romans, for example, can be arranged as follows:

Paul, a servant of Jesus Christ
(called to be an apostle)

All God's beloved in Rome
(who are called to be saints)

Grace to you and peace from God our Father and the Lord Jesus Christ.

First, I thank my God through Jesus Christ for all of you.

....

....

....

Timothy, my fellow worker, greets you. . . .

Paul

P:t[12]

Number and Dates of the Letters Paul was an inveterate letter writer. The products of his pen preserved in the New Testament evidently comprised only a fraction of a much more voluminous correspondence. In Corinthians 5:9, he mentions a letter he had previously sent to that church. In II Corinthians 2:4, he refers to still another letter he wrote to that congregation, and the thumbnail description of its nature makes clear that it was not I Corinthians. In Colossians 4:16 he calls attention to "the letter from Laodicea," by which he presumably means the letter he had written to that church. In addition, there is evidence that some of Paul's communications contain parts of letters we do not otherwise possess. Note the abrupt break in the train of thought at II Corinthians 6:14

---

[11]Presumably both the Severe Letter (II Cor. 10–13) and the Conciliatory Letter (II Cor. 1–9) were carried to Corinth by Titus (II Cor. 7:6–8; 8:17–18), Philippians was carried by Epaphroditus (Phil. 2:25), Colossians by Tychicus and Onesimus (Col. 4:7–9), and Romans 16 (a separate letter) to Ephesus by Phoebe (Rom. 16:1).
[12]"P" stands for Paul and "t" for his amanuensis, Tertius. Our outline is partly based on D.J. Selby, *Toward the Understanding of St. Paul* (Englewood Cliffs, N.J.: Prentice-Hall, Inc., 1962), p. 240.

and 10:1. Philippians 3:2–4:1 appears to be an interpolation from some other writing of Paul. Romans 16 seems to be a separate letter.

Number Editors of the King James Version of the New Testament attribute fourteen letters to Paul:

Romans	Colossians
I and II Corinthians	I and II Thessalonians
Galatians	I and II Timothy
Ephesians	Titus
Philippians	Philemon

Hebrews

In the Revised Standard Version of the New Testament, the number of Paul's letters is reduced to thirteen by eliminating Hebrews from the list. This act was not arbitrary. As early as the second century, scholars began to doubt that Hebrews should be assigned to Paul. Origen opined that only God knows who wrote the book.[13] It makes no claim to have been written by Paul, and modern specialists are nearly unanimous in affirming its non-Pauline character. Many scholars also strike Ephesians from the list. Although it may well have been written by a devoted disciple of the Apostle to the Gentiles, differences of vocabulary, style, and theological content would seem to preclude Paul's authorship.[14] A considerable cloud of suspicion hangs over Colossians, too, but we judge the letter to be genuine. I and II Timothy and Titus, commonly called the pastorals because they emphasize pastoral and ecclesiastical concerns, claim to have been written by Paul. Considerations of vocabulary, style, and the use of Pauline words and phrases with altogether different meanings render the claim most unlikely. In Paul's genuine letters, for example, "faith" means trust in God, but in the Pastorals it means a body of knowledge to be protected and preserved.[15] The nine letters that remain cannot be dated apart from a chronology of Paul's career.

Chronology of Paul's Career The few indications of time provided by Paul's letters simply date events in relation to other events. For an absolute chronology, if such can be secured, we must turn to Acts. On the basis of Jewish or Roman sources, only five references in Acts can be assigned even approximate dates.

[13]Eusebius, *Ecclesiastical History*, VI, 14, 25.
[14]See C.L. Mitton, *The Epistle of the Ephesians, Its Authorship, Origin, and Purpose* (Oxford: Clarendon Press, 1951).
[15]See J.C. Beker, "The Pastoral Letters," in George A. Buttrick, ed., *The Interpreter's Dictionary of the Bible* (New York: Abingdon Press, 1962), K–Q 668–675.

Acts 12:23	Death of Herod Agrippa I	44 A.D.[16]
Acts 11:28	Palestinian famine during reign of Claudius	46 A.D.
Acts 18:2	Edict of Claudius banning Jews from Rome	49 A.D.
Acts 18:12	Gallio arrives in Corinth as Roman proconsul	51 A.D.
Acts 24:27	Festus arrives in Caesarea as Roman proconsul	59 A.D.

Only two of these dates are at all helpful in arriving at a time that ties in with Paul's autobiographical references—the edict of Claudius and Gallio's arrival in Corinth. Neither of these happenings, however, can be assigned a date with complete confidence. Dio Cassius (150–235 A.D.), a reputable Roman historian, refers to the Edict of Claudius along with events that occurred in 41 A.D., and the Delphi inscription (which permits a rather close dating of Gallio's arrival in Corinth) is badly mutilated and subject to more than one interpretation. If these limitations are discounted, both happenings point to the probability that Paul began his Corinthian campaign about 50 A.D. With this as a "fixed point," it is possible to reckon backward and forward, utilizing notes of time and place in the letters and in Acts, and establish a tentative chronology for Paul's career.

The establishment of a fixed date from which to reconstruct Paul's career presents many problems, but it does not exhaust the supply. Although Luke provides a few specific time indications (Acts 18:11; 19:8, 10), most of his references are decidedly imprecise (Acts 14:28, 19:23).[17] He gives no clues as to how long Paul spent on his journeys, and he drops few hints as to the time the apostle spent in the cities of Galatia and Macedonia. Do the "fourteen years" Paul mentioned in Galatians 2:1 include or exclude the "three years" referred to in 1:18? What is the relation of Acts to Paul's letters? It makes a great deal of difference in the chronology of Paul's life whether the Jerusalem visit of Galatians 2 is identified with Acts 11:30–12:25, or Acts 15:1–29, or Acts 18:22.[18]

Various reconstructions of Paul's life have been made, despite the hazards involved. Our own estimate of key happenings in his career is presented below:

Birth (Acts 22:3)	A.D. 10–15
Conversion (Acts 9, 22, 26; Gal. 1:15–16)	33
First Jerusalem Visit (Acts 9:26–29; 22:17–21; Gal. 1:18–19)	36
Famine Visit (Acts 11:30; 12:25)	46

---

[16]Some scholars date Agrippa's death at 41 A.D.
[17]Compare Acts 9:23 with Galatians 1:18.
[18]An excellent discussion of this subject is presented by Caird, "The Chronology of the New Testament," in *The Interpreter's Dictionary of the Bible*, A–D, 603–607.

First Missionary Campaign (Acts 13–14)	47–48
Summit Conference in Jerusalem (Acts 15; Gal. 2)	49
Second Missionary Campaign (Acts 15:36–18:21)	49–52
Arrival in Corinth (18 months)	50
Third Missionary Campaign (Acts 18:23–21:17)	52–56
Arrives in Ephesus (three years)	53–56
Winters in Corinth (Acts 20:3)	56
Voyage to Jerusalem with the Collection (Acts 20:3–21:17; Rom. 15:25–28)	57
Arrest and Imprisonment (Acts 21:18–23:30)	57
Prisoner in Caesarea (Acts 23:31–35; 24:27; 26:32)	57–59
Paul before Festus (Acts 24:27–26:32)	59
Voyage to Rome (Acts 27:1–28:16)	60
Prisoner in Rome (Acts 28:17–31; Col. 4:18; Phm. 13; Phil. 1:7)	60–62

Dates of the Genuine Letters

The letters attributed to Paul in the Revised Standard Version do not appear in chronological order. They are arranged according to length—from the longest to the shortest, first to communities (Romans through II Thessalonians) and second to individuals (I Timothy through Philemon).[19] Innumerable efforts have been made to place the letters in their proper historical sequence. The motive, aside from simple curiosity, has been to determine whether or not Paul's thought underwent development. The results have been no more unanimous than voting in the Security Council of the United Nations. Some scholars regard Galatians as the first of Paul's letters, while others place it near the time of Romans. Three other letters, Philippians, Colossians, and Philemon, were written from prison (Phil. 1:12–13; Col. 4:3, 10, 18; Phm. 1), but scholars cannot agree where they originated. Was it a prison at Ephesus, Caesarea, or Rome? Whichever place is chosen decidedly affects the date of these writings.

It is perilous to pontificate when scholars are divided, but some sort of judgment is required. If allowance is made for a modest margin of error, the following chronological arrangement of the nine genuine letters of Paul is probably no more vulnerable than any other:

Letter	*Origin*	*A.D.*
I Thessalonians	Corinth	50
II Thessalonians	Corinth	50
I Corinthians	Ephesus	54–55
II Corinthians	Macedonia	55–56
Galatians	Ephesus or Corinth	56
Romans	Corinth	56–57

[19]The only exception is Ephesians, which is slightly longer-than Galatians.

Colossians	Rome	61
Philemon	Rome	61
Philippians	Rome	62

Campaign Strategy and Handicaps

Acts indicates that Paul went to the local synagogue as soon as he reached a given city. He preached to the assembled congregation as long as they permitted him to do so. When opposition grew intense, he withdrew to a nearby house or gathering place where he continued to speak to converts and interested prospects (Acts 16:11–15, 18:1–8). No such procedural pattern, however, is evident in Paul's letters.

Self-support

It was apparently against Paul's principles to accept money on a regular basis for preaching. In a letter to the church at Corinth, he mentions that he worked with his own hands (I Cor. 4:12; 9:6). According to Acts, he was a tentmaker by trade (18:3). This probably meant that he worked with leather rather than cloth. We know that rabbis were urged to learn a trade, but Paul made no claim to rabbinic training. Whatever his means of making a living, he chose to exercise it in order not to burden the fledgling churches that he had founded (I Cor. 9:12, 15, 18). Probably another motive was to blunt the charge that he proclaimed the gospel for personal gain. One known exception to Paul's practice of self-help, though, can be cited. In a note near the end of his letter to the Philippians, he gratefully acknowledged their repeated material assistance at the beginning of his work in Macedonia. "Not that I seek the gift," he carefully explained to his benefactors, "but I seek the fruit which increases to your credit. I have received full payment, and more; I am filled, having received from Epaphroditus the gifts you sent, a fragrant offering, a sacrifice acceptable and pleasing to God" (Phil. 4:17–18).

Fellow Workers

According to Mark, Jesus assembled the Twelve and sent them out "two by two" (6:7). This pattern appears frequently in Acts—Paul traveled first with Barnabas (13:2) and then with Silas (15:40). The sudden shifts in the narrative from "they" to "we" have also suggested to many scholars that Paul was accompanied on his journeys by an anonymous companion (Luke?) who wrote the travel document that was later preserved in Acts (16:10–17, 20:5–15; 21:1–18; 27:1–28:16). Paul also sent out workers in pairs (19:22).

Paul did not usually remain long in one place. He did stay eighteen months in Corinth and about three years in Ephesus, but these extensive periods were exceptions to the rule. His aim was to preach the gospel where the name of Christ was not yet known (Rom. 15:20). Again and again in his letters he exhibited an eagerness to press on to virgin territory. When he dictated Romans about midpoint in his writing career, he disclosed plans to go beyond Rome to Spain, where Christian preachers had not yet penetrated (Rom. 15:24). He relied heavily on his fellow workers not only in the founding of new churches, but also in their growth and consolidation after he had left for new fields to conquer. Priscilla and Aquila had first assisted him at Corinth. Near the close of Romans, he mentioned them with special fondness: "Greet Prisca [Priscilla] and Aquila, my fellow workers in Christ Jesus, who risked their necks for my life, to whom not only I but also all the churches of the Gentiles give thanks; greet also the church in their house" (Rom. 16:3–5a). He then went on to greet a long list of people, many of whom are called "fellow workers" (Rom. 16:5b–16). Timothy and Titus also performed yeoman's service for Paul (Phil. 1:1; II Cor. 7:5–16). Clearly he could not have executed his task effectively apart from the company of such an able and devoted group of associates.

Handicaps   *The message* of Paul to the Gentiles was the early Christian kerygma, the essence of the gospel. Although he engaged in various "secular" tasks, such as tentmaking and fund raising, his overarching concern was evangelism. "For I *delivered* to you as of first importance what I also *received*," he wrote to the Corinthians, "that Christ died for our sins in accordance with the scriptures, that he was buried, that he was raised on the third day in accordance with the scriptures, and that he appeared to Cephas, then to the twelve."[20] The odds against this message making favorable headway in the ancient world were so fantastic that professional gamblers would probably have declined to quote them. Even Paul acknowledged that what he preached suffered from two almost insurmountable handicaps. It was "a stumbling-block to Jews and folly to Gentiles" (I Cor. 1:23).

Jesus did not fit common Jewish expectations. He was not a king. His parentage and birthplace did not conform to prophecy. He assumed authority unmerited either by training or by office, and he exercised that authority to subvert such sacred Jewish institutions as Sabbath observance and separation from Gentiles. He even predicted the destruction of the Temple, the center of Jewish worship. Although he lived his entire life in occupied territory, he advocated payment of taxes to Caesar and unrelenting love of one's enemies. It is not surprising that the nation's leaders despised him and happily conspired to bring about his death. His postresurrection followers added insult to injury when they boldly proclaimed that they, not the unbelieving Jews, had correctly interpreted the Jewish Scripture. Jesus was God's Messiah who had been rejected by the very people who should have welcomed him with open arms!

[20] I Corinthians 15:3–5; italics added.

The Greeks were galled by the gospel, too, but for different reasons. Since they were "very religious," they were keenly aware of the claims made in behalf of Dionysus, Attis, Adonis, Osiris, and others. These claims conformed to a single pattern: a divine being assumes human form, dies, is restored to life, and becomes the savior of those who believe in him.[21] But this was a far cry from the Christian assertions concerning Christ. A man born of humble parents in an obscure village in a remote Roman province was duly tried and executed as a common criminal by order of the provincial governor and with the enthusiastic endorsement of his own religious leaders. This same man was then resurrected from the dead and is the savior of the world. To the Greeks, such claims were sheer nonsense.

The messenger who delivered the gospel to the Gentiles suffered from some sort of physical handicap. Paul never disclosed what the handicap was, but he did refer to it metaphorically as "a thorn . . . in the flesh" (II Cor. 12:7). Several diagnoses of the malady have been suggested. Some scholars think it was epilepsy, and others declare in favor of malaria. Still others believe it was an eye ailment, because the Galatians were willing to pluck out their eyes and give them to him and because he wrote with such large letters (Gal. 4:15; 6:11). Whatever the disorder, it was an abiding annoyance for Paul. Three times he prayed for release from the illness, but his petitions were denied. "My grace is sufficient for you," the Lord declared, "for my power is made perfect in weakness" (II Cor. 12:9). Paul concluded that the purpose of his affliction was to keep him humble (II Cor. 12:7), but other judgments were not so charitable. Paul's detractors delighted in calling attention to his weak bodily appearance and his ineffectual speech (II Cor. 10:10). Even fellow Christians were embarrassed by his physical presence. Paul made quite a point of commending the Galatians for their ability to overlook his handicap: "You know it was because of a bodily ailment that I preached the gospel to you at first; and though my condition was a trial to you, you did not scorn or despise me, but received me as an angel of God, as Christ Jesus" (Gal. 4:13-14).

Correspondence with Thessalonica

About 50 A.D., in the Greek city of Corinth, Paul received news concerning friends in Thessalonica, Macedonia, about whom he had been exceedingly anxious. He had founded the church there not long before, but he was soon forced to flee the city to prevent violence to himself and his friends.[22] His concern for his converts increased daily. At least twice he tried to return to them, but Satan hindered him

[21]See pp. 17-20.
[22]See p. 239.

(I Thess. 2:18). When he could endure the tension no longer, he sent Timothy back to Thessalonica from Athens (I Thess. 3:1-2, 5). Timothy returned in due course with good news. Paul's friends had not forgotten him. They still honored him and the gospel he had preached. They believed that Jesus was God's Messiah, and they eagerly awaited his return from heaven. They hoped to see their spiritual mentor again soon.

Paul was overjoyed by Timothy's report, and he dictated a letter to his friends to express his gratitude. He also dealt with several problems that had arisen in the church that called for counsel and admonition. The letter he wrote was I Thessalonians, the first New Testament book to be composed. Not many weeks later, he found it necessary to write a second letter to these same Christians. Somehow they had concluded that the day of the Lord, for which they had been instructed to be prepared, had already arrived. Some had substituted contemplation for work. Others, in their idleness, had brought scandal to the church. Paul composed this second communication to correct their mistaken theology and to improve their morality.

Not all scholars would agree with our conclusions concerning Paul's correspondence with the church at Thessalonica. The authenticity of I Thessalonians is generally recognized, but both the genuineness of II Thessalonians and its relationship to the other letter have been frequently questioned. The eschatology of the second letter is said to be inconsistent with that of the first. In I Thessalonians, the day of the Lord is imminent. Readers are warned that it will come as a thief in the night. They should be expectant and prepared. In II Thessalonians, however, the day of the Lord is postponed to the indefinite future. It will not occur until "the rebellion" takes place and the "man of lawlessness" is revealed. How could two such contrary views be endorsed by the same author at about the same time? The similarity and the difference in language and style pose another problem. Parts of II Thessalonians so closely resemble I Thessalonians that they appear to be paraphrases. Why would Paul have written almost identical letters to the same church within such a short time interval? Why, also, would he so markedly vary the tone of the two letters? I Thessalonians is warm, personal, and affectionate, whereas II Thessalonians is cool, official, and detached.

Several solutions have been suggested to solve the difficulties connected with Paul's letters to Thessalonica. (1) II Thessalonians was written much later than I Thessalonians and by someone other than Paul. (2) Both letters were authored by Paul, but II Thessalonians was written first. (3) The two letters were composed at the same time, but I Thessalonians was addressed largely to the Gentile wing of the church and II Thessalonians to the Jewish wing. (4) Paul delegated Silvanus or Timothy to write one or the other of the letters. Absolute certainty concerning matters of authorship, date, and destination is beyond our human grasp, but most (although by no means all) contemporary scholars affirm the authenticity of both letters and believe that they were written in their canonical order.[23]

I Thessalonians   Paul begins his letter with an extended thanksgiving for the faithfulness of the Thessalonians. They have become compelling examples for all the believers in Macedonia and Achaia. The apostle recalls his labors among them, their loyalty to him, and compares their persecutions with those of the Judean churches. His longing to see them has been intensified by Timothy's return and favorable report. He prays that they may be directed by God to increase their love for one another and for all men, so that they may be perfected in holiness when Christ comes (1–3).

Paul devotes the remainder of his letter to special problems that have arisen in the church. He warns his converts, who are only one step removed from paganism, to abstain from sexual immorality. He urges them to work at their trade in order to win the respect of the community and to avoid becoming objects of charity. He implores them to love and esteem their religious leaders who admonish them. Apparently some of the faithful have died since he left them, and the Thessalonians are concerned about the status of the deceased at Christ's coming. Paul assures his readers that "the dead in Christ will rise first; then we who are alive, who are left, shall be caught up together with them in the clouds to meet the Lord in the air" (4:16b–17). He reminds his converts that the day of the Lord will come "like a thief in the night" (5:2). As "sons of the day," they are to remain sober, "put on the breastplate of faith and love, and for a helmet the hope of salvation" (5:8). He brings his letter to a close with a brief summary of his exhortations, a benediction, and a command that the letter be read to "all" the brethren.

II Thessalonians   Not many weeks after Paul's first letter had been dispatched, he learned that the situation in Thessalonica was more serious than he had supposed. Two problems in particular had persisted and grown more acute. Since their treatment constitutes the distinctive part of II Thessalonians and probably provided the occasion for its composition, we shall confine our discussion to them.

[23]For a more detailed treatment of the issues involved, see Selby, *Toward the Understanding of St. Paul*, pp. 250–252; J.W. Clarke, "Exposition, I & II Thessalonians," in George A. Buttrick, ed., *The Interpreter's Bible* (New York: Abingdon Press, 1955), XI, 249–251.

The Thessalonians had the idea that the eagerly awaited day of the Lord had already arrived. Paul does not seem to know how this erroneous conclusion was reached. It may have been caused by a misinterpretation of a prophetic utterance, a Christian tradition, or a letter purporting to be from Paul (2:1-2). Whatever the source, the idea is without foundation, and Paul hastens to set his readers right. He forthrightly declares that that day will not come "unless the rebellion comes first, and the man of lawlessness is revealed, the son of perdition, who opposes and exalts himself against every so-called god or object of worship, so that he takes his seat in the temple of God, proclaiming himself to be God" (2:3-4).

Paul had previously explained the essence of Christian eschatology to the Thessalonians in some detail, but his words had been imperfect-ly understood (I Thess. 5:1-2; II Thess. 2:5). His repeated instructions on this subject in II Thessalonians may well have enlightened his converts, but some of his references puzzle modern scholars. The "rebellion" he mentions alludes to the popular apocalyptic notion that apostasy would precede the day of the Lord. But what is "the mystery of lawlessness already at work?" Who or what "restrains" it (2:7)? Who is the "man of lawlessness" who enthrones himself in the Temple and claims to be God?[24]

The second vexing problem that cried for correction in Thessalonica was that of idleness. It was nothing novel, and Paul had dealt with it briefly in his first letter. Now the notion that the day of the Lord had already come placed a premium on laziness. Some of the faithful quit work and wallowed in idleness. They were mere "busybodies." Paul instructs his followers to have nothing to do with them. He worked when he was in their midst, and he ate no one's bread without paying for it. As an apostle, he had every right to live at their expense, but he elected to work in order that they might have an example to imitate. "If any one will not work," he declared, "let him not eat" (3:10).

The two letters to Thessalonica are not path-breaking in their theologi-cal thrust. Except for the teaching on eschatology, they contain little

---

[24]Some scholars think that the man of lawlessness was a Roman emperor and the mystery of lawlessness was the Roman empire. Pitted against the two are the unidentified restraining force and the restrainer. Other scholars believe that the man of lawlessness was a Jewish religious leader (perhaps a wicked high priest), the mystery of lawlessness was Judaism, the restraining force was the Roman empire, and the restrainer the em-peror. Still others suggest that Paul was the restrainer, and the restraining force was the Christian gospel, which must be preached to the Gentiles before the End arrived. None of these explanations is wholly satisfactory. Paul probably had historical people and situations in mind, but his vision is not limited to them.

that is distinctive. They do reveal much, however, about Paul's marvelous personal and pastoral qualities and the strengths and weaknesses of a community which had recently embraced the Christian religion.

The Corinthian
Correspondence

The Corinthian correspondence is the most voluminous in the collection of Paul's letters, and in some respects it is the most valuable. Along with Romans and Galatians, it is a fertile source of knowledge concerning the apostle's thought. It paints the best picture of a first-century Christian church available. Its Hymn of Love is one of the most widely heralded and deeply revered passages of any scripture (I Cor. 13). Its treatment of the resurrection is the earliest and most systematic (I Cor. 15).

The casual reader of the New Testament is likely to conclude that Paul wrote only two letters to Corinth, I and II Corinthians. A more careful examination of the record, however, suggests that this was not the case. In I Corinthians 5:9–11, the apostle refers to a letter he had previously written to that church that dealt with the problems of associating with immoral men. In II Corinthians 2:3–4 and 7:8, he mentions a "severe letter," the description of which coheres neither with the letter mentioned in I Corinthians nor with I Corinthians itself.

Some scholars believe that the letters mentioned in I and II Corinthians have been lost. Others suggest that parts of these communications have been preserved in the Corinthian correspondence with which we are familiar. In II Corinthians, 6:14–7:1 rudely interrupts the text. When this passage is removed, the material before it fits perfectly with what follows. Since the content of the dislocated passage deals with a subject strikingly similar to that of the letter described in I Corinthians 5:9–11, it seems reasonable to conclude that the intruding passage is a fragment of the letter referred to in I Corinthians. An even more startling break in both tone and content occurs after II Corinthians 9:15. Up to this point the letter is conciliatory. There had been grave trouble in the church at Corinth, and Paul's leadership had been repudiated. But the insurrection had been quelled, and Paul is attempting to bridge the gulf that had developed between him and his Corinthian converts. The subject of the last two chapters before the break is that of the collection to be completed for the poor saints in Jerusalem. Except for Paul's customary greetings and benediction, 9:15 seems to bring the letter to a close: "Thanks be to God for his inexpressible gift!" But what happens in chapters 10–13 constitutes an abrupt about-face. Paul excoriates his opposition with unrelenting zeal. It is as though the insurrection were still in full force. Chapters 10–13 appear to be a separate letter, minus the formal introduction, which can be equated with the "severe letter" mentioned in II Corinthians 2:3–4 and 7:8. This hypothesis is strengthened by the likelihood that chapter 10 was written from Ephesus and chapters 7–9 from Macedonia.[25] A comparison of passages in chapters 10–13 with similar material in the preceding chapters convincingly demonstrates that chapters 1–9 (excepting 6:14–7:1) were written after the severe letter of 10–13.[26]

There are other places in the Corinthian correspondence where breaks occur.[27] Several scholars have made a more extensive reconstruction of the letters on the basis of these additional interruptions than we have proposed.[28] Since the additional breaks are less pronounced than the instances we have discussed, most critics attribute them to the sudden shifts of mood and thought that characterized the author. Although there is no manuscript support for the four-letters-to-Corinth proposal, it is preferable to accepting I and II Corinthians as they are or reducing them to a hodgepodge. Our reconstruction of the known communications between Paul and the Corinthians, which receives substantial scholarly support, can be summarized as follows:

1. *Paul's first letter*, mentioned in I Corinthians 5:9–11 and partially preserved in II Corinthians 6:14–7:1, was written from Ephesus.
2. Corinthians visited Paul at Ephesus (I Cor. 1:11; 16:17) and he received a letter from Corinth (I Cor. 7:1).
3. *Paul's second letter*, also written from Ephesus, is our I Corinthians.
4. Paul made a "painful visit" to Corinth, precipitated perhaps by unfavorable news (II Cor. 12:14; 13:1–2; 2:1), and then returned to Ephesus.
5. *Paul's third letter*, the "severe letter," largely preserved in II Cor. 10–13, was written in Ephesus. Titus took it to Corinth. Paul subsequently proceeded to Troas (II Cor. 2:4; 7:8).
6. Titus failed to appear in Troas as expected. Paul grew apprehensive and went on to Macedonia where Titus appeared with the welcome news that the insurrection was over (II Cor. 2:13; 7:13).
7. *Paul's fourth letter*, the "conciliatory letter," largely preserved in II

[25]Paul writes of his intention to preach the gospel "in lands beyond you" in II Corinthians 10:16. The "lands" refer to Italy and Spain (Rom. 1:5; 15:28)—an appropriate expression for one writing from Ephesus to Corinth, but not from Macedonia to Corinth. II Corinthians 7:5, 8:1, and 9:2, however, suggest that those parts of the letter originated in Macedonia.
[26]Compare II Corinthians 10:6, 13:2, and 13:10 with II Corinthians 2:9, 1:23, and 2:3.
[27]I Corinthians 9, for example, appears to be uncomfortable in its surroundings.
[28]A critical summary of these efforts is presented in A.H. McNeile, *An Introduction to the Study of the New Testament*, 2nd ed., rev. C.S.C. Williams (Oxford: Clarendon Press, 1953), pp. 132–142.

Corinthians 1:1–6:13; 7:2–9:15, was written from Macedonia to express his thankfulness.[29]

The First Letter (I Cor. 5:9–11)

The scope of Paul's first known letter to Corinth is uncertain. According to I Corinthians 5:9, the communication contained a warning to his Corinthian converts: "I wrote to you in my letter," the apostle recalled, "not to associate with immoral men." Perhaps this was the main burden of the letter. If so, its contents (except for the usual opening, thanksgiving, and closing) are probably preserved in II Corinthians 6:14–7:1. Such a short letter is not impossible, as Paul's letter to Philemon proves.

The theme of this letter is stated in its first extant line: "Do not be mismated with unbelievers." The five rhetorical questions that follow (all of which are to be answered in the negative) underscore the point. There can be no partnership between righteousness and iniquity, light and darkness, Christ and Satan, believer and unbeliever, the Temple and idols. Christians are the Temple of God, and a mosaic of Old Testament quotations is cited to show that God will dwell with them if they shun evil. They are to cleanse themselves "from every defilement of body and spirit, and make holiness perfect in the fear of God" (II Cor. 7:1).

The Second Letter (I Cor. 1–16)

Paul's first letter to Corinth failed to accomplish its purpose. The original problem persisted and others sprang up to keep it company. Word of the developing difficulties reached Paul from two sources—Chloe's people and a letter from the church.[30] The apostle's reply discusses the issues in that order. The dividing line comes at the end of chapter 6, where he turns from the problems raised by Chloe's people to those mentioned in the letter he has received.

Divisiveness (I Cor. 1:10–17; 3:5–15).[31] The once thriving and charismatic Christian community at Corinth had fallen victim to the virus of disunity. Some of its members championed the cause of Apollos, who had been instructed by Paul's Ephesian converts prior to Apollos'

---

[29]Scholars who accept the unity of the Corinthian correspondence hold that the "earlier letter" and the "severe letter" have been lost. The various partition theories, they argue, exaggerate the differences between the alleged intrusions and the material which surrounds them. II Corinthians 12:14–18, moreover, appears to have been written *after* II Corinthians 8:16–24. II Corinthians 12:14, 21 and 13:1, which are found in the "severe letter," anticipate a visit of Paul to Corinth for which the "severe letter" is supposed to be a substitute. Such arguments cannot easily be brushed aside. Yet, on balance, it seems to us that the partition theory we have advanced is to be preferred.

[30]See I Corinthians 1:11 and 7:1, respectively.

[31]The customary salutation and thanksgiving are found in 1:1–9.

successful ministry at Corinth. They took delight in making unfavorable comparisons between the dazzling oratory of the Alexandrian and the more pedestrian performance of Paul. Others supported Cephas (Peter). Still others honored Paul, their spiritual father. The words "I belong to Christ" (1:12) are probably a gloss. Some pious scribe, noting the conflicting loyalties at Corinth, wrote the sentence in the margin of the manuscript as his own declaration of loyalty. A later copyist, thinking that it had been placed in the margin by Paul as a correction, incorporated it into the text.[32] In any case, neither the party of Cephas nor the party of Christ receives attention in the discussion that follows. The real rivalry evidently involved the devotees of Paul and Apollos.

Paul tactfully reminds his readers that Christ cannot be divided. The church is his body, and none of its leaders can stand in Christ's place. It was through his death and resurrection that the redemption of the world was made possible. Although Paul founded the Christian community at Corinth, he did not attempt to make its members Paulinists. Even those few whom he had baptized stand in no special relationship to him (1:15). He and Apollos are simply servants through whom the Corinthian Christians believed. Paul planted, Apollos watered, and God gave the increase. All evangelists are subordinate to Christ. They are not competitors but "fellow workmen for God," who alone passes judgment upon the relative merits of their work (3:9).

Worldly wisdom (I Cor. 1:18–31; 2:6–3:4). Paul did not preach to the Corinthians with eloquent wisdom—an indirect put-down, perhaps, of the lustrous language of Apollos. Not many of the congregation were wise, powerful, or of noble birth. Besides, secular sophistication would rob the cross of Christ of its power. Jews demand "signs" (divine public confirmation of the gospel's claims), and the Greeks seek "wisdom" (rational justification). But Paul and his fellow workers preach "Christ crucified, a stumbling-block to Jews [who believe the Messiah will live forever] and folly to Gentiles [who view a crucified criminal as ethically offensive and evidence of weakness]" (1:22–23). God chose what was "foolish," "weak," and "despised" in the world so that no one might boast in His presence. "He is the source of your life in Christ Jesus," Paul writes the Corinthians, "whom God made our wisdom, our righteousness and sanctification and redemption; therefore, as it is written, 'Let him who boasts, boast of the Lord'" (1:30–31).

---

[32]An alternative view is that the Christ party was composed of those who claimed direct visions of Christ and repudiated all human leaders.

Paul is not adverse to the use of sophisticated language when his audience can comprehend it. "Among the mature," he declares, "we *do* impart wisdom, although it is not a wisdom of this age or of the rulers of this age. . . . We impart a secret and hidden wisdom of God."[33] These words call to mind the wisdom speculation current in the Judaism of Paul's day. Personified wisdom was pictured as the agent through whom the world was created and through whom knowledge of God was given.[34] The Christian kerygma, which has been revealed by the Spirit that is from God, can be understood only by those whom the Spirit has enlightened. "Unspiritual men," those who are governed by worldly wisdom, cannot receive the gifts of the Spirit. When Paul first spoke to the Corinthians, he did not address them as spiritual men because they had not yet been touched by the Spirit of God. "I fed you with milk, not solid food," he writes, "for you were not ready for it; and even yet you are not ready, for you are still of the flesh. For while there is jealousy and strife among you, are you not of the flesh, and behaving like ordinary men? For when one says, 'I belong to Paul,' and another, 'I belong to Apollos,' are you not merely men?" (3:2–4).[35]

Immorality (I Cor. 5:1–6:20). Word reached Paul of a notorious case of incest in the Christian community at Corinth. A man was living with his stepmother. Such shocking immorality, which was forbidden to Jews on the pain of death, made even pagans blush (Lev. 18:8; Deut. 22:30; 27:20). Yet the church had done nothing about it. Corinth issued many invitations to immorality. Brothels serviced sailors, and sacred prostitution flourished in connection with the love goddess, Aphrodite. The tiny Christian community could not be expected to elevate its environment significantly, but it could maintain internal standards of purity. Paul ordered that the member guilty of incest be excommunicated: "You are to deliver this man to Satan for the destruction of the flesh, that his spirit may be saved in the day of the Lord Jesus" (5:5). When Paul wrote in his first letter for his converts "not to associate with immoral men," he did not mean the immoral of the world. He meant the immoral in the church. He had nothing to do with judging outsiders—God judges them. But Christians are to drive out the wicked from their midst. Some converts had so rationalized their freedom from the Law as to indulge in sexual intercourse with prostitutes. Such a practice ignored the fact that a Christian's body is not meant for immorality. "Do you not know," the apostle inquires, "that your body is a temple of the Holy Spirit within you, which you have from God?" (6:19).

[33] I Corinthians 2:6–7, italics added.
[34] Note, for example, the Wisdom of Solomon 7:7, 21–22.
[35] Some commentators hold that Paul is combating a Gnostic viewpoint in these passages, but the wisdom-foolishness conflict with which he deals does not seem to be of the esoteric Gnostic kind. Anyway, Gnosticism appears to have been of a later vintage (see pp. 14–15).

Another behavior pattern of the Corinthian church rankled the apostle. Members took one another into courts where they proceeded to wash their dirty linen before pagan judges. "Do you not know that the saints [believers] will judge the world?" Paul inquires. "And if the world is to be judged by you, are you incompetent to try trivial cases?" (6:2). Surely there were people in the brotherhood who were wise enough to adjudicate disputes. It would have been better to suffer wrong or be defrauded than to parade their disunity in public.

Marriage and celibacy (I Cor. 7) The first question raised by the letter from the Corinthian church to Paul concerned marriage and celibacy. Although some church members divorced sex from morality, others argued for asceticism. They regarded marriage as a state to be avoided if at all possible. Paul acknowledges that celibacy is preferable, but marriage is perfectly proper for those sorely tempted to immorality. Husbands and wives should not deny each other their conjugal rights unless it is done by mutual consent and for the purpose of prayer.[36] Continence should continue only for a season, though, lest Satan take advantage of their situation. A husband should not divorce his wife, and she should not separate from her husband. Christians married to pagans should not seek to shed their mates but work for their conversion.

Paul's preference for celibacy did not stem from a myopic view of marriage. His approval of the wedded state is shown by his prohibition of divorce and his use of the analogy of marriage to depict the relation of Christ to the church (II Cor. 11:2). The apostle's controlling thought sprang from his eschatology. He believed that the End of the Age would soon appear. In view of this "impending distress," it is well that a person remain as he is. If he is single, he should stay that way. If he should marry, though, it would be no sin. The one state is not holier than the other. But the single person has fewer obligations and is thus abler to devote himself to "the affairs of the Lord." Those who have wives should live as though they had none. Maintenance of the status quo enables everyone to give his "undivided devotion to the Lord" (7:35).

Food offered to idols (I Cor. 8:1–11:1). The second problem raised by the letter from Corinth concerned food sacrificed to pagan deities. Many cults besides Judaism engaged in animal sacrifices. Part of the animals was burned, and part was consumed by the priests and by lay worshipers. If meat remained, which was usually the case in public services sponsored by city magistrates, it was sold in the

---

[36]The idea of sexual abstinence as a preparation for cultic rites was a familiar practice in paganism.

market place. Could Christians eat such meat in good conscience? The issue was complicated by the common conviction that the spirit of the gods possessed men when they ate food that had been sacrificed. Some Corinthian Christians, reveling in their newly discovered knowledge that "an idol has no real existence" and "there is no God but one," cast caution to the winds and gleefully purchased the sacrificial meat (8:4). Less knowledgeable brothers believed that the libertines were in some sense participating in the pagan sacrifices when they ate such meat. The consternation caused in the minds of potential converts by these grossly inconsistent views and practices can scarcely be imagined.

Paul reminds his readers that liberty is disciplined by love. Although he heartily agrees with the emancipated that idols have no real existence, he is acutely aware that not everyone has this knowledge. Weaker brethren in the church, recent converts from paganism, actually eat food "as really offered to an idol" (8:7). Out of consideration for these people, Paul urges "the strong" to exercise responsibility toward the weak. It is a sin against Christ to encourage a Christian to act contrary to his conscience, no matter how absurd his scruples may be. "If food [offered to idols] is a cause of my brother's falling," the apostle declares, "I will never eat meat, lest I cause my brother to fall" (8:13). Then he cites his own situation as an example. As an apostle, he has certain privileges. He has the right to marry and to receive material benefits from his converts. But he has deliberately refrained from using his prerogatives lest people suspect his motives: "I have become all things to all men, that I might by all means save some" (9:22).

Idolatry was a constant temptation for Corinthian Christians, and Paul goes to great length to warn them against it. His allusion to the Israelites in their wilderness wanderings and "the Rock [Christ] which followed them" may have mystified Gentile Christians as much as it has modern ones. The point he attempts to make, however, is a cogent one. Supernatural food and drink did not immunize the Israelites against sin. Many of them were destroyed. The Corinthians faced a comparable danger from the heathen influences around them. Pagan worship is of demonic origin. People who participate in pagan ceremonial meals become partners with demons. Christians cannot "partake of the table of the Lord and the table of demons" (10:21). Meat sold in the market place can be purchased with impunity, but care should be taken not to offend another person's conscience. All should be done for the glory of God without offense to Jew, Greek, or the church.

Worship disorders (1 Cor. 11:2–14:40).[37]   Women of the church were taking advantage of their new found freedom to pray and prophesy during worship services with their heads uncovered. Such behavior was shocking to Paul on two counts. No respectable woman appeared unveiled outside her home. The apostle was fearful lest members of the first Ladies' Aid Society be mistaken for prostitutes. Moreover, the quest of the women for emancipation and equality violated the hierarchic principle that prevails in the universe. All are not equal. A divine order was fixed at creation. The "head" of a woman (the one to whom she is subordinate) is her husband. (If she is seen in church with her head uncovered, that is, without the veil which symbolizes her dependence, she dishonors her husband.) The head of a man is Christ, and the head of Christ is God. The head is the one to whom obedience is due. In the Christian community, of course, women are not disadvantaged. "For as woman was made from man, so man is now born of woman" (11:12).

Disorder also characterized the Lord's Supper. The Jerusalem-type celebration prevailed in Corinth. Fellowship rather than commemoration dominated the common meal (Acts 2:46).[38] Just as the Risen Christ had become known to the Emmaus-bound disciples in the breaking of the bread, so Christians in the Holy City saw their meal as an extension of the fellowship they had experienced with the incarnate Christ (Lk. 24:35). As they ate the food, they anticipated the time when they would feast with Christ again in the kingdom of God (Mk. 14:25). But fellowship at Corinth had degenerated into frolic. People ate as soon as they arrived. Early birds gorged themselves and drank to excess. The poor, whose duties prevented early arrival, stared in disbelief at empty tables while their hunger mounted (11:21). Paul pleads that the meal be understood as a memorial to Jesus' death. The broken bread represents the broken body, and the blood symbolizes his life offered up to God.[39] The apostle also insists that the meal should be *repeated* ("Do this") and be regarded as the *new* covenant spoken of by the prophet Jeremiah (31:31–34). Paul has no quarrel with those who view the meal as the precursor of the Big Banquet in which the People of God will participate in the Age to Come. Until that glorious time arrives, however, he thinks

[37]Since this section is not introduced by "now concerning," it is unclear whether the matters discussed were raised by the letter from Corinth or by other reports Paul had received.

[38]For a discussion of the Jerusalem and Pauline types of celebration of the Lord's Supper in the early church, see Hans Leitzmann, *Mass and Lord's Supper* (Leiden: E.J. Brill, 1953).

[39]See Genesis 9:4. Cyprian (*c.* 200–258) was the first to connect the sacrifice in the death of Christ with the sacrifice of the Mass. In Paul's day, drinking the cup was not considered to be drinking the blood of God in order to share his life.

that the Corinthians should replace their first-come, first-served community potluck with a eucharistic meal of a memorial character. For those of a contrary conviction, he has a word of warning: "When you come together to eat, wait for one another—if any one is hungry, let him eat at home—lest you come together to be condemned [by God] (11:33–34).

Worship services were further disrupted in Corinth by the practice of speaking in tongues.[40] Members of the congregation vied with one another for the privilege of articulating the ecstatic gibberish that they attributed to the activity of the Spirit of God. Paul does not question the validity of their inspiration or their right to exercise it. He claims to speak in tongues more than any of them. But this virtue should not be flaunted as a mark of superiority. There are varieties of gifts. All are inspired by the same Spirit. On the apostle's value scale, though, speaking in tongues ranks only eighth. "For one who speaks in a tongue speaks not to men but to God; for no one understands him, but he utters mysteries in the Spirit. On the other hand, he who prophesies speaks to men for their upbuilding and encouragement and consolation. He who speaks in a tongue edifies himself, but he who prophesies edifies the church" (14:2–4). Tongues repel potential proselytes and leave church members so bewildered they don't know when to say "Amen." If tongues are spoken, only two or three should do so at a meeting, they should speak in turn, and someone should interpret. It is better, however, to utter five comprehensible words than ten thousand in a tongue. "God is not a God of confusion but of peace . . . ; all things should be done decently and in order" (14:33, 40).

The urgent need of the Christian church in Corinth was unity. Party divisions had earlier prompted Paul to appeal to his converts to be "united in the same mind and the same judgment" (1:10). This theme is stressed again in chapters 12–14. In the course of his discussion, the apostle develops his famous metaphor of the church as the body of Christ. The church, like the human body, has many members. Each has its own valid function, and each is necessary for the proper operation of the whole. "If one member suffers, all suffer together; if one member is honored, all rejoice together" (12:26). The unity of the body of Christ stems from the spirit: "For by one Spirit we were all baptized into one body—Jews or Greeks, slaves or free—and all were made to drink of one Spirit" (12:13). From the human perspective, however, the bond of unity is love. This love is not sexual attraction (*eros*) or friendship (*philia*), but selfless and patient concern for the welfare of those who are without merit. This "more excellent

[40]The issue was raised in the letter Paul received from Corinth. See pp. 214–216.

way" dampens discord and pulverizes pride in spiritual gifts. Love is ultimate. Faith will be replaced by knowledge, and hope will be realized. But love will never be surperseded—for "God is love" (I John 4:8). Christians, therefore, should make love their aim.

Resurrection of the Dead (I Cor. 15:1–58). The amount of space devoted to this final major topic in Paul's letter suggests that the resurrection of the dead was a hotly debated issue in the Corinthian church. Apparently some of the faithful had downgraded the importance of the resurrection or denied it completely. Those of Greek background were repelled by any concept of physical survival after death. They believed that the body lies "moldering in the grave" while the soul "goes marching on."

Paul readily acknowledges that "flesh and blood" cannot inherit the kingdom of God, but he insists that belief in the resurrection is basic: "If Christ has not been raised, your faith is futile and you are still in your sins" (15:17).[41] This cornerstone of the kerygma has been attested to by a host of witnesses, among whom is the apostle himself. Paul predicates the resurrection of the dead on the resurrection of Christ, and he communicates this predication by an implied analogy. Faithful Israelite farmers habitually bring the first fruits of their harvest and present them to the Lord. Jesus in like fashion presented himself before God as "the first fruits" of the heavenly harvest (15:23). God raised Jesus from the dead not simply to bring the dead back to life but to establish a new order of humanity. Death came through Adam and disobedience; life comes through Christ and obedience. "For as in Adam all die," Paul declares, "so also in Christ shall all be made alive" (15:22). The eschatological sequence of events is spelled out. (1) Christ was the first fruits. (2) At Christ's (second) coming, those who belong to him will be resurrected. (3) Christ rules until he subdues all of his enemies. (4) Then comes the end when he delivers the kingdom to God and personally becomes subject to the Father.

Paul introduces the idea of the "spiritual body" to describe the nature of the resurrection. Although he does not precisely define what he means by the term, it is clear that it constitutes a repudiation of the Jewish notion of a resuscitated corpse and the Greek concept of a disembodied spirit. "Spiritual" indicates that the new life is nonphysical, and "body" suggests that the individual is resurrected in his wholeness. The spiritual body is *given* to the dead. For the living, it is the result of a complete metamorphosis. "We shall not

[41]Compare I Corinthians 15:50.

all sleep [die]," Paul assures his converts, "but we shall all be *changed*."[42] The spiritual body is imperishable, glorified, and powerful—ideally suited to the Age to Come.

The final chapter of I Corinthians is devoted to the collection for Jerusalem and a few personal notes and greetings. The collection, an issue raised by the Corinthians, is a matter of genuine concern to Paul. He regards it as a symbol of the unity of the church, a tangible way in which the Gentile converts can share in the life and work of Mother Church in Jerusalem. Paul advises the Corinthians to accumulate the collection in weekly installments in order that it will be ready when he arrives. "Be watchful, stand firm in your faith, be courageous, be strong," he advises. "Let all that you do be done in love" (16:13–14).

The Third Letter (II Cor. 10–13) [43] Paul's second letter to Corinth was a failure. The moral laxity that he had roundly condemned continued unabated (12:21). Instead of discounting their differences and uniting in love, the factions united against Paul. Their revolt was apparently assisted by certain Jewish Christians who appeared in Corinth with letters of recommendation and a strong determination to exercise leadership.[44] One Corinthian in particular flaunted Paul's authority (11:4).[45] The apostle paid a personal visit to Corinth to quell the rebellion, but it was to no avail (2:1; 12:14). He could not persuade the Corinthians to expel the insurrectionists who were subverting his leadership. With a warning that he would soon return and set things right, he went back to Ephesus.

Defeat at Corinth did not plunge Paul into despair. He made one final effort to recover his lost leadership by writing a stern letter to the church (2:4; 7:8, 12). Its contents are largely preserved in II Corinthians 10–13. Paul's enemies had claimed that they were Hebrews, servants of Christ, apostles, and workers on a par with him. Paul retorts with ironic boasts about his authority, endowments, and achievements. His authority has been received from the Lord for the upbuilding of his converts. He has not acted in worldly fashion. His concern for the Corinthians is genuine. Has he not betrothed them to Christ? Has he not preached the gospel to them without compensation? While he can boast more than any of them about hardships, visions, and revelations, he much prefers to speak about his weaknesses "that the power of Christ may rest upon me" (12:9).

[42]I Corinthians 15:51, italics added. See pp. 195–196.
[43]The letter is largely preserved in these chapters.
[44]See II Corinthians 11:22; 3:1; 11:5, respectively.
[45]Compare II Corinthians 2:5–11.

He threatens vengeance on the rebels and warns them that he will come to Corinth soon to exert his power.

The letter was dispatched to Corinth by the hand of Titus. Paul was left with the hardest task such an active and vigorous man can have—waiting for the results.

The Fourth Letter (II Cor. 1:1–6:13; 7:2–9:15) [46] When Titus failed to return from Corinth, Paul was plagued with anxiety. Had he erred in sending the severe letter? Had his missive widened the breach? Soon the apostle left Ephesus for Troas, where he preached the gospel with power and effectiveness. His mind was not at rest, though, because he did not find Titus there (2:13). He crossed the Aegean to Macedonia. There, at length, he met Titus. To Paul's immense relief, he learned that the severe letter had produced the desired effect. The Corinthians had acknowledged that Paul was an authentic apostle and that his way with them had been upright and honorable. They had vented their wrath against their misleaders, especially against the ringleader. They eagerly awaited Paul's arrival in Corinth so that they could assure him of their confidence and affection. The apostle expressed his relief and satisfaction at the unexpected turn of events in his fourth and final Corinthian letter known to us.

The opening words of this letter recall one of the initial verses of Isaiah 40. Paul reminds the Corinthians that God is "God of all comfort [consolation, encouragement, and strength], who comforts us in all our affliction, so that we may be able to comfort those who are in any affliction, with the comfort with which we ourselves are comforted by God" (1:3–4). The apostle nearly died in Asia, but his extremity was God's opportunity. God delivered him from a deadly peril. "You also must help us by prayer," he entreats the Corinthians (1:11). He explains that it is to spare them that he has refrained from coming to Corinth. He has not wanted to make them another painful visit. Paul displays uncommon magnanimity toward the chief offender. He urges the Corinthians to forgive and "reaffirm your love for him. . . . Any one whom you forgive, I also forgive" (2:8, 10).

The audacious affirmations of the severe letter are reversed or restated in a more conciliatory tone. Paul will not "commend" himself. The Corinthians are his "letters of recommendation." His "sufficiency is from God." He is a minister of a new covenant in the Spirit (3:1–6).

---

[46] The letter is largely preserved in these passages.

The treasure he has is in earthen vessels, but this does not cause him to lose heart. "This slight momentary affliction is preparing for us an eternal weight of glory beyond all comparison, because we look not to the things that are seen but to the things that are unseen; for the things that are seen are transient, but the things that are unseen are eternal" (4:17–18).

Paul views his ministry as one of reconciliation. He regards no one from a human viewpoint. If anyone is "in Christ," he is a new creation. God through Christ "reconciled us to himself and gave us the ministry of reconciliation" (5:18). The Corinthians are not restricted by Paul, but they are restricted in their affections toward him. "Widen your hearts also," he counsels them (6:12). Both he and Titus have rejoiced at their repentance. While the apostle once was sorry that he had sent the severe letter, this is no longer the case (7:6–16).

The last two chapters of Paul's fourth letter concern the collection for the Christian poor in Jerusalem. The Macedonian churches had implored the apostle to permit them to participate, and their resultant generosity set a superb example for the Corinthians to emulate. Titus, the letter-bearer, and two others of spotless reputation are being sent to assist the Corinthians in raising their share of the relief funds. The project had begun earlier in Corinth, but it probably ground to a halt when relations with Paul ruptured. The apostle insists that the collections be resumed at once, and he appeals to numerous motives to achieve this goal (8:8–15). He seeks to allay any suspicion that the funds will be misappropriated. "So give proof, before the churches," he urges, "of your love and of our boasting about you to these men" (8:24).[47] The collection symbolizes both the repentance of the Corinthians and the unity of the church. Paul's final words seem to express not only his gratitude to God for His Son, but also his relief at the improved situation: "Thanks be to God for his inexpressible gift!" (9:15).

[47]Since chapter 9 also deals with the collection, repeating some matters as though they had not already been discussed, some scholars regard it as a separate note sent to Corinth later. The repetition, though, could have been made for emphasis.

XI

Paul's Correspondence
(Galatians,
Romans,
Colossians,
Philemon,
Philippians)

The two most influential letters of Paul are Galatians and Romans. They were probably written only a few months apart, and they can best be understood in connection with each other. Together they present the apostle's most distinctive understanding of the Christian kerygma.

Galatians

Paul's authorship of Galatians is unmistakable. The occasion, purpose, and message of the communication are transparent. Less clear are the date of the letter, where the apostle was at the time, and to what churches the missive was directed. Galatians offers no direct information concerning these issues, and Paul's other letters provide little help. The account in Acts is fragmentary and of dubious historical accuracy. Some scholars believe that Galatians was Paul's earliest letter and date it about 49 A.D.[1] Others argue for the 52–54 A.D. range or for 56 A.D.[2] The divergencies stem from the uncertainties as to whether Paul's Jerusalem visit of Galatians 2:1 should be identified with Acts 11:30 or 15:2 and on which one of Paul's "missionary journeys" the churches were founded. Two views of the destination of Galatians have resulted—the North and South Galatians theories.

Destination

What was the location of "the churches of Galatia" to which Paul's letter was addressed? "Galatia" is an ambiguous term with two possible meanings. A group of Gauls invaded Asia Minor in the third century B.C. They were ultimately confined to a tract of land in the northern part of the central plateau, and the territory became known as Galatia. Its chief towns were Ancyra, Pessinus, and Tavium. During the Roman conquests, Galatia was annexed and enlarged. In 25 B.C., it became a Roman province. This greater Galatia included not only Galatia proper but parts of Phrygia, Pisidia, and Lycaonia, and the southern cities of Antioch, Iconium, Lystra, and Derbe.

[1]Albert E. Barnett, *The New Testament: Its Making and Meaning* (New York: Abingdon Press, 1946), pp. 25–29, with Syrian Antioch as the place of composition.
[2]See E.J. Goodspeed, *Paul* (Philadelphia: The John C. Winston Co., 1947), pp. 105–112, and J.H. Ropes, *The Singular Problem of the Epistle to the Galatians* (Cambridge, Mass.: Harvard Univ. Press, 1929), p. 46, respectively. Where Paul was (Antioch? Ephesus? Rome?), of course, depends on when the letter was written.

Advocates of the *North Galatians theory* maintain that Paul used "Galatia" in its original sense. He founded churches there at the beginning of his second journey and revisited them on his third (Acts 6:16; 18:23).[3] Protagonists acknowledge that Luke says nothing about the founding of churches in Acts 16:6. This omission is attributed to his eagerness to advance Paul to Troas and Europe. Luke does not refer to Antioch, Iconium, Lystra, and Derbe as cities of Galatia. Paul, moreover, used geographical rather than political designations to describe land areas (Gal. 1:21; I Thess. 2:14). Like Luke, then, when he used "Galatia," he must have meant North Galatia.

Since the latter part of the eighteenth century, scholars have increasingly favored the *South Galatians theory.* Now they constitute a consensus. They hold that two obscure references in Acts (16:6; 18:23) are sandy soil on which to build a case. The "region of Galatia" that these verses mention need not include all of the Galatian territory. No evidence exists in Acts or elsewhere that Paul ever founded churches in North Galatia. His purpose was to pass through the region rather than to preach in it. When Paul spoke of a *group* of churches, such as those in Galatia, it was his custom to call them by the Roman province in which they were located (I Cor. 16:19a; II Cor. 1:1b; 8:1). He spoke of the provinces of Judea, Syria, Cilicia, Asia, Macedonia, and Achaia, but not of Phrygia, Pisidia, and Lycaonia. The latter were merely geographical regions. "Galatia" was the only term that would have included all the cities that he had evangelized on his first journey. Luke, contrary to his usual practice, mentions no churches in Acts 16:6–8 and 18:23. In the latter verse, all the *disciples* were strengthened, whereas elsewhere it was the *churches* that were strengthened (Acts 14:23; 15:41; 16:5).[4]

Date If Paul's letter to "the churches of Galatia" was directed to Christians in Antioch, Iconium, Lystra, and Derbe, what was the year of its composition? Available evidence does not decisively fix the time. The communication, as we have seen, has been located at several junctures in Paul's career. The North Galatians theory requires a date after the journey mentioned in Acts 18:23, since Galatians 4:13 indicates that Paul had visited Galatia twice prior to writing the letter. If this was the case, the place of composition was probably Ephesus

---

[3]The last two words of Galatians 4:13 may mean either "formerly" or "the former of two times." If the latter is preferable, Paul had visited the Galatians twice before he wrote to them.

[4]If Acts is not a reliable historical guide, as we believe, it should not be used as a basis for confident theorizing. The facts that the churches mentioned in Acts have no letters written to them by Paul and that the letters Paul wrote to churches in Asia Minor are not mentioned in Acts suggest something about the authenticity of Acts.

and the date about 52 A.D.[5] The South Galatians theory enables Galatians to be assigned to the same period, but other dates are also possible. Some place it at 49 A.D. after Paul's return to Syrian Antioch at the end of his first journey (Acts 14:26). Although this view cannot be completely ruled out, it requires the rather awkward notion that Paul's two visits to Galatia took place on his first journey and the improbable identification of the Jerusalem visit of Galatians 2:1 with Acts 11:30. If Galatians was written in 49 A.D., why do the Thessalonian letters that shortly followed contain no marks of the faith-works controversy? It seems to us that Galatians cannot be forced to conform to Acts. Paul's letter is the primary source. It demonstrates strong thought affinities with Romans and discusses issues akin to certain concerns in the Corinthian correspondence. We believe that it was written in Ephesus or Corinth on Paul's third journey about 56 A.D.

The Troublemakers
The fomenters of discord in Galatia are commonly identified as "Judaizers"—Jewish Christians who regarded circumcision as essential to salvation and insisted that Christians adhere to the ceremonial laws of Judaism. They believed Paul's gospel was incomplete and needed to be supplemented by legal exactitude. They openly attacked his apostolic authority, and they impugned the motives of his missions. References to "certain men" who "came from James" to Antioch and objected to Jewish Christians eating with Gentiles and to "those who unsettle you" have caused many to conclude that the troublemakers were emissaries from the Jerusalem church to Galatia (2:4, 12; 5:12).[6] But there is no evidence that Jerusalem Judaizers hounded Paul during his campaigns for Christ. If such a delegation had arrived in Galatia, Paul would not have been in the dark as to their identity, yet in Galatians 5:10 he refers to one of the troublemakers as "whoever he is." There were enough native Jews in Galatia to account for the enthusiasm for the Law that the churches evidenced.[7]

Another group attacked Paul from a different angle. They were antilegalists who wanted to abandon the Old Testament and its prophetic insights. They accused Paul of supporting the old legalism and preaching circumcision (2:18; 5:11).

---

[5]The "so quickly" of Galatians 1:6, of course, does not need to be taken so literally.
[6]See also Galatians 3:1; 4:17; 5:10; 6:12–13. The idea reflects the Tübingen theory that a basic antagonism prevailed between Paul and the Jerusalem apostles.
[7]Johannes Munck, in his book *Paul and the Salvation of Mankind* (Richmond, Va.: John Knox Press, 1959) has advanced the novel notion that the troublemakers were not Jewish Christians but Gentile converts who came to their convictions by studying the Septuagint. They appealed to the position of the Twelve (whom they came to know through Paul) over the head of the apostle himself. Their error was the idealization of Judaism.

Galatians is unique among Paul's letters in the abruptness with which it plunges into the heart of its message. The letter is devoid of the customary felicitations, thanksgivings, and compliments. Only the formal grace and peace are retained. Indeed, the first point of Paul's argument intrudes into the introduction: "Paul an apostle—not from men nor through man, but through Jesus Christ and God the Father, who raised him from the dead" (1:1). The letter itself divides naturally into three parts.

Declaration of independence from Judaism (Gal. 1:6–2:21). Paul was astonished that the Galatians had so quickly deserted the gospel he preached to them. The innovations that they had introduced from Judaism amounted to another gospel. Paul was called to be an apostle by Christ. Like Isaiah and Jeremiah before him, he was chosen before birth. He conferred with no one after his conversion, and it was three years before he went up "by revelation" to Jerusalem and had limited conversations with some of the Twelve. His Greek companion, Titus, was not "compelled" to submit to circumcision. Peter, James, and John "added nothing" to him. On the contrary, they endorsed his gospel by extending to him "the right hand of fellowship." When Peter arrived in Antioch, he readily participated in table fellowship with Gentiles. But pressure from Jerusalem Judaizers prompted him to abandon the practice. Paul reprimanded Peter when he saw that he was not straightforward about the truth of the gospel and reminded the Rock that "a man is not justified by works of the law but through faith in Jesus Christ" (2:16).

Priority and superiority of faith (Gal. 3:1–5:12). After Paul had established the divine origin of his apostleship and the legitimacy of his gospel, he determined to teach the truth of his gospel and prevent its perversion by the Judaizers. He turns first to the experience of the Galatians themselves. They have received the Spirit not by works of the Law but by hearing with faith. Why then should they want to return to the Law? The Law was never intended to be the ideal basis of man's relationship to God. Abraham, father of the Hebrews, had received righteousness by faith 430 years before the Law was given. "So you see," declares the apostle, "that it is men of faith who are the sons of Abraham" (3:7). God's promise to Abraham makes plain that Gentiles are included: "In thee shall all the nations [the Gentiles] be blessed" (3:8). By the subtle treatment of a collective noun as singular, Paul later shows that the promise is realized through Christ: "Now the promises were made to Abraham and to his offspring. It does not say, 'And to offsprings,' referring to many; but, referring to one, 'And to your offspring,' which is Christ" (3:16).

All who rely on works of the Law are under its curse, because the Law requires perfect obedience. Its purpose was to expose human sinfulness and to keep men dependent on God's prior promise to Abraham. The Law was a temporary and provisional means of discipline intended to bring people to Christ. But now that faith has come, the Law is passé. Believers in Christ are free from its tutelage. For the Galatians to practice circumcision and conform to ceremonial Judaism would be to submit to bondage. Once they were slaves "to the weak and beggarly elemental spirits"—invisible demons or world rulers. Do they think that devotion to the Law will immunize them against the pernicious influences of the spirit world?

After a parenthetical appeal to the Galatians for a restoration of their former loyalty to him, Paul climaxes his argument with an allegory based on Abraham's two sons. It was not the son of Hagar, the slave, but the son of Sarah, the free woman, who became Abraham's heir. Christians, like Sarah's son, Isaac, are "children of promise" (4:28). Through Christ, they are free. If they insist on remaining under the Law, however, they will be like Hagar's son, Ishmael, who was cast out. "For in Christ Jesus," Paul persists, "neither circumcision nor uncircumcision is of any avail, but faith working through love" (5:6).

Freedom of Spirit-led men (Gal. 5:13–6:10). This third section of Galatians emphasizes the responsible use of freedom by those who are guided not by the Law but by the Spirit. Christian freedom requires neighbor-love rather than selfish indulgence. The whole Law is fulfilled in the command, "You shall love your neighbor as yourself." The apostle lists the works of the flesh and contrasts them with the fruit of the Spirit. "And those who belong to Christ Jesus," he asserts, "have crucified the flesh with its passions and desires" (5:24). He warns Christians against self-conceit, provocation of one another, and envy. Those "who are spiritual" should practice gentle forbearance toward offenders and not grow weary in well-doing.[8]

Some of the arguments in Galatians sound strange to modern ears. Some of the issues, such as circumcision, have long since been resolved in favor of freedom. But Paul's stress on Christianity's independence from the Law, the priority and superiority of faith, and the freedom of Spirit-led men remain at the core of the Christian faith.

---

[8]Those "who are spiritual" need not refer to a group other than the Judaizers. Paul has earlier attacked those who have begun in the Spirit and are ending in the flesh. Now near the close of his letter he continues his opposition to those "who would compel" the Galatians to be circumcised and thereby exalt the flesh (6:12).

The scholars who question that Paul wrote Romans, or at least the bulk of it, are rare. The latter's style and vocabulary are comparable to I & II Corinthians and Galatians. The subjects dealt with fit the churches at mid-century, the doctrinal development coheres with Paul's day, and the communication is found in every known list of Pauline letters, orthodox or heretical.

Textual Variations When Paul's letter left his hand, it bore no title. This was doubtless an addendum of a later date derived from references in Romans 1:7 ("to all God's beloved in Rome") and 1:15 ("to you also who are in Rome"). In two manuscripts, however, the word Rome does not appear and chapters 15 and 16 are missing.[9] The doxology, moreover, is a floater. It is found in most of the best manuscripts in its canonical position at 16:25–27, in the majority of manuscripts at the end of chapter 14 (either alone or in addition to its canonical position), in one prized manuscript (called P46) at the end of chapter 15, and in a few manuscripts it is missing entirely.

These facts have given rise to numerous conjectures. (1) Paul wrote the shorter form of Romans (without the words "in Rome" of 1:7, 15) to the churches as a general letter that he later enlarged and dispatched to Rome. (2) The church edited Paul's full-length letter for general use. (3) Marcion, influential second-century reformer and devotee of Pauline Christianity, shortened Paul's letter. Assumptions that Romans was a general letter are ruled out by the author's repeated assertion of his intention to visit the addressees (1:13; 15:22–23). There seems to be nothing in chapters 15–16 to which Marcion would have objected. Perhaps the best explanation of the existence of the shorter version is that the last chapters were lost from the end of the manuscript. This would account for the floating nature of the doxology, a composition that most scholars consider non-Pauline both in style and content. According to the list of Paul's letters in the Muratorian fragment (a portion of a corrupt Latin manuscript comprising the greater part of the Christian writings accepted as canonical, perhaps by someone at Rome in the second century A.D.), Romans once stood at the end of the collection. The doxology was probably a post-Paul composition designed to provide a suitable conclusion for the collection as a whole. It would be only natural, then, for these verses to appear in different places where one or another of the forms of the letter ended.

Destination and Date The deletion of the words "in Rome" in Romans 1:7, 15 continues to perplex scholars. The only plausible reason would be to make

---

[9]Codices Fuldensis and Amiatinus.

Romans a general letter, but such a designation ill befits this writing. Besides, everything in Romans (except chapter 16, which is discussed below) confirms that address.

The date of Romans, like all the other letters, is a matter of dispute. This is true despite the fact that Paul provides us with some solid clues. The apostle is near the close of his career. He has fully preached the gospel from Jerusalem to Illyricum, and he no longer has any room in these regions. He wants to go to Spain, since Italy is already being evangelized and he is reluctant to build on another man's foundation, but he would like to visit the Roman church en route. He cannot do so at once, though, because he must first visit Jerusalem with aid for the saints. For some time he has been engaged in taking a collection among the churches of Macedonia and Greece. The venture is now virtually complete, and he feels compelled to deliver the collection in person lest the wrong interpretation be placed on it. When he has accomplished this task, he will go to Spain by way of Rome (15:19–29). In lieu of an immediate visit, he writes a letter to the Roman Christians.

The occasion for Paul's collection for the Jerusalem poor is mentioned in Galatians 2:10. This labor of love is in process in I Corinthians 16:1–4 and II Corinthians 8–9. By the time Romans 15:25–28 was written, the collection is almost ready to be delivered. Paul plans to end his work on the collection in Corinth, according to I Corinthians 16:3–4. This intention is about to be realized and the apostle is actually on his way to that city in II Corinthians 9:3–5. It is natural to conclude, then, that he wrote Romans in Corinth. The date was 56 A.D. according to our reckoning. Paul spent three months there on the eve of his departure for Jerusalem at the close of his third journey. Shortly thereafter he would be in the Holy City and suffer his final imprisonment (Acts 20:2–3; 21:33; 24:17).

A Letter to Ephesus? Chapter 16 of Romans begins with an introduction of Phoebe, a deaconess of the church at Cenchreae and bearer of the letter. This introduction is followed by a long list of names of people to whom the author wants greetings conveyed. Next comes a warning against those who create dissensions and difficulties. Greetings to the church from some of Paul's associates then lead to the doxology that we have already discussed.

There is much about this chapter to cause one to question its relationship to Romans. Paul's principal purpose in writing Romans was to explain his version of the gospel to a church of which he had no firsthand knowledge. Yet in 16:3–16, he mentions twenty-six people by name. How did he know so many people so well in a church he had never visited? The polemical tone of 16:17–20 clashes with the benign character of the rest of Romans. How did Paul, moreover, learn about the troublemakers to whom these verses refer? Such doubts are sustained by the witness of the Chester Beatty papyrus, the oldest known manuscript of Romans. It places the doxology (16:25–27) at the end of chapter 15.

If chapter 16 is Romans' foster child, who was its natural father? Many experts believe that it is a genuine note of Paul originally addressed to Ephesus. In the process of collecting and editing the Pauline correspondence, they allege, the small missive became attached to the letter to Rome.[10] The theory, while not without its difficulties, has much to commend it. Paul had lived at Ephesus longer than anywhere else on his missions, and he would have been intimately aware of that church and its needs. The pastoral tone of the letter would be altogether appropriate under the circumstances. When Prisca and Aquila were last mentioned they were in Ephesus, where a church met in their house (I Cor. 16:19; Rom. 16:5; Acts 18:18, 26). Epaenetus is mentioned as "the first convert in Asia for Christ" (Rom. 16:5). Although the other names have no such connection with Asia or Ephesus, they might well be found there.[11]

Purpose   Romans seems to erase all doubt as to why Paul wrote it. In the introduction, the apostle mentions his long-standing desire to visit the Romans. He wants to impart "some spiritual gift to strengthen" them and to "reap some harvest" among them as well as among the rest of the Gentiles (1:11–13). In the final chapter, Paul returns to his reasons for writing: "I hope to see you in passing as I go to Spain, and to be sped on my journey there by you, once I have enjoyed your company for a little" (15:24).[12] His purpose is clear. He wants to visit the Romans briefly, enrich them while he is there, and then go on to Spain to accomplish his principal task.

[10]E.J. Goodspeed, *An Introduction to the New Testament* (Chicago: Univ. of Chicago Press, 1937), pp. 85–86.
[11]Opponents of the Ephesus hypothesis point to the fact that Paul does not greet a single person by name in any letter of his addressed to a church he knows. They also wonder why, after so short a time away from Ephesus, it is necessary for Paul to remind the Ephesians of the noble deeds of Prisca and Aquila, the status of Epaenetus, etc. Some scholars, therefore, regard chapter 16 as a second-century pseudonymous addition to Romans. For an excellent discussion of the various theories, see John Knox, "The Epistle to the Romans: Introduction," in George A. Buttrick, ed., *The Interpreter's Bible* (New York: Abingdon Press, 1954), IX, 365–368.
[12]Compare 15:28. Some scholars see a shift of emphasis between chapters 1 and 15. In the former, Paul views Rome as a field of pastoral activity and does not mention Spain; in the latter, Rome is pictured simply as a way station on his journey to Spain.

Many commentators question the adequacy of these motivations for the composition of Romans. "Why should Paul write such an extensive theological document," they ask, "simply to introduce himself and to announce his forthcoming 'tourist stop' en route to Spain? He would be there shortly. A brief note would have sufficed and been more appropriate." Consequently, a host of hidden motives have been suggested to supplement or supplant those already mentioned. (1) Paul wanted to secure the endorsement and support of the Roman church for his Spanish mission. (2) He wanted to set forth a compendium of his gospel. (3) He wished to refute the charge that he had neglected such an important church. (4) He sought to contradict false suppositions concerning the nature of his ministry. (5) He wanted to safeguard Roman Christians against dangers other churches had experienced. (6) He wanted to clear up the trouble that existed between Jewish and Gentile Christians. (7) He wrote to restate the principles of his gospel for the Gentiles in its relation to Judaism. Perhaps the fact that he had not founded the church at Rome accounts for his rather lengthy statement.

Message The theme of Romans is stated in 1:16–17: The Gospel "is the power of God for salvation to every one who has faith, to the Jew first and also to the Greek. For in it the righteousness of God is revealed through faith for faith; as it is written, 'He who through faith is righteous shall live.' " Every aspect of salvation that is to be discussed is foreshadowed in these verses. The source of salvation is God's gracious action. Salvation is open to the Jews and the Greeks. Faith is its sole prerequisite, and forgiveness ("justification") and life are its certain consequences.

Universal predicament: sin (Rom. 1:18–3:20). Paul develops the thesis of Romans by first focusing on the Gentiles. Ever since the creation of the world God's invisible nature has been clearly perceived in His works, yet men have refused to honor Him. Instead, they have resorted to idolatry. Their punishment has been appropriate. God has given them up to impurity—shameless lusts, violent and unruly passions, and lack of natural affections. While the Jews delight in passing judgment on the Gentiles, the Jews are in no sense superior. They have done the same things and will suffer the same condemnation. The notions that God's goodness and his favoritism will cancel their deserved punishment are false. Although the Law is a mark of privilege for the Jews, it is also the standard by which they will be judged. It cannot save them, because they have not kept it. It serves only to increase their responsibility and deepen their despair. "All who have sinned without the law," Paul declares, "will also perish without the law, and all who have sinned under the law will be judged by the law" (2:12). What advantage, then, do Jews have? They were entrusted with the oracles of God. However, this did not make them immune to sin. All men are under the power of sin. The Law is powerless to rescue them from this situation, for no human being can be justified in God's sight by works of the Law "since through the law comes knowledge of sin" (3:20). The universal predicament calls for a universal remedy.

Universal remedy for sin: justification by faith (Rom. 3:21–4:25). The Gentiles have tried wisdom, and the Jews have tried Law. Neither has proved to be an effective antidote for sin. "But now the righteousness of God has been manifested apart from law," Paul asserts, ". . . through faith in Jesus Christ for all who believe. For there is no distinction; since all have sinned and fall short of the glory of God, they are justified by his grace as a gift, through the redemption which is in Christ Jesus, whom God put forward as an expiation by his blood, to be received by faith. This was to show God's righteousness, because in his divine forbearance he had passed over former sins; it was to prove at the present time that he himself is righteous and that he justifies him who has faith in Jesus" (3:21–26).

These verses make use of legal and religious terms that were quite familiar to Jews and Greeks in the ancient world, but they require some explanation for modern readers. *Righteousness*, in English usage, normally indicates a moral quality of uprightness and justice attributable either to God or man. The cognate verb, *to justify*, means to make or to declare right. To justify God is to prove His righteousness; to justify man is to pronounce him morally right or to make him so. Righteousness is a moral quality. In Hebrew thought, however, it was not primarily a quality but an activity. How did an Israelite judge justify one who had been accused? He did not implant in him the quality of uprightness. Neither did he publicly announce that the man was innocent of wrong. He rectified the situation and restored the accused to his rightful place in society. Similarly, when Paul speaks of "the righteousness of God," he is not simply describing His character. Neither is he implying that God instills His own moral qualities into particular people. The apostle is asserting that God has taken the initiative in restoring a man to his proper place among men and before Him.

God's justifying activity is centered in the death of Jesus on the cross. Paul views that death as a ransom, the primary meaning of the Greek word translated "redemption" (3:24).[13] The form of the word, how-

---

[13]Compare Mark 10:45.

ever, stresses the act of ransoming rather than the ransom itself. The apostle does not intend to suggest that God paid a price to Satan to loosen his grip on men. God dealt with His adversary not to appease him but to defeat him and to destroy his power. The ransom metaphor speaks to man's hopeless condition. He is bound by sin and death, and he lacks both the power and opportunity to escape. God in Christ came to the rescue. He suffered and died on the cross to set men free. Men are thus justified by God's "grace as a gift, through the redemption which is in Christ Jesus" (3:24). *Grace* is the spontaneous and unmerited kindness, mercy, and love that God displays toward men. Nothing man can do will call it forth. It is wholly gratuitous, as the word "gift" makes plain.

Jesus was the agent of God's justifying act. God put him forward "as an expiation by his blood, to be received by faith" (3:25). The quotation may suggest to some that God is vengeful and must be appeased by the sacrificial slaughter of His Son. The use of "propitiation" instead of "expiation" in the King James Version strengthens this notion. But the regular Septuagint usage of the term in question denotes the removal of guilt that separates man from God. If man is the agent, the proper rendering is *"expiation."* If God is the agent, the proper translation is *"forgiveness."*[14] "Blood," in Hebrew thought, stood for "life." According to Paul, Jesus offered up his life to God. This act of abnegation removed the barrier that sin had built between men and their Maker. Prior to Jesus' death, God had been forgiving toward men and forbearing toward their sins. But their guilt had grown like weeds until it blinded them to God's true nature. Then they exchanged the glory of the immortal God for images (1:23). Jesus' dedication to God even unto death, the last of a long series of obediences, was God's great gesture of reconciliation. It made it possible once again for men to see what God is really like. He hates sin, loves sinners, and takes the initiative in bringing men into a right relationship with Himself. In response to what God has done in Christ, men are expected to trust God and to depend for their salvation on His justifying act. The cross discloses the costliness of sin, and it dispels the idea that divine forgiveness means moral indifference. Consequently God can freely forgive anyone who unreservedly commits his life to Him no matter what the level of his moral attainment at the time.

How is justification by faith related to God's former revelation to Israel? The Law, based on the principle of works, permitted boasting, but the principle of faith pulverizes pride. God accepts a man not

[14]See C.H. Dodd, *The Epistle of Paul to the Romans* (New York: Harper & Row, 1932), pp. 48–61, for a helpful discussion of the significant words of this passage.

on the basis of what he has done, but on the basis of what God has done for him in Christ. The Law distinguished between Jew and Gentile, but that distinction is no longer valid. Both must approach God on the ground of faith. Does faith, then, overthrow the Law? Certainly not. Faith upholds the Law. Note the case of Abraham. He "believed God, and it was reckoned to him as righteousness" (4:3). Circumcision was not required of him until after he had trusted God and been accepted by Him. "He received circumcision as a sign or seal of the righteousness which he had by faith while he was still uncircumcised. The purpose was to make him the father of all who believe without being circumcised and who thus have righteousness reckoned to them, and likewise the father of the circumcised who are not merely circumcised but also follow the example of the faith which our father Abraham had before he was circumcised" (4:11–12). The promise to Abraham and his descendants that they would inherit the world came not through the Law but through the righteousness of faith. Since the promise rests on grace, it is guaranteed to all—not only to the Law-abiders but also to those who share Abraham's faith (4:13–25).

New life that results from justification by faith (Rom. 5:1–8:39). Up to this point, Paul has been concerned with justification—the need for it and the ground for it in God's action in Christ. Now the apostle moves on to the new life that results from God's justifying act. Those who are justified by faith have peace with God. They rejoice in their hope of sharing God's glory and in their sufferings. Justification (God's gracious removal of guilt and condemnation) and *reconciliation* (the resultant restoration of warm personal relationships) are present realities, but *salvation* (which is closely linked with the resurrection in Paul's thought) is still in the future: "Since, therefore, we are now justified by his blood, much more shall we be saved by him from the wrath of God. For if while we were enemies we were reconciled to God by the death of his Son, much more, now that we are reconciled, shall we be saved by his life" (5:9–10). "His life" refers to the continuing reality of Christ, his lordship of the Christian community.

Paul mirrored popular Jewish thought when he wrote that "sin came into the world through one man and death through sin" (5:12). Since Adam was the first man, he was seen not simply as a symbol of the human race, but also as its representative. When he violated God's command, all of his descendants were somehow involved in his transgression and its consequent penalty—death. Did Paul, then, believe in inherited sin? Sometimes he seems to say so. "By one man's disobedience," he declared, "many were made sinners" (5:19). Yet in other passages, he appears to attribute death's universality not to Adam's sin but to the sin of subsequent men. "Death spread to all men," he wrote, "because all men sinned" (5:12). Such statements make it difficult, if not impossible, to discern Paul's attitude concerning sin as a hereditary disease. Of one thing, however, we can be comfortably certain. He believed that sin came into the world when Adam set himself against God, and its effects were continued and compounded by the sins of subsequent generations. His concern was primarily with the corporate reality of sin, not with its origin, and for this he had a surefire solution: "As by one man's disobedience [Adam's] many were made sinners, so by one man's obedience [Christ's] many will be made righteous" (5:19). Through faith in Christ, men are lifted into a new order of life characterized by justification, redemption from the power of sin, and victory over death.

Paul was convinced that the Law served to heighten men's sin and their sense of sin, "but where sin increased, grace abounded all the more" (5:20). At this point the apostle's doctrine of justification by faith laid him open to a serious charge. Should men continue to sin that grace may abound? "By no means!" Paul resolutely responded. "How can we who died to sin still live in it?" (6.2). The three analogies that follow, although not as apt as they might be, are designed to clarify his thought. (1) When a person is "baptized into Christ," he dies to sin. The figure of speech was probably suggested to Paul by the resemblance between immersion and burial. He saw Christ's death as a symbol of the old order and his resurrection as the beginning of the new. Sin ruled the old community headed by Adam, but sin has no power in the new community headed by Christ. To be "in Christ" is to be a "new creature" in the newly created community. "Those who belong to Christ Jesus," Paul wrote the Galatians, "have crucified the flesh with its passions and desires" (Gal. 5:24). (2) When a person is a slave, he is a slave of the one whom he obeys—"either of sin, which leads to death, or of obedience, which leads to righteousness" (6:16). The Romans were once slaves of sin, but Christ liberated them and they are now slaves of righteousness. (3) A married woman, according to the Law, is bound to her husband as long as he lives. If he should die, however, she is free to marry another man. So it is with Christians. We were formerly married, as it were, to sin, but we have died to the Law (which aroused our sinful passions) through the death of Christ. Now we are free to marry another husband, Christ, to whom we really belong. Once we bore "fruit for death"; now we bear "fruit for God" (7:1-6).

Did Paul, then, consider that the Law is sin? So it might seem. He thought that the Law provides knowledge of sin, increases the trespass, and arouses sinful passions. But the apostle shrank from saying that the Law is sin. Nothing that comes from God can be tainted. The Law "is holy and just and good" (7:12). Its failure stems not from its purpose but from man's perverseness. "If it had not been for the law," Paul declared, "I should not have known sin. I should not have known what it is to covet if the law had not said, 'You shall not covet.' But sin, finding opportunity in the commandment, wrought in me all kinds of covetousness. . . . The very commandment which promised life proved to be death to me" (7:7–10). Paul poignantly described the intolerable tension that sin created in him: "I can will what is right, but I cannot do it. For I do not do the good I want, but the evil I do not want is what I do. Now if I do what I do not want, it is no longer I that do it, but sin which dwells within me" (7:18b–20).

By faith the believer is freed of condemnation. "For the law of the Spirit of life in Christ Jesus has set me free from the law of sin and death. For God has done what the law, weakened by the flesh, could not do: sending his own Son in the likeness of sinful flesh and for sin [that is, to deal with sin], he condemned sin in the flesh, in order that the just requirement of the law might be fulfilled in us, who walk not according to the flesh but according to the Spirit" (8:2–4). The Spirit, the self-validating presence and power of God in the world, is the experiential ground of faith and hope. This Spirit bridges the span between the believers' past (justification and reconciliation) and their future (salvation). As "heirs of God and fellow heirs with Christ," they eagerly await the future glory when all creation "will be set free from its bondage to decay" (8:17,21). They are "more than conquerors" through him who loved them. Paul's credo was theirs: "For I am sure that neither death, nor life, nor angels, nor principalities, nor things present, nor things to come, nor powers, nor height, nor depth, nor anything else in all creation, will be able to separate us from the love of God in Christ Jesus our Lord" (8:38–39).

The place of Jew and Gentile in God's purpose (Rom. 9–11). Chapters 9–11 constitute such an independent unit that one eminent scholar maintains they were originally a sermon by Paul that he incorporated into his letter to the Romans.[15] While one may question whether the apostle wrote out his sermons so carefully and filed them for ready reference, it is worth asking why he included such a self-contained discussion in this letter. The answer is not too difficult to surmise. He would shortly depart for Palestine with the collection taken among predominantly Gentile churches for the support of their Jewish brethren in Jerusalem. He doubtless hoped that the offering would moderate the controversy that had raged for years concerning

[15]Dodd, *The Epistle of Paul to the Romans,* pp. 148–150.

the relation of Christians to Jewish Law and concerning the calling and destiny of the Jewish people. Because the apostle was himself a Jew, such problems had a special poignancy. It would be only natural at this stage of his career that he would want to record his own mature position on subjects so critical to the church. If, as some suspect, Paul had been pictured to the Romans as one who despised his religious heritage, the Roman church (which was fond of the Jews) might well have been offended. This would explain why the apostle felt uncertain about the kind of reception he would receive in Rome and why he explained in detail his attitude toward the Jewish nation and his view of the place of Jews in God's plan.

In a brief introduction to the thought of chapters 9–11, Paul expressed "great sorrow and unceasing anguish" for his kinsmen who had failed to respond affirmatively to the gospel despite their abundant privileges (9:1–5). Then he plunged into the heart of his argument. (1) The failure of the Jewish nation as a whole to accept Christ (even if that dereliction should prove to be permanent) would not constitute a failure of God's promise. His promise was not made to the nation per se, but only to individuals or groups within the nation—such as Isaac (Not Ishmael) and Jacob (not Esau) and their descendants. He chose these people, moreover, before they had done anything "either good or bad, in order that God's purpose of election might continue, not because of works but because of his call" (9:11). (2) God's selection of some to be heirs of the promise and His rejection of others suggest that He is arbitrary. If so, he is not unjust. "Has the potter no right over the clay," Paul asked, "to make out of the same lump one vessel for beauty and another for menial use?" (9:21).[16] (3) God's choice of a remnant was in fact not arbitrary at all; it was based on the Israelite nation's failure to call on Him *in faith.* "Gentiles who did not pursue righteousness have attained it," Paul asserted, "that is, righteousness through faith; but . . . Israel who pursued the righteousness which is based on law did not succeed in fulfilling that law. Why? Because they did not pursue it through faith, but as if it were based on works" (9:30–32). (4) God's rejection of the Jews was not final. Sin had for a time separated them from their Maker. This estrangement had provided the Gentiles with an opportunity to hear and accept the gospel. The "hardening" that had afflicted part of Israel was temporary. It would prevail "until the full number of Gentiles" came in. Then "all Israel" would be saved (11:25–26).

Did Paul believe in universal salvation? Such verses as 11:32 would seem to say so: "God has consigned all men to disobedience, that

[16]Compare Jeremiah 18:6.

he may have mercy upon all." But much depends on what Paul meant by "all." If the word included every person, universal salvation was intended. This interpretation is supported by the apostle's teaching of salvation by faith through the grace of a loving God. But Paul may have used "all" in the corporate sense.[17] If so, then he meant that salvation was available both to the Greek and Jewish worlds. The scales are weighted in favor of this latter view by his acute consciousness of sin *and* judgment and his strong conviction that the recalcitrant demonic powers would be destroyed.

The Roman Forum. The plain rectangular building near the upper center of the picture is the Curia, where the Senate met. To the left of the Curia stands the Arch of Septimius Severus. Behind the Arch can be seen the roof of a small church that was constructed over the ruins of the Mamertine Prison. According to tradition, Peter and Paul were imprisoned here. In the center of the picture are three columns of Castor's temple. To the far left of the three columns are the column bases of Basilica Julia, one of the colonnaded porticoes used for the transaction of business in ancient Rome. [Courtesy of Frederic Lewis, Inc.]

[17]See, for example, I Corinthians 15:24–26.

Ethical exhortations make up much of the remainder of Romans (12:1–15:13). Paul urges his readers to present themselves as living sacrifices to God, avoid conformity to the world, eschew self-righteousness, let their love be genuine, bless their enemies, and strive to live peaceably with everyone.

The Christian's proper attitude toward the state is delineated in Romans 13. "Let every person be subject to the governing authorities. For there is no authority except from God, and those that exist have been instituted by God. Therefore he who resists the authorities resists what God has appointed, and those who resist will incur judgment. For rulers are not a terror to good conduct, but to bad" (13:1–3a). Such an equation of government and God offends modern sensitivities and forces experts to foster understanding by citing Paul's experiences. He has been the beneficiary of Roman law and order on numerous occasions. He has traversed land and sea with comparative safety. Although these considerations cannot be overlooked, it is doubtful that the apostle makes his church-state pronouncement on the grounds of personal convenience or expediency. He is aware, moreover, that governors can be arbitrary and ruthless. Two sources of his injunction are his theology and his eschatology: "There is no authority except from God" and "Salvation is nearer to us now than when we first

A Reconstruction of the Roman Forum. [Courtesy of Historical Pictures Service—Chicago]

believed" (13:1,11). Christians are, consequently, to pay their taxes and give honor to whom honor is due. This view of the state as a God-infused instrument for good, however, did not long go unchallenged. Near the close of the first century, the author of the book of Revelation used cryptic language to convince his readers that they should actively resist the Roman Empire as an instrument of Satan.

Paul assures the Romans that love of neighbor fulfills the law. A Christian should respect another man's conscience. Although the apostle is persuaded that in the Lord Jesus nothing is unclean in itself, "it is wrong for any one to make others fall by what he eats" (14:20). Those who are strong ought to bear the burdens of the weak and welcome one another as Christ has welcomed them (15:1,7). After Paul has taken the collection to Jerusalem, he informs the Romans, he will visit them on his way to Spain. He solicits their prayers for a safe and favorable reception "so that by God's will I may come to you with joy and be refreshed in your company. The God of peace be with you all. Amen" (15:32–33). Thus ends what some have called the most influential letter ever written.[18]

Correspondence from Prison

Four of Paul's letters were ostensibly penned in prison—Ephesians (3:1; 4:1; 6:20), Philippians (1:7, 13–14), Colossians (4:18), and Philemon (9). Tradition has decreed that the captivity correspondence originated while the apostle languished in a Roman jail awaiting the outcome of his appeal to Caesar. If this was the case, these letters constitute Paul's last known witness to the church before his martyrdom.[19] Recent scholarship, however, has clouded this picture. Paul's authorship of Ephesians is usually denied, and some experts contest the genuineness of Colossians. Among those who accept the authenticity of Philippians, Colossians, and Philemon, a significant number favor Ephesus over Rome as the place of composition, and a few opt for Caesarea. We cannot deal with these issues in detail, but the genuineness and place of origin of the imprisonment letters have serious implications for Pauline chronology and theology.

Where was Paul when he wrote Philippians, Colossians, and Philemon? A brief imprisonment, such as the one he suffered at Philippi, would not have provided sufficient time for the work and travel involved (Acts 16:22–40). This leaves three remaining possibilities: the apostle's two-year imprisonments in Caesarea and Rome and his alleged incarceration in Ephesus (Acts 24:27; 28:30–31; II Cor. 1:8–9,

[18]See D.J. Selby, *Toward the Understanding of St. Paul* (Englewood Cliffs, N.J.: Prentice-Hall, Inc., 1962), p. 291.
[19]This judgment assumes that I & II Timothy and Titus are from a later hand.

11:23–24). Since Chrysostom wrote in the fourth century, church tradition has supported the Roman origin of the captivity communications. *Rome* was probably suggested to the early commentators by two references in Philippians. Paul states that his imprisonment for Christ has become known "throughout the whole praetorian guard" and he sends greetings to the Philippians from "those of Caesar's household" (1:12–13; 4:22). Colossians' advanced Christology (which outdistances any of Paul's uncontested letters) also points to a date at least as late as that which a Roman origin would provide. A third support for Rome is deduced from the apostle's attitude toward his imprisonment. He no longer seems to think of it as a passing problem but as a semi-settled state (Phm. 13; Col. 4:18). His situation at Caesarea (Ephesus?) might easily have been altered by a bribe or an appeal to Caesar, but at Rome such options were obsolete. There he could anticipate only a prolonged detention before a verdict from Nero's court.

The traditional view of the imprisonment letters has suffered some erosion of support. Recent discovery of inscriptions and papyri reveal that "the praetorian guard" and "those of Caesar's household" were not terms covered by an exclusive Roman patent. "The praetorian guard" frequently referred to the military headquarters in many important provincial cities and "those of Caesar's household" described Roman civil servants who were found in all parts of the empire. Another difficulty is the time required to travel the nearly 800 miles between Rome and Philippi. Philippians suggests that Paul has been in close touch with its readers for some time. Four trips between the apostle's prison and the Macedonian city are indicated and a fifth is in the offing. A one-way excursion would have required more than seven weeks. Perhaps ten months would have been required for the trips already made when Paul wrote Philippians. Although distance makes Rome a more difficult hypothesis, it by no means rules out the Eternal City.

Advocates of *Ephesus* as the place of composition of the captivity correspondence point out that travel between Ephesus and Philippi would have required no more than a dozen days. Paul's presence in Ephesus would make the frequent comings and goings much more easily understood. It is further argued that a fugitive slave from Colossae (Phm. 10, 16) would probably have sought refuge in the nearby city of his own province rather than in distant Rome. Epaphras (Paul's friend and fellow worker who faced a crisis in the church he had evangelized) would have been more likely to seek Paul's counsel and aid at Ephesus than to absent himself from the threatened congregation for the long period a journey to Rome would have necessitated. Paul's request that a guest room be prepared for him would make more sense if he was just a few days away rather than in Rome (Phm. 22). Each of these points can be countered, of course, but the most damaging datum against the Ephesus hypothesis is that there is no hard evidence that Paul suffered imprisonment in Ephesus. Even if he did, there is no proof that it was of the duration and nature to permit the literary activity and communication that his letters presuppose.

The case for *Caesarea*, which has a few staunch supporters, makes much of the commonality of names of Paul's associates in Colossians and Philemon: Timothy, Luke, Aristarchus, Tychicus, Epaphras, and Onesimus. If Luke authored the "we-sections" of Acts, he accompanied Paul to Rome and may well have been with him in Caesarea. Timothy, Tychicus, and Aristarchus had gone with Paul to Jerusalem, according to Acts 20:4, and probably followed him to Caesarea after his arrest. (This same coincidence-of-names argument has also been used to bolster the Ephesus origin of the letters.) It is further urged that Paul customarily traveled through territories he had already conquered for Christ before he embarked on a new field of labor. While the apostle was in Caesarea, he had his heart set on going to Rome. It would be quite natural that from Caesarea he would inform the Philippians that he hoped to visit them shortly and the people of Colossae that they should prepare a guest room for him (Phil. 2:24; Phm. 22). But it is improbable that the premonition of death, contained in Philippians, loomed on the near horizon for Paul at Caesarea. Why, since the apostle had recently visited Philippi twice, would he want to go there again so soon (Acts 20:1, 3-6)?

Where, then, were the imprisonment letters composed? No answer can be given with full assurance. In our judgment, Caesarea has little to recommend it. Ephesus has possibilities, but the absence of a documented imprisonment of Paul in that city militates against it. We see no reason to abandon the traditional view, despite some minor difficulties, that Philippians, Colossians and Philemon originated during Paul's long incarceration in Rome. On this assumption, the letters were probably written between 60 and 62 A.D. Consensus places Philippians, with its death threat, last although some scholars put it first because of its literary affinities with Romans.

Colossians   Colossae was located on the Lycus River, a tributary of the Meander, about ten miles southeast of the twin cities of Laodicea and Hierapolis. It was over a hundred miles southeast of the famous city of Ephesus, capital of the Roman province of Asia. This town of bygone eminence lay within the western border of ancient Phrygia, a region noted for the spawning of ardent cults and avant-garde prophets. Paul had never visited the area. Colossae and its neighboring cities had evidently been evangelized by his colleague, Epaphras. He visited the apostle in jail, informed him of the success of the campaign for Christ, and made known to Paul and his associates the Colossians' "love in the Spirit" (1:7-8). Colossians was Paul's response. He wrote to confirm the truth of the gospel according to Epaphras and to combat the rival "philosophy" that sorely tempted the Colossian converts (2:8).

Authorship. Although a majority of modern scholars continue to affirm that Paul wrote Colossians, there are those who doubt its authenticity. Their skepticism has three major sources. (1) The style of Colossians (long, involved sentences, measured liturgical cadences) differs from Paul's other letters. (2) The thought of Colossians is markedly different from that of Paul's undisputed letters. The Christology is akin to that of the Gospel of John and Hebrews. The saving significance of Christ is overshadowed by cosmological considerations. The noun translated "faith" seems to be used to describe a collection of doctrines to be believed rather than personal trust in God. (3) Colossians and Ephesians are closely related. Goodspeed states that three-fifths of Colossians is reflected in Ephesians.[20] The two works repeatedly contain verbally identical phrases. A passage used in one often appears in the other in only slightly modified form. If Ephesians is post-Paul, how can such a closely related letter as Colossians be accepted as authentic?

These objections to Paul's authorship of Colossians are serious, but they are not necessarily crucial. Style alone provides a precarious basis on which to form a judgment. The subject matter and the situation can affect style profoundly, and in the instance of Colossians they are sufficient to account for the stylistic differences between it and Paul's other letters. The thought of Colossians was also influenced by the situation that prompted Paul to write the missive. The letter's blood relationship to Ephesians can be accounted for if the author of Ephesians made extensive use of Colossians. Although Paul's authorship of Colossians falls short of demonstration, we concur with scholarly consensus that the letter is genuine.

The "philosophy." It is common to call the religious teaching at Colossae that Paul opposed a "heresy," but the designation is anachronistic. Heresy requires the presence of formal standards of or-

[20]Edgar J. Goodspeed, *The Meaning of Ephesians* (Chicago: Univ. of Chicago Press, 1933), p. 8. The most convincing case for the postapostolic authorship of Colossians is found in Eduard Lohse, *Die Briefe an die Colosser und an Philemon* (Göttingen: Vandenhoeck & Ruprecht, 1968). Lohse's views are summarized in his "Pauline Theology in the Letter to the Colossians," *New Testament Studies* XV, no. 2 (1969), 211–220.

thodoxy, and in the apostolic age no such standards existed. Christianity was characterized by a remarkable variety of thought and activity. Novel interpretations of the gospel were not abruptly dismissed as "heretical" but judged on their respective merits. Paul's description of his opponent's thought as a "philosophy" is far more accurate but not much more enlightening. The letter offers nothing in the way of a direct account of the tenets of the philosophy. We don't even know whether its devotees were disciples of Christ or those who merely sought to make room for him in a system that they believed to be more inclusive than Christianity. Their ideas must be deduced from a number of allusions in the letter.

The Colossian philosophy apparently gave a central position to angelic beings ("the elemental spirits of the universe") who were to be worshiped (2:8,18). It was believed that these cosmic powers were organized in a heavenly hierarchy with appropriate titles to signify their respective ranks: "thrones . . . dominions . . . principalities . . . authorities" (1:16). They functioned as mediators between men and the highest deity. Together they constituted the *pleroma* ("fullness") of divine attributes and activities (1:19; 2:9).[21] The redemption that they made available to men clashed with the Christian gospel because it was not conveyed through Christ or predicated on the forgiveness of sins (1:14). Whether these concepts were pre-Gnostic or simply syncretistic teachings is an open question. Traces of Jewish asceticism and legalism, however, are readily detectable. Paul's opponents went beyond the requirements of the Law (which dealt only with food) and became greatly exercised about "questions of food *and* drink." They prescribed that the sacred seasons of the Jewish calendar ("a festival or a new moon or a sabbath") be observed.[22] Some of the legal requirements they fashioned into a set of taboos ("do not handle, do not taste, do not touch") that resembled a manual of discipline. They attempted to promote the "rigor of devotion and self-abasement and severity to the body" (2:21, 23). The influence of the mystery religions is seen in the frequent reference to the Christian gospel as a "mystery" and the description of the leader of the group as one who took "his stand on visions" (2:18).[23]

Message.   After his customary thanksgiving and prayer, Paul moves quickly to the main purpose of his letter. His words are designed to expose the weakness of the "philosophy" that threatened Colossae.

[21]Compare Zoroastrian thought.
[22]Colossians 2:16, italics added.
[23]For a concise discussion of the various problems connected with Colossians, one to which we are indebted, see Francis W. Beare, "The Epistle to the Colossians: Introduction," in *The Interpreter's Bible*, XI, 133–146.

The apostle begins by defining Christ's relationship to God, to the cosmos, and to the church. Christ "is the image of the invisible God," he declares, "the first-born of all creation" (1:15). He is, also, the sole mediator of both creation and redemption. "In him all things were created, in heaven and on earth, visible and invisible. . . . He is the head of the body, the church; he is the beginning, the first-born from the dead" (1:16–18). As head of the new creation, he occupies a preeminent position. "In him all the fullness of God was pleased to dwell" (1:19). This fullness is not, as in the philosophy, distributed among a host of mediators. The cosmos, rent by man's rebellion and disobedience, is restored to harmony "by the blood of his cross" (1:20). Those Colossians who "continue in the faith, stable and steadfast, not shifting from the hope of the gospel" are promised a part in the cosmic reconciliation (1:23).[24]

A strange statement appears in connection with Paul's ministry of suffering. "I rejoice in my sufferings for your sake," he tells the Colossians, "and in my flesh I complete what is lacking in Christ's afflictions for the sake of his body, that is, the church" (1:24). Some have concluded that the apostle believed that his sufferings provided satisfaction for the sins of others.[25] That he suffered vicariously cannot be denied, but there is no hint in his words that he thought Christ's sufferings were insufficient to accomplish redemption. What Paul wished to underline is that suffering is an integral part of a Christian's vocation. The servant is no greater than his Master. He who afflicts the church, afflicts Christ. His sufferings include not only what he suffered in the flesh, but also what he continues to suffer in his "body," the church.

Paul describes the gospel as "the mystery hidden for ages and generations but now made manifest to his saints" (1:26). The word *mysterion* shares with pagan cults the idea that something was given to men through revelation. For Paul, however, the term has shed its connection with initiatory rites and secrets known only to the few. The Christian "mystery" is proclaimed to every man, and its benefits are unrelated to ascetic discipline, mystical contemplation, or prescribed cultic rites. The apostle's primary concern is to present every man "mature in Christ" (1:28).

---

[24]Since no parallel for such a cosmic Christ can be found in Paul's uncontested letters, some scholars attribute this passage (or the entire composition) to an unknown author of a later period. But Paul may have been compelled to enter the field of cosmic speculation because of the false notions being propagated at Colossae. He may even have used a pre-Pauline hymn as the basis of his argument.
[25]This interpretation has been used to support the Roman Catholic teaching of the "treasury of merits."

Paul directly attacks the philosophy that exalts the elemental spirits instead of Christ and affirms once again that in Christ "the whole fullness of deity dwells bodily" (2:9). Christians possess in Christ all that is falsely promised them as reward for worshiping the angelic powers. Christ is the head of all such powers. In him Christians experience a spiritual circumcision that makes the physical operation obsolete. This spiritual circumcision is symbolized by baptism in which the participants die to the old life and rise to the new with their past sins freely forgiven. This forgiveness cancels "the bond which stood against us with its legal demands" and disarms "the principalities and powers . . . , triumphing over them in him" (2:14–15).

The apostle attacks the taboos and cultic observances so dear to the hearts of the devotees of the Colossian philosophy. He declares that they are "only a shadow of what is to come; but the substance belongs to Christ" (2:17). While such practices create the appearance of wisdom, piety, and self-denial, they are of no value in curbing the indulgence of the flesh. Christians have risen with Christ to a new life, and they are to "seek the things that are above" and "put to death" all immorality and selfishness (3:1, 5). There are no longer any distinctions of race or class for "Christ is all, and in all" (3:11). His followers must "put on love" with all of its attributes and "do everything in the name of the Lord Jesus" (3:14,17).

Paul applied these general principles of Christian conduct to household relationships—of husbands and wives (3:18–19), children and parents (3:20–21), and slaves and masters (3:22–4:1).[26] Injunctions to watchfulness and prayer follow, and an appeal is made for wise conduct toward non-Christians. The apostle concludes his communication by introducing his friend Tychicus, bearer of the letter, and Onesimus, who will return to Colossae in his company. He relays the greetings of several of his associates, instructs the Colossian church to exchange letters with the church at Laodicea, and urges the Colossians to encourage Archippus (who is included among those to whom Philemon is addressed) to fulfill his ministry. Colossians ends with a personal greeting in Paul's own handwriting.

Philemon   Philemon is unique among the letters of Paul. It is not only the briefest contribution to the collection, occupying little more than a single page, but its character and content are also distinctive. The other communications are addressed primarily to churches and are

---

[26]Since the bulk of this section is addressed to the slaves, it has been conjectured that Paul introduces the table of domestic duties because of his concern for the slave, Onesimus.

concerned with appropriate church problems. Philemon, on the other hand, is addressed primarily to an individual, seems to be concerned with a purely personal matter, and is devoid of forthright ethical and theological content. Its style and vocabulary (so similar to those of Romans, Corinthians, Galatians, and Philippians) shout its genuineness.

This letter was occasioned by Paul's concern for Philemon's slave, Onesimus. Paul was a prisoner in Rome (according to our reckoning) where Onesimus had been his associate for some time. How the slave had happened to be in Rome is something of a mystery. According to tradition, he had run away from Philemon after he had stolen funds with which to make good his escape. He eventually came in contact with Paul and was converted. After a period of fruitful association, Paul sent Onesimus home to Colossae with the letter we now call Philemon. The letter asks Philemon to forgive his runaway slave and accept him as a Christian brother. As for anything Onesimus may have filched, the apostle magnanimously declared, "Charge that to my account" (18). It was a calculated risk to send a runaway slave back to his master. Philemon could have punished Onesimus in any manner he saw fit. The law permitted even the supreme penalty under the circumstances. To mitigate this danger, Paul had Tychicus accompany Onesimus (Col. 4:7–9).

This traditional understanding of Philemon has been seriously questioned in recent decades. Even if, as alleged, Onesimus was a runaway slave, it does not necessarily follow that Paul's letter was simply an appeal in behalf of Onesimus. The ideas we would expect to be emphasized in such a communication are strangely missing. There is no mention of repentance on the part of Onesimus, and no explicit appeal is made to Philemon for forgiveness. Some scholars, consequently, assert that the real purpose of this letter is revealed in the not-so-subtle hint found in verses 13–14:

I would have been glad to keep him with me, in order that he might serve me on your behalf during my imprisonment for the gospel; but I preferred to do nothing without your consent in order that your goodness might not be by compulsion but of your own free will.

What Paul deeply desired was to have Onesimus returned to him for further evangelistic work. This is why he stressed his own imprisonment, his need for Onesimus, and his confidence that Philemon would do even more than the apostle requested (21).

Professor Knox, who has made an intensive study of Philemon, has introduced some novel touches. He believes that the owner of Onesimus was not Philemon but Archippus, whose house was the meeting place for the Colossian church. He also argues that Paul's strange words in verse 17 were designed to enlist the support of the Colossian church in his effort to secure the services of Onesimus. The letter was addressed to Philemon because he had succeeded Epaphras as leader of the churches in the area. Knox further theorizes that Philemon is actually "the letter from Laodicea" mentioned in Colossians 4:16. Philemon's home was probably in Laodicea, and our letter was brought to him first and subsequently delivered to Archippus and the Colossian church.[27] Professor Goodspeed takes a different tack. He holds that all of the people addressed in Philemon were Laodiceans. Paul urged the exchange of letters to secure the help of the nearby Colossian church in the realization of his purpose.[28] It is just as likely, though, that all were Colossians and that the traditional notion that both Philemon and Colossians were addressed to Colossae is correct. The apostle's injunction to exchange letters makes more sense when it is related to the primary concern of Colossians (the refutation of the dangerous "philosophy") rather than to Onesimus (whose role in Philemon was both little and late).

Ignatius, bishop of Syrian Antioch, wrote seven letters during his trip to Rome in the early part of the second century. In one of the letters he indicates that the bishop of the church at Ephesus at the time was a man named Onesimus. Professor Knox accepts the tradition that equates this Onesimus with the one mentioned in Philemon. If Onesimus was bishop about 110 A.D., Knox reasons, he probably occupied that office a score of years earlier. If so, he was at Ephesus when Paul's letters were collected and published. Indeed, the project may have been completed under his sponsorship and supervision.[29]

Although theories that espouse the deeper purpose of Paul's letter to Philemon and the identification of the Onesimus of that letter with the later bishop of Ephesus fall short of demonstration, they cannot be lightly dismissed. They deserve to be classified as plausible conjectures. If they should one day be proved correct, they would explain how such a brief and seemingly personal note became canonical and comprise a valuable chapter in the unfolding story of how our New Testament developed.

[27]John Knox, *Philemon Among the Letters of Paul*, 2nd. ed. rev. (New York: Abingdon Press, 1959). See also his "Philemon: Introduction," in *The Interpreter's Bible*, XI, 555–560.

[28]Goodspeed, *An Introduction to the New Testament*, pp. 119–120.

[29]John Knox, "Philemon: Introduction," in *The Interpreter's Bible*, XI, 559. See also Goodspeed, *An Introduction to the New Testament*, pp. 121–124.

Authenticity and integrity. The authenticity of Philippians is generally accepted, but some doubt exists concerning its integrity. Why would Paul use the later terms "bishops and deacons" to refer to church leaders instead of his usual and more general designations—"the outstanding men" or "those who rule among you" (1:1)? The force of this question, however, is cushioned considerably when it is realized that the apostle does not imbue these terms with their developed ecclesiastical meanings. A more pressing matter is the alleged composite nature of the letter. A sudden break occurs between 3:1 and 3:2. In the very act of saying farewell, Paul resumes his letter with a vengeance. Opponents that he has treated with commendable restraint are now pounced upon with unremitting fury: "Look out for the dogs, look out for the evil-workers, look out for those who mutilate the flesh" (3:2). The words in 3:1 suggest that the apostle has sent a previous communication to this congregation, and this suspicion is supported by a reference Polycarp (bishop of Smyrna in the latter half of the second century) made in a letter to the Philippians to the *letters* Paul had written to that church.

Several theories have been proposed to solve the problem posed by Philippians. Some scholars think that this letter is composed of parts of several letters. Others believe that 3:2–4:1 is a part of a letter originally addressed to another church. An increasingly popular view is that 3:2–4:23 is an early letter that gratefully acknowledges the arrival of Epaphroditus and 1:1–3:1 is the missive that Paul sent with Epaphroditus as he subsequently returned to Philippi.[30] The division of Philippians into two or more letters, however, is based on flimsy evidence. The reference to "the same things" in 3:1 may be to what Paul is about to write (not to a previous letter), and Polycarp's reference may be to Paul's collected letters. The expression of gratitude in 4:14–19 coheres with the reference to Epaphroditus in 2:25–30, and the allusions to those who "preach Christ from envy and rivalry" and insincerely "proclaim Christ out of partisanship" prepare the reader for the outburst in 3:2 (1:15, 17). If we were to chop Paul's letters into separate communications wherever he digresses or suddenly shifts gears, his literary log would soon be shattered into a pile of kindling. Without more evidence than we now possess, it would seem wiser to treat Philippians as a single letter.

Occasion. The circumstances that propelled Paul to write Philippians are usually gleaned from the letter itself. When the Philippians learned of the apostle's imprisonment, they dispatched Epaphroditus

---

[30]See Goodspeed, *An Introduction to the New Testament*, pp. 90–92. Compare F.W. Beare, *A Commentary on the Epistle to the Philippians* (Harper & Row, 1959), pp. 1–3, 24–26, 100–102, 150–151.

with a sum of money to aid him. Epaphroditus remained to assist Paul, but during this period he became acutely ill. News of his indisposition reached the Philippians, and their anxiety escalated—much to the distress of Epaphroditus. When he recovered sufficiently to be able to travel, Paul sent him home with the letter of thanks to the Philippians for their generous help. But if this is Paul's primary purpose in writing Philippians, it seems odd that he should wait until the letter is nearly finished before even mentioning the gifts. Stranger still is the apostle's apparent willingness to remain silent for several months before acknowledging the gifts at all. Consequently, modern scholars are inclined to think that Paul thanked the Philippians soon after he received their charity, and that he now writes to them for two different purposes. (1) He wants to insure Epaphroditus a good reception. As a result of his illness, Epaphroditus is returning to Philippi much earlier than his church expects. Paul is eager to indicate that it is because of the apostle's own desire that his assistant is on his way back. Perhaps this is why Paul addresses the bishops and deacons specifically. As officers of the church, they are the ones to whom their representative, Ephaphroditus, will deliver Paul's letter to confirm the completion of his mission. (2) He wants to deal effectively with certain troubles that plague the church at Philippi. It is divided by personal animosities, perfectionist tendencies, and the seductive advances of Judaism. The apostle would like to deal with the menacing situation personally, but this imprisonment prevents this for the time being. He plans to send Timothy, his most trusted associate and a founder of the Philippian church, as soon as he can be spared. Meanwhile, Epaphroditus is coming. He will act in Paul's stead. The letter Epaphroditus bears, which we believe was written in Rome about 62 A.D., will convince the Philippians that he is Paul's ambassador.

Message. The letter opens with one of the heartiest expressions of thanksgiving and appreciation found in any of Paul's writings. This is followed by a brief reference to the author's imprisonment. Contrary to what one might expect, Paul's imprisonment has actually advanced the gospel and emboldened most of the brethren to proclaim the word of God without fear. Some, though, preach Christ from envy and rivalry. The apostle does not know what the outcome of his incarceration will be. At times, he thinks that his deliverance is likely and he confidently makes plans for the future (1:19, 22, 24–26; 2:24). At other times, the future is clouded by uncertainty (2:17; 3:10). He wants to depart and be with Christ, but he feels obligated to remain on account of his converts (1:23–24). He exhorts the Philippians to "stand firm in one spirit" when faced with opposition and suffering (1:27). They are to do nothing from selfishness or conceit but humbly regard others as better than themselves. The example of humility Christ set for them is to be their standard. Although he was in the form of God, he emptied himself, took the form of a servant, and was born in the likeness of men. "And being found in human form he humbled himself and became obedient unto death, even death on a cross" (2:8).[31] The Philippians are to work out their salvation with fear and trembling, do all things without grumbling, and hold fast to the word of life.

Paul turns next to the immediate purpose of his letter. After declaring his hope to send Timothy to the Philippians soon and his desire to follow his associate shortly, the apostle explains the circumstances of Epaphroditus' return to Philippi. He evidently fears that the Philippian church will conclude that its emissary has been derelict in his duty. Paul is writing Philippians to insure Epaphroditus a cordial welcome. "Receive him in the Lord with all joy;" Paul commands his converts, "and honor such men, for he nearly died for the work of Christ, risking his life to complete your service to me" (2:29-30).

The abrupt transition at 3:1 suggests that Paul also has other reasons for writing to the Philippians. Their church is so troubled that the apostle feels that the presence of one of his trusted associates is required. Jewish propagandists have taken their toll. Paul lashes out at the proselytes who pounce on his converts like ravenous dogs. He warns his readers to look out for the dogs, the evil-workers, and those who mutilate the flesh (3:2). If any man has reason for "confidence in the flesh," it is Paul (3:4). He is a birthright Hebrew—"as to the law a Pharisee, as to zeal a persecutor of the church, as to righteousness under the law blameless" (3:5-6). Yet whatever gain he has he counts as loss for the sake of Christ who revealed to the apostle "the righteousness from God that depends on faith" (3:9).[32]

Paul's disclaimer of personal perfection in 3:12 may strike some readers as an expression of histrionic humility. Not so. The apostle looks upon the frank recognition of his own weakness and imperfection as a mark of Christian maturity. He probably also attempts by indirection to deal with another problem that troubled the Philippian Christians. Some evidently claimed that they had attained perfection

---

[31]The poetic character of 2:5-11 suggests that it is a Christian hymn composed by Paul or used by him. Of particular importance is the phrase in 2:7 that asserts that Christ "emptied himself, taking the form of a servant." From the third or fourth century theologians used the word "*kenōsis*" ("emptying") to describe the idea expressed here. Christ voluntarily stripped himself of the insignia and prerogatives of deity. He did not masquerade as man but submitted to all of the conditions and limitations of human life.

[32]Compare Galatians 1-2.

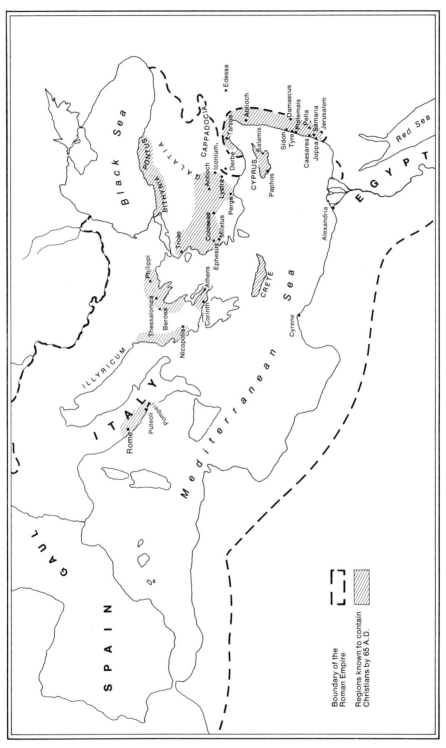

THE CHURCH AT THE CLOSE OF PAUL'S MINISTRY (c.65 A.D.)

Boundary of the
Roman Empire

Regions known to contain
Christians by 65 A.D.

in this life. The resultant mood of complacency dampened their enthusiasm for further effort. Paul, the earthly agent of their faith, reminds them that he finds it necessary to forget what lies behind and press on toward the goal "for the prize of the upward call of God in Christ Jesus" (3:14). In solemn language he exhorts the Philippians to imitate him in this pursuit.

Paul's plea for the restoration of harmony between two feuding women is a model of tact. He urges Euodia and Syntyche to agree in the Lord, and he asks one of their comrades to act as intermediary. After a fresh attempt to terminate the letter, the apostle expresses his gratitude to the Philippians for their generosity. His acknowledgment is not motivated by self-concern. He has long ago learned the secret of living with either plenty or hunger. He is pleased, though, that his converts have opted to share his troubles. "Not that I seek the gift; but I seek the fruit which increases to your credit" (4:17). With greetings and a benediction, Paul brings to a close what some scholars have called his richest and most self-revealing letter.

From the moment Paul encountered Christ until his martyred blood was spilled, he was possessed by a consuming passion. He was Christ's captive. His incredible ministry was burdened by toils and tribulations that would have felled a lesser man. No one, save Christ himself, has made as deep an impression on succeeding centuries. The inspiration of his indefatigable labors, the compelling character of his ethical principles, and the insightfulness of his theology fully justify the title history has reserved for him—Peerless Apostle of Jesus Christ.

4

Conflict and Consolidation in the Christian Community

James, brother of Jesus and head of the Jerusalem church, was stoned to death in 62 A.D. Shortly thereafter Christians from Jerusalem fled to the Gentile city of Pella in Perea to escape the imminent Jewish revolt against Roman rule.[1] According to tradition, Peter and Paul met martyrdom in the mid-sixties in Rome. The ill-fated Jewish revolt, begun in 66 A.D., precipitated the destruction of Jerusalem and the Temple. By the end of the decade most (if not all) of the apostles were dead.

The several decades that followed Jerusalem's destruction are commonly called "the postapostolic age." The term is admittedly imprecise. Since the fate of most of the apostles is larded with legend, we do not know when the age actually began; since there is no sharp demarcation at the other end, it is difficult to know when the age came to a close. Despite its blurred edges, "the postapostolic age" has proved to be a convenient designation for the post-Paul period in the Christian community's development.

We have discovered, in our study of the Synoptics and (Luke-) Acts, some of the crises that confronted the Christian community in the postapostolic age. (1) The passing of the apostles amplified fears that information about Jesus might perish with them. (2) The delayed parousia of Jesus forced the community to take historical time seriously. (3) Debates about the nature and practice of the faith created confusion. (4) The rapid growth of the fellowship intensified the demand for written records for evangelistic and educational purposes. (5) Hostility between the Christian community and the synagogue intensified. (6) There began to appear on the horizon signs of impending trouble with the Roman government.

It is sometimes assumed that the most pressing problem confronting

[1]See Josephus, *Antiquities*, XX, 9, 1; Eusebius, *Ecclesiastical History*, III, 5, 2–3.

the Christian community in the postapostolic age was the external one of persecution, but this was not the case. Although persecution was a constant concern, it was too spasmodic and unsystematic to be the most formidable foe. Far more crucial was the internal situation created by the demise of those who "from the beginning were eyewitnesses and ministers of the word" and the appearance of "false" apostles, prophets, and teachers (Lk. 1:2). The Christian community, freed from the restraints imposed by the Law, was a fertile field for the growth of all sorts of ideas designed to accommodate the apostolic faith to its surrounding culture. Chief planters of alien notions were probably the Gentile converts themselves. Somehow the church managed to surmount its internal problems, develop safeguards for its faith, invest that faith with apostolic authority, and yet maintain sufficient flexibility to permit theological development.

The precise pattern by which the Christian community marched toward its eventual catholicity cannot be discerned. Sources dealing with the postapostolic period are few and fragmentary. Later generations were not inclined to preserve writings for posterity that were unsuited to the needs of their day or handicapped by the stigma of "heresy." Earlier Christians were too preoccupied with the parousia to pay attention to record-keeping. The relatively few sources that have survived pose problems for scholars. Their dates and places of origin are often in doubt, and many of them fly under false colors.

As we study the remainder of the New Testament, we shall continue our interest in the special problems connected with the origin and interpretation of the writings. The books will be treated in groups rather than in some presumed chronological order. Special attention will be focused on the relation of the Christian community to the state, the development of forms of organization to cope with altered circumstances, and types of apology used to extend and defend the faith.

XII

The Paulinists
(Ephesians, I and II
Timothy, Titus)

It was a common practice in ancient times for one writer to borrow heavily from another without permission, payment, or embarrassment. The author of Matthew, we have noted, reproduced 90 percent of Mark without any hint of indebtedness. It was also common for one person to write under the name of another. Such tactics would be considered unseemly today, but they were perfectly proper in a society unacquainted with printing presses and copyright laws.

Manuscripts written under the names of other persons are called "pseudonymous," from the Greek for "under a false name." Most of the Jewish apocalyptic writings fall into this category. Authors who cannot be dated earlier than the second century B.C. wrote under the names of such ancient worthies as Adam, Enoch, Baruch, and Daniel. This familiar literary device had a fourfold virtue. It paid tribute to the venerable figure, conferred authority on the writing, guaranteed the writing an instant readership, and focused attention on the message rather than the messenger. Solomon was another name frequently used in pseudonymous writings. The king's reputation for sagacity prompted a whole body of wisdom literature to be developed under his name.[1]

Pseudonymous writings also found their way into the New Testament. Second- and third-generation Christians were inspired by Paul's life, and his letters were copied and quoted as authoritative documents. It was only a matter of time until someone capitalized on allusions found in I and II Corinthians to produce III Corinthians—an alleged exchange of correspondence between the apostle and his Corinthian converts. Someone else, taking his cue from Colossians 4:16, composed an Epistle to the Laodiceans, drawing freely from the authentic Philippians. Still another writer fashioned correspondence between Paul and the Roman philosopher Seneca that revealed the mutual-ad-

---

[1]See Proverbs, Ecclesiastes, Wisdom of Solomon, Psalms of Solomon, etc.

miration society the two had formed.[2] Fortunately, none of these works was included in the Christian canon, but the writings of other Paulinists were. In this chapter we shall consider four pseudonymous New Testament books—Ephesians, I and II Timothy, and Titus.[3]

Ephesians

Ephesians is noted for its stress on the oneness in Christ and the sharp differences of opinion among scholars concerning the letter's authorship, destination, and occasion.

Authorship

The letter "to the Ephesians" purports to be by Paul (1:1; 3:1), and its mention of Tychicus in language virtually identical to Colossians suggests that Paul wrote Ephesians shortly after Colossians (Eph. 6:21-22; Col. 4:7-8). From the second century to the nineteenth, Ephesians was accepted as a genuine work of the apostle—written during his Roman imprisonment and taken along with Colossians by Tychicus on the journey to Asia.

Many modern scholars question the genuineness of Ephesians. They regard the letter as pseudonymous, the product of a gifted Paulinist. (1) Its style and vocabulary differ from Paul's accepted letters. Style and vocabulary, of course, are influenced by subject matter and audience. But the devotional nature of Ephesians and its unrelatedness to a local church are deemed insufficient to account for its peculiarities. Ideas in Paul's accepted writings cascade through the penned page like water from a broken dam, but their development in Ephesians is at a glacier's pace. Eighty-two words in Ephesians cannot be found in Paul's authentic letters, and common Pauline words are frequently put together in uncommon ways. (2) Although its central concepts are Pauline, Ephesians contains a number of advanced theological notions. Paul spoke of Christ as the sole foundation of the church, but Ephesians has Christ share this honor with "the apostles and prophets" (I Cor. 3:11; Eph. 2:20). Paul spoke of Christ's burial, but Ephesians deduces from Christ's ascension his descent "into the lower parts of the earth" and makes this doctrine necessary to the completion of his mission. His death is consistently subordinated to his exaltation (4:9-10).[4] Paul usually pictures God as the reconciler of men, but Ephesians makes Christ the reconciler (2:14-16).[5] Spiritual gifts are not bestowed by the Spirit but by the ascended Christ, and they are not primarily related to individual Christians but to

---

[2]See M.R. James, trans. *The Apocryphal New Testament* (Oxford: Clarendon Press, 1955), pp. 288-291; 478-484.
[3]Some scholars would add I Peter to the writings of the Paulinists, and others would include the Gospel of John and Hebrews.
[4]Compare I Corinthians 15:3-11.
[5]Compare Romans 5:10-11; II Corinthians 5:18-19.

the leaders of the church—apostles, prophets, evangelists, pastors, and teachers (4:7–14).[6] Those who accept Ephesians as genuine, however, counter these arguments by affirming that Paul simply developed in Ephesians the deeper implications of his earlier teachings. (3) The historical situation of Ephesians postdates Paul. The apostle regarded Gentile Christians as a small minority in the church. He compared them to "a wild olive shoot" grafted into the "olive tree" of Israel (Rom. 11:17). The author of Ephesians, on the other hand, thought of the church as composed largely of Gentile Christians (2:11). The tension and antagonism that characterized relations between Jewish and Gentile Christians in Paul's day are entirely absent from Ephesians. The church is no longer threatened by Judaism but by paganism (4:17–5:15). Paul's emphasis on the coming of the Lord has vanished, and his peer-level attitude toward the apostles has escalated to outright veneration (Gal. 2:11; Eph. 3:5).

The determination of Ephesians' authorship is not a simple matter. There are weighty arguments on both sides of the issue. The role played by subjective factors looms large no matter which conclusion is embraced. It is our judgment that Ephesians was written by a Paulinist immersed in the apostle's thought (especially of Colossians) who was himself a theologian of merit and discernment. This view is increasingly held by modern scholars.[7]

Destination All of Paul's authentic letters mention their recipients directly: "To all the saints . . . who are at Philippi," "To the church of God which is at Corinth," etc. This is not true, though, of the letter "to the Ephesians." It is addressed in a very general way: "To the saints who are also faithful in Christ Jesus" (1:1).[8] "At Ephesus" does not appear in any Greek manuscript prior to the fourth century, and the *Revised Standard Version* has properly relegated the phrase to a footnote. It is unlikely, moreover, that Paul could have written such a letter to the church *at Ephesus*. He had labored in that city for three years, yet he writes as though he is a perfect stranger. He makes no mention of his personal relations to the church or of his old friends. Indeed, he seems to imply that they know each other only by hearsay (1:15; 3:1).

[6]Compare I Corinthians 12:7–11.
[7]F.J.A. Hort, *Prolegomena to St. Paul's Epistles to the Romans and the Ephesians* (London: The Macmillan Co., 1895) presents strong arguments in defense of Paul's authorship of Ephesians. Edgar J. Goodspeed, *The Meaning of Ephesians* (Chicago: Univ. of Chicago Press, 1933) offers the most convincing case against Paul's authorship. A brief and balanced treatment of the subject is made by F.W. Beare, "Ephesians, Introduction," in George A. Buttrick, ed., *The Interpreter's Bible* (New York: Abingdon Press, 1953), X, 597–601.
[8]Compare Philippians 1:1; I Corinthians 1:2.

Two principal solutions have been suggested. (1) Ephesians was a circular letter designed to be carried from place to place by a single courier. Perhaps the author left a blank space in the superscription for the reader to supply the appropriate address. But such a letter is without parallel in ancient literature. More likely, copies of the letter would have been made with the name of a particular place inserted into each. If so, why weren't some of the names preserved in the manuscript? (2) Some second-century scribe recalled a statement in II Timothy and provided the letter with its title.[9] Someone else later brought the letter into conformity with its traditional title and the superscriptions found in Paul's authentic letters by supplying the words "at Ephesus."

Whatever the merit of these theories, "To the Ephesians" and its counterpart in the superscription are without significance. The author writes not for any particular church but for the church as a whole. This explains why his thought is unconcerned with parochial matters such as discipline, administration, and the purity of doctrine. His focus is on the unity of the total organism.

Occasion   If Ephesians was composed by a Paulinist and addressed to all faithful Christians, what prompted the author to write it? Professor Edgar J. Goodspeed has advanced a seminal suggestion.[10] He believes that Ephesians was written to introduce Paul's collected works. Paul's letters had fallen into disuse once the problems with which they dealt had been resolved, but the "publication" of Acts about 90 A.D. revived interest in the great apostle. Some Christian (probably from Asia and perhaps Onesimus—once a runaway slave and now bishop at the church in Ephesus) was moved to find as much of Paul's correspondence as possible. Acts led him to the churches in Galatia, Philippi, Thessalonica, Corinth, and Rome. He discovered that the abandoned letters were not only insightful but that they contained a vital message for the contemporary church. He soon resolved to make the collected letters available to the entire church, and he composed Ephesians in letter form to introduce the collection. Since he was best acquainted with Colossians and Philemon, they influenced the introduction the most. But Paul's representative ideas were gleaned from the whole collection and organized around a theme of compelling significance for the church.

Goodspeed's hypothesis has numerous positive features. It provides a believable setting and motivation for the writing of Ephesians by

[9]II Timothy 4:12: "Tychicus I have sent to Ephesus."
[10]See Goodspeed, *The Meaning of Ephesians.*

a Paulinist, accounts for the marked influence of Paul's accepted letters on Ephesians, and explains why the post-Paul composition has always been a part of the collection. Some aspects of the theory, however, are less than convincing—the "lost" letters of Paul, the alleged influence of Acts, and the introductory liturgical and mosaic character of Ephesians. Many scholars doubt that Paul's letters fell into disuse, question the motivational influence of Acts, believe that Paul's letters were only gradually assembled into a single collection, and argue that Ephesians is a self-contained composition only partially dependent on Paul's letters. Despite these reservations, though, they accept the Goodspeed hypothesis in large outline and the assumption that Ephesians is the product of a Paulinist.

A post-Paul Ephesians can be dated from 75 to 100 A.D. The author's closeness to Paul's situation suggests a date not far removed from the apostle's death. The alleged influence of Acts and allusions to Ephesians in the writings of the Apostolic Fathers favor a later date. Our estimate is about 90 A.D. If I Peter was influenced by Ephesians, as a number of scholars claim, then the date could be reduced by a decade.

Message Ephesians has the form of a letter, but its contents resemble a tract. Its theme is the unity of all things in Christ, with the church as the visible symbol of that unity. This idea is expounded in the first three chapters, and the remainder of the letter is devoted to the ethical consequences of this concept for the Christian in the world.

The unity of all things in Christ. The salutation reveals that Ephesians is addressed to all Christians. This universal note prepares the reader for the exposition of a doctrine of cosmic significance. In a hymn of adoration that recounts the multitude of spiritual blessings God has showered upon His people, the author introduces the letter's theme. God has revealed in Jesus Christ His primordial purpose—"to unite all things in him, things in heaven and things on earth" (1:10). Man's sin, the cause of the world's disunity, has prevented him from realizing God's intention (1:7). But God's purpose will progressively prevail in the Jews, who now find their messianic hopes fulfilled, and the Gentiles, who hear the gospel proclaimed and receive the gift of the Holy Spirit (1:11–14).

God has shown his power by raising Christ from the dead and placing him over all earthly authority. These mighty acts have a parallel in the spiritual experience of the readers. God has raised them from the death of sin to share the heavenly life of Christ himself (1:15–

2:10). Gentile Christians are reminded that they were once separated from Christ and alienated from God's chosen people, but now they enjoy a privileged status as members of the household of God. Their altered status resulted from Christ's death on the cross. He broke down "the dividing wall of hostility [which separated the inner court of the Temple, open only to Jews, from the outer court to which Gentiles were admitted], by abolishing in his flesh the law of commandments and ordinances [the system of legal observances, symbolized by the dividing wall, that prevented fellowship between Jew and Gentile], that he might create in himself one new man in place of the two [a new humanity unmarked by the ancient divisions of religion and race], so making peace, and might reconcile us both to God in one body [the Christian community] through the cross, thereby bringing the hostility to an end" (2:14–16).[11] Christ preached peace both to Gentiles and Jews, and there resulted a new community that is the true Temple of God, with Christ as its chief cornerstone (2:17–22).

A prayer for the spiritual progress of the readers barely begins before it is interrupted by an account of Paul's preeminent position as the divinely appointed herald of the gospel to the Gentiles and as an interpreter of the mystery of Christ (3:2–13). Then the prayer resumes with a series of petitions on behalf of the readers. The author asks that they be strengthened through the Spirit "that Christ may dwell in your hearts through faith; that you, being rooted and grounded in love, may have power to comprehend with all the saints what is the breadth and length and height and depth, and to know the love of Christ which surpasses knowledge, that you may be filled with all the fullness of God" (3:17–19).

The ethical consequences of Christian unity. The second half of Ephesians begins with a plea for its readers to lead a life worthy of their calling "with all lowliness and meekness, with patience, forbearing one another in love, eager to maintain the unity of the Spirit in the bond of peace" (4:1–3). This general concern is then made specific by exhortations related to four particular areas of life—the church (4:4–16), paganism (4:17–5:20), the family (5:21–6:9), and the spiritual forces of evil in the universe (6:10–20).

The church bears witness to the truth that its unity is based on the belief in "one Lord, one faith, one baptism, one God and Father

[11]Some scholars believe that the breaking down of "the dividing wall of hostility" would not have suggested itself to a Christian writer prior to the destruction of the Temple in 70 A.D. Others hold that as a symbol of hostility the phrase would have more meaning if the wall was still standing.

of us all, who is above all and through all and in all" (4:5–6). God has given the church a ministry that will eventually lead to unity of thought and action. Then its members will be insulated against every wind of doctrine. They will speak the truth in love and fulfill their mission in the world.[12]

Readers are warned that they must no longer live as the Gentiles do, but must shun the immorality of their former lives. They are to speak the truth, curb their anger, perform honest work, be kind to one another, "forgiving one another, as God in Christ forgave" them (4:32). They are to imitate God, walk as children of the light, and try to discern what is pleasing to the Lord. They are to take no part in the works of darkness, avoid drunkenness, be filled with the Spirit, and worship in thankfulness (5:1–20).

Wives are obligated to obey their husbands, and husbands must love their wives—for marriage is a symbol of Christ and the church. Children must obey their parents, but fathers must not provoke their children to wrath. Slaves must obey their masters, and masters must treat their slaves kindly, because both have a Master in heaven (5:21–6:9).

The author of Ephesians brings his letter to an appropriate climax with the striking analogy of the panoply of a Roman soldier. He urges his readers to put on "the whole armor of God" that they may be able to stand against "the wiles of the devil" (6:11). The apocalyptic image of the final conflict has been changed. "The evil day" does not refer to the gathering of the forces of evil for the decisive conflict (Armageddon) prior to the End but to "this present darkness" (6:12–13).[13] Christians are called to arm themselves for unremitting warfare against the moral and intellectual climate of the pagan world. An exhortation to continual prayer, including prayer for the author, a personal note concerning Tychicus, and a benediction conclude the communication (6:13–23).

Perhaps no book in the Bible is better suited to our times than Ephesians. We are divided by the conflicts of culture, class, color, and commitment. This letter assures us that this will not always be so. In the fullness of time God will unite all things in Christ. The pledge

[12]The emphasis on "one faith, one baptism" and the contribution of church officials to the desired unity reflect a post-Paul period—as does the notion in 4:8–9 that Christ descended into the lower parts of the earth and ascended far above all the heavens leading "a host of captives."
[13]Compare II Thessalonians 2:8–10.

of this ultimate unity is the church, which will increasingly include both Jews and Gentiles. She is the spiritual entity that must expand until it unites all mankind under Christ's rule.[14]

The Pastorals   The three remaining letters in the Pauline collection were purportedly written by Paul and addressed to Timothy and Titus, two of his assistants, rather than to particular churches. Because they were composed by a chief "pastor" (shepherd or spiritual overseer), intended for pastors, and emphasize pastoral and ecclesiastical matters, I and II Timothy and Titus have been called the Pastorals since the eighteenth century.[15]

Authorship   The Pastorals are missing from Marcion's collection of Paul's writings and from Papyrus 46, the earliest codex. Not much can be concluded from these data, however. Marcion regularly rejected writings that condemned heresies, and the papyrus codex is minus its ending. If there are allusions to the Pastorals in the writings of the Apostolic Fathers, as seems reasonably certain, the pre-Marcion origin of the Pastorals is established. In the early manuscripts and canon lists they are always present or missing together. This fact, coupled with their commonality of style, vocabulary, and ideational content, makes the assumption of common authorship mandatory.

From the late second century until modern times, it was generally believed that Paul wrote the Pastorals. It was assumed that the apostle's appeal to Caesar eventually resulted in his acquittal. After his release he resumed his campaign for Christ in the East, where he wrote I Timothy and Titus. He was subsequently arrested and returned to Rome, where he wrote II Timothy.

A preponderance of modern scholars, though, regard the Pastorals as the product of a Paulinist of the postapostolic period. Their case rests largely on internal evidence. It is not necessary to present the data fully in order to understand their cumulative effect.

The situation reflected in the Pastorals cannot be accounted for in Paul's ministry unless he was released from his Roman imprisonment and permitted to engage in campaigning for Christ in Asia Minor,

---

[14]See Beare, "Ephesians, Introduction," in *The Interpreter's Bible*, X, 607, to whose illuminating study we are indebted. Mitton, *The Epistle to the Ephesians, Its Authorship, Origin, and Purpose* (Oxford: Clarendon Press, 1951), emphasizes the liturgical interests of Ephesians.

[15]Although this designation has been questioned, especially for II Timothy, no better term has been devised.

Macedonia, Crete, Greece, and perhaps even Spain. Yet evidence for such a campaign is derived almost solely from the Pastorals themselves—a circuitous kind of reasoning that carries little conviction.

The style of the Pastorals differs from that of Paul's accepted writings. The apostle wrote with vigor and emotional intensity, and his works exhibit a wide range of mood. Sudden shifts from humility to boldness, from love to anger, from hope to despair are commonplace. The thought is rich and the aptness of image and metaphor distinctive. But none of these things can be said about the Pastorals. They move at a snail's pace and are fond of repetition and colorless expressions.

The vocabulary of the Pastorals differs markedly from Paul's writings. More than one-third of the words they use (excluding proper names) are not used in the letters of Paul. Over 170 words in the Pastorals cannot be found in the rest of the New Testament. However, nearly one-fourth of the vocabulary of the Pastorals (although absent from Paul's letters) is commonly used by second-century Christian authors. Where the Pastorals do make use of standard Pauline words or phrases, it is often done with a radically different meaning. "Faith," which for Paul has the dynamic meaning of trust, becomes the simple acceptance of a body of doctrine in the Pastorals.[16]

The church organization is more rigid and highly developed in the Pastorals than in Paul's letters. The "apostles, prophets, and teachers" of the earliest church have been succeeded by the bishop and elders (or elder-bishops) and deacons.[17] The positions held by "Timothy" and "Titus" and the prerogatives they possess suggest that they are bishops despite the missing title. They outrank the elders whom they have appointed and whom they supervise and discipline. If they were in fact bishops, then the author of the Pastorals evidently exercised the powers subsequently held by archbishops or metropolitans. Since our author habitually uses "bishop" in the singular and "elder" and "deacon" in the plural, it is often assumed that the monarchical episcopacy prevailed in his churches. If so, it would reflect a period well after Paul's day.

---

[16]The most exhaustive study of the vocabulary is P.N. Harrison, *The Problem of the Pastoral Epistles* (London: Oxford Univ. Press, 1921). The results are summarized and evaluated by F.D. Gealy, "Introduction," in *The Interpreter's Bible*, XI, 360–363. Although Harrison's statistical methods have been questioned, his main conclusions have been widely accepted.

[17]Bishops and deacons are mentioned in Philippians 1:1, of course, and there are numerous references in Paul's writings to various offices in the church that point to a definite structure. Yet the usage in the Pastorals is different.

Advocates of Paul's authorship of the Pastorals are not mute in the face of these claims. They point out that the Pastorals were written at least seven years after the latest of Paul's earlier letters. The passage of time is believed to have had a mellowing effect on the apostle. When this is combined with a change of subject matter and persons addressed, it is argued, there is sufficient grounds to account for the fresh vocabulary of the Pastorals. Besides, each of Paul's accepted letters is noted for its linguistic peculiarities.[18]

The case for a Paulinist as author of the Pastorals is convincing to us. Its main obstacle is the presence in these writings of passages allegedly manifesting the style and vocabulary of the apostle. Some of the passages are said to echo parts of Paul's accepted letters, and others seem to be new material so characteristically Pauline that they may be fragments of his genuine letters no longer extant. The presumed fragments appear to be personal notes composed by Paul at different times and under different circumstances and addressed to Timothy and Titus. It has been suggested that they were used as the framework for the Pastorals themselves.[19] Since there is no agreement among scholars as to the identification or origin of the fragments, however, they do not constitute a serious roadblock to the postapostolic authorship of the Pastorals.

If the author of the Pastorals was a Paulinist, his identity is known to us only through his letters. Perhaps the most perceptive suggestion is that he was a convert from Hellenistic Judaism who held a position of prominence in the Pauline churches of Asia Minor. He was a man devoted to the apostle and the care of his churches. His Jewish background is reflected in his nonspeculative nature, practical piety, notion that women's true vocation is in the home (the training ground of church leaders), nonascetic attitude toward food and drink, attitude toward Scripture, and eschatology. The language of the Pastorals, though, is Hellenistic Greek of a higher literary level than the popular koine employed by Paul.

Date and Sequence The Pastorals have been dated anywhere between 61 and 180 A.D., and disagreement as to their order of composition is just as great. Although Titus follows the two Timothys in the New Testament, virtually no scholar believes it was written last. Those who hold that Paul wrote the letters in their entirety think that the order was I Timothy, Titus, and II Timothy. Since there is no hint of persecution in I Timothy and Titus, they are commonly dated before the winter

[18]The most cogent defense of Paul's authorship of the Pastorals has been made by C. Spicq, *St. Paul: les Epitres Pastorales* (Paris: J. Gabalda, 1947).
[19]See Harrison, *The Problem of the Pastoral Epistles*, part III, pp. 87–135.

of 64 A.D. II Timothy is assigned a somewhat later date. Although this sequence is endorsed by some who reject Paul's authorship, the majority of critics prefer the following order: II Timothy, Titus, and I Timothy. They claim that this arrangement reveals clear development in church government, progressively increased opposition to "heretics," and a lessening of the purely personal data concerning Paul.

The dates of the Pastorals are largely determined by such factors as the identity of the "heretical" teaching that the author opposed, the alleged parallels between the Pastorals and the writings of the Apostolic Fathers, and the type of church organization reflected in the Pastorals. Since we believe that the situation, style, and vocabulary of the Pastorals point to the postapostolic period, what is the most likely date of composition? A significant group of scholars suggest a date somewhere between 90 and 110 A.D. A second group extend the time somewhat farther into the second century. Those who regard the Pastorals as anti-Marcionite works favor 140–180 A.D. Choosing from these options is hazardous. Since we do not think the "heresy" was Marcionite, we prefer the 100–130 A.D. range.

The "Heresy"   It is exceedingly difficult to identify specifically the doctrinal deviates against whom the author of the Pastorals inveighed. They are often called "Gnostics" and sometimes associated with a particular heretic like Marcion. But Gnosticism, as we have observed, was such a varied and complex movement as to defy definition or description.[20] Despite these seemingly insuperable obstacles, we shall attempt to discover the character and ideological bent of the people condemned by the Pastorals.

They constitute a danger from within the church, not from outside, as was the case with persecution. They are Christians who have rejected the "sound doctrine" transmitted by the apostles in favor of "the godless chatter and contradictions [*antitheses*] of what is falsely [*pseudōnymou*] called knowledge [gnōsis]" (I Tim. 6:20).[21] "Pseudonymous gnosis" are the very words used by Irenaeus to characterize the entire Gnostic movement, and this raises the suspicion that those opposed in the Pastorals were infected by some form of Gnosticism. The similarity of Marcion's *Antitheses*, which appeared about 140 A.D., to the "contradictions" mentioned in I Timothy has led some scholars to the conclusion that the Pastorals are anti-Marcionite documents. This is a dubious identification, however. The Old Testament was

[20]See pp. 12–15.
[21]Compare I Timothy 1:10; 6:3; II Timothy 1:13; Titus 1:9, 2:1.

anathema to Marcion, but the dispensers of "false knowledge" betray definite Jewish proclivities. Some of them, at least, are of "the circumcision party" (Tit. 1:10). They give "heed to Jewish myths" (Tit. 1:14).[22] They desire "to be teachers of the law, without understanding either what they are saying or the things about which they make assertions" (I Tim. 1:7).

They advocate asceticism. They "forbid marriage and enjoin abstinence from foods which God created to be received with thanksgiving by those who believe and know the truth" (I Tim. 4:3). Since these prohibitions characterized Gnostic thought, it is tempting to call those condemned in the Pastorals "Gnostics." Gnostics regarded creation and procreation as impediments to salvation because they involved contact with a corrupt and evil world. But asceticism was widespread in the ancient world, and it was practiced by such Jewish groups as the Essenes. Its un-Jewish association in the Pastorals with the ban against marriage suggests that asceticism was an aspect of the cultural context that shaped Gnostic and Marcionite ethics.

They "occupy themselves with myths and endless genealogies which promote speculations rather than the divine training that is in faith" (I Tim. 1:4).[23] Some take this to be a reference to Gnostic treatment of Old Testament texts. Gnostics were particularly prone to engage in speculation on the Pentateuchal genealogies with reference to Gnostic aeons and other figures of the pleroma. However, the reference need not be so interpreted. The author frequently lapses into abusive language. He may have accused his opponents of nothing more than having an attachment to foolish tales.

They permit women to play a significant role in the public life of the church.[24] This, too, harmonizes with Gnostic practice. According to Irenaeus, Simon Magus was always accompanied by a prostitute named Helena whom he called his first *ennoia* or mental conception. Gnostic writings picture women as teachers, preachers, and recipients of revelation. Women evidently found gnostic concepts so attractive that the author of Pastorals was impelled to warn against their seductive onslaught (II Tim. 3:6–7).

There are other factors besides the endorsement of asceticism, fondness for myths, and the privileged position accorded women that seem to point to Gnostics as the false teachers condemned in the pastorals.

[22]Compare I Timothy 1:4.
[23]Compare II Timothy 4:4; Titus 1:14.
[24]Otherwise, the stinging rebuke found in I Timothy 2:9–12 would have been pointless.

They think that "the resurrection is past already" (II Tim. 2:18). From the Pastor's strong emphases, moreover, it may be concluded that his opponents believe the opposite of what he champions. The Pastor stresses that "everything created by God is good" (I Tim. 4:4). In the same letter he declares that God desires "all men" to be saved and to come to the knowledge of the truth (I Tim. 2:4).

Despite the Gnostic-like characteristics of the false teachers in the Pastorals, it is impossible to identify them with any of the important Gnostic systems. The Pastor's penchant for polemics is partly responsible. He substitutes denunciation for debate. Opponents are condemned in terms of traditional ethical lists popular in philosophical schools. The catalog of vices attributed to them is couched in such general terms as to mask their identity. They are "lovers of self, lovers of money, proud, arrogant, abusive, disobedient to their parents, ungrateful, unholy, inhuman, implacable, slanderers, profligates, fierce, haters of good, treacherous, reckless, swollen with conceit, lovers of pleasure rather than lovers of God, holding the form of religion but denying the power of it" (II Tim. 3:2–5). Evidently the "heresy" the Pastor opposed was not peculiar to his own situation. Its resemblance to the spurious teachings Paul combatted in Colossians has frequently been noted. In both cases, Jewish and Gnostic ideas and practices seem to have been fused into a faith that cannot be defined precisely.

Church Organization Church organization was an issue of considerable magnitude in the postapostolic Christian community. The postponed parousia, the gradual loss of charismatic leadership, the burgeoning of faulty interpretations of the faith, and the external pressure from the state combined to make an officially ordained ministry a necessity. Otherwise, who could act as the credentialed interpreter of Scripture and guardian of apostolic teaching? The church ultimately adopted a threefold criterion to protect the purity of its faith: (1) an "apostolic" ministry, (2) an "apostolic" creed, and (3) an "apostolic" canon. Although the Pastorals permit us to view this development in church organization from its initial stages, it is our conviction that threefold apostolic ministry (of bishops, elders, and deacons) postdates their composition.[25]

The author of the Pastorals evidences marked interest in such matters as the standards for ordination and the offices of bishops, elders,

[25]For an illuminating discussion that contends that the Pastorals assume a more advanced and highly differentiated type of church organization than we have depicted or the relevant texts themselves suggest, see Gealy, "Introduction," in *The Interpreter's Bible*, XI, 345–348.

deacons, and widows. What he meant by these titles is by no means certain. Far more attention is paid to the prerequisites for the offices than to the duties of the occupants. Even the moral standards required are so stock as to raise the suspicion that they were secured from contemporary community lists. Despite these difficulties, we shall attempt to discover what the Pastor meant when he used the terms in question. Bishop stems from the Greek *episcopos*, and in the Septuagint and the Hellenistic world it most frequently meant "overseer." Its first usage in Christian literature suggests the administration of local churches.[26] *Elders* translates the Greek *presbuteroi*, and in the Jewish congregations and communities they often performed administrative duties (Acts 21:18). How, then did bishops and elders differ? Sometimes the terms were used as synonyms,[27] but in the Pastorals, a separation seems to be under way. Although the two terms are not yet distinct, they never occur together, and "bishop" appears only in the singular. Evidently the bishops are about to emerge from the elders and assume increased leadership.[28] *Deacon* comes from the Greek *diakonos* and means "servant." Paul used the term frequently in a generic sense. The appointment of the Seven "to serve [*diakonein*] tables" suggests that the office sprang from the desire to meet the physical needs of disadvantaged widows (Acts 6:2). The association of "bishops and deacons" in Paul's writing and in subsequent Christian usage is commonly understood to imply hierarchical subordination (Phil. 1:1). Deacons are those who "assist" the bishop in his work.[29] *Widows* seem to form an order, too, but their duties are not defined.

Message of I Timothy   The superscription of I Timothy bears the marks of postapostolic authorship. "Paul" supposedly informs his intimate disciple, "Timothy," that his mentor is an apostle of Jesus Christ by "command" of God. This is a stronger word than "will," and it dovetails nicely with the Pastor's interest in ministerial "orders." "God our Savior" cannot be paralleled in the early Pauline letters, and "Christ our hope" was a favored phrase of a later day (I Tim 1–2).

"Timothy's" purpose at Ephesus is to combat heresy.   The gospel Paul

---

[26]Philippians 1:1, where it is linked with "deacons."

[27]In Acts, "elders" (20:17) and "guardians" (20:28) both translate "*episcopoi*."

[28]In the Epistles of Ignatius, which may reflect an idealized account of the actual situation, a threefold hierarchical ministry is depicted. The bishop is the real leader of the congregation and of the battle against heresy. Deacons are subordinate both to bishops and presbyters. Although the role of the presbyters is indistinct, they are closely associated with the bishop and supportive of him, but their leadership function is clearly limited. Precisely how the monarchical bishop emerged remains a mystery. Perhaps one man became president of a college of presbyters and was assigned the title of "bishop," or perhaps there were several bishops and their duties were consolidated and given to one man.

[29]The concept of "assistants" is primary when Epaphras, Tychicus, and Timothy are called "deacons" in Colossians 1:7, 4:7, and I Thessalonians 3:2 respectively.

preached is being perverted by people who "occupy themselves with myths and endless genealogies" and who desire "to be teachers of the law" (I Tim. 1:4, 7). The Law is good if used lawfully, but it is no substitute for the gospel. Christians have advanced beyond the Law's function. Their need now is for "sound [that is, "correct"] doctrine" (I Tim. 1:10). The stress is the Pastor's, not Paul's. The gospel is no longer a spirit religion but a body of proper teaching.

It is easy to see from the paragraph that follows why the Pastor wrote in Paul's name. The apostle was clearly his hero, the foremost interpreter of the Christian tradition. The genuineness of the language and the logic of verse 15 have been questioned, but the verse rings true as a devoted follower's tribute to the apostle.

The charge to "Timothy" (I Tim. 1:18–6:19). The Pastor's "bill of particulars" is prefaced by a statement suggesting the proper credentials for church leaders. Like Paul, and unlike the two heretics named, these leaders are to be men "holding faith and a good conscience" (I Tim 1:19).[30]

The paragraphs that follow are often characterized as early church manuals primarily concerned with church offices. Although the Pastorals do contain instructions regarding public worship and the qualifications of church officers and of other church groups, the description does justice neither to their contents nor their commanding interest.

"Timothy," who is addressed as one in charge of public worship, is told that prayer is to be offered for all men because God desires all men to be saved. Women are to exercise no leadership in public worship. They are to dress modestly and remain silent. Their subordinate status stems from the order of creation: Adam was formed first, then Eve. "I permit no woman to teach," the Pastor pontificates, "or to have authority over men" (I Tim. 2:12).[31]

The Pastor evidently assumed that "Timothy" was well acquainted with the functions of bishops, elders, and deacons. Consequently, he focuses his attention on their qualifications for office. They must be men of conventional morality and mature faith because the church is "the pillar and bulwark of the truth" (I Tim. 3:15). It is her task to protect the faithful from "deceitful spirits and doctrines of demons." Those who are afflicted by these twin evils are ascetics "who forbid

[30]Since the treatment of the heretics here is so much more final than in II Timothy 2:17 and 4:14, some scholars argue that II Timothy was written before I Timothy.
[31]Compare I Corinthians 14:34–35, a probable interpolation.

marriage and enjoin abstinence from foods which God created to be received with thanksgiving" (I Tim. 4:1–3).[32]

If "Timothy" presents these instructions to the brethren, he will be a good minister of Jesus Christ, his salvation will be assured, and his example will result in the salvation of his hearers (I Tim. 4:6–16). His conduct toward persons of different ages and sexes is prescribed, and instructions concerning the treatment of widows and the remuneration, discipline, and selection of elders are given. A warning against abstinence and some proverbial sayings conclude the chapter (I Tim. 5:1–25).

Slaves are commanded to honor their masters. If masters are also "brethren," they should be served all the better. The marks of false teachers and the desirability of godliness are followed by comments concerning the perils of wealth. The "man of God" shuns such temptations and aims at "righteousness, godliness, faith, love, steadfastness, gentleness" (I Tim. 6:11). The wealthy are to be rich in good deeds. The final appeal is a warning to "Timothy" to preserve the deposit of faith entrusted to him and to avoid "the godless chatter and contradictions of what is falsely called knowledge" (I Tim. 6:20–21).

Message of II Timothy The form of II Timothy recalls Paul's accepted letters more than I Timothy and Titus, but striking differences in vocabulary and situation belie its authenticity.[33]

"Timothy" is admonished to emulate Paul's life and be true to the gospel. The Pastor remembers the addressee constantly in his prayers, is cognizant of his sincere faith, and urges him to rekindle the gift of God that he received through the laying on of hands. He should never be ashamed of witnessing to the Lord, of Paul's suffering, or of suffering for the gospel himself. He should follow the pattern of "sound words" and "guard the truth that has been entrusted" to him (II Tim: 1:13–14). This personal appeal for "Timothy's" complete loyalty is made poignant by a reference to the disaffection of "all who are in Asia," and the contrasting devotion of Onesiphorus (II Tim. 1:15–18). "Timothy" is to bear suffering "as a good soldier of Christ" (II Tim. 2:3). To die with Christ is to live with him.

"Timothy" is instructed to remind his ministers to keep the received faith and to teach correct doctrine in love. Godless chatter will merely foster more ungodliness. Two people in particular have already

---

[32]See I Timothy 5:17–22 for the remuneration and discipline of elders.
[33]See Gealy, "Introduction," in *The Interpreter's Bible*, XI, 460–461.

swerved from the truth by asserting that the resurrection is already past. This denial of the general resurrection has controverted Pauline teaching and created confusion among some of the faithful. The Lord's representatives should be tactful, not contentious, correcting their opponents with gentleness in order to win them over (II Tim. 2:14–26).

Stress will appear in the last days. Men will be more concerned with themselves than with God, and they will cherish the form of religion but deny its power. Such people should be avoided. "Timothy" has observed Paul's unflinching faith, patience, and love in the face of suffering. Since all who desire to live a godly life in Christ will be persecuted, "Timothy" should emulate the apostle's selfless devotion. "Timothy" has been acquainted with the sacred writings from childhood. The Christian faith is guaranteed by its inspired Scriptures. They constitute the standard "for teaching, for reproof, for correction, and for training in righteousness, that the man of God may be complete, equipped for every good work" (II Tim 3:16–17).

"Timothy" is charged to preach the word in season and out of season. The time is approaching when people will not abide sound teaching. They will have "itching ears" and affection for teachers who tell them what they want to hear. Such circumstances demand that the addressee "fulfill the ministry" (II Tim. 4:1–5).

"Paul" declares that his death is imminent. He has fought the good fight, finished the race, and kept the faith. Now he looks forward to the crown of righteousness that the Lord will give him on that Day. "Timothy" is to exert every effort to come to him, with Mark, before winter. Only Luke is by his side. A few greetings bring the letter to a close (II Tim. 4:6–22).

Message of Titus Titus is the briefest of the Pastorals, but it has the longest salutation. Its formal and liturgical character clashes with a supposedly personal letter. The Pastor has a clear-cut view of his own ministry. He has been entrusted "by command of God" with the apostolic kerygma. His right to command derives from his Commander, and his thesis is that knowledge of the truth and perfect piety are as inseparable as a boy and his dog. He makes no effort to identify the addressee as the Titus of Paul's letters. Neither should we. It would also be fruitless to attempt to recover the historical setting of the Cretan mission. The ministry of "Titus" stands for the type of ministry that succeeded that of the apostles in any church.[34] Wherever the work

---

[34]See Gealy, "Introduction," in *The Interpreter's Bible*, XI, 525.

of the apostles has deteriorated it is to be restored, and the church is to establish a qualified ministry.

The qualities and duties of elders and bishops. "Paul" left "Titus" in Crete to amend what was defective and to appoint elders in every town. They were to be blameless men, married only once, with believing children, nonprofligate and subordinate. A bishop had to pass an even stricter test of character and conduct. His function was to maintain "sound doctrine and also to confute those who contradict it" (1:9). There were many insubordinate men in Crete, the most deceptive of whom were those of the circumcision party. They had to be silenced (1:10–16).

The duties of a minister to his congregation. A minister should teach what befits sound doctrine to various groups within the church. The ethical injunctions echo Paul's counsel conditioned by conventional morality, and they are rooted in God's grace that has appeared for the salvation of all men. The phrase, "our great God and Savior Jesus Christ," has evoked spirited theological discussion (2:13). The Pastor customarily writes of "God the Savior" and refers separately to Christ. Perhaps this innovative phrase stems from church worship that reacted to the claims made in the mystery religions and emperor cults.

Christian conduct in a non-Christian society. Christians should submit to rulers and authorities, be obedient, and be ready for any honest work. They should speak evil of no one, avoid quarreling, be gentle, and show courtesy toward all. Except for the grace of God, they would be like their neighbors. These teachings could well have come from Paul, but at two points the Pastor departs from his mentor. The Pastor sees salvation as a past event, and he views baptism as "the washing of regeneration" (3:5). Developments such as these strongly suggest that the Pastorals are moving theology in the direction of later catholic Christianity.

Titus ends on a note that is loudly trumpeted in the book of James: genuine faith is known not by its words but by its works. The message was perfectly suited to the society of the day.

The Pastor who chose to write under the pseudonym of "Paul" fought the good fight in the Apostle's name. Our understanding of the church at the time the Pastor wrote is considerably greater because of his pious and well-intentioned "forgeries."

**Catholic
Concerns**
(I Peter, Hebrews,
James, Jude, II
Peter)

From the fourth century A.D. the word "catholic" has been used to describe seven letters found in our New Testament—James, I and II Peter, I, II, and III John, and Jude.[1] The term was derived from the Greek (*katholikos*) and meant "general." It was intended to describe writings composed for the church as a whole in contradistinction to those addressed to particular persons or local congregations. Although the designation is somewhat inexact (since III John is an authentic personal letter), it does serve a useful purpose. Whenever "catholic" can be applied appropriately, it points to the open-letter character of the compositions. We are no longer dealing with letters (which have specific audiences) but with epistles (which have general audiences).

Since apostolic authorship was an "open sesame" to enshrinement in the Christian canon, it is not surprising that letters were attributed to the three "pillars" of the church in Jerusalem (Peter, James, and John) and to the Apostle Jude (Gal. 2:9). But the gradual and rather late acceptance of these seven letters by the church is surprising. Although I Peter, I John, and perhaps James were known in some areas of the church at a relatively early date, no hint of the others exists before the end of the second century. At the beginning of the fourth century Eusebius listed only I Peter and I John among the "undisputed" works. The others were not accepted in the West until the end of the fourth century, and even then II Peter's authenticity remained in grave doubt. The fifth-century Peshitta Version, official Bible of the Syrian Church, included only I Peter, I John, and James among its accepted letters.

It is difficult to discover a convincing chronological arrangement of the Catholic Epistles. Scholars vary widely in their assignment of dates to the specific writings. We shall begin with the most important work (I Peter), continue with Hebrews (which has sometimes been

---

[1]Eusebius, *Ecclesiastical History*, II, 23; III, 25, 1–3.

called a general epistle but may well merit a classification of its own), and conclude with James, Jude, and II Peter. The three letters of John will be considered in the next chapter together with the Gospel of John.

I Peter

This brief work purports to have been written by the apostle Peter (1:1) with Sylvanus playing some part either in its composition or delivery (5:12). Perhaps no other New Testament book has earlier or better attestation. Some scholars think that Clement of Rome, who wrote about 96 A.D., reflects its influences. Polycarp and Irenaeus, writing in the latter part of the second century, were markedly influenced by I Peter. In the fourth century, Eusebius included it among the "accepted" sacred writings. With such usage and support, I Peter's authenticity seemed assured.

Authorship

It was not until modern times that Peter's authorship of I Peter was challenged. (1) How could an Aramaic-speaking Galilean fisherman have written such fine Greek? I Peter was composed in fluent and idiomatic Greek that is considerably superior to that found in Paul's letters. (2) The author was dependent upon Paul's published works. Paul's central thesis that Jesus' death atoned for sin and resulted in righteousness is echoed in I Peter 1:18–19 and 2:24. Paul's concept of being "in Christ" is found in 3:16 and 5:10, 14, and his attitude toward the state (Rom. 13:1–7) is strikingly paralleled in 2:13–14. If Peter died in Rome in the 60's, how could he have known Romans, possibly Ephesians, and probably Paul's collected letters? (3) The letter displays too little knowledge of Jesus' life and teaching to have been written by an apostle. (4) The letter betrays a postapostolic time period. I Peter 4:15–16 suggests that it was a crime simply to profess Christianity. Yet there is no solid evidence that such was the case until the time of Trajan (98–117 A.D.).[2] Pliny's letter to Trajan originated in one of the provinces to which I Peter was addressed, and many scholars regard his communication as strong support for a second-century dating of I Peter. Furthermore, the theology of I Peter is too advanced to have come from Peter's pen.

Modern defenders of Petrine authorship acknowledge the cogency of some of these criticisms, but they continue to find sufficient evidence to maintain the traditional view. They assert that the first two objections can be accounted for by the role played by Sylvanus. "By Sylvanus . . . I have written briefly to you" strongly suggests that Sylvanus, as Peter's secretary, actually composed the letter in its present form (5:12). This would explain the author's dependence upon

[2]See pp. 71–72.

Paul. But if Sylvanus is the same person as Silas in Acts 15:22, 32 (as is commonly supposed), he was an Aramaic-speaking Palestinian like Peter. The first objection, therefore, would remain. The third objection to Peter's authorship is often flatly denied. There are numerous passages that seem to support the author's awareness of Jesus' mission and message (1:8; 2:21-24; 5:1, 2, 5). But it is a moot question whether such passages reveal intimate knowledge of Jesus or of the traditions of the church concerning him. The fourth objection is countered by a different interpretation of the references to suffering and persecution in the letter (1:6; 2:12, 15; 4:12-19; 5:9). These are seen not as "the slings and arrows of outrageous fortune" inflicted by the state in the second century but as the result of public abuses that were experienced by Christians almost from the beginning. Even if some passages are understood as references to persecution by the state, there is no conclusive evidence that Christians escaped persecution "for the name of Christ" until the time of Trajan.

Advocates of the Petrine and of the second-century authorship of I Peter fought to a draw. Other scholars sought to break the impasse by proposing a third possibility. Professor Edgar J. Goodspeed, for example, accepted the pseudonymous character of I Peter, but he assigned it to a different time period. According to Goodspeed, the letter originated in Rome about 95 A.D., late in the reign of Domitian. Hebrews (5:12) had urged the Roman Church to become the teacher of the churches. The book of Revelation had created a serious moral problem in the churches of Asia Minor. Although it had stimulated those churches to meet persecution heroically, it had heightened their temptation to hate their enemies. Paul's collected letters had sponsored a more moderate position toward the state, and Ephesians (which was composed to introduce the collection) had made plain the possibilities of the encyclical. After the appearance of Revelation and Hebrews, I Peter became a virtual necessity. A representative of the Roman Church composed the epistle in the name of the church's patron, Peter.[3] In so far as this theory supplies a motive for pseudonymity, it has strength. But its Achilles' heel is the lack of evidence that Domitian persecuted Christians "for the name of Christ."

Although no completely convincing account of the origin of I Peter exists, our evaluation of the data supports pseudonymous authorship and a date in the days of Trajan. Correspondence between the emperor (98-117 A.D.) and Pliny the Younger, who was Trajan's imperial legate in the province of Pontus-Bithynia, shows that Trajan had prohibited secret meetings of unapproved societies. The emperor,

---

[3]Edgar J. Goodspeed, *An Introduction to the New Testament* (Chicago: Univ. of Chicago Press, 1937), pp. 265-266.

threatened by an invasion from Parthia, feared that such societies in Asia Minor might become subversive. Pliny wrote to Trajan, asked how he should treat the Christians, and sketched the procedure he had followed to date. If a Christian persisted in his faith, Pliny executed him. If he recanted and invoked the state gods and worshiped the emperor's statue, he was home free. Trajan's reply approved of Pliny's procedure. The emperor indicated that no special effort should be made to find Christians, but if they were accused, they should be punished.

The Trajan-Pliny exchange, it seems to us, rather accurately depicts the situation reflected in I Peter. Christianity was an illegal religion. People were suffering "for the name of Christ." However, their persecution was individual, not general.

Date and Destination If the letter was composed by Peter, it was written in the 60's, and the suffering to which it refers arose from Nero's persecution. But Nero's repression occurred in Rome, not in Asia Minor (to which I Peter is addressed). Besides, victims of Nero's maltreatment were not punished "for the name of Christ" but because they were believed to be arsonists and disturbers of the peace.

If the letter was not authored by Peter, then it originated either about 95 A.D. (soon after the appearance of Revelation and Hebrews and near the date of I Clement) during the persecution of Domitian or about 112 A.D. during the reign of Trajan. For reasons already indicated we prefer the latter dating.

The letter is addressed to Christians in Pontus, Galatia, Cappadocia, Asia, and Bithynia. These four Roman provinces (Pontus and Bithynia counted as one) probably stand for Asia Minor as a whole, and they encompass the territory of Pliny's actions. The addressees are called "exiles," and the frequent allusions to their past "futile ways" strongly suggest that they were once Gentiles (1:14, 18; 2:9–10; 3:6; 4:3).

Character The author reveals no direct personal relations with his readers, and he does not deal with questions raised by a particular community. These characteristics suggest that I Peter is a general letter intended for at least limited public circulation. A sharp break in the text (between 4:11 and 4:12—with doxology and new address), repetition before and after the break, and a difference in the timing of the readers' suffering (which is potential in 1:6 and 3:14 and actual in 4:12) cause some scholars to divide the letter into two parts: 1:3–4:11 and 1:1–2; 4:12–5:14. It is alleged that the first part is not really a letter, but a baptismal sermon. The author addresses himself to new converts, and baptismal terminology permeates the whole.[4] Although some scholars regard the second part as a genuine letter designed to comfort Christians in time of persecution, others claim that it simply reproduces a closing service for the entire congregation.[5] Still other scholars attribute the broken character of I Peter to two letters that were fused. The author composed 1:3–4:11 with a closing greeting to some churches where persecution was acute and 1:1–2 and 4:12–5:14 to other churches where persecution was only potential. When the apostolic writings were later assembled, the two "inserts" were copied continuously within the shared framework of salutation and farewell.[6]

Occasion I Peter probably originated in Rome. The clue is provided in 5:13: "She who is at Babylon . . . sends you greetings." "She" stands for the local church from which the author wrote, and "Babylon" is a Christian code name for Rome.[7] The author's object was to fortify Christians in Asia Minor so that they would hold fast to their faith despite the suffering that beset them. The cause of this suffering is much disputed. Some scholars absolve the state of any responsibility and attribute the suffering to a caustic environment created by a nonconforming minority.[8] But if the addressees suffered "as Christians" and were threatened by "the fiery ordeal," something more than general community hostility was involved (4:16; 4:12). Our conclusion is that they lived under circumstances comparable to those described in the Pliny correspondence. They did not seek a confrontation with the state, and the Roman authorities did not deliberately hunt for them. The conflict arose naturally as a result of the rapid growth of the Christian community and of the peculiar convictions of its members. The Empire was not concerned with the content of the Christian faith but with its consequences. When *Pax Romana* was threatened, no stone was left unturned to preserve the established order.

Message In the salutation the author addresses the Asia Minor Christians,

[4]See 1:12; 2:2; 4:3–4 and 1:23; 2:2; 3:21 respectively.
[5]For support of the baptismal-service nature of I Peter see H. Preisker, in the appendix to the commentary by Hans Windisch, *Die Katholischen Briefe*, 2nd ed., *Handbuch zum Neuen Testament*, vol. XV (Tübingen: J.C.B. Mohr, 1951), pp. 156–160; F.L. Cross, *I Peter; A Paschal Liturgy* (London: Mowbray, 1954); F.W. Beare, *The First Epistle of Peter*, 2nd ed. (Oxford: Blackwell, 1958). Criticism of this theory is ably presented by C.F.D. Moule, "The Nature and Purpose of I Peter," in *New Testament Studies*, vol. III (Cambridge: At the University Press, 1956–1957), pp. 1–11.
[6]See W.C. van Unnik, "The Teaching of Good Works in I Peter," in *New Testament Studies*, vol. I (Cambridge: At the University Press, 1955), pp. 92–93.
[7]See Revelation 14:8; 18:2.
[8]See W.C. van Unnik, "Peter, First Letter of," in George A. Buttrick, ed., *The Interpreter's Dictionary of the Bible* (New York: Abingdon Press, 1962), K–Q, 762.

reminds them of their election and consecration, and prays that their grace and peace may be multiplied (1:1–2). From this point the letter falls into three convenient sections.

The blessings of God's redeemed people (I Peter 1:3–2:10). The author praises God for Christ's resurrection, which sparked a living hope in a heavenly inheritance. Fellow believers in Asia Minor should see their present trials as a test of the validity of their faith. If they pass the test, their reward will be the final salvation to which the prophets pointed. They should avoid the passions of their past, live holy lives, and earnestly love one another. As newborn children of God, they should shun malice and grow up to salvation. Christ is the cornerstone of their spiritual temple. They are the people of God summoned to proclaim the wonderful deeds of Him who called them out of darkness into light.

The conduct of God's redeemed people (I Peter 2:11–4:11). Christians are urged to behave properly among the Gentiles in order to silence their criticism and to elicit their eventual praise of God. They are to be subject to civil authorities as divinely ordained. Servants are to obey their masters even if it results in unjust suffering. Such conduct brings God's approval. It is also an emulation of Christ, whose innocent afflictions have redeemed them from their sins. Wives should be submissive to their husbands, dress with due modesty, and cultivate a gentle and quiet spirit. Husbands should be considerate of their wives and bestow honor on them as members of the weaker sex. All should have unity of spirit, sympathy, and love of the brethren. Those who suffer for righteousness' sake are blessed. Readers should be ever ready to defend their faith with gentleness. Christ, who died for sins, was made alive in the spirit "in which he went and preached to the spirits in prison" (3:19).[9] The saving of Noah's household during the flood has a counterpart in Christian baptism. Christians should no longer live for the flesh but for doing the will of God. If their pagan neighbors are surprised at their abstinence from wild profligacy and abuse them, Christians should leave such people to the Judge of the living and the dead. The end is near. Sobriety and prayer are essential—and love is even more so. Gifts from God should be used for men's service and God's glory.

[9]Compare I Peter 4:6. I Peter 3:19 is one of the most enigmatic in the New Testament. When combined with 4:6, its simplest meaning is that Christ, between his death and resurrection, descended into Hades to preach to certain imprisoned spirits. Were they the fallen angels of Genesis 6:1–4 or the rebels of Genesis 6:6–7 who perished in the flood? In any case, the statements in I Peter are designed to answer two questions that bothered early Christians: (1) Where was Christ's spirit while his body was in the tomb and (2) what was the fate of those who had died before Christ came?

The tribulations of God's redeemed people (I Peter 4:12–5:11).
Readers are cautioned against being surprised at their coming ordeal. They should rejoice insofar as they share Christ's sufferings. If they are reproached because they bear his name, they are blessed. Judgment is beginning with the faithful, and if it starts with the church, what will happen to unbelievers? As a fellow elder and a witness of Christ's suffering, the author implores the elders in Asia Minor to tend the flock willingly, eagerly, and selflessly. When the chief Shepherd appears, he will reward them. Younger members of the congregations should be subject to the elders. All should be humble, carefree, sober, and watchful. Since the devil stalks the earth, they should be vigilant and ready to suffer with their fellow Christians throughout the world. After a little while God will restore and strengthen them. This remarkable letter closes with a commendation of Sylvanus and greeting from Christians in "Babylon."

A primary focus of I Peter is Christian ethics—although this may be obscured by the author's deep concern for the suffering of his addressees. The new life bestowed by God through the Holy Spirit is the central message of the church. Although the end is believed to be near, Christians are presently called upon to live "in the world." This forces them to formulate an ethical code to prevent the new life from being engulfed by the old. How should they relate to the state? Jesus counseled the payment of taxes to Caesar, and Paul commanded that everyone be subject to the governing authorities.[10] Our author, unlike the author of Revelation, adopts a similar stance. On such matters as government authority and slavery, our author advocates accommodation to the world. In the area of "personal" ethics he calls Christians to obedient work and witness in the world without surrendering themselves to the world's standards and demands.

Hebrews Sometime during the second half of the first century a Christian leader wrote to fellow Christians to buoy up their faith. His communication came to be known as "The Letter to the Hebrews," but it is such a puzzling product that it has often been called "the riddle of the New Testament." Hebrews names neither its author nor its intended readers. It gives no explicit information about its origin, destination, or date of composition. Even its form is an enigma. It begins like a treatise and ends like a letter. Although the first twelve chapters are closely related, it is an open question whether the thirteenth (in whole or in part) can claim the same parentage.

---

[10]See Mark 12:17 and Romans 13:1 respectively.

All efforts to identify the author of Hebrews rest on tradition or on inferences from the letter itself. It was ascribed to numerous authors, especially to Paul, but his authorship was questioned even in the early centuries. I Clement, although addressed to the church Paul founded in Corinth, does not mention him as author of quotations apparently taken from Hebrews.[11] Pantaenus, the Alexandrian scholar of about 185 A.D., accepts Paul's authorship, but Clement of Alexandria and Origen deny that the style of the letter belongs to the Apostle.[12] Nevertheless, after Origen, critical doubts concerning Paul's authorship declined in the East. By the fourth century the Alexandrian tradition began to influence the West, and over the centuries it gradually prevailed. There were notable dissenters, of course, and numerous alternative authors proposed—including Luke, Barnabas, Silas, Apollos, and Clement of Rome. But in 1546 the Council of Trent finalized the Roman Catholic position by including Hebrews among the letters of Paul. This does not mean, according to the Pontifical Bible Commission of Rome in 1914, that the faithful are obligated to believe that Paul gave the letter its final form.

The great majority of Protestant scholars, including Luther and Calvin of Reformation days, deny Paul's authorship of Hebrews. They point to the marked differences in style (which the Alexandrian scholars noted), ideas, arrangement of materials, and thought patterns between this letter and Paul's authentic writings. Hebrews knows nothing of such characteristic Pauline concepts as justification, reconciliation, and mystical union with Christ. Shared ideas, moreover, are used in diverse ways. "Faith," for Paul, is trust in God and receptivity to the gospel, but in Hebrews it is loyalty to invisible realities honored by worthies of the past. Paul speaks of "the Law" primarily in its moral aspects, but Hebrews stresses its ritualistic requirements. Nowhere in Paul's writings can one find the interweaving of closely reasoned argumentation and earnest exhortation that makes Hebrews so distinctive.

If Paul did not author Hebrews, who did? Origen's celebrated answer, although intended to apply only to the literary style of the letter, is relevant to the entire composition: "in truth, God knows."[13] What we know about the author must be inferred from his work. He wrote good Greek, and his language and style strongly suggest that he was educated in the Hellenistic tradition. He was familiar with Platonic thought, as his two-story view of reality suggests, and he reveled in the work of Philo. His interest in word study, his use of Jewish Wisdom

---

[11] See I Clement 17:1, 5; 19:2; 27:2; 36:1–5; 43:1; 56:2–4.
[12] Eusebius, *Ecclesiastical History*, VI, 14, 2–3 and 25, 11–12.
[13] Eusebius, *Ecclesiastical History*, VI, 25, 13–14.

Literature, and his exegesis of Scripture point to the apologist from Alexandria. Yet he was also acquainted with the rabbinical way of interpreting sacred writ. He was assuredly a Christian—whether of Jewish or Gentile heritage we cannot say—who came to the faith under the tutelage of the Judaism of the Diaspora.

Origin and Destination

The only parts of Hebrews that purport to inform readers of the origin of the letter are the title, "To the Hebrews," and the closing salute in 13:24, "Those who come from Italy send you greetings." Although the title was early attested by Pantaenus and Tertullian, it was originally outside the rolled papyrus and probably never copied. The present title appears to have been derived from the contents of the communication. Moreover, the derived title is ambiguous. Who are "the Hebrews"? The closing salutation is suspect since it may be the work of another hand. But even if it is genuine, the Greek is grammatically uncertain. It may mean Christians living in Italy or Italians abroad who join the author in greeting their countrymen in Italy. If Italy is the place of origin, what is the destination? If the destination is Italy, where is the place of origin?

Despite these considerable difficulties, most scholars have concluded that Hebrews was written to Rome or its vicinity. The first witness to the existence of the letter is I Clement, which tradition indicates originated in Rome. The absence of any early Western references to Paul's authorship of Hebrews suggests that its actual origin was unknown. The dearth of Pauline ideas points to an area where the Apostle had not campaigned, and the curious fusion of early Christian and Hellenistic Christian thought could easily arise in a cosmopolitan community like Rome. Exhortations in Hebrews that refer to past and present persecution of the readers and their need for steadfastness can also be used to support the Roman destination of the letter (10:32–33; 12:3–4).

The premise that Hebrews was written for readers at Rome is doubtless the easiest to defend, but it is a far cry from certainty. Alexandria, Palestine, and (more specifically) Jerusalem also have their advocates. If Hebrews was written to Rome, it is reasonable to assume that the author was an esteemed elder in that church who wrote the letter while he was away. It is futile to speculate about where he was at the time.

Date and Occasion

Some scholars assign Hebrews a date as early as 60 A.D. They buttress their claim by declaring that neither Nero's persecution nor the Temple's destruction (70 A.D.) is mentioned, and the author writes about Temple worship in the present tense. What they fail to see is that the author is not concerned with happenings in Jerusalem but only with the original pattern of worship revealed to Moses on Mt. Sinai (8:5). Moreover, the present tense was customarily used in interpreting the Jewish Law, as an examination of Josephus' writings, the Mishna (a collection of oral laws) and the Talmud will reveal. Hebrews discloses no personal knowledge of Temple worship anyway.

Most interpreters date Hebrews between 85 and 95 A.D., and there are many references that seem to justify this. The author is a second-generation Christian, and so are his readers (2:3). They have lost the enthusiasm that came with their conversion and enabled them to endure suffering, public exposure, and affliction (under Nero?), and they are in danger of drifting away (10:32–33; 2:1). Their present temptation to apostasy (6:4–6; 10:26; under Domitian?) has not yet resulted in bloodshed, but it has caused shame and obloquy (12:2–4). They need to hold fast (10:23) until the end (6:11) with endurance (10:36) and perseverance (12:1) and not lose hope (6:19). They should have been teachers by this time, instead of students in need of instruction (5:12). The parousia (perhaps postponed) is sure (9:28) so they should exhort one another daily (3:13).

This situation seems to place Hebrews in the time of Domitian (81–96 A.D.). If, as some scholars claim, the author quotes extensively from I Clement (which is usually dated about 96 A.D.), this date would constitute the *terminus ad quem*. But an end-of-the century birthday for Hebrews is by no means certain. The dating of I Clement (not to mention who wrote it) is debatable, and its introductory reference to "sudden and successive misfortunes and disasters that have overtaken us" need not be to Domitian's persecution, which itself lacks substantial documentation. Although the author of Hebrews warns against apostasy, he does not directly attribute his readers' "drifting away" to overt persecution. His reminder of "former days" when his readers "endured a hard struggle with sufferings" coheres with Nero's persecution, but one wonders why there is no mention of martyrs (10:32–34).

Clearly Hebrews can be dated anywhere between 60 and 95 A.D. Since the author and his readers are second-generation Christians and the letter deals with problems of the postapostolic period and reveals a close relationship to I Clement, we think that the 85–95 A.D. range is the best possible estimate of its date.

The occasion of Hebrews is no more certain than its date. Until modern times it was generally assumed that the author wrote to prevent Jewish Christians from reverting to Judaism. The assumption was based on the title of the letter, the author's sustained argument that Christianity is superior to Judaism, and his extensive use of the Old Testament (Septuagint). But such reasoning is suspect. The title is not native to the letter. The author expounds the superiority of Christianity in a calm, reasoned, and nonpolemic manner without any hint that his readers are disturbed by Jewish teaching. Their problem seems to be quite the opposite. They are sluggish, inattentive, and dull—in danger of drifting away from what they had embraced (2:1). "Take care, brethren," the author warns, "lest there be in any of you an evil, unbelieving heart, leading you to fall away from the living God" (3:12). And his generous use of the Old Testament proves nothing. It was the Bible of both Jewish and Gentile Christians.

Another theory, less popular now than a couple of decades ago, holds that Hebrews is addressed to a community threatened by persecution. Christians were in danger of apostasy because of the hostility they experienced from the government under Domitian. The author wrote to fortify a faith that was under fire.[14] There are passages in Hebrews, as we have noted, that give this notion some plausibility.[15] The overall benign tone of the letter, its failure to attribute its readers' condition to overt persecution, and the limited knowledge we have about Domitian and the church make the theory somewhat less convincing than its zealous exponents realize.

It may be that Hebrews was written to combat some kind of Jewish-Christian or Gnostic speculation. The Roman church may have developed from a Hellenistic Jewish synagogue, and numerous parallels between Philo's thought and Hebrews have been discovered in certain pre-Christian Gnostic writings.[16] But Hebrews does not appear to be a refutation of any kind of speculation, Jewish-Christian or Gnostic. Until further evidence comes to light, we must rest content with a declaration of the letter's positive purpose. It was designed to arouse its readers from advancing lethargy by asserting the finality of the Christian faith.

Literary Form Since Hebrews contains a sonorous opening and much closely reasoned argumentation, it has been called a treatise. Its extensive exhortations have stimulated still others to call the communication a sermon or homily. None of these designations is altogether artless, and none is wholly satisfactory. Hebrews is as unique in literary form as it is in thought content.

[14]See H. C. Kee, F. W. Young, and K. Froehlich, 2nd ed., *Understanding the New Testament*, (Englewood Cliffs, N. J.: Prentice-Hall, Inc., 1965), p. 429.
[15]See p. 346.
[16]See E. Dinkler, "Letter to the Hebrews," in *The Interpreter's Dictionary of the Bible*, E–J, 573–575.

The question of why Hebrews was composed in such a unique form has spawned several theories. (1) The author wrote with a particular group in mind, and the entire "letter" was intended for their benefit. (2) The author wrote for one group and later dispatched the same communication to another group with the personalia added. (3) Someone other than the author sent the communication to a definite group after he had added the epistolary ending. (4) Hebrews 1–12 (or 1:1–13:17) constituted the original work, and another hand added the concluding material to simulate Paul's authorship and thereby win acceptance of the whole.[17]

None of these notions is immune to criticism. If the author originally wrote for one group and later made additions and sent the missive to another group, why didn't he delete the inappropriate personal references in 6:10 and 10:32–34? If the original author (or another) added the final chapter to make Hebrews appear to be Pauline, why was Paul's name omitted from it? Striking verbal parallels exist between chapter 13 (but not the rest of Hebrews) and Paul's letters. This fact gives plausibility to the hypothesis that chapter 13 was added by another hand.[18] But any conjecture that rejects the unity of Hebrews lacks textual support. This leaves the first theory as the most likely. The author wrote to a group he knew well. His exhortations are direct throughout. His failure to treat purely local matters in the course of his argumentation and exhortation suggests that he had an "open letter" in mind—suitable both for a given group and for a general audience.

Message

The author's habit of interweaving argument and exhortation makes a simple outline of his work a deceptive affair. Although his Christological passages are regularly followed by hortatory ones, he frequently introduces admonitions into the doctrinal sections themselves. A relatively uncomplicated arrangement of Hebrews can only be discerned when this limitation is kept in mind.

The *general* theme of Hebrews is sounded in its sonorous prologue: the finality of God's revelation in Jesus Christ. God had spoken previously through the prophets, but in these "last days" He has spoken fully and finally by a Son. The Son was both heir and agent of creation. He radiated God's glory because he bore "the very stamp of his nature, upholding the universe by his word of power." After

[17]See Alexander C. Purdy, "Hebrews, Introduction," in George A. Buttrick, ed., *The Interpreter's Bible* (New York: Abingdon Press, 1955), XI, 577–595, on whose stimulating insights we have been partially dependent.
[18]Compare 13:23 with Philippians 2:19, 23–24; 13:16 with Philippians 4:18; 13:21 with Philippians 4:20.

he had made "purification for sins," he was given a seat at God's right hand where he outranks the angels (1:1-4). The finality of God's revelation in Jesus Christ is suggested in two ways: the Son appeared in the "last days," and the Son shared the very nature of God. Previous revelations were not denigrated, but they lacked finality because the prophets had been only vehicles of the verity. The idea of the Son as the agent of creation had its counterpart in Judaism (Wisdom) and in Hellenism (the Logos). Our author assuredly expressed himself in borrowed terms, but it is idle speculation to assign these terms to specific sources. They were common to the culture of his day.

The superiority of the Son (1:5-4:13). The author's argument really begins in the prologue. There he asserts that the Son is superior to angels (1:4). He then documents this thesis from the Old Testament. God never referred to angels as "Son," appointed them the righteous ruler of His kingdom (1:8-9), or gave them the seat of honor (1:13). On the contrary, He called them "servants" (1:14) and commanded that they worship the Son (1:6).

The readers are urged to pay close attention to the superior revelation declared first by Jesus, attested to by those who heard him, and affirmed by subsequent Christians (2:1-4). While it is not yet so, in the Age to Come all things will be subject to man, not the angels (2:5-8). The Son was temporarily subordinate to the angels in order that through his suffering and death he might become the pioneer of man's salvation and have sympathy with man as his high priest (2:9-18).

The Son is also superior to Moses. Moses called the House of Israel into being, but as Israel's representative he was simply a servant. What he said and did as a servant merely foreshadowed what Jesus would say and do as the Son. The substance outranks the shadow (3:1-6a).

The author again urges his readers to hold fast to their confidence in Christ by whom the true household of God has been established. He quotes Psalm 95 to show that a whole generation of Israelites perished in the wilderness because they doubted God's promise that He would provide them with a New Land. As long as it is "today" ("these last days," 1:2), our author assures his readers that this "rest" (no longer the Promised Land of Moses but "salvation," the heavenly "sanctuary," or "the city of the living God" of the church) is still open (2:3; 10:19; 12:22). The wilderness generation failed to obtain the promised rest because of their lack of faith. They were destroyed, but the promise of entering God's rest remains. There is a sabbath rest for the people of God. "Let us therefore strive to enter that restm" our author pleads, "that no one fall by the same sort of disobedience" (4:11). To fall short of that rest is to incur the judgment of God, who discerns the inward thoughts of men (3:6b–4:13).

The high priesthood of the Son (4:14–7:28). With 4:14 the *specific* theme of Hebrews is introduced. The notion is not new (2:17, 3:1), but it is now clothed in formal dress: "We have a great high priest . . . , Jesus, the Son of God." His qualifications merit comparison with those of the Levitical priests. (1) Both Jesus and the priests are human. They can understand and sympathize with human weakness. Even though Jesus has "passed through the heavens," he has known every temptation that flesh is heir to. But unlike the Levites, he has never yielded to sin (4:14–16). (2) Both are appointed by God to act on behalf of men in relation to God, to offer gifts and sacrifices for sins (5:1). But the Levitical priest is a sinner. He must offer sacrifices for himself as well as for the people (5:2–3). Since Jesus, though fully human, is without sin (4:15), he does not need to offer sacrifices for himself. (3) Both are called to their office by God, but the offices and the length of service differ. The Levites are called to the Aaronic priesthood for life; Christ is a priest forever "after the order of Melchizedek" (5:4–6).

Our author is the only New Testament writer who refers to the order of Melchizedek, an order we shall discuss shortly. His object is to demonstrate that Christ's order of priesthood is superior to that of the Levites (7:1–28). Before the author discusses Christ's high priesthood, however, he again exhorts his readers (5:11–6:20). He rebukes them for their dullness of hearing. Although they ought to be teachers, they need someone to teach them the first principles of God's word. Despite their penchant for milk, he proposes that they abandon the elementary teachings of Christ and go on to maturity by adopting a diet of solid food.[19] There is no second repentance for the enlightened if they commit apostasy.[20] In the readers' case, the author feels sure of better things. God will not overlook their work. Abraham obtained the promise of posterity through patient endurance. Christians should seize the hope God has set before them. It lies in the inner shrine behind the curtain of the tabernacle. Jesus has entered that shrine on their behalf—as a high priest after the order of Melchizedek.

[19]Is "solid food" the author's view of Christ as a priest forever, or is it some esoteric knowledge about Christ possessed by the "mature"?
[20]This distinctive teaching, which concerns the willful denial of Christianity rather than sins that arise from weakness and ignorance, stems from the author's conviction that Christ is God's full and final revelation. He offered himself once and for all for the purification of sins. His priestly ministry provided the only access to God. Compare the concepts of "unforgivable sin" (Mk. 3:29) and "new creature" (II Cor. 5:17).

The author develops the idea of Jesus' high priesthood from two Old Testament sources, Genesis 14:17-20 and Psalms 110:4. According to the Genesis account, Melchizedek, king of Salem and priest of the Most High God, met Abraham returning from a battle to free Lot from captivity. Melchizedek blessed the patriarch and accepted from him a tenth of all that he had. The fact that neither passage supports our author's specific thesis (4:14-16) may seem strange to modern readers, but his method of interpretation was common in his day. His object is to establish the superiority of Christ's priesthood. He begins his argument by affirming the dignity of Melchizedek, the prototype of Christ. Melchizedek is king of righteousness and peace. He is without father, mother, genealogy, birthday or death day. Like the Son of God, he is a priest forever (7:1-3). He is superior to Abraham, since the patriarch paid a tithe to him. He is also superior to Levi and the Levites since it could be said that Levi paid tithes through Abraham (7:4-10). If perfection had been attainable through the Levitical priesthood, there would have been no need for the other order of priesthood through Melchizedek. When there is a change in the priesthood, the Law that established that priesthood is superseded (7:11-14). Christ's priesthood is not validated by Levitical descent but by his indestructible life (7:15-19). His priesthood is guaranteed by the divine oath and carries with it a better covenant (7:20-22). The Levitical priests were numerous, but death eventually terminated their service. Christ's priesthood is permanent. He is able at all times to save those who seek his help (7:23-25). How fitting it is that Christians have a high priest who is holy and blameless, devoid of any need to offer daily sacrifices for his own sins, a high priest who made a once-for-all sacrifice when he offered up himself (7:26-28)!

The superiority of the Son's sanctuary, covenant, and sacrifice (8:1-10:39). Once our author has established that Christ's priesthood was after the order of Melchizedek, he does not mention that mysterious personage again. He moves on to the climax of his theological argument: the superiority of Christ's sanctuary, covenant, and sacrifice to those of the Levitical priesthood.

Christ ministers in the "true tent" or "the heavenly sanctuary" set up by God, whereas the Levitical priests operate in a man-made earthly sanctuary that is only "a copy and shadow" of the heavenly sanctuary. Throughout his discussion the author has in mind the tent that ancient Israel set up in the wilderness rather than the Jerusalem Temple, which he may never have seen. His two-world idea of reality cannot be precisely documented.[21] Modified forms of Plato's dualism

[21]Note how frequently the author uses such words as "copy" (8:5; 9:23, 24) and "shadow" (8:5; 10:1) in contrast to "true" (8:2; 9:24; 10:1), "perfect" (9:11) and "real" (10:1).

had permeated the Hellenistic world, and Philo had spoken of the Temple as a symbol of the true temple.[22] The only source our author cites specifically is the Old Testament. The concept of the heavenly tabernacle was common in late Judaism (8:1–5).

Christ's ministry in a superior sanctuary is accompanied by a better covenant. If the first covenant (which God made with Israel during the Exodus) had been faultless, there would have been no need for a second. Yet through the prophet Jeremiah, God promised a *new* covenant to Israel—one that would be written on their hearts. According to the author of Hebrews, God regards the old covenant as obsolete. The new covenant is superior because it rests on better promises (8:6–13).[23]

The author next describes the earthly sanctuary with its ineffective priesthood and sacrifices (9:1–14).[24] In order to follow his reasoning it is important to recall some features of Israel's worship. In the Tabernacle there were two inner tents, the Holy of Holies and the Holy Place. The Holy Place, the outer of the two, was open to the priests but not to the people. It was the area where the daily sacrifices were offered. The Holy of Holies, the inner tent, could be entered only by the High Priest once a year on the Day of Atonement (9:6–7). At that time he would sprinkle sacrificial blood on the mercy seat—the blood of a bull for his own sins and those of his fellow priests and the blood of a goat for the sins of the people (Lev. 16). These animal sacrifices, our author argues, dealt only with infractions of the Law that concerned ritual purity ("food and drink and various ablutions," 9:10). Their efficacy was limited. When the worshiper sinned again, as he surely would, they would need to be repeated. They were incapable of perfecting the conscience of the worshiper (9:9). But when Christ appeared as the true high priest, he entered "once for all" into the heavenly sanctuary not with the blood of goats and calves but with his own blood, thus securing "an eternal redemption." He who was "without blemish" offered himself to God to purify "your conscience from dead works to serve the living God" (9:11–14).

Christ's sacrifice was superior to those of the Levitical priests not only because it was nonrepeatable but also because it made Christ

---

[22]See E.R. Goodenough, *By Light, Light* (New Haven, Conn.: Yale Univ. Press, 1935), pp. 108–109, 116–117.
[23]Our author's use of Jeremiah 31:31–34 is highly selective. It ignores completely the prophet's stress on the purely spiritual and inward aspects of religion. But our author is intent on making a single point: the new antiquates the old. Unlike Jeremiah, he assumes that the priestly principle is at the core of real religion.
[24]See Purdy, "Hebrews, Exegesis," in *The Interpreter's Bible*, XI, 685–687, for discrepancies between his description and the account that begins in Exodus 25.

the mediator of a new covenant (9:15). A will (or covenant) takes effect only at death (9:17). Even the first covenant was ratified with blood (9:18). Under the Law nearly everything is purified with blood, and without bloodshed there is no forgiveness of sins (9:22). As it was necessary for the "copies" of reality to be purified by such rites, "heavenly things" require a better sacrifice (9:23). At the end of the age Christ appeared to put away sin by the sacrifice of himself (9:26). When he comes a second time, it will not be to deal with sin but to save those who eagerly wait for him (9:28).

Since the Law is but a shadow of reality, the continual sacrifices it requires cannot make anyone perfect (10:1). By putting words from Psalm 40 in Christ's mouth our author has Christ declare that he came to terminate all other kinds of sacrifice by doing God's will. In his death Christ consecrated once for all those who believe (10:5–10). By his single offering he perfected for all time those who are consecrated. His death ratified the new covenant and made any further offering for sin superfluous (10:11–18).

The section on the superiority of the Son's sanctuary, covenant, and sacrifice is concluded with an exhortation designed to demonstrate the implications of Christ's priesthood for the readers (10:19–39). Although the Jewish High Priest could enter the Holy of Holies (where God resided) only once a year, Christ's "brethren" have confidence that they can enter the heavenly sanctuary by the blood of Jesus (10:19). They should hold fast their confession of Christ, stimulate one another to love and good works, meet together, and encourage one another—for the Day of Judgment is drawing near (10:20–25). If they deliberately sin after they have received the truth, there is no longer any sacrifice for sins. Only judgment awaits them, and it is a fearful matter to be judged by the living God (10:26–31). After their enlightenment they endured a hard struggle with sufferings, public exposure to abuse and affliction, and even joyfully accepted the plundering of their property because they knew that they had a better and abiding possession. They should continue steadfast in confidence and good works lest they lose their promised reward. Christ will come soon. They should not shrink back and suffer destruction but have faith and keep their souls (10:32–39).

The nature of faith and the meaning of discipline (11:1–13:21). Chapter 11 is a rhetorical masterpiece that ranks with the finest passages in the New Testament. It caps the climax of our author's argument. He has proved from Scripture that Jesus Christ is God's final revelation. Now he turns his attention to a purely practical matter. How can men avail themselves of this perfect revelation? They can do so by developing an attitude and action that he calls faith. Faith is "the assurance of things hoped for, the conviction of things not seen" (11:1). This definition, the only explicit one on the subject in the New Testament, is couched in language familiar to Hellenistic philosophers. The unseen realities have independent and objective validity. Men live in a shadow world that is a mere copy of reality. It is through faith, our author reasons, that the real world is apprehended. Faith gives assurance of things hoped for. But faith is more than hope. Faith makes hope operative as a present and prospective motive for action. Faith breeds conviction and—to the extent that it does—it is evidence of things unseen. By faith the men of old received God's approval (11:2).

The author's roll call of the Old Testament witnesses to faith is intended to strengthen and inspire his readers by reminding them that they do not stand alone in their struggles. Abel was the first witness because he was the first to receive "divine approval" (11:2). Enoch, Noah, Sarah, and Abraham are then cited. Abraham is the *cause célèbre*. He journeyed into a strange country without any map to guide him. He *trusted* God and His promise. Moses, Gideon, Barak, David, and a host of others were well attested by their faith, but none received what was promised (11:4–40).

The object of faith, which the "cloud of witnesses" had only dimly perceived, is a crystal-clear reality for the readers of Hebrews. They should lay aside, therefore, every weight and sin, run the race set before them with perseverance, and look to Jesus "the pioneer and perfecter of our faith, who for the joy that was set before him endured the cross, despising the shame, and is seated at the right hand of the throne of God" (12:1–2). His victory came through the discipline of suffering. If he suffered and died, the readers ought not to "grow weary or faint-hearted" (12:3). They should persist in their struggle against sin even if it should cost them their lives (12:4). Have they forgotten that discipline is both scriptural (Prov. 3:11–12) and parental (12:9)? When it is administered by "the Father" it is more endurable, of short duration, and for the good of the recipients. It enables them to share God's holiness (12:9–11).

Once again our author warns his readers against weariness. They should strive for peace among men and for the consecration required to see the Lord (12:12–14). The dire consequences of failing to obtain the grace of God are underscored by analogies from the fate of Esau (12:15–17) and the fate of those who violated the sanctity of Sinai (12:18–21). As awesome and dreadful as was the giving of the Law to Moses on Mt. Sinai, it cannot be compared to the New Covenant mediated by Jesus on Mt. Zion, the city of the living God, the heavenly

Jerusalem (12:22-24). If the people who failed to obey Moses did not escape, how much worse will be the fate of those who reject him who warns from heaven! The readers should be grateful that they have received an unshakable kingdom and offer to God acceptable worship (12:25-29).

The final chapter of Hebrews contains a series of specific admonitions about brotherly love, hospitality to strangers, compassion for prisoners and the ill-treated, the honor due to marriage, freedom from the love of money, and respect for and obedience to leaders, as well as a warning against "diverse and strange teachings" (13:1-17). After a request that his readers pray for his restoration to them, the author concludes with one of the most beautiful benedictions in the New Testament (13:18-21). A postscript and a briefer benediction are appended.

The Epistle to the Hebrews is today probably one of the least read major works of the New Testament. Its closely reasoned and sometimes labored argumentation and its preoccupation with priesthood, sacrifice, and ceremony have a strange ring to modern ears. But it is easy to imagine how compelling its message of encouragement was for its first readers. They lived in a shadow world whose institutions were believed to be only copies of the divine originals. For our author to remind such people that God's full and final revelation is found in Jesus Christ, who made purification for sins and now sits in the seat of honor in the real sanctuary, is to write words of supreme relevance. The message, without the medium, still strikes a responsive chord. Small wonder that our author's work is valued today for far more than the profound influence it has had upon the language of our prayers and our hymns.

James   The Letter of James is one of the most disputed writings in the New Testament. Critics of conservative and liberal persuasion disagree among themselves on such matters as authorship, date, setting, first readers, and literary character. Some question its religious value and dispute its place in mainstream Christianity. Their reticence or rejection is not without precedent. No writer before Origen attributed the letter to James, the brother of Jesus, and Origen seems to have had qualms about its authority. Eusebius observed that not many of the ancients mentioned James, and he listed the letter among the "disputed books."[25] Although Martin Luther acknowledged that James contained many good sayings, he was disturbed by its alleged non-Pauline interpretation of faith. He called the book an epistle of straw and threw it into the Elbe River.

[25]Eusebius, *Ecclesiastical History*, II, 33.

Authorship The author identifies himself simply as "James, a servant of God and of the Lord Jesus Christ" (1:1) who is a teacher (3:1). Attempts to equate him with the apostle James, son of Zebedee, or with the apostle James, son of Alphaeus (Mk. 3:17–18), have long since been abandoned, but the idea that he was James, brother of Jesus (Mk. 6:3), has persisted for centuries. The letter's supposed Jewish tone, the primitive simplicity of its Jewish Christianity, and its stress on Law and Lawgiver are cited as confirming evidence.

There are many features of James, however, that render authorship by Jesus' brother implausible. (1) Prior to Origen, the letter was evidently unknown beyond its place of birth. Although "apostolicity" quickly became a compelling credential for canonicity, James was accepted with reluctance in Syria and the West. (2) James lived in Nazareth and must have been intimately acquainted with his brother and his mission, message, death, and resurrection. Yet no book in the New Testament tells us less about Jesus. His sayings are never cited directly and rarely indirectly. (3) James' native tongue was Aramaic. Although he may well have developed a carpenter's command of Greek, our author thought and taught in Koine Greek. He not only evidenced a fine style and varied vocabulary, but he made use of the Hellenistic paraenesis and diatribe.[26] (4) Josephus indicates that James was martyred by order of the High Priest, Annas II, after the death of Festus but prior to the arrival of his successor, Albinus.[27] This would place James' death about 60–62 A.D.

It is possible, of course, that the letter was written by some unknown James who was later identified as Jesus' brother. The most likely hypothesis, though, is that James is a pseudonymous writing, a view that Jerome indicates was not uncommon in the ancient church. It was customary for people to write in the name of revered figures of the past. Witness Enoch, Baruch, and Ezra in Judaism and Paul, Peter, and John in Christianity. Because the name of James had been popularized by Galatians and perhaps by Acts, it is not at all surprising that it would be used in accordance with current literary practice.

Origin and Destination There is no sure way to tell where James was written because its author makes no reference to the subject. His stress on the "good life" (3:13) and obedience to "the perfect law" as its foundation (1:25) remind one of Matthew and the Didache and suggest Syrian Antioch. But the reluctance of the Syrian canon to accept James punctures

---

[26]A paraenesis is a collection of somewhat similar ethical exhortations cast in the second person and directed toward an individual or group. A diatribe imitates the style of a speaker who is engaged in a lively oral debate with an opponent.
[27]Josephus, *Antiquities*, XX, 9, 1.

this proposal. Caesarea has been suggested, and this is as good a guess as any. It fits the relatively early acceptance of James in the East, but it is lacking in certitude.

The destination of James is nearly as vague as its place of origin: "To the twelve tribes in the dispersion" (1:1). Some commentators have taken the phrase quite literally and have concluded that the letter is addressed to Jewish Christians. But there is nothing in the rest of the letter that deals specifically with Jewish-Christian problems. It is better to regard "the twelve tribes" as the spiritual Israel (all Christians) and "the dispersion" as the hostile world in which they live. This is in keeping with the impersonal nature of James (no greetings, no farewell message) and the universal character of its ethical teachings. James is not addressed to any particular community; it is a genuine catholic communication.

Date and Occasion   If James was written by Jesus' brother, it must be dated before 62 A.D. (or 66 A.D. according to Hegesippus, a Christian writer of the latter half of the second century). If the letter is postapostolic, as we believe, a date anywhere between 70 A.D. and 150 A.D. is possible. The author knew Romans—as a comparison of James 2:14–16 and Romans 4 suggests. A letter ascribed to James would have been written only after his death and the passage of sufficient years to permit him to be recognized as an authoritative figure of bygone days. These considerations suggest a date no earlier than 80 A.D. On the other hand, our author's eschatological hopes are still high (5:8), and the type of church organization he depicts is relatively simple (5:14). All in all, a date between 80 A.D. and 100 *A.D.* seems most likely for James.

Our author does not specifically indicate why he wrote his catholic communication, but some of his reasons are not difficult to discern. He wanted to remind his readers of the Christian code of conduct. He was not so much concerned with the formulation of "ethics for exiles" as he was its fruition. "What does it profit," he asked, "if a man says he has faith but has not works?" (2:14). He also wanted to refute a current distortion of Paul's teaching about love and faith. Love does not condone "partiality" (2:1–13) or sanction inertia by equating faith with mere intellectual assent to correct beliefs (2:14–26). If religion is not relevant to the whole of life, it is dead. There may be some merit to the suggestion by some scholars that 1:2–4 and references to "enduring trial" (1:12) and possible "suffering" (5:13) indicate a time of persecution, but the language of these verses is exceedingly general. The problems faced by the readers of James are from within the Christian community rather than from without.

Apart from its opening verse, James does not read like a letter. It has no customary ending, and its contents consist of miscellaneous topics. Whatever unity it has is derived not from its subject matter but from its practical purposes.

The trials of life and the pursuit of pure religion (1:2–27). The readers should rejoice when their faith is tested because only a tested faith is perfect and complete (1:2–4). Only those who pray for wisdom in faith will receive it (1:5–8). Riches are a curse (1:9–11), but those who endure trial will receive "the crown of life" (1:12). Temptation comes from human desire and leads to sin and death, but every good endowment and perfect gift come from God (1:13–18). Self-control and meekness are necessary virtues (1:19–20). Doers of the word, not those who merely hear it, are blessed (1:21–25). A religious man controls his tongue, or his religion is in vain. Pure religion consists of visiting orphans and widows and remaining unstained from the world (1:26–27).

Right relations with men and God (2:1–5:6). To show partiality toward the rich is contrary to the gospel, a sin against the royal law (2:1–13). Faith without works is dead (2:14–26). A tamed tongue is a mark of the perfect man, especially of a teacher (3:1–12). Jealousy and selfish ambition are contrary to the wisdom from above (3:13–18). Passion and desire (two Stoic evils) have led to dire results. The readers should realize that friendship with the world means enmity with God. They should cleanse their hands and purify their hearts (4:1–10). Brethren should not speak evil of one another (4:11–12). Christians should not become so concerned with making a living that they neglect the Author of Life (4:13–16). It is a sin to know the right and fail to do it (4:17). The injustices of the rich will shortly cause them mighty miseries (5:1–6).

The need for patience, honesty, and health (5:7–20). No matter what the hardship, the readers should be patient as were the prophets and Job (as depicted in the prose framework of Job). The end of the world is at hand, and the righteous will soon receive their reward (5:7–11). Oath-taking is forbidden and honesty enjoined (5:12). If one of the brethren is sick, he should call for the elders of the church. They will pray for him and anoint him with oil, and he will be healed. The prayer of righteous people has great power, as the acts of Elijah bear witness. If a brother wanders from the truth and someone brings him back, both the sinner and the savior will benefit.

Two themes in James require special comment: the author's attitude toward "the rich" and "the poor" and his view of "faith" and "works."

Despite his stark warning against "partiality," the author betrays a marked antipathy toward the rich. Some commentators interpret this term quite literally—for them, the rich are "the wealthy." However, our author does not deride the rich because they have mountains of mammon. He chastises them because they "oppress" the poor, "drag them into court," "blaspheme" Christ or his followers (2:6-7), and keep "back by fraud" the wages of their field hands (5:4). They delight in their pleasure-prone, luxury-laden life style while they condemn men to death by depriving them of their livelihood (5:5-6). "Has not God chosen those who are poor in the world," our author asks, "to be rich in faith and heirs of the kingdom which he has promised to those who love him?" (2:5).

A similar interpretation of rich and poor appears in Luke, where the author revels in the ultimate reversal of their roles (1:51-52; 6:20-21; 12:16-21; 16:19-26). The notion was not new. Judaism had long been acquainted with the equation of the poor and the pious (Ps. 86:1-2). James should be understood in the same vein, although his interests are purely pragmatic. The rich are the godless, and the poor are the righteous. He never meant to suggest that the rich could not repent, mend their ways, and become righteous or that the poor of pocket were righteous *per se.*

Our author seems to take a stance directly opposite to that of Paul on the subject of faith and works. In Romans 3:28 Paul declares that "a man is justified by faith apart from works of law," but James 2:24 asserts that "a man is justified by works and not by faith alone." The differences between the two, however, are more apparent than real. What James was attacking was not Paul's teaching, but a perversion of it. The faith-not-works formula was introduced into the Christian community by Paul, and distortions of it evidently continued to plague the church in postapostolic times (II Peter 3:15-17).

The notion that James opposes Paul's teaching on faith and works may stem from the failure to recognize their different circumstances and use of words. When Paul speaks of "works," he means the moral and ritual requirements of the Law. That kind of "works" does not lead to justification. James suggests that "works" are love in action. The two could not be in closer agreement. By "faith" Paul means surrender of the whole self to the God revealed in Christ. When James states that a man is not justified by faith alone, he uses "faith" in the sense of mere intellectual assent to some doctrine such as "God is one" (2:19). Such a faith is "barren" or "dead" (2:20, 26). Paul would have approved. He viewed faith as active in love and the works of love as "the fruit of the Spirit" (Gal. 5:6, 22-23).

All of this is not to affirm that James plumbed the depths of Paul's great teaching on justification by faith. For Paul, justification was the initial act in the salvation drama by which God accepts the believer, forgives him, and starts him on his way. For James, justification lay much farther down the road, and heaven is reserved for those who have faith and good works. His grasp of the full significance of Paul's doctrine was doubtless deficient, but his emphasis on an ethical code derived from faith served as a needed antidote to those "Christians" who relished a faith divorced from the cries of those who are "ill-clad and in lack of daily food" (2:15).

Jude

Jude occupies the last place among catholic communications in the Christian canon. Its brevity and seemingly irrelevant subject matter, however, prompt modern Christians to wonder why it was included at all. But many of the New Testament writings were composed to meet crises faced by the early church. Their preservation was due, in part, to the importance of the issue they treated. This factor accounts for the longevity of Jude.

Authorship

The superscription identifies the author as "Jude [Judas], a servant of Jesus Christ and brother of James," and therefore of Jesus (1). But it is highly unlikely that this Jude wrote the tract, since he probably died before 70 A.D.[28] The phrase, "brother of James," may have been an editorial addition, or the letter may have been the work of an unknown Jude. Scholarly consensus holds that Jude is a pseudonymous work, and it was probably recognized as such from the start.

Origin and Destination

Jude may have originated in Rome, but evidence to support this conjecture is slim indeed. There is equal uncertainty about any particular locality to which Jude's first readers belonged. The salutation fits any Greek-speaking community. The "heresy" with which the letter deals suggests the churches of Asia Minor, but the author's message is appropriate for any and all churches threatened by the unacceptable teachings and immoral practices that are condemned. Jude is clearly encyclical in character.

Date and Occasion

Neither the author of Jude nor his readers were first-generation Christians. The author wrote of "the predictions of the apostles" as though they had been made long ago. The apostles had predicted that "in the last time" (a time that has now actually arrived) there would be "scoffers" who would follow "their own ungodly passions" (17–18). The author spoke of faith as a deposit "once for all delivered to

---

[28]Eusebius, *Ecclesiastical History*, III, 20, 1–2.

the saints" (3), and he asked his readers to build themselves up on their "most holy faith" (20). These factors, when combined with Jude's alleged affinities with the Gospel of John and I and II John, suggest a date between 120 A.D. and 150 A.D. The latter date is usually assigned to II Peter, which reproduces (in one form or another) at least 19 of Jude's 25 verses. Perhaps a date of about 125 A.D. is the most likely for Jude.

The author of Jude originally intended to write a treatise on "our common salvation," but he was diverted from this purpose by a crisis in the church. The very foundations of sound doctrine and morality had been placed in jeopardy. He therefore discarded his treatise idea in favor of a tract. He appealed to his readers "to contend for the faith which was once for all delivered to the saints" (3).

Message   With the completion of the superscription and justification for writing, our author begins the main thrust of his brief letter. He assumes that his readers know the content of both "the faith" he urges them to defend and the false teaching that endangers it. His object, therefore, is not to inform as much as it is to arouse.

The character and condemnation of the heretics (5–16).[29]   God condemns people who were once spiritually privileged but who have fallen into sin. Three Old Testament examples are offered as proof: the experience of the unbelieving Israelites in the desert, the fallen angels, and the people of Sodom and Gomorrah (5–7). In this passage and those that follow (9–12, 14–15) our author borrows from the Assumption of Moses, Enoch, and the Old Testament to elaborate on his theme of judgment. The highly-touted spirituality of the heretics (which is based on dreams or visions believed to mediate divine revelation) is spurious. Instead of generating moral conduct, it leads to licentiousness, rejection of authority, and scorn of the glorious ones (8). Michael exercised great restraint even while dealing with the devil, but the heretics court disaster by relying on their animal instincts as a guide to spiritual reality (9–10). Woe to them! They are like Cain (who cared only about himself), Balaam (who used others for gain), and Korah (who rebelled against the authority of Moses). To these three analogies from Scripture the author adds five metaphors to highlight the iniquity of the heretics. They are "blemishes" on the love feasts of the church, "waterless clouds, carried along by winds," "fruitless trees in late autumn, twice dead, uprooted," "wild waves of the sea, casting up the foam of their own shame," and "wandering stars for whom the nether gloom of darkness has been reserved for ever" (11–13). The judgment that Enoch prophesied the Lord would execute on the "ungodly" was intended to include the heretics—"grumblers, malcontents, following their own passions, loud-mouthed boasters, flattering people to gain advantage" (14–16).[29]

The "most holy faith" is the sure foundation (17–23). The readers are living "in the last time" when scoffers follow "their own ungodly passions" (18) and "set up divisions" because they are "devoid of the Spirit" (19). How should Christians conduct themselves with such people in their midst? They should recall "the predictions of the apostles" (17) and build themselves up to their "most holy faith." They should "pray in the Holy Spirit," keep themselves "in the love of God," wait patiently for the blessings that will be theirs when Christ comes again, and seek the redemption of those who have succumbed to false teaching—without condoning their sin (20–23).

The Heretics   Identification of the heretics is complicated by the author's general description of them and by the confused and confusing nature of the text. Are they outsiders or members of the church? At one point the author suggests that they are outsiders who have "secretly" gained admission to the church (4), but at another point he describes them as church members who are "blemishes" on its love feasts. Since they "look after" themselves, they may be separatists who refuse to submit to apostolic authority (12). A reconstruction of the ambiguous verse 23 suggests that the church is preparing to excommunicate them.

Despite their clandestine entrance into the Christian community, the heretics have gained significant support for their teachings. Their "licentiousness" probably stems from their gospel of freedom. Since they have access to divine revelation through their dreams or visions, they feel liberated from the ethics of earthbound mortals (8, 12, 16). Our author's stress on the judgment and the parousia suggests that the heretics may have been believers in a spiritual resurrection that denied these cardinal concepts of the church. In any case, the invectives of Jude seem to be directed toward some form of gnosis. It would be hazardous, however, to equate that gnosis with any of the well developed systems of the second century described by Irenaeus, Hippolytus, or Epiphanius.

The vitriolic vituperation of Jude is redeemed by its several virtues. Its majestic benediction is inspirational (24–25). It insists that the Christian community's security against error is derived from the grace

[29]"Heresy" and "orthodoxy" are used proleptically. There could have been no real heretics until there existed a fully-developed orthodoxy from which they had deviated. That kind of orthodoxy was embodied in the creeds of Christendom that were formulated after the books of the New Testament were written.

of God and "the faith which was once for all delivered to the saints." It provides a window on the developing struggle between orthodoxy and heresy—as do Revelation, the Johannine letters, the Ignatius letters, the Pastorals, and II Peter.

II Peter This catholic communication not only reproduces most of Jude, but it is directed against a similar (although somewhat more developed) type of heresy.

Authorship The author claims to be the Apostle Peter (1:1), and he reinforces this notion at stated intervals in his brief letter. He alludes to Jesus' prediction of Peter's martyrdom (1:14), asserts that he was with Jesus "on the holy mountain" during the Transfiguration (1:17–18), implies that he wrote I Peter (3:1), and calls Paul his "beloved brother" (3:15). His zeal to establish the letter's authenticity inspires incredulity rather than confidence—an incredulity strongly supported by both external and internal evidence.

The first explicit reference to II Peter is made by Origen (217–251 A.D.), who classifies it as "doubtful."[30] Its canonical history is probably the weakest of any New Testament work. If I Peter is thought to be authentic, it would take an ingenious theory of secretarial aid to account for the stark differences in style and language between it and II Peter. Why would the Apostle Peter include most of Jude in his second chapter (of II Peter)? Why would he imply that he belongs to a generation of Christians to whom the church founders are known by tradition (3:2, 4)? Why would he refer to Paul's letters (which did not circulate as a group until about 95 A.D.) as "scripture" and allude to their abuse by "the ignorant and unstable" (3:16)? Clearly II Peter is a postapostolic pseudonymous writing.

Origin and Destination Rome has been suggested as the place of origin for II Peter. This is a deduction from the author's strident opposition to heresy, his reference to Peter's martyrdom (1:14), the benign picture he paints of Peter's relations with Paul, and his provision that after Peter's death the readers will be able "at any time" to recall what he has taught (1:15)—a transparent reference to the tradition that Mark wrote down what he remembered of Peter's preaching. Such speculation is intriguing, but it cannot yield certainty.

The communication is addressed to "those who have obtained a faith of equal standing" with the apostles "in the righteousness of our God

---

[30]Origen, *Commentary on John*, V, 3.

and Savior Jesus Christ" (1:1). They have previously received I Peter from the author (3:1), and they accord Paul's collected letters the same status as "the other scriptures" (3:16). The author has no particular church in mind. His message is intended for Christians everywhere whose true faith is under attack by false teachers.

Date and Occasion   Most scholars think that II Peter was the last New Testament book to be written, and they date it about 150 A.D. Their reasoning is cogent and compelling. (1) First-generation Christians have died, and false teachers whom "many" follow endanger the church (2:2). (2) The author's style and language have been decidedly influenced by Hellenistic culture. (3) He reproduces most of Jude. (4) The false teaching he opposes appears to be more developed than in Jude. (5) He stoutly defends orthodoxy and appeals to apostolicity (Peter, the Twelve, and Paul) and a recognized ministry. (6) He calls Paul's letters "scripture." (7) He is acquainted with a rather extensive body of Christian literature—the fourfold gospel (1:14),[31] the collected letters of Paul and twisted interpretations of them (3:16), Jude, I Peter (3:1), and perhaps Hebrews (2:20–21).[32]

The virulent attack that false teachers had launched against orthodoxy impelled our author to write his letter. He was particularly distressed by the heretics' denial of the parousia with its accompanying judgment (3:3–13) and the distortion of Paul's teaching on Christian freedom (3:16). If these "destructive heresies" (2:1) should prevail, the faith of "the fathers" would be doomed (3:4).

Message   In the salutation (1:1–2) the author of II Peter states his credentials ("servant and apostle"), designates his audience ("those who have obtained a faith of equal standing" with the apostles, that is, the church at large), and prays that "grace and peace be multiplied" to them.

Apostolic faith leads to the eternal kingdom (1:3–21). When Christ disclosed knowledge of himself to his disciples, he gave them the truths that have to do with salvation. People became partakers of "the divine nature" through moral and spiritual fellowship with him (1:3–4). For this reason, the readers should make every effort to supplement their faith by appropriating seven suggested virtues (1:5–7). If these virtues are possessed in abundance, believers are saved from being ineffective or unfruitful in knowledge of Christ. They should be zealous to confirm their "call and election." If they

[31]Compare John 21.
[32]Compare Hebrews 6:4–8; 10:26–31.

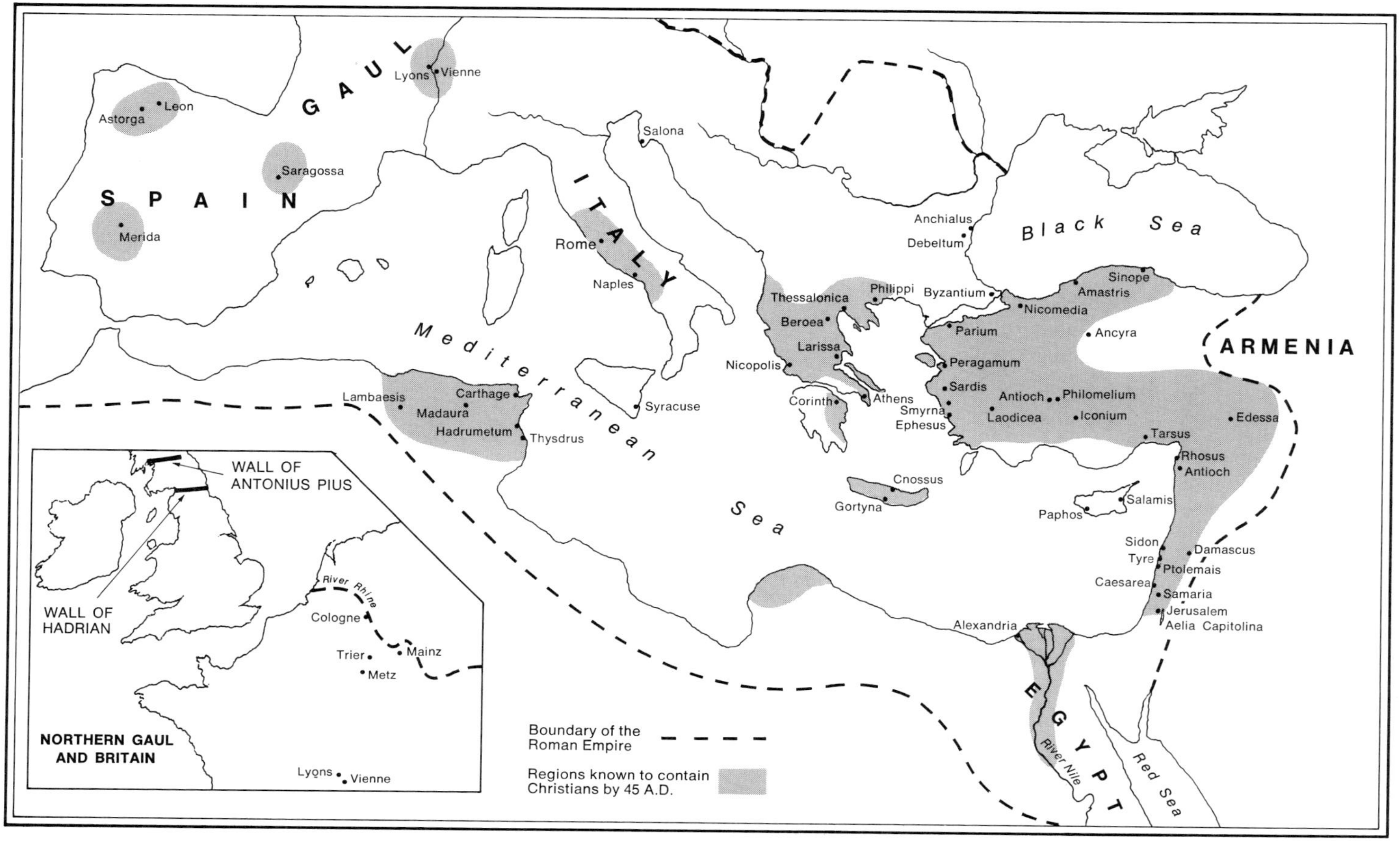

THE CHURCH IN THE TIME OF IRENAEUS (c.185 A.D.)

ARMENIA

Black Sea

Red Sea

EGYPT

River Nile

Edessa

Rhosus
Antioch
Damascus
Ptolemais
Samaria
Sidon
Tyre
Caesarea
Jerusalem
Aelia Capitolina

Tarsus

Salamis

Paphos

Alexandria

Sinope
Amastris
Ancyra
Nicomedia
Philomelium
Iconium

Byzantium
Parium
Peragamum
Sardis
Antioch
Philadelphia
Laodicea
Smyrna
Ephesus

Anchialus
Debeltum

Philippi
Thessalonica
Beroea
Larissa
Athens
Corinth
Nicopolis

Cnossus
Gortyna

Mediterranean Sea

Salona

Syracuse

Naples
Rome
ITALY

Carthage
Madaura
Lambaesis
Hadrumetum
Thysdrus

GAUL

Lyons Vienne

SPAIN

Saragossa

Leon
Astorga
Merida

- - - Boundary of the
Roman Empire

Regions known to contain
Christians by 45 A.D.

NORTHERN GAUL
AND BRITAIN

River Rhine

Cologne
Mainz
Trier
Metz
Lyons Vienne

WALL OF
ANTONIUS PIUS

WALL OF
HADRIAN

do this, they will never fall, and their entrance into the eternal kingdom of Christ will be assured (1:8–11). The author introduces Christ's prediction of Peter's death and "Peter's" witness of the Transfiguration to support his claim to be the Apostle Peter and to undergird his witness to the truths of the apostolic message (1:12–21).

The author of II Peter reminds one of Jude when he uses faith as a synonym for a body of beliefs—the truths that make up the message of salvation derived from Christ and proclaimed by the apostles. But there is an active aspect of faith in II Peter that should not be overlooked. The kerygma must be appropriated and developed by human effort. Salvation, of course, is not man-made. It depends upon God's initiative and power. Yet men must "confirm" their call and election by possessing and developing the seven virtues enumerated (1:10).

A description and denunciation of the false teachers (2:1–22). Since our author reproduced virtually all of Jude in this chapter, it would be redundant to discuss the material again here.[33] He evidently felt that Jude's description and denunciation of the false teachers was eminently suited to his own antagonists. It is evident that II Peter borrowed from Jude instead of *vice versa* from the fact that Jude is intelligible without reference to II Peter while parts of II Peter make no sense apart from a knowledge of Jude. The reference to angels in II Peter 2:11, for example, is an enigma without the reference to Michael in Jude 9.

A defense of the parousia (3:1–18a). Our author has laid the groundwork for "an apology of early Christian eschatology."[34] He has established the legitimacy and authority of his witness, condemned the "myths" of the false teachers and their devotees, and denounced the "spiritual freedom" that made them slaves of corruption. Now that he has defanged their biting denial of the parousia, he presents a fourfold defense of this historic Christian teaching. (1) The argument that "all things have continued as they were from the beginning of creation" (3:4) is disproved by the Biblical story of the deluge. Just as the earth once perished by flood, it will be consumed by fire in the future (3:5–7). (2) God's time and man's time are different, as Psalm 90:4 clearly shows. With the Lord one day is a thousand years, and a thousand years, one day. What the heretics called a delayed parousia has, according to the Creator's clock, already occurred (3:8).

---

[33]See pp. 361–363.
[34]See Ernst Käsemann, "An Apologia for Primitive Christian Eschatology," in *Essays on New Testament Themes*, trans. W.J. Montague, *Studies in Biblical Theology*, vol. XLI (London: SCM Press, 1964), pp. 169–195.

To God, all events are present, including the parousia. (3) The Lord does not telescope the time until the End but stretches it out, because He is merciful and wants to give everyone opportunity to repent (3:9). (4) The certainty of the parousia, with its accompanying cosmic catastrophe, makes godliness a necessity—as Paul's letters show (3:10–18).

The Christian community was ill equipped to enter the postapostolic period, and its prospects for survival appeared to be chancy. In many respects the church resembled a rudderless, pilotless ship laden with precious cargo but buffeted by a gathering storm from without and threatened by mutiny from within. The priceless cargo of the church was the faith that had once for all been delivered to the apostles. But that faith, which formerly had simply been proclaimed, now had to be protected. False teachers had secretly gained admission to the church, won converts, and perverted the grace of God into licentiousness and a denial of Jesus Christ (Jude 3–4). At the same time a parallel conflict with the state was incipient. Christians constituted a minority, and (like minorities everywhere) they were subject to social ostracism and political discrimination and disfavor. To be a Christian was to invite suspicion and risk suffering "for the name of Christ" (I Peter 4:14). Survival prompted the church to reformulate its faith in order to combat the challenge of false teachers. The orthodoxy that gradually emerged, however, proved to be only a partial guarantee against heresy. The church also found it necessary to develop a regular ministry and endow it with authority to curb the excesses that resulted from the freedom of the Spirit. Although these safeguards served to minimize the hazards encountered by postapostolic Christianity, they by no means eliminated them. The problems faced by the church in Catholic Concerns continue in Johannine Literature.

**Johannine
Writings**
(The Gospel of
John; I, II, and III
John)

Five books were admitted to the Christian canon partly because they
were believed to have been written by one of Jesus' intimate disciples—John, the son of Zebedee. These books are the Gospel of
John, the three Letters of John, and Revelation. The tradition of
the Apostle's authorship was endorsed by Irenaeus (Bishop of Lyons
in the latter half of the second century) who reported that the Apostle
John was active at Ephesus until Trajan's time.[1] Irenaeus' views, with
some exceptions, prevailed generally with respect to the authorship
of Revelation, the Fourth Gospel, and I John.[2] II John traveled a
more tortuous road to respectability. Except for Rome, its authorship
and canonicity were disputed as late as the fourth (and, in some places,
the fifth) century. No explicit reference to III John can be found
prior to the third century, when its authenticity was questioned.

This brief summary suggests that authorship of the Johannine writings
cannot be determined decisively by an appeal to church tradition.
It must be supplemented by a critical examination of the works themselves. When attention is focused on the respective communications,
a surprising fact is uncovered. Of the five books, only Revelation
discloses that its author's name is John. At no time does the author
assert that he is an apostle or make any claim to apostolic authority.
The two lesser letters, II and III John, were composed by a man
who calls himself "the elder," and the Fourth Gospel and I John
are anonymous.

John was a common name in the ancient world. If the author of
Revelation was not the Apostle John, it would have been natural
for the early church to assume that he was. The historical, literary,
and theological similarities of the five compositions—despite their
considerable differences—could easily have inspired the assumption

[1]Eusebius, *Ecclesiastical History*, III, 23, 1–4.
[2]Muratorian canon; Clement of Alexandria (Eusebius, *Ecclesiastical History*, VI, 14,
7), and Origen (Eusebius, *Ecclesiastical History*, VI, 25, 9–10).

that the generic John of Revelation was the Apostle John who also authored the Gospel and the Letters. The tradition that he had survived the martyrdom of his brother James and had borne witness to his faith at Ephesus until the time of Trajan would endow the inspiration with temporal feasibility.

The Johannine writings constitute one of three major collections of New Testament books ascribed to a single author. (The other two are Paul's letters and Luke-Acts.) Although modern scholars draw differing conclusions concerning the Johannine literature, on one point they are in general agreement. The tradition that associates these works with a church or churches in Asia Minor is probably correct. For this reason, if no other, they should be thought of as a unit. Of these five books remaining in our study of the New Testament, four will be discussed in this chapter and Revelation in the final chapter.

The Gospel of John

The Gospel of John is at once the simplest and most substantial writing in the New Testament. Its subtle blend of history and interpretation defies separation. Although its presuppositions are Hebraic, its propositions are packaged in a phraseology designed to interest the Hellenist. No other gospel poses so many perplexing questions or permits so few acceptable solutions.

Authorship

By the second half of the second century the church was nearly unanimous in ascribing the Fourth Gospel to John, son of Zebedee, one of the Twelve. The star witness for this tradition, as noted above, was Irenaeus, Bishop of Lyons. As a boy he had lived in Ephesus and had seen and heard Polycarp. In his mature years Irenaeus recalled Polycarp's assertion that the Apostle John had composed his Gospel while living in Ephesus. This secondhand witness would be altogether credible if it were not for the silence of Ignatius. He wrote to the church at Ephesus while he was on his way to Rome to be martyred. He invoked the example and influence of Paul in his letter, but he never mentioned John. Moreover, there is no reference to the Fourth Gospel in Polycarp's Letter to the Philippians, although he quoted from I John. Justin Martyr, a second century author who appears to quote from the Fourth Gospel, did not designate John as its author, although he did attribute Revelation to John. An argument from silence, of course, is never decisive, but it is peculiar that the Gospel and its author are not mentioned in writings that would be expected to contain them—*if* the Gospel enjoyed apostolic authorship and authority.[3]

---

[3]See J.N. Sanders, *The Fourth Gospel in the Early Church* (New York: The Macmillan Co., 1943), pp. 27-28.

Some conservative second-century Christians in Asia Minor did dispute the apostolic authority of the Gospel of John because they took umbrage at its teaching concerning the Holy Spirit. About two centuries later Epiphanius referred to a group (which he called the Alogi or "anti-Word people") who attributed the Gospel and Revelation to a Gnostic teacher named Cerinthus. That the authority of the Gospel could be impugned by faithful Christians at so late a date arouses suspicion about its alleged apostolic origin.

The possible early martyrdom of the Apostle John also undermines the claim that he authored the Fourth Gospel. According to Mark 10:39, Jesus forewarned Zebedee's sons that they would suffer the same fate as he would. Acts 12:1-2 indicates that James was put to death by Herod Agrippa I (41-44 A.D.). It has been argued with considerable cogency that Mark would not have preserved Jesus' prediction of the martyrdom of James and John if John's death had not occurred by the time Mark wrote his Gospel. In the fifth century Philip of Side quotes Papias to the effect that John the Divine and his brother James were killed by Jews, and a similar statement was made by Georgius Monachus in the ninth century. Two lists of Christian martyrs, dated about 411 A.D. and 505 A.D. respectively, suggest that John suffered the same fate as James, perhaps at the same time.[4]

The authorship of John cannot be determined by an appeal to external evidence alone. We must discover what data the Gospel itself yields on the subject. Nowhere does the Gospel name John, son of Zebedee, as its author. The work is patently anonymous. If early church tradition had not attributed it to John, some commentators reason, it is doubtful that anyone today would think of him in connection with it. Yet others argue that the Gospel points unerringly in John's direction. He presents himself under the guise of the disciple "whom Jesus loved" (13:23; 19:26). The phrase, according to Mark 9:2 and 14:33, suggests one of Jesus' three intimate associates—Peter and Zebedee's sons, James and John. Since James had been martyred by Herod Agrippa I and Peter is differentiated in the narrative from "the disciple whom Jesus loved," only John remains. But it is strange that a Gospel so "pointedly" apostolic was not known as Johannine or widely quoted until the end of the second century. And it is stranger still that an authentic apostle would be so coy as to refrain from specifically identifying himself as the author of such a splendid writing—or so crass as to refer to himself repeatedly as "the beloved disciple".

There can be little doubt that those who first commended the Fourth

---

[4]See C.K. Barrett, *The Gospel According to St. John* (London: S.P.C.K., 1955), pp. 86–87.

Gospel to the world in some way regarded the Apostle John as its authority, but such an identification was not necessarily the intent of its author. On balance, we conclude that the Gospel is exactly what it appears to be—an anonymous work.[5] All we can know about the author must be gleaned from his work.

Religious Background   Some commentators have stressed the idea that our author was a Palestinian Jew, and there is much in the Gospel to sustain their viewpoint. Its Greek has an Aramaic flavor, and its author displays extensive knowledge of the customs and geography of the area. He is familiar with rabbinical methods of interpretation, and he relies heavily on the Old Testament and apocryphal literature.[6] Confirmation of the Palestinian origin of the Fourth Gospel, some scholars hold, has been provided by recent archaeological discoveries. Some of the Gospel's words and ideas are hauntingly similar to those found in the Qumran Scrolls. Both are addicted to a fundamental dualism that contrasts light and darkness, truth and falsehood, and good and evil, and both share such distinctive phrases as "do the truth," "sons of light," and "the spirit of truth."[7]

Other commentators have found the unmistakable imprints of the Hellenistic mystery religions in John. Our author's sacramental concept, his emphasis on rebirth and eternal life, and his call for union with Christ are all believed to be mystery-religion derivatives. Still other scholars have found strong Gnostic influences in this Gospel. Rudolf Bultmann, for example, attributed parts of the prologue and most of the sayings to Gnostic sources, although he recognized that our author had Christianized their meaning when he incorporated them into his Gospel.[8] The writings of the Mandaeans (whose name means "knowers"), which date from the seventh and eighth centuries but have their roots in the first, suggest that John was also influenced by the Gnostic notion of a divine redeemer who descended from heaven to show men the way of salvation. But other authorities attribute the Gnostic influence in the Gospel to the Hermetic writings of the third or fourth century, which were derived from earlier Egyptian traditions.[9] Both the Mandaean and Hermetic literature exhibit

[5]For the sake of convenience we shall refer to the author of the Fourth Gospel as John.
[6]See C.H. Dodd, *The Interpretation of the Fourth Gospel* (Cambridge: At the University Press, 1953), pp. 74–96.
[7]See Raymond E. Brown, "The Qumran Scrolls and the Johannine Gospel and Epistles," in Krister Stendahl, ed., *The Scrolls and the New Testament* (New York: Harper & Row, 1957), pp. 183–207.
[8]Bultmann's source analysis is discussed by Robert M. Grant, *Historical Introduction to the New Testament* (New York: Harper & Row, 1963), pp. 159–162. Bultmann's own work, *Das Evangelium des Johannes* (Göttingen: Vandenhoeck & Ruprecht, 1956) has not been translated into English.
[9]See Dodd, *The Interpretation of the Fourth Gospel*, pp. 115–130 and 10–53 respectively.

371   **Johannine Writings (The Gospel of John; I, II, and III John)**

a style markedly similar to that found in parts of John. This may prove nothing more, however, than the contention that our author reflected a style common to his Hellenistic environment. His consummate skill in homogenizing his material makes identification of his sources virtually impossible.

Relation to the Synoptics The four gospels seem to have much in common. They introduce Jesus' ministry with an account of John the Baptist. They record the calling of the Twelve and Jesus' popular mission in Galilee. The Fourth Gospel repeats familiar stories found in one or more of the Synoptics: the Temple Cleansing, the Feeding of the Five Thousand, the Stilling of the Storm, Jesus' Anointing, the Triumphal Entry, the Last Supper, the Trials, and the Crucifixion.

The differences between the Fourth Gospel and the Synoptics are both more numerous and more striking than the similarities. John omits about 90 per cent of the Synoptics—including the genealogy, the births of John and Jesus, the baptism, temptation, transfiguration, and the agony in Gethsemane. When it does relate incidents treated in the Synoptics, it often reflects a later stage in the tradition's transmission.[10] It contradicts the Synoptics in the length of Jesus' ministry (four years vs. about one), the place of his main mission (Judea vs. Galilee), and the time of the Temple Cleansing (at the beginning vs. the end of his ministry). It contains no messianic secret and no parables. Instead, allegories usually expand a series of "I am" sayings. It transforms the very speech of Jesus. The peasant-prophet-Messiah of the Synoptics is replaced by the preexistent Son of God who is a stranger to humility and limited knowledge. The succinct sayings, similes, and parables are discarded for long discourses and dialogues on extended themes. The themes are eternal life, truth, light, darkness, and glory, not the ones made familiar by the Synoptics (the parousia, the kingdom of God, the need for forgiveness, righteousness, and watchfulness). John makes extensive use of symbols (bread, door, vine, way, word, water) and words with double meanings (*anōthen*, 3:3, can be translated either "anew" or "from above"). It also makes effective use of dramatic devices such as artistic form, concentrated action, contrasts (light-darkness, life-death, love-hate), symmetry, variety, and irony.[11]

Some scholars attribute the similarities of the Gospels to the use of Mark and Luke (and perhaps Matthew) by the author of John, but

[10]Compare Matthew 8:5–13 and Luke 7:1–10 with John 4:46–54; Mark 14:46–47 and Luke 22:49–51 with John 18:4–11.
[11]See C. Milo Connick, "The Dramatic Character of the Fourth Gospel," *Journal of Biblical Literature*, LXVII, Part II (1948), 159–169.

others claim that he did not have access to the Synoptics. They hold that he made use of certain oral traditions that were eventually incorporated into the Synoptics. Still other scholars assert that the Fourth Gospel differs so radically from the Synoptics that its author must have relied on sources that developed independently of the Synoptic tradition.[12] Our own conclusion is that he did rely on Mark and Luke in their written form. The unity of his composition in language, style, and theology stems not from his independence of the Synoptics and other sources but from his creative imagination and the sovereign freedom with which he handled his "raw" material.

Relation to the Letters   Many scholars believe that the similarity of thought and language between the Gospel of John and I, II, and III John demonstrates common authorship.[13] But equally reputable interpreters have pointed out significant differences. The Letters are said to reflect a more conventional eschatology and a closer connection with Gnosticism than does the Gospel.[14] Perhaps the data can best be explained by the hypothesis that the author of the Letters edited the Gospel.[15] At this stage of Johannine studies, though, caution is a virtue. It seems reasonably certain that the Gospel and the Letters spring from the same school of thought, but identity of authorship is still an open question.

Unity   A distinguished scholar of the nineteenth century italicized the literary unity of the Fourth Gospel by calling it a "seamless robe" that had been woven from top to bottom, but many of his modern counterparts think of it as a "patchwork quilt" whose innumerable pieces were stitched together by a variety of "seamstresses." One does not have to delve deeply into the text to discover why. Even the casual reader is impressed by the abrupt transitions, chronological incongruities, and parenthetical comments. These peculiarities have spawned a multitude of theories concerning partition, displacement, and redaction of the original text.[16] A few illustrations will suffice. (1) The story of the Adulterous Woman (7:53–8:11) is not found in the best manuscripts, and modern editions of John relegate it to footnote status.

---

[12]See C.H. Dodd, *Historical Tradition in the Fourth Gospel* (Cambridge: At the University Press, 1963).

[13]See A.E. Brooke, *Critical and Exegetical Commentary on the Johannine Epistles*, International Critical Commentary (New York: Charles Scribner's Sons, 1912), pp. ii–xi; W.F. Howard, "The Common Authorship of the Johannine Gospel and Epistles," *Journal of Theological Studies*, XLVIII (1947), 12–25.

[14]C.H. Dodd, "The First Epistle of John and the Fourth Gospel," *Bulletin of the John Rylands Library*, XXI (1937), 129–156.

[15]See J.N. Sanders, "John, Gospel of," in George A. Buttrick, ed., *The Interpreter's Dictionary of the Bible* (New York: Abingdon Press: 1962), E–J, 938, 945.

[16]For a discussion of this extensive topic see W.F. Howard, *The Fourth Gospel in Recent Criticism and Interpretation*, 4th ed., rev. C.K. Barrett (London: Epworth Press, 1955).

(2) Chapters 5 and 6 are transposed, since 6:1 follows 4:54 better than 5:47. (3) The abruptness of 10:1 is relieved by placing 10:1–18 after 10:29. (4) Chapter 12:36–43 (from "When Jesus had said this") should follow 12:50 to prevent the interruption of Jesus' speech by the evangelist's reflections.

These rearrangements (as well as a host of others) have been predicated on the propositions that the author of John was acutely concerned with chronological sequence and the logical progression of thought. The speculative nature of the reconstructions is indicated by the great diversity of the various reconstructions and by their almost total lack of textual support. The credibility of some of the "reshuffling of the leaves of the Gospel" would be enhanced if the passages assigned to editors and redactors did not so conveniently dispose of ideas that are offensive to the "shufflers." Although we acknowledge with alacrity the existence of editorial additions to the Gospel and the secondary character of its final chapter, we view with unmixed skepticism the wholesale reconstruction of the author's work. His Gospel possesses an intrinsic unity. It cannot be dissected and disarranged without inflicting upon it the fate of a house of cards.

Date and Occasion

Some nineteenth-century scholars believed that John was written in the second half of the second century, but such a late date was vitiated in this century by the discovery of three papyrus fragments, dated about 130–150 A.D., that contain portions of the Gospel.[17] Specialists who stress the Hellenistic nature of the Gospel tend to date it near the close of the first century (90–100 A.D.). Those who accept the Apostle John's authorship and those who find frequent affinities between the Fourth Gospel and the Qumran Scrolls often advocate an earlier date. However, those who sponsor a date prior to Mark are confronted with seemingly insuperable problems. What circumstances prompted the author to write at such an early stage in the development of the Christian community? Why did he use the gospel form? And, perhaps most importantly, can a convincing New Testament chronology be constructed that does not assume the priority of Mark?

Although it is much easier to decide on a date than to defend it, it seems to us that the most suitable one for the Gospel of John is about 100 A.D. This is based on the likely but not indisputable assumption that our author knew and used Mark and Luke in their written form. It is supported by the Gospel's emphasis on the presence of Christ and eternal life and his subordination of the parousia and the consummation of the kingdom of God. It is also buttressed by the author's attitude toward the Jews and their Law. The hostility

[17]Papyrus Egerton 2, the Rylands fragment (P52), and Papyrus Bodmer II (P66).

evidenced between the church and the synagogue suggests a period somewhat later than Matthew, and the semishift from conflict over the Law to conflict over the person of Christ and his relation to God argues for a similar time slot.

The author openly declares his reason for composing the Fourth Gospel: "These [signs] are written that you may believe that Jesus is the Christ, the Son of God, and that believing you may have life in his name" (20:31). Such a succinct and straightforward statement would seem to settle the issue once and for all. Instead, it has simply served as a starting point. Who are the people addressed as "you"? Are they Christians who need their faith confirmed? Converts who cry for instruction? Or unbelievers, Jewish or Gentile, who need to be convinced? Why is a particular confession emphasized—"Jesus is the Christ, the Son of God"? Were there other and less complimentary titles being assigned to him?

Few experts doubt that the central purpose of our author was to provide a faith-producing testimony to Jesus as God's Son in order that his readers might possess the life eternal promised in Christ's name. But some authorities profess to find in the Gospel definite apologetic interests as well. The author, they claim, wrote to defend the Christian message against its adversaries. The hostility of the synagogue can be inferred from the frequent and unfavorable references to "the Jews" in Jesus' discourses in Jerusalem. The marked subordination of John the Baptist to Jesus suggests the existence of a John-the-Baptist sect that imperiled the true faith. The incipient heresy called Docetism (from *dokein*, meaning "to seem"), which disparaged the physical body and deprecated matter as inherently evil, is deflated by the declaration that "the Word became flesh" (1:14) and by repeated references to Jesus' hunger, thirst, sorrow, suffering and death.[18] No doubt our author's motives in writing were multiple. This fact, though, should not be permitted to obscure his basic aim. He wrote to reinterpret Jesus' mission and message in the light of his conviction that the Man from Nazareth was none other than God's eternal Son. This is why he repeated so little of the Synoptics. He assumed that his readers were familiar with the "facts" of Jesus' marvelous ministry. Although his Gospel contains hard information, it was not his intent simply to record historical data. Like Joshua of old, he wanted his generation to answer the question, "What do these stones *mean*?"[19] It was as an *evangelist* and *theologian* that he wrote, and his *interpretation* of Jesus' person, words, and works is more meaningful and more moving than any other Christian composition.

[18]See E.C. Colwell, *John Defends the Gospel* (New York: Willett, Clark and Co., 1936).
[19]Joshua 4:21, italics added.

Where the Fourth Gospel originated is as much a puzzlement as other problems that plague this publication. Three separate cities have been proposed: Ephesus, Syrian Antioch, and Alexandria. The Alexandrian hypothesis is based on the affinities of this Gospel to the writings of Philo and Hermetic literature and the strong appeal John made to the Alexandrian Gnostics. One of their number, Heracleon, composed the first commentary on this Gospel. The Antioch suggestion stems from the close connection between Johannine thought and the letters of Ignatius, Bishop of Antioch. A Syrian fragment attached to the Armenian translation of Ephrem's commentary on Tatian's *Diatessaron* states that John wrote his Gospel in Greek at Antioch. The most popular theory, though, is that the Fourth Gospel originated in Ephesus. This city had a potent Jewish community, was the reputed home of a John-the-Baptist sect (Acts 18:24), and hosted countless currents of Hellenistic culture and thought. We believe that the author was a Christian of Jewish extraction whose faith had once been fashioned by the Diaspora synagogue. He was profoundly influenced by Hellenistic (including Gnostic) and Qumran-type speculation as well. But his cultural conditioning—from whatever direction and at whatever place—never overpowered his Christian convictions. His sources and his social experience were transformed by the kerygma of the church.

The identity of the Fourth Gospel's intended audience is also contested. Is the Gospel addressed to Jews, Jewish Christians, or Christians in general? Recent converts or longstanding ones? The unconverted pagan world? Perhaps the author had more than one group in mind. Efforts to pinpoint the audience in terms of a specific cultural or religious group have not been crowned with success.

Message   John consists of a prologue (1:1–18), the main narrative (1:19–20:31), and an epilogue (21) that is usually ascribed to a later hand. The main narrative is divided into two parts. The first part deals with the public ministry of Jesus that begins with the witness of the Baptist and ends with the judgment of the word (1:19–12:50). The second part begins with Jesus washing the disciples' feet and ends with a statement of the author's purpose (13:1–20:31). Its first chapters depict the private phase of Jesus' ministry during which he instructs his disciples (13–17), and the final ones describe the passion and the resurrection (18–20).

Prologue (1:1–18). The first few words of John are eye-catching: "In the beginning was the *Logos*."[20] The Greek term, usually translat-

---

[20]John 1:1, italics added.

ed "Word," signified not only the word in the mind (idea, plan, or reason) but the word spoken (idea, plan, or reason actualized)—the deed. Old Testament prophets often prefaced their pronouncements with the phrase, "Hear the word of the Lord" (Isa. 1:10). For them God's Word consisted not only of His thought that the prophet articulated, but also of the series of happenings that were triggered by the prophet's words and works.

The Gospel's prologue was custom-made for the conceptual world of its first readers. It would have reminded Jews who read their Scripture in the Greek (the Septuagint) of the first chapter of Genesis. The Logos refers to the Word of God through which He created the universe. This marvelous event occurred when God *spoke*. In time men concluded that it was by God's Logos that all things came into being. Logos in the Wisdom Literature of the Old Testament and the Apocrypha was sometimes equated with Wisdom as God's creative agent. Since the Law was regarded as the embodiment of God's Wisdom and Word, there was also the tendency to assign all of their attributes to the Law.[21] For Gentiles, like the Stoics and others, the Logos was the rational principle that pervaded and controlled the universe. They would understand our author's words to be a reaffirmation of their convictions that ultimate reality is reason, and man, by virtue of the reason that resides in him, can comprehend all things visible and invisible. For those who already shared the author's viewpoint, his words would be comprehended as a distinctive statement of the kerygma: at a time of his own choosing God had disclosed His purpose in history.

The prologue reaches its climax with the declaration, "And the *Logos* became *flesh*."[22] Our author's usage is unique. He identifies the Logos with Jesus Christ. The miracle of the incarnation confronts Jews, pagans, and Christians alike. Jesus did not simply *speak* the Word of the Lord; he *was* himself the Word. To the Jew he was the one "of whom Moses in the law and also the prophets wrote" (1:45). To the Greek, who believed that the way to truth was through the mind and that to know the truth was to follow it, our author asserts that "the true light that enlightens every man" has already come into the world (1:9). But man's knowledge of this was not arrived at by mental speculation or mystical contemplation: "No one has ever seen God; the only Son . . . has made him known" (1:18). To Christians, tempted by the Docetic doctrine that denied Jesus' human-

[21]For a penetrating discussion of this subject, see J.D. Rylaarsdam, *Revelation in Jewish Literature* (Chicago: Univ. of Chicago Press, 1946).
[22]John 1:14, italics added.

ity, our author declares that "the Word became *flesh*"—a truth to which the apostles bore witness as they "beheld his glory."[23]

The paucity of the appearances of Logos in the rest of the Gospel has prompted much speculation. Was the prologue an original part of the Gospel, or was it added as an afterthought? Was it pre-Christian or Christian in origin? Was it authored by someone else and adapted by the evangelist, or was he the actual composer?[24] Perhaps the most satisfactory solution is to regard the prologue as a Christian hymn that the evangelist annotated and incorporated into his Gospel. The prologue's poetic character is clearly evident in Greek, especially when the text is printed in strophic form, but something of its solemn and pregnant quality can be discovered in an English translation.[25] Its poetic structure is interrupted several times—twice by references to John the Baptist (1:6–8, 15). Other probable intrusions are 1:13 and 17–18.[26] The author doubtless discontinued his use of Logos because he did not want it to be understood in terms of its other associations. For him the Logos was defined in the light of Jesus and no other. The prologue's link to the remainder of the Gospel, though, is not trivial or tenuous. Its main motifs are part of the warp and woof of the whole composition: light and darkness, life coming into the world, witness and belief, to receive, to be born of God, truth, and the only Son.

Witness of the Baptist and of the disciples (1:19–51). The author of the Fourth Gospel, like those of the Synoptics, begins Jesus' ministry with an account of John the Baptist. He makes no attempt to tell of the Baptist's work in its own right. In passage after passage he subordinates John's role to that of Jesus. The poetry of the prologue is twice broken to depreciate the priest turned prophet. "He was not the light, but came to bear witness to the light" (1:8). The Baptist is even forced to testify to his own inferiority: "He who comes after me ranks before me, for he was before me" (1:15). The Baptist's message is omitted completely. When an embassy from Jerusalem asks him who he is, he states that he is nothing but a "voice" (1:23). His sole task is to identify Jesus as "the Lamb of God, who takes away the sin of the world" (1:29, 36) and as the Son of God (1:34). The Baptist's disciples, apparently at their leader's suggestion, become

[23]John 1:14, italics added.
[24]See W.F. Howard, *Christianity According to St. John* (Philadelphia: The Westminster Press, 1946), from p. 47.
[25]See R.E. Brown, *The Gospel According to John (I–XII)*, in The Anchor Bible (Garden City, N.Y.: Doubleday Co., 1966), pp. 3–4.
[26]Compare C.F. Burney, *The Aramaic Origin of the Fourth Gospel* (Oxford: Clarendon Press, 1922) and J.R. Harris, *The Origin of the Prologue to St. John's Gospel* (Cambridge: At the University Press, 1917).

followers of Jesus. The Baptist is further subordinated to Jesus when the contrast between a water baptism and a Spirit baptism, simply stated in the Synoptics (Mt. 3:11; Mk. 1:7–8; Lk. 3:16), is heightened in the Fourth Gospel (1:26, 28, 31, 32–34; 3:23; 10:40). All tributes to the Baptist are omitted. Since our author was presumably acquainted with Mark and Luke, it cannot be argued that he did not know that "among those born of women none is greater than John" (Lk. 7:28) or that the baptism of John was "from heaven" (Mk. 11:30; Lk. 20:4). These would appear to be calculated omissions.

There was a point to the Fourth Gospel's portrayal of the Baptist as an inferior. A sect that revered John the Baptist evidently existed in the first century. Indeed, such a group has survived to the present day—the Mandaeans in modern Iraq regard the Baptist as their redeemer.[27] When our author downgraded the Baptist, he was doubtless deflating members of a rival movement in Asia Minor composed of devotees of John.[28] But the Baptist is not the only figure in the Gospel whose status the author deliberately shrank. He tended to treat every character in his composition as a foil in a drama designed to enhance the perceptivity and profundity of Christ.[29] The Baptist spoke not only for himself but for Nicodemus, the Jews, the Samaritan woman, and many others when he declared, "He must increase, but I must decrease" (3:30).

The Baptist does not know who Jesus is in the Synoptics (except in Matthew), but in the Fourth Gospel God discloses Jesus' identity to the Baptist through the Spirit (1:31–33). This "historical" statement is based on a theological principle that the author will develop more completely in the remainder of his work: Jesus' identity is made known by God, through the Spirit, to those who believe. Jesus is the one on whom the Spirit descends *and* remains; he is the one who baptizes with the Spirit.[30] The Baptist's assertion that Jesus is "the Lamb of God" (1:29, 36) is another statement reserved for later elaboration. Jesus' death, unforeseen in the early stages of the Synoptics, is alluded to at the very beginning of this Gospel. It is crucial to the comprehension of who Jesus is and what he is about. He is, as our author subsequently reveals, the sacrificial lamb.

The call of the disciples in the Fourth Gospel (1:35–51), when com-

[27]See E.L. Drower, *The Mandaeans of Iraq and Iran* (Leiden: E.J. Brill, 1962). For an excellent discussion of the priest-prophet, see C.H. Kraeling, *John the Baptist* (New York: Charles Scribner's Sons, 1951).
[28]See Acts 18:24–19:7.
[29]See footnote 10 of this chapter.
[30]How appropriate that E.C. Colwell and E.L. Titus entitled their discerning study of the Fourth Gospel *The Gospel of the Spirit* (New York: Harper & Row, 1953).

pared to the Synoptics, contains additional surprises. Jesus is recognized as the Messiah at the beginning of his ministry (1:41) rather than near its close (Mk. 8:29). Simon is nicknamed "the Rock" (Cephas in Aramaic) at his call (1:42) rather than at his confession (Mt. 16:18). The climax comes in the account of Nathanael's call, the first of a series of dialogues between Jesus and various people who have symbolic significance. Nathanael is a Jew with "no guile." He can find nothing in his heritage to support Philip's claim that Jesus is the Messiah. Certainly no prophet has ever predicted that the Messiah would come from Nazareth. But despite his doubt he accedes to Philip's invitation to "come and see." For our author such pragmatic open-mindedness is the prerequisite of faith. Nathanael is astounded at Jesus' seemingly superhuman knowledge of him and swiftly declares that Jesus is the Son of God. Jesus counters with the promise that Nathanael's faith will one day rest on a firmer foundation: "You will see heaven opened, and the angels of God ascending and descending upon the Son of man" (1:51). The singular pronoun "you" of 1:50 is changed to the plural in 1:51. Nathanael stands for all men of faith. After Jesus' death and resurrection they will realize that he is the "ladder" (as in Jacob's dream, Gen. 28:10–12) by which men are led to God and by which God discloses Himself to men.

New life from Christ (2:1–25). In chapters 2 through 12 our author presents his version of Jesus' public ministry. According to the Synoptics Jesus labored largely in Galilee, but in this Gospel his earlier work oscillates between Galilee and Jerusalem (2:1–6:71) and his later mission is confined to Judea (7:1–12:50). The evangelist organizes his material around six miracle stories,[31] a series of discourses and dialogues, and several journeys to Jerusalem at festival seasons. No fixed pattern is followed, though. This is why "outlines" of these chapters are so diverse.

Several times our author refers to miracle stories as "signs." Some scholars suspect that he had access to a collection of such stories—a so-called "Book of Signs."[32] His interest in miracles is not in the physical phenomenon (history) but in what the physical phenomenon signifies (event). Small wonder that scholars are fond of saying that in the Fourth Gospel the apparent meaning is never the real meaning. The *first sign* highlights the theme of Jesus' entire ministry (2:1–11). The scene is a wedding feast in Cana of Galilee. The celebration

[31]Some scholars count seven by including the account of Jesus Walking on the Water (6:16–21). John does not emphasize this story as much as Matthew (14:22–23), though, and to count it destroys the symbolism we believe John intended. See p. 381.
[32]Dodd, *The Interpretation of the Fourth Gospel,* from p. 297.

lasted a week, with new guests arriving daily. Wine flowed freely at such festivals, and on this occasion it was all consumed before the marriage was consummated. When Jesus' mother informs him of the depletion, he remarks, "My hour has not yet come" (2:4). The surface meaning is simple: "I must wait for the right opportunity." But the evangelist has a deeper meaning in mind. For him "hour" refers not to a hand on a clock, so to speak, but to Jesus' death and resurrection when God's revelation will be fully finished (12:23–25). Mary may have been mystified by her son's response, but her composure suggests otherwise. She instructs the servants to follow his wishes. Jesus has them fill six large stone jars with water, and then he miraculously changes the water into wine. Its quantity (over 52 gallons) is matched by its quality.

This story, which is found only in John, bristles with difficulties. Did Jesus have the power to turn water into wine? If so, would he have used his power for such a mundane purpose? Matthew (4:3–4) and Luke (4:3–4) report that he refused to turn stones into bread. Why did he make so much wine so late in the week? However appropriate these questions are for modern minds, they probably never occurred to the author of John. He very likely saw in the story the symbolic suggestion that the religion of the Spirit is superior to the religion of the Law, but his primary interest lay in the evidence it provided of the glory of the Son of God. It was this factor that induced the disciples to believe (2:11). "Glory," for the evangelist, stands not only for God's supernatural power but also for the power perceived in Christ—the power that produces salvation: "We have beheld his glory, glory as of the only Son from the Father" (1:14). In each of the signs the Son reveals the Father's power by doing the Father's works (5:36; 9:3). The fact that there are six signs, one less than the perfect number, is significant. They point to the final and perfect sign: the death and resurrection of Jesus. This sign constitutes the climax of this Gospel and the completion of God's revelation. It is the sign through which the meaning of the other six is mediated.

The story of the Cleansing of the Temple raises additional questions (2:13–22). The Synoptics place the incident in the final days of Jesus' ministry. Were there two cleansings? Would Jesus deliberately have provoked the authorities at the inception of his work? Some scholars think that the passage originally appeared late in the Fourth Gospel, and they attribute its present position to displacement. However, consensus holds that the author puts the cleansing at the beginning for dramatic and theological reasons. By shifting the cleansing to the beginning of Jesus' ministry the author stressed that the Spirit that was calling into being a new community of worshipers was present in Jesus from the start. The climax of the cleansing is reached in

Jesus' words to the Jews: "Destroy this temple, and in three days I will raise it up" (2:19). The language is deliberately ambiguous. "Temple" is used both for a religious shrine and for the body (I Cor. 3:16 and 6:19). "Destroy" is used both for the demolition of buildings and the dissolution of the body. "Raise" can be used for the erecting of a structure or the resurrection from the dead.[33] The Jews, like the other foils in this Gospel, misunderstand Jesus. They think he is referring to the Temple building. Our author interprets Jesus' words symbolically. Jesus is predicting his death and resurrection, which will happen shortly ("in three days"). Then the risen Christ will replace the Temple as the place where men discover God. The true worshipers, as Jesus will later tell the Samaritan woman, are those who "worship the Father in spirit and truth" (4:23).

The author of John, as we have noted, arranges the chronology of Jesus' ministry around a series of Jewish festivals. He begins with the cleansing of the Temple at Passover (2:13) and closes with the crucifixion at a later Passover (19:14). In the interim Jesus makes profound pronouncements in or near the Holy City on other festival occasions. The arrangement is designed to show that Jesus supplanted the festivals of Judaism with a new and better way of worship.

The new birth (3:1-36). This chapter purports to relate a conversation between Jesus and Nicodemus, a distinguished Pharisee, but some scholars suspect that it is John's reinterpretation of the Synoptic account of Jesus' encounter with the Rich Young Ruler (Mk. 10:17-22). In John the dialogue (3:2-15) changes into a monologue or discourse (3:16-21) that constitutes the author's commentary on the conversation. The topic of the conversation is entrance into the kingdom of God. Jesus informs Nicodemus that the passport to the kingdom is for him to be born *anōthen*. John's choice of this ambiguous word was deliberate. It can mean born "anew" or "from above." Nicodemus takes the literal meaning (physical birth), but John intends the symbolic one ("from above," meaning "of the Spirit," 3:6). All men are born of the flesh, but only those born of the Spirit can enter the kingdom. This new birth has been made possible by the Son of Man who descended from heaven and ascended again (3:13). Those who believe in him "have eternal life" (3:15).[34]

The dialogue with Nicodemus is written in retrospect. It presupposes not only Jesus' ministry, death, and resurrection (3:13-14), but also

---

[33]See. W.F. Howard, "The Gospel According to St. John, Introduction and Exegesis," in George A. Buttrick, ed., *The Interpreter's Bible* (New York: Abingdon Press, 1952), VIII, 499, to which we are indebted.
[34]Compare John 1:12-13.

the faith of the early church. John's shift from the first person singular to the first person plural suggests that he is spokesman for the Christian community: "Truly, truly, *I* say to you [singular, Nicodemus], *we* speak of what we know, . . . but you [plural, the Jews whom Nicodemus symbolizes] do not receive our testimony."[35] Christian baptism, which John saw as the sacramental rite that consummated rebirth, is referred to in the saying, "Unless one is born of water and the Spirit, he cannot enter the kingdom of God" (3:5).

Although the dialogues in John seem to flow on spontaneously, they tend to follow a set pattern. (1) Someone asks a question or makes a statement. (2) Jesus replies with a profound pronouncement. (3) The pronouncement, often capable of a double interpretation, is misunderstood and its spiritual significance is missed. (4) Jesus corrects the mistake. (5) If a second question shows that he has done so successfully, Jesus then gives further, more detailed instruction on the subject.[36] The constant misunderstanding of Jesus' conversants serves to underscore their mental sluggishness and to stress the sagacity of Jesus' sayings. Moreover, Jesus, Nicodemus, the Samaritan woman, and others all speak in the same style. It is sometimes impossible to determine, furthermore, where Jesus ends his conversation and the commentary of John begins. Clearly the author had no intention of recording the *ipsissima verba* spoken on a given occasion.[37]

The discourse that follows Jesus' dialogue with Nicodemus represents John's reflections (3:16–21). His capsule declaration of the purpose of Jesus' mission is a Christian classic. Luther referred to verse 16 as the gospel in miniature: "God so loved the world that he gave his only Son, that whoever believes in him should not perish but have eternal life." The Son was not sent to judge the world but to save it. Nevertheless, judgment was a by-product of his appearance: "The light [Christ] has come into the world, and men loved darkness rather than light, because their deeds were evil" (3:19). Judgment is a present reality: "He who believes in him is not condemned; he who does not believe is condemned already" (3:18). Unbelief is the unforgivable sin for John. God is true. The Son whom He has sent "utters the words of God" (3:34). He is "the way, and the truth, and the life; no one comes to the Father" except by him (14:6). If one believes that Jesus is the Son of God, trustfully enters into a personal relationship with him, and obeys his commands, he has "eternal life" (3:36).

---

[35]John 3:11, italics added.
[36]See John 3:2–15; 4:31b–34; 6:48–58; 8:31b–36; 11:21b–26a.
[37]See Connick, "The Dramatic Character of the Fourth Gospel," *Journal of Biblical Literature*, LXVII, Part II (1948), 167–168.

Two emphases in the Fourth Gospel deserve special comment. (1) The adjective "eternal," seldom found in the Synoptics, has a distinctive meaning for John. It accents the qualitative rather than the quantitative nature of life with God. (2) That life is primarily a present reality rather than a future prospect (3:18–21; 5:24, 25, 36; 12:31).[38] Eternal life has already penetrated history in the person of Jesus Christ, and it is now available to all who believe that he is the Son of God (1:14; 3:16, 36). Baptism is not simply a symbol of repentance in expectation of the advent of the kingdom; it is a sacrament of rebirth to the heavenly world of the Spirit. "Son of Man" no longer stands for an apocalyptic figure who will come with the clouds of heaven to judge the world; the Son of Man has come, and final judgment is in process. John has significantly altered Synoptic eschatology by his notions of the heavenly Son of Man and the Preexistent Logos.

The world's Savior (4:1–54). The scene shifts to Samaria. After a long journey Jesus is resting at Jacob's well. A Samaritan woman approaches to draw water, and Jesus asks her for a drink. The woman is perplexed not only by his request (since the Jews and the Samaritans have been cold-war antagonists for centuries) but also by his reference to "living water." He claims that he can supply water that becomes "a spring of water welling up to eternal life" (4:14). Old Testament writers frequently used "water" to symbolize God's life-giving activity (Ps. 23:2; Zech. 14:8–9). Jeremiah spoke of God as "the fountain of living waters" (2:13). Jews baptized converts in *running* water because it was proof of God's presence.[39] It was only natural, then, for John to use water as a metaphor for the Spirit (7:38–39).

When Jesus discloses details of the Samaritan woman's private life, she calls him a prophet. She then asks him to settle a subject that has long been a bone of contention between their peoples: Where is the proper place to worship—the Temple in Jerusalem (favored by the Jews) or the Temple on Mt. Gerazim in Samaria (supported by her people)? Jesus opts for neither. He declares that "the hour is coming, and now is, when the true worshipers will worship the Father in spirit and truth" (4:23). The woman replies that when the Messiah comes, "he will show us all things" (4:25). In response to her maturing faith Jesus says, "I who speak to you am he" (4:26). The woman hurries into the city of Sychar, shares her exhilarating experience, and muses whether Jesus might be the Christ. Many of the inhabitants believe in Jesus because of the woman's testimony.

[38]Contrast John 5:28–29; 12:48.
[39]Even today, Roman Catholics do not consider water baptism valid unless the water *moves.*

Samaritan Priests. These men, distant relatives of the Samaritan woman who conversed with Jesus at Jacob's Well, exhibit a copy of the Samaritan Pentateuch. Only a few hundred Samaritans are alive today. About half of them live in the shadow of Mt. Gerizim near Nablus, ancient Shechem.

At their invitation he spends two days in Sychar. Many more converts result—not because of the woman's words but because the people have heard for themselves. "We know," they declare, "that this is indeed the Savior of the world" (4:42).

It is by design that John locates the dialogue between Jesus and the woman in Samaria. The conversion of the Samaritans suggests the scope of Jesus' mission. He did not come to sponsor local shrines or to save select people. As the Samaritans so quickly saw, he came to foster worship "in spirit and truth" and to be "the Savior of the world." Even the vocabulary betrays a cosmopolitan flavor. "Savior" has far more religious significance for Gentiles than the Jewish term

"Messiah." The disciples want to delay the true worship until the kingdom comes (4:35), but the Jesus of John is not advocating an eschatological hope. The time for universal worship is *now* for those who slake their thirst with the water that wells up to eternal life (4:14, 23).

The *second sign* of Jesus follows the incidents in Samaria and stresses the same point (4:46–54). Jesus is in Cana in Galilee, where he made the water wine. A Roman official stationed in Capernaum comes and begs Jesus to heal his son who is near death. Instead of commending the man's faith Jesus chides him for seeking signs to bolster it. Then Jesus says, "Go; your son will live" (4:50). The official takes Jesus at his word, and when he arrives home he discovers that his son's fever vanished at the very hour Jesus assured him his son would live. The story is similar to the episode of the centurion's servant told in Matthew (8:5–13) and Luke (7:1–10). The fact that the official is a Roman emphasizes again the universal nature of Jesus' saving work.

The work of the Father and the Son (5:1–6:71). The healing of a man in Jerusalem at the sheep-gate pool is the *third sign* of Jesus (5:2–9). It appears to be a variant of the healing of the paralytic in Matthew (9:1–8), Mark (2:1–12), and Luke (5:17–26). It is Jesus' forgiveness of sins that arouses the ire of the Jews in the Synoptics, but in John they are disturbed "because he not only broke the sabbath but also called God his Father, making himself equal with God" (5:18). The meaning of the sign is disclosed in the extended discourse that follows (5:19–47). The Son can do nothing on his own; he simply does what he sees the Father doing. The Father loves the Son, and He will show him greater works than the one at the sheep-gate pool. That sign points to the Father's final work: He "raises the dead and gives them life." The Son also "gives life to whom he will" (5:21). He who hears the Son's word and believes the Father who sent him "has eternal life; he does not come into judgment, but has passed from death to life" (5:24). Once again the evangelist emphasizes his "realized eschatology." Eternal life is a present reality for those who believe. Since this thought seems to clash with references in John to a future resurrection and judgment, some authorities assign the latter to a later hand. Such an assignment lacks textual support. We believe that John retained the traditional resurrection hope while highlighting the present possession of eternal life for those who believe that Jesus was "sent" from God.

John's frequent use of the Greek word translated "sent" is significant (5:23, 24, 30, 37). It comes from the same root as the word "apostle" (5:36) and means one who is commissioned by God to speak or act in His stead. It reminds one of the Old Testament prophets who spoke or acted in God's name (Isa. 37:21). Gnosticism also knew of heavenly agents and their earthly counterparts who were "sent" to proclaim divine truth. But Jesus, according to John, is no mere messenger. He not only speaks for God and acts in His behalf, but the words he speaks *are* God's words, and the works he does *are* God's works.

Jesus' judgment is valid because it is based on divine authority, and it is just because it coheres with God's will (5:30–47). His self-witness is suspect, but there are other credible witnesses. The Father bears witness to the Son, and Jesus knows that His testimony is true. It is internal, though, and therefore is unacceptable to the Jews. There is the testimony of the Baptist. There are the works that the Father enables the Son to do. Finally, there is the testimony of the Scriptures. Since only two witnesses are needed to confirm a fact in a Jewish court, they should have been convinced. But they did not receive Jesus.

The *fourth sign* is John's version of the Synoptic story (Mt. 14:13–21; Mk. 6:30–44; Lk. 9:10–17) of the Feeding of the Five Thousand (6:1–14). The significance of the sign is found in its sequel. After Jesus has fed the multitude, they proclaim that he is "indeed the prophet who is to come into the world" (6:14). But they misunderstand his mission, as Jesus perceives. They intend to "take him by force to make him king" (6:15). The sign is a symbol of heavenly food that gives life to the world, as Jesus makes plain in the synagogue at Capernaum on the following Sabbath (6:25–59). The crowd fails to grasp who Jesus really is and that his kingship "is not of this world" (18:36).

Jesus withdraws to the hills, and his disciples get into a boat to go to Capernaum. The story of Jesus Walking on the Water, seen by some as a fifth sign,[40] differs markedly from the Synoptic account (Mt. 14:22–23; Mk. 6:45–52). John states that it was dark "and Jesus had not yet come to them" (6:17). The disciples had rowed three or four miles before he did appear (6:19). When they took him into the boat, "immediately the boat was at" the Capernaum shore (6:21). The climax of the story comes with Jesus' words to the frightened disciples who see him walking on the water toward their boat: "It is I" (6:20). These words translate the Greek *egō eimi*, which literally means "I am." In the Septuagint version of the Old Testament these same Greek words had been used as a name for God (Isa. 41:4).

---

[40]See p. 380, n. 31, and p. 381.

For John they signify God's presence in the person of Jesus. His ability to walk on water indicates that the power of the incarnate Logos knows no limit.

Jesus' mention of heavenly bread prompts his listeners to request some for themselves (6:32–34). This sets the stage for the first of a series of sayings by Jesus that are unique to this Gospel. They begin with the words "I am" and continue with a phrase of supreme symbolic significance such as "the bread of life" (6:35), "the light of the world" (8:12), "the door of the sheep" (10:7), "the good shepherd" (10:11), "the resurrection and the life" (11:25), "the way, and the truth, and the life" (14:6), and "the true vine" (15:1). The form of these pronouncements is not found elsewhere in Christian literature, but it had been used for centuries in the East as a verbal vehicle for deity. The crass egotism of the "I am" sayings clashes mightily with Jesus' kingdom-centered declarations in the Synoptics. The discrepancy is dissolved, however, if "I am" is replaced by "He is." The sayings are not the court-recorded words of the man from Nazareth. They embody the thinking of the author and the church or churches he represents. Jesus is for them "the bread of life" (6:35). Those who come to him shall hunger no more, and those who believe in him shall never thirst. He came down from heaven to do his Father's will: to give eternal life to those who see the Son and believe in him (6:38–40).

The Jews raise two objections to Jesus' claim that he is the bread that came down from heaven (6:41–59). They point to his human parentage.[41] Then they voice doubt that he can give them his flesh to eat. Jesus' reply must have confounded them the more: "Unless you eat the flesh of the Son of man and drink his blood, you have no life in you; he who eats my flesh and drinks my blood has eternal life. . . . [He] abides in me, and I in him . . . He who eats me will live because of me. This is the bread which came down from heaven. . . ." (6:53–58).

The very thought of drinking a man's blood was repulsive to the Jews. They went to great lengths, in keeping with the Law, to remove all blood from the animals they were permitted to eat. Many of Jesus' own followers took offense at the saying, and his lucid explanation failed to soothe their ruffled feelings: "It is the spirit that gives life, the flesh is of no avail; the words that I have spoken to you are spirit and life" (6:63). This discourse, as well as the Feeding

[41]The virgin birth of Jesus is not noted in John.

of the Five Thousand that precedes it, suggests the eucharistic teaching of the early church. As the faithful ate the bread and drank the wine, they became aware that he who had lived as a man in their midst now shared his life with them. He had done this before his death, of course, but it was not until his resurrection and dispatch of the Spirit that the full force of his life-giving activity was felt (6:62–63). Those who ate the meal abode in him and he in them (6:56). This mystical union between Christ and the believer, which will be developed more fully in John 14–17, is close to Paul's concept of being "in Christ" (I Cor. 15:22). It also calls to mind language used in Hellenistic religious thought. John doubtless availed himself of Hellenistic notions and nomenclature when he commented on the eucharist, but he never succumbed to some of the Hellenists' erroneous presuppositions: the magical powers of the meal, the deification of the devotee, the assimilation of the devotee by the deity.

The children of light (God) and the children of darkness (the devil), 7:1–10:42. Chapters 7 and 8 of John purportedly describe a controversy that raged between Jesus and the Jews concerning Sabbath observance. Both the timing and the topic are faulty. The controversy really reflects the hostility that existed between the church and the synagogue when this Gospel was composed, and the true topics are Jesus' alleged messiahship (7:40–52) and sonship (8:1–59).

Jesus is at the feast of Tabernacles in Jerusalem when he utters his second "I am" saying: "I am the light of the world; he who follows me will not walk in darkness, but will have the light of life" (8:12).[42] The Pharisees accuse him of bearing self-witness, which is inadmissible in court. Jesus acknowledges the self-witness claim, but he asserts that his testimony is true, nonetheless, "for I know whence I have come and whither I am going" (8:14). To be sure, he continues, the Law requires the harmonious testimony of two witnesses to establish a truth, but Jesus meets this test. "I bear witness to myself," he declares, "and the Father who sent me bears witness to me" (8:18). When the Pharisees ask, "Where is your Father?" (8:19) they betray the fact that they know neither Jesus nor his Father. The two are inseparable. Jesus declares to the world what he has heard from the Father (8:26). Many of the Jews place their faith in Jesus (8:31); others give intellectual assent but withhold their faith (8:32).[43] Since unbelief is the cardinal sin in John, Jesus calls those who withhold their faith slaves of sin (8:34). Their destination is death (8:24). They

---

[42]John 7:53–8:11, footnoted in the RSV, is a floating tradition that has been inserted after John 7:52, at the end of John, or after Luke 21:38. Its vocabulary is non-Johannine, and the passage is found in no Greek manuscript prior to the sixth century.
[43]This distinction in the Greek is not made in the English translation.

claim to be descendants of Abraham (8:33, 39), but their desire to kill Jesus discloses their true pedigree. They are children of the devil. He was a murderer from the start, and there is no truth in him. Jesus, on the other hand, tells the truth. The children of God hear his words (8:39–47).

The *fifth sign,* according to our reckoning, concerns the miraculous restoration of sight to a man born blind (9:1–41), and it is intended to illustrate Jesus' claim to be the light of the world (8:12). The narrative falls into five parts: (1) the physical healing and the interest it arouses (9:1–12); (2) the division of opinion among the Pharisees (9:13–17); (3) examination of the sighted man by skeptical Jews (9:18–23); (4) the recollection of the sighted man and his dialogue with the Jews (9:24–34); (5) the development of insight and faith in the sighted man and Jesus' denunciation of the blindness of the Pharisees (9:35–41).

The scene is Jerusalem at the feast of Tabernacles. The appearance of a man blind from birth prompts Jesus' disciples to inquire about the relationship between physical suffering and sin: "Rabbi, who sinned, this man or his parents, that he was born blind?" (9.2). Jesus rejects both horns of this dilemma and seizes the occasion to demonstrate the works of God. He anoints the blind man's eyes with a mixture of spittle and clay and sends him to wash in the pool of Siloam. Since the pool was a large reservoir that drew its water through a subterranean canal, it was called in Hebrew a name that meant "sender." John treats the word as a passive participle ("sent") so he can suggest one of his favorite designations for Jesus: "He who was sent."[44] The blind man goes and washes and comes back sighted. Those who have known him before are astounded.

We miss the meaning of this sign, as well as the others, if we focus our attention on the physical healing. It is what the healing signifies that is important. The disciples are concerned about the cause of the man's physical disability, and his acquaintances are curious about how his handicap is cured. But our author is oblivious of optics. He has eyes only for the eyes of faith. The climax of this story comes when the sighted man becomes insightful. Jesus identifies himself as the Son of Man, and the man born blind makes his confession: "Lord, I believe" (9:38). Then he worships Jesus.

Some of the Pharisees are a study in contrast. A cryptic statement

[44]According to Howard, "The Gospel According to St. John: Introduction," in *The Interpreter's Bible,* VIII, 438, the phrase is spoken by Jesus 26 times in John, and a synonymous verb is used 18 times for the Son's mission from the Father.

by Jesus causes consternation: "For judgment I came into this world, that those who do not see may see, and that those who see may become blind" (9:39). The Pharisees ask, "Are we also blind?" (9:40). The man born blind, Jesus says in effect, represents all men. Spiritually speaking, all men are blind at birth. They grope in darkness that no man can dissipate—only God can do that. If men acknowledge their blindness, He will flood their world with light. The sin of these Pharisees is their smugness. They have closed their eyes to God's revelation in Christ. To them Jesus is a man possessed by demons (8:46). They know what the Christ will be like when he comes, and Jesus does not fit their preconceived pattern. It is their claim to sight that makes them blind and brings judgment upon them. They are children of the devil because they love the darkness. Christ is the light of the world (8:12; 9:5). Those who believe in him are the children of light (God).

John next depicts Jesus as "the good shepherd" who cares for his sheep (10:1-39).[45] The shepherd-sheep figure was a familiar one to Jews (Ps. 23; 78:70; Isa. 40:10-11; Ezek. 34; 37:24), and it was common coin in the Gentile world as well. It was a title for deity in the religions of Egypt, Babylonia, and Persia, and in some Hermetic literature the shepherd is described as the sole revealer of truth. According to John, Jesus is "the door of the sheep" (10:7). Like the literal shepherd, he stands (or sleeps) at the entrance of the sheepfold (a pen or cave) to protect the flock (10:9). Anyone who enters the fold another way "is a thief and a robber."[46] The sheep know the shepherd's voice and follow him out of the fold, but they are stone deaf to strangers (10:3-5). The shepherd gives life to the sheep by laying down his own life (the crucifixion) that he may take it up again (the resurrection). His sheep consist not only of believing Jews but also of future Gentile converts.[47] The goal is one flock and one shepherd (10:11-17). The sheep know both the shepherd and the Father, because the shepherd and the Father are one (10:30). The Father gives the sheep to the shepherd, and from the shepherd they receive eternal life. Since the Father is the ultimate source of life, the sheep are secure indeed (10:25-29).

The resurrection and the life and the hour for glorification (11:1–12:50). Chapter 11 is largely devoted to the *sixth sign* of Jesus' public

[45]Scholars who think the text is dislocated suggest the following rearrangement: 10:19–21 (which logically follows Jesus' charge of blindness against some Pharisees at the close of chapter 9); 10:1–18; 10:30–42. John 10:22–29 reflects a different situation, the feast of Dedication, two months after the feast of Tabernacles, when the allegory of the good shepherd was delivered.
[46]John 10:1, 10, which may be a reference to heretics who endanger the church in Asia Minor.
[47]The church in John's day was predominantly composed of Gentile converts.

ministry: the raising of Lazarus from the dead (11:1–44). Like all of the other signs it is performed for the glory of God and the glorification of the Son (11:4) and points to the seventh and perfect sign: the death and resurrection of Christ. The story is peculiar to John, and its historicity has often been questioned. The Synoptics relate the raising of Jairus' daughter, and Luke tells of the restoration of the widow's son at Nain,[48] but the difference between revival shortly after death and four days after death (when putrefaction is present) boggles the mind. Some scholars suggest that John's account is a literal reinterpretation of Luke's parable of the Rich Man and Lazarus (16:19–31). There the point is made that some Jews would not be convinced if someone returned from the dead and testified to the truth. A comparable consequence stems from the resurrection of Lazarus. It stimulates not the conversion of the Jews but the final conflict (11:53).[49] But whatever the source of John's story, one thing seems certain—he prized it for its symbolic meaning.

Lazarus and his two sisters, Mary and Martha, reside in Bethany. When Lazarus becomes ill, the sisters send word to their good friend, Jesus. He declares that "the illness is not unto death" and delays two days before taking action. Only when he is convinced that Lazarus is dead ("sleep" is a Semitic euphemism for "death") does he depart for Bethany (11:4–15). Martha meets him with a poignant reproach: "Lord, if you had been here, my brother would not have died" (11:21). When Jesus assures her that Lazarus will rise again, she voices the conventional pharisaic belief in the resurrection "at the last day" (11:24). Jesus promptly corrects and contemporizes Martha's eschatology: "I am the resurrection and the life," he declares, "he who believes in me, though he die, yet shall he live, and whoever lives and believes in me shall never die" (11:25–26). Jesus, according to John, gives eternal life *now* to those who believe in him. When he asks Martha if she believes she replies in the affirmative and assigns to Jesus three messianic titles: "Yes, Lord; I believe that you are the Christ, the Son of God, he who is coming into the world" (11:27). By the third title John asserts that the Messiah's work has already begun on earth. The powers of the age to come are present in the person and performance of Jesus.

This "I am" saying and Martha's confession constitute the verbal climax of this story, and they suggest the symbolic meaning of the sign. The glory of God disclosed in Lazarus' restoration to physical life is only a sample of the glory that is revealed in God's gift of

---

[48]See Matthew 9:18–26; Mark 5:22–43; Luke 8:41–55 and 7:11–17 respectively.
[49]See Alan Richardson's penetrating study, *The Miracle-Stories of the Gospels* (London: SCM Press, 1941), from p. 120.

eternal life through his Son. The complete disclosure of this life will be made in the death and resurrection of Jesus. Lazarus represents all men. Alienated from Christ, they are already dead; united with him, they have eternal life now.

John's interest in symbolism is evident throughout the story. Lazarus has been dead "four days" when Jesus approaches the tomb. This is one day beyond the number that stands for "completeness." "Four days" serves to magnify the miracle that follows. Martha's remark that "by this time there will be an odor" enhances the miracle even more (11:39). It also suggests John's awareness of a rabbinical tradition that the soul hovers near the grave for three days, hoping to reunite with the body, but permanently departs at the first sign of decomposition. Surely the language of symbolism is used to describe Lazarus' exit from the sepulcher. He comes out, "his hands and feet *bound* with bandages, and his face *wrapped* with a cloth." Then Jesus commands some onlookers, "*Unbind* him, and let him go."[50] Even the cunning High Priest Caiaphas is made to utter words that have a surface and a symbolic significance. Members of the Sanhedrin fear that Jesus' mushrooming popularity will evoke the wrath of the Romans and trigger the destruction of their Temple and nation. "You do not understand," Caiaphas counters, "that it is expedient for you that one man should die for the people, and that the whole nation should not perish" (11:50). His political sagacity is no match for his unwitting religious prophecy. How like John to make the man whose carnal policy led to Jesus' death the spokesman not only for the truth of universal atonement but for the eventual unity of the gathered and scattered children of God (11:51–52)!

Chapter 12 concludes the public ministry of Jesus. The Passover season has arrived, and Jesus is reclining at supper in the home of Lazarus. Mary, apparently in gratitude for her brother's restoration, anoints Jesus' feet with a costly ointment of pure nard and dries them with her hair. Judas rebukes her for the extravagance and complains that the ointment should have been sold on behalf of the poor. Jesus defends Mary's action on the grounds that the poor are always present and she can keep the remainder of the nard for the day of his burial. The story shows some dependence on the Synoptics (Mt. 26:1–13; Mk. 14:1–9; Lk. 7:36–50), but John's account differs in many ways. The most important deviation is what the anointing means to him. Mark sees it as a preparation for Jesus' burial. John mentions this, to be sure, but the emphasis is on Jesus' anointment as a king. When Jesus enters Jerusalem, the crowd hails him "the King of Israel" (12:13). No one really understands the proclamation until after Jesus'

---

[50]John 11:44, italics added.

death and resurrection (12:16). His kingship, after all, is "not of this world" (18:36). The title affixed to his cross in three different languages informs the witnesses of the charge against Jesus, but to John it also indicates who he really is: "Jesus of Nazareth, the King of the Jews" (19:19).

The apprehension of the chief priests and the Pharisees concerning Jesus' exploding popularity (11:47–48) was not the product of paranoia. "Look," the Pharisees now exclaim, "the world has gone after him" (12:19). No sooner said than shown. Some Greek converts or God-fearers who were attending the Passover ask to see Jesus. John, who writes from the vantage point of one who has seen the church develop into a ubiquitous and cosmopolitan institution, interprets the request as a prophecy of the global spread of Christianity. Again and again it has been stated in this Gospel that Jesus' "hour" has not yet come (2:4; 7:6, 30; 8:20). But when Jesus is informed of the Greeks' desire to see him, he declares, "The hour has come for the Son of man to be glorified" (12:23). There is a difference, of course, between the hour *for* the glorification and the hour *of* the glorification. The condition *for* glorification (the appearance of the Greeks) is here; the time *of* glorification (Jesus' death and resurrection) is near.[51] Jesus' death will bring judgment on the world, and its ruler (the devil) will be cast out. When Jesus is "lifted up" (resurrected), he will "draw all men to" himself (12:31–32). Eternal life is not given indiscriminately in John. It is bestowed only on those who believe.

The mark of discipleship (13:1–38).   Prior to the feast of the Passover, Jesus withdraws from his public ministry for a period of close association with his disciples. The Last Supper of the Synoptics is not found in this Gospel, but the evening meal with its foot-washing episode seems to be John's substitute for it. John's dating, twenty-four hours in advance of the Synoptics, is usually preferred by scholars. This is true despite the convenient coincidence of Jesus' death and the slaying of the Passover lambs—thus making Jesus "the Lamb of God, who takes away the sin of the world," the Lamb whose bones may not be broken (1:29; 19:36).[52] As the original Passover led the Israelites from Egyptian slavery to freedom, the death of Christ leads men from the devil and his world of darkness into eternal life.

During the supper Jesus leaves the table and begins to wash the

---

[51]See Alfred Loisy, *Le Quatrième Evangile*, 2nd ed. rev. (Paris: Emile Nourry, 1921), p. 371.
[52]See C. Milo Connick, *Jesus: The Man, the Mission, and the Message* (Englewood Cliffs, N.J.: Prentice Hall, Inc., 1963), pp. 360–364, for a summary of the relevant data on dating.

disciples' feet. It was the duty of a slave to do this as the guests reclined at table before the meal began. Evidently the courtesy had been neglected. None of the disciples cares to compromise his claim to a free man's status by performing the menial task, so Jesus takes it upon himself. Peter vehemently protests, but when Jesus says, "If I do not wash you, you have no part in me" (13:8), he changes his mind in a hurry and requests more of an ablution than had been proffered. The key to the foot-washing is found in the evangelist's opening words concerning Jesus: "Having loved his own who were in the world, he loved them to the end" (13:1). "The end" is a phrase that carries a double meaning: "completely" or "until death." John probably had both ideas in mind. When Jesus washes the disciples' feet, he illustrates the kind of love that characterizes true disciples: "If I then, your Lord and Teacher, have washed your feet, you also ought to wash one another's feet" (13:14). A disciple's love is complete. It knows no limit. "A servant," Jesus continued, "is not greater than his master" (13:16).

The second meaning of "the end" is suggested by Jesus' comment to the disciples that they "are not all clean" (13:11) and his quotation of Psalm 41:9: "He who ate my bread has lifted his heel against me" (13:18). Even so, his disciples appear to be shocked when Jesus states that "one of you will betray me" (13:21). When pressed for the identity of the betrayer, Jesus dips a morsel in a dish and hands it to Judas. The other disciples don't understand Jesus' disclosure, because the act is an Oriental custom that evidences friendship. The evangelist knows, though, because he writes that after Judas receives the morsel "Satan entered into him. . . . He immediately went out; and it was night" (13:27, 30). The reference is not to nocturnal darkness. It depicts the blackness of unbelief of one who fails to find in Jesus the source of light and life. The imminence of Jesus' death prompts him to give his disciples a "new commandment"—that they love one another as he has loved them (13:34). Such love leads to humble service and perhaps even to death. It is the indelible mark of a true disciple.

Farewell discourses (14:1–16:33). The meal at which Jesus washed his disciples' feet was also the occasion for a series of extended discourses (14–16) and a protracted prayer (17). Since chapter 14 ends with the command, "Rise, let us go hence," some scholars think that the text has been displaced. The close content connection of chapters 14–17, though, decrees that they be regarded as one. (We shall treat chapter 17 in our next section.) The discourses concern Jesus' departure from his disciples and his return. Nothing like them appears in the Synoptics, although the subject matter suggests that the discourses constitute John's reinterpretation of such Synoptic apocalyptic expectations as Mark 13. Several themes are scattered throughout the chapters.

Chapter 14 begins with words of consolation: "Let not your hearts be troubled." They are designed to calm minds made anxious by Jesus' announcement in 13:33: "Yet a little while I am with you. . . . Where I am going you cannot come." When Jesus asserts that to know him is to know the Father (14:7), Philip responds, "Lord, show us the Father, and we shall be satisfied" (14:18). The request sets the stage for the development of a dominant theme of the discourses: the relationship of the Father and the Son. Jesus is "in the Father" and the Father is "in" him. The words Jesus speaks and the works he performs are derived from the Father (14:10–11). The Father is greater than Jesus (14:28) since Jesus has assumed the limitations of life on earth. This distinction will vanish, however, when the Son returns to the Father. Then his disciples will do greater works because he has gone to the Father (14:12). The unity of the Father and Son is not so much metaphysical as it is motivational. It springs from love. The Father stays with the Son to the very end (16:32), and the Son faithfully obeys the Father's commands—even unto death (14:31; 15:10). It is at Jesus' death and resurrection (the seventh sign) that the two loves become one. When tragedy (the death) is turned to triumph (the resurrection), the perfect love of Christ and the perfect love of God are revealed.

God's love cannot be completely disclosed, according to John, until Jesus goes to the Father. Jesus repeatedly refers to his departure both in connection with his death and his resurrection (14:3, 28; 16:17). A promise that he will return is often coupled with these references. "When I go and prepare a place for you," he tells his disciples, "I will come again and will take you to myself, that where I am you may be also" (14:3). This aspect of his coming coheres with the several references to his future resurrection. But there is another mode of Christ's coming that dominates these discourses. It is in the promised presence of the Holy Spirit. In four passages John speaks of the Spirit as *Paraclete*, an English transliteration of the Greek *paraklētos* (14:15–17, 25–26; 15:26–27; 16:5–11), and in a fifth (16:12–15) he uses "the Spirit of truth" as a synonym (14:17).[53] The term usually means "advocate" in the Greek, one who pleads the case of another in court. The RSV translates the word as "Counselor." This is the proper meaning in 14:15–17. On other occasions John uses the term to describe one who convinces or convicts the world (16:5–11) or who guides people to all the truth (16:12–15; 14:26).

[53]Some scholars think that the *Paraclete* passages are from a later hand. See Howard, *Christianity According to St. John*, pp. 74–80.

Sometimes it is the Father who will send the Paraclete (14:16, 26) and sometimes it is the Son (15:26; 16:7). But since the Father and Son are one (10:30), the problem is one of semantics only. If the Son does not go away, the Paraclete will not come (16:7). When the Paraclete (who is the Spirit of truth) does come, he will bear witness to the truth about Christ (15:26)—the truth that the disciples could not "bear" during his ministry (16:12). Then they will know that he is "the way, and the truth, and the life" and that "no one comes to the Father" except by him (14:6–7). The Spirit will also generate the Christian community because apart from the Spirit Jesus' followers will not know that he still lives. "Because I live," he has assured them, "you will live also" (14:18–19).

The allegory of the vine is the supreme expression of the mystical union that exists between Christ and those who believe in him (15:1–11). It combines in a remarkable way Paul's thought expressed in the figure of one body with many members (I Cor. 12:12–26) and John's emphasis on love as the hallmark of a Christian (15:9–10). Christ is the vine, and Christians are the branches that owe their life to the vine. If the branches do not bear fruit, they are cast forth and wither away. Both the fruitfulness and the life of Christians depend on union with Christ. If they abide in Christ and his words abide in them, their prayers will be answered affirmatively (15:7), God will be glorified through their service and character (15:8), and they will be filled with Christ's joy (15:11).

Christians can expect to be persecuted because the world persecuted their master (15:18–22). Persecution will be their lot because the world does not know the Father or the Son (16:3). When the Paraclete comes, the sin of the world—its rejection and persecution of Christ—will be judged (16:7–11). Soon the disciples will be scattered, and they will leave Jesus alone. But he will not really be alone; God will be with him. His followers will have tribulation in the world, but they should be of good cheer. Jesus has overcome the world (16:32–33)!

The Petitionary Prayer (17:1–26). This chapter has often been called Jesus' "High Priestly Prayer" because in it he purportedly consecrates himself before offering his life as the perfect and complete sacrifice for the sins of the world (17:1–5). He then consecrates his disciples that they may effectively carry on his work (17:6–19) and prays for the church that its witness may win the world to God (17:20–26). Close examination of the chapter, however, suggests that the real author is not Jesus but John. The prayer reflects his thought and language, and in one instance it even refers to Jesus in the third person: "This is eternal life," Jesus tells the Father, "that they know thee the only true God, and *Jesus Christ* whom thou hast sent."[54]

The prayer's nonauthentic nature does not impair its beauty or its value. It provides a splendid shorthand account of Jesus' accomplishments according to John. Jesus has done the work that God assigned to him. His death has glorified God, and God has glorified Jesus by his resurrection. Through his Spirit it has been revealed that eternal life is to know the one true God and Jesus Christ whom He sent (17:1–5). Jesus has revealed the nature and purposes of God to the church, and the church has faithfully preserved and proclaimed the revelation (17:6). The church knows that Jesus' words and works have come from God and that he is God's emissary (17:7–8). The Spirit, which has continued with the Christian community since its arrival, has convinced the faithful that they are under God's care. This conviction is the cause of their unity and joy (17:9–13). Their faithfulness to God's word revealed in Christ has separated them from the world and evoked its hatred. Although they are not of the world, since they have eluded the evil one, they are in it. Christ has sent them into the world to proclaim the truth that he disclosed to them (17:14–19). Their evangelistic efforts have been eminently successful. Many new converts have joined the Christian community, where they have discovered the love of God that is eternal (17:20–26).

Jesus' death and resurrection: the sending of the Spirit (18:1–20:31). The prayer we have just considered constitutes the theological summit of this Gospel. The one who prays is not the Jesus of history but the Christ of faith. He speaks from the perspective of the Christian community near the turn of the century. Jesus' passion is past. His work is accomplished, and his "hour" has come. He has glorified the Father, and the Father has glorified him. His resurrection has made possible the coming of the Spirit, and the Spirit has long been at work in the world—convincing the faithful of God's love in Christ and converting the unbelievers.

Jesus' Petitionary Prayer, then, serves both as a prelude and a postlude to his Passion (18–20). The account of his death and resurrection immediately follows the prayer, and yet the prayer presupposes that these momentous events have already occurred. The limitations of space prevent a detailed treatment of John's version of the Passion. We have observed how frequently he assumes the tradition preserved in the Synoptics. Nowhere is this more noticeable than in his Passion narrative. Although he introduces some novel notions, such as the

[54]John 17:3, italics added.

appearance of a squad of Roman soldiers in the story of Jesus' arrest (18:3, 12), he often hews the Synoptic line. The distinctiveness of his record, aside from some data of high historical probability, lies in his interpretations.

The central theme of the Passion is Jesus' kingship. It is introduced at the trial before Pilate (18:33) and becomes the catalyst for a pronouncement of Jesus that reveals John's understanding of Jesus' mission: "My kingship is not of this world" (18:36). Jesus does not deny his kingship, but he makes crystal clear that it is not of earthly origin or of a political character. His sovereignty stems from his witness to truth, and those who acknowledge the truth are his subjects.

Throughout John's account the volitional nature of Jesus' death is emphasized. When the soldiers appear to arrest him, he twice identifies himself to them (18:4-8). Their early involvement with Jesus suggests that the whole world is arrayed against him. Jesus carries his own cross to Golgotha (19:17). This observation not only underscores his initiative, but it combats Docetic tendencies in the church of John's day. Jesus' "I thirst" accomplishes the same purpose and fulfills Scripture as well (19:28).

Jesus' final words from the cross contain John's customary double commentary (19:30). "It is finished" marks not only the end of Jesus' physical life, but also the end of the *earthly* mission of the Incarnate Logos. Christ's *life* is not over, of course, and his full *mission* has not yet been accomplished. He gives "up his spirit" (19:30) in order that he may give his Spirit to the world (20:19-23). The close timing of Jesus' ascension and Pentecost is one of the striking features of this Gospel. The shepherd who laid down his life for his sheep is not long separated from his flock. As he promised, the Paraclete has come to dwell with them forever (14:16-17).

John's final words reiterate a prominent theme in his Gospel. The resurrected Jesus appears to his disciples assembled behind closed doors and challenges Thomas to touch him. Thomas was absent when Jesus first appeared to the disciples, and he refused to accept second-hand evidence of Jesus' resurrection. This time Thomas has no doubt. He confesses the creed of the Christian church of John's day: "My Lord and my God!" (20:28). Then Jesus, also speaking for the author, declares, "Blessed are those who have not seen and yet believe" (20:29). The words are intended for John's own generation, but they are capable of bridging any generation gap. All men are blessed whose faith enables them to find Christ in the community of believers.

It was through the revelation and inspiration of the Spirit that John wrote his entire Gospel. The authors of the Synoptics also wrote from a postresurrection perspective, but John's interpretative proclivity is far more pronounced. His Gospel is not devoid of facts; sometimes he is more factual than the Synoptics. His overriding interest, though, is not history but the meaning of history. He is convinced that the full truth about Jesus' historic ministry is not disclosed by a recital of what Jesus said and did. It is revealed by understanding Jesus' mission and message in terms of the insights supplied by the living Christ to the ongoing Christian community. These insights began with Jesus' dispatch of the Spirit, and they have continued to this very day. The tremendous appeal of John's Gospel is partly due to his disdain of historicism and his facile use of language, but it is largely attributable to the tutelage of the Paraclete who taught him "all things" and brought to remembrance all that he had said in the days of his flesh (14:26).

The Letters of John

The three remaining Catholic epistles are I, II, and III John. III John is not really an epistle, but a private letter addressed to a particular person, Gaius (1). II John is addressed to "the elect lady and her children, whom I love in the truth" (1). No name is assigned to the addressees, and the admonitions that follow seem to be directed to a congregation. (Note the change to the second person plural from verse 6 on.) It is probable that "the elect lady and her children" stands for a congregation or the church as a whole. I John lacks both epistolary introduction and conclusion, yet it reflects some of the marks of a letter (2:1). The author seems to know his readers and their situation. He writes to them with warmth and authority, although his discussion of the Christian life is somewhat general. Various metaphors have been used to describe his style—such as spiral and cyclical. One commentator even compared it to the Meander River. The composition as a whole is usually referred to as a tract or homily.

Authorship

The authorship of the Letters is related to the entire "Johannine question." Since we have devoted considerable space to the authorship of the Gospel of John and that Gospel's connection with the Synoptics and the Letters, only minimal attention to authorship will be given here.[55] The similarities between John's Gospel and I John are impressive. They exhibit a special fondness for dualistic terminology: light–darkness, truth–falsehood, God–the Evil One, love–hate, life–death. Identical phrases appear in both: "knowing [or doing] the truth," "walking in," "abiding in," "of the truth," "of God," "of the world." They share the same basic concepts of God, the Son,

[55]See pp. 369–373.

love, and rebirth, and their style invites positive comparison. I and II John are bound together by content and linguistic likeness. II and III John share an epistolary framework and authorship by one who calls himself the Elder. The unity of the Letters is difficult to deny.[56] The facts that I John is quoted early in the second century and II and III John are not mentioned until decades later suggest to some that the Letters don't belong together. Irenaeus, to be sure, mentions only "the epistle of John," but he quotes from both I and II John.[57] He, as well as the Muratorian fragment (which mentions "two epistles" of John), may have referred to the whole corpus.[58]

Differences between the Gospel of John and I John should not be discounted. They are sufficient to raise grave doubt in the minds of many able commentators as to their common authorship. I John introduces the non-Gospel concept of the antichrist. It emphasizes the expiatory nature of Jesus' death and repeatedly connects it with the forgiveness of sins, whereas the Gospel usually links Jesus' death with his resurrection and the consequent sending of the Spirit. The Epistle seldom refers to the Old Testament, and its concepts of the parousia and final judgment are untouched by "realized" eschatology.[59]

Tradition holds that the Letters, like the Gospel, were written by the Apostle John, but apostolic authorship for the Letters has been widely abandoned by modern scholars. Most of the reservations made in connection with the Gospel's authorship apply to the Letters as well. There was a prominent Asian church leader called John the Elder who lived near the close of the first century or the beginning of the second.[60] It has been suggested that he is the John who wrote the Gospel and the Letters, since the author of II and III John calls himself "the Elder." Perhaps so, but the speculators seem to be clutching at straws. II and III John are so brief that they provide virtually no clues as to their origin. Their similarities to I John seem to us to make common authorship a reasonable hypothesis, although the author's identity continues to remain a mystery. II John appears to presuppose and oppose the same heretical views resisted by I John.

[56]For a concise and cogent discussion which assumes the scholarly consensus that the Letters have a common but nonapostolic author, see A.N. Wilder, "I, II, and III John, Introduction," in *The Interpreter's Bible*, XII, 209–216.

[57]Irenaeus, *Against Heresies*, III, 16, 8.

[58]E.J. Goodspeed, *An Introduction to the New Testament* (Chicago: University of Chicago Press, 1933), p. 324.

[59]See Dodd, "The First Epistle of John and the Fourth Gospel," *Bulletin of the John Rylands Library*, XXI (1937), 129–156, and his *The Johannine Epistles*, Moffatt New Testament Commentary (New York: Harper & Row, 1946), pp. xlvii–lvi.

[60]Eusebius, *Ecclesiastical History*, III, 39, 3–7.

At least on the surface, though, this problem is not discussed by III John. We believe that the Gospel and the Letters reflect somewhat similar milieus, although the Letters express a more orthodox eschatology and attack a more highly developed heresy. Assertions of their identical authorship, however, fall far short of scholarly consensus.

Origin, Occasion, Destination, and Date

The earliest evidence for the existence of the Letters appears in writing that originated in Asia Minor—Polycarp's Letter to the Philippians and the works of Papias.[61] The tradition of their Asian origin is strengthened by the special use of the title "Elder" in that area. Evidently there was a time there when people could write under the title of "the Elder" without the necessity of adding their own names or other symbols of authority.

If the Letters have a common author, as we assume, I John is illuminated by the other two communications. It is a pastoral letter or homily directed to the churches within "the Elder's" sphere of influence. It was delivered by itinerant missionaries under his direction. It deals with the same error combatted in II John (7) and the same divisiveness reflected in III John (9–10). On one of their trips the missionaries presumably took with them II and III John, whose similar conclusions suggest that they were sent at the same time. Their purpose was to enable the missionaries to cope effectively with particular church emergencies. II John warns a specific church against the subversive activities of a rival group that was dedicated to Docetic doctrine (7). Since the Elder had already dealt with the errorists in II John, there was no need for him specifically to mention the doctrinal disturbance in his letter to Gaius (III John). In view of the situation described in I and II John, however, it is likely that the troublemakers mentioned in III John (9–10) were fellow errorists.[62]

A precise dating of the Letters is impossible. Their type of church organization antedates the one presupposed by Ignatius and coheres with the one at Corinth about 96 A.D. when Clement of Rome wrote to the church there. Since the Letters betray no hint of persecution, they cannot be assigned a date coincident with that of Revelation. A date of 100–110 A.D. for the Letters is as defensible as any.

Message

III John is a private letter dispatched by the Elder to a "beloved Gaius" (1). The Elder praises him for his hospitality to itinerant missionaries and encourages him to continue his entertainment of such travelers (5–8). A certain Diotrephes, who thinks of himself first, has slandered the Elder, rejected his authority, boycotted his emis-

[61]Eusebius, *Ecclesiastical History*, III, 39, 3–7.
[62]See Wilder, "I, II, and III John, Introduction," in *The Interpreter's Bible*, XII, 209–10.

saries, and excommunicated from the church any who wanted to welcome the missionaries (9–11). With a word of commendation for Demetrius (who may have headed a band of missionaries that had been subjected to shabby treatment) and the expressed hope that he will see them soon, the Elder closes his brief communication (12–15).

The Elder attributes Diotrephes' insubordination to a self-serving motive rather than to erroneous teaching. Yet the extreme measures that Diotrephes resorted to and the caustic nature of the Elder's rebuke suggest a more crucial cause of the rift. We believe that Diotrephes is the conscientious leader of a vigorous group of errorists with representatives in various churches. The Elder feels no need to define the error in III John because he has already done so in his accompanying letter, which we call II John.

II John is addressed to "the elect lady and her children," a thinly-disguised figure for a particular church (1). It carries the greeting of the Elder and a sister church. The author's stress on "truth" in the superscription suggests that he is moved to write by a threat to it (1–2). Some members of the congregation are devoted to the truth (4). All are reminded of their obligation to love one another, which means that they should keep the commandments (5–6). This emphasis on love and the commandments probably indicates that the errorists are guilty of unchristian practices. "Many deceivers have gone out into the world," the Elder warns his readers, "men who will not acknowledge the coming of Jesus Christ *in the flesh.*"[63] They are devotees of the Docetic doctrine that denies the incarnation. Perhaps they are followers of Cerinthus of Ephesus, a Gnostic and tradition-designated adversary of St. John, who was active about 100 A.D. He taught that Jesus was the biological son of Mary and Joseph. The heavenly "Christ" descended on Jesus at the baptism and empowered him to preach the mysteries of the true God. But before the crucifixion, Cerinthus argued, "Christ" left him. The "Christ" never suffered; he just *seemed* to suffer. It was Jesus who suffered and was resurrected.[64] In any case, the Elder urges his readers to be on guard against the errorists, who are called the antichrist, lest their doctrine cause the true believers to lose their full reward (8). Then he advocates a boycott against the deceivers: "If any one comes to you and does not bring this [true] doctrine [of Christ], do not receive him into the house [church] or give him any greeting; for he who greets him shares his wicked work" (10–11).

[63]II John 7, italics added.
[64]Irenaeus, *Against Heresies*, I, 26, 2; compare III, 3, 4. Positive identification of the errorists with Cerinthus cannot be made because none of his writings has survived, and accounts of him in the early Fathers are vague and conflicting.

I John is elucidated by the two briefer letters. As missionaries like Demetrius traveled about Asia Minor, they carried with them this longer letter. In it the Elder (who does not mention himself or use the letter form) deals with the same error referred to in II John and the same divisive situation reflected in III John.

The cyclical nature of I John makes it exceedingly difficult to discern the author's plan of organization. In the course of developing a theme he sometimes returns to the starting point—or so it seems. There may be a slight shift of thought, which supplies a springboard for the elaboration of a new theme. Sometimes he treats an already-discussed idea from a slightly different vantage point. It is not surprising, then, that a standardized "outline" of his work is nonexistent. Our treatment calls attention to the two major tests of "the truth"—one doctrinal and the other ethical—that constitute the foci of I John.[65]

The doctrinal test. The errorists in I John are not named, but their description leaves little doubt as to their identity. They claim to *know* God (2:4), be *born* of Him (5:18), and *love* Him (4:20), but their claims are spurious. They cannot know God because they deny "that Jesus is the Christ" (2:22). It is the supporters of the Elder who know the Father and the Son (2:13–14, 21, 29). Like the errorists in II John 7, these deceivers are false prophets who have gone out into the world to proclaim that Jesus Christ did not come *in the flesh.* They belong not to God, but to the antichrist (4:2–3). There are "many antichrists" at work (2:18; 4:3).[66] This is why "it is the last hour" (2:18). Once the errorists embraced the Christian faith and fellowship, but now they have departed from both (2:19).

The Elder appeals to the Christian kerygma in his doctrinal duel with the Docetists. Although he shares much of their outlook and language, he sets them right on the fundamentals. Christianity is the true *gnosis* (2:13, 14, 21, 29). If this is not so, then Christ is only one of many saviors. "Every spirit which *confesses* that Jesus Christ has come *in the flesh*," the Elder declares, "is of God"[67] His

---

[65]See A.H. McNeile, *An Introduction to the Study of the New Testament* (Oxford: Clarendon Press, 1953), pp. 300–301. For a threefold emphasis, see C. Milo Connick, *The Message and Meaning of the Bible* (Belmont, Calif.: Dickenson Publishing Co., 1965), pp. 172–173.
[66]The word "antichrist" appears here for the first time in Christian writings. The Elder's use of the plural form and his identification of it with the errorists are noteworthy. Jewish apocalyptic writings (including those at Qumran) were well acquainted with "Belial," the personification of evil connected with the End of the Age. For a history of the antichrist idea, see Martin Rist, "Antichrist," in *The Interpreter's Dictionary of the Bible*, A–D, 140–143.
[67]I John 4:2, italics added.

use of the word "confess" (1:9; 2:23; 4:2, 15) suggests that his appeal rests on creedal constructions, and his accent on Christ's death as "the expiation" for "the sins of the whole world" confirms it (2:2; 1:7). Forgiveness does not come from esoteric knowledge and participation in the mysteries but from Christ's blood and propitiation alone.

The ethical test. Gnosticism tended to produce antinomianism, the notion that knowledge (or "faith" for the Christian) makes the moral law null and void. Antinomianism, in turn, tended to foster libertinism. Paul had his problems with people who thought that freedom from the Law meant freedom for sin (Rom. 6:1, 15), and the heretics in Jude 4 and II Peter 2:2 stood condemned because they had lapsed into licentiousness and enticed others to do likewise (II Peter 2:18). We do not know that the errorists in the Letters were guilty of sexual sins. They *could* have indulged in bodily vices because, according to their creed, their higher state of *gnosis* rendered such behavior unimportant and Jesus' death for human sin meaningless. What we do know about them is that they displayed a superior attitude toward the less sophisticated devotees of Christ. The Elder repeatedly chastises them for their lack of brotherly love. People cannot love God and hate their brothers. If they do not love their brothers whom they have seen, it is impossible to love God whom they have not seen (4:20). Love is the foundation of the Christian code of conduct. It is not a concept to be admired but a commandment to be obeyed. Love is the infallible ethical test. It separates the sinners from the saints, the Docetists from the Doers (3:18). Christians should follow Jesus' example (2:6). As he laid down his life for them, they should lay down their lives for the brethren (3:16). "If any one has the world's goods and sees his brother in need, yet closes his heart against him," the Elder asks in summing up his kerygmatic defense, "how does God's love abide in him?" (3:17).

The Johannine Letters constitute a trenchant example of the difficulties encountered by churches governed solely by the Spirit. When conscientious but conflicting groups of Christians claim to have the *true* spirit, how can a correct choice be made between them? The spirits themselves need to be tested "to see whether they are of God" (4:1). The Elder's doctrinal and ethical tests go far toward resolving this difficult and recurring dilemma.

We turn now to the final Johannine writing, the Book of Revelation.

XV

**A New Heaven
and a New Earth**
(Revelation)

The book of Revelation has the dubious distinction of being the most misunderstood composition in the New Testament. Many readers don't know what to make of the writing, and others make altogether too much of it.[1] This is not very surprising. The author describes one series of cataclysmic events after another with symbols and images that are frequently foreign to modern minds. His work is further complicated by the fact that he purports to be relating things he has seen in visions. Are the visions to be taken literally, or are they simply literary devices? Perhaps some of the confusion about Revelation can be eliminated if we comprehend what kind of writing it really is.

Revelation is frequently called "The Apocalypse," a transliteration of a Greek word which, in the infinitive form, means "to uncover" or "to reveal." It is the only thoroughgoing apocalyptic composition in the New Testament. Daniel is its Old Testament counterpart. Apocalyptic passages appear in other Biblical books, of course, such as Zechariah, Joel, Ezekiel, the Synoptics, and I and II Thessalonians. Apocalyptic writings are largely (although not exclusively) Jewish and Christian. They are both dualistic and eschatological in nature. They reflect a belief in two conflicting cosmic powers (God and Satan or his equivalent) and two distinct ages (the present and the future). The present temporal age of human history is seen as wholly evil. It is under the firm control of Satan and his demonic and human associates who oppress the righteous. In the near future, however, God will directly intervene in human history. He will overthrow Satan and his agents and create a new, perfect, and eternal age for the enjoyment of His righteous followers.

This type of thinking evidently originated in Persian Zoroastrianism. It was transmitted to Judaism in the exilic and postexilic periods and

---

[1]See James L. Price, *Interpreting the New Testament* (New York: Holt, Rinehart, & Winston, 1961), p. 518.

through Judaism to early Christianity. None of the ancient apocalyptic writers attempted to forecast detailed happenings that would occur in medieval and modern times. They didn't believe that the world would *have* an extended history. As the author of Revelation repeatedly points out, the supernatural events that he predicts "must *soon* take place."[2] If readers keep this qualifying condition in mind, they will avoid the inappropriate and misleading use of Revelation as an infallible textbook of contemporary and future international relations. It is a book about the *first century*, even though it has a message for the twentieth. Its basic concern is with a *religious* matter, although it impinges on political affairs as well.

Authorship Revelation is the only New Testament book that claims to have been written by John. About the middle of the second century Justin Martyr identified this John as the Apostle John.[3] This view came to be widely held in the early church, and it is still not without its advocates. Certain Christians in the second and third centuries, however, either hesitated to accept Revelation's apostolic origin or denied it outright. The first serious scholar to argue that the book could not have been written by the Apostle John was Dionysius, Bishop of Alexandria (247–264 A.D.). He pointed out that the style, grammar, and ideas of Revelation differ markedly from those of the Fourth Gospel, which he considered to be apostolic. Eusebius was impressed by Dionysius' views, and he concluded that Revelation was written by a certain John the Elder whom Papias had distinguished from the Apostle John. The historian acknowledged, though, that some rejected Revelation and others counted it among the recognized books.[4]

The evidence that Revelation itself supplies does not support its apostolic authorship. Although the author calls himself "John" (1:1, 4, 9; 22:8), he never declares that he is an apostle or lays claim to apostolic authority. (This is a rather clear indication that the book is not pseudonymous.) He is God's "servant" (1:1) and his first readers' "brother" (1:9). He considers himself a Christian prophet and views his message as prophecy (1:3; 22:6–7, 9–10, 18–19). Nowhere does he indicate that he has seen Jesus in the flesh or been associated with him in his ministry. Nearly everything he says about Christ clashes with what we know about the Carpenter. His statement that the city wall has twelve foundations inscribed with the names of the twelve apostles implies that he is not one of the Twelve and that the apostolic age is past (21:14). Evidence that the Apostle John, like his brother James, suffered an early martyrdom must also be

[2]Revelation 1:1; 22:6, italics added. Compare 2:16; 3:11; 22:7, 10, 12, 20.
[3]Justin Martyr, *Dialogue with Trypho*, 81; Eusebius, *Ecclesiastical History*, IV, 18, 8.
[4]Eusebius, *Ecclesiastical History*, III, 39, 6; III, 24, 18, and 25, 4.

reckoned with. The radical differences between Revelation and the Fourth Gospel in style, vocabulary, and perspective, of course, are pertinent only for those who accept the apostolic origin of the Gospel. There were many Johns in the early church. At a time when Revelation was a disputed work its supporters doubtless desired apostolic sanction for their "protégé." It would have been an easy thing for them to equate the inspired writer of Revelation with the Apostle who bore the same name. However well intentioned this identification may have been, we conclude that it was mistaken. The man who wrote Revelation was John, but he was not an apostle. He may have been John the Elder (which we doubt) or some other John. All we really know about him is found in his book.

Origin, Occasion, and Destination

John was on the island of Patmos in the Aegean Sea about sixty miles southwest of Ephesus. He had shared "the tribulation" with his Christian brothers on the mainland. Scholars have long wished that he had described this persecution in depth. What was its date, duration, extent, and precise nature? Such details would have saved endless discussion and debate. But the author's parsimonious description has one redeeming feature. It provides proof positive that he wrote for his own people rather than for posterity. He didn't include such information because his readers already possessed it. He had shared with them "the kingdom and the patient endurance" with which they had met their plight. It was "on account of the word of God and the testimony of Jesus" that John had been banished to Patmos (1:9).

John described his divine commission as a prophet and seer as others had done before him. It was "the Lord's day" (Sunday) and John was "in the Spirit" (a state of mystical ecstasy) when he heard a loud trumpetlike voice say, "Write what you see in a book and send it to the seven churches" of Asia Minor (1:10–11). Visitors to Patmos today are shown a cleft in the roof of John's cave where, it is alleged, the loud voice broke through the rock. John may well have had visions. They were the stock-in-trade of prophets and seers.[5] The book he wrote, however, appears to be the product of careful literary composition. It is fashioned in the form of a letter to the seven churches, with appropriate salutation (1:4–5) and benediction (22:21). Each of the churches is addressed by name and appropriately commended and condemned (2–3). The letter form is abandoned after chapter 3, though, in favor of the finest apocalyptic writing in existence. The encouragement the author offers his readers rests on something different from that of Jewish apocalypses. Instead of heralding the *coming* of the Messiah he declares that the Messiah *has come.* He has conquered death and redeemed the faithful by his death.

[5]See Isaiah 6; Ezekiel 1–3.

He will soon return to reign with the martyrs in a new and heavenly Jerusalem on earth for a thousand years. This millennium will be a prelude to Christ's complete conquest of his enemies, God's final judgment, the destruction of evil men and powers, and the establishment of the kingdom of God and Christ where the saints shall reign for ever and ever.

Date The earliest authorities commonly assigned Revelation to the closing years of Domitian's reign. Somewhat later a few scholars argued that the situation described in Revelation suggested the reign of Claudius, Nero, or Trajan.[6] Modern scholarship exhibits a similar range of opinion, but consensus focuses on Domitian's time and about the year 95 A.D.

There are references in Revelation that to some scholars seem to point to a time prior to 70 A.D. John is instructed to measure the Temple (11:1). This implies that the Temple is still standing. Perhaps so, but no other verse in Revelation does. John is experiencing a vision, and visions have a habit of utilizing destroyed buildings. Besides, Hebrews and other postapostolic works also refer to the Temple as though it were still there. The flight of the woman into the wilderness (12:13–14) is seen by some as a reference to the escape of Christians to Pella in Perea before Jerusalem's fall. It could also refer to the flight of Mary, Joseph, and their babe into Egypt to avoid the machinations of Herod—which would make Revelation a very early book indeed! Most scholars who support a date earlier than 70 A.D. believe that Revelation was written during the reign of Nero (54–68 A.D.). But Nero persecuted Christians as arsonists, not because they refused to worship him. Moreover, his persecutions did not extend beyond Rome. And how could the myths mentioned in Revelation (13:3, 12, 14; 17:8, 11) to the effect that Nero would be restored to life to lead an army from the east against Rome have originated before his death?

Other scholars maintain that the five fallen kings (17:10) should be reckoned from Augustus. This would make Vespasian (69–79 A.D.) the reigning king of Revelation. But Vespasian didn't take his divinity very seriously, and according to Tertullian (a vigorous Christian apologist of the late second and early third centuries) he did not persecute the Christians. Trajan (98–117 A.D.) was the first emperor to have Christians put to death *as Christians*, as Pliny the Younger's correspondence with him proves.[7] It is difficult to identify Trajan with

[6]See R.H. Charles, *The Revelation of St. John*, International Critical Commentary (New York: Charles Scribner's Sons, 1920), I, xci ff.
[7]See pp. 71–72.

the beast who "is" or Trajan's successor (Hadrian, 117–138 A.D.) with the one who will "remain only a little while" (17:10). The latter, however, fits Nerva (96–98 A.D.), Domitian's successor, perfectly.

Domitian had both personal and political reasons for stressing emperor worship. As a youth he played second fiddle to his brother, Titus, who was the favorite of their father Vespasian and of the public. Despite the fact that his father and brother were emperors before him, Domitian's plebeian background and lack of notable personal accomplishments proved to be considerable handicaps. When he ascended the throne, he encountered the strenuous opposition of Roman aristocrats and influential Stoic philosophers. Under the circumstances it was only natural that he should zealously cultivate the cult of the Flavian house (the house of his father) in order to establish the divine nature of his family. As the descendant of the divine Vespasian he could claim heavenly parentage and require citizens and subjects of the empire to extend to him the loyalty, obedience, and worship due one of his divine status. He commanded public sacrifices to his "genius" and oaths by it. He referred to his bed as the couch of a god and ordered his household to call him Lord and God. Many of the coins struck during his reign display the cult image of Domitian sitting in the holy place or on the throne of a god. Those made in Smyrna present him as father of the gods, and an inscription from Laodicea exalts the incarnate Jupiter in the doxology: "to Zeus the Supreme, the Savior, the Emperor Domitian."[8] His huge marble statue graced the new imperial temple at Ephesus and served as the fulcrum for emperor worship in Asia.

Before the time of Domitian, divine honors had been granted only to deceased sovereigns. But the divinity tradition for emperors had been long in the building, and Domitian's innovations were readily accepted, especially in the provinces. Jews and Christians, of course, were scandalized by his claims. People who refused to perform religious ceremonies honoring him along with the state gods could be found guilty on both civil and religious grounds. Domitian accused many people of "atheism" and loyalty to Jewish customs in 95 A.D. Flavius Clemens, the Roman consul, was executed. His wife, Flavia Domitilla (Domitian's niece) was exiled "with many others" to the island of Pontia, a fate similar to that of the author of Revelation.[9] Perhaps "the sudden and repeated misfortunes" mentioned in I Clement 1:2 refer to these happenings, yet there is no evidence that Domitian ever issued an edict against either Christians or Jews. When

[8]See Ethelbert Stauffer, *Christ and the Caesars*, trans. K. and R.G. Smith (Philadelphia: The Westminster Press, 1955), pp. 147–191; Martin Rist, "The Revelation of St. John the Divine, Introduction and Exegesis," in George A. Buttrick, ed., *The Interpreter's Bible* (New York: Abingdon Press, 1957), XII, 354–356.
[9]Eusebius, *Ecclesiastical History*, III, 18, 3–4.

John wrote Revelation it is probable that Christians were being persecuted here and there in Asia Minor for refusing to participate in the public ceremonies that proclaimed Domitian divine. It should not be assumed, however, that the persecution was widespread or that it was against Christians *as Christians.* Systematic efforts to eradicate the church did not occur until the time of Decius (249–251 A.D.). Persecution of Christians *as Christians,* so far as we know, first took place under Trajan (98–117 A.D.), but even then it was isolated and spasmodic—and not initiated by the state. From the time of Trajan, however, the security threshold of the church dropped lower and lower.

The author of Revelation had not been put to death. He had been banished or imprisoned like some of his friends. "Do not fear what you are *about* to suffer," he cautioned the Christians in Smyrna. "Behold, the devil is *about* to throw some of you into *prison*, that you may be tested."[10] But from his position of imprisonment John augured the worst. The cases of harassment and martyrdom in Asia Minor and elsewhere were a cloud no larger than a man's hand, but they certified the approach of a terrible storm. The empire was full of temples, shrines, altars, and statues designed to foster emperor worship, and a well-established priesthood existed to supervise the patriotic and religious rites. The Christian community was poorly prepared to meet the crisis created by such a powerful competitor. Some of its members capitulated and participated in the compromising ritual. They may have rationalized their act by claiming that it was only a formality. Others had become so lukewarm about their faith that they may not have given the matter a second thought (3:16). But there was at least one man who had. He had been banished to the island of Patmos. On the Lord's day, as he meditated on the worship of the church from which he was separated, he saw the significance of the critical times in which he lived. He was so convinced that his insight was correct that he wrote a letter to each of the seven leading churches of Asia Minor. The letters grew into a book. He could not write plainly because his communication contained a bitter attack on the government under which he and his readers lived. So he resorted to the cryptic language of Jewish apocalypticism. His purpose was to stiffen the spine of his readers against the temptations of compromise and apostasy, and his promise was a divine reward "to him who conquers" (2:7, 11, 17).[11]

---

[10]Revelation 2:10, italics added.
[11]For a discussion of the plan of Revelation see the various outlines presented by A.H. McNeile, *An Introduction to the Study of the New Testament,* rev. ed. (Oxford: Clarendon Press, 1953), from p. 254. The impact of church liturgy on John's mind is shown in G.E. Wright and R.H. Fuller, *The Book of the Acts of God* (Garden City, N.Y.: Doubleday & Co., 1960), pp. 376–377. Lucetta Mowry, "Revelation 4–5 and Early Liturgical Usage," *Journal of Biblical Literature,* LXXI (1952), 75–84, utilizes prayers and other liturgical material in Revelation as sources for the reconstruction of postapostolic church worship.

St. John on the Island of Patmos. This engraving pictures John on the Island of Patmos writing the Book of Revelation. [Courtesy of The Bettmann Archive]

Message John sees the immediate crisis not primarily as a clash between the church and the state but as a decisive period in the final conflict between God and the forces of evil. The present ordeal is the beginning of the End—the "woes" of the Messiah. If Christians remain steadfast in their faith even unto death, they will receive the crown of life and witness God's total realization of His purpose in creation.

The formal preface of Revelation suggests that it is addressed to Christians assembled for worship (1:1–3). The author declares that God is the ultimate source of the book's content, and he stresses that what it reveals must soon take place. He pronounces a benediction on the presiding reader, the congregation, and all who heed the book's message. In a covering letter (1:4–20), antiphonal choruses praise God and Christ, and John relates his situation and reason for writing.

Letters to the seven churches (2:1–3:22). Each of the seven major churches of Asia Minor is addressed in turn. John knows the churches well, and he does not hesitate to point out their strengths, weaknesses, and possibilities. Christians at *Ephesus*, for example, have shown patient endurance in the face of persecution. They hate evil men and the works of the Nicolaitans. But they have abandoned their first love (of Christ?). If they do not recover it, their lampstand (church) will be removed. If they repent and do the works that they did at first, they will eat the fruit from the tree of life in the paradise of God (the new Eden).

John follows a similar format in letters to the remaining churches, which are addressed in an order whose outline on the map resembles a sitting duck. His knowledge of their situation never falters. Christians at *Smyrna* are bothered by persecution, poverty, and the "synagogue of Satan"—Jews who inform on them to Domitian's supporters (2:9). *Pergamum* Christians dwell where "Satan's throne is," a reference not only to that city's status as promoter of emperor worship in the East, but also to its sponsorship of the cult long before it became fashionable in Rome (2:13). Some Christians in *Thyatira* have succumbed to immorality and idolatry under the influence of a false prophetess whom John appropriately calls Jezebel. Others have been enticed by "the deep things of Satan," an incipient Gnosticism (2:24). The church at *Sardis* is known for its robust Christians, but they are really only nominal (asleep). John warns them to wake up because Christ will come "like a thief" (3.3). This reference should alert them. Sardis was once considered an impregnable city, but the Persians penetrated the acropolis through a small crevice while the celebrated King Croesus basked in the "security" of his splendid palace. *Philadelphia*, like Smyrna, is troubled by Jewish informers. *Laodicea* is reputed to be a wealthy city. Evidently people in the church there like to boast about their city's blessings. John castigates them for their claim and the pride that sired it. They should exchange the black wool clothing derived from their sheep for the white garments of martyrs. Then the shame of their nakedness would be covered with righteousness and their worldly wealth transmuted into heavenly treasures. The "blindness" of the Laodicean Christians was ironic, and John's recommendation that they anoint their eyes with "salve" to regain their sight was particularly pointed (3:18). Their city prided itself in its splendid hospital dedicated to the god of healing, Aesclepius, and in its famed Phrygian powder (salve) that was supposed to cure blindness.

Visions of God and Christ (4:1–5:14). John's fondness for the number seven is one of the most memorable features of his work.

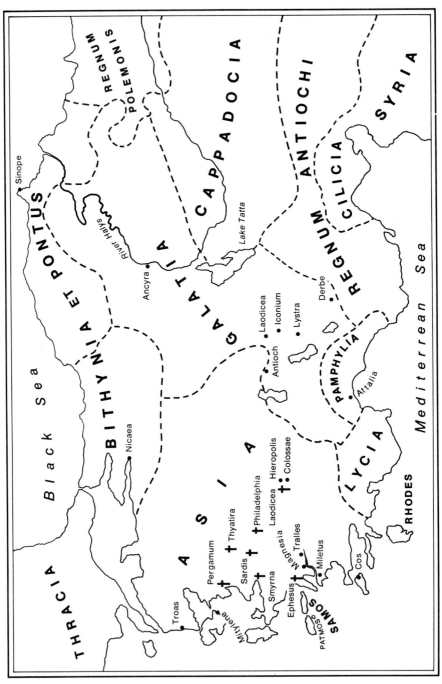

ASIA MINOR

He presents the main message of his book in a series of seven eschatological visions, each one of which has seven visions in itself. The entire series of visions is appropriately introduced by visions of God (4:1–11) and Christ (5:1–14). Both God and Christ are seen in heaven in all of their majesty, splendor, and power. In deference to Jewish sensibilities on the subject God is not pictured, but his throne and its surroundings are described in detail. Although God is in heaven, His authority is universal. The four living creatures "full of eyes in front and behind" suggest that nothing escapes His attention (4:6). "I will show you what must take place," a voice has declared to John (4:1). God is in control of history even though Satan may seem to be in the driver's seat at the moment.

The second prefatory vision introduces the dominant figure of the Apocalypse. He is, paradoxically, both heavenly and humble, aggressive and submissive, Lion (5:5) and Lamb (5:6). John does not disclose his personal name, but it is perfectly clear that he is none other than Jesus Christ. He alone is able to unroll the seven-sealed scroll that reveals God's judgment on the world and its unrighteous inhabitants (5:2,5). The chorus of the twenty-four elders indicates why:

Worthy art thou to take the scroll and to open its seals,
for thou wast slain and by thy blood didst ransom men for God
from every tribe and tongue and people and nation,
and hast made them a kingdom and priests to our God,
and they shall reign on earth. (5:9–10)

These two visions are calculated to reassure Revelation's readers. God and Christ are presently far removed from the earth and from its inhabitants, who suffer from the domination of Satan and his demonic agents. But the sufferers should take heart. Their Heavenly Overseers are aware of their desperate situation, concerned about their sorrows and afflictions, and have the power and resolve to rescue them from their adversaries. The visions suggest that soon the Heavenly Ones will intervene in human affairs, defeat Satan and his followers, and establish a new age for the benefit of those who have kept the faith.

A few words of caution are in order before we begin a limited discussion of the principal visions. It is easy to become mystified by Revelation's celestial calculations and bizarre beasts. Most of these figures are borrowed from late Jewish apocalyptic works. These writings provide an initial context for their interpretation. John takes these well-known materials and reworks them in terms of the crisis of faith that he sees hanging heavy on the horizon. The historical situation (actual or impending) is the master key to understanding the visions. Their meaning is more easily grasped, moreover, if their cyclical nature is respected. John does not arrange his prophecies chronologically. He describes the coming of the End with one figure after another: seven seals, seven trumpets, etc. After the seventh seal is broken, there is "silence in heaven for about half an hour" (8:1). The suspense builds. Then he describes the coming of the End, using the figure of the trumpet. Revelation is to John what the parables are to Jesus. Both present one theme with ever-changing imagery.

Seven visions with seven visions (6:1–21:8). The main part of Revelation consists of seven groups of visions, each one of which consists of seven visions—with a few interludes interspersed here and there. There are seven seals (6:1–8:6), seven trumpets (8:7–11:19), seven visions of the dragon's kingdom (12:1–13:18), seven visions of worshipers of the Lamb and worshipers of the beast (14:1–20), seven bowls (15:1–16:21), seven visions of the fall of Babylon (17:1–19:10), and seven visions of the end of Satan's evil age and the beginning of God's righteous age (19:11–21:8). All of the visions are designed to disclose God's plan for the world and its inhabitants. Since the passages are highly repetitious, we shall confine our comments to some of the more significant signs and scenes.

1. The seven seals (6:1–8:6). The Lamb (Jesus Christ) is the only one worthy to open the seven-sealed scroll. Frightful consequences arise on earth with the breaking of each seal: war (the white horse, 6:2), civil strife (the red horse, 6:3–4), famine (the black horse, 6:5–6), and death (the pale horse, 6:8). These, in popular parlance, are the Four Horsemen of the Apocalypse. The opening of the fifth seal reveals the martyrs in heaven crying out for vengeance: "How long," they ask the Lord, "before thou wilt judge and avenge our blood on those who dwell upon the earth?" (6:10). God informs them that this will not happen until they are joined by the rest of their brethren on earth who bear witness to their faith unto death.[12] The breaking of the sixth seal is followed by cosmic disturbances (6:12–17). They suggest to the readers of Revelation that all creation is involved in the accomplishment of their destiny. A great persecution on earth before the End will provide the necessary number of martyrs (6:11). As a consequence, the woes stop for a time until those who are to become martyrs are sealed (7:1–3). The sealed martyrs number 144,000, twelve thousand for each of the twelve tribes of Israel. They

[12]Martyr, a transliteration of a Greek infinitive, originally meant "to witness." When Christians who witnessed to their faith were put to death, the word acquired its modern connotation.

are not really Jews, though, as John's allegory soon shows. 1 are the true Israel: Christians drawn from every people and na (7:9). God's mark of ownership is placed on the foreheads of potential martyrs to protect them from spiritual death.[13] The sc suddenly shifts from earth to heaven and from the present to future. The full complement of martyrs are assembled in their p mised white robes (3:5) in the presence of God and the Lamb. 1 prophet praises God's faithful witnesses in poetry.

Therefore are they before the throne of God,
  and serve him day and night within his temple;
  and he who sits upon the throne will shelter them with his presenc
They shall hunger no more, neither thirst any more;
  the sun shall not strike them, nor any scorching heat.
For the Lamb in the midst of the throne will be their shepherd,
  and he will guide them to springs of living water;
and God will wipe away every tear from their eyes. (7:15–17)

2. The seven trumpets (8:7–11:19). The sealing of the martyrs and their proleptic glorification in heaven are two interludes that set the stage for the climactic act in the apocalyptic drama. Readers have every right to expect that with the breaking of the seventh seal there will follow the conquest of Satan, the end of the age, the resurrection, and final judgment. Not so! The breaking of the seventh seal is followed by a dramatic pause: silence in heaven for about half an hour. Then seven angels initiate a second series of woes: the seven trumpets. Hail and fire consume a third of the earth. Blazing objects fall from the heavens and turn a third of the sea to blood and make a third of the rivers and fountains of water brackish (8:8–11). A third of the sun, moon, and stars are darkened (8:12). Locusts with the sting of scorpions torture all except the prospective martyrs (9:3–5). Jerusalem is judged, and the prophets of God bring drought upon the land (11:1–6). The sounding of the seventh trumpet (11:15) triggers a series of seven visions of the dragon's kingdom (12:1–13:18).

3. The heavenly pregnant lady and the dragon (12:1–17). A woman "clothed with the sun, with the moon under her feet, and on her head a crown of twelve stars" appears in heaven (12:1). She is heavy with child, and birthpangs cause her to cry out in anguish for delivery. A red, seven-headed dragon also appears in heaven. He is a composite creature made up of aspects of earlier apocalyptic models. His identity

---

[13]Compare the mark God placed on Cain in Genesis 4:15.

and history are disclosed in the prior-in-time passage of 12:7-12. A war in heaven between Michael and his angels and the dragon and his angels resulted in defeat for the latter. The defeated dragon (now identified as the devil and Satan, 12:9) and his angels were cast out of heaven. As the devil falls to earth, his tail sweeps down a third of the stars (12:3-4). The dragon stands near the heavenly woman (who is now apparently on earth also) to devour her child as soon as it is born. The woman gives birth to a son (the preexistent Messiah) who is destined to rule the world with an iron rod. It is this prediction that accounts for the dragon's deadly hostility and his desire to kill the child. But the child is caught up to God and his throne, and the woman flees into the wilderness to a place God has prepared for her. There she will be nourished for about three and one-half years (12:5-6). The devil's time is short (12:12). He has only half of the perfect number (seven years) to accomplish his work.

John's story of the heavenly pregnant woman is a "flashback." He relates an event that occurred in the past as though it were just taking place. The account is not derived from any known Jewish source. It seems to be based on a wide-spread myth of the divine child whose life is jeopardized by those whose power he endangers. John's version, with its astral aspects, reminds one of the myth about Horus' birth.[14] The identity of the dragon is no mystery, but who are the woman and child? Some scholars claim that they are Mary and Jesus. According to astral thought, though, everything that occurs on earth has already happened in heaven. John tells of the birth (perhaps before creation) of a *heavenly* Messiah to a *celestial* woman. The hostility of the dragon (Satan) toward the child *in heaven* prefigures the animus that the dragon will later have toward him. John's interest is not focused on the historical Jesus here any more than it is in the rest of his book. He makes a subtle and characteristic shift in symbolism. The heaven-mother of the preexistent Messiah is the preexistent church and her offspring are the Christians, as 12:17 indicates. Although her children are to be persecuted for about three and one-half years, she (the church) will not be harmed. She will be nourished in a safe place prepared by God. This, of course, is intended as a sign of encouragement for her children (the faithful Christians). Their ultimate (spiritual) safety is assured!

4. The two beasts (13:1-18). John's visions of the two beasts are companion pieces of his visions that involve the dragon (12:1-17). Indeed, the beast from the sea resembles the dragon. He has "ten

[14]See Rist, "The Revelation of St. John the Divine, Exegesis," in *The Interpreter's Bible*, XII, 452.

horns and seven heads" (13:1). The ten horns stand for the ten Roman emperors (Tiberius through Domitian) who have ruled since Jesus' public ministry began. The seven heads represent the seven major emperors of that period excluding the three occupants of the throne (Galba, Otto, and Vitellius in 68–69 A.D.) whose brief rules had only slight significance. The blasphemous name upon the beast's seven heads (a contrasting counterpart to God's mark on the foreheads of the martyrs) probably refers to the divine titles the emperors claimed for themselves. The dragon (Satan) gives his power, throne, and authority to the beast, making him a semi-Satan incarnate, rival of the incarnate Logos (13:2). The dragon's beneficence is designed to lure the unsuspecting into worshiping the beast on the supposition that he is divine.

One of the beast's seven heads appears to have a mortal wound that has been healed (13:3). This is a thinly-disguised reference to Nero, who was responsible for the death of many Christians including, perhaps, Peter and Paul. Nero was condemned to death for his crimes by the senate in 68 A.D., but he fled to his villa where, it was reported, he committed suicide by stabbing himself in the throat. The mysterious circumstances surrounding his death and the awesome power he wielded during his life soon mated and gave birth to a rumor. Nero had not died, it was alleged, but had gone into hiding in the East. He would return at the head of the armies of Parthia, Rome's traditional and terrifying enemy, to devastate the empire. This rumor later underwent marked modification. Nero's reported death was accepted as factual, but it was believed that in due time he would be restored to life. Then he would lead enemy armies (presumably Parthian) to ravage the empire. Eventually Nero *redivivus* was equated with the antichrist. When he and his armies invaded the empire, they would be defeated and destroyed by a heaven-sent king (God's Messiah).[15]

The first beast comes from the sea (13:1), but the second beast comes from the land. He has two horns like a lamb, but his Christ-like appearance is deceptive. He is really satanic, because he speaks like a dragon (13:11). He exercises the authority of the first beast and makes all people worship the first beast whose mortal wound was healed (13:12). For perceptive first-century readers Revelation's mystery fades as the masks of the dragon and the two beasts fall. The second beast symbolizes the imperial priesthood that vigorously fosters emperor worship with authority derived from the emperors. The one whose fatal wound is now healed is not Nero (who had been dead

[15]Compare the Sibylline Oracles 5:361–367 (4:119–127, 137–139) and 5:106–110 (5:33–34) respectively.

for decades when John wrote) but Nero *redivivus*, symbol of all the Caesars worshiped as gods—and especially, for John, the symbol of *his* emperor.

The number of the second beast is 666 (or 616 in a few texts), John discloses, in what may seem like a sop to slow learners (13:18). Far too much has been made of this figure. It has been applied to nearly every rogue in history. It has also been assigned to some who were rather righteous but who sponsored a different political or religious viewpoint from the designators. Among those who have been nominated to bear the number of the beast are Mohammed, Luther, Pope Benedict IX, Napoleon, Mussolini, and Franklin D. Roosevelt. In the early days of former President Roosevelt's New Deal, merchants were required to display the Blue Eagle emblem to signify compliance with the NRA (National Recovery Act). Some Biblical literalists and "economic royalists" who were opposed to the program claimed that the Blue Eagle was the mark of the beast of Revelation 13:17. During World War II many people were convinced that Hitler was the beast. Someone proved it by assigning numbers to the alphabet in this fashion: $A = 100, B = 101, C = 102$, etc. The letters in HITLER, then, added up to 666.[16] But this is rather like proving Shakespeare to be the author of Psalm 46. If a person counts down forty-six words in Psalm 46 in the King James Version, he comes to the word "shake." If he counts up forty-six words, he comes to the word "spear." If he allows for a slight variation in spelling, he has "indisputable" proof that Shakespeare wrote Psalm 46!

The assignment of numerical value to letters of the alphabet is not as farfetched as it may seem. Neither the Hebrews nor the Greeks had special numerical symbols. They used the letters of their respective alphabets as numbers. This practice suggests that the clue to the meaning of the number of the beast in Revelation 13:18 may be found in some person's name.[17] It is impossible to determine with certainty which person John had in mind, since the number of names that add up to 666 is nearly infinite. The connection of the beast with Nero *redivivus*, though, has caused most scholars to find the solution in his name. If the Greek letters for Neron Caesar are transliterated into Hebrew and given numerical equivalents, their sum is 666. If Neron is written without the final "n" (in keeping with its Latin form), the sum is 616—the variant reading previously noted.[18] The likelihood that Domitian was the emperor John intended to indict

[16]See Thomas S. Kepler, *The Book of Revelation* (New York: Oxford Univ. Press, 1957), p. 147.
[17]Revelation 13:18 (King James Version) states that the number "is the number of a man."
[18]See Rist, "The Revelation of St. John the Divine, Exegesis," in *The Interpreter's Bible*, XII, 466–467; Kepler, *The Book of Revelation*, p. 148.

raises no insurmountable difficulties. It was the habit of apocalyptists to reuse materials from earlier times without updating them. It heightened the mystery to mention the emperor by number rather than by name, and it minimized persecution of Christians by followers of the antichrist. If John had explicitly referred to Nero *redivivus*, the lot of his readers would have been worsened. He knew that his symbolism would not be lost on his first readers. They were familiar with cryptic writings, and no one needed to inform them about the gravity of their situation. Their emperor claimed to be "Lord and God," and imperial priests zealously proclaimed this "truth." For Christians in Asia Minor about 95 A.D., John's indirect reference to the Nero *redivivus* myth would have been a code word for Domitian.

5. The great harlot and the bride of Christ (14:1–19:10). All of the leading characters of John's apocalyptic drama have now appeared on stage except for the great harlot (17:4), the bride of Christ (19:7), and Gog and Magog (20:8). With the beginning of chapter 14 John turns from a description of the dragon's kingdom (12:1–13:18) to another series of seven visions. Christ is pictured as the Lamb with the martyrs on Mt. Zion (14:1–5). Separate angels admonish the worship of God (14:6–7), pronounce the doom of Babylon (14:8), and condemn the worship of the beast (14:9–12). The martyrs are blessed (14:13). The Son of Man announces and executes the judgment (14:14–16), and an angel tramps out the grapes of God's wrath in the same way that people stamp out the juice of grapes in the winepress with their feet (14:17–20).

After a beautiful hymn of praise to God for His mighty deeds and unmatched holiness (15:3–4) John extends the tapestry of God's judgment with the visions of seven bowls, filled with God's wrath, that are poured out on the earth in a vain effort to evoke repentance (15:5–16:21). They are similar in character and purpose to the plagues of the seven seals (6:1–8:6) and the seven trumpets (8:7–11:19). The seven bowls "are the last, for with them the wrath of God is ended" (15:1). They are followed by seven visions that depict the fall of Babylon, a code name for Rome (17:1–19:10). Rome was the scourge of first-century Christians as Babylon was for the people of God in the prophetic period. Rome is called "the great harlot" (17:1). She is dressed in passionate purple and sumptuous scarlet as befits her imperial status, and she is bedecked with gold and precious stones to suggest the enormous wealth of her empire. All of her surface splendor, however, cannot erase the fact that at heart she is a prostitute endeavoring to seduce the world to worship of the emperor. John's apt and graphic figure owes much to the Hebrew prophets who frequently saw adultery and idolatry as associated evils.[19]

[19]See Nahum 3:1–4; Isaiah 1:21; Ezekiel 16:15; Hosea 2:5.

A taunting, exultant dirge proleptically celebrates the utter destruction of the city situated on seven hills:

Fallen, fallen is Babylon the great!
It has become a dwelling place of demons,
  a haunt of every foul spirit,
  a haunt of every foul and hateful bird;
  for all nations have drunk the wine of her impure passion. . . .
Alas, alas, for the great city
  that was clothed in fine linen, in purple and scarlet,
  bedecked with gold, with jewels, and with pearls!
In one hour all this wealth has been laid waste. (18:2–3a, 16–17a)

John's figure of Christ as the bridegroom and faithful Christians as the bride is eschatologically oriented (19:7–8).[20] The marriage date is scheduled for the Second Advent. The Lamb and his bride "clothed with fine linen, bright and pure" (19:8) are a stark contrast to the imperial beast and his prodigal prostitute attired in purple and scarlet and bedecked with jewels. The eternal city (the church) is more than a match for the temporal city (Rome) that many people mistakenly considered to be eternal.

6. Gog and Magog (19:11–21:8). The six series of seven visions each have ended, and the seventh and final series now begins. These seven visions describe the end of the age of Satan and his agents and the opening of the new age of God and the faithful. The eschatological pattern presented by the visions is reasonably clear. The conquering Christ comes from heaven with his heavenly army (19:11–16). He defeats the beast and his false prophet and casts them both into the lake of fire. He also annihilates the rest of the people on earth, those who have supported the antichrist (19:17–21). Satan is bound and locked in the bottomless pit. While his rule is suspended, the martyrs are restored to life, and they alone reign with Christ for a millenium (20:1–6). At the end of this blessed period (which would have provided tremendous motivation for the proleptic martyrs to remain faithful) Satan is unbound. He deceives Gog and Magog, personifications of the nations at the four corners of the earth,[21] and induces them to attack the saints in the holy city. (This gathering of the nations overlooks their previous destruction, along with the

---

[20]The symbolism may well have been influenced by both Jewish and Hellenistic thought. See Isaiah 54:5–6; 62:5; Ezekiel 16:6–14; Hosea 2:19–20; Matthew 25:1–13; Mark 2:19–20; John 3:29. In Hellenistic mystery religions, the initiation was often seen as a sacred marriage uniting the devotee and the deity.
[21]Compare Ezekiel 38–39.

two beasts, prior to the millennium!) Gog and Magog are defeated, and Satan is cast into the fiery lake to be company for the two beasts. His age is ended for ever (20:7–10). The earth over which he reigned disappears along with the sky. The second and general resurrection takes place, and all the dead except the martyrs are judged before the throne of God. Death and Hades are thrown into the lake of fire (the second death) along with all whose deeds are evil (20:11–15).

A new heaven and a new earth 21:1–22:5). The seventh vision of the seventh series (21:1–8) is elaborated in the following scene (21:9–22:5). The two must be treated as one. The first earth and the first heaven have passed away, and a new heaven and a new earth have been created. John sees the new Jerusalem come down from heaven and the beginnning of God's perfect and eternal age:

I heard a great voice from the throne saying,
'Behold, the dwelling of God is with men.
He will dwell with them, and they shall be his people. . . . ;
he will wipe away every tear from their eyes, and death shall be no
*   more,*
neither shall there be mourning nor crying nor pain any more, . . .
Behold, I make all things new. . . .
To the thirsty I will give water without price from the fountain of the
*   water of life.*
He who conquers shall have this heritage,
and I will be his God and he shall be my son. . . .

Then he showed me the river of the water of life,
bright as crystal, flowing from the throne of God and of the Lamb
*   . . . ;*
also, . . . the tree of life with its twelve kinds of fruit,
yielding its fruit each month; and the leaves of the tree
were for the healing of the nations. . . .

And night shall be no more; they need no light
of lamp or sun, for the Lord God will be their light,
and they shall reign for ever and ever.
*   (21:3–4, 5a, 6c–7; 22:1, 2b–d, 5)*

NEW TESTAMENT TIME CHART

Roman Emperors	Judean Procurators	Christian Writings
Augustus, 27 B.C.–14 A.D.		
Tiberius, 14–37 A.D.	Coponius, 6–9 A.D. Ambibulus, 9–12 A.D. Annius Rufinus, 12–15 A.D. Valerius Gratus, 15–26 A.D. Pontius Pilate, 26–36 A.D.	
Gaius Caligula, 37–41 A.D.	Marcellus, 36–37 A.D. Marullus, 37–41 A.D.	
Claudius, 41–54 A.D.	Cuspius Fadus, 44–46 A.D. Tiberius Alexander, 46–48 A.D. Ventidius Cumanus, 48–52 A.D.	I and II Thessalonians, 50 A.D. I Corinthians, 54–55 A.D.
Nero, 54–68 A.D.	M. Antonius Felix, 52–60 (?) A.D.	II Corinthians, 55–56 A.D. Galatians, 56 A.D. Romans, 56–57 A.D. Colossians, 61(?) A.D. Philemon, 61 A.D.
	Porcius Festus, 60–62(?) A.D. Albinus, 62–64(?) A.D. Gessius Florus, 64–66 A.D.	Philippians, 62 A.D. Mark, 65–70 A.D.
Galba, 68–69 A.D. Otho, Vitellius, 69 A.D. Vespasian, 69–79 A.D. Titus, 79–81 A.D. Domitian, 81–96 A.D.		Matthew, 80–85 A.D. James, 80–100(?) A.D. Luke-Acts, 80–90 A.D. Ephesians, 90(?) A.D.
Nerva, 96–98 A.D. Trajan, 98–117 A.D.		Hebrews, 85–95(?) A.D. Revelation, 95 A.D. I Clement, 90–100(?) A.D. John, 100(?) A.D. I, II, III John, 100–110(?) A.D. Peter, 112(?) A.D. Didache, 100–130(?) A.D. I and II Timothy and Titus, 100–130(?) A.D. Shepherd of Hermas, 100–140(?) A.D.
Hadrian, 117–138 A.D.		Epistles of Ignatius, 110–117(?) A.D. Jude, 125(?) A.D. II Peter, 150(?) A.D.

NEW TESTAMENT TIME CHART

Important Christian Happenings	Jewish Writings	Important Jewish Happenings
		Maccabean Revolt, 168 B.C.
	Testament of the XII Patriarchs, 109–106(?) B.C.	Dead Sea Sect at Qumran, 105 B.C.(?)–66 A.D.
		Pompey Captures Jerusalem, 63 B.C.
	Psalms of Solomon, 48(?) B.C.	Herod the Great (King of Judea, Mt. 2:1, 19), 37 B.C.–4 B.C.
	Wisdom of Solomon, 50 B.C.–10(?) A.D.	
Birth of Jesus, 8–4 B.C.	Fragments of a Zadokite Work, 18–8(?) B.C.	Herod Antipas (Tetrarch of Galilee, Mt. 14:1), 4 B.C.—39 A.D.
Ministry of John the Baptist, 27–29(?) A.D.		Herod Archelaus (Ethnarch of Judea, Mt. 2:22), 4 B.C.–6 A.D.
Ministry of Jesus, 29–33(?) A.D.	Assumption of Moses, 7–29(?) A.D.	Herod Philip (Tetrarch of Iturea), 4 B.C.–34 A.D.
Crucifixion-Resurrection, 30–33 A.D.	IV Maccabees, 63 B.C.–38(?) A.D.	Caiaphas, High Priest, 18–36 A.D.
Paul's Conversion, 33–35(?) A.D.	First Century, A.D., II Enoch	Theudas' Revolt, 40(?) A.D.
Peter imprisoned by Herod Agrippa, 41–44(?) A.D.	I, II, III Baruch	Herod Agrippa I (King of the Jews, Acts 12:1–2), 41–44 A.D.
Martyrdom of James (and John?), son of Zebedee, 44 A.D.	Martyrdom of Isaiah Books of Adam and Eve IV Ezra (II Esdras)	Claudius banished Jews from Rome, 49(?) A.D.
Paul in S. Galatia, 47–49(?) A.D.		
Paul in Corinth, 50–51 A.D.		
Paul in Ephesus, 52–54 A.D.		
Paul arrested in Jerusalem, 56 A.D.		
Paul in Rome, 60 A.D.		
Death of Jesus' brother, James, 62 A.D.		
Flight of Christians to Pella, 66–67 A.D.		War with Rome, 66–73 A.D.
		Temple and Holy City destroyed, 70 A.D.
		The so-called Council of Jamnia, 90(?) A.D.
Martyrdom of Ignatius, 117(?) A.D.		Fall of Jerusalem, 134 A.D.

425

Chapter I   A brief but illuminating article by S. Vernon McCasland, "The Greco-Roman World" is presented in George A. Buttrick, ed., *The Interpreter's Bible* (New York: Abingdon Press, 1951), VII, 75–99. More
definitive treatments of this subject are found in Samuel Angus, *The
Environment of Early Christianity* (New York: Charles Scribner's Sons,
1920); T.R. Glover, *The World of the New Testament* (Cambridge:
At the University Press, 1931); and F.C. Grant, *Roman Hellenism
and the New Testament* (New York: Charles Scribner's Sons, 1962).
Representative texts from Greco-Roman and Jewish sources are presented in C.K. Barrett, *The New Testament Background: Selected Doc-
uments* (New York: The Macmillan Co., 1957). Helpful discussions
of the religions of the time are available in H.R. Rose, *Religion in
Greece and Rome* (New York: Harper & Row, 1959); Samuel Angus,
The Religious Quests of the Greco-Roman World (London: John Mur-
ray, Ltd., 1929); T.R. Glover, *The Conflict of Religions in the Early
Roman Empire*, 12th ed. (London: Methuen Co., Ltd., 1932); F.C.
Grant, ed., *Hellenistic Religions: The Age of Syncretism* (New York:
Liberal Arts Press, 1953); H.R. Willoughby, *Pagan Regeneration* (Chi-
cago: University of Chicago Press, 1929); and Morton S. Enslin, *Chris-
tian Beginnings* (New York: Harper & Row, 1938). Also useful is
A.N. Sherwin-White, *Roman Society and Roman Law in the New
Testament* (London: Oxford University Press, 1962). Three penetrat-
ing and suggestive studies of Gnosticism are R. McL. Wilson, *Gnosis
and the New Testament* (Oxford: Basil Blackwell, 1968); Hans Jonas,
The Gnostic Religion (Boston: Beacon Press, 1958); and Robert M.
Grant, *Gnosticism and Early Christianity* (New York: Columbia University Press, 1959). Rudolf Bultmann, *Primitive Christianity in Its
Contemporary Setting*, trans. R.H. Fuller (New York: Meridian Books,
1956), provides an excellent survey of the religious and cultural milieu
of early Christianity.

Chapter II   Morton S. Enslin's article, "Palestine," in George A. Buttrick, ed.,
The Interpreter's Bible (New York: Abingdon Press, 1951), VII,
100–109, presents a succinct and graphic account of the Jewish world

from Alexander the Great through 135 A.D. Elias Bickermann, *From Ezra to the Last of the Maccabees* (New York: Schocken Books, 1962) is also very useful. Nigel Turner's treatment of the Hasmoneans in George A. Buttrick, ed., *The Interpreter's Dictionary of the Bible* (New York: Abingdon Press, 1962), E–J, 529–535, is concise and convincing. Roman rule from 63 B.C. to 66 A.D. is ably covered by R.H. Pfeiffer, *History of New Testament Times* (New York: Harper & Row, 1949), pp. 24–40. Political conditions in Palestine just prior to and during Jesus' lifetime are vividly portrayed by Joseph Klausner, *Jesus of Nazareth*, trans H. Danby (New York: The Macmillan Co., 1925), pp. 135–173. A comprehensive study has been made by Werner Foerster, *From the Exile to Christ: A Historical Introduction to Palestinian Judaism*, trans. G.E. Harris (Philadelphia: Fortress Press, 1964). Early and useful data are also provided by Josephus, *Antiquities*, XIV–XIX, and *Wars*, I–II.

Chapter III Excellent treatments of the Jewish religion are found in Bernhard W. Anderson, *Understanding the Old Testament*, 2nd ed. (Englewood Cliffs, N.J.: Prentice-Hall Inc., 1966) and H. Keith Beebe, *The Old Testament: An Introduction to Its Literary, Historical, and Religious Traditions* (Belmont, Calif.: Dickenson Publishing Co., 1970). Informative articles dealing with such topics as the Temple, the synagogue, scribes, Pharisees, Sadducees, Essenes, Zealots, eschatology, and apocalypticism are found under the appropriate headings in George A. Buttrick, ed., *The Interpreter's Dictionary of the Bible* (New York: Abingdon Press, 1962). Louis Finkelstein, *The Pharisees*, 2 vols. (Philadelphia: The Jewish Publication Society of America, 1962), is excellent. A comprehensive collection of ancient Jewish and pagan writings appears in C.K. Barrett, *The New Testament Background: Selected Documents* (New York: The Macmillan Co., 1957). A convenient collection of translated sources for Jewish religion is S.W. Baron and J.L. Blau, eds., *Judaism: Postbiblical and Talmudic Period* (New York: Liberal Arts Press, 1954). Lawrence E. Toombs, *The Threshold of Christianity* (Philadelphia: The Westminster Press, 1960) provides a nontechnical coverage of intertestamental literature. Two penetrating studies concerning the Qumran community are Millar Burrows, *The Dead Sea Scrolls* (New York: Viking Press, 1955) and F.M. Cross, Jr., *The Ancient Library of Qumran and Modern Biblical Studies* (Garden City, N.Y.: Doubleday & Co., 1958). A. Dupont-Sommer, *The Essene Writings from Qumran* (New York: Meridian Books, 1961) furnishes a fine translation of the documents, but his conclusions are often suspect. Krister Stendahl, *Introduction to the Scrolls and the New Testament* (New York: Harper & Row, 1957), Geza Vermes, *The Dead Sea Scrolls in English* (Baltimore: Penguin Books, 1962), and Theodor Gaster, *The Dead Sea Scriptures* (Garden City, N.Y.: Doubleday & Co., 1956) are useful collections. "The Dead Sea

Scrolls," by F.M. Cross, Jr., in *The Interpreter's Bible* (New York: Abingdon Press, 1957), XII, 645–667, is a concise but valuable discussion. Helmer Ringgren, *The Faith of Qumran* (Philadelphia: Fortress Press, 1961) is a choice work, and John C. Trever's *Untold Story of Qumran* (Westwood, N.J.: Fleming H. Revell Co., 1965) is a handsomely illustrated eyewitness account of the discovery of the Scrolls and the intrigue that surrounded their purchase and publication.

Chapter IV   Various theories concerning Jesus' existence, their sources, and the non-Christian and Christian evidence against them (excepting the Gospels) are found in Maurice Goguel, *The Life of Jesus*, trans. O. Wyon (London: George Allen & Unwin, Ltd., 1933), pp. 37–133. Frederick C. Grant, *The Gospels: Their Origin and Their Growth* (New York: Harper & Row, 1957) is a fine general introduction, as is Vincent Taylor, *The Gospels: A Short Introduction*, 7th ed. (London: Epworth Press, 1952). See also A.M. Perry, "The Growth of the Gospels," in George A. Buttrick, ed., *The Interpreter's Bible* (New York: Abingdon Press, 1951), VII, 60–74. The classic treatment of the problem of Synoptic relations and sources is B.H. Streeter, *The Four Gospels: A Study of Origins*, rev. ed. (London: The Macmillan Co., 1930). Articles that introduce the different gospels and the accompanying commentary in *The Interpreter's Bible* (New York: Abingdon Press, 1951–1952), VII, VIII and in *Harper's New Testament Commentaries* are instructive. F.W. Beare, *The Earliest Records of Jesus* (New York: Abingdon Press, 1962) provides excellent nontechnical commentary on the Synoptics. Choice studies of individual gospels include Willi Marxsen, *Mark the Evangelist*, trans. R.A. Harrisville (New York: Abingdon Press, 1969). Ernest Best, *The Temptation and the Passion in Mark* (Cambridge: At the University Press, 1965); R.M. Lightfoot, *The Gospel Message of Mark* (Oxford: Clarendon Press, 1952); J.M. Robinson, *The Problem of History in Mark* (Naperville, Ill.: Alec R. Allenson, 1957); Curtis Beach, *The Gospel of Mark* (New York: Harper & Row, 1959); D.M. and G.H. Slusser, *The Jesus of Mark's Gospel* (Philadelphia: The Westminster Press, 1967); Günther Bornkamm, Gerhard Barth, and H.J. Held, *Tradition and Interpretation in Matthew* (Philadelphia: The Westminster Press, 1963); G.D. Kilpatrick, *The Origin of the Gospel According to St. Matthew* (Oxford: The Clarendon Press, 1946); Krister Stendahl, *The School of St. Matthew* (Philadelphia: Fortress Press, 1968); H.J. Cadbury, *The Making of Luke-Acts* (New York: The Macmillan Co., 1927); Hans Conzelmann, *The Theology of St. Luke*, trans. Geofrey Buswell (New York: Harper & Row, 1960). The works of two pioneer form critics are paramount—Martin Dibelius, *From Tradition to Gospel*, trans. B.L. Woolf (New York: Charles Scribner's Sons, 1935) and Rudolf Bultmann, *History of the Synoptic Tradition*, trans. John March (New York: Harper & Row, 1963). B.S. Easton, *The Gospel Before the Gospels* (New York: Charles

Scribner's Sons, 1928) evaluates form criticism from a conservative viewpoint. Vincent Taylor, *The Formation of the Gospel Tradition* (London: The Macmillan Co., 1938) offers a well-balanced view. Classic essays dealing with form criticism appear in paperback form in R. Bultmann and K. Kundsin, *Form-Criticism*, trans. F.C. Grant (New York: Harper & Row, 1962). Also useful are F.C. Grant, ed., *Form Criticism* (New York: Harper & Row, 1962) and E.V. McKnight, *What is Form Criticism?* (Philadelphia: Fortress Press, 1969). Perhaps the best treatment of redaction criticism is Joachim Rohde, *Rediscovering the Teachings of the Evangelists*, trans. Dorothea M. Barton (Philadelphia: The Westminster Press, 1968). Norman Perrin, *What is Redaction Criticism?* (Philadelphia: Fortress Press, 1969) is also instructive.

Chapter V Stout defenders of the virgin birth of Jesus are J.G. Machen, *The Virgin Birth of Christ* (New York: Harper & Row, 1930) and G.H. Box, *The Virgin Birth of Jesus* (London: I Pitman, 1916), a more moderate and persuasive work. E. Worcester, *Studies in the Virgin Birth of the Lord* (New York: Charles Scribner's Sons, 1932) takes a critical stance. The most dispassionate treatment of the subject is made by Vincent Taylor, *The Historical Evidence of the Virgin Birth* (Oxford: Clarendon Press, 1920). The finest work in English on Jesus' prophetic predecessor is Carl H. Kraeling, *John the Baptist* (New York: Charles Scribner's Sons, 1951). Classical treatments of Jesus' career include Maurice Goguel, *The Life of Jesus*, trans. O. Wyon (London: George Allen & Unwin, Ltd., 1933) and H.D.A. Major, T.W. Manson, and C.J. Wright, *The Mission and Message of Jesus* (New York: E.P. Dutton & Co., 1938). Two penetrating studies from Jewish specialists are Joseph Klausner, *Jesus of Nazareth*, trans. H. Danby (New York: The Macmillan Co., 1925) and C.G. Montefiore, *The Synoptic Gospels*, rev. ed., vols. I and II (London: The Macmillan Co., 1927). More recent and more popular treatments are presented by Vincent Taylor, *The Life and Ministry of Jesus* (New York: Abingdon Press, 1955) where realized and futuristic eschatology are combined; Ethelbert Stauffer, *Jesus and His Story* trans. R. and C. Winston (New York: Alfred A. Knopf, Inc., 1960) where a conservative and historical reconstruction of Jesus' life is attempted; Morton S. Enslin, *The Prophet from Nazareth* (New York: McGraw-Hill Book Co., 1961), which presents Jesus as a prophet akin to those of the Old Testament. A more complex book, written in the Bultmann tradition, is Günther Bornkamm, *Jesus of Nazareth*, trans. I. and F. McLuskey with J.M. Robinson (New York: Harper & Row, 1960). A comprehensive work, which presents Jesus as viewed from different theological perspectives, is C. Milo Connick, *Jesus: The Man, the Mission, and the Message* (Englewood Cliffs, N.J.: Prentice-Hall, Inc., 1963). A briefer treatment in a more specialized vocabulary is Ernest W. Saunders, *Jesus in the*

Gospels (Englewood Cliffs, N.J.: Prentice-Hall, Inc., 1967). A highly readable study of the Synoptic Gospels and the rest of the New Testament from a Jewish viewpoint is Samuel Sandmel, *A Jewish Understanding of the New Testament* (Cincinnati: Hebrew Union College Press, 1957). Reputable and rather exhaustive studies, which often arrive at "radical" conclusions, are Charles Guignebert, *Jesus*, trans. S.H. Hooke (London: Kegan, Paul, Trench, Trubner & Co., 1935) and W.E. Bundy, *Jesus and the First Three Gospels* (Cambridge, Mass.: Harvard University Press, 1955).

Chapter VI   Pioneering work on the parables was done by A.B. Bruce, *The Parabolic Teaching of Christ* (New York: A.C. Armstrong, 1892) and Adolf Jülicher, *Die Gleichnisreden Jesu*, vols. I and II (Leipzig: J.C.B. Mohr, 1888–1899). A path-breaking study by C.H. Dodd, which appeared in 1936, is currently available in a revised edition, *The Parables of the Kingdom* (New York: Charles Scribner's Sons, 1961). The finest book on the subject, first published in 1947, is Joachim Jeremias, *The Parables of Jesus*, rev. ed., trans. S.H. Hooke (New York: Charles Scribner's Sons, 1963). A.M. Hunter, *Interpreting the Parables* (Philadelphia: The Westminster Press, 1960) is a popular treatment with a conservative orientation. T.W. Manson, *The Teaching of Jesus* (Cambridge: At the University Press, 1963), is the best book on this subject.

Scholars will find Martin Dibelius, *The Sermon on the Mount*, trans. C.H. Kraeling (New York: Charles Scribner's Sons, 1940) a rewarding study. Dibelius sees the Sermon's demands as signs of the eternal kingdom—they spur us on toward the divine likeness, but they cannot be realized in our age. Hans Windisch, *The Meaning of the Sermon on the Mount*, trans. S.M. Gilmour (Philadelphia: The Westminster Press, 1951), another book for specialists, argues for the "fulfillability" of the Sermon's teachings. A.N. Wilder, *Eschatology and Ethics in the Teachings of Jesus*, rev. ed. (New York: Harper & Row, 1950) is difficult but fructifying reading. Wilder holds that the most significant factor in Jesus' ethical teachings is the eschatological: the teachings are an emergency ethic not of the interim but of Jesus' mission. Harvey K. McArthur, *Understanding the Sermon on the Mount* (New York: Harper & Row, 1961) adopts a more moderate position on the eschatological nature of the Sermon and provides a splendid summary of the different ways Christians have interpreted the Sermon during the history of the church. C. Milo Connick, *Build on the Rock, You and the Sermon on the Mount* (Westwood, N.J.: Fleming H. Revell Co., 1960) presents a popular but scholarly-based view of the Sermon's teaching and its relevance to the contemporary world. Dietrich Bonhoeffer, *The Cost of Discipleship* (New York: The Macmillan Co., 1957) is an existential treatment of the Sermon by one who died a martyr under Hitler.

The mighty works of Jesus have recevied close attention. J.M. Thompson, *Miracles in the New Testament* (London: Edward Arnold & Co., 1912) provides rational explanations for the "miracles" but retains belief in the supernatural. J. Wendland, *Miracles and Christianity* (London: Hodder & Stoughton, Ltd., 1911) argues that miracles have their own proper law. Other works that reflect varied viewpoints include F.R. Tennant, *Miracle and Its Philosophical Presuppositions* (Cambridge: At the University Press, 1925); C.J. Wright, *Miracle in History and in Modern Thought* (New York: Henry Holt & Co., 1930): Alan Richardson, *The Miracle Stories of the Gospels* (London: SCM Press, 1941); C.S. Lewis, *Miracles* (New York: The Macmillan Co., 1947); R.M. Grant, *Miracle and Natural Law in Graeco-Roman and Early Christian Thought* (Amsterdam: N. Holland Publishing Co., 1952). The contributions of modern psychotherapy to the understanding of Jesus' healings are competently discussed by S.V. McCasland, *By the Finger of God* (New York: The Macmillan Co., 1951). The current critical-but-appreciative approach to the miracles is reflected in Reginald H. Fuller, *Interpreting the Miracles* (Philadelphia: The Westminster Press, 1963).

The literature dealing with the messianic question is voluminous and the viewpoints are varied. Rudolf Bultmann, *Theology of the New Testament*, vol. I, trans. K. Grobel (New York: Charles Scribner's Sons, 1951), is an impressive work. R.H. Fuller, *The Mission and Achievement of Jesus* (Naperville, Ill.: Alec R. Allenson, 1954) provides a critical evaluation of Bultmann's position. Rudolf Otto, *The Kingdom of God and the Son of Man*, rev. ed. (Boston: Beacon Press, 1943) is a classic work on the subject that has influenced all subsequent studies. T.W. Manson, *The Servant-Messiah* (Cambridge: At the University Press, 1956) is a popular presentation of thas author's widely known position. Wm. Manson, *Jesus the Messiah* (Philadelphia: The Westminster Press, 1946) pays particular attention to form criticism. Günther Bornkamm, *Jesus of Nazareth*, trans. I. and F. McLuskey with J.M. Robinson (New York: Harper & Row, 1960), pp. 169–178 and Appendix III, reflects Bultmann's thought. Oscar Cullmann, *The Christology of the New Testament*, (Philadelphia: The Westminster Press, 1959) gives an extensive account of the titles of Jesus.

For a fuller treatment of the message and the messenger than was possible in this chapter see C. Milo Connick *Jesus: The Man, the Mission, and the Message* (Englewood Cliffs, N.J.: Prentice-Hall, Inc., 1963), pp. 197–313.

Chapter VII   Perceptive treatments of Jesus' Jerusalem journey and ministry are provided by Joseph Klausner, *Jesus of Nazareth*, trans. H. Danby (New York: The Macmillan Co., 1925), pp. 304–355; H.D.A. Major,

T.W. Manson, and C.J. Wright, *The Mission and Message of Jesus* (New York: E.P. Dutton & Co., 1938); and Vincent Taylor, *The Life and Ministry of Jesus* (New York: Abingdon Press, 1955), pp. 161–224. More recent discussions can be found in C. Milo Connick, *Jesus: The Man, the Mission, and the Message* (Englewood Cliffs, N.J.: Prentice-Hall, Inc., 1963), pp. 317–421, and E.W. Saunders, *Jesus in the Gospels* (Englewood Cliffs, N.J.: Prentice-Hall, Inc., 1967), pp. 233–312. A reconstruction of Jesus' ministry from the Transfiguration to the Triumphal Entry is presented by Maurice Goguel, *The Life of Jesus*, trans. O. Wyon (London: Allen & Unwin, Ltd., 1933), pp. 400–428.

An excellent summary of the factors leading to Jesus' death is presented in Martin Dibelius, *Jesus*, trans. C.B. Hedrick and F.C. Grant (Philadelphia: The Westminster Press, 1946), chapter 9. Wm. Manson, *Jesus the Messiah* (Philadelphia: The Westminster Press, 1946), chapter 7, relates Jesus' death to his total ministry. Jesus' trial is ably discussed by M. Radin, *The Trial of Jesus of Nazareth* (Chicago: Chicago University Press, 1931); S. Zeitlin, *Who Crucified Jesus?*, 2nd ed. (New York: Harper & Row, 1947), pp. 144–179; F.J. Powell, *The Trial of Jesus Christ* (Grand Rapids, Mich.: Eerdmans Publishing Co., 1949). The latest and most perceptive treatment on the subject is by the knowledgeable Jewish scholar, Paul Winter, *On the Trial of Jesus* (Berlin: Walter de Gruyter & Co., 1961).

Fruitful considerations of the resurrection are found in Kirsop Lake, *The Historical Evidence for the Resurrection of Jesus Christ* (New York: G.P. Putnam's Sons, 1907), pp. 57–202; C.R. Bowen, *The Resurrection in the New Testament* (New York: Putnam, 1911), pp. 150–373; J.M. Shaw, *The Resurrection of Christ* (Edinburgh: T. & T. Clark, 1920), pp. 44–94, 123–207; S. Vernon McCasland, *The Resurrection of Jesus* (New York: Thomas Nelson & Sons, 1932), pp. 15–74, 169–198; and Michael Ramsey, *The Resurrection of Christ* (London: Geoffrey Bles Ltd., 1946). A well-balanced account of the relevance of psychical research to the Easter faith is contained in M.C. Perry, *The Easter Enigma* (London: Faber & Faber, Ltd., 1959).

Chapters VIII and IX A stimulating study of the origin of the Christian movement is the five-volume work edited by F.J. Foakes-Jackson and Kirsopp Lake, *The Beginnings of Christianity* (London: The Macmillan Co., 1920–33). A path-breaking book on the literary and historical background is H.J. Cadbury, *The Making of Luke-Acts* (New York: The Macmillan Co., 1927; London: S.P.C.K., 1961). Martin Dibelius, *Studies in the Acts of the Apostles*, ed. H. Greeven, trans. M. Ling (New York: Charles Scribner's Sons, 1956) presents more detailed essays based on form criticism. C.S.C. Williams, *A Commentary on the Acts* *of the Apostles* (New York: Harper & Row, 1957) is very useful. The most perceptive and penetrating treatment of Luke-Acts as a theological treatise is Hans Conzelmann, *Theology of St. Luke*, trans. Geoffrey Buswell (New York: Harper & Row, 1960). A critique of Conzelmann's threefold time schema is found in Helmut Flender, *St. Luke: Theologian of Redemptive History* (Philadelphia: Fortress Press, 1967). For those who read German, Ernst Haenchen, *Die Apostelgeschichte* (Göttingen: Vandenhoeck & Ruprecht, 1959) will prove richly rewarding. A useful survey of research on Luke-Acts is provided by C.K. Barrett, *Luke the Historian in Recent Study* (London: Epworth Press, 1961). L.K. Keck and J.L. Martyn, eds., *Studies in Luke-Acts* (New York: Abingdon Press, 1966) contains vital essays by leading scholars on the current status and probable future of Lukan studies. L.E. Keck, *Mandate to Witness: Studies in the Book of Acts* (Valley Forge, Pa.: Judson Press, 1964) is an up-to-date study book. G.H.C. Macgregor, "Introduction and Exegesis of Acts," in George A. Buttrick, ed., *The Interpreter's Bible* (New York: Abingdon Press, 1954), IX, 3–352, is unusually helpful.

Chapters X and XI Nontechnical but reputable treatments of Paul's life and thought are provided by F.W. Beare, *St. Paul and His Letters* (New York: Abingdon Press, 1962), M. Dibelius and W.G. Kuemmel, *Paul*, trans. Frank Clarke (Philadelphia: The Westminster Press, 1953), and A.D. Nock, *St. Paul* (New York: Harper & Row, 1968). A more comprehensive work is James S. Stewart, *A Man in Christ* (New York: Harper & Row, n.d.). John Knox, *Chapters in a Life of Paul* (New York: Abingdon Press, 1950) stresses the unreliability of Acts as history and the slim chance that its data can be reconciled to Paul's letters. C.H. Dodd, *The Meaning of Paul for Today* (New York: Meridian Books, 1957) is very instructive. A recent but more traditional stance is presented in D.J. Selby, *Toward the Understanding of Paul* (Englewood Cliffs, N.J.: Prentice-Hall, Inc., 1962). A.M. Hunter, *Paul and His Predecessors*, rev. ed. (Philadelphia: The Westminster Press, 1961), discusses the Apostle's debt to those before him and to the early Christian tradition. His relationship to the Jerusalem church is thoroughly explored by W.L. Knox, *St. Paul and the Church of Jerusalem* (Cambridge: At the University Press, 1925). W.D. Davies, *Paul and Rabbinic Judaism*, rev. ed. (London: S.P.C.K., 1955) offers a technical study of Paul's thought as related to first-century rabbinic teaching. H.J. Schoeps, *Paul: The Theology of the Apostle in the Light of Jewish Religious History*, trans. H. Knight (Philadelphia: The Westminster Press, 1961) breaks somewhat similar ground. Joseph Klausner, *From Jesus to Paul*, trans. W.F. Stinespring (Boston: Beacon Press, 1961) is insightful. Maurice Goguel, *The Birth of Christianity* (New York: The Macmillan Co., 1954) discusses Paul's break with Jewish Christianity at length. C.K. Barrett, *From First Adam to Last* (New York: Charles Scribner's Sons, 1962) deals effectively with Paul's

Christology. Herbert M. Gale, *The Use of Analogy in the Letters of Paul* (Philadelphia: The Westminster Press, 1964), is a helpful study. W.A. Beardslee, *Human Achievement and Divine Vocation in the Message of Paul* (Naperville, Ill.: Alec R. Allenson, 1961) presents a scholarly discussion of Paul's apostolic vocation. The Corinthian situation is explored in two recent works by J.C. Hurd, *The Origins of I Corinthians* (New York: The Seabury Press, 1965) and W. Baird, *The Corinthian Church: A Biblical Approach to Urban Culture* (New York: Abingdon Press, 1964).

A stimulating and insightful (although highly technical) study of Paul's theology is Rudolf Bultmann, *Theology of the New Testament*, trans. K. Grobel (New York: Charles Scribner's Sons, 1951), I, 185–352. A more recent coverage is V.P. Furnish, *Theology and Ethics in Paul* (New York: Abingdon Press, 1968), which also surveys modern interpretations of Paul's ethics. J.A. Fitzmyer, *Pauline Theology: A Brief Sketch* (Englewood Cliffs, N.J.: Prentice-Hall, Inc., 1967) is succinct and useful. D.E.H. Whiteley, *The Theology of St. Paul* (Philadelphia: Fortress Press, 1964) is also valuable.

The introductory articles and exegesis pertaining to Paul's letters in *Harper's New Testament Commentaries* (New York: Harper & Row, 1960–) and in George A. Buttrick, ed., *The Interpreter's Bible* (New York: Abingdon Press, 1953–1955), vols. IX, X, XI, are of considerable helpfulness. Karl Barth, *The Epistle to the Romans*, 6th ed., trans. E.C. Hoskyns (London: Oxford University Press, 1933) is a classic. F.J. Leenhardt, *The Epistle to the Romans, A Commentary*, trans. H. Knight (London: Lutterworth Press, 1961), and F.F. Bruce, *The Epistle of Paul to the Romans* (Grand Rapids, Mich.: Wm. B. Eerdmans Publishing Co., 1963), are also of real value.

Chapter XII *Ephesians.* E.J. Goodspeed, *The Meaning of Ephesians* (Chicago: University of Chicago Press, 1933), is a technical work that espouses the view that Ephesians was written by a disciple of Paul as an introduction to Paul's collected letters. C.L. Mitton, *The Epistle to the Ephesians: Its Authorship, Origin, and Purpose* (Oxford: Clarendon Press, 1951), reflects a similar viewpoint. Goodspeed's position on the origin of Ephesians is developed by John Knox, *Philemon Among the Letters of Paul*, rev. ed. (New York: Abingdon Press, 1959). F.W. Beare, "Introduction and Exegesis of Ephesians," in George A. Buttrick, ed., *The Interpreter's Bible*, vol. X (New York: Abingdon Press, 1953), is an insightful commentary. E. Best, *One Body in Christ* (London: S.P.C.K., 1955) offers a fine theological discussion of the unity of the church.

The Pastorals: I & II Timothy and Titus. P.N. Harrison, *The Problem of the Pastoral Epistles* (Oxford: Humphrey Milford, 1921) argues that the Pastorals in their present form could not have been written by Paul. Three splendid commentaries are C.K. Barrett, *The Pastoral Epistles in the New English Bible* (Oxford: Clarendon Press, 1963); J.D.N. Kelly, *The Pastoral Epistles* (New York: Harper & Row, 1963); and B.S. Easton, *The Pastoral Epistles* (New York: Charles Scribner's Sons, 1947). F.D. Gealy, "Introduction and Exegesis to I & II Timothy and Titus," in *The Interpreter's Bible* (New York: Abingdon Press, 1955), XI, 342–551, is also valuable. J.C. Beker, *The Church Faces the World: Late New Testament Writings* (Philadelphia: The Westminster Press, 1960) is a well-written introduction. Maurice Goguel, *The Primitive Church* (New York: The Macmillan Co., 1964), treats the development in church organization and theology. B.H. Streeter, *The Primitive Church* (London: The Macmillan Co., 1929) is an earlier work of continuing value. Eduard Schweizer, *Church Order in the New Testament* (Naperville, Ill.: Alec R. Allenson, 1961) is instructive. C.F.D. Moule, *Worship in the New Testament* (Richmond, Va.: John Knox Press, 1961) is an excellent book on the subject.

Chapter XIII   *I Peter.* For a discussion of historical problems and insightful commentary see A.M. Hunter, "Introduction and Exegesis," in George A. Buttrick, ed., *The Interpreter's Bible* (New York: Abingdon Press, 1957), XII, 77–159. F.W. Beare, *The First Epistle of Peter: The Greek Text with Introduction and Notes*, rev. ed. (Oxford: Basil Blackwell, 1958) is also very useful. On the historical figure of Peter see Oscar Cullmann, *Peter: Disciple-Apostle-Martyr*, rev. ed., trans. F.V. Filson (Philadelphia: The Westminster Press, 1962). Bo Reicke, *The Epistles of James, Peter and Jude*, The Anchor Bible, vol. XXXVII (Garden City, N.Y.: Doubleday & Co., 1964), is an easy-to-read, popular commentary. The ethical teachings of I Peter are probed in W.C. van Unnik, "The Teaching of Good Works in I Peter," *New Testament Studies*, I, no. 2 (November 1954), 92–110. See the same author's "Peter, First Letter of," in *The Interpreter's Dictionary of the Bible*, (New York: Abingdon Press, 1962), K–Q, 758-766. E.G. Selwyn, *The First Epistle of Peter* (London: The Macmillan Co., 1946) is another helpful study.

Hebrews. A comprehensive commentary on the English text, from a generally conservative viewpoint, is F.F. Bruce, *The Epistle to the Hebrews*, The New International Commentary on the New Testament (Grand Rapids, Mich.: Wm. B. Eerdmans Publishing Co., 1964). Alexander C. Purdy presents a concise treatment of the historical, literary, and theological problems and an illuminating commentary in "The Epistle to the Hebrews, Introduction and Exegesis," in *The*

Interpreter's Bible (New York: Abingdon Press, 1955), XI, 577–763. W. Manson expounds some atypical notions about the purpose of the letter in *The Epistle to the Hebrews: An Historical and Theological Reconsideration* (London: Hodder & Stoughton, 1951), and his thinking is reflected in the popular and brief commentary by W. Neil, *The Epistle to the Hebrews* (London: SCM Press, 1955). E. Dinkler, "Letter to the Hebrews," in *The Interpreter's Dictionary of the Bible* (New York: Abingdon Press, 1962), E–J, 571–575, is a short but thoughtful summary. Older works of continuing value are E.F. Scott, *The Epistle to the Hebrews* (Edinburgh: T. & T. Clark, 1922), Hans Windisch, *Der Hebräerbrief*, 2nd ed. (Tübingen: J.C.B. Mohr, 1931), and F.V. Filson, *Yesterday, A Study of Hebrews in the Light of Chapter 13* (London: SCM Press, 1967).

James. Joseph B. Mayor, *The Epistle of St. James*, 3rd ed. (London: The Macmillan Co., 1910), an older but comprehensive commentary, is of indispensable value if supplemented by more modern works. James Moffatt, *The General Epistles*, Moffatt New Testament Commentary (New York: Harper & Row, n.d.; London: Hodder & Stoughton, 1928) is a concise and useful work. Hans Windisch, *Die Katholischen Briefe*, 3rd ed., reworked by H. Preisker, *Handbuch zum Neuen Testament* (Tübingen: J.C.B. Mohr, 1951), XV, makes use of Arnold Meyer's insights as well as those of many other commentators. B.S. Easton, "The Epistle of James, Introduction and Exegesis," in *The Interpreter's Bible* (New York: Abingdon Press, 1957), XII, 3–74, is very instructive. C.L. Mitton, *The Epistle of James* (Grand Rapids, Mich.: Wm. B. Eerdmans Publishing Co., 1966) is a recent and extensive commentary. A fine popular commentary is Bo Reicke, *The Epistles of James, Peter and Jude*, The Anchor Bible, vol. XXXVIII (Garden City, N.Y.: Doubleday & Co., 1964). R.V.G. Tasker, *The General Epistle of James* (Grand Rapids, Mich.: Wm. B. Eerdmans Publishing Co., 1956) provides a compact review of Roman Catholic and Protestant attitudes toward James. The development of ethical teaching from a theological perspective is ably treated by Rudolf Bultmann, *Theology of the New Testament*, trans. K. Grobel (London: SCM Press, 1955), II, 203–231, and W. Beach and H.R. Niebuhr, *Christian Ethics* (New York: The Ronald Press Co., 1955), pp. 46–57.

Jude and II Peter. Several older works provide valuable background for and interpretation of these letters: J.B. Mayor, *The Epistle of St. Jude and the Second Epistle of St. Peter* (London: The Macmillan Co., 1907); James Moffatt, ed., *The General Epistles*, Moffatt New Testament Commentary (New York: Harper & Row, n.d.; London: Hodder & Stoughton, 1928); J.W.C. Wand, *The General Epistles of St. Peter*, Moffatt New Testament Commentary (New York: Harper & Row, n.d.; London: Hodder & Stoughton, 1928). More recent studies of special worth are Hans Windisch, *Die Katholischen Briefe*, 3rd ed., reworked by H. Preisker, *Handbuch zum Neuen Testament* (Tübingen: J.C.B. Mohr, 1951), XV, and Ernst Käsemann, "An Apologia for Primitive Christian Eschatology," in *Essays on New Testament Themes*, trans. W.J. Montague, *Studies in Biblical Theology*, XLI (London: SCM Press, 1964), pp. 169–195.

Chapter XIV *The Gospel of John.* Three brief but thoughtful books are E.C. Colwell and E.L. Titus, *The Gospel of the Spirit* (New York: Harper & Row, 1956), E.L. Titus, *The Message of the Fourth Gospel* (New York: Abingdon Press, 1957), and W.F. Howard, *Christianity According to St. John* (Philadelphia: The Westminster Press, 1946). E.C. Colwell, *John Defends the Gospel* (New York: Willett, Clark, & Co., 1936), depicts the polemic nature of this Gospel. C.H. Dodd, *The Interpretation of the Fourth Gospel* (Cambridge: At the University Press, 1965), C.H. Dodd, *Historical Tradition in the Fourth Gospel* (Cambridge: At the University Press, 1963), Ernst Käsemann, *The Testament of Jesus*, trans. Gerhard Krodel (Philadelphia: Fortress Press, 1968), and J.L. Martyn, *History and Theology in the Fourth Gospel* (New York: Harper & Row, 1968), are compelling interpretations. E.C. Hoskyns, *The Fourth Gospel*, ed. F.N. Davey (London: Faber & Faber Ltd., 1947) is a comprehensive, useful commentary. R.H. Lightfoot, *St. John's Gospel* (New York: Oxford University Press, 1960) is an excellent popular study, as is Alan Richardson, *The Gospel According to St. John* (New York: Collier Books, 1962). W.F. Howard, "Introduction and Exegesis to the Gospel of St. John," in George A. Buttrick, ed., *The Interpreter's Bible* (New York: Abingdon Press, 1952), VIII, 435–811, is very helpful. R.E. Brown, *The Gospel According to John*, a two-volume work in The Anchor Bible (New York: Doubleday & Co., 1966 and 1970), is probably the best commentary to date.

J.L. Martyn, *History and Theology in the Fourth Gospel* (New York: Harper & Row, 1968) suggests that this Gospel arose out of a severe dispute between Judaism and the early church. An interpretation of the Fourth Gospel against the background of the sacraments is presented by Oscar Cullmann, *Early Christian Worship*, trans. A.S. Todd and J.B. Torrance (Naperville, Ill.: Alec R. Allenson, 1953). Amos Wilder, *New Testament Faith For Today* (New York: Harper & Row, 1955), pp. 142–164, treats the Fourth Gospel's literary method and theological viewpoint with rare perception.

The Johannine Letters. Amos Wilder, "Introduction and Exegesis, The First, Second, and Third Epistles of John," in *The Interpreter's Bible* (New York: Abingdon Press, 1957), XII, 207–313, is instructive.

C.H. Dodd, *The Johannine Epistles,* Moffatt New Testament Commentary (New York: Harper & Row, 1946) is incisive.

Chapter XV   Three popular but solidly-based interpretations are Thomas Kepler, *The Book of Revelation* (New York: Oxford University Press, 1957); Hans Lilje, *The Last Book of the Bible* (Philadelphia: Muhlenberg Press, 1957); and J.W. Bowman, *The Drama of the Book of Revelation* (Philadelphia: The Westminster Press, 1955). R.H. Charles, *The Revelation of St. John*, vols. I & II, International Critical Commentary (New York: Charles Scribner's Sons, 1920), presents a comprehensive, technical treatment of the book. William Ramsay, *The Letters to the Seven Churches* (New York: A.C. Armstrong & Sons, 1905) surveys the historical situation of Revelation. Commentaries of genuine merit are M. Kiddle, *The Revelation of St. John* (New York: Harper & Row, 1940) and in the Harper series, G.B. Caird, *A Commentary on the Revelation of St. John the Divine* (New York: Harper & Row, 1966). Martin Rist, "Introduction and Exegesis of the Revelation of St. John the Divine" in George A. Buttrick, ed., *The Interpreter's Bible* (New York: Abingdon Press, 1957), XII, 345–613, is concise and very illuminating. Another interesting study is M. Rissi, *Time and History*, trans. G.C. Winsor (Richmond, Va.: John Knox Press, 1966). A helpful study of apocalyptic literature of the period is D.S. Russell, *The Method and Message of Jewish Apocalyptic: 200* B.C.–A.D. *100* (Philadelphia: The Westminster Press, 1964). H.A. Guy, *The New Testament Doctrine of Last Things* (London and New York: Oxford University Press, 1948), deals with the development of eschatology. Its existential dimensions are expounded by Rudolf Bultmann, *The Presence of Eternity* (New York: Harper & Row, 1957).

Revelation raises the questions of church-state relations, persecution, and martyrdom. These subjects are probed by Oscar Cullmann, *The State in the New Testament*, rev. ed. (London: SCM Press, 1963). R.M. Grant, *The Sword and the Cross* (New York: The Macmillan Co., 1955) makes a similar study but gives more attention to non-Christian sources. Ethelbert Stauffer, *Christ and the Caesars*, trans. K. & R. Smith (Philadelphia: The Westminster Press, 1955), is also pertinent. An extensive and scholarly work is W.H.C. Frend, *Martyrdom and Persecution in the Early Church* (Oxford: Basil Blackwell, 1965).

Mosaic Law (*see* Law of Moses)
Moses, 48–9, 83, 130, 136, 145–6, 177, 181, 346, 349, 354, 377
Mount of Olives, 185
Mt. Gerizim, 45
Mt. Sinai, 55, 136
Muratorian Canon, 86
Mystery cults, 15–22, 243–4, 306, 371

Nag-Hammadi manuscripts, 13–14
Nathanael, 380
Nature wonders, 155
Nazareth, 106–8, 125–6
Nebuchadnezzar, 44
Nehemiah, 45
Nero, 72, 78, 87, 303, 340, 346, 409, 419
redivivus, 420–1
New age, 180
New covenant, 65, 183–4
Nicodemus, 382–3
Noah, 354

Onesimus, 304, 308–10, 322
Origen, 81, 344, 355, 363
Ormazd, 52

Pantaenus of Alexandria, 344
Papias, 75, 77, 81, 86, 370, 402, 407
Papyrus, 46, 326
Parables, 96, 121, 137–45, 148
Paraclete, 396–7 (*see also* Holy Spirit)
Parousia, 180, 235, 317–8, 331, 346, 366–7
Passion
predictions, 135
story, 94–5, 184–92, 398–9
Passover, 117, 181
Pastor, 326, 331–6
Pastorals, 326–36, 363
Patmos, 408, 411
Paul, 9, 11–2, 15, 57, 69–70, 73–4, 77–8, 86–7, 108, 183, 195–7, 208–13, 215, 220, 226–33, 237–323, 326–7, 332–6, 359, 363–4, 367, 369, 397, 405, 419
authority, 259–60
conversion, 223–5
dates, career, 264–6
handicaps, 268
Pentateuch, 58
Pentecost, 214
Holy Spirit, 214–6
Pergamum, 413
Pericope, 94
Persian Empire, 51
Peshitta Version (Syrian Bible), 337
Peter, the apostle, 74, 77–8, 135–6, 208–10, 216–7, 221, 258, 288, 317, 337–9, 356, 363, 370, 395, 419
confession, 131–2
disputed position, 132–5
Gentile mission, 225–8

Peter (I), book of, 337–43
Peter (II), book of, 337, 361, 363–7, 405
Petitionary Prayer, 397–8
Pharaoh, Egyptian, 39, 181
Pharisees, 27–8, 58–61, 63, 122–4, 149, 176, 178–9, 251, 389, 390–1, 394
Philadelphia, 413
Philemon, 309–10
Philemon, book of, 260, 265–6, 274, 308–10, 322
Philip the Evangelist, 75, 221–3, 250, 396
Philip of Side, 370
Philippi, 238–9, 303, 311, 313, 322
Philippians, book of, 263, 265–6, 302–4, 311–15, 319
Philo Judeus, 48, 61, 344, 352, 376
Phoebe, 291
Phrygia, 304–5
Pilate, Pontius, 33, 34–5, 72, 157, 165, 186–9, 192–3, 399
Plato, 10, 12, 351–2
Platonic thought, 344
Pliny the Elder, 61
Pliny the Younger, 71–2, 338–41, 409
Polybius, 210
Polycarp (Bishop of Smyrna), 311, 338, 369, 402
Pompey, 8, 28–9
Pope John XXIII, 133
Pope Paul VI, 193
Postapostolic age, 317–8
Prayer, 150
Priests, Jewish, 55–6
Prince of Peace, 147
Priscilla (Prisca), 243, 245, 246, 267, 292
Procurators, Roman, 33–5
Pronouncement, 95, 124 (n. 76), 176
Psalm (22), 192
Psalm (46), 420
Psalm (95), 349
Psalm (110), 351
Psalms of Solomon, 53–4
Pseudepigrapha, 47, 48
Pseudonymous writings, 47, 319–20
Ptolemy I, 6
Publicans, 34

Q, Gospel source, 74–5, 81, 83, 88–9, 90–3, 159, 234
Qumran, 61, 64, 113
inhabitants, 63
scrolls, 57, 110, 371, 374
writings, 48, 61–3

Rabbis, 137
Redaction criticism, 100–2
Renaissance, 155–6
Repentance, 119–20, 137
Resurrection, 177, 281–2
of Jesus, 194–6
Resuscitations, 154–5
Revelation, book of, 340, 343, 363, 368, 402, 406–23
seven visions, 416–23

Roman Catholic Church, 133–4, 344
Roman Empire, 6–9
Romans, book of, 262, 263, 265, 272, 285, 287, 290–301, 309, 357
Rome, 6, 255–6, 265–7, 290–1, 302–4, 309, 322, 326, 341, 345, 363, 369, 409, 421–2
Roosevelt, Franklin D., 420
Rule of the Community (Essene writing), 64

Sabbath, 61, 65, 85, 123–4
Sacrifice, animal, 41–2
Sadducees, 27, 58–9, 63, 177
Salome, 31
Samaria, Samaritans, 42–3, 45, 221, 384–5
Sanhedrin, 34, 56, 59, 161, 165, 186–8, 251–2, 393
Satan, 52, 114–6, 118, 218, 274, 277, 294, 395, 406, 413, 415, 417–9, 422–3
Sayings of Jesus, 95–6
Schweitzer, Albert, 118–9
Scribes, 57, 122–4, 137, 139, 142, 177–9
Seleucus I, 6
Seneca, 11, 319
Septuagint, 5, 46, 48, 82
Sermon on the Mount, 121, 145–51
Sermon on the Plain, 145
Servant of the Lord, 163–4
Seven, The, 218–9
Shakespeare, William, 420
Shema, 57, 118
Silas, 237–9, 241, 244, 266
Simeon, 214
Simon ben Kosibah, 36
Simon of Cyrene, 190
Simon, Jewish leader, 26
Simon Magus, 14, 330
Simon Peter (*see* Peter)
Simony, 221
Sin, sinners, 122–3, 147, 293–8
Smyrna, 413
Solomon, 41, 319
Son of God, 162–3, 348–51
Son of Man, 53, 135, 158–62
Spain, 267, 291–3, 301
"Speaking in tongues" (*see* Glossolalia)
Spiritual body, 195, 281–2
Stephen, 208, 219–20
Stilling of the Storm, 155
Stoicism, 10–11
Streeter, B.H., 92
Suetonius, 72
Synagogue, 56–8
Synoptic gospels, 90–3, 103, 406
  oral sources, 93–4
  source dates, 100
Sylvanus, 237, 270, 338–9, 343–4

Tacitus, 72
Talmud, 60, 73, 346

Tarsus, 223, 227
Taylor, Vincent, 95, 152
Teacher of Righteousness, 57, 61, 63, 66
Temple of Jerusalem, 41, 44–5, 54–6, 250, 345–6, 409
  cleansing, 173–5, 381–2
  destruction prophecy, 179–80
Tertius, 260, 262 (n. 12)
Tertullian (North Africa), 201, 345, 409
Testaments of the Twelve Patriarchs, 178
Testimonia Document (Essene writing), 65–6
Theophilus, 87, 89, 201, 213
Thessalonians (I), book of, 245, 260, 265, 268–70, 406
Thessalonians (II), book of, 245, 265, 269, 270–2, 406
Thessalonica, 239, 268–9, 322
Thomas, the disciple, 399
Thucydides, 210
Thyatira, 413
Tiberius, 35, 72, 419
Timothy, 237, 241, 244, 269–70, 304, 312–3, 326–7, 332–5
Timothy (I), book of, 263, 320, 326, 328–34
Timothy (II), book of, 212, 263, 320, 322, 326, 328, 330–1, 334–5
Titus, 237, 263, 273, 283, 288, 326, 327, 335
Titus, book of, 320, 326, 328–9, 335–6
Torah, 60, 63, 68
Trajan, 36, 71–2, 338–40, 368–9, 409, 411
Transfiguration, 135–6
Twelve, The, 126–7, 219, 225, 257–8, 288, 364
Tychicus, 304, 308–9, 320, 325

United Kingdom, 49
Unleavened bread, festival, 181–2

Valentinius, 13, 14
Vatican I, 133
Vespasian, 36, 47, 409–10
Vita (Josephus), 47

War Scroll, 62
Wesley, John, 133
Windisch, Hans, 150–1, 231–2

Yahweh, 52

Zealots, 67–8
Zechariah, 45, 85, 171, 214, 406
Zeno, 10
Zeus, 15, 16, 17, 410
Zoroastrianism, 52, 406

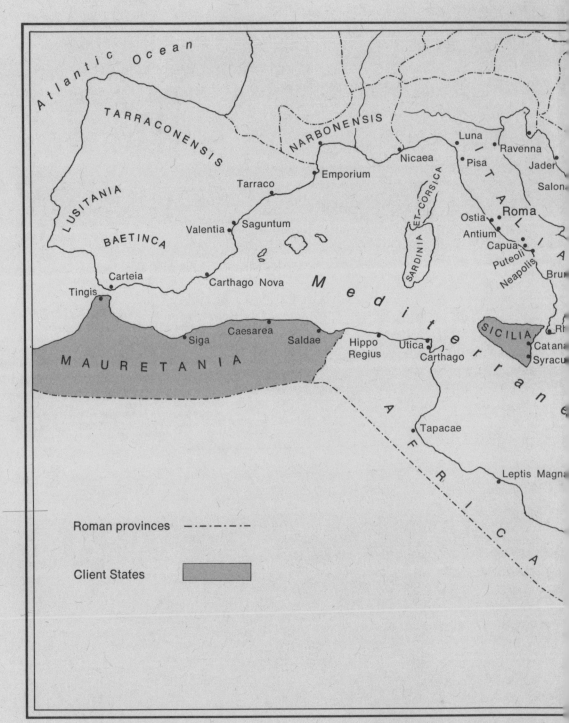

THE MEDITERRANEA